T0190006

Lecture Notes in Computer Science   13334

More information about this series at https://link.springer.com/bookseries/558

Xiaowen Fang (Ed.)

HCI in Games

4th International Conference, HCI-Games 2022
Held as Part of the 24th HCI International Conference, HCII 2022
Virtual Event, June 26 – July 1, 2022
Proceedings

Springer

Editor
Xiaowen Fang
DePaul University
Chicago, IL, USA

ISSN 0302-9743   ISSN 1611-3349 (electronic)
Lecture Notes in Computer Science
ISBN 978-3-031-05636-9   ISBN 978-3-031-05637-6 (eBook)
https://doi.org/10.1007/978-3-031-05637-6

This Springer imprint is published by the registered company Springer Nature Switzerland AG
The registered company address is: Gewerbestrasse 11, 6330 Cham, Switzerland

Foreword

Human-computer interaction (HCI) is acquiring an ever-increasing scientific and industrial importance, as well as having more impact on people's everyday life, as an ever-growing number of human activities are progressively moving from the physical to the digital world. This process, which has been ongoing for some time now, has been dramatically accelerated by the COVID-19 pandemic. The HCI International (HCII) conference series, held yearly, aims to respond to the compelling need to advance the exchange of knowledge and research and development efforts on the human aspects of design and use of computing systems.

The 24th International Conference on Human-Computer Interaction, HCI International 2022 (HCII 2022), was planned to be held at the Gothia Towers Hotel and Swedish Exhibition & Congress Centre, Göteborg, Sweden, during June 26 to July 1, 2022. Due to the COVID-19 pandemic and with everyone's health and safety in mind, HCII 2022 was organized and run as a virtual conference. It incorporated the 21 thematic areas and affiliated conferences listed on the following page.

A total of 5583 individuals from academia, research institutes, industry, and governmental agencies from 88 countries submitted contributions, and 1276 papers and 275 posters were included in the proceedings to appear just before the start of the conference. The contributions thoroughly cover the entire field of human-computer interaction, addressing major advances in knowledge and effective use of computers in a variety of application areas. These papers provide academics, researchers, engineers, scientists, practitioners, and students with state-of-the-art information on the most recent advances in HCI. The volumes constituting the set of proceedings to appear before the start of the conference are listed in the following pages.

The HCI International (HCII) conference also offers the option of 'Late Breaking Work' which applies both for papers and posters, and the corresponding volume(s) of the proceedings will appear after the conference. Full papers will be included in the 'HCII 2022 - Late Breaking Papers' volumes of the proceedings to be published in the Springer LNCS series, while 'Poster Extended Abstracts' will be included as short research papers in the 'HCII 2022 - Late Breaking Posters' volumes to be published in the Springer CCIS series.

I would like to thank the Program Board Chairs and the members of the Program Boards of all thematic areas and affiliated conferences for their contribution and support towards the highest scientific quality and overall success of the HCI International 2022 conference; they have helped in so many ways, including session organization, paper reviewing (single-blind review process, with a minimum of two reviews per submission) and, more generally, acting as goodwill ambassadors for the HCII conference.

This conference would not have been possible without the continuous and unwavering support and advice of Gavriel Salvendy, founder, General Chair Emeritus, and Scientific Advisor. For his outstanding efforts, I would like to express my appreciation to Abbas Moallem, Communications Chair and Editor of HCI International News.

June 2022   Constantine Stephanidis

HCI International 2022 Thematic Areas and Affiliated Conferences

Thematic Areas

- HCI: Human-Computer Interaction
- HIMI: Human Interface and the Management of Information

Affiliated Conferences

- EPCE: 19th International Conference on Engineering Psychology and Cognitive Ergonomics
- AC: 16th International Conference on Augmented Cognition
- UAHCI: 16th International Conference on Universal Access in Human-Computer Interaction
- CCD: 14th International Conference on Cross-Cultural Design
- SCSM: 14th International Conference on Social Computing and Social Media
- VAMR: 14th International Conference on Virtual, Augmented and Mixed Reality
- DHM: 13th International Conference on Digital Human Modeling and Applications in Health, Safety, Ergonomics and Risk Management
- DUXU: 11th International Conference on Design, User Experience and Usability
- C&C: 10th International Conference on Culture and Computing
- DAPI: 10th International Conference on Distributed, Ambient and Pervasive Interactions
- HCIBGO: 9th International Conference on HCI in Business, Government and Organizations
- LCT: 9th International Conference on Learning and Collaboration Technologies
- ITAP: 8th International Conference on Human Aspects of IT for the Aged Population
- AIS: 4th International Conference on Adaptive Instructional Systems
- HCI-CPT: 4th International Conference on HCI for Cybersecurity, Privacy and Trust
- HCI-Games: 4th International Conference on HCI in Games
- MobiTAS: 4th International Conference on HCI in Mobility, Transport and Automotive Systems
- AI-HCI: 3rd International Conference on Artificial Intelligence in HCI
- MOBILE: 3rd International Conference on Design, Operation and Evaluation of Mobile Communications

List of Conference Proceedings Volumes Appearing Before the Conference

1. LNCS 13302, Human-Computer Interaction: Theoretical Approaches and Design Methods (Part I), edited by Masaaki Kurosu
2. LNCS 13303, Human-Computer Interaction: Technological Innovation (Part II), edited by Masaaki Kurosu
3. LNCS 13304, Human-Computer Interaction: User Experience and Behavior (Part III), edited by Masaaki Kurosu
4. LNCS 13305, Human Interface and the Management of Information: Visual and Information Design (Part I), edited by Sakae Yamamoto and Hirohiko Mori
5. LNCS 13306, Human Interface and the Management of Information: Applications in Complex Technological Environments (Part II), edited by Sakae Yamamoto and Hirohiko Mori
6. LNAI 13307, Engineering Psychology and Cognitive Ergonomics, edited by Don Harris and Wen-Chin Li
7. LNCS 13308, Universal Access in Human-Computer Interaction: Novel Design Approaches and Technologies (Part I), edited by Margherita Antona and Constantine Stephanidis
8. LNCS 13309, Universal Access in Human-Computer Interaction: User and Context Diversity (Part II), edited by Margherita Antona and Constantine Stephanidis
9. LNAI 13310, Augmented Cognition, edited by Dylan D. Schmorrow and Cali M. Fidopiastis
10. LNCS 13311, Cross-Cultural Design: Interaction Design Across Cultures (Part I), edited by Pei-Luen Patrick Rau
11. LNCS 13312, Cross-Cultural Design: Applications in Learning, Arts, Cultural Heritage, Creative Industries, and Virtual Reality (Part II), edited by Pei-Luen Patrick Rau
12. LNCS 13313, Cross-Cultural Design: Applications in Business, Communication, Health, Well-being, and Inclusiveness (Part III), edited by Pei-Luen Patrick Rau
13. LNCS 13314, Cross-Cultural Design: Product and Service Design, Mobility and Automotive Design, Cities, Urban Areas, and Intelligent Environments Design (Part IV), edited by Pei-Luen Patrick Rau
14. LNCS 13315, Social Computing and Social Media: Design, User Experience and Impact (Part I), edited by Gabriele Meiselwitz
15. LNCS 13316, Social Computing and Social Media: Applications in Education and Commerce (Part II), edited by Gabriele Meiselwitz
16. LNCS 13317, Virtual, Augmented and Mixed Reality: Design and Development (Part I), edited by Jessie Y. C. Chen and Gino Fragomeni
17. LNCS 13318, Virtual, Augmented and Mixed Reality: Applications in Education, Aviation and Industry (Part II), edited by Jessie Y. C. Chen and Gino Fragomeni

18. LNCS 13319, Digital Human Modeling and Applications in Health, Safety, Ergonomics and Risk Management: Anthropometry, Human Behavior, and Communication (Part I), edited by Vincent G. Duffy

19. LNCS 13320, Digital Human Modeling and Applications in Health, Safety, Ergonomics and Risk Management: Health, Operations Management, and Design (Part II), edited by Vincent G. Duffy

20. LNCS 13321, Design, User Experience, and Usability: UX Research, Design, and Assessment (Part I), edited by Marcelo M. Soares, Elizabeth Rosenzweig and Aaron Marcus

21. LNCS 13322, Design, User Experience, and Usability: Design for Emotion, Well-being and Health, Learning, and Culture (Part II), edited by Marcelo M. Soares, Elizabeth Rosenzweig and Aaron Marcus

22. LNCS 13323, Design, User Experience, and Usability: Design Thinking and Practice in Contemporary and Emerging Technologies (Part III), edited by Marcelo M. Soares, Elizabeth Rosenzweig and Aaron Marcus

23. LNCS 13324, Culture and Computing, edited by Matthias Rauterberg

24. LNCS 13325, Distributed, Ambient and Pervasive Interactions: Smart Environments, Ecosystems, and Cities (Part I), edited by Norbert A. Streitz and Shin'ichi Konomi

25. LNCS 13326, Distributed, Ambient and Pervasive Interactions: Smart Living, Learning, Well-being and Health, Art and Creativity (Part II), edited by Norbert A. Streitz and Shin'ichi Konomi

26. LNCS 13327, HCI in Business, Government and Organizations, edited by Fiona Fui-Hoon Nah and Keng Siau

27. LNCS 13328, Learning and Collaboration Technologies: Designing the Learner and Teacher Experience (Part I), edited by Panayiotis Zaphiris and Andri Ioannou

28. LNCS 13329, Learning and Collaboration Technologies: Novel Technological Environments (Part II), edited by Panayiotis Zaphiris and Andri Ioannou

29. LNCS 13330, Human Aspects of IT for the Aged Population: Design, Interaction and Technology Acceptance (Part I), edited by Qin Gao and Jia Zhou

30. LNCS 13331, Human Aspects of IT for the Aged Population: Technology in Everyday Living (Part II), edited by Qin Gao and Jia Zhou

31. LNCS 13332, Adaptive Instructional Systems, edited by Robert A. Sottilare and Jessica Schwarz

32. LNCS 13333, HCI for Cybersecurity, Privacy and Trust, edited by Abbas Moallem

33. LNCS 13334, HCI in Games, edited by Xiaowen Fang

34. LNCS 13335, HCI in Mobility, Transport and Automotive Systems, edited by Heidi Krömker

35. LNAI 13336, Artificial Intelligence in HCI, edited by Helmut Degen and Stavroula Ntoa

36. LNCS 13337, Design, Operation and Evaluation of Mobile Communications, edited by Gavriel Salvendy and June Wei

37. CCIS 1580, HCI International 2022 Posters - Part I, edited by Constantine Stephanidis, Margherita Antona and Stavroula Ntoa

38. CCIS 1581, HCI International 2022 Posters - Part II, edited by Constantine Stephanidis, Margherita Antona and Stavroula Ntoa

39. CCIS 1582, HCI International 2022 Posters - Part III, edited by Constantine Stephanidis, Margherita Antona and Stavroula Ntoa
40. CCIS 1583, HCI International 2022 Posters - Part IV, edited by Constantine Stephanidis, Margherita Antona and Stavroula Ntoa

http://2022.hci.international/proceedings

Preface

Computer games have grown developed to become beyond simple entertainment activities. Researchers and practitioners have attempted to utilize games in many innovative ways, such as educational games, therapeutic games, simulation games, and gamification of utilitarian applications. Although a lot of attention has been given to investigate the positive impact of games in recent years, prior research has only studied isolated fragments of a game system. More research on games is needed to develop and utilize games for the benefit of society.

At a high level, a game system has three basic elements: system input, process, and system outcome. System input concerns the external factors impacting the game system. It may include, but is not limited to, player personalities and motivations to play games. The process is about game mechanism and play experience. System outcome includes the effects of game play. There is no doubt that users are involved in all three elements. Human Computer Interaction (HCI) plays a critical role in the study of games. By examining player characteristics, interactions during game play, and behavioral implications of game play, HCI professionals can help design and develop better games for the society.

The 4th International Conference on HCI in Games (HCI-Games 2022), an affiliated conference of the HCI International Conference, intends to help, promote and encourage research in this field by providing a forum for interaction and exchanges among researchers, academics, and practitioners in the fields of HCI and games. The Conference addresses HCI principles, methods and tools for better games.

This year, researchers from around the world have contributed significant amounts of work in multiple themes. Regarding system processes, the papers present research about gameplay and game mechanics, a major constituent of the overall gaming experience that needs to be carefully crafted. For system outcomes, studies about user experience, player behavior, and gamified interactions have been conducted, shedding light on how a game is perceived and experienced by its target users, the players. Research has also expanded to a broad range of disciplines and application domains, such as games in education and learning, serious games, as well as augmented and virtual reality games.

One volume of the HCII 2022 proceedings is dedicated to this year's edition of the HCI-Games Conference and focuses on topics related to gameplay and game mechanics design, user experience in games and gamified interactions, player behavior and games' impact, games in education and learning, serious games, as well as augmented and virtual reality games.

Papers of this volume are included for publication after a minimum of two single–blind reviews from the members of the HCI-Games Program Board or, in some cases, from members of the Program Boards of other affiliated conferences. I would like to thank all of them for their invaluable contribution, support and efforts.

June 2022

Xiaowen Fang

4th International Conference on HCI in Games
(HCI-Games 2022)

Program Board Chair: **Xiaowen Fang,** DePaul University, USA

- Amir Zaib Abbasi, King Fahd University of Petroleum and Minerals, Saudi Arabia
- Dena Al-Thani, HBKU, Qatar
- Abdullah Azhari, King Abdulaziz University, Saudi Arabia
- Ikram Bououd, KEDGE Business School, France
- Barbara Caci, University of Palermo, Italy
- Darryl Charles, Ulster University, UK
- Benjamin Ultan Cowley, University of Helsinki, Finland
- Khaldoon Dhou, Texas A&M University-Central Texas, USA
- I. Scott MacKenzie, York University, Canada
- Daniel Riha, Charles University, Czech Republic
- Owen Schaffer, Bradley University, USA
- Jason Schklar, UX is Fine, USA
- Fan Zhao, Florida Gulf Coast University, USA
- Miaoqi Zhu, Sony Pictures Entertainment, USA

The full list with the Program Board Chairs and the members of the Program Boards of all thematic areas and affiliated conferences is available online at

http://www.hci.international/board-members-2022.php

HCI International 2023

The 25th International Conference on Human-Computer Interaction, HCI International 2023, will be held jointly with the affiliated conferences at the AC Bella Sky Hotel and Bella Center, Copenhagen, Denmark, 23–28 July 2023. It will cover a broad spectrum of themes related to human-computer interaction, including theoretical issues, methods, tools, processes, and case studies in HCI design, as well as novel interaction techniques, interfaces, and applications. The proceedings will be published by Springer. More information will be available on the conference website: http://2023.hci.international/.

General Chair
Constantine Stephanidis
University of Crete and ICS-FORTH
Heraklion, Crete, Greece
Email: general_chair@hcii2023.org

http://2023.hci.international/

Contents

Gameplay and Game Mechanics Design

Movement Control Methods for Mobile Devices: An Empirical Study
of Displacement Interfaces 3
  Elias Bestard Lorigados, I. Scott MacKenzie, and Melanie Baljko

Assessing the Comprehensiveness of the Co-operative Performance
Metric: A Mixed-Method Analysis Using Portal 2 22
  Gregory Gorman and Conor Linehan

Auto Generating Maps in a 2D Environment 40
  Lazaros Lazaridis, Konstantinos-Filippos Kollias, George Maraslidis,
  Heraklis Michailidis, Maria Papatsimouli, and George F. Fragulis

Spell Painter: Motion Controlled Spellcasting for a Wizard Video Game 51
  Daniel MacCormick and Loutfouz Zaman

Dynamic Difficulty Adjustment in Digital Games: Comparative Study
Between Two Algorithms Using Electrodermal Activity Data 69
  Ian Nery Bandeira, Vitor F. Dullens, Thiago V. Machado,
  Rennê Ruan A. Oliveira, Carla D. Castanho, Tiago B. P. e Silva,
  and Mauricio M. Sarmet

Playable Characters Attributes: An Empirical Analysis Based
on the Theoretical Proposal from Katherine Isbister and Ernest Adams 84
  Tânia Ribeiro, Gonçalo Ribeiro, and Ana Isabel Veloso

Guidance is Good: Controlled Experiment Shows the Impact
of Navigational Guidance on Digital Game Enjoyment and Flow 101
  Uday Sai Reddy Ambati, Gregory Brandt, and Owen Schaffer

Slow, Repeat, Voice Guidance: Automatic Generation of Practice Charts
to Improve Rhythm Action Games 119
  Shio Takidaira, Yoshiyuki Shoji, and Martin J. Dürst

User Experience in Games and Gamified Interactions

Conveyance of Narrative Through Digital Game Environments 141
  Michael Brandse

Design of Emotion-Driven Game Interaction Using Biosignals 160
   Yann Frachi, Takuya Takahashi, Feiqi Wang, and Mathieu Barthet

Frankenhead - Exploring Participatory Engagement and Play as a Cultural
Event 180
   *Andreas Kratky, Joanna Shen, Hesiquio Mendez Alejo, Rong Deng,
   and Fabian Bock*

Targeting IMPACT: A New Psychological Model of User Experience 196
   Leah Kurta and Jonathan Freeman

Practical Considerations on Applications of the Popularity of Games:
The Case of Location-Based Games and Disaster 213
   Nicolas LaLone, Phoebe O. Toups Dugas, and Konstantinos Papangelis

Research on the User Experience of Affordance of the Cube Game
Interface Design 234
   Hongyu Li and Chien-Hsiung Chen

Online Social Games in the Eyes of Children and Teens: A Systematic
Review 245
   Sean Li, Erin Li, and Xiaojun Yuan

Artistic and Communication Strategies of Creating Playful Experiences
in New Media Arts: A Reconnaissance 256
   Anna Maj

Apples and Oranges: A Study of "Tend & Befriend" as a Phenomenon
in Digital Games 269
   Zoë O'Shea, Richard Bartle, Xueni Pan, and Jonathan Freeman

Design Implications for a Gamified Recycling House 289
   *Adam Palmquist, Ole Goethe, Jeanine Krath, Joacim Rosenlund,
   and Miralem Helmefalk*

Player Behavior and Games Impact

Social Anxiety Strategies Through Gaming 309
   Matthew Copeman and Jonathan Freeman

Does Gamification Increase Purchase Intention? A Systematic Review 327
   Yichen Gao and Zhanwei Wu

How is Video Game Playing Time Linked to Parent-Child Communication
Frequency? A Longitudinal Cross-Lagged Analysis 340
    Jiawen Gou, Lihanjing Wu, and Hui Li

A Study on Player Experience in Real-Time Strategy Games Combined
with Eye-Tracking and Subjective Evaluation 354
    Jiawei Jiao, Jinchun Wu, and Chengqi Xue

First Person vs. Third Person Perspective in a Persuasive Virtual Reality
Game: How Does Perspective Affect Empathy Orientation? 375
    Asha Kambe and Tatsuo Nakajima

Does "Left-Behind" Cause Rural Adolescents to Spend More Time
Playing Video Games in China? Evidence from China Education Panel
Survey 387
    Siyuan Wang, Lihanjing Wu, and Xiao Liang

Games in Education and Learning

Validating Learning Games, a Case Study 399
    Alessandro Canossa, Alexis Lozano Angulo, and Luis Laris Pardo

Do We Speak the Same Language? The Effect of Emojis on Learners
in an Online Learning Environment 414
    Wad Ghaban

Multisensory Collaborative Play: Online Resources for Parents of Children
with Autism Spectrum Disorder 427
    Mohamad Hassan Fadi Hijab, Bilikis Banire, and Dena Al-Thani

Students' Status Toward the New Gamified Learning Method:
An Exploratory Study 444
    Lan Jiang, Fan Zhao, Xiaoxue Wang, and Jingshun Zhang

Understanding School Children's Playful Experiences Through the Use
of Educational Robotics - The Impact of Open-Ended Designs 456
    Jeanette Sjöberg and Eva Brooks

Videogame Design Using a User-Centered Approach to Teaching
Projectile Motion 469
    Julian F. Villada and Maria F. Montoya

Serious Games

A 'Serious Games' Approach to Decisions of Environmental Impact
of Energy Transformation 487
  Jakub Binter, Silvia Boschetti, Tomáš Hladký, Hermann Prossinger,
  Timothy Jason Wells, Jiřina Jílková, and Daniel Říha

A Configurable Serious Game for Inhibitory and Interference Control 496
  Houda Chabbi, Sandy Ingram, Florian Hofmann, Vinh Ngyuen,
  and Yasser Khazaal

AWATO: A Serious Game to Improve Cybersecurity Awareness 508
  Lauren S. Ferro, Andrea Marrella, Tiziana Catarci, Francesco Sapio,
  Adriano Parenti, and Matteo De Santis

Designing Social Exergame to Enhance Intergenerational Interaction
and Exercise 530
  Emiran Kaisar, Shi Qiu, Rui Yuan, and Ting Han

Toward the Design of a Gamification Framework for Enhancing Motivation
Among Journalists, Experts, and the Public to Combat Disinformation:
The Case of CALYPSO Platform 542
  Catherine Sotirakou, Theodoros Paraskevas, and Constantinos Mourlas

FIST FIX: Soft Hard Combination Product Design for Hand Rehabilitation
After Stroke 555
  Tianyu Zhou and Ting Han

Augmented and Virtual Reality Games

An Augmented Reality Update of a Classic Game: "Where in the World is
Carmen Sandiego?", Case Study 569
  Annette Marie Chabebe Rivera, Wenyu Wu, and Chengqi Xue

A Data-Driven Design of AR Alternate Reality Games to Measure
Resilience 586
  Reza Habibi, Sai Siddartha Maram, Johannes Pfau, Jessica Wei,
  Shweta K. Sisodiya, Atieh Kashani, Elin Carstensdottir,
  and Magy Seif El-Nasr

Implicit Interaction Mechanisms in VR-Controlled Interactive Visual
Novels 605
  Cristóbal Maldonado, Francisco J. Gutierrez, and Victor Fajnzylber

LegionARius - Beyond Limes 618
   David A. Plecher, Andreas Wohlschlager, Christian Eichhorn,
   and Gudrun Klinker

Research Status and Trends of the Gamification Design for Visually
Impaired People in Virtual Reality 637
   Shufang Tan, Wendan Huang, and Junjie Shang

DropAR: Enriching Exergaming Using Collaborative Augmented Reality
Content 652
   Kieran Woodward, Eiman Kanjo, and Will Parker

Author Index 665

Gameplay and Game Mechanics Design

Movement Control Methods for Mobile Devices: An Empirical Study of Displacement Interfaces

Elias Bestard Lorigados[✉], I. Scott MacKenzie, and Melanie Baljko

York University, Toronto M3J 1P3, Canada
{elias39,mack,mb}@cse.yorku.ca

Abstract. We conducted a user study to compare four displacement interfaces on mobile devices. An Android application was developed with four displacement methods: Soft Joystick, up-down-right-left Buttons, Tilt Sensors, and Dual Soft Joystick. The study involved 12 participants using the four interfaces to control an object from a starting point to a goal point in five trials having different paths. The time (s), number of wall hits, efficiency (%), and out-of-path movement (%) per trial were logged to compare the methods. There was a significant effect of Displacement Method and Path on each dependent variable ($p < .005$). The Button method had 95.5%, 90.4%, and 84.2% less out-of-path movement than the Soft Joystick, Tilt Sensors, and Dual-Soft-Joystick methods, respectively. Also, the number of times the object missed the path using Buttons represented 10% of the total, followed by Dual-Soft-Joystick with 20% of the total. Tilt Sensors was 2.8% faster than Buttons (second fastest) in time per trial. Button reported the best numbers for efficiency with 58.8% on average per trial being 12% more efficient than Soft Joystick as the second best. In addition, there were statistical differences in post hoc tests ($p < .005$) between Button, the best overall method, and the remain interfaces on all dependent variables results. The participants indicated Buttons as the most comfortable method overall and Tilt Sensor as the best and most promising method.

Keywords: Displacement · Movement control · Joystick · Sensors · Buttons · Up-down-right-left Buttons · Mobile user interface

1 Introduction

Mobile devices are broadly used by all generations in daily life. The use of these gadgets varies depending on the needs, impediments, interests, and even preferences of each person. Individuals who suffer from certain physical or social impediments might use a cell phone, tablet, or any other specific interface to facilitate their interaction with the external world in order and exploit the device sensors for movement simulation. On the other hand, other individuals primarily use these devices for entertainment, such as filling leisure time with activities like playing video games, where motion is present most of the time. Nowadays, almost every person commonly interacts with and uses these devices for a combination of the aforementioned purposes. Therefore, the study and development of new user interfaces have become a necessity.

If we examine specific interfaces, we can focus on the displacement or movement of an object from a starting point to a goal point. Examples include moving a cursor, virtual ball, or playing card, as well as controlling virtual racing cars, space ships, or other objects, including players, in games scenarios, such as shooting games, role-playing video games (RPG), sports games, etc. For the purpose of this research, we refer to "displacement" as the movement of an object from a starting point to another point. Displacement is commonly found in games, but we aim to target all applications that use displacement in some way or another.

This study focuses specifically on an empirical comparison of displacement from a starting point to a goal point in mobile devices. We aim to collect data using different game-like interfaces to control an on-screen object's motion and use that information for a comparison of the interfaces with a set of participants. We will examine which input method is better for movement control, which one is easier or more intuitive for users, and if these input methods can be improved. This comparison can help to enhance several areas of research and development of mobile user interfaces, particularly for games. The results will help to determine situations where one interface or another is preferable for users. Also, these data will facilitate the selection of a preferred interface for future mobile application development or game development.

1.1 Related Work

Plenty of work has been conducted in the area of displacement control interfaces. Research progress is particularly evident in the use of joysticks, arrow buttons, tilt sensors, and key pads on mobile computing devices for gaming. Examples of these improvements were studied by Chu and Wong in evaluating participant experience on hard and soft keypads [3]. They found that the input device directly affected the gaming experience, and offered a list of game genres best suited to various input modalities.

Constantin and MacKenzie performed a user study examining tilt-control to move an object in a maze [4]. They compared the control of a ball using velocity-control and position-control. They found position-control 16% faster, with similar accuracy compared to velocity-control. On the other hand, the participants preferred velocity-control.

Medryk and MacKenzie compared gaming performance during gameplay using tilt-control and touch-based input system [5]. They observed better results using touch input during gameplay. On the other hand, participants preferred tilt-control since it brought more challenges to the games. Similarly, Browne and Anand conducted a study evaluating mobile interfaces specifically in video games [2]. They performed a study with 36 participants using three interfaces, where they had a combination of accelerometer sensors, buttons, and a touchscreen-based interface. The reported that users preferred sensors over joysticks and buttons.

Other studies compared on-screen game-pad designs with sensor-controlled designs for mobile devices on video games. Baldau et al. conducted a comparison of four game-pad controllers using traditional input methods [1]. They specifically compared directional buttons, a directional pad, a floating joystick. And tilt control and observed that directional buttons were the most precise for direction-restricted navigation. Additionally, unintentional movements occurred while using the joystick and the use of tilt was rejected for some tasks.

In addition, Teather and MacKenzie evaluated the tilt-control method on mobile devices [6]. They investigated the performance of cursor control using devices with built-in accelerometers, different levels of tilt gain, and two selection modes. This study reported a tilt gain range of 50–100 to obtain optimal performance for movement time.

Similarly, Teather et al. proposed the use of tilt sensors coexisting with touch control in mobile devices [8]. They used two soft joysticks to independently control the moving and aiming in shooting games and included a standard dual analog control scheme. They also tested two options using tilt control in lieu of touch control for either movement or aiming, and a tilt-only control scheme. Conclusively, they report that touch-based control offered the best performance but tilt-based was a comparable interface.

Zhang et al. worked on an interface to control games based on different sensors [9]. Their results in the games studied indicate better performance using a joystick. However, participants still preferred using the sensors, which provided more freedom controlling the movement.

Input using a tilt sensor has also shown good results in comparison with touch-based interfaces in a study on motion sickness while gaming [7]. In the cited study, motion sickness was commonly seen with users who spend many hours gaming. This is an additional reason for testing the use of a tilt sensor in the present study. All the cited studies support velocity-control using a tilt sensor as an input method and stress the importance of studying the differences between movement interfaces. They inspired us to examine traditional and novel methods to control the movement of objects in mobile devices. Thus, the optimal values for tilt gain obtained by Teather and MacKenzie [6] were relevant to the development of our Android application. It was also found that directional buttons and the use of joysticks are common in the literature.

2 Method

A user study was conducted to compare four different movement interfaces in terms of performance differences and user preferences. Each participant completed five trials, each using a different path pattern, on the four different movement interfaces (see apparatus section for a description of the interfaces).

2.1 Participants

Twelve participants were selected to conduct the study and evaluation of the experiment. They were divided into four groups to counterbalance learning effects. Aiming to include variety, the study included daily smartphone users, avid gamers, and those who do not tend to play video games. Ages ranged from 18 to 35 years, with most of the participants between 21–30 years old. Six of the participants were male, six were female. The participants were selected from the local university campus and received $25 compensation for their assistance.

2.2 Apparatus

The study was conducted on an LG *G4* smart phone running the Android 8 operating system. The device had 5.5-in. display with a resolution of 1440 × 2560 pixels and 538 ppi density (Fig. 1).

Fig. 1. Mobile device used in the user study, LG *G4*.

The software[1] was developed on Android Studio (4.1.1) using Java as the programming language for the main activities and XML for the graphical interfaces.

The application contains four interfaces for displacement control:

– Soft Joystick, Fig. 2(a)
– Dual Soft Joystick, Fig. 2(b)
– Up-down-right-left Buttons (Buttons), Fig. 2(c)
– Tilt Sensors.

Each interface controls the movement of an on-screen object differently. The Soft Joystick and Tilt Sensors interfaces give a 360° of movement control of the object while the Dual Soft Joystick and Buttons interfaces are limited to

---

[1] The software was developed using Demo_TiltBall as the starting point.

moving an object up, down, left, right, and diagonally. The Tilt Sensors interface uses the device's built-in tilt sensor and the tilt of the device to control the direction and speed of the object. Additionally, the Soft Joystick presents a wide circle containing a smaller circle in the center as shown in Fig. 2(a). This interface directs the object to where the smaller circle is positioned within the larger circle. The speed of object movement is computed by the distance of the smaller circle to the center of the joystick. Maximum speed is reached when the smaller circle touches the circumference of the joystick. The Buttons interface is maybe the most commonly seen interface for displacement control, see Fig. 2(c). It functions simply by moving the object in the direction of the pressed button. When pressing two buttons, such as right+up, movement is diagonal in the up-right direction. Finally, the Dual Soft Joystick interface is composed of two Soft Joysticks, as seen in Fig. 2(b). The left joystick moves the object up-down while the right joystick moves the object left-right. Similarly to the Buttons interface, when using both joysticks simultaneously, the object moves in a diagonal direction.

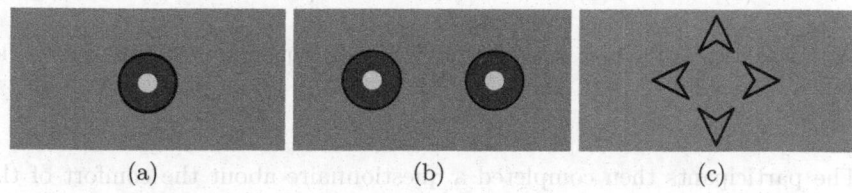

(a)   (b)   (c)

Fig. 2. Displacement interfaces: (a) Soft Joystick, (b) Dual Soft Joystick control, (c) Updown-right-left buttons.

The flow of the application is shown in Fig. 3. First, there was a setup state where the user chose the movement method to use during the trials. Users were asked to try the movement method using a test mode before starting the experiment. This allowed them to become familiar with the input methods. When the test ends the application returns to the setting state. This was followed by the experimental state, where the users completed five movement patterns or paths with each interface. Each path completed is consider a trial. See Fig. 4. The name of each path was given after its shape or directions they follow (N-North, S-South, E-East, W-West).

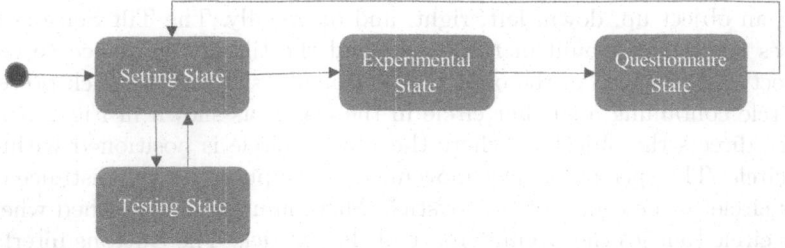

Fig. 3. Flow chart of the application showing how each state interacts with the next one.

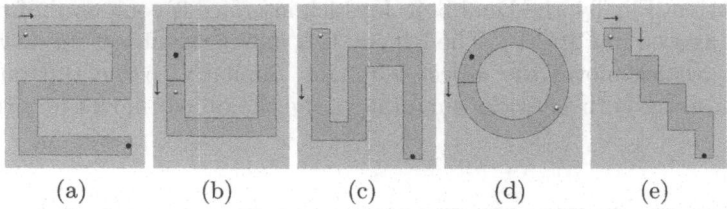

| (a) | (b) | (c) | (d) | (e) |

Fig. 4. Paths used in the user study: (a) ESWSE, (b) Square, (c) SENES, (d) Circle, (e) Stairs.

The participants then completed a questionnaire about the comfort of the displacement method after finishing with each input method. Lastly, data were collected, and the users were then directed to either the setting state to choose the next interface method to continue the experiment or to exit if they completed all interfaces. Each participant complete the five path trials with each displacement method.

The experiment interface was presented in a View panel where the participants could see and control an object – a virtual ball. There was a starting point (where the object originally starts), a path to follow, and a goal point. At the bottom, there was a panel with the input method for controlling the movement. Figure 5 shows a screenshot of the application layout during a demo run. The task involved controlling the object by moving it from the starting point to a goal point and returning to the starting point. The device vibrated each time the object touched the path borders while the object is inside the path. When the object completed the out-and-back movement, a sound was emitted and a dialog appeared indicating the beginning of the next trial, which started after the user pressed "OK".

The timing of the trial began when the experiment state started and ended when the object touched the goal point on its way back. The logged data for each trial contained the method of displacement control, the time per trial, the optimal time for each path, the number of times the ball hit the path wall, the time the object was outside the path, the percentage of time the object was outside the path, and a set of coordinates tracking the ball movement. Notably,

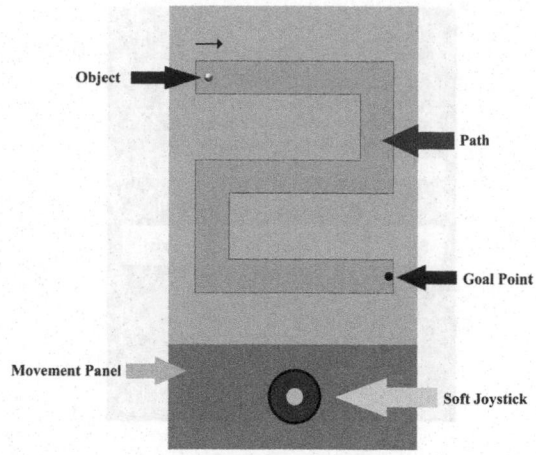

Fig. 5. Experiment state interface using Soft Joystick.

this percentage of time the object was outside the path was calculated by dividing the time outside the path by the time to complete the path multiplied by 100. The optimal path of each path is defined as the fastest time the object can complete each path following a line in the middle of the path.

After the five trials were completed with a chosen displacement method, the interface entered a questionnaire state where the participant indicated from 0 to 10 how comfortable they felt using the method, with 10 being the most comfortable (Fig. 6). The users saved their results and either went back to the setup state to continue the experiment with another displacement interface or exit the application. When they finished all interfaces, after closing the app, they answer a set of questions about the procedure.

2.3 Procedure

For the procedure, we ensured each participant understood the purpose of the experiment, what to do/expect, how long it would take for them to complete the experiment and which group they belonged to (see design section for a description of each participant group). They were asked to do one practice test with each interface so as feel comfortable with the displacement method. Participants were assigned to a group (for counterbalancing) and started the experiment with no breaks in between. When they finished the five trials on each input method, they saved the data by clicking a save button and continued with the next interface until they were done. After finishing all trials, participants indicated which method they liked the most and which one they felt would become the most practical after additional practice. The experiment took about 20 min per

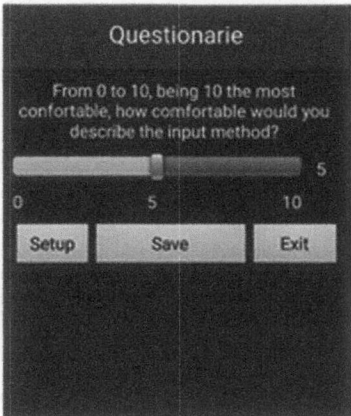

Fig. 6. Questionnaire state.

participant to use the four input methods. We did not allow trial repetitions or incomplete experiments when performing the analysis. Figure 7 shows an example of a participant performing the experiment using the Dual Soft Joystick interface.

2.4 Design

The user study was a 4 × 5 within-subjects design with the following independent variables and levels:

- Displacement method: Soft Joystick, Dual Soft Joystick, up-down-right-left Buttons, Tilt Sensors
- Path: ESWSE, Square, SENES, Circle, Stairs.

In addition, we gathered subjective responses at the end with a questionnaire asking participants to indicate from 0 to 10 how comfortable they found each displacement method (higher scores better). Also, participants indicated their preferred method and the method they felt would work best after sufficient practice. The experiment took about 20 min per participant.

The dependent variables were time per trial (seconds), the number of wall hits per trial, the efficiency of each trial (%) defined in Eq. 1, and the percentage of out-of-path movement time for each trial (%).

$$Efficiency = \frac{OptimalTime}{Laptime} \times 100 \qquad (1)$$

Participants were divided into four groups to counterbalance the testing order, thereby cancelling the learning effects using a balanced Latin square. The first group used the input methods in the following order: Tilt Sensor, Soft Joystick, Buttons, and Dual Soft Joystick. The second group used the order Buttons, Tilt Sensor, Dual Soft Joystick, and Soft Joystick. The third group used

Fig. 7. A Participant performing the experiment using Dual Soft Joystick in path ESWSE.

the interfaces in the reverse order of the first group, while the last one used them in the reversed order of the second group. The total number of trials was 240 (= 12 participants × 4 displacement methods × 5 paths).

3 Result and Discussion

3.1 Time per Trial

The grand mean for time per trial was 26.0 s. Most trials (81 out of 240) took between 15.7 and 22.0 s to complete when 11.1 s was the optimal time average. Then, the effects of displacement method and path were statistically significant on the time per trial as expected, ($F_{3,24} = 5.78, p < .005$) and ($F_{4,32} = 20.57, p < .0001$) respectively. Additionally, the overall mean time for Tilt Sensor was 22.8 s having the fastest average of time per trial. The second fastest was reported by Buttons with an average of 23.50 s, followed by Soft Joystick with 26.3 s, and lastly Dual Soft Joysticks with 31.51 s. Thus, Tilt Sensor was 2.8% faster than Buttons and 27.5% faster than the slowest one. Figure 9 shows the mean time per trial (s) on each different displacement method.

It was observed that the time per trial on each path showed a similar behavior with all four displacement methods. Buttons and Tilt Sensors were the two fastest methods per path with the exception of the Circle path where the Buttons and Dual Soft Joystick were slowest. This result was interesting since both methods of movement control (Buttons and Dual Soft Joystick), as part of their intrinsic characteristics, can only control the object in a specific direction (right, left, up, down, and diagonals). Also, the circular shape of this path might affect the time participants take using those two movement interfaces. On the other hand, Tilt Sensors and Soft Joystick can direct the object in any direction from 0 to 360°, making them easier to control the object in a circular path Fig. 4(d). Figure 8 shows the time per trial (s) of each different movement control interface for each path.

A Bonferroni-Dunn post hoc test ($p < .05$) showed that Buttons-Dual Soft Joystick and Dual Soft Joystick-Tilt Sensor comparisons were the only significantly different pairs in terms of the time per trial. In addition, the times of ESWSE-Stair and Circle-Stair were the only two path pairs that differed significantly.

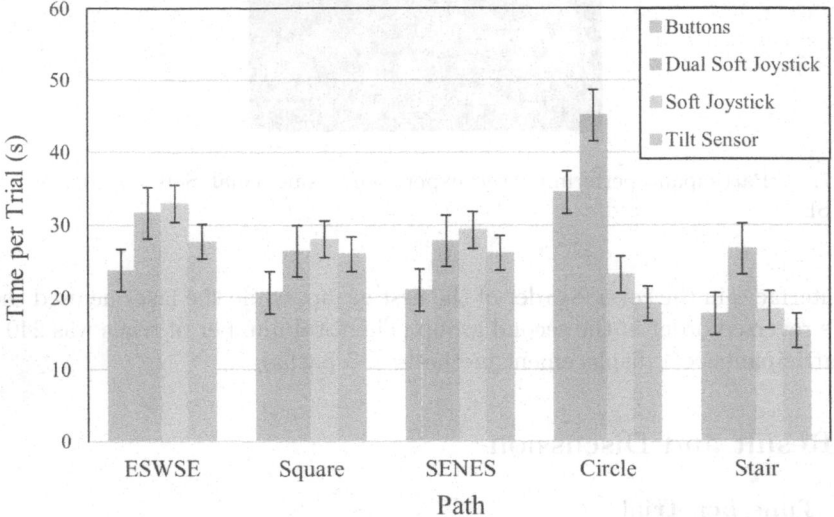

Fig. 8. Time to complete each trial (s) per displacement interface. Error bars show ±1 SD.

Figure 9 shows trace examples of participant trials. Figure 9(a) shows the fastest time of all trials made in 9.37 s by participant 8 in the Stair path using Soft Joystick. Figure 9(b) shows an average time of a trial by participant 8. It is interesting to observe an example of the use of Dual Soft Joystick on the Circle path. We can see that the control of the object become more complicated in circular shaped paths taking more time for the participant to complete the path and worsening the overall results. This example was completed in 23.9 s with 10 wall hits and 1.46% out-of-path movement. On the other hand, Fig. 9(c) shows the result of the same participant in the same path using Soft Joystick showing a better result of time, 14.3 s, 0% out-of-path movement, and smooth control of the object.

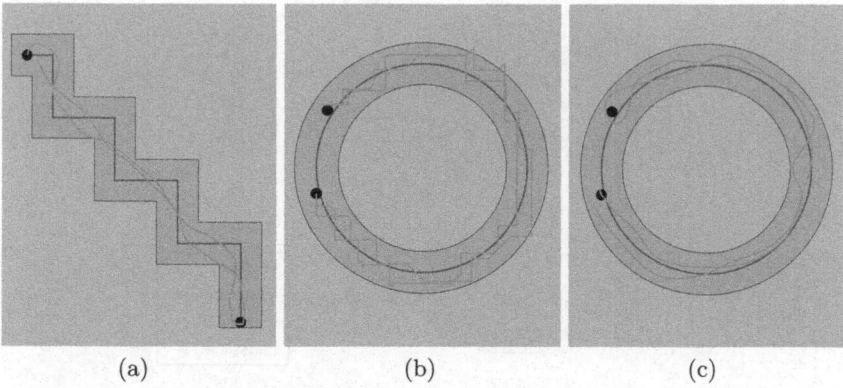

(a)   (b)   (c)

Fig. 9. Trace examples of a participant's trials. (a) Trace of the fastest trial, (b) Trace of trial in Circle path performed using Dual Soft Joystick, and (c) Trace showing a trial in Circle performed using Soft Joystick.

3.2 Number of Wall Hits

The study consisted of 240 trials with 40 trials per displacement method. The total number of times the object touched the wall (border of a path) was 701. Only 67 of this number happened with Buttons, representing 10% of the total. Dual Joystick reported 142 missed paths, which represents 20% of the total. Tilt Sensors and Soft Joystick reported 31% and 39% of the times the object touched the wall, 218 and 274 times respectively. See Fig. 10.

Number of Wall Hits per Trial. The grand mean number of wall hits per trial was 2.92 while most trials (93 out of 240) had between 0–2 wall hits. Analyzing the effects of the independent variables on number of wall hits, both (Displacement Method, Path) were statistically significant as expected ($F_{3,24} = 19.4, p < .0001$) and ($F_{4,32} = 7.52, p < .0005$) respectively. Buttons had the best performance, only touching the borders with a mean of 1.12 times per trial, and it is followed by Dual Soft Joystick with a mean of 2.37 times per trial. On the other hand, Tilt Sensors and Soft Joystick reported 3.63 and 4.57 wall hit times per trial. Thus, Buttons performed 75.5% better than Soft Joystick and 52.8% better than Dual Joystick as second best. See Fig. 11.

Over the five paths, it is interesting to point out that Buttons and Dual Soft Joystick performed similarly again in the number of missed paths per trial. Similarly, to time per trial, Buttons and Dual Soft Joysticks have a representative peak of missed paths on trial number four, which has a circular shape, as already mentioned. On the other hand, it is interesting how Tilt Sensor behaved over the trials in average. This method steadily decreased its number of wall hits per trial with a significant decrements in the Circle path and went up again as its usual values in the Stair path. Soft Joystick performed poorly when analysing each path separately. It decreased the wall hits for the middle paths but started

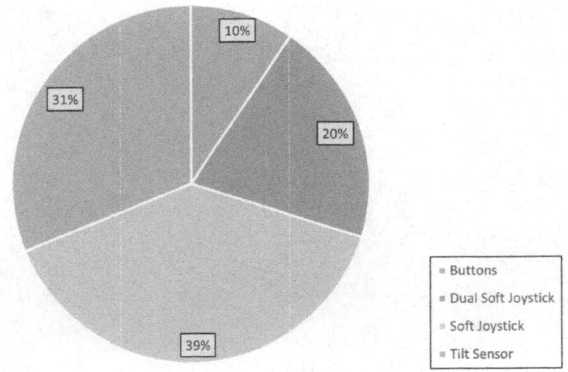

Fig. 10. The number of times the object missed the path as a percentage of the total.

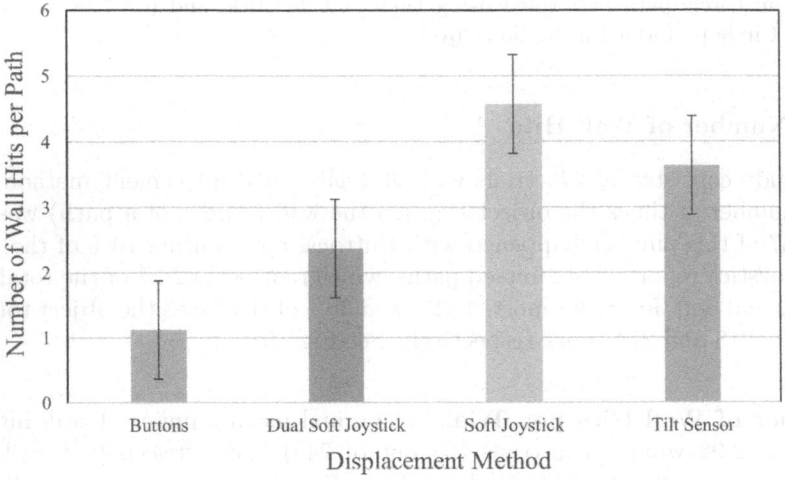

Fig. 11. Mean of the number of wall hits by displacement method. Error bars show ± 1 *SE*.

to increase at Circle path. Overall, both, Buttons and Dual Soft Joystick, show improvements in the first three paths while Soft Joystick and Tilt Sensor perform better in the middle path and worst in the first and last path. See Fig. 12.

After conducting a Bonferroni-Dunn post hoc test ($p < .05$) it was shown that the pairs Buttons-Soft Joystick, Buttons-Tilt Sensor, and Dual Soft Joystick-Soft Joystick comparisons were significantly different. Additionally, the wall hits in the path pairs Square-Circle, Square-Stair, SENES-Circle, and SENES-Stair were significantly different.

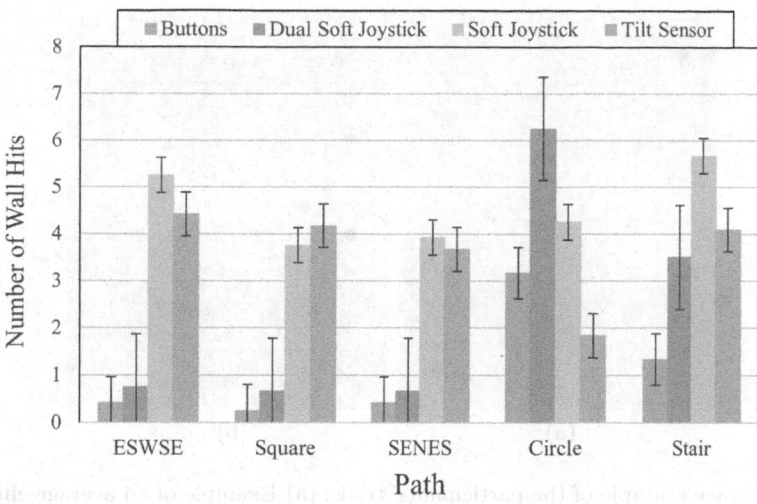

Fig. 12. The number of wall hits per trial by displacement method. Error bars show ±1 *SD*.

3.3 Efficiency

When analysing the efficiency of all displacement methods Tilt Sensor was removed because its results were not comparatively representative with the other methods. The results show extreme values when comparing the time participant took to complete the trials with respect to the possible optimal time for each path. Finally, most results of Tilt Sensor when analysing the efficiency are almost 0%.

The grand mean for efficiency per trial was 51.0% with most trials (63 out of 240) between 8% and 23% efficient. For both independent variables, displacement method and path, the effect on efficiency was statistically significant with $(F_{3,24} = 88.3, p < .0001)$ and $(F_{4,32} = 53.2, p < .0001)$, respectively. The average efficiency for Buttons was 58.8% which represents the best overall performance. The second one was reported by Soft Joystick with 52.5%, followed by Dual Soft Joystick with 43.9%. Thus, Buttons was 34% more effective than Dual Soft Joystick and 12% more effective than Soft Joystick.

Figure 13 shows trace examples of participant trials. Figure 13(a) shows an example of a trial with average efficiency performed by participant 4 using Soft Joystick and obtaining 48.3% of effectiveness with two wall hits. In addition, Fig. 13(b) shows the best efficiency obtained in the experiment by participant 9. It is interesting to highlight that this trial broke the estimate of optimal time of the Square path (16.5 s) using Buttons in 15.3 s with no wall hits – a perfect trial! Both had 0% out-of-path movement.

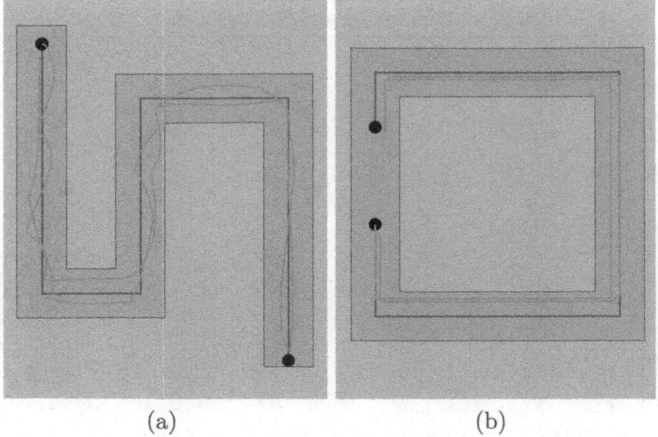

(a)   (b)

Fig. 13. Trace example of the participants' trials. (a) Example of an average efficiency trial, (b) Trace of the trial with best efficiency.

It was observed that the efficiency on all four different methods was decreasing overall. Soft Joystick seems to be more conservative about the effectiveness and stayed balanced around 50% on each different path. On the other hand, Dual Soft Joystick and Buttons showed similar results with their highest efficiency numbers in path number two and then a constant decrease with their lowest number in path number four. This also arguments that these two displacement methods do not perform well with circular shapes. See Fig. 14.

When analysing each pair of displacement method with respect to their efficiency conducting a Bonferroni-Dunn post hoc test it was found that the pairs Buttons-Dual Soft Joystick, Buttons-Tilt Sensor, Dual Soft Joystick-Tilt Sensor, and Soft Joystick-Tilt Sensor were significantly different between them. Similarly, the pair of paths ESWSE-Circle, Square-Circle, Square-Stair, and SENES-Circle were significantly different of each other. We can see how Circle path showed a difference with respect of most paths which is an interesting result to further study.

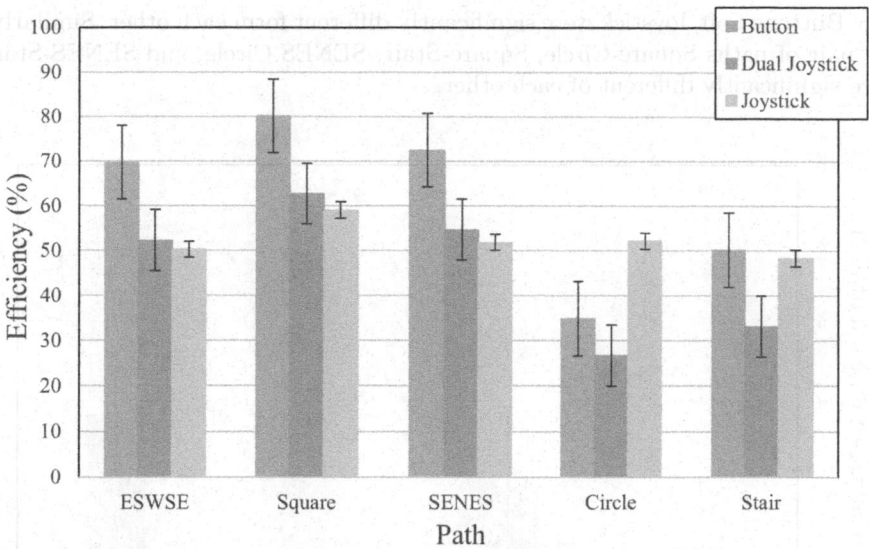

Fig. 14. The efficiency per trial by displacement method. Error bars show ±1 *SD*.

3.4 Percentage of Out-of-Path Movement Time

The grand mean of percentage of out-of-path movement time was 3.5% with the great majority (188 out of 240 trials) between 0% and 4.9% of out-of-path movement. The displacement method with best results in average was Buttons with only 0.4% of out-of-path movement while Soft Joystick reported an average of 7.9%. Dual Soft Joystick and Tilt Sensor presented similar results with 2.2% and 3.7%. Thus, Buttons was the most accurate overall being 95.5% more accurate than Soft Joystick (with the worst results) and 84.2% more accurate than Dual Soft Joystick. See Fig. 15.

There is a notary difference between Buttons and Dual Joystick over the five trials. After analyse the effects of displacement method and paths on the percentage of out-of-path movement, both were statistically significant ($F_{3,24} = 4.20, p < .05$) and ($F_{4,32} = 6.99, p < .0005$) respectively. The first method had an overall almost zero percent of out-of-path movement in all paths with zero in ESWSE and Stair. On the other hand, Soft Joystick oscillated between percentages above 10% and 3.7% as the lowest result in Square. The other two methods have a similar tendency over the five paths, they start decreasing and reported a spike in path number four and finished with a low percentage of out-of-path movement. It is worth highlighting that Buttons and Dual Soft Joystick had 0% average of out-of-path movement in two of the five paths for all trials. Figure 16 shows the overall percentages of out-of-path movement path on each trial.

When analysing each pair of displacement method with respect to their out-of-path movement conducting a Bonferroni-Dunn post hoc test it was found that only Buttons-Soft Joystick were significantly different form each other. Similarly, the pair of paths Square-Circle, Square-Stair, SENES-Circle, and SENES-Stair were significantly different of each other.

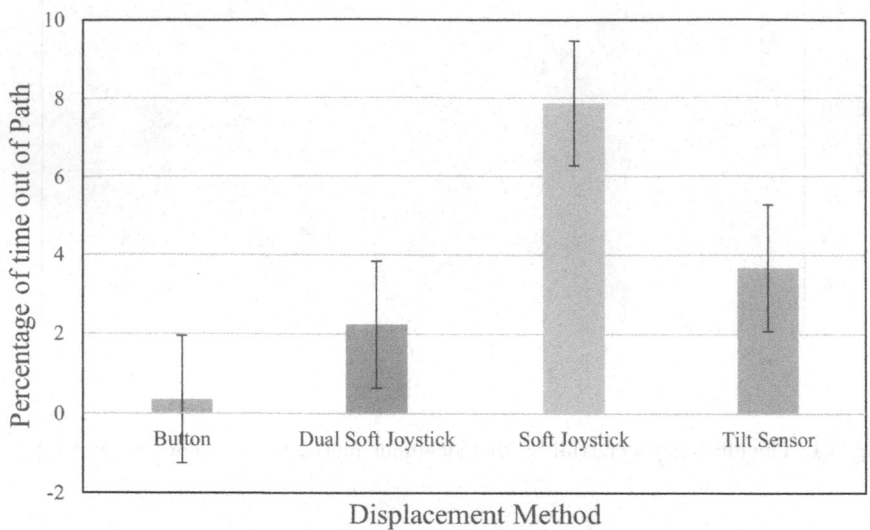

Fig. 15. Out-of-path movement (%) by displacement method. Error bars show ±1 *SE*.

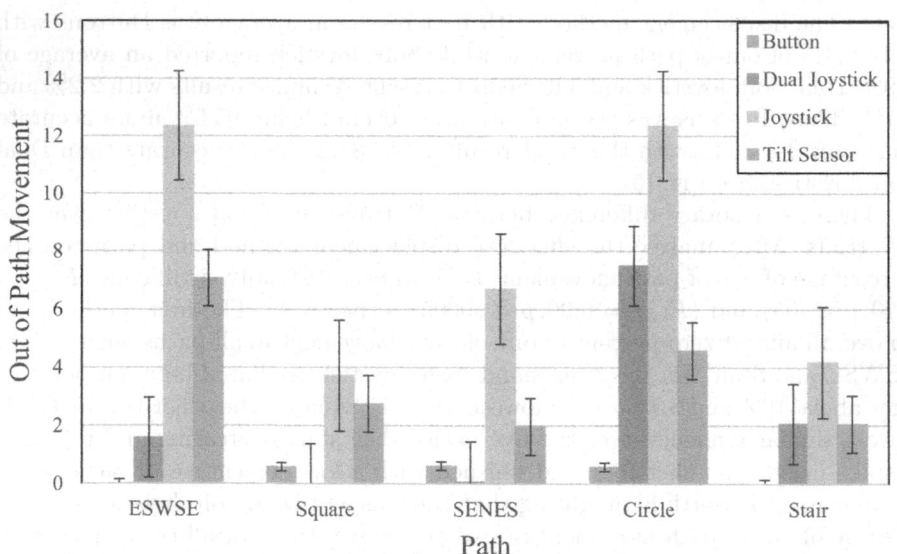

Fig. 16. Out-of-path movement (%) per trial by displacement method. Error bars show ±1 *SD*.

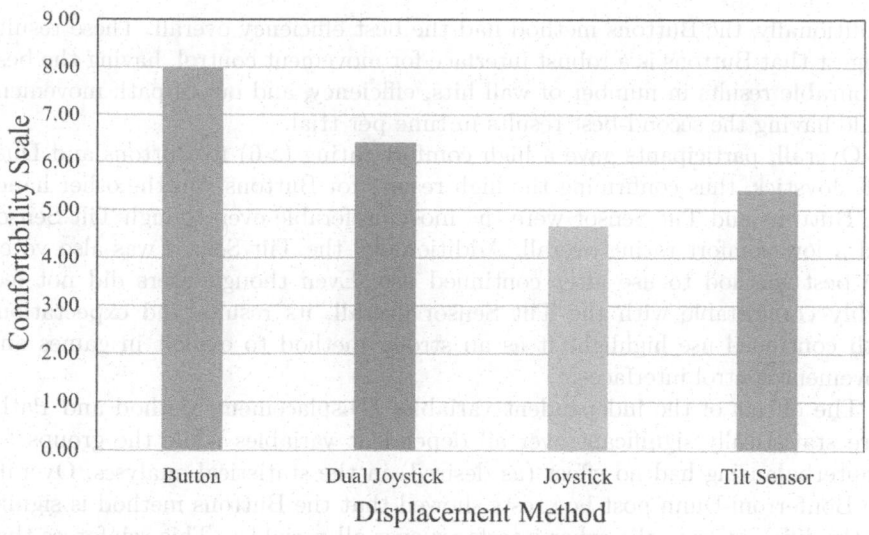

Fig. 17. Subjective comfort by displacement method.

3.5 Questionnaire

Each participant was asked to complete a questionnaire after they completed the five trials with each displacement method as well as they complete the experiment. The questionnaire asked how comfortable the participants felt from 0 to 10 with each method used right after they finished the five trials with each method. It also asked after the experiment ended which method they prefer and which method they felt will become better to use after time with practice. The most comfortable method was Buttons with a mean of 8.8 out of 10. It is followed by Dual Soft Joystick and Tilt Sensor with a mean of 6.4 and 5.42, respectively. Lastly, the least comfortable interface overall was Soft Joystick with a mean of 4.7 out of 10. See Fig. 17.

When analysing the preferences of each participant, Buttons and Tilt Sensor were the ones most preferable with five votes each. Then, Tilt Sensor was vote as the best method to used after time of practice followed by Buttons and Soft Joystick with three votes each.

4   Conclusions

A user study was conducted comparing four interfaces that control the movement of an object in mobile devices (Soft Joystick, Up-down-right-left Buttons, Tilt Sensors, and Dual Soft Joystick). The study revealed that Tilt Sensors (fastest time per trial method) was 2.8% faster than Buttons (the second fastest) in time per trial. On the other hand, the Buttons method had the lowest number of wall hits overall, outperforming Tilt Sensors as the third method with less wall hits.

Additionally, the Buttons method had the best efficiency overall. These results suggest that Buttons is a robust interface for movement control, having the best favourable results in number of wall hits, efficiency, and out-of-path movement while having the second-best results in time per trial.

Overall, participants gave a high comfort rating (>6) to Buttons and Dual Soft Joystick, thus confirming the high results for Buttons. On the other hand, the Buttons and Tilt Sensor were the most preferable even though Tilt Sensor had a low comfort rating overall. Additionally, the Tilt Sensor was also voted the best method to use after continued use. Even though users did not feel highly comfortable with the Tilt Sensor overall, its results and expectations with continued use highlight it as an strong method to exploit in games and movement control interfaces.

The effects of the independent variables (Displacement Method and Path) were statistically significant over all dependent variables while the groups for counterbalancing had no effect (as desired) in the statistical analyses. Overall, the Bonferroni-Dunn post hoc tests showed that the Buttons method is significantly different from the other interfaces over all variables. This reinforces that Buttons should be considered an irreplaceable option for displacement methods in different environments.

The study also revealed interesting patterns for the displacement interfaces. For example, Buttons and Dual Joystick performed similarly over all dependent variables in different path shapes while they showed significant differences in half of the dependent variables. This similarity is mostly seen as degraded performance in the Circle path while the Soft Joystick and Tilt Sensors performed consistently in all paths. These performance issues in the Circle path with respect to movement-control with the Buttons and Dual Soft Joystick raise questions regarding to their utility in different path shapes. Additionally, the post hoc analyses showed that the results with the Circle path are significantly different from the other paths in the study. This noteworthy observation could lead to future changes in evaluation strategies. Future work could examine participant performance on a greater variety of path shapes to determine which interface is better for each path shape. Furthermore, future studies should include additional methods of displacement control, more complicated scenarios, and consider a transition from 2D to 3D where a combination of different methods can bring new perspectives and opportunities to the game-development industry.

References

1. Baldauf, M., Fröhlich, P., Adegeye, F., Suette, S.: Investigating on-screen gamepad designs for smartphone-controlled video games. ACM Trans. Multimed. Comput. Commun. Appl. **12**(1s), 1–21 (2015)
2. Browne, K., Anand, C.: An empirical evaluation of user interfaces for a mobile video game. Entertainment Comput. **3**, 1–10 (2012). https://doi.org/10.1016/j.entcom.2011.06.001
3. Chu, K., Wong, C.Y.: Mobile input devices for gaming experience. In: 2011 International Conference on User Science and Engineering (i-USEr), pp. 83–88. IEEE, New York (2011). https://doi.org/10.1109/iUSEr.2011.6150542

4. Constantin, C.I., MacKenzie, I.S.: Tilt-controlled mobile games: velocity-control vs. position-control. In: 2014 IEEE Games Media Entertainment, pp. 1–7. IEEE, New York (2014). https://doi.org/10.1109/GEM.2014.7048091
5. Cuaresma, J., MacKenzie, I.S.: A comparison between tilt-input and facial tracking as input methods for mobile games. In: 2014 IEEE Games Media Entertainment, pp. 1–7. IEEE, New York (2014). https://doi.org/10.1109/GEM.2014.7048080
6. MacKenzie, I.S., Teather, R.J.: FittsTilt: the application of Fitts' law to tilt-based interaction. In: Proceedings of the 7th Nordic Conference on Human-Computer Interaction - NordiCHI 2012, p. 568. ACM, New York (2012). https://doi.org/10. 1145/2399016.2399103
7. Stoffregen, T.A., Chen, Y.C., Koslucher, F.C.: Motion control, motion sickness, and the postural dynamics of mobile devices. Exp. Brain Res. **232**(4), 1389–1397 (2014)
8. Teather, R.J., Roth, A., MacKenzie, I.S.: Tilt-Touch synergy: input control for "dual-analog" style mobile games. Entertainment Comput. **21**, 33–43 (2017)
9. Zhang, D., Cai, Z., Chen, K., Nebel, B.: A game controller based on multiple sensors. In: Proceedings of the International Conference on Advances in Computer Entertainment Technology, ACE 2009, pp. 375–378. ACM, New York (2009). https://doi. org/10.1145/1690388.1690464

Assessing the Comprehensiveness of the Co-operative Performance Metric: A Mixed-Method Analysis Using Portal 2

Gregory Gorman [ID] and Conor Linehan[(⊠)] [ID]

University College Cork, Cork T12 K8AF, Ireland
ggorman@ucc.ie

Abstract. The Co-operative Performance Metric (CPM) is the only existing tool for evaluating co-located game play experiences but has not yet been extensively studied. To observe how effectively the CPM captured co-located and co-operative player behaviour, this study investigates the comprehensiveness of the CPM by comparing a CPM analysis of co-located gameplay with a much more time-consuming video ethnographic analysis. Five pairs of participants played the puzzle game *Portal 2* for one hour, while their interactions were video recorded and analysed. Results indicate that the CPM successfully captures many co-operative behaviours relating to player experience, with some exceptions. The most important missing components were the social effects; 1) prior experience playing the game, and 2) whether players were friends. Thus, with some small modifications, the CPM can function as a quick but comprehensive assessment of co-operative player behaviour, social effects, and game genre.

Keywords: Co-located gameplay · Co-operative gameplay · Evaluating co-operative game design · Mechanics · Dynamics and aesthetics · Video ethnography

1 Introduction

Co-located play refers to two or more players occupying the same physical space while playing a game together. We do not yet have well-validated instruments for measuring and visualising the quality of co-located player experiences. One promising tool that could achieve this is the Co-operative Performance Metric (CPM) [1]. The CPM is a brief and easy to administer tool that allows game designers and researchers to describe co-located player behaviour, and to link the frequency of different behaviours to features of game design and player experience [1]. Game designers can use the tool to evaluate whether their designs are promoting the intended player experiences, and to assess what might need to be changed to create a desired player experience.

In the small number of studies where it has been used, the CPM has evidenced both utility and construct validity. For example, in a pilot study for the development of the CPM [1], the authors demonstrated that varying game designs were reliably scored as distinct based on observed behaviours, indicating different experiences for player

X. Fang (Ed.): HCII 2022, LNCS 13334, pp. 22–39, 2022.
https://doi.org/10.1007/978-3-031-05637-6_2

groups based on game design. Secondly, in a study of the platform game 'Geometry Friends' (2015), the CPM, and in particular, in the metric component 'worked out strategies', reliably discriminated between varying extents of cooperative behaviours that were influenced by how challenging level designs were and whether levels necessitated cooperation to complete [2]. Emmerich & Masuch [3] utilised components within the CPM components to detect discrete patterns of cooperative behaviour in a 2D platform game, where interdependence was manipulated. Findings suggest that interdependent game designs resulted in better communication and less frustration, and shared control schemes increased frustration and lowered perceived competence and autonomy [3], with each of the conditions being reflected in distinct CPM scores.

Beyond the mentioned studies, the CPM has not been extensively evaluated and since the CPM is relatively brief and simple, it is possible that a CPM-based evaluation of a game may miss a lot of the rich character of interpersonal interaction during co-located and co-operative gameplay. Thus, this paper sets out to examine whether a CPM analysis comprehensively captures data on interpersonal interaction. We do so by comparing results of a CPM analysis with those derived from a much more detailed video ethnography. Additionally, this research will comment on the strengths and limitations of the CPM and suggest potential improvements.

2 Background

To better understand the factors impacting player behaviour/experience and the results of both the CPM and video ethnographic analyses, the following section will review literature on; 1) game design, 2) puzzle game design, 3) co-operative gameplay and player experience, 4) social effects, 5) the Co-operative Performance Metric.

2.1 Game Design

Games are comprised of interaction patterns, wherein implemented game elements produce intended in-game behaviours and experiences [4], and many scholars have attempted to catalogue specific game elements to indicate the effects they have on player behaviour. For example, games have been described in terms of design patterns [5], narrative [6], skill scaffolding [7], design features [8] and lenses [9].

'The Mechanics, Dynamics and Aesthetics (MDA) Framework' [10] is useful for analysing game design by ignoring distracting details, while still accounting for numerous game elements that capture general player activity and player affect. The MDA framework separates games into hierarchical elements constituting player experience [10], breaking games down to 1) their core gameplay mechanics (the obstacles, objects, abilities, rules and goals), 2) how they combine to form in-game dynamics/behaviours and; 3) how together they shape aesthetics [or player experiences; see Fig. 1]. This framework was utilised in this study to supplement the video ethnographic analysis with compact descriptions of Portal 2 game design, and player behaviour/experience.

Fig. 1. Game elements/mechanics culminate to impact player behaviour and experience [10].

2.2 Puzzle Game Design

Since *Portal 2*, a co-operative first-person puzzle game is examined in this study, it is important to understand how puzzle game genre and related game designs impact player behaviour. Previous research has analysed and documented common features in the design of puzzles. Iacovides et al. [11] suggest that puzzle games create their unique player experience through presenting challenges that encourage problem solving behaviours, such as breakdowns, breakthroughs, trial and error and hypothesizing. They suggest that a 'breakdown' begins when a player does not know how to progress or solve a puzzle. In attempting to surmount the obstacle, a player usually begins problem solving, i.e. 'trial and error,' to see if anything of consequence occurs from actions taken, 'hypothesizing' a solution when players increase their understanding of game mechanics which is followed by a 'breakthrough' once a new strategy is adopted and a problem is solved [11].

Lundgren et al. [12] described 7 aesthetics as gameplay ideals (i.e. gameplay that produces a type of player experience), 2 of which, *camaraderie* and *emergence* could aid understanding of how co-operative puzzle games are experienced by players. *Camaraderie* refers to how players work together to achieve mutual goals while adopting a shared perspective and *emergence* refers to consistent rules enable players to understand and utilize to progress. Bergström et al. [13] expanded on the aesthetic of *camaraderie* and associated co-operative gameplay dynamics such as: coordination, strategising, playful mischief and 'guilting' (to stop certain activities) [13].

2.3 Co-operative Gameplay and Player Experience

Co-operative gameplay relies on game design patterns that establish how the game elements cause intended co-operative interactions among players [14]. For example, Beznosyk et al. [15] identified typical co-operative game mechanics in casual co-operative games and identified them as either being 'closely-coupled games' or 'loosely coupled games'. Closely-coupled games' relied on game mechanics such as limited resources, complementary abilities and interaction with the same object, while 'loosely coupled games' utilised shared puzzles that were solved individually, or shared goals while acting independently to complete them. To illustrate the impact of co-operative game design on player experience and interaction, Beznosyk et al. [15] compared several player outcomes for closely and loosely coupled games which led to different reported levels of enjoyment and in game behaviours [15].

Additionally, game design patterns impact how players communicate to accomplish goals, as seen in previous work on co-operative first person shooters that found information is often communicated within the virtual space itself using the in-game objects, and interface [i.e. visual pings highlighting a point of interest; [14, 16], or if players are co-located, through bodily gesturing and pointing [14]. However, much of the communication was verbal (oftentimes with the use of tactical "call-outs" and was enhanced through pinging locations [14, 17].

In our study, we anticipate that *Portal 2* will adhere to a closely coupled game design, with frequent verbal communication that makes use of pinging. Beyond game design, the social context may change how a game is played. We refer to social contexts influencing player experience/behavior as 'social effects'.

2.4 Social Effects

Social effects refer to behavioural outcomes that are impacted by social contexts and are an often-overlooked aspect of player experience frameworks [18]. Poels et al. [18] developed a broad categorization of player experience, that included 'social presence', which comparatively, the CPM does not incorporate [1]. Additional considerations known to impact player experience/behavior are the history the player has with the game, the attitude of the player (casual or hard-core) and whether or not players are friends [19]. As such whether pairs of players are friends or have previous experience playing the game are considered in this study.

2.5 The Co-operative Performance Metric

Numerous techniques have been developed to evaluate 'Game User Experience' (GUX). However, the Co-operative Performance Metric (CPM) is one of the only measures that attempts to evaluate GUX by gauging co-located behaviour to evaluate co-operative game designs by analysing recorded game sessions [1]. To create the CPM, Seif El-Nasr et al. [1] conducted an analysis on the design of popular co-operative video games at the time and based CPM components on the identified co-operative game designs and co-operative designs identified by Rocha et al. [20] before them. The pilot study was conducted utilizing the CPM and attempted to gauge the impact to cooperative game designs had on player behavior from documented player responses. The CPM succeeded in displaying divergent frequencies, means, and confidence intervals of observed player behaviours between games, which enabled discussion about the influence of co-operative game designs on behaviour [1].

Despite the merits in successfully delineating different player behaviours and experiences as seen in previous studies [1–3], there are limitations in the pilot study [1]. Firstly, in relying on broad co-operative design differences between game genres to illustrate the utility of the metric, it is possible that the CPM loses data that is specific to game genre, since genre influences game designs and player experience. Secondly, the study inconsistently had 2 to 4 players per session, meaning social effects were not controlled (i.e. certain behaviour/player experience outcomes that occur because of social effects). Further indicating potential shortcomings in the metric was Emmerich & Masuch's [3] research which combined CPM with other metric components on social behaviours which the CPM remits. In building from Seif El-Nasr et al.'s study [1], this research will only examine one game (and game type) along with more fixed social contexts by only having two people play together at one time. This study aims to: 1) evaluate the comprehensiveness of the CPM by comparing output to a video ethnographic analysis, 2) comment on the strengths and limitations of the CPM and, 3) suggest improvements to the metric.

3   Methods

3.1   Participants

10 participants (9 men, 1 woman; M age = 23, SD = 4.1) were conveniently sampled from a university and were recruited with in-class announcements, with the selection criteria being that they played at least one hour of video games per week. Participants were assigned into pairs using a random number generator. There were a total of 5 trials, with each trial consisting of two participants. To assess social effects, participants' were identified as either having previous experience playing *Portal 2* or not and each pair was identified as either being friends or not (see Table 1).

Table 1. Descriptive characteristics of participant pairs in each trial.

Trials	Categories of experience and friendship	Genders
Trial 1	One experienced and one inexperienced participant	Two men
	Who are friends	
Trial 2	Two inexperienced participants	Two men
	Who are not friends	
Trial 3	Two inexperienced participants	Two men
	Who are friends	
Trial 4	Two inexperienced participants	One man and one woman
	Who are friends	
Trial 5	Experienced and inexperienced participant	Two men
	Who are not friends	

3.2   Portal 2

Portal 2 [21] is a first-person puzzle platformer game from Valve which supports co-operative multiplayer. In co-operative mode, players inhabit the robots P-Body and Atlas and embark to solve physics-based puzzles set as a series of obstacle courses.

3.3   Study Design

This experiment was set up in a quasi-natural environment. Two chairs were placed in front of a desktop computer within a computer lab and individuals were seated and given a joy pad to play *Portal 2* for an hour within a computer lab, while their backs faced the camera. Before recording, players were given 5 min to become familiar with the controls and recording began at the start of the first co-operative level.

3.4 The Co-operative Performance Metric

Recordings were first analysed using the CPM. The CPM is a tool to detect co-operative game design impact on player experience by observing co-located behaviours that are influenced by game designs [1].

These scored observed behaviours are: 1) Laughter and Excitement Together: when players laugh simultaneously, express enjoyment or excitement at the same game event; 2) Worked Out Strategies: verbal expressions of plans and problem solving and navigating the game world together; 3) Helping: when players teach each other's how to play, use controls or save/rescue others and giving unreciprocated instruction on how to navigate the world/obstacle; 4) Global Strategies: events where players take different roles during gameplay that complement each other's responsibilities and abilities; 5) Waited for Each Other and; 6) Got in Each Other's Way: events where one player leads and the other lags behind, or when both players want to do different actions. An inter-rater agreement was performed in El-Nasr et al.'s (2010) pilot study and kappa values were produced; four of the CPM components had almost perfect agreements ranging from .84 (Helping) to .94 (Laughter and Excitement Together), and two of the CPM components had substantial agreements ranging from .69 (Worked Out Strategies) to .71 (Waited for Each Other) [22].

3.5 Video Ethnographic Analysis and the Supplementary MDA Analysis

There were two steps in the video ethnographic analysis; 1) an MDA analysis of the game in order to produce a concise description of the game context with which our participants were interacting, and 2) the analysis of players interacting with that game. The first author (GG) conducted the MDA analysis by playing through the first hour of the game 4 times with a friend, and writing out a formal MDA analysis after each playthrough. Gameplay was described according to Hunicke et al.'s [10] hierarchical elements of mechanics, dynamics and aesthetics which enabled the generation of descriptive patterns between gameplay and behaviour without overwhelming data. The broad description of gameplay was vital since there are currently no established methods for succinctly describing video games in a video ethnographic analysis.

Video ethnography observes people and technology in complex environments, to provide naturalistic (i.e. nonexperimental or quasi-experimental conditions) analyses of work and Human Technology Interaction [23]. Since co-operative co-located game play shares many characteristics as co-operative co-located work, this method was deemed appropriate to gather nuanced data on how social contexts and the video game being played impact behaviour. The use of recordings provides access to specific conduct, conversation, and participant engagement with technology, objects, and artefacts [24], which provides insight into how contextual artefacts can shape behaviour, therein obtaining nuanced findings to compare with the CPM results. This analysis broke down: conversation, actions, the context and time [see Fig. 2]. The video game dynamics and aesthetics that were coded for in the MDA analysis were used in the video ethnographic analysis. Game dynamics (reoccurring behaviours with game elements) were CAPITALISED and game aesthetics were *italicised*.

Conversation	Michael: We were struggling so much at the beginning... what's that doing? George: wait press it.. look these signals are corresponding to the button.. from X to dot..It looks like we have to go upstairs..What happens when I press that? Michael: I can go up and press that.... George: oh they were orange now blue they change colour, press it again. Yeah see... oh a timer?... what? Michael: So they all need to be clicked
Action	Both players EXPLORE, TRIAL & ERROR with mechanics and DISCOVER/ INVESTIGATE cause and effect.
Context	The introduction of a new mechanics brings both players to INVESTIGATE what the mechanics (buttons) do. Once they learn it is a timer, they quickly HYPOTHESIZE a correct solution *reasoning* and *emergence*
Time	11:55-13:51

Fig. 2. An example of trial 3 from the video ethnographic analysis, to demonstrate how conversation, in-game action/behaviour, context, and time were each documented across a horizontal table as they co-occur. The entireties of all trials were documented in this format.

3.6 Synthesizing Results

This mixed-methods analysis was designed to detect frequently occurring player dynamics that are shaped by both game design and social effects leading to diverging aesthetics/experiences in each of the paired participants. In order to synthesize results across both analyses, we compare and consolidate results from the CPM and video ethnographic analysis (which is facilitated with the MDA framework, see Fig. 3).

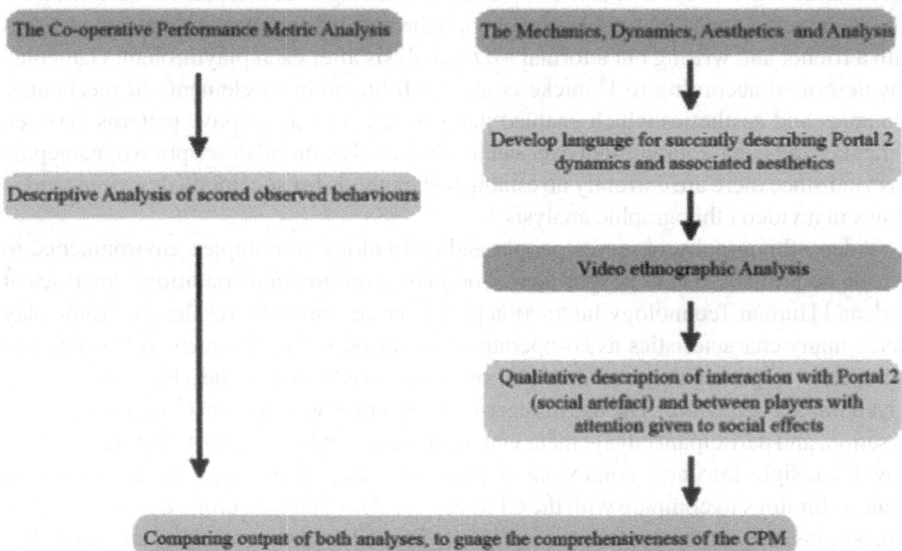

Fig. 3. Blue signifies the analyses, green the output, and the orange, the synthesis of outputs.

3.7 Ethics

Ethics was obtained from the School of Applied Psychology's Ethics Committee board on 18/02/2020. Once transcriptions were complete, the original video files had been deleted and only the transcript files were kept on encrypted university servers. Pseudonyms were given to participants to ensure anonymity in transcripts.

4 Results and Discussion

4.1 CPM Results

Video footage was scored by each individual pair according to the six CPM behavioural metrics, as seen in Table 2.

Table 2. Scores, means and standard deviations of each metric component across all trials.

	Laughter & Excitement together	Worked Out Strategies	Helping	Global Strategies	Waited for Each Other	Got in Each Other's Way
Trial 1	59	51	60	2	15	12
Trial 2	15	108	40	1	1	0
Trial 3	37	116	70	2	1	0
Trial 4	28	80	63	2	2	1
Trial 5	3	38	81	0	2	0
M	28.4	78.6	62.8	1.4	5.6	2.6
SD	15.0	34.2	23.2	0.5	5.9	5.3

The two highest scoring metrics are Worked Out Strategies (M = 78.6) and Helping (62.8), both of which successfully capture frequently occurring dynamics elicited by the game's design. The metric Worked Out Strategies captured when players navigated the world together or spoke aloud about it and how to solve a shared obstacle/puzzle. Helping mostly occurred with players unreciprocated instruction about the correct sequence of actions to take, which was particularly frequent if that player had prior experience of playing *Portal 2*, as seen in Trial 1 and Trial 5 scoring the higher in Helping than in Worked Out Strategies when pairing experienced players with inexperienced players. While the CPM was very functional in identifying Worked Out Strategies and had a very clear definition for it, the component of Helping was less clear in the original study whether a single instruction or a string of instructions are scored differently on the metric [1]. This analysis scored Helping with every conjunction used (e.g. Do X and then do Z after Y would count as three scores).

Laughter and Excitement Together was most prominent among friends with one player having experience of playing the game (Trial 1 scoring 59), as opposed to friends without experience scoring (Trial 3 scoring 37, and Trial 4 scoring 28). It was much lower amongst those who weren't friends (Trial 2 scoring 15) and was lowest among strangers when one player had experience and the other did not (Trial 5 scoring 3). These results indicated that behaviour was socially mediated, with both experience and friendship status playing important roles.

Global Strategies refer to in-game mechanics wherein player roles and abilities complement each other, and players strategize around that and scored low in this analysis since the game gave players identical abilities. Waited for Each Other and Got in each other's scored lowly and highlighted the lack of 'loss' condition or skill requirement, since problems could be overcome through instruction of a sequence of actions rather than waiting on a player if the game demanded high skill execution.

4.2 MDA Analysis

The aesthetics identified in the MDA analysis are repeatedly referred to throughout video ethnographic results, and described as a combination of behaviours/dynamics which are CAPITAISED, while the aesthetics are *italicised*. These aesthetics are:

Camaraderie: How players achieve more working as a group than individually. Especially important in forming this experience are MUTUAL GOALS and a SHARED PERSPECTIVE, although somewhat abstract when observing this game alone, it becomes more salient when considering research on 'closely-coupled games' or 'loosely coupled games' based on their co-operative game design, with reliably different experiences based on mechanics that require close team play, such as, INTERACTING WITH THE SAME OBJECT (which occurs in *Portal 2*) compared to distant teamplay when solving problems independently [15]. Given that Portal 2 is a 'closely coupled game', the *Camaraderie* experience is similar to the *Co-operative Challenge*, however there are loosely co-operative puzzle games could score these differently if players have independent goals when working apart.

Co-operative Challenge: The LIMITED RESOURCES (only one exit and entrance portal per player) along with SIMULTANEOUS CHALLENGES ensures that both players must understand their tasks. This encourages INTERACTION for player success as players must each perform the correct sequence of actions to solve puzzles (this is related to *Emergence* as RULE CONSISTENCY is needed for communication and verbalized HYPOTHESES to be meaningful). This meant players had to overcome the same obstacles to reach the same goals through team strategy and interpersonal communication with players providing feedback and information to one another.

Emergence: as an aesthetic ideal stresses the importance of simplicity and RULE CONSISTENCY wherein players predict the consequences of actions and understand cause and effect of mechanics. *Emergence* is made evident with players forming HYPOTHESES and achieving BREAKTHROUGHS.

Fellowship: refers to social affiliative behaviours that are not goal orientated. This was the least prominent aesthetic but did consistently result from participants reflecting on shared game related experience during DOWNTIME or made comments unrelated to the game and resisted the incorporeal and mocking AI named GLaDOS.

Humour: refers to how game designs facilitate *Humour* (both GAME GENERATED, and PLAYER GENERATED). Game generated humour referred to uncontrollable or scripted game events that made players laugh (in this case, character designs and dialogue from the AI GLaDOS), while player generated was more linked to player behaviour, especially when players PLAYFULLY SABOTAGED one another, made MISTAKES when LEARNING about new game mechanics or witnessed something unexpected or RANDOM.

Reasoning: The game has consistent mechanics to navigate puzzles that use momentum, gravity, objects, and portals. In order to LEARN these mechanics, a process of EXPLORATION, ANALYSIS, TRIAL & ERROR and BREAKDOWN occurred until eventually mechanics were UNDERSTOOD, and *Emergence* could occur.

4.3 Ethnographic Analysis of Each Trial

Video ethnographic results are presented with a short account of each trial and document the behaviours that were impacted by social effects in this experiment.

Trial 1. Brendon and Carlos were friends and Brendon had previous experience playing the game while Carlos did not. This opened up the possibility for Brendon to engage in PLAYFUL MISCHIEF with prior knowledge of how to utilise the game mechanics. Game design supported PLAYFUL MISCHIEF with a LACK OF PENALTY upon player death and NO TIME PRESSURE, which resulted in the trial with the most *Humour*. There was intermitted DISTRUST, but MUTUAL GOALS reinforced by game mechanics that utilized LIMITED RESOURCES kept them playing co-operatively despite frequent MISCHIEF. It is also worth noting that Brendon never betrayed his co-player's trust excessively and did not subvert the lusory attitude. At times, Carlos' playfully GUILTED, Brendan for his PLAYFUL SABOTAGE [laughing] *"What the hell man!"*.

Brendan's previous experience also negated a lot of EXPLORATION, DISCOVERY, TRIAL & ERROR, HPYOTHESISING and BREAKDOWN and BREAKTHROUGHS since he was already familiar with the game, thereby changing Carlos's experience of the game through a lot of INSTRUCTION, as evident with the frequent series of directions given by Brendon *"Now right hit the thing"*, resulting in less LEARNING and UNDERSTANDING (less *Reasoning* and *Emergence*) compared to other trials. DOWNTIME, like other trials led to REFLECTION on performance, but since they were friends, they also JOKED about the MISCHIEF during the level which increased *Fellowship*. This trial had higher levels of *Humour* and *Fellowship* and moderate *Camaraderie, Co-operative Challenge, Emergence* and, *Reasoning*. The one-sided INSTRUCTION lowered the experience of *Co-operative Challenge, Emergence*, and *Reasoning*.

Trial 2. Stephan and Tim were strangers and both were inexperienced at Portal 2. Being strangers impacted how the game was played, with both players strictly trying to solve puzzles. As every new puzzle began, they EXPLORED, ANALYZED, set about TRIAL & ERROR and HYPOTHESIZED before achieving the correct sequence of actions. They LEARNED the mechanics as the game intended through puzzles slowly increasing in difficulty. DOWNTIME featured silence or comments on game quality or comments in response to the AI. The response to the AI encouraged some *Fellowship* in resisting the AI's attempts to, as Tim put it *"to pit us"* against each other, and facilitated *humourous* interactions between the two *"watch by the end of the hour we'll be killing each other. [Laughing]"*. In this trial, the game is functional but other aspects of game dynamics are not present due to the social context, such as the opportunity for playful sabotage since both players are strangers and inexperienced to the game which kept the lusory attitude related to in-game goals [13]. Here the aesthetic experiences were high in *Camaraderie, Co-operative Challenge, Emergence, and Reasoning,* moderate in *Fellowship,* and low in *Humour.*

Trial 3. George and Michael were both friends and new to the game. Almost every puzzle involved EXPLORATION, ANALYSIS, TRIAL & ERROR, HYPOTHESIS, LEARNING, TEAM STRATEGY IDENTIFACTION and MUTUAL GOALS. The process of co-operatively solving problems and using newly introduced game mechanics contributed to an experience of *Camaraderie, Co-operative Challenge, Reasoning,* and *Emergence. Humour* and *Fellowship* were facilitated by their friendship which enabled a more light-hearted play through with self-deprecating jokes during DOWNTIME, and some MISCHIEF. However, there was less *Humour* when compared to the first trial, since in that trial, one player had prior experience and engaged in a lot more MISCHIEF due to his familiarity with game mechanics, suggesting an interaction between the effect of 'experience' and 'friendship' and game design.

Trial 4. Ryan and Sinead were both friends without previous experience of playing Portal 2. This was a similar social context to trial 3 with George and Michael and resulted in similar behavioural outcomes. Their friendship enabled a more light-hearted play through with exaggerated resistance to GLaDOS during DOWNTIME, achieving both *Fellowship* and *Humour, "They're trying to break down our teamwork. Don't listen to her [GLaDOS][Both laughing]"*.

Trial 5. Sean and Brian were both strangers and Brian was new to the game while Sean had previous experience. This resulted in moments when Sean would knowingly progress or instruct Brian, while Brian did not get the opportunity to UNDERSTAND game mechanics *"I have no idea what is going on"*. Many of Sean's attempts to converse were not reciprocated resulting in a lot of silences or one-sided laughter (which does not score on the CPM as a 'laughter' event) [1]. It is very plausible that the game experience of *Camaraderie, Co-operative Challenge, Emergence,* and *Reasoning* was disrupted due to Sean's history of playing *Portal 2* which contributed to his excessive INSTRUCTION. Furthermore, they did not have a base to socially relate on since they were not friends which reduced experiences of *Humour* and *Fellowship.* As the game progressed and Brian got more experience and was able to help Sean during a BREAKDOWN and began ANALYZING and HYPOTHESIZING more; resulting in a slightly more engaged co-operative experience as the experience gap was lessened.

4.4   The Impact of Social Effects

The social factors in this analysis were explored in the video ethnographic analysis and summarised in Fig. 4 below.

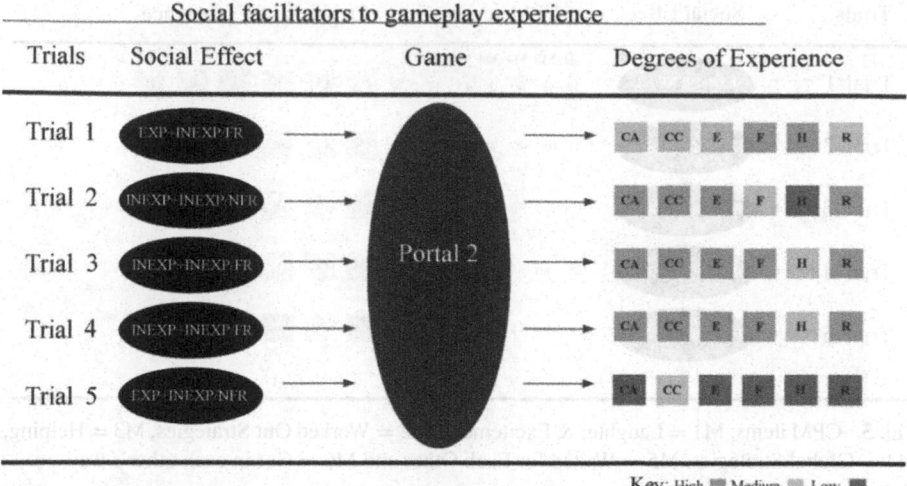

Fig. 4. The social factors incorporated in this analysis were EXP/INEXP (Experienced/Inexperienced) and FR/NFR (Friends/Not Friends) which seemed to have impacted how participants engaged with the game and therein, the six types of aesthetics and associated behaviours detected in the MDA analysis. These aesthetics are: *Camaraderie (CA), Co-operative Challenge (CC), Emergence (E), Fellowship (F), Humour (H),* and *Reasoning (R).* The interpretation of 'high', 'moderate' and 'low' degrees of experience was subjectively judged, based on the video ethnographic analysis.

4.5 Comparing the CPM and Video Ethnographic Results

This section compares and synthesizes both CPM and video ethnographic findings, then identifies the strengths and weaknesses of the CPM in detecting co-located behavioural data relating to player experience and co-operative game design. As such, this section discusses what the CPM detected and what puzzle specific behaviours were missing in the CPM. We recommend referring to Fig. 5 to visually consolidate this synthesis as we describe how CPM scores relate to gameplay behaviours/aesthetics.

The CPM component Helping detected dynamics revolving around unreciprocated INSTRUCTION about gameplay mechanics or controls, and was associated with *Co-operative Challenge*, while Worked Out Strategies detected dynamics surrounding EXPLORATION, MUTUAL GOALS, SHARED PERSPECTIVES, TEAM STRATEGY IDENTIFICATION and SIMULTANEOUS CHALLENGES and was tied to feelings of *Camaraderie* and *Co-operative Challenge*. The CPM component Worked Out Strategies successfully detects dynamics relating to the aesthetic of *Camaraderie* that results in a 'closely coupled game', relying on dynamics like VIRTUAL CO-PRESENCE (as opposed to not occupying the same virtual space), MUTUAL GOALS and SHARED LEARNING [12]. CPM scores that were high in Worked Out Strategies and low in Helping were associated with numerous experiences of *Camaraderie* and *Co-operative Challenge* (trials 2, 3 and 4) whereas those scoring high on Helping but low on Worked Out Strategies were associated with high *Co-operative Challenge* but low *Camaraderie*, indicating a less fun experience (trial 1and trial 5). The video ethnographic analyses

Trials	Social Effect	CPM scores	Degrees of Experience

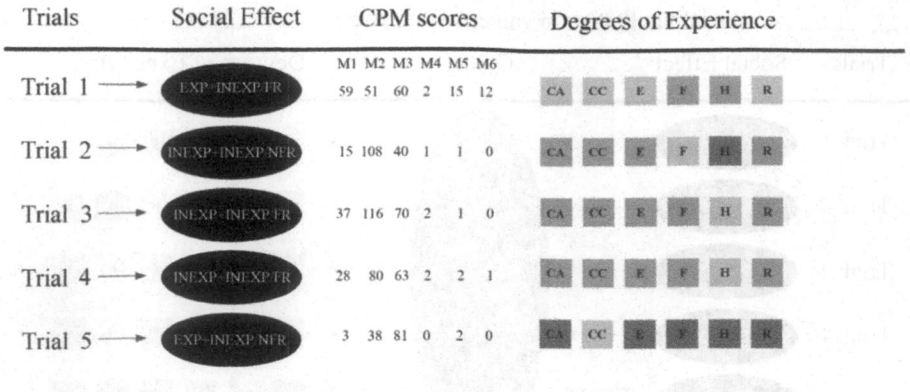

| | | M1 M2 M3 M4 M5 M6 | |

Trial 1 → EXP-INEXP/FR   59 51 60 2 15 12   CA CC E F H R

Trial 2 → INEXP-INEXP/NFR   15 108 40 1 1 0   CA CC E F H R

Trial 3 → INEXP-INEXP/FR   37 116 70 2 1 0   CA CC E F H R

Trial 4 → INEXP-INEXP/FR   28 80 63 2 2 1   CA CC E F H R

Trial 5 → EXP-INEXP/NFR   3 38 81 0 2 0   CA CC E F H R

Fig. 5. CPM items: M1 = Laughter & Excitement, M2 = Worked Out Strategies, M3 = Helping, M4 = Global Strategies, M5 = Waited for Each Other and M6 = Got in each other's way.

suggests these divergent results manifested due to previous experience playing the game (social effects) wherein the SHARED EXPERIENCE of LEARNING game mechanics is restricted due to excessive INSTRUCTION, and resulted in lower *Camaraderie, Co-operative Challenge, Emergence*, and *Reasoning* (trial 1 and 5). Zabal et al. [25] noted a cooperative game degenerates into a single player game when one player begins performing or directing all the games' actions and consequently becomes boring; these results suggest gaps in player experience with a game could exaggerate this tendency in co-operative games.

The component Laughter and Excitement Together captures the several dynamics that shaped player behaviour to encourage *Humour*, which were GAME GENERATED HUMOUR (often through refuting or enjoying the snarky AI, GLaDOS and humorous avatar design and animations) or PLAYER GENERATED HUMOUR which occurred through a variety of non-goal orientated behaviour (PLAYFUL MISCHIEF and PLAYFUL SABOTAGE) or RANDOMNESS when engaging with novel mechanics. This could justify splitting CPM component of laughter and excitement as either player generated or computer generated.

Humour as scored in the MDA analysis or 'Laughter and Excitement Together' in the CPM analysis was mostly mediated by the social effects, with the highest score being achieved in Trial 1 (EXP + INEXP/FR group). This was mediated by prior knowledge of game mechanics and a friendship that allowed for MISCHIEF and non-goal orientated behaviour to alter the lusory attitude and a game 'well-played' for mostly humorous aesthetic ideals [19]. Those who were friends without experience still utilised game mechanics with *humorous* intent, especially compared to those who were not friends (trials 1,3,4 compared to trials 2 and 5). These results support research that found social norms are adhered to less when players are more familiar with one another, allowing for more fun and 'bending of social rules' [19].

The remaining three metric components, Global Strategies, Waited for Each Other, Got in each other's way each scored very lowly, but still highlight game mechanics that did not provide complementary roles, had low skill execution requirements, and lacked the possible tension of getting in one another's way since there was unlimited time and no punishment when making mistakes.

The behaviour reflecting *Reasoning* reoccurred across all trials and is an indicator of the process involved with LEARNING the rules to navigate puzzles, these were: 1) EXPLORATION AND ANALYSIS; 2), TRIAL AND ERROR and 3) BREAKDOWNS. *Emergence* also reoccurred across trials and was a demonstration of behaviours that reflected UNDERSTANDING, these were 1) HYPOTHESIS and 2) BREAKTHROUGH, which manifested as actions and verbal explanations (or planning) that show the players' understanding of the game and ability to estimate cause and effect based on the rules established in the game. *Portal 2* engaged both of these processes and are worth including in the metric when analysing puzzle games.

In the CPM, the metric component worked out strategies could comprise both *Emergence* and *Reasoning* however, we recommend breaking the component worked out strategies into two aspects, '*Emergence*' and '*Reasoning*', which could be more revealing in a game analysis. High scores in *Reasoning* and low scores in *Emergence* could also serve as an indicator for frustration, due to excessively random TRIAL & ERROR along with a lack of UNDERSTANDING and BREAKDOWN; whereas high scores in *Emergence* and a low score in *Reasoning* could indicate that the game is too easy with puzzles that do not necessitate LEARNING.

Moreover, the aesthetic of *Fellowship* was facilitated by the lack of punishment for failure (lack of frustration) and mechanics supporting PLAYER GENERATED HUMOUR. Furthermore the antagonistic AI encouraged positive social interaction between players and DOWNTIME encouraged REFLECTION or more personal communication unassociated with problem solving.

Put briefly, the strengths of the CPM lie in its success in capturing dynamics associated with *Camaraderie*, *Co-operative Challenge*, and *Humour* with the metric components worked out strategies and laughter and excitement together. However, improvements could be made by adding social categories that impact game experience, such as previous experience with the game and whether players are friends. Additionally, splitting the component worked out strategies into *Emergence* and '*Reasoning*' could be useful to capture the experience of different stages of solving puzzles.

5 General Discussion

This research set out to evaluate the comprehensiveness of the CPM by comparing output with a video ethnographic methodology across five pairs of participants playing *Portal 2*. Ideally, the CPM could be used to document consistent co-located co-operative behaviours with associated game designs, and to effectively analyse how a game orchestrates behaviour, and assess what might need to be changed to create a desired player experience. CPM results were compared to a video ethnographic analysis which had descriptive game data organised using an MDA analysis, so moment-to-moment video game contexts could be succinctly described. Six aesthetics were observed in the MDA analysis: *camaraderie, cooperative challenge, emergence, fellowship, humour* and *reasoning*. No new aesthetics were identified in follow up playthroughs by different players, suggesting that the identified aesthetics from the MDA analysis were valid and reliable for these trials.

This study identified strengths of the CPM, wherein the components could successfully detect co-operative aesthetics and game designs based on the six observable behaviours it was scored on. The fact that there were parallels between the CPM and video ethnographic results in detecting *camaraderie, co-operative challenge* and *humour* demonstrates impressive efficacy, despite being such a brief and easy to use tool. However, some shortcomings in the CPM were identified, the first being the lack of consideration for social effects. The 'social effects' identified in this study were 'previous experience' (playing the game) and 'friendship status', and should be considered if game designers wish to evaluate co-operative game designs, since outcome behaviours are not isolated from social context and seemed to impact how the game was played in this study. Additionally, the CPM did not account for social behaviours relating to solidarity between players which was covered in the aesthetic of *'Fellowship'*. Furthermore the CPM did not differentiate *'Humour'* as being computer generated (i.e. scripted events in game) or player generated (scenarios that encourage humour through gameplay), which could be useful to inform which elements of Humour a game designer might wish to improve upon.

Moreover, co-operative puzzle game behaviours were found to be related to the CPM component worked out strategies. However this component could be improved by splitting the component into two aspects, *'Emergence'* and *'Reasoning'*. This way, game designers could more easily identify which aspect of a puzzle game design is functioning as intended, with *'Reasoning'* capturing the behaviours around the learning process and *'Emergence'* relating to behaviours when a puzzle is understood. Worked out strategies alone does not capture these differences, and they are useful in documenting if puzzles are too difficult (i.e. too high in *'Reasoning'* and associated behaviours of breakdown and trial and error) or too easy (too high in *'Emergence'* or understanding of rules/game elements). Future research could conduct MDA analyses on different game genres and appropriately factor these components into a modified version of the CPM to capture associated niche behaviours relating to game genre. For example, incorporating *'Emergence'* and *'Reasoning'* into a modified version of the CPM to detect niche behaviours for puzzle games could be named the CPM-PZ (The Co-operative Performance Metric-Puzzle).

Finally, it is worth noting that Emmerich & Masuch's [3] previous research used both CPM components and social components items to annotate videotaped gaming sessions and included friendly behaviours such as 'shared success and failure' and 'off-topic' that could arguably be included under the single construct of *'Fellowship'*. Their work also included several other useful items to indicate player frustration, with behaviours like swearing. We recommend including these additional behaviours into a metric for increased accuracy. For example, when all aspects are included for a puzzle modified CPM, the metric would include: game generated humour, player generated humour, excitement, worked out strategies (scored aspects beingreasoning and emergence), waited for each other, got in each others way, global strategies, fellowship and frustration, along with nominal categories on the social effects of friendship and experience with the game. Furthermore, there was little physical behaviour during the gameplay sessions, with players almost exclusively behaving in the game, meaning this metric could be applied to online gaming sessions in future studies.

6 Strengths, Limitations and Recommendations

This study utilized a mixed methods design to view whether the CPM was a comprehensive metric by comparing CPM and video ethnographic outputs to identify the CPM's strengths and weaknesses in detecting player experience and associated behaviours. The video ethnographic analysis succeeded in uncovering puzzle game effects and social effects that mediated player behaviour and experience.

This research has a potential limitation in the hour-long trial format which could have exaggerated the impact of a disparity of experience with the game, wherein hour-long trials would not observe how inexperienced players would behave as they familiarised themselves with the game. Additionally, due to the scrupulous nature of video ethnography, only a small sample size was obtained, meaning that observations in this study can only infer a possible pattern, and not describe an established pattern between social effects and niche game designs that cause reliable behavioural outcomes. Future research can investigate whether social effects and game genre explain statistically significant variance by incorporating them into a modified CPM as nominal variables and analysing data from larger sample sizes which could be conducted online using voice communications and recordings of in-game behaviour.

7 Conclusion

Overall, the six CPM components captured aspects of behaviour that was influenced by co-operative game design. However, to effectively compare games within the same genre, as indicated by video ethnographic results, it is important to distinguish behaviours that are unique to specific game genres, as highlighted by the suggestion to split the CPM component 'worked out strategies' into two aspects, *reasoning* and *emergence* for puzzle games. Furthermore, the social context (prior experience playing the game and whether players were friends) has a pronounced impact on behavioural outcomes and we recommend adding these as nominal categories to the CPM (e.g., EXP/INEXP and FR/NFR) in future studies along with a humour component that discriminates between player generated and computer-generated humour, and finally the inclusion of *fellowship*, indicating behaviours of solidarity.

Acknowledgments. We appreciate the participants for their time and agreement to participate in this study. There was neither funding nor conflicts of interest for this study.

References

1. Seif El-Nasr, M., et al.: Understanding and evaluating cooperative games. In: Elizabeth M., Don, S., Geraldine, F., Scott, H., Keith, E., Tom, R. (eds.) Proceedings of the SIGCHI CONFERENCE on Human Factors in Computing Systems, pp. 253–262. Atlanta, Georgia (2010). https://doi.org/10.1145/1753326.1753363
2. de Passos Ramos, R.V.: Procedural Content Generation for Cooperative Games. M.A Thesis, Instituto Superior Técnico, Lisbon (2015)

3. Emmerich, K., Masuch. M.: The impact of game patterns on player experience and social interaction in co-located multiplayer games. In: Proceedings of the Annual Symposium on Computer-Human Interaction in Play. Association for Computing Machinery, pp. 411–422. New York, NY, USA (2017). https://doi.org/10.1145/3116595.3116606

4. Kreimeier. B.: The Case For Game Design Patterns. Blog (2002). https://www.gamasutra.com/view/feature/132649/the_case_for_game_design_patterns.php?print=11. Accessed 05 April 2020

5. Björk, S., Holopainen, J.: Patterns in Game Design. Charles River Media, Hingham MA (2005)

6. Jenkins. H.: Game design as narrative architecture. In: Wardrip-Fruin, N., Harrigan, P. (eds.) First Person: New Media as Story, Performance, and Game. pp. 118–130. MIT Press, Cambridge, MA (2004)

7. Linehan, C., Bellord, G., Kirman, B., Morford, Z. H., Roche, B.: Learning curves: analysing pace and challenge in four successful puzzle games. In: Proceedings of the first ACM SIGCHI annual symposium on Computer-human interaction in play, pp. 181–190. Association for Computing Machinery, New York, USA, (2014). https://doi.org/10.1145/2658537.2658695

8. Deterding, S., Dixon, D., Khaled, R., Nacke, L.: From game design elements to gamefulness: defining "gamification". In: Proceedings of the 15th International Academic MindTrek CON-FERENCE: Envisioning Future Media Environments. Association for Computing Machinery, pp. 9–15. New York, NY, USA (2011). https://doi.org/10.1145/2181037.2181040

9. Schell, J.: The art of game design: a book of lenses. Morgan Kaufmann Publishers Inc., San Francisco, CA, USA (2008)

10. Hunicke, R., LeBlanc, M., Zubek, R.: MDA: A formal approach to game design and game researchss. In: Proceedings of the AAAI Workshop on Challenges in Game AI in the Game Design and Tuning Workshop at the Game Developers CONFERENCE, pp. 1–5. California, San Jose, USA (2004)

11. Iacovides, I., Cox, A.L., McAndrew, P., Aczel, J., Scanlon, E.: Game-play breakdowns and breakthroughs: exploring the relationship between action, understanding, and involvement. Hum.–Comp. Inter. 30(3–4), 202–231 (2015). https://doi.org/10.1080/07370024.2014.987347

12. Lundgren, S., Bergström, K., Björk, S.: Exploring aesthetic ideals of gameplay. In: DiGRA CONFERENCE Exploring Aesthetic Ideals of Gameplay: Breaking New Ground: Innovation in Games, Play, Practice and Theory. London, UK (2009)

13. Bergström, K., Björk, S., Lundgren S.: Exploring aesthetical gameplay design patterns: cama-raderie in four games. In: Proceedings of the 14th International Academic MindTrek Con-ference: Envisioning Future Media Environments, pp. 17–24. Association for Computing Machinery, New York, USA (2010). https://doi.org/10.1145/1930488.1930493

14. Toups, Z.O., Hammer, J., Hamilton, W.A., Jarrah, A., Graves, W., Garretson, O.: Garretson. A framework for cooperative communication game mechanics from grounded theory. In: Proceedings of the first ACM SIGCHI annual symposium on Computer-human interaction in play. Association for Computing Machinery, pp. 257–266. New York, USA (2014). https://doi.org/10.1145/2658537.2658681

15. Beznosyk, A., Quax, P., Lamotte, W., Coninx, K.: The Effect of Closely-Coupled Interaction on Player Experience in Casual Games. In: Herrlich, M., Malaka, R., Masuch, M. (eds.) ICEC 2012. LNCS, vol. 7522, pp. 243–255. Springer, Heidelberg (2012). https://doi.org/10.1007/978-3-642-33542-6_21

16. Cheung, V., Chang, Y.L.B., Scott, S.D.: Communication channels and awareness cues in collocated collaborative time-critical gaming. In: Proceedings of the ACM 2012 conference on Computer Supported Cooperative Work. Association for Computing Machinery, pp. 569–578. New York, NY, USA (2012). https://doi.org/10.1145/2145204.2145291

17. Tang, A., Massey, J., Wong, N., Reilly, D., Edwards, W.K.: Verbal coordination in first person shooter games. In: Proceedings of the ACM 2012 conference on Computer Supported Cooperative Work. Association for Computing Machinery, pp. 579–582. New York, NY, USA (2012). https://doi.org/10.1145/2145204.2145292
18. Poels, K., De Kort, Y., IJsselsteijn, W.: Identification and categorization of digital game experiences: a qualitative study integrating theoretical insights and player perspectives. Westminst. Pap. Commun. Cult. 9(1), 107–129 (2012)
19. Kirman, K.: Playful Networks: Measuring, Analysing and Understanding the Social Effects of Game Design. Ph.D. Dissertation. University of Lincoln, Lincoln, United Kingdom (2011). ID Code: 15079
20. Rocha, J.B., Mascarenhas, S., Prada, R.: Game mechanics for co-operative games. In: The Proceedings of the ZDN Digital Games Conference, pp. 73–80. Anaheim, California (2008)
21. Valve Corporation, CyberFront Corporation. 1996. Portal 2. Game [PlayStation 3, Xbox 360, Microsoft Windows, Classic Mac OS, Linux]. Kirkland, Washinton, United States (2011). Last Played Feb 2020
22. Cohen, J.: A coefficient of agreement for nominal scales. Educ. Psychol. Measure. 20(1), 37–46 (1960). https://doi.org/10.1177/001316446002000104
23. Heath, C., Paul, L.P.: The naturalistic experiment: Video and organizational interaction. Organ. Res. Methods 21(2), 466–488 (2018). https://doi.org/10.1177/1094428117747688
24. Heath, C., Hindmarsh, J.: Analysing interaction: video, ethnography and situated conduct. In; May, T. (ed.) Qualitative Research in Action. pp. 99–120. Sage, London (2002). https://doi.org/10.4135/9781849209656.n4
25. Zagal, J.P., Rick, J., Hsi, I.: Collaborative games: lessons learned from board games. Simul. Gaming 37(1), 24–40 (2006). https://doi.org/10.1177/1046878105282279

Auto Generating Maps in a 2D Environment

Lazaros Lazaridis⬛, Konstantinos-Filippos Kollias⬛, George Maraslidis⬛,
Heraklis Michailidis⬛, Maria Papatsimouli⬛, and George F. Fragulis⁽✉⁾⬛

Department of Electrical and Computer Engineering,
University of Western Macedonia, Kozani, Greece
gfragulis@uowm.gr

Abstract. Methods of algorithmic data generation, also known as Procedural Content Generation (PCG), consist of a striking vision within the gaming development industry. It is a way of creating enormously unique and diverse content, something that exponentially increases the game replayability. Although PCG in video games has a long history, there are also plenty of methods that have already been applied to levels, maps, models and textures among others. There is a variety of methods that have been used in video games, each with its own advantages and disadvantages. In the current study, an algorithm which generates 2D maps filled with rooms and some decorating items is presented. Map generation in commercial games heavily relies on constructive algorithms which do not evaluate and regenerate the output if something goes wrong. They do not demand heavy processing power and they can be used in real time situations, such as generating big worlds with fauna and flora. However, the playability of the generated map is examined by an agent which is usually created to access every corridor, room, and the start to finish pathway.

Keywords: Computer games · Two dimensional display maps · Game content generation · Procedural dungeon generation · Algorithms · Replayability · PCG · Entertainment industry

1 Introduction

Algorithmic generation of data, usually referred as Procedural Content Generation (PCG), is a method that has been used for creating random content for several occasions such as maps, loot, item attributes and so on [30], in contrast with manual creation. A game is often evaluated by its replayability, how lavish content has, play hours etc. Game content of good quality usually demands manual generation and a lot of effort by a considerably large team consisted of designers and developers, something that is expensive and severely time-consuming. Large studios, as well as publishers are capable of affording such concepts. On the other hand, this luxury cannot be afforded by independent (indie) developers, so an alternative way has to be found. PCG content has long history in electronic gaming and many games have relied on it, such as games that have been heavily based on replayability in order to hold player's interest. Some popular games which utilise PCG methods are: *The Binding of Issac* [7] which randomly generates rooms (Fig. 1), *Minecraft* [22] in which its universe is procedurally generated and each asset is placed in a unique arrangement, every time a new game is loaded so that no two players' worlds resemble. In *APEX Legends* [8] the weapons' spawn location is fully randomized, albeit the whole map is divided into areas and each area has different percentage of special weapon spawn. An important side effect of PCG methods is the fact that the final game size on disk is significantly reduced as the content which is generated by the game engine, is not stored somewhere but it is created on-the-fly, so a better resource management is also achieved.

The purpose of this paper is the presentation of an algorithm creating a top-down open-air level map filled with rooms of three sizes and a fountain in a random arrangement that changes every time the map is loaded. The same algorithm is possible to be used in several other applications such as the interior of a dungeon or a room [10]. In other instances, it could be used to randomly arrange loot and/or weapons along with random range attributes throughout a map or to add details such as vegetation, doors, clouds and so on [21]. Nevertheless, such methods do not intend on replacing any work in the illustration field but aim more at being used as helper applications [17]. The rest of our paper includes four sections ordered as follows: Sect. 2 introduces some basic methods and strategies regarding PCG. An analysis of the rules which have to be taken into consideration by the algorithm and the algorithm itself are presented in Sect. 3. In Sect. 4, some limitations and possible solutions as well as our future plans are reported and finally in Sect. 5 an overall conclusion and discussion about PCG are presented.

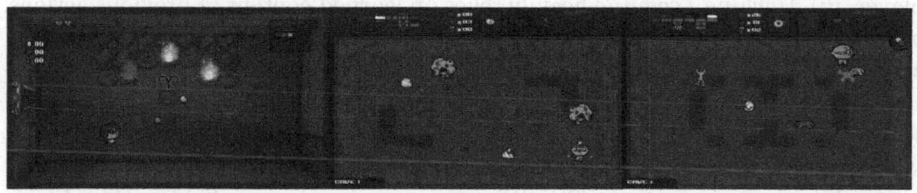

Fig. 1. Binding of Isaac is a game where all rooms are generated and decorated randomly.

2   Concepts of PCG

Throughout the years, several methods of PCG have been developed that significantly differ from each other in terms of how to achieve it [11]. There are usually methods which generate the game content before the game level is loaded (*Offline*) [5], while other methods, less popular such as the *Online* one, create game content during gameplay according to various criteria such as player's performance. A major difference between methods is whether an algorithm is constructive or not. *Constructive* algorithms [14, 19] do not demand any evaluation regarding the playability of the final content, as opposed to *generate-and-test* algorithms [12, 24] in which an agent is also created in order to test for instance if a level can be successfully completed. The algorithm that will be shown in this paper is an *Offline* one in which the map is created before the game level begins. It is also a constructive one without the need of an agent to be present as it is based on a ruleset that prevents the final map to be unplayable and the final content is being created each time from scratch [4]. Furthermore, although it relies on its generative rules to build varied level maps every time is loaded it is not considered as *random seed* [25] entirely as it can be accepted a minor input in order a little higher degree of complexity to be added by defining some *parameters*.

2.1   Solutions for PCG

A whole game can be built by only using PCG methods regarding the content of each asset (difficulty, loot, map, room interior, weapons etc.) that can be generated randomly each time by following some rules according to game progress. Specifically, the most common techniques rely on i) *Markov Models* [23] which are quite fast in PCG generation, ii) *Cellular Automata* [1, 9] that follows a ruleset in a grid map and examines if the neighbor cells can be used for a potential asset or not. This method is well-known for cavern-like level creations. iii) *Generative Grammar* [28] is basically a grammatical rule system which is traditionally used by parsers to strictly define what is possible to be done and what is not. It is widely used by games which require action by the user and depending on his options either different game progress is achieved, or different quests are generated, or if a Non-Playable-Character (NPC) member team will follow the player. iv) *Machine Learning* heavily relies on learned content of previous actions or of an initially standard dataset [26]. Although this approach is very fast, it cannot guarantee that the final game will be completely playable especially if the final result is a room. However, several solutions have been proposed that soothe the problem presented above based on Generative Adversarial Networks (GAN) [15, 29], Reinforcement Learning (RL) [6, 16, 27] and Deep Learning [20]. v) *Evolutionary Algorithms* [2], although a newly growing field within PCG, they have been used in 3D landscape modelling, to improve strategy game maps and assist in dungeon creation [13]. They have some vulnerabilities related to natural aesthetic or some conflicts between some objects. Therefore, they can be used for specific operations for the time being. Our algorithm uses the Cellular Automata (CA) strategy as grid space is a better fit for our needs.

3   The Spawn Algorithm

In this section, a Spawn Algorithm will be presented and analyzed. It is based on a 2D Grid Map which helps on the creation of random maps filled with three types of rooms in three different sizes. The room entrances do not face the same direction and especially the small rooms can rotate in 360°. Also, a fountain is placed at the end to decorate the area a bit more. The four elements by which the level map consists of are shown in Fig. 2, while the final result is a small scale minimap that can be later translated into a playable one, retaining the arrangement as shown in Fig. 3. It is based on Cellular Automata (CA) technique and the graphics engine *Unity* was selected as the basic software while the algorithm was implemented in the C# programming language.

The concept primarily relies on special rules as the avoidance of any collisions between rooms is critical. Something that must be noted is the fact that the algorithm is designed for the outdoor environment. The same method, with minor changes, could be used for arranging things of any kind for indoor purposes something that is out of scope in our research. Even though no movement was predicted and the defined rules prevent any collision, bounding boxes and in particular hitboxes that will be used for collision detection in later use are applied on all game assets. AABB hitboxes were used for rooms and the outer wall, while a spheroidal one was used for the fountain [18].

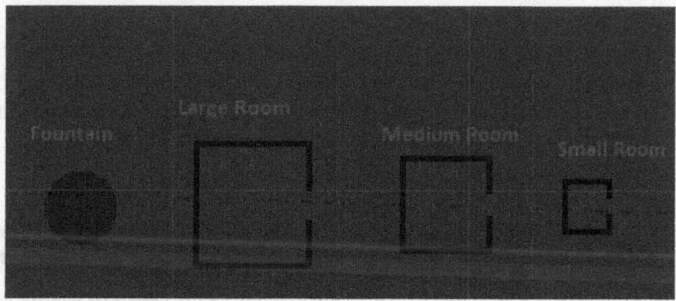

Fig. 2. There are four constant sized distinct elements that could be put on the level map.

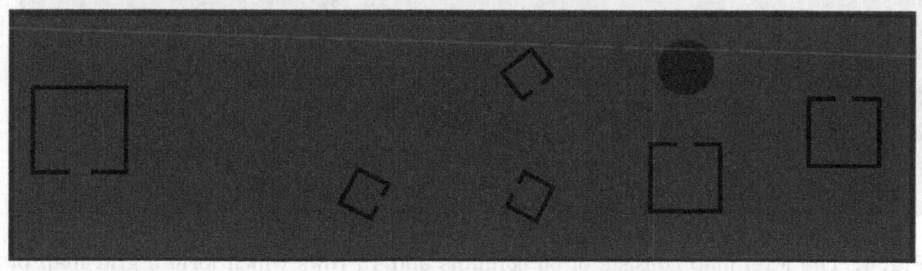

Fig. 3. An example of a final outcome. This minimap later can be translated into a full 2D landscape and also be decorated with non-collide elements such as grass, flowers, loot, items etc.

3.1 Rules Specification

As a constructive algorithm, it does not use an agent to check if the final result is playable, so a set of strict rules must be set and applied while the final result must resemble natural or hand-crafted. In addition, the rules must be somehow flexible especially in terms of room number of each kind. On initial levels the amount of rooms could be less dense while later ones could be considerably denser. Additionally, the capability of specific rooms can be excluded if special conditions are present. Finally, although the algorithm seems to be built for one level map each time, it can also be used to multi-level maps by creating two or more level maps [3] before the game is loaded, connecting them with some kind of stairs in case we desire more than one connecting points on the same level. The rules are presented:

1. The large rooms are placed first (if the generator selects one - chances not to be present are rather small)
2. The medium rooms are placed second (if the generator selects one)
3. The small room are placed third (if the generator selects one)
4. The developer can define the maximum rooms of each type
5. The fountain is placed last
6. In case a large room is present, it must be single on its column
7. Large and medium rooms can be rotated only in 0°, 90°, 180° and 270°
8. Medium rooms should not be placed in a previous and a next column where a large room is located
9. A minimum distance between assets must be calculated

These rules ensure that there will be no overlap between two rooms or no rooms will be placed very close to each other. The map is initially divided into small grids (Fig. 4) and then into large ones with each one enclosing a group of small grids. In general, grid term refers to a large one.

Fig. 4. The level map consists of 50 columns and 15 rows which form a grid map of 750 tiles overall.

Each game asset has its pivot point exactly in its center and it can be moved anywhere in its selected large grid as shown in Fig. 5. For our research the level map has 10 columns and 3 rows which form a large grid map of 30 tiles. In this space, an asset according to its center can be moved anywhere within a large grid. The large room that invades the other three adjacent large grids is the worst-case scenario and it is allowed while the algorithm must predict this behavior and act accordingly.

Fig. 5. The grid map is divided into larger grids with each one concludes 5 × 5 small grids. In this instance two large rooms are placed and their pivot points are located exactly in the center of shape.

By definition, if the pivot point of an asset is placed in the edge of a large grid then the asset will take space from the adjacent large grid(s). This is not forbidden and the algorithm must take it into account to set a minimum distance between them if an asset is selected to be placed in such a way covering some space of the adjacent grid(s). In our research, the maximum number of large rooms is set to one as this room takes a lot of space, medium rooms are set to two and small rooms are set to three.

3.2   2D Map Creation Algorithm

In the following algorithm, a vector is used to create a grid area consisting of small tiles. Vector is a very useful data structure as in the same "record" can be saved two, three, or more dimensional information. The algorithm uses two and three-dimensional vectors with each of the first two attributes representing x rows and y columns respectively, while the third one (if needed) sets the rotation.

Input: 15 rows × 50 columns grid area, maximum number of large, medium and small rooms is set 1, 2 and 3 respectively.

   2 dimension vectors: map[x, y]

   Variables: i, j as counters.

   Random values: 0 → large room, 1 → medium room, 2 → small room, 3 → no room

```
1. for i = 1 to maxColumns(50) do

2.    for j = 1 to maxRows(15) do
3.        map[i, j] = new Vector2(x, y)
4.        y = y + 1 (+1 tile in the row)
5.    end do (j)
6.    y = 0 (initiate the row tile)
7.    x = x + 1 (+1 tile in the column)
8. end do (i)

9. for i = 1 to largeColumns(10) do

10.   for j = 1 to largeRows(3) do
11.       randomGenerator = randomValue 0 to 3
12.       if randomGenerator == 0 and maxNumberLargeRoom != 0 and noP-
resenceOfAnotherLargeRoom
13.          choose a direction other than no face wall
14.          create a large room as Vector3(map[i,j].x, map[i,j].y, direction)
15.          reduce the maxNumberLargeRoom by 1 16.      end if
17.   end do (j)

18.   for j = 1 to largeRows do
19.       randomGenerator = randomValue 0 to 3
20.       if randomGenerator == 0 and maxNumberMediumRoom != 0 and noP-
resenceOfAnotherLargeRoom
21.          choose a random direction
22.       create a medium room as Vector3(map[i,j].x, map[i,j].y, direction)
23.          reduce the maxNumberMediumRoom by 1 24.      end if
25.   end do (j)

26.   for j = 1 to largeRows do
27.       randomGenerator = randomValue 0 to 3
28.       if randomGenerator == 2 and maxNumberSmallRoom != 0 and noP-
resenceOfAnotherLargeRoom
29.          choose a freely random direction
30.          create a small room as Vector3(map[i,j].x, map[i,j].y, direction)
31.          reduce the maxNumberSmallRoom by 1 32.      end if
33.   end do (j)

34.   for j = 1 to largeRows do
35.       randomFountainGenerator = randomValue 0 to 1
36.       if randomFountainGenerator == 1 and maxNumberFountain != 0
37.          create a fountain as Vector3(map[i,j].x, map[i,j].y, direction)
38.          reduce the maxNumberFountain by 1
39.       end if
```

40.   end do (j)

41. nextPointerLargeGridX = 0
42. nextPointerLargeGridY = nextPointerLargeGridY + stepY (10)
43. end do (i)

The algorithm is divided into five main sections. The first one {1...8} creates a conceivable grid map of small tiles. The remaining loops {9...43} group the small tiles into large ones. The next three sections {11...17}, {18...25} and {26...33} essentially scan the whole map area, column by column, to decide if a selected room can be placed or not. Large rooms have the highest priority, followed by medium and small ones. The fourth section {34...35} scans the map to find a suitable place for the fountain. Numbers in parentheses declare the actual values that they used for this instance. Any value can be used both for map tiles and the amount of every room type depending on what we would like to achieve, such as a map with few rooms or a large map with dense contents not all of them be visible (secret or underground rooms).

4 Limitations and Future Work

The Spawn algorithm has some limitations which in future work will be considered and fully resolved. The first one is the frequency with which the rooms are placed, especially the large ones. During the first scanning, the large rooms have the tendency to choose the first two columns whereas the possibility to be placed in the last column is majorly reduced. In general, the algorithm always scans from the first column to the last and in each step, it decides if a large room can be placed. As the entire grid is empty at the first scanning, it is importantly more possible for the first pair of columns to be selected. A viable solution could be to let the algorithm initially choose a random column (equal opportunities for each column) and finally choose a random row. However, in this case, there will be an increase in complexity as the other room loops should be properly informed to save extra information about reserved positions and a new communication model among scanners has to be created.

Another minor limitation is that medium rooms occasionally appear in the left column of a large room while the exact opposite does not happen. This happens because of the scanning technique, as the algorithm scans the entire map column by column. In case a medium room is selected to be initially placed upon an empty column, there is no information of what will be placed in the next column as the corresponding loop still scans the current one. In the next cycle though, it is possible for a large room to be placed, as the current column is empty but in this case, the previous column contains at least one medium room. Although it is not considered a major fault, the environment becomes quite dense in this specific area. In a later implementation, this will be fixed by setting a condition in the large room cycle.

In our future work, the algorithm will be improved in terms of the number of cycles. In the current release, there are instances in which extra cycles are executed and as a result, the upcoming loading screens will be increasingly growing in a slower rate while there is a map expansion, so a more refined approach is needed. Also, the rooms will not have a standard size but they will be as much variable as possible using clearly defined limits.

Future editions of the algorithm will be expanded in other areas of the game, as well. For instance, the same algorithm, with minor changes, can be used for decorating the interior of each room according to its size. There can be standard decoration items from bookcases, stashes, tables to even villains and contraptions that will affect other rooms or a piece of the outdoor area. It is also planned to incorporate a random generator for item properties which can be picked up from a player character as well as the difficulty of villains depending on the character's stats or score. Although this will ostensibly take place in real-time, it will certainly happen during gameplay.

5   Conclusion

Even though research on Procedural Content Generator has a long history, many issues still remain. Several contemporary games are trying to fully simulate a specific environment in the best way to increase the end-user immersion. The creation of these environments demands a lot of effort, workforce, and considerably a big chunk of the overall amount of time. PCG methods can contribute to this effort by building ready-to-play or in more complex situations ready-to-decorate environments. The concept behind PCG is not to diminish the corresponding workforce but to be used as a tool to create more complex environments, conditions, or decorations with more speed. On the other hand, independent developers appraise such kinds of methods as they save them valuable time from designing other parts of the game.

References

1. Adams, C., Louis, S.: Procedural maze level generation with evolutionary cellular automata. In: 2017 IEEE Symposium Series on Computational Intelligence (SSCI), pp. 1–8. IEEE (2017)
2. Alvarez, A., Dahlskog, S., Font, J., Togelius, J.: Empowering quality diversity in dungeon design with interactive constrained map-elites. In: 2019 IEEE Conference on Games (CoG), pp. 1–8. IEEE (2019)
3. Antoniuk, I., Rokita, P.: Procedural generation of multilevel dungeons for application in computer games using schematic maps and L-system. In: Bembenik, R., Skonieczny, Ł, Protaziuk, G., Kryszkiewicz, M., Rybinski, H. (eds.) Intelligent Methods and Big Data in Industrial Applications. SBD, vol. 40, pp. 261–275. Springer, Cham (2019). https://doi.org/10.1007/978-3-319-77604-0_19
4. Bontrager, P., Togelius, J.: Learning to generate levels from nothing. In: 2021 IEEE Conference on Games (CoG), pp. 1–8. IEEE (2021)

5. De Kegel, B., Haahr, M.: Procedural puzzle generation: a survey. IEEE Trans. Games **12**(1), 21–40 (2019)
6. Delarosa, O., Dong, H., Ruan, M., Khalifa, A., Togelius, J.: Mixed-initiative level design with RL brush. In: Romero, J., Martins, T., Rodríguez-Fernández, N. (eds.) EvoMUSART 2021. LNCS, vol. 12693, pp. 412–426. Springer, Cham (2021). https://doi.org/10.1007/978-3-030-72914-1_27
7. McMillen, E., Himsl, F.: The Binding of Isaac. https://bindingofisaac.fandom.com
8. Electronic-Arts: Apex legends. https://www.ea.com/games/apex-legends
9. Flores-Aquino, G.O., Ortega, J.D.D., Arvizu, R.Y.A., Muñoz, R.L., Gutierrez-Frias, O.O., Vasquez-Gomez, J.I.: 2D grid map generation for deep-learning-based navigation approaches. arXiv preprint arXiv:2110.13242 (2021)
10. de Freitas, V.M.R.: Procedural generation of cave-like maps for 2D top-down games (2021)
11. Gellel, A., Sweetser, P.: A hybrid approach to procedural generation of rogue-like video game levels. In: International Conference on the Foundations of Digital Games, pp. 1–10 (2020)
12. Gisslén, L., Eakins, A., Gordillo, C., Bergdahl, J., Tollmar, K.: Adversarial reinforcement learning for procedural content generation. In: 2021 IEEE Conference on Games (CoG), pp. 1–8. IEEE (2021)
13. Gravina, D., Khalifa, A., Liapis, A., Togelius, J., Yannakakis, G.N.: Procedural content generation through quality diversity. In: 2019 IEEE Conference on Games (CoG), pp. 1–8. IEEE (2019)
14. Green, M.C., Khalifa, A., Alsoughayer, A., Surana, D., Liapis, A., Togelius, J.: Two-step constructive approaches for dungeon generation. In: Proceedings of the 14th International Conference on the Foundations of Digital Games, pp. 1–7 (2019)
15. Gutierrez, J., Schrum, J.: Generative adversarial network rooms in generative graph grammar dungeons for the legend of Zelda. In: 2020 IEEE Congress on Evolutionary Computation (CEC), pp. 1–8. IEEE (2020)
16. Khalifa, A., Bontrager, P., Earle, S., Togelius, J.: PCGRL: procedural content generation via reinforcement learning. In: Proceedings of the AAAI Conference on Artificial Intelligence and Interactive Digital Entertainment, vol. 16, pp. 95–101 (2020)
17. Lai, G., Latham, W., Leymarie, F.F.: Towards friendly mixed initiative procedural content generation: three pillars of industry. In: International Conference on the Foundations of Digital Games, pp. 1–4 (2020)
18. Lazaridis, L., Papatsimouli, M., Kollias, K.-F., Sarigiannidis, P., Fragulis, G.F.: Hitboxes: a survey about collision detection in video games. In: Fang, X. (ed.) HCII 2021. LNCS, vol. 12789, pp. 314–326. Springer, Cham (2021). https://doi.org/10.1007/978-3-030-77277-2_24
19. Liapis, A.: 10 years of the PCG workshop: past and future trends. In: International Conference on the Foundations of Digital Games, pp. 1–10 (2020)
20. Liu, J., Snodgrass, S., Khalifa, A., Risi, S., Yannakakis, G.N., Togelius, J.: Deep learning for procedural content generation. Neural Comput. Appl. **33**(1), 19–37 (2020). https://doi.org/10.1007/s00521-020-05383-8
21. Minini, P., Assuncao, J.: Combining constructive procedural dungeon generation methods with wavefunctioncollapse in top-down 2D games. In: Proceedings of SBGames (2020)
22. Persson, M.: Minecraft. https://www.minecraft.net/en-us
23. Snodgrass, S., Ontanón, S.: Learning to generate video game maps using Markov models. IEEE Trans. Comput. Intell. AI Games **9**(4), 410–422 (2016)

24. Song, A., Whitehead, J.: TownSim: agent-based city evolution for naturalistic road network generation. In: Proceedings of the 14th International Conference on the Foundations of Digital Games, pp. 1–9 (2019)
25. Summerville, A.: Expanding expressive range: evaluation methodologies for procedural content generation. In: Fourteenth Artificial Intelligence and Interactive Digital Entertainment Conference (2018)
26. Summerville, A., et al.: Procedural content generation via machine learning (PCGML). IEEE Trans. Games **10**(3), 257–270 (2018)
27. Sutton, R.S., Barto, A.G.: Reinforcement Learning: An Introduction. MIT Press, Cambridge (2018)
28. Thompson, T., Lavender, B.: A generative grammar approach for action-adventure map generation in the legend of Zelda (2017)
29. Torrado, R.R., Khalifa, A., Green, M.C., Justesen, N., Risi, S., Togelius, J.: Bootstrapping conditional GANs for video game level generation. In: 2020 IEEE Conference on Games (CoG), pp. 41–48. IEEE (2020)
30. Viana, B.M., dos Santos, S.R.: Procedural dungeon generation: a survey. J. Interact. Syst. **12**(1), 83–101 (2021)

Spell Painter: Motion Controlled Spellcasting for a Wizard Video Game

Daniel MacCormick and Loutfouz Zaman[✉]

Ontario Tech University, Oshawa, ON, Canada
loutfouz.zaman@ontariotechu.ca

Abstract. Motion controlled video games were popular with the release of the original *Nintendo Wii,* but that popularity faded over time as new peripherals were released. While the *Wii*'s success demonstrated the interest that customers have in motion controls, motion controls too often rely on expensive external hardware. In this work, we present *Spell Painter*, a fully motion-controlled spell dueling game that can be played with only a webcam. We present the game and its implementation, as well as two preliminary evaluations, which suggest the system has an accuracy between 80%–90%.

Keywords: Hand tracking · Gesture recognition · Video game · Control system

1 Introduction

Within the last few decades, the video game industry has seen massive growth and is now worth more than 150 billion USD globally [35]. Alongside this growth, games have become exponentially larger and more complex, driving their costs higher as well [33]. This growth has also spurred rapid innovation within the field, allowing developers to try out novel ideas within all areas of game development.

One such area that has seen innovation in the game development field has been immersive technologies [36]. Immersive technologies attempt to bring the player metaphorically closer to the game, minimizing the interface barriers between them. In 2006, Nintendo released the *Wii* [37], which was one of the first truly mainstream immersive technologies for games. The main selling point of the *Wii* was its motion controls. Players had to physically move their bodies to control the games, making gestures that were mirrored by their in-game avatar. The motion controls proved to be incredibly popular, as the *Wii* became one of the highest selling video game consoles of all time [34]. The enthusiasm and excitement around the system clearly showed an interest in motion controls for mainstream video games. Later, competing video game companies Sony and Microsoft released their own motion control systems, known as the *PlayStation Move* [38] and *Kinect* [39], respectively. Microsoft also later released an updated version of the *Kinect,* known as the *Kinect* for *Xbox One* [40]. Despite the enthusiasm for the *Wii*'s motion controls, neither the *PlayStation Move* nor the *Kinect* were able to replicate its success, with both falling short of expectations [8]. After these systems, motion controls became largely forgotten and less prevalent in mainstream gaming. Recently, they were

X. Fang (Ed.): HCII 2022, LNCS 13334, pp. 51–68, 2022.
https://doi.org/10.1007/978-3-031-05637-6_4

brought back in some part due to the rise of virtual reality (VR) systems like the *Oculus Rift* [41] and the *HTC Vive* [42], as well as peripherals such as the *Leap Motion* [43].

While difficult to pinpoint exactly why competing motion control systems had trouble replicating the *Wii*'s success, one factor is likely cost. Cost is currently seen as one of the aspects holding back VR – and therefore motion controls – from becoming mainstream [32]. Nearly all motion control systems rely on specialized external hardware, which can cost hundreds of dollars. As a result, it becomes an interesting question to consider how one can create a motion-controlled game that is affordable and accessible to everyone. One possible answer is webcams.

Webcams are practically ubiquitous – they are integrated into nearly every laptop and smartphone on the market. As such, they are accessible to nearly everyone, and they come at effectively no extra cost [30]. Therefore, they can be a strong target for making motion-controlled video games without many of the hurdles present for other devices. To make a webcam-based motion-controlled game, computer vision techniques for hand or body tracking can be used.

There are several possible approaches for creating motion gesture recognition in computer vision. Hidden Markov Models [29] and finite state machines [9] are two examples. Gesture spotting [10] is another technique that is used to help identify the start and end of a motion gesture. There are also techniques that are useful for isolating the user's body from the background, such as background subtraction [17] and image segmentation [5]. After a body has been isolated, pose estimation [25] can be used to interpret full body gestures. In lieu of full body gestures, hand gestures can also be identified and utilized [3, 19, 20]. In summary, there are many useful computer vision techniques that can be employed to create a motion-controlled system using only a webcam. This work primarily focuses on hand gestures.

In this work, *Spell Painter* – a novel motion-controlled video game that only requires a webcam – is introduced. The game makes use of hand gesture identification. The game's premise is simple: the player takes on the role of a wizard and attempts to defeat their opponent in a best-of-five duel. The player paints glyphs in the air, representing the spells they want to cast. They control the painting via hand gestures. This simple game serves as an introductory exploration into webcam-based motion-controlled video games.

Two preliminary user evaluations, designed to evaluate the accuracy of the hand tracking and glyph identification system, are also introduced and discussed. Furthermore, a future comparative evaluation that can be performed to further understand the effectiveness of the gesture control techniques, is discussed. In short, this work makes the following contributions:

- the introduction of a novel spellcasting video game called *Spell Painter*, and
- an exploration of motion-control using only a webcam and hand gesture detection.

2 Related Work

2.1 Computer Vision Techniques

Freeman et al. [4] presented a number of computer vision techniques for interactive computer graphics. They utilized hand tracking and gestures to control a toy robot. They also developed a 3D magic carpet game that is controlled via leaning, with the ability to cast a spell by raising one's arm. They even created a simple rock paper scissors game that is controlled with hand gestures. Much of their implementation makes use of histograms of oriented gradients (HOGs) which make it robust to lighting changes.

Stergiopoulou et al. [23] combined several existing techniques to try and make hand tracking as accurate as possible. They combined motion detection and morphological features with a novel skin colour classifier, resulting in an accuracy of over 98%. Okkonen et al. [15] also combined several techniques together to better recognize hand gestures. They chose to use background subtraction and colour recognition, in combination with support vector machines (SVM) to identify the gestures. They performed an experiment in three uniquely lit and cluttered environments to evaluate the robustness of their approach, achieving an 89% accuracy.

2.2 Gesture-Controlled Utility Applications

Buades Rubio et al. [2] designed a system to track the user's hands and face for use in a VR application. Their system required submitting a photo of the user and manually highlighting regions that represent skin colour. The system uses this data as the basis for the tracking, computing a probability that each pixel in the image represents skin. They adapted their system to work with stereo cameras and used it to place an avatar of the user's head and hands into 3D space.

Wu et al. [28] used a *Kinect* sensor to control a program called *MeiTuKanKan*. Their approach relied on the depth information from the *Kinect*, as they assumed that the object in the foreground would be the hand. They then utilized HOGs to identify hand gestures. They connected different gestures within their gesture alphabet to certain actions in the program, allowing users to control the system fully using motion gestures. Rautaray and Agrawal [19] created a system that can be controlled with hand gestures, using techniques such as CAMShift [1] and Haar cascades [26]. They connected their gesture alphabet to controls in a simple image browser, allowing users to move, zoom, and rotate images.

Sabab et al. [21] introduced *Hand Swifter*, which is a gesture control system that can be used to navigate a computer. The system relies on a webcam as well as a *Leap Motion*. It has three distinct modes that can be switched between using gestures. They performed a preliminary user evaluation and received promising results.

2.3 Gesture-Controlled Video Games

Wilson and Salgian [27] created a webcam gesture-based control system for a first person shooter game. Their approach relied on background subtraction, skin detection, hand and face tracking, and gesture recognition. Their gesture alphabet is primarily based on full-body gestures, with a total of nine unique gestures. They performed a preliminary user evaluation to understand the system's accuracy and planned to later connect the system to *Quake II* [44]. Kang et al. [10] combined gesture spotting with gesture recognition to develop a system that identified motion gestures from a user's upper body. They completed the integration of their system into Quake *II* and were able to achieve an accuracy of 93%.

Zhu and Yuan [31] used the *Kinect* as the basis for their system which was able to recognize both one- and two-handed gestures. Their approach used template matching as well as colour and depth segmentation. They also made use of support vector machines (SVMs) to identify the difference between an open palm and a closed fist. They connected their system to both *PowerPoint* [45] and *Need for Speed* [46], as a way of demonstrating its robustness with both slow- and fast-paced tasks.

Doe-Hyung Lee and Kwang-Seok Hong [3] created a Chinese chess game that was controlled with hand gestures. Their approach used stereo cameras to calculate depth and assumed foreground objects were the hands. They also made use of difference image entropy as part of their method for hand recognition. Sriboonruang et al. [22] created a chess game that is controlled by gestures, where the player can pinch to "grab" a piece and release to let it go. Their approach made use of skin colour segmentation to identify the hand.

Yeh et al. [30] created a simple virtual ball catching game that was controlled with hand tracking and gestures. The user would close their hand to "catch" the ball. They used background subtraction and colour detection techniques. They chose to build their system to work with webcams since they are inexpensive and accessible. Khalaf et al. [11] performed a comparative evaluation between the *Leap Motion, Kinect,* and *Intel RealSense* [47] to compare performance, cognitive demand, comfort, and player experience. To facilitate this, they made a simple object grabbing game where the goal was to catch the object as quickly as possible. They found that participants both preferred and performed the best with the *Leap Motion*. Similarly, Pirker et al. [18] performed a comparative evaluation between *Leap Motion* control and standard keyboard and mouse control for a small game. They found that participants generally preferred *Leap Motion* and had an enjoyable experience with it, but also found it to be exhausting over an extended period.

Rautaray and Agrawal [19] developed a simple game where the player is stationary and defends themselves against enemy birds. The game is controlled via a webcam. The player can use different hand gestures to trigger attacks and defenses in-game. Manresa et al. [13] created a system to identify hand gestures for use in a video game. Their approach used image segmentation and convexity defect identification to determine gestures and they achieved a 98% accuracy. They did not actually connect their system to a game but could quickly do so given their system correctly maps gestures to action identifiers.

2.4 Commercial Motion Controlled Spellcasting Games

There are several similar commercial games that make use of hand tracking as well. *Harry Potter and the Deathly Hallows: Part 1* [48] optionally supported the *Kinect* sensor for casting spells. Similarly, *Fable: The Journey* [49] is a spellcasting game for the *Kinect* where the player can use gestures and motions to cast spells. Finally, *Spellpunk VR* [50] is a VR game released recently that serves as the primary inspiration for this work. In the game, players duel with magic spells which they can cast by drawing glyphs in 3D space with the VR system's motion controls.

2.5 Summary

Hand tracking and gesture identification have been studied extensively, having been used for both video games and utility applications. Some systems make use of external sensors such as the *Kinect* or *Leap Motion*, while others rely on webcams. It can be seen that webcams are a viable medium for creating motion-controlled games, but it has not been fully explored. *Spellpunk VR* provides an immersive approach for casting spells by drawing shapes in 3D space but is restricted by the expensive VR systems required to play the game. In this work, we present an approach that combines the immersive interaction of *Spellpunk VR* with the accessibility and affordability of webcams.

3 Spell Painter

Fig. 1. A screenshot of *Spell Painter*. Note the different sub-windows.

Spell Painter was built in *Python*. A screenshot showing all the aspects of the game can be seen in Fig. 1. The game screen is split into several important sub-windows. The top sub-window is where most of the game's effects and feedback appear. The game's theming is that of a medieval festival, where the wizards duel on a field, like a jousting match. The player controls the blue wizard on the left side of the screen and the artificial intelligence (AI) controls the red wizard on the right side. Each wizard has three coloured hearts above them, representing their remaining health. If the heart is brightly coloured, they still have that health, whereas if it is darkened, that health is lost. The player's goal is to bring the AI's health down to 0 before their own health is depleted.

Below the top window is the spell painting canvas. This is a live feed of the player's webcam with two tutorial overlays on it. The top overlay informs the player of the combat interactions and the glyphs that are needed to be painted for each of the three spells (fire, water, and lightning). The combat is based on a triangular system where each spell defeats one other spell and is defeated by another (water defeats fire, lightning defeats water, fire defeats lightning). The bottom overlay informs the player of the hand gestures that are required for controlling the painting. If the player holds up just their index finger, they can paint by moving their hand in front of the screen, with the "paint" emanating from the tip of their index finger. If they hold up three fingers, they can clear the screen. This is important so they can choose to cast a different spell or fix a mistake in their painting. Finally, if they hold up all five of their fingers, they will cast the spell. The clearing and casting are not instant, requiring ½ of a second of holding the gesture, to ensure that the player is certain they want to perform that action.

The game's internal systems can be broken into four major components: the hand detection and tracking, the hand gesture recognition, the glyph painting and detection, and finally the game logic.

3.1   Hand Detection and Tracking

There are two primary sub-components to the hand detection and tracking. They are background subtraction and hue-saturation-value (HSV) histogram backprojection [24]. Background subtraction is performed first to reduce some of the noise in the image and provide the backprojection algorithm with a smaller search space.

Background Subtraction. *Spell Painter's* background subtraction is implemented using *OpenCV*'s [51] default features. The *MOG2* subtractor algorithm was used, as it provided the clearest results without affecting performance substantially compared to the others (e.g., *KNN, CNT*, etc.). In the future, it would likely be worthwhile to further evaluate the performance of the different subtractors to select the best method for *Spell Painter*.

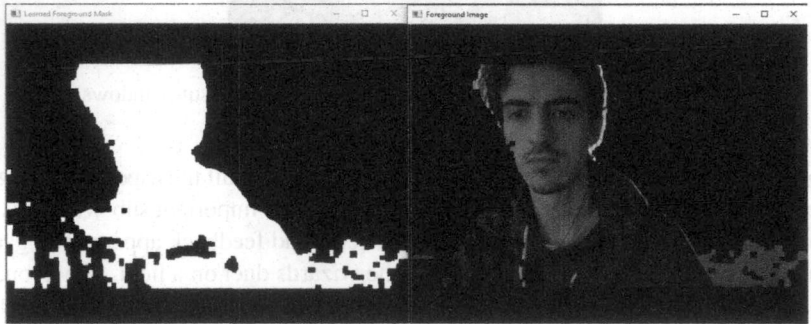

Fig. 2. Background subtraction. (Left) The background subtraction mask, after the convolution operations. (Right) The mask applied to the webcam to illustrate what has been identified as the foreground.

The output of this stage is a mask that is on the range of 0–1, where 0 indicates the pixel is the background and 1 indicates the foreground. *OpenCV*'s filtering is then used to smooth out the mask, helping to remove some of the holes in it. At this point, the background subtraction is complete. The results can be seen in Fig. 2 where the mask has been applied to the webcam image as well, for illustrative purposes. Normally, the player would not see either of these images.

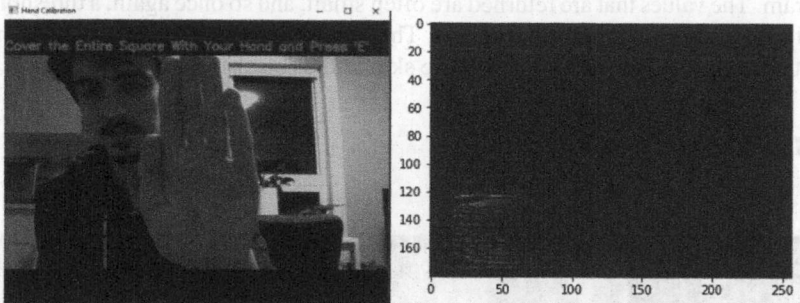

Fig. 3. (Left) A user placing their hand into the ROI. (Right) The histogram generated using the user's skin tone as reference. The X-axis is saturation and the Y-axis is hue. Note the higher values in the bottom left of the image.

HSV Histogram and Backprojection. The second stage in the hand detection and tracking involves a technique called histogram backprojection, which was initially introduced by Swain and Ballard [24]. In essence, backprojection is an algorithm that computes the probability of a given pixel belonging to a given histogram. When applied across an entire image, it results in a greyscale image, which can be treated as a mask when thresholded.

When the game first launches, it instructs the user to place their hand in front of the webcam such that it completely fills a rectangle on screen (see Fig. 3). This rectangle is a region of interest (ROI) which is then used to generate a histogram shortly thereafter. The histogram is a plot that depicts the concentration of colours in an image (see Fig. 3). The areas of the histogram that have the highest counts represent the range of colours that best represent the user's skin tone.

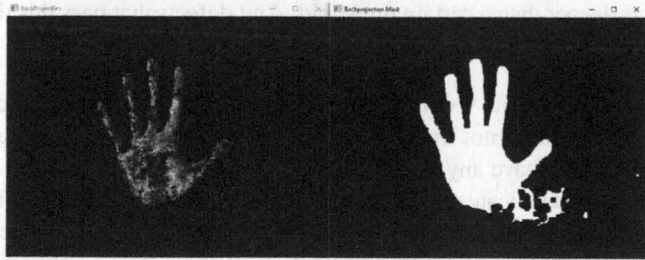

Fig. 4. The results of the backprojection. (Left) The initial results. (Right) The thresholded version, resulting in the final mask.

After the histogram is generated, it is passed to another of *OpenCV*'s functions, which performs the actual backprojection. It performs the algorithm on the result of the background subtraction since, in theory, the player's hand should be part of the foreground and therefore the background items are irrelevant. It uses the histogram as reference and determines the probability for each pixel belonging to the generated histogram. The values that are returned are often small, and so once again, a thresholding operation is applied to binarize it (Fig. 4). The result of this operation is a mask that is 1 (white) wherever there is perceived to be skin and 0 (black) where there is not.

3.2 Hand Gesture Recognition

Fig. 5. Counting fingers. Convex hulls are red, contours are blue, defects are green circles. (Left) Two defects have been identified, thus three fingers. (Right) Four defects have been identified, thus five fingers.

Counting Fingers. After the skin pixels have been identified with backprojection, *OpenCV*'s built-in functionality is used to determine the largest contour (assumed to be the hand) and convert it into a convex hull. After the hull is defined, its convexity defects are determined with *OpenCV*. When someone holds up their hand with their fingers splayed apart, the hull generated around the tips of the fingers would only be perturbed by the spaces between the fingers themselves (assuming no noise). As such, it can be assumed that defects are spaces between fingers (Fig. 5). In reality, there are often many more defects that are very small due to noise. Therefore, it is best to only consider defects deeper than a certain threshold. Any defects that pass this threshold are assumed to be related to fingers.

Following a simple logic, the number of fingers is the number of defects plus one. The only case where this is not true is when the user is holding up a single finger. The generated hull does not have any significant defects at all in this case. One can assume that zero defects would indicate one finger held up, but this does not differentiate between one finger held up and a closed fist. As such, in the cases where no defects are discovered, the system determines the highest point of the hull. If the distance between the highest point and the centroid is greater than a certain value, it can be assumed that one finger is being held up. Otherwise, it is assumed the hand is actually a closed fist. After the number of fingers has been determined, the game logic uses the information to control the painting according to the gesture alphabet.

Fig. 6. The gesture alphabet.

The Gesture Alphabet. *Spell Painter* has a simple gesture alphabet, with only three gestures (Fig. 6). If the user holds up one finger, they enter painting mode and can paint with the tip of their index finger. Holding up three fingers will clear the painting, allowing the user to erase anything they have painted and correct mistakes. Finally, holding up all five fingers will cast the spell, triggering the glyph detection and the subsequent game logic.

3.3 Glyph Painting and Detection

The glyph detection system is built around a convolutional neural network (CNN). The CNN is built with *PyTorch* [52] and trained using a synthetic dataset.

Creating the Glyph Dataset. In order to use the CNN to evaluate the player-painted glyphs, the CNN first had to be trained. We chose to generate synthetic dataset as it allowed us to train with many images.

Fig. 7. The base symbols for the three spells. From left to right: fire, lightning, water.

The first step to creating the synthetic dataset was to define the base symbols for each of the spells. The base symbols were created manually in a photo editing software and exported into 64 × 64 RGB images (Fig. 7).

After the base symbols were defined, a script using a free library called *Pillow* [53] was created to generate a set of 5,000 images for each spell type. The images were generated by applying random transformations to the symbols and exporting the results to new 64 × 64 images. Some example results can be seen in Fig. 8.

Training the CNN. The glyph detection CNN was created in PyTorch. It has three convolutional layers that utilize min pooling and ReLU [14] as the activation function. It also has two fully connected layers which also use ReLU. The first layer takes in a 64 × 64 image as input and the final layer has three possible outputs: fire, water, or lightning.

Fig. 8. Example generated images for each of the spells.

All 15,000 images were randomly shuffled and used in the process: 90% for training and 10% for testing. The training relies on the ADAM [12] optimizer with a learning rate of 0.001. It uses a batch size of 100 images. Initially, it was trained with 3 epochs, but overfitting was observed. The in-sample accuracy reached 100% but the network performed poorly with out-of-sample data (the hand-painted glyphs in-game). The final version was trained with only 1 epoch, which seems to still potentially be overfitting by reaching a 100% in-sample accuracy. It performs better in-game, however.

After the CNN was trained, the model was deployed and saved out to a file. It is loaded into *Spell Painter* when the game is launched so it can be used for analysis.

Fig. 9. The glyph painting. (Left) The glyph painted on top of the webcam seen by the user. (Right) The painting mirrored to the hidden canvas, unseen by the user.

Painting Within OpenCV. In order to use the CNN in-game, there must be something to pass as input, which is where the glyph painting comes in. When the game determines the user is holding up a single finger, it is set to painting mode. In this mode, it identifies the highest point on the hull and assumes it is the tip of the user's finger. From there, *OpenCV* is used to draw a small coloured circle onto the webcam image at that location. This allows the user to see what they are painting. At the same time, it also places a white circle onto a hidden canvas that is the same size as the webcam. More circles are placed every frame as the user moves their finger, which over time creates a painting (Fig. 9).

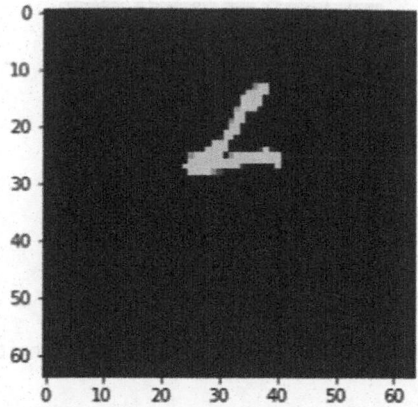

Fig. 10. The hidden canvas shown in the earlier figure, resized to 64 × 64 so it can be sent to the CNN.

Merging Painting with the CNN. When the game detects the user has held up five fingers for the required amount of time, it must attempt to identify the spell glyph. To facilitate this, the hidden canvas is resized to be 64 × 64 (Fig. 10), which is the input size of the CNN. It is then converted to a tensor and passed to the CNN. The largest of the three CNN output values is considered its single prediction, which is the spell that is cast. After the prediction is made, the canvas is cleared for the next spell.

3.4 Game Logic

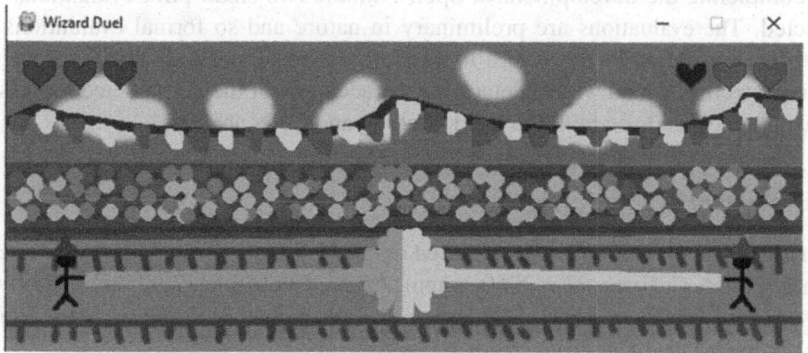

Fig. 11. The main game view, created with *PyGame*.

The game itself is simple. It was created in *PyGame*, which is a free library for making games in Python. The main game view, which is the top part of the game window (see Fig. 11), is all drawn with *PyGame* sprites. The bottom of the window is the result of the OpenCV webcam operations, and it is converted into a format that works with *PyGame*. Finally, PyGame sprites are used to overlay the tutorial images above the webcam output.

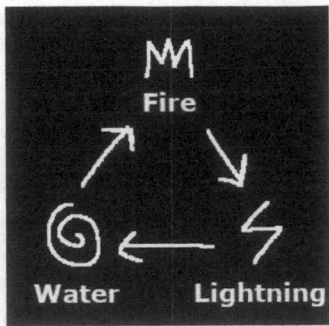

Fig. 12. The triangular spell system. The spell at the tail of the arrow defeats the spell at the tip of the arrow.

When the player casts a spell, the game displays the corresponding effect in the main game view. At the same time, it randomly selects a spell for the enemy AI to cast, with an equal 33.3% chance for each spell. It displays that effect as well and then determines the "winner" of the round. The winner is defined according to a simple triangular interaction (see Fig. 12) where every spell can defeat one other spell. If both spells that are cast are identical, no damage is done and the round ends. If there is a winner however, the winner deals one damage to the opponent, represented by the hearts in the interface. The game will end when one of the two wizards has completely run out of health. After this, the game will simply restart.

4 Evaluations

After completing the development of *Spell Painter*, two small pilot evaluations were conducted. The evaluations are preliminary in nature and so formal evaluations will need to be performed in the future to validate the results. The evaluations had one primary objective, which was to determine the accuracy of the glyph detection system. The accuracy depends on both the hand tracking and CNN analysis.

4.1 Evaluation 1

Apparatus. The evaluation was performed on an *MSI* laptop with Microsoft *Windows* 10, an NVIDIA *GeForce RTX* 2060 graphics card, Intel *Core* i7-9750H @2.60 GHz processor, and 16 GB of RAM. The laptop was positioned with the webcam facing a neutral-coloured wall with even overhead lighting.

Participants. Four participants were recruited via convenience sampling.

Design & Procedure. Each participant was introduced to *Spell Painter* before playing. The game, its mechanics, and its input method were explained. Then, a short demo was performed where one spell of each type was cast by the researcher. Any questions participants had were then answered. This was to ensure participants understood how to interact with the game and took roughly 5 min.

When participants were ready to begin, they launched the game themselves and placed their hand into the ROI as detailed earlier. They then began the game. A list of 30 spells, 10 of each type, were randomly shuffled. The first spell was read aloud to the participant and they proceeded to paint the corresponding spell glyph with the hand tracking and gesture system. Participants were free to clear the screen if they desired. After they were satisfied with their glyph, they cast the spell. The invigilator then recorded if the spell that was actually cast by the wizard matched the requested one. This was repeated for the remaining 29 spells in the list, until all 10 of each type had been cast. The full session took approximately 15 min.

Table 1. Results from evaluation 1.

Fig. 1. Participant ID, Dominant Hand	Fig. 2. Fire Correct (/10, %)	Fig. 3. Water Correct (/10, %)	Fig. 4. Lightning Correct (/10, %)	Fig. 5. Total Correct (/30, %)
Fig. 6. 1, Left	Fig. 7. 10, 100%	Fig. 8. 10, 100%	Fig. 9. 5, 50%	Fig. 10. 25, 83.3%
Fig. 11. 2, Right	Fig. 12. 10, 100%	Fig. 13. 9, 90%	Fig. 14. 8, 80%	Fig. 15. 27, 90.0%
Fig. 16. 3, Right	Fig. 17. 10, 100%	Fig. 18. 7, 70%	Fig. 19. 3, 30%	Fig. 20. 20, 66.7%
Fig. 21. 4, Right	Fig. 22. 10, 100%	Fig. 23. 10, 100%	Fig. 24. 6, 60%	Fig. 25. 26, 86.7%
Fig. 26. **Average**	Fig. 27. **10, 100%**	Fig. 28. **9, 90%**	Fig. 29. **5.5, 55%**	Fig. 30. **24.5, 81.7%**

Results of Evaluation 1. The results of the preliminary evaluation are detailed in Table 1. The participant's handedness was recorded to make sure it would work with both left and right hands. It was expected that this would not make a difference since the employed convexity defect approach for determining hand gestures is an analytical method that does not consider the underlying image information, and this is what was found within the small sample size.

It is interesting to note the accuracies. Fire was identified correctly 100% of the time. Water was slightly less reliable, with an accuracy of 90%. Lightning, however, averaged 55% accuracy which is quite poor in comparison.

Post-Evaluation 1 System Modifications. The following changes were made to the system to improve accuracy:

- glyph rotation was randomized within full range of 360° (was previously only 30°),
- learning rate was lowered from 0.001 to 0.0005,
- epochs were increased to 5, and

- batch size was changed to 32.

These changes resulted in an in-sample accuracy of 54.6% after a single epoch (previously was 100% after a single epoch) and a final in-sample accuracy of 96.7%.

4.2 Evaluation 2

The apparatus and procedure were identical to the ones that were used in the first evaluation. The participants were re-used for the second evaluation. The following changes were made to the system to improve accuracy after the first evaluation:

Table 2. Results from Evaluation 2.

Fig. 31. Participant ID, Dominant Hand	Fig. 32. Fire Correct (/10, %)	Fig. 33. Water Correct (/10, %)	Fig. 34. Lightning Correct (/10, %)	Fig. 35. Total Correct (/30, %)
Fig. 36. 1, Left	Fig. 37. 10, 100%	Fig. 38. 8, 80%	Fig. 39. 8, 80%	Fig. 40. 26, 86.7%
Fig. 41. 2, Right	Fig. 42. 10, 100%	Fig. 43. 9, 90%	Fig. 44. 8, 80%	Fig. 45. 27, 90.0%
Fig. 46. 3, Right	Fig. 47. 9, 90%	Fig. 48. 10, 100%	Fig. 49. 8, 80%	Fig. 50. 27, 90.0%
Fig. 51. 4, Right	Fig. 52. 10, 100%	Fig. 53. 10, 100%	Fig. 54. 9, 90%	Fig. 55. 29, 96.7%
Fig. 56. Average	Fig. 57. 9.75, 97.5%	Fig. 58. 9.25, 92.5%	Fig. 59. 8.25, 82.5%	Fig. 60. 27.25, 90.8%
Fig. 61. Change from Evaluation 1	Fig. 62. −0.25, −2.5%	Fig. 63. +0.25, +2.5%	Fig. 64. +2.75, +27.5%	Fig. 65. +2.75, +9.1%

Results of Evaluation 2. The results of the evaluation can be seen in Table 2. The overall accuracy in this evaluation was slightly above 90%, which shows a roughly 9% increase. In this evaluation, there was an instance where fire was incorrectly identified, thus showing a decrease in accuracy. This is expected, as over a large enough sample size, the system is unlikely to be 100% accurate for any symbol type. Water had a similarly small increase in accuracy, which can again likely be attributed to random variations.

The largest difference is within the lightning detection, as the accuracy increased by 27.5%. It is possible that the performance increase can be most directly attributed to the rotations applied to the synthetic dataset. The CNN was possibly mis-identifying the lightning symbols as slightly rotated fire symbols. Training on more heavily rotated data seems to have mitigated this effect somewhat. That said, lightning still has the lowest accuracy and so can be further improved.

5 Limitations

This work has several limitations. Firstly, the most obvious is the participant sample size within the evaluations. A proper evaluation would likely require at least 10 or more participants to have a strong enough sample size. Reusing the participants for both evaluations could also have biased the results, as the accuracy increase could potentially be partially attributed to the participants making better glyphs due to their previous experience with the system. In addition, the participants were recruited using convenience sampling within the demographic that does not go against the social distancing norms. It would be better to have a broad assortment of participants. It would also be valuable to perform the evaluation in front of several backgrounds, with varying light conditions and clutter, similar to Okkonen et al. [15]. This would give a better idea of the robustness of the system.

6 Future Work

There are numerous ways this work could be built upon in the future. To begin with, the hand gesture identification system could be converted to working with a CNN to improve robustness. Afterwards, both CNN's could be finely tuned to achieve the highest possible accuracy. The game could also be expanded, with the introduction of many new spells. This would require a rebalancing of the combat system, but it would likely become more engaging as a result. Similarly, the game could be made multiplayer, either locally or via networking. It would also be interesting to connect the game to full body gestures, instead of just hand gestures. This could potentially be accomplished by using the *Kinect* sensor, or by implementing a deep neural network-based pose estimation system like *DeepPose* [25].

Furthermore, formal user studies can be performed to properly evaluate the system. This would involve an extension of the preliminary evaluations discussed in this paper. It could also involve an additional user evaluation, with a different procedure. This evaluation would be similar to those performed by Pirker et al. [18] and Khalaf et al. [11] in that it would compare the game when played with different input methods. Comparing the current version of the game with one that uses the mouse to paint spells could be one consideration, another could use the keyboard to cast them, and potentially one that uses another peripheral like the *Leap Motion*. We could also compare against cutting-edge VR input systems such as the *Sensoryx VR Glove* [54].The comparison would follow recommendations from Pettersson et al. [16], in that it would include multiple methods of data collection. Accuracy metrics, a standard questionnaire such as the NASA-TLX [6, 7], and a semi-structured interview can all be employed. The goal of the evaluation would be to identify which spell input method is preferred by users.

7 Conclusion and Future Work

In this paper, we presented *Spell Painter*, a simple spellcasting game controlled by painting spell symbols with hand gestures. The game can be played with only a webcam, mitigating the need for users to purchase expensive external hardware devices. The results of two preliminary evaluations were presented, suggesting that the spell detection is between 80%–90% accurate. In the future we will use this method for different games and perform comparative user studies with a larger set of participants.

Acknowledgements. We would like to thank our friend and colleague, Dr. Faisal Qureshi, for his guidance throughout this project. His assistance was invaluable in sparking the project's development.

References

1. Bradski, G.R.: Computer vision face tracking for use in a perceptual user interface (1998)
2. Buades Rubio, J.M., Perales, F., Varona, J.: Real Time Segmentation and Tracking of Face and Hands in VR Applications, pp. 259–268 (2004)
3. Lee, D.H., Hong, K.-S. Game interface using hand gesture recognition. In: 5th International Conference on Computer Sciences and Convergence Information Technology, pp. 1092–1097 (2010)
4. Freeman, W.T., et al.: Computer vision for interactive computer graphics. IEEE Comput. Graph. Appl. **18**, 42–53 (1998). https://doi.org/10.1109/38.674971
5. Haralick, R.M., Shapiro, L.G.: Image segmentation techniques. Comput. Vision Graph. Image Process. **29**, 100–132 (1985)
6. Hart, S.G.: Nasa-Task Load Index (NASA-TLX); 20 Years Later. Proc. Hum. Factors Ergon. Soc. Annu. Meet **50**, 904–908 (2006). https://doi.org/10.1177/154193120605000909
7. Hart, S.G., Staveland, L.E.: Development of NASA-TLX (task load index): results of empirical and theoretical research. In: Hancock, P.A., Meshkati, N. (eds.) Advances in Psychology. North-Holland, pp. 139–183 (1988)
8. Hester, B.: All the money in the world couldn't make Kinect happen. In: Polygon. https://www.polygon.com/2020/1/14/21064608/microsoft-kinect-history-rise-and-fall (2020). Accessed 9 Dec 2020
9. Hong, P., Turk, M., Huang, T.S.: Gesture modeling and recognition using finite state machines. In: Proceedings Fourth IEEE International Conference on Automatic Face and Gesture Recognition (Cat. No. PR00580). IEEE, pp. 410–415 (2000)
10. Kang, H., Lee, C.W., Jung, K.: Recognition-based gesture spotting in video games. Pattern Recogn. Lett. **25**, 1701–1714 (2004). https://doi.org/10.1016/j.patrec.2004.06.016
11. Khalaf, A.S., Alharthi, S.A., Dolgov, I., Toups, Z.O.: A comparative study of hand gesture recognition devices in the context of game design. In: Proceedings of the 2019 ACM International Conference on Interactive Surfaces and Spaces. Association for Computing Machinery, New York, NY, USA, pp. 397–402 (2019)
12. Kingma, D.P., Ba, J.: Adam: A Method for Stochastic Optimization. arXiv:14126980 [cs] (2017)
13. Manresa, C., Varona, J., Mas, R., Perales, F.J.: Hand tracking and gesture recognition for human-computer interaction. ELCVIA Electron. Lett. Comput. Vision Image Anal. **5**, 96–104 (2005). https://doi.org/10.5565/rev/elcvia.109
14. Nair, V., Hinton, G.E.: Rectified linear units improve restricted Boltzmann machines. In: ICML (2010)
15. Okkonen, M.-A., Kellokumpu, V., Pietikäinen, M., Heikkilä, J.: A visual system for hand gesture recognition in human-computer interaction. In: Ersbøll, B.K., Pedersen, K.S. (eds.) SCIA 2007. LNCS, vol. 4522, pp. 709–718. Springer, Heidelberg (2007). https://doi.org/10.1007/978-3-540-73040-8_72

16. Pettersson, I., Lachner, F., Frison, A.-K., Riener, A., Butz, A.: A Bermuda triangle?: a review of method application and triangulation in user experience evaluation. In: Proceedings of the 2018 CHI Conference on Human Factors in Computing Systems. ACM, New York, NY, USA, pp. 461:1–461:16 (2018)
17. Piccardi, M.: Background subtraction techniques: a review. In: 2004 IEEE International Conference on Systems, Man and Cybernetics (IEEE Cat. No. 04CH37583). IEEE, pp. 3099–3104 (2004)
18. Pirker, J., Pojer, M., Holzinger, A., Guetl, C.: Gesture-Based Interactions in Video Games with the Leap Motion Controller (2017)
19. Rautaray, S.S., Agrawal, A. Interaction with virtual game through hand gesture recognition. In: 2011 International Conference on Multimedia, Signal Processing and Communication Technologies, pp. 244–247 (2011)
20. Rautaray, S.S., Kumar, A., Agrawal, A.: Human computer interaction with hand gestures in virtual environment. In: Kundu, M.K., Mitra, S., Mazumdar, D., Pal, S.K. (eds.) PerMIn 2012. LNCS, vol. 7143, pp. 106–113. Springer, Heidelberg (2012). https://doi.org/10.1007/978-3-642-27387-2_14
21. Sabab, S.A., Islam, S.S., Hossain, M., Shahreen, M.: Hand swifter: a real-time computer controlling system using hand gestures. In: 2018 4th International Conference on Electrical Engineering and Information Communication Technology (iCEEiCT), pp. 9–14 (2018)
22. Sriboonruang, Y., Kumhom, P., Chamnongthai, K.: Visual hand gesture interface for computer board game control. In: 2006 IEEE International Symposium on Consumer Electronics, pp. 1–5 (2006)
23. Stergiopoulou, E., Sgouropoulos, K., Nikolaou, N., Papamarkos, N., Mitianoudis, N.: Real time hand detection in a complex background. Eng. Appl. Artif. Intell. **35**, 54–70 (2014). https://doi.org/10.1016/j.engappai.2014.06.006
24. Swain, M.J., Ballard, D.H.: Indexing via color histograms. In: Active Perception and Robot Vision. Springer, pp. 261–273 (1992)
25. Toshev, A., Szegedy, C.: DeepPose: Human Pose Estimation via Deep Neural Networks, pp. 1653–1660 (2014)
26. Viola, P., Jones, M.: Rapid object detection using a boosted cascade of simple features. In: Proceedings of the 2001 IEEE Computer Society Conference on Computer Vision and Pattern Recognition, CVPR 2001. IEEE, p. I–I (2001)
27. Wilson, R., Salgian, A.: Gesture Recognition for a Webcam-Controlled First Person Shooter (2008)
28. Wu, X., Yang, C., Wang, Y., Li, H., Xu, S.: An intelligent interactive system based on hand gesture recognition algorithm and Kinect. In: 2012 Fifth International Symposium on Computational Intelligence and Design, pp. 294–298 (2012)
29. Yamato, J., Ohya, J., Ishii, K.: Recognizing human action in time-sequential images using hidden Markov model. In: CVPR, pp. 379–385 (1992)
30. Yeh, C.-H., et al.: Vision-based virtual control mechanism via hand gesture recognition. J. Comput. **21**, 55–66 (2010)
31. Zhu, Y., Yuan, B.: Real-time hand gesture recognition with Kinect for playing racing video games. In: 2014 International Joint Conference on Neural Networks (IJCNN), pp. 3240–3246 (2014)
32. Virtual reality is too expensive. In: Game Rant. https://gamerant.com/virtual-reality-too-expensive-305/ (2016). Accessed 9 Dec 2020
33. The cost of games. In: VentureBeat. https://venturebeat.com/2018/01/23/the-cost-of-games/ (2018). Accessed 6 Dec 2020
34. The Bestselling Consoles of All Time. In: Digital Trends. https://www.digitaltrends.com/gaming/bestselling-consoles-of-all-time/ (2020). Accessed 9 Dec 2020

35. Video Game Market Size, Share, Industry Report, 2020–2027. https://www.grandviewres earch.com/industry-analysis/video-game-market. Accessed 6 Dec 2020
36. Incredible Advances in Gaming Technology Enhancing Gamer Immersion. In: UKTN (UK Tech News). https://www.uktech.news/incredible-advances-in-gaming-technology-enh ancing-gamer-immersion. Accessed 9 Dec 2020
37. Nintendo Wii, Console and Games. In: Encyclopedia Britannica. https://www.britannica.com/ topic/Nintendo-Wii. Accessed 9 Dec 2020
38. PlayStation Move. In: PlayStation. https://www.playstation.com/en-ca/explore/accessories/ vr-accessories/playstation-move/. Accessed 9 Dec 2020
39. Kinect for Xbox 360. https://marketplace.xbox.com/en-US/Product/Kinect-for-Xbox-360/ 66acd000-77fe-1000-9115-d8025858084b. Accessed 9 Dec 2020
40. Kinect – Windows app development. https://developer.microsoft.com/en-us/windows/kinect/. Accessed 9 Dec 2020
41. Oculus Rift, Oculus. https://www.oculus.com/rift/. Accessed 9 Dec 2020
42. VIVE^{TM} Canada, Discover Virtual Reality Beyond Imagination. https://www.vive.com/ca/. Accessed 9 Dec 2020
43. Tracking, Leap Motion Controller. Ultraleap. https://www.ultraleap.com/product/leap-mot ion-controller/. Accessed 7 Oct 2020
44. QUAKE II on Steam. https://store.steampowered.com/app/2320/QUAKE_II/. Accessed 9 Dec 2020
45. Download PowerPoint, Try PowerPoint, Free, Microsoft 365. https://www.microsoft.com/ en-ca/microsoft-365/powerpoint. Accessed 10 Dec 2020
46. Need for Speed Video Games – Official EA Site. https://www.ea.com/games/need-for-speed. Accessed 10 Dec 2020
47. Intel® RealSense^{TM} Technology. In: Intel. https://www.intel.com/content/www/us/en/archit ecture-and-technology/realsense-overview.html. Accessed 10 Dec 2020
48. Harry Potter and the Deathly Hallows^{TM} – Part 1. https://marketplace.xbox.com/en-ie/ Product/Harry-Potter-and-the-Deathly-Hallows-Part-1/66acd000-77fe-1000-9115-d80245 4108f9. Accessed 2 Dec 2020
49. Fable: The Journey. https://marketplace.xbox.com/en-CA/Product/Fable-The-Journey/66a cd000-77fe-1000-9115-d8024d530a1a. Accessed 7 Oct 2020
50. SpellPunk VR on Steam. https://store.steampowered.com/app/1258980/SpellPunk_VR/. Accessed 7 Oct 2020
51. OpenCV: In: OpenCV. https://opencv.org/. Accessed 2 Dec 2020
52. PyTorch: https://www.pytorch.org. Accessed 2 Dec 2020
53. Pillow: Python Imaging Library (Fork)
54. Sensoryx – VRfree® glove – intuitive VR interaction. https://www.sensoryx.com/. Accessed 1 Feb 2021

Dynamic Difficulty Adjustment in Digital Games: Comparative Study Between Two Algorithms Using Electrodermal Activity Data

Ian Nery Bandeira[1], Vitor F. Dullens[1], Thiago V. Machado[1],
Rennê Ruan A. Oliveira[1], Carla D. Castanho[1], Tiago B. P. e Silva[2(✉)],
and Mauricio M. Sarmet[3]

[1] Department of Computer Science, University of Brasilia, Brasília, Brazil
iannerybandeira@gmail.com
[2] Department of Design, University of Brasilia, Brasília, Brazil
tiagobarros@unb.br
[3] Federal Institute of Education, Science and Technology of Paraíba, Paraíba, Brazil

Abstract. With the increasing reach of digital games, it is beyond doubt that the gaming experience should be pleasurable while at the same time appropriately challenging. In this context, the Dynamic Difficulty Adjustment (DDA) technique is used to adapt the difficulty level as a function of the player's ability. In this work, electrodermal activity (EDA) data were used to infer the arousal levels and affective states of each player in order to use them as input in the comparison of two DDA algorithms: Data Subset Analysis (DSA) and Real-Time Arousal Set (RTA). A blind experiment was conducted with 60 participants, implementing these algorithms within the game *Asteroids: in the 2nd and 1/2th Dimension* and collecting data through game metrics, algorithm adjustments, and through questionnaires regarding the participants' perception of the experiments, such as game difficulty and their joy while playing the game. Our findings indicated that the DSA algorithm could detect the player's excitement level more adequately when compared to the RTA algorithm. This allows for finer adjustments to the game's difficulty, creating a more enjoyable experience for players.

Keywords: Affective Dynamic Difficulty Adjustment (Affective DDA) · Electrodermal activity (EDA) · Digital games

1 Introduction

The gaming industry has a constant growth in the entertainment of people of various ages and profiles. Currently, much is being studied about balancing game difficulty [9,10], since people with different profiles can play the same game, strengthening the idea that it is essential to have mechanisms that adjust the game to the player's skill level.

© The Author(s), under exclusive license to Springer Nature Switzerland AG 2022
X. Fang (Ed.): HCII 2022, LNCS 13334, pp. 69–83, 2022.
https://doi.org/10.1007/978-3-031-05637-6_5

The Dynamic Difficulty Adjustment (DDA) technique aims to adjust the difficulty of a given game based on player data, either performance data or affective data. A performance DDA [10] uses only data provided from the gameplay to adjust the game difficulty, e.g., the number of times the player has died to a specific enemy. On the other hand, the affective DDA [10] aims to infer the player's emotional state from physiological data by sensing whether a player is angry, bored, frustrated, among other affective states, and from those inferences, adjust the game difficulty for the player to enjoy it better.

There are several DDA algorithms, whether based on Performance data, Affective data or Hybrid that were used in previous works [5,10,14,16]. This study analyzes two Affective DDA algorithms based on electrodermal activity (EDA) [2]: the *Data Subset Analysis* (DSA) [12] which was later adapted by Imre [10] and the *Real-Time Arousal Set* (RTA) [3] later adapted by Rosa [16]. The Data Subset Analysis (DSA) is an algorithm with a simple yet robust design, based on the work of authors Fairclough and Gilleade [4] and Leiner, Fahr and Früh [12]. The Real-Time Arousal Set (RTA) algorithm, based on Dawson's description [3], uses minimum and maximum values of skin conductance, making it possible to extract the tonic (slow changes) and phasic (peaks) components of the user's EDA.

The main goal of this work is to compare the DSA and RTA algorithms for affective DDAs, which use electrodermal activity data as the input signal to perform the fitting calculations. To this end, a practical experiment was conducted with a population of 60 participants.

The rest of this manuscript is organized as follows. Section 2 presents the main theoretical concepts involved in this research, such as: emotion and affective states, electrodermal activity, dynamic difficulty adjustment, among others. Section 3 details the methodology used to carry out the empirical experiment. The results have been compiled and are presented in Sect. 4. The Conclusion is found in Sect. 4.

2   Fundamental Concepts

This section introduces the main concepts related to this work, such as Affect, Electrodermal Activity (EDA), Dynamic Difficulty Adjustment (DDA), and DDA Algorithms.

2.1   Affect

According to Russell [17], affect can be described by combining two independent scales: Arousal and Valence. The Arousal scale corresponds to the intensity of a sensation, i.e. when the arousal is low, it represents tiredness or drowsiness, while high arousal represents panic or surprise. Valence corresponds to the positivity or negativity inherent to the emotion, i.e., it corresponds to pleasure when positive and displeasure when negative.

From these two scales, Russell proposed a Circumplex Model of Affect (Fig. 1). From this model, it is possible to represent any affect in a two-dimensional form from the coordinates of Arousal, which corresponds to the y-axis of the model, and Valence corresponding to the x-axis.

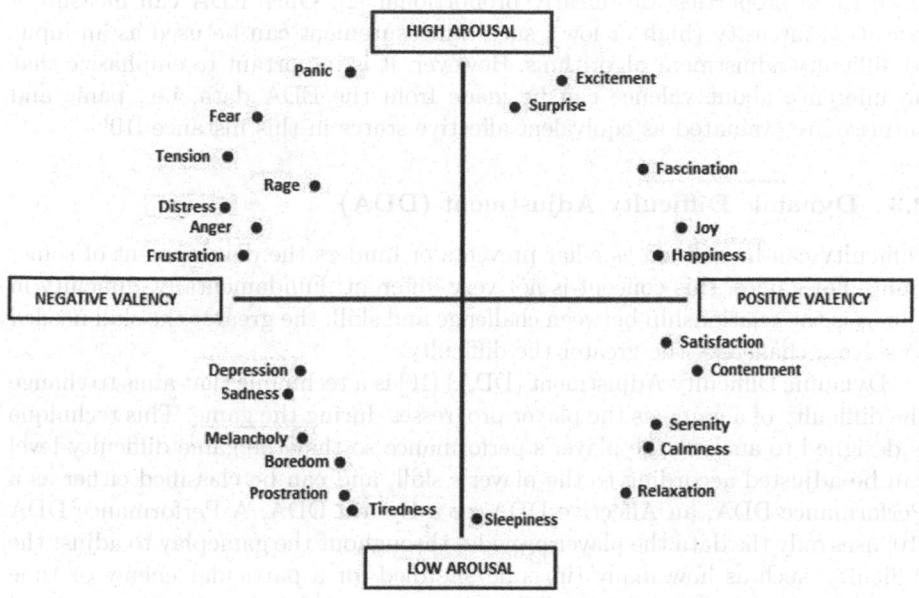

Fig. 1. Circumplex model of affect, proposed by Russell. (Adapted from [17])

The proposed model fits into the context of this work as it allows the player's affective state to be estimated from two variables, that is, the player's arousal and valence degrees are collected and treated as input to the algorithms that manipulate them to adapt the difficulty of a game.

2.2 Electrodermal Activity (EDA)

Affective states can be perceptible beyond those who feel them [11] - they can be perceived through physiological signs such as heartbeat, change in skin tone, sweat, and agitation, among others. In this context, Electrodermal Activity (EDA), also known as Galvanic Skin Response (GSR), is described as the property of the human body that causes continuous variations in the electrical characteristics of the skin and can be detected through sensors that apply an electrical potential and measure the resulting electric current flow between them.

According to Braithwaite [2], two main components describe the EDA: the tonic-level, which correlates to slower changes and secondary features of the signal (slow rises and slopes over time, its overall level), which is commonly measured by the Skin Conductance Level (SCL); and the EDA phasic-level, which refers to rapid changes in the signal, i.e., the Skin Conductance Response (SCL) from unexpected, relevant, and aversive events. Recent evidence suggests that both are essential components and may rely on different neural mechanisms [3].

From the electrodermal activity (combination of tonic and phasic components), it is possible to infer the arousal intensity of a person (x-axis of Fig. 1) since these properties are linearly proportional [2]. Once EDA can measure a sensation intensity (high or low), such a measurement can be used as an input to difficulty adjustment algorithms. However, it is important to emphasize that no inference about valence can be made from the EDA data, i.e., panic and surprise are evaluated as equivalent affective states in this instance [10].

2.3 Dynamic Difficulty Adjustment (DDA)

Difficulty can be defined as what prevents or hinders the development of something. For games, this concept is not very different. Fundamentally, difficulty in games is the relationship between challenge and skill; the greater the skill needed to solve a challenge, the greater the difficulty.

Dynamic Difficulty Adjustment (DDA) [10] is a technique that aims to change the difficulty of a game as the player progresses during the game. This technique is designed to analyze the player's performance so that the game difficulty level can be adjusted according to the player's skill, and can be classified either as a Performance DDA, an Affective DDA, or a Hybrid DDA. A Performance DDA [10] uses only the data the player provides throughout the gameplay to adjust the difficulty, such as how many times he/she died for a particular enemy or time spent in a phase. An Affective DDA [10] tries to infer the player's emotional state from physiological data, detecting whether a player is angry, bored, or frustrated, for example, and from these inferences, it adjusts the game to improve the player's experience. The Hybrid DDA [10] uses both, performance data and the player's affective data, to ajust the difficulty.

2.4 DDA Algorithms

There are several DDA algorithms, whether by Performance, Affective or Hybrid that were used in previous works [5,10,14,16]. This study analyzes two Affective DDA algorithms based on electrodermal activity (EDA)[2]: the *Data Subset Analysis* (DSA) [12] which was later adapted by Imre [10] and the *Real-Time Arousal Set* (RTA) [3] later adapted by Rosa [16].

The Data Subset Analysis (DSA) is an algorithm with a simple yet robust design, based on the work of authors Fairclough and Gilleade [4] and Leiner, Fahr, and Früh [12]. It takes only the last two EDA measurements and computes the difference between them, adding the result to a final amount. This process is repeated a certain predetermined number of times, and, based on the obtained result, the algorithm detects if any change in the player's excitation state has occurred. If the change is detected, the game adjustment is performed.

Based on Dawson's description [3], the Real-Time Arousal Set (RTA) algorithm uses the minimum and maximum values of skin conductance, making it possible to extract the tonic (slow changes) and phasic (peaks) components of the user's EDA. These components make it possible to establish the general excitement level in a window between 0 and 1000. This process is repeated throughout the game session and is saved after a certain amount of time. Then, a comparison between the excitation value found and the previously calculated excitation value is performed, and the adjustment is made from the result.

3   Methodology

The main goal of this research is to compare the DSA and RTA algorithms for affective DDAs using electrodermal activity data as an input to perform the difficulty adjustment calculations. Therefore, a practical experiment was conducted in a controlled environment at the University of Brasília with 60 participants using the game *Asteroids: in the 2nd and 1/2th Dimension* with both implementations (Fig. 2).

The game *Asteroids: in the 2nd and 1/2th Dimension* (Fig. 2) has a license for non-commercial use and is open source, allowing the necessary changes to be made to the DDA implementation. Moreover, the game has a straightforward goal – to pass trough an entire level while dodging asteroids – and its difficulty can be modified just by changing the speed of the asteroids. On each level, the player must control a ship to cross a finish line after a field of asteroids without colliding with them. It is also possible for the player to shoot the asteroids to destroy them. The distance required to complete a level is shown on screen and the player starts each level with a shield that absorbs only the first collision with an asteroid. If the player's ship collides with another asteroid and is destroyed, the player will return to the beginning of the level.

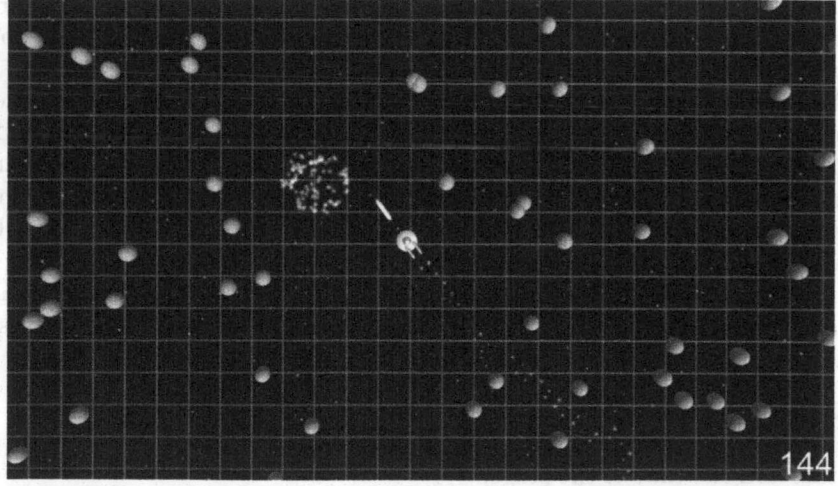

Fig. 2. Scene from the game *Asteroids: in the 2nd and 1/2th Dimension*

In order to avoid bias favoring a specific DDA algorithm, the experiment participants were randomly and blindly divided into three groups: those who played the game with the RTA algorithm-based DDA (n = 20); those who played the game with the DSA algorithm-based DDA (n = 20); and those who played the game without using any DDA algorithm (control group, n = 20). For real-time acquisition of the player's EDA data (tonic and phasic components) the wristband sensor *Empatica E4* was used (Fig. 3).

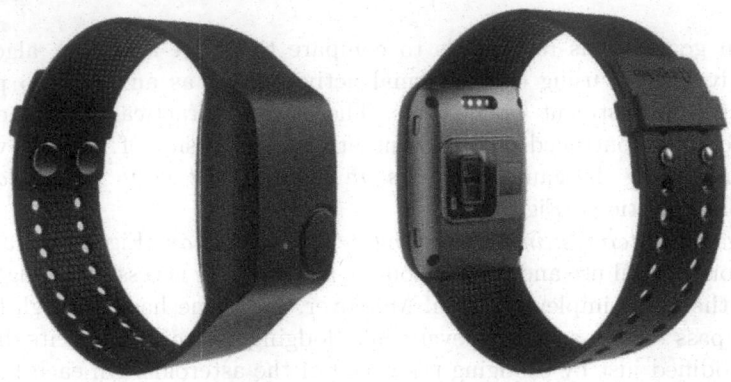

Fig. 3. Empatica E4 Wristband

Each participant received and signed an Informed Consent Form detailing the objectives of the experiment and how it would be conducted. Also, the participants received an initial questionnaire to collect demographic data and information regarding expertise with games. Then, the participants played six levels of the game. After each level, the participants were requested to answer a brief questionnaire (available at Table 1) on their perception of difficulty, boredom, frustration, and fun for that specific stage.

At the end of each game session, another questionnaire was applied to collect the participant's general perceptions about the gameplay (available at Table 2). Both the questionnaires involving the participants' perception on each game level (Table 1) and the general gameplay impressions (Table 2) only contained close-ended questions with a scale from 1 to 10 or a Likert scale [1] as possible answers.

In addition to the EDA data, the following metrics regarding the game and the algorithms were captured, which could provide a baseline for comparison between the two algorithms:

- Number of asteroids;
- Minimum and maximum speed of the asteroids;
- Start and end time of the stage;
- Stage duration;
- Average time per life;

Table 1. Questionnaire questions for each level

ID	Question
Q1.1	On a scale from 1 to 10, how difficult was this level?
Q1.2	This level was tedious
Q1.3	This level was frustrating
Q1.4	This level was fun

Table 2. Questionnaire questions on general gameplay

ID	Question
Q2.1	On a scale from 1 to 10, how do you rate your performance in the game?
Q2.2	The game was challenging
Q2.3	I was able to overcome all the presented challenges
Q2.4	The game difficulty was appropriate
Q2.5	I enjoyed the experience of playing this game
Q2.6	My attention was entirely focused on the game
Q2.7	At several moments I found myself doing things automatically, without having to think
Q2.8	I lost track of time while playing the game

- Whether the player has completed the phase;
- Time in which the player died;
- The moment and amount of adjustments that were made by the DDA algorithms.

4 Results

4.1 Demographic Profile of the Participants

Regarding their age, 4% of the participants are less than 18 years old, 26% are between 18 and 22, 58% are between 23 and 27, 2% are between 28 and 32, and 10% of the players are over 32 years old. Regarding gender, 72% of the participants identify themselves as male, and 28% identify themselves as female.

Concerning the participants' experience with video games, on a scale of 1 to 5, where 1 refers to having no experience and 5 refers to having a lot of experience, 64% of the participants reported to have some experience with games (between 4 and 5), and the other 36% reported to have little experience (between 1 and 3). Regarding how much the participants like 2D games, on a scale of 1 to 5, where 1 represents no liking and 5 represents liking 2D games a lot, 69.7% chose between 1 and 3;

Regarding familiarity with gaming devices, 50% of the participants reported that they are most familiar with playing on desktops computers, 30% on consoles, 15% on smartphones, and 5% on portable consoles.

About the preferred difficulty setting for games, 33.3% of the participants reported that when they play a game, it is usually set on hard difficulty, 51% are set on medium, and 15.7% are set on easy.

With the data from this questionnaire, we have that the audience participating in the experiment is primarily male, with a high experience playing games. It can also be observed that the study population is dispersed concerning preferred difficulty setting. Most respondents do not like 2D games, and the device most used by the participants to play is a desktop computer.

4.2 Comparative Analysis Between DSA and RTA Algorithms

To effectively compare the described algorithms, we analyze the data regarding the player's performance (i.e. average deaths per level and average duration of each phase); data regarding the algorithms behavior (i.e. average number of adjustments performed by each algorithm at each level); and data regarding the players perceptions collected by the questionnaires.

About the number of deaths per level, the Fig. 4 shows that the participants that played with the RTA algorithm display a higher number of deaths than the other groups. In contrast, the group with the DSA algorithm has a lower average than the control group and the RTA algorithm group, particularly in the last three stages. Regarding the average stage duration per level, presented in Fig. 5, it can be seen that there is relative maintenance of the average time, with the RTA group increasing slightly faster than the others.

These data alone has little relevance since the death in games not necessarily means a bad indicator for the functioning of the algorithms adjustment. Death is often used as a core mechanic that enhances both gameplay and narrative [15] in several game genres, including souls-like [6,7,15], platformer [13], and rogue-like games [7,8,18]. However, considering the analysis of the number of adjustments made by the algorithms at each level, presented by Fig. 6, we can see that the number of adjustments performed by the DSA algorithm was higher than those performed by the RTA algorithm. This finding might indicate that the DSA algorithm perceives difficulty settings better, especially in the game's early stages where the low difficulty can let the player unmotivated without an adjustment.

The pattern observed in the average amount of adjustments for the DSA algorithm over the stages may indicate a potential convergence in the number of adjustments, while the pattern observed in the RSA algorithm adjustments appears to be erratic. This behavior is positively reflected in the analysis of perceived difficulty collected at the end of each level, presented in Fig. 7, where the trend line of the DSA algorithm remained more constant on the difficulty axis when compared to the RTA algorithm and the control group. This suggests that the difficulty increased more steadily when analyzing the group using the DSA algorithm rather than the other two.

When looking at the Fig. 6, the adjustments of the DDA using the RTA algorithm are higher in levels 1, 2, 3, and 5 when compared to the levels 4 and 6. This reflects on the data of Figs. 5 and 4, staying in a similar metric to that observed in the analyses of the group that used the DSA algorithm. However, this pattern is not reproduced in stages 4 and 6, which, when compared to their respective previous levels, the RTA algorithm performed few adjustments. Thus, we can infer that, with the thresholds proposed by Oliveira [14], the RTA algorithm works punctually but does not have a consistent behavior throughout the test, strengthening the idea that these thresholds should be changed for greater consistency of the results.

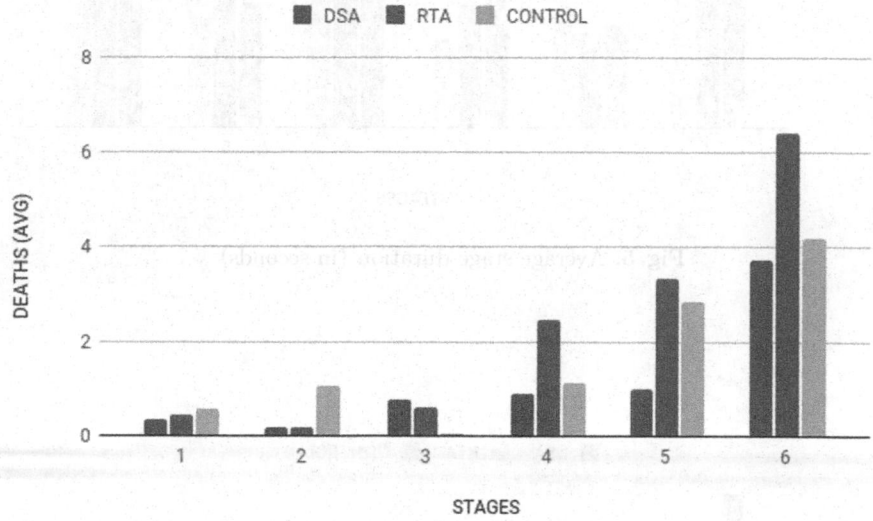

Fig. 4. Average deaths per level

A punctual analysis of the positive and negative adjustments of each algorithm in a specific stage also enlightens us about the functioning of the algorithms, whereas positive adjustments refer to the ones that increase the asteroid speed, while negative adjustments refer to the ones that decrease the asteroid speed. To allow such analysis using varying lengths of stage duration, the data was normalized into 12 time quantiles, as presented in Figs. 8, 9, and 10. They represent the results for the first, the middle, and the last stages of the experiment, respectively.

In Fig. 8, referring to the analysis of the first and easiest level, the amount of positive adjustments is higher than the number of negative adjustments, especially for the DSA algorithm, which performs a more significant amount of increments in speed than the RSA algorithm. Similar to the level 6 analysis, presented in Fig. 10, in which the difficulty is greater because the levels are built based on the final velocity of the previous level plus a fixed velocity, the DSA algorithm

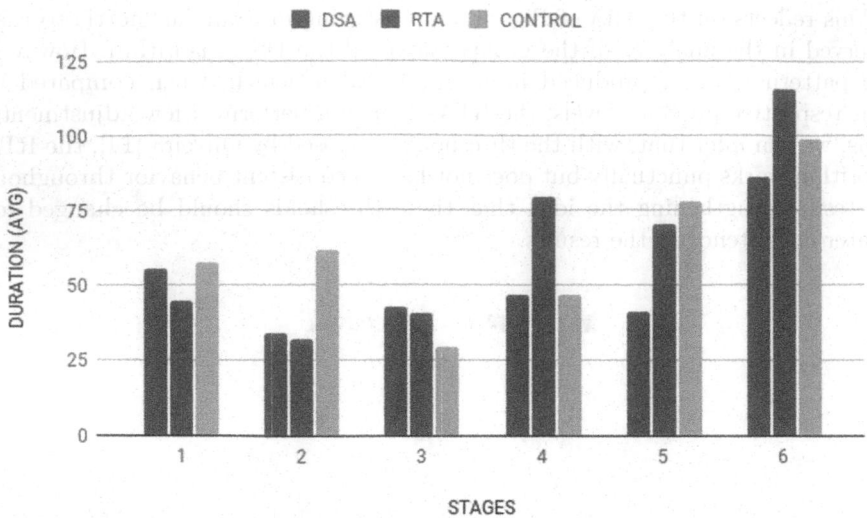

Fig. 5. Average stage duration (in seconds)

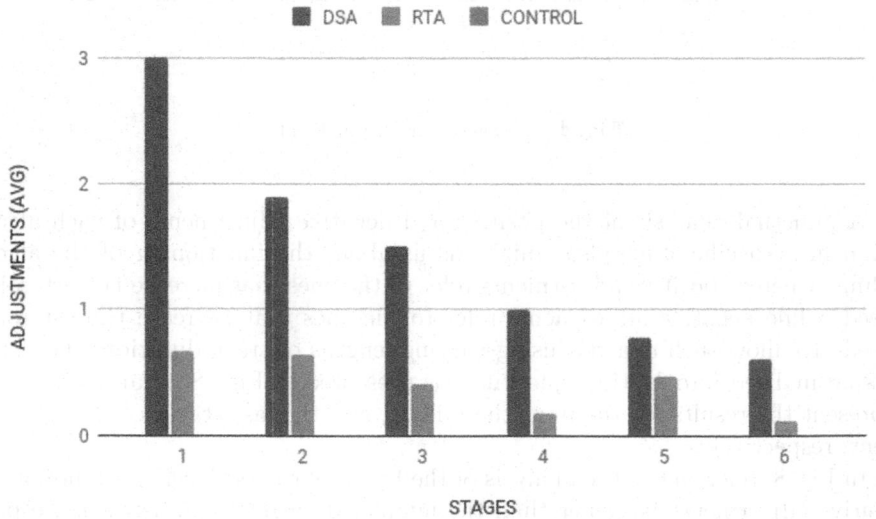

Fig. 6. Average number of adjustments performed by the algorithms per level

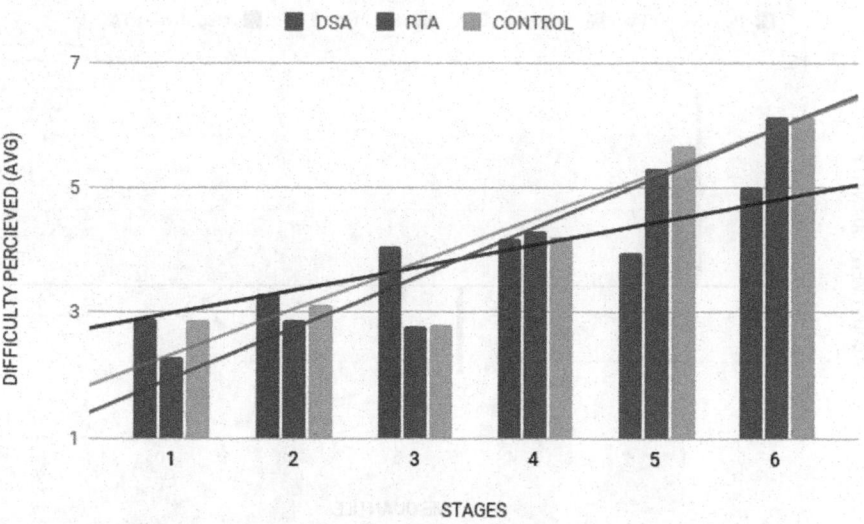

Fig. 7. Average reported difficulty per level (Question Q1.1)

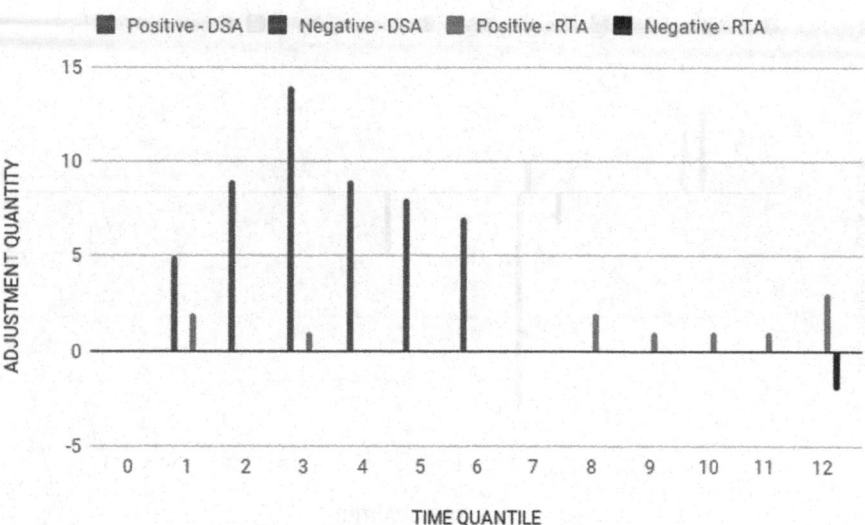

Fig. 8. Total amount of adjustments per stage duration - Stage 1

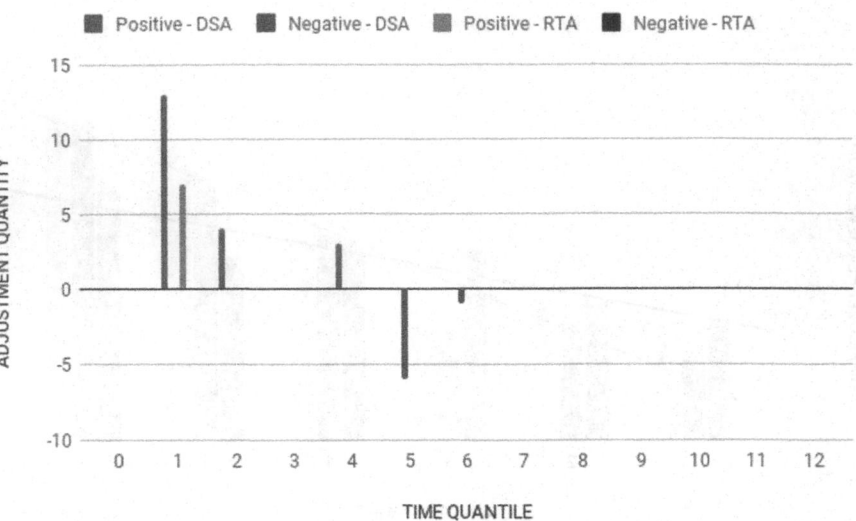

Fig. 9. Total amount of adjustments per stage duration - Stage 3

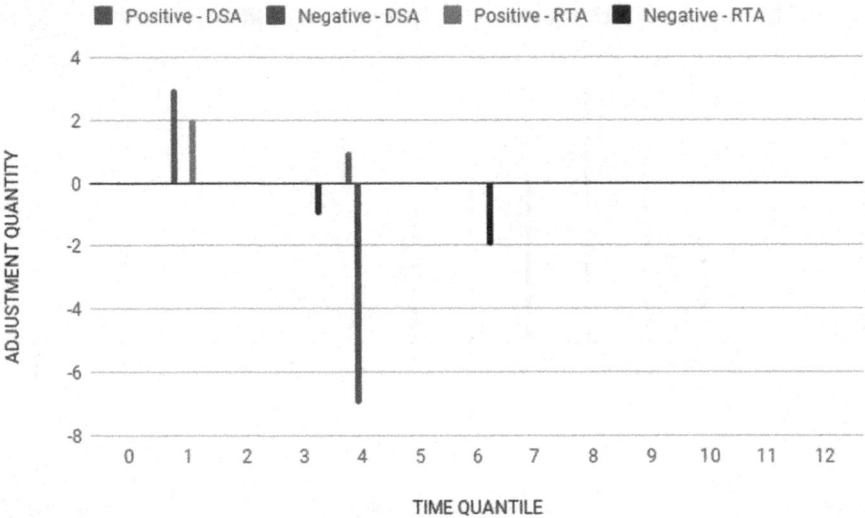

Fig. 10. Total amount of adjustments per stage duration - Stage 6

performs a much larger amount of negative adjustments than the RTA algorithm, which also performs them in a later period besides having a smaller amount of adjustments to reduce the velocity of the asteroids.

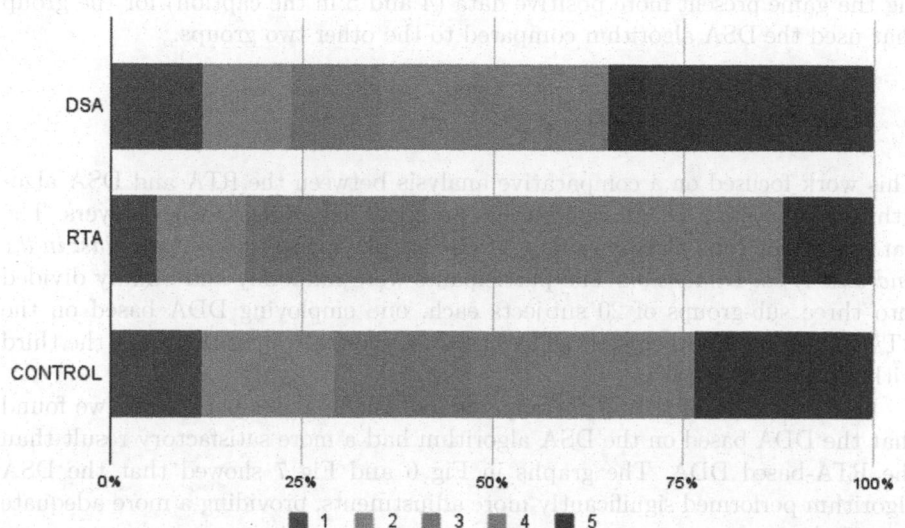

Fig. 11. Respondents' perception regarding whether the difficulty was appropriate or not (Question Q2.4)

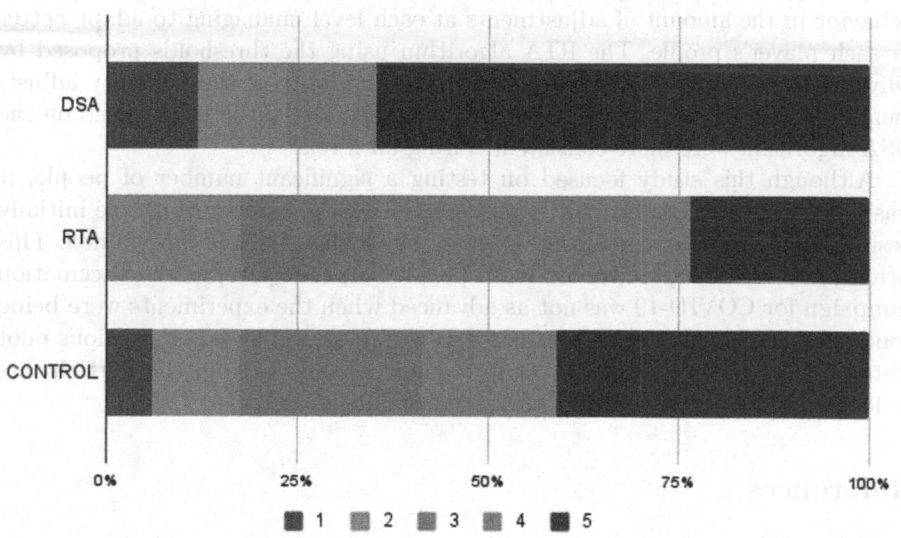

Fig. 12. Respondents' perception into whether they enjoyed the game or not (Question Q2.5)

From the data collected on each participant's perception in the general game-play questionnaire, presented in Table 2, we found that questions Q2.4 and Q2.5, presented in Figs. 11 and 12, corroborate our earlier findings. The perception of players regarding the overall difficulty of the game and their enjoyment of playing the game present more positive data (4 and 5 in the caption) for the group that used the DSA algorithm compared to the other two groups.

5 Conclusion

This work focused on a comparative analysis between the RTA and DSA algorithms for affective DDAs, conducting practical experiments with players. The data collection took place with 60 participants playing the game *Asteroids: in the 2nd and 1/2th Dimension*. The participants were randomly and blindly divided into three sub-groups of 20 subjects each, one employing DDA based on the RTA algorithm, another with DDA based on the DSA algorithm, and the third without any DDA.

From the data of the 60 participants and the analyses performed, we found that the DDA based on the DSA algorithm had a more satisfactory result than the RTA-based DDA. The graphs in Fig. 6 and Fig. 7 showed that the DSA algorithm performed significantly more adjustments, providing a more adequate game balance.

Therefore, it can be concluded that the DSA algorithm performed better in the tests. This happens, mainly, because the DSA algorithm is able to more adequately detect the player's excitement level. In addition, it has a convergent behavior in the amount of adjustments at each level, managing to adapt better to each player's profile. The RTA algorithm using the thresholds proposed by Oliveira [14] presented inconsistencies in the regularity of the difficulty adjustments for some game levels. The participants who tested the DDA based on the DSA algorithm were more consistent during all levels.

Although this study focused on testing a significant number of people, it was not possible to conduct the experiments with the number of people initially desired, given the pandemic conditions in which this study is constrained. This situation made it impossible for more people to participate, as the vaccination campaign for COVID-19 was not as advanced when the experiments were being conducted. Although the number of levels was increased based on previous pilot tests, it was still not sufficient, as it was not feasible to hold the participants inside the collection room for a prolonged period.

References

1. Allen, I.E., Seaman, C.A.: Likert scales and data analyses. Qual. Prog. **40**(7), 64–65 (2007)
2. Braithwaite, J.J., Watson, D.G., Jones, R., Rowe, M.: A guide for analysing electrodermal activity (EDA) & skin conductance responses (SCRs) for psychological experiments. Psychophysiology **49**(1), 1017–1034 (2013)

3. Dawson, M.E., Schell, A.M., Filion, D.L.: The electrodermal system (2017)
4. Fairclough, S.H., Gilleade, K.: Advances in Physiological Computing. Springer, London (2014). https://doi.org/10.1007/978-1-4471-6392-3
5. Fernandes, M.V.: Dynamic difficulty adjustment in digital games: a comparative case study between affective and performance-based models. Technical report, University of Brasilia, November 2021. https://bdm.unb.br/handle/10483/29227
6. Gandolfi, E.: Enjoying death among gamers, viewers, and users: a network visualization of dark souls 3's trends on Twitch.tv and steam platforms. Inf. Vis. **17**(3), 218–238 (2018). https://doi.org/10.1177/1473871617717075
7. Genovesi, M., et al.: I passed away, but i can live again: the narrative contextualization of death in dead cells and Sekiro: shadows die twice. Acta Ludolog. **4**(2), 32–41 (2021)
8. Godfirnon, M.: Mythologie et narration DANs le rogue-like: analyse de hades, 14 May 2020. http://hdl.handle.net/2268/251398
9. Hunicke, R.: The case for dynamic difficulty adjustment in games. In: Proceedings of the 2005 ACM SIGCHI International Conference on Advances in Computer Entertainment Technology, pp. 429–433 (2005)
10. Imre, D.: Real-time analysis of skin conductance for affective dynamic difficulty adjustment in video games. Bachelor's dissertation (2016). http://danielimre.com/wp-content/uploads/2016/03/Imre-Real-Time-Analysis-of-Skin-Conductance-for-Affective-Dynamic-Difficulty-Adjustment-in-Video-Games.pdf
11. Lang, P.J.: The emotion probe: studies of motivation and attention. Am. Psychol. **50**(5), 372 (1995)
12. Leiner, D., Fahr, A., Früh, H.: EDA positive change: a simple algorithm for electrodermal activity to measure general audience arousal during media exposure. Commun. Methods Meas. **6**(4), 237–250 (2012)
13. Melcer, E.F., Cuerdo, M.A.M.: Death and rebirth in platformer games. In: Bostan, B. (ed.) Game User Experience And Player-Centered Design. ISCEMT, pp. 265–293. Springer, Cham (2020). https://doi.org/10.1007/978-3-030-37643-7_12
14. Oliveira, R.R.A.: Analysis of different dynamic difficulty adjustment algorithms using electrodermal activity data in digital games. Technical report, University of Brasilia, October 2021. https://bdm.unb.br/handle/10483/28952
15. Petralito, S., Brühlmann, F., Iten, G., Mekler, E.D., Opwis, K.: A good reason to die: how avatar death and high challenges enable positive experiences. In: Proceedings of the 2017 CHI Conference on Human Factors in Computing Systems, CHI 2017, pp. 5087–5097. Association for Computing Machinery, New York (2017). https://doi.org/10.1145/3025453.3026047
16. Rosa, M.P.C.: Hybrid dynamic difficulty setting in a platform game genre. Technical report, University of Brasilia, July 2020. https://bdm.unb.br/handle/10483/25301
17. Russell, J.A.: A circumplex model of affect. J. Pers. Soc. Psychol. **39**(6), 1161 (1980)
18. Wilson, J.B.: Roguelife: digital death in videogames and its design consequences. Ph.D. thesis, Massachusetts Institute of Technology (2019)

Playable Characters Attributes: An Empirical Analysis Based on the Theoretical Proposal from Katherine Isbister and Ernest Adams

Tânia Ribeiro(✉) ⓘ, Gonçalo Ribeiro ⓘ, and Ana Isabel Veloso ⓘ

DigiMedia, University of Aveiro, Aveiro, Portugal
ribeirotania@ua.pt

Abstract. The research aims to test the attributes proposed by the authors Katherine Isbister, *Better game characters by design: a psychological approach* (2006) and Ernest Adams in *Fundamentals of Game Design* (2006). The Playable Characters analyzed were retrieved from the most played digital games from the *Entertainment Software Association* (ESA) reports between 2008 e 2017 and fit the following inclusion criteria: be a third person character; the aesthetical look of the Playable Character had to remain unchanged throughout the game; be a single-player game and the Playable Character from the digital game has to be the protagonist.

Considering the inclusion criteria, the Playable Characters analyzed are Niko Bellic from the digital game *Grand Theft Auto IV*, John Marston (*Red Dead Redemption*), Batman (*Batman: Arkham City*), Edward Kenway (*Assassin's Creed IV: Black Flag*), Joel Miller (*The Last of Us*), Aiden Pearce (*Watch Dogs*) and Link (*The Legend of Zelda: Breath of the Wild*). The characters mentioned were selected based on their commercial success – retrieved from ESA sales reports and analyzed based on their physical and psychological attributes. The attributes were tested through 110 participants through an online survey – comparing the perception between respondents who played and did not play the games in analysis. The results show that the character perception of the respondents about physical and psychological attributes is similar regarding their gaming experience.

Keywords: Digital games · Playable characters · Physical attributes · Psychological attributes

1 Introduction

Digital games and digital games-related media – such as gamified applications – are a subject with a wide range of applicability covering health, education, marketing, and so on [1]. In addition, digital games-related industries nowadays have a substantial economic impact, currently considered one of the most lucrative entertainment industries [2].

The person's identification with a character – from a game or other medium – impacts the individual's social persona, a phenomenon that in some cases promotes the creation of

X. Fang (Ed.): HCII 2022, LNCS 13334, pp. 84–100, 2022.
https://doi.org/10.1007/978-3-031-05637-6_6

social groups around these characters or digital games [3]. Several authors [4–6] reported this phenomenon and dedicated research to digital games-related subjects. Furthermore, there is a lack of empirical research to test the off-the-shelf Playable Character attributes and the player's perceptions about Playable Characters from games.

The purpose of this paper is to test the attributes presented by the authors Katherine Isbister in the book *Better game characters by design: a psychological approach* (2006) [5] and by Ernest Adams, in the book *Fundamentals of Game Design* [6] through an online survey.

This paper is organized as follows: Sect. 2 explains the attributes proposed by the authors Katherine Isbister and Ernest Adams that motivates this research; Sect. 3 is about the survey design and dissemination strategy; Sect. 4 presents the results, divided into four subsections, sample characterization; the survey results are detailed regarding the respondents' perception of the characters they had played; the respondents' perception of characters they hadn't play, and finally the discussion of the results, where an overview of the results is made, confronting the data collected about the characters' perception in analysis. This paper ends with conclusions, research limitations, and future work.

2 Playable Characters Attributes Characterization

Physical attributes generally affect how one perceives and treats a person. From a social standpoint, the previous sentence is sometimes an uncomfortable truth since, at a young age, we have been told that "beauty is only skin deep." Nevertheless, it is true that sometimes we, as a society, misunderstand a person based on their appearance. It is the subject of countless fictional works: the infantile fairy tale *The Ugly Duckling,* the computer-animated comedy film *Shrek,* and *The Elephant Man* are examples of popular culture portraying this phenomenon [5].

According to the author Katherine Isbister in the book *Better game characters by design: a psychological approach* (2006) [5], the same principles can be applied to Playable Characters, and for that matter, Isbister highlights three key attributes – *Attractiveness, Babyfaces,* and *Stereotypes* – that may affect the player's first impressions of digital game characters.

Attractiveness refers to aesthetic values related to possessing features that arouse interest in others. These qualities are related to being good-looking, beautiful, healthy-looking, good posture, body and facial symmetry, and the right height. Players tend to consider characters with these attributes dominant, intelligent, stronger, kinder and tend to be more sympathetic towards the character. The opposite effect happens when the visual qualities are reversed, which can be used, for example, to create more disgusting antagonists. This characteristic is also called the *halo effect* or *halo error* [7].

Babyfaces refer to characters with infant-like facial features. These characters tend to have big eyes and pupils, small chin, high eyebrows and forehead, small nose, and full lips and cheeks, all resembling an adult's face and body. The human bias assumes that those who have babyfaces will be warmer and more trustworthy. These characters may also be more dependent, less responsible, and more submissive and manipulable [5].

The last attribute proposed is Stereotypes. These characters are powerful social tools that guide unconscious decisions perpetuating an inequitable situation. For this matter, stereotypes are a sensitive subject. Stereotypes can be defined as schemas or preconceptions in your memory that associate a pattern of cues with a typical set of qualities in a person. It refers to physical attributes like style, gender, ethnicity, posture, manner of speaking and moving, and the company in which a person is seen. So, being good-looking, healthy-looking is a sign of intelligence, good companies, and so on. Stereotypes can help players make rapid character evaluations in a digital game. Still, stereotypes can withdraw value in a more complex character and lead to a personality misunderstanding [5].

Once that player gets to know the character – by playing with them; understanding the character's background and motivations – the player comes to see the personality depth of his character [6]. In the book *Fundamentals of Game Design* [6] (2077), Ernest Adams classified a character's psychological depth in four dimensions, namely zero-dimensional (0d), one-dimensional (1d), two-dimensional (2d), and three-dimensional (3d):

The most rudimentary characters are the zero-dimensional (0d) characters: they have binary antagonistic emotional states with no mixed feelings, like happy and sad. The one-dimensional (1d) characters have only a single variable to characterize a changing feeling or attitude, like a non-binary zero-dimensional. Still, these two antagonistic emotions can change in a spectrum: like happy and sad and a bit sad, fully happy, and so on. The two-dimensional (2d) characters are described by multiple variables expressing their impulses. Still, those do not conflict between them, like antipathy or sympathy, hate or love. They can feel antipathy and hate simultaneously, but never antipathy and love because these feelings are each other's opposite. The most complex characters are three-dimensional (3d): they have multiple emotional states that can produce conflicting impulses. These characters are not just black and white. They have doubts and mixed feelings. According to the author, these characters are the rarest in digital games because they are the most difficult to implement in technical terms [6].

The definition attributes were coded to be utilized and conveyed so that the non-academic public can understand (Table 1).

Table 1. Research key concepts coded to be instrumentalized in the survey:

Author concept	Key concepts (coded)
Attractiveness; *Babyfaces* and *Stereotypes* [5]	Intelligence
	Charisma
	Physical robustness
	Kindness
	Player sympathy towards the character
	Dependence (dependent on other characters)
	Responsibility
	Manipulation (manipulable by other characters)

(*continued*)

Table 1. (*continued*)

Author concept	Key concepts (coded)
	Submission (submissive towards other characters)
	Trustworthiness
	Psychological robustness
0d character [6]	The character has one emotional state at a time, with no transition in between emotional states
1d character [6]	The character is divided between two dichotomous/binary emotional states
2d character [6]	The character shows a change of attitude or feelings regarding a single variable throughout the whole game
	The character behaves erratically (expresses emotion and acts in a contradictory way)
3d character [6]	The character distinguishes moral values
	The character is psychologically complex

3   Methods: Survey Design and Dissemination

As previously mentioned, the research aims to test the attributes proposed for the authors Katherine Isbister in *Better game characters by design: a psychological approach* (2006) and Ernest Adams in *Fundamentals of Game Design* (2006). So, after the attributes were coded (Table 1), they were transformed into survey questions to test the respondents' perception of selected characters.

The Playable Characters tested were retrieved from the most played games from the *Entertainment Software Association* (ESA) reports between 2008 e 2017 [8–14] that fit in the following four inclusion criteria: i) be a third person character; ii) the aesthetical look of the character had to maintain unchanged throughout the game; iii) be a single-player game, and iv) the playable character from the digital game has to be the protagonist.

In order to test the player's perception of the characters, a five-section survey was designed to do the data collection, where each group had different aims as systematized in Table 2.

Table 2. Survey design:

Section:	Questions	Typology
1. Sample characterization	Age	Multiple choice

(*continued*)

Table 2. (*continued*)

Section:	Questions	Typology
	Education level	Multiple choice
	Nationality	Open question
2. Gaming habits characterization	Digital Games Played (Hours/week)	Multiple choice
	Life period when spending more time playing (Hours/week)	Multiple choice
	Gaming Platforms	Multiple choice
	Three digital games were played and finished	Open question
	Typology player-playable character [15]	Ranking
3. Games played	Digital game genres which respondents ever played (from the characters in the study)	Open question
4. Played character perception analysis	Resorting to your memory of the [character], do you consider that character] shows the usual behavior (stereotypical) of a playable character belonging to an action-adventure game?	Multiple choice: Yes or No
	How would you rate the characterization of [Character image] regarding Physical appearance; Physiognomy/Countenance; Movement	Linkert scale: (1 Less usual (stereotypical) – 4 More usual (stereotypical))
5. Played characters dimensionality [6]	5a. This [Character] one emotional state at a time, with no transition in between emotional states	Linkert scale: 1 Do not Agree – 4 Strongly Agree
	5b. This [Character] is divided in between two dichotomous/binary emotional states (Peace/Fury)	
	5c. This [Character] shows a change of attitude or feelings regarding a single variable throughout the game	
	5d. This [Character] behaves erratically (expresses emotion and acts in a contradictory way)	
	5e. This Character distinguishes moral values (right/wrong)	
	5f. This Character is psychologically complex	

(*continued*)

Table 2. (*continued*)

Section:	Questions	Typology
6. Non-played character perception analysis	Focusing exclusively on the pictures above, rate: Intelligence; Charisma; Physical robustness; Psychological robustness; Kindness; Friendliness; Your sympathy towards this Character; Dependence (dependent on other characters); Responsibility; Manipulation (manipulable by other characters); Submission (submissive towards other characters); Trustworthiness	Linkert scale: 1 Less – 4 More

Being set the inclusion criteria, the Playable Characters analyzed were: Niko Bellic from the digital game *Grand Theft Auto IV* [16]; John Marston (*Red Dead Redemption*) [17]; Batman (*Batman: Arkham City*) [18]; Edward Kenway (*Assassin's Creed IV: Black Flag*) [19]; Joel Miller (*The Last of Us*) [20]; Aiden Pearce (*Watch Dogs*) [21] and Link (*The Legend of Zelda: Breath of the Wild*) [22]. The characters mentioned were selected based on their commercial success – retrieved from ESA sales reports [2] and analyzed based on their physical and psychological attributes. These attributes were retrieved based on the authors Katherine Isbister, explicit in the book *Better game characters by design: a psychological approach* (2006) and Ernest Adams *Fundamentals* of Game Design (2006).

The survey structure changes accordingly to the progress of respondents, such as whether respondents had played the games in analysis or not to properly evaluate their perception. When a Playable Character is mentioned in the survey sections, an image of the character is displayed in three photographic plans: medium shot, close up, and full shot [23] (from the front and the back of the character). These images displayed (screenshots) were retrieved from each character in the referent game.

4   Results

The survey was available from June 18th, 2020, to July 18th, 2020, in private digital game-related social groups in social networks (Facebook and Discord) and distributed via e-mail throughout University of Aveiro students and Staff.

This section presents the survey results, divided into four subsections. In the first section, sample characterization is made. Then, in Subsect. 4.2, the survey results are detailed regarding the respondents' perception of the characters they had played, followed by the respondents' perception of characters they hadn't played. In the last section of this section, the results are discussed, confronting the data collected about the characters in the analysis.

4.1 Sample Characterization

The questionnaire had 217 valid responses – 107 (49.31%) from female respondents and 110 (50.60%) from male respondents. Additionally, most of the respondents (N = 104) came were Portuguese's (94.55%).

In Sect. 2 of the survey, regarding the question about three games played, 110 respondents declared having played at least 3 games in their life. For that reason, these respondents were considered gamers and selected for further analysis. The remaining respondents were eliminated for not being considered gamers once they did not have enough familiarity with the medium [24–27].

110 participants declared having played at least 3 games in their life: 34 female respondents and 76 male respondents. The data collected about respondents' characterization, referent to the first two survey sections, is systemized in Table 3.

In the question where the participant identified the genres of digital games for which they have the greatest preference, the action-adventure games were selected by N = 66 (64.7%) of the respondents followed by role-playing games (RPG) (62.7%, N = 64) and shooters (61.8%, N = 63). Only one respondent declared not to identify digital games by genre.

The last question of the third survey section was as if the respondent had played 3 digital games throughout their life. A total of 110 respondents (54.46%) had played. For that reason, they were eligible to respond to Sect. 3 (played the game) and Sect. 4 of the survey (played but did not finish):

i)   *Grand Theft Auto IV:* N = 34 played the game, N = 7 never played the game, N = 37 played but did not finish;

ii)   *Red Dead Redemption:* N = 21 played the game, N = 66 never played the game, N = 23 played but did not finish.

iii) *Batman: Arkham City:* N = 24 played the game, N = 60 never played the game, N = 26 played but did not finish;

iv)   *Assassin's Creed IV: Black Flag:* N = 32 played the game, N = 47 never played the game, N = 31 played but did not finish;

v)   *The Last of Us:* N = 29 played the game, N = 61 never played the game, N = 20 played but did not finish;

vi)   *Watch Dogs:* N = 13 played the game, N = 61 never played the game, N = 36 played but did not finish;

vii) *The Legend of Zelda: Breath of the Wild:* N = 19 played the game, N = 64 never played the game, N = 27 played but did not finish (Fig. 1).

The number of players who played but did not finish impacts the survey last section since the survey questions are different regarding the respondent's gaming experience. As previously mentioned, the responses of "Played but not finished" were discarded once these respondents had contact with the character and game narrative, but they didn't experiment with all interaction, which may influence their perception.

Table 3. Sample characterization:

Survey section	Questions	Responses	Representation
1. Sample characterization	Biological sex	Female	N = 34 (30.91%)
		Male	N = 76 (69.09%)
	Age	21–25 years old,	N = 43 (39.09%)
		26 and 30 years	N = 28 (25.45%)
		Other ages	N = 39 (35.46%)
	Education level	Bachelor's degree or equivalent	N = 53 (48.18%)
		High school	N = 24 (21.82%)
		Master's degree	N = 22 (20%)
		Other education levels	N = 11 (10%)
	Nationality	Portugal	N = 104 (94.55%)
		Other nationalities	N = 6 (5.45%)
2. Gaming habits characterization	Digital Games Played (Hours/week)	1 to 4 h playing	N = 29 (26.36%)
		5 to 10 h playing	N = 24 (21.82%)
		11 to 15 h playing	N = 24 (21.82%)
		16 to 20 h playing	N = 18 (16.36%)
		More than 20 h playing;	N = 20 (18.18%)
	Life period when spending more time playing (Hours/week)	Childhood	N = 4 (3.64%)
		Preadolescence	N = 9 (8.18%)
		Teenage years/adolescence	N = 50 (45.45%)
		Young adulthood	N = 39 (35.45%)
		Twenties and thirties	N = 8 (7.27%)
	Gaming Platforms	Personal Computer (PC)	N = 57 (51.82%)
		PlayStation (PS)	N = 26 (23.64%)
		Mobile devices	N = 11 (10%)
		Other platforms	N = 16 (14.54%)

(*continued*)

Table 3. (*continued*)

Survey section	Questions	Responses	Representation
	Typology player-playable Character [15]	Explorers	N = 56 (50.91%)
		Achievers	N = 24 (21.82%)
		Killers	N = 20 (18.18%)
		Socializers	N = 10 (9.09%)

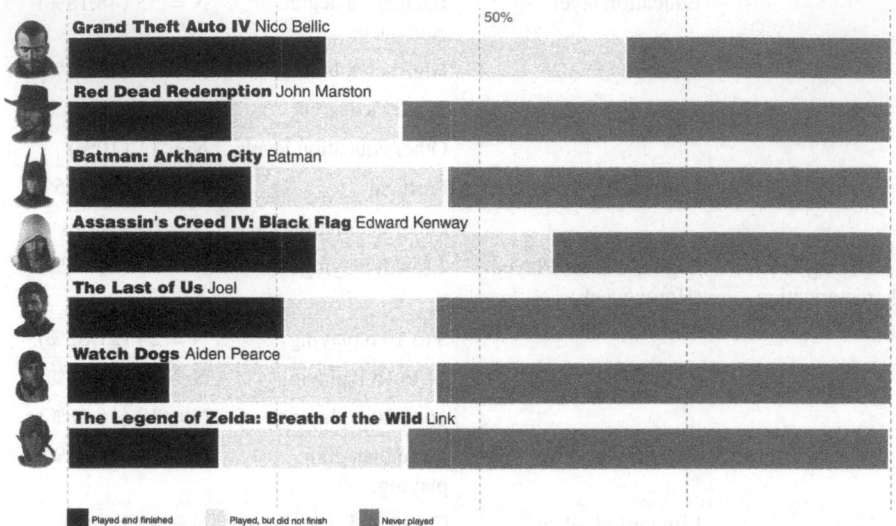

Fig. 1. Respondent's gaming experience and his characters from top to bottom: Grand Theft Auto IV, Red Dead Redemption; Batman: Arkham City; Assassin's Creed IV: Black Flag; The Last of Us; Watch Dogs; The Legend of Zelda: Breath of the Wild

4.2 Characters Perception: Played Games

Regarding the respondents' universe, the number of valid responses of the survey section four and five scenario varies depending on whether respondents had played the games under analysis, as said in the previous section.

Suppose the respondent had played and finished the game in analysis (Table 2 – Sect. 3), the respondent was asked to answer two questions about the Playable Character (Table 2 – Sect. 4).

Overall, the respondents find the characters stereotypical since more than half responded "Yes" to the question. The less stereotypical Character is Nico Bellic 18/34; followed by Aiden Pearce 8/13; Link 14/19; Edward Kenway 26/32; Joel 24/29; Batman 21/24; being John Marston 20/21, the character that had more affirmative answers.

Regarding the specific question about the stereotypes, where respondents were asked to rate on a Likert scale – 1 Less usual (stereotypical); 4 More usual (stereotypical) –the average score and correspondent standard deviation can be consulted in Fig. 2.

The value that appears most frequently – Mode (Mo) of Physical appearance – the characters Nico Bellic Mo = 2; John Marston Mo = 4; Batman Mo = 4; Joel 4; Aiden Pearce 3; Link Mo = 2 and Mo = 4. The character Edward Kenway has a bimodal score of Mo = 3 and Mo = 4 as well the Character Link Mo = 2 and Mo = 4. The tendency of the responses (mean and standard deviation) regarding the character's physical appearance is in Fig. 2a).

Concerning Physiognomy/Countenance: Nico Bellic Mo = 3; John Marston Mo = 4; Batman Mo = 4; Joel Mo = 4; Aiden Pearce Mo = 4; Link Mo = 2. The Character Edward Kenway presents a bimodal score of Mo = 3 and Mo = 4, mean and standard deviation can be compared in Fig. 2b).

Regarding Movement (the way the character moves in the animations of its different actions): Nico Bellic Mo = 2; John Marston Mo = 4; Batman Mo = 4; Edward Kenway Mo = 4; Joel Mo = 4; Aiden Pearce Mo = 3; Link Mo = 4. The other statistically relevant values regarding Movement perception of the characters are systematized in Fig. 2c).

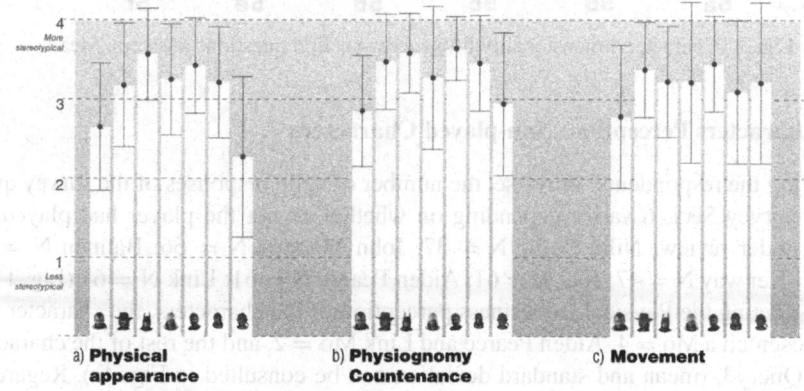

a) Physical   b) Physiognomy   c) Movement
   appearance   Countenance

Fig. 2. Stereotypes, mean and standard deviation.

According to the respondents' opinions (Mean), the most psychologically complex character (Fig. 3 – 5f) is Joel Miller from the digital game *Last of Us*, followed by John Marston, Batman, Edward Kenway, Niko Bellic, and Aiden Pearce. According to the respondents' opinion, the least psychologically complex character is Link.

In the Mo analysis of the responses: the characters John Marston, Batman, Edward Kenway, and Joel Miller show a Mo = 4, then Niko Bellic Mo = 3, the Character Aiden Pearce present a bimodal score of Mo = 2 and Mo = 3 and then Link Mo = 1.

Regarding the psychological aspects of the characters, as it is possible to inspect in Fig. 3, the responses do not show any tendency in the respondents' answers.

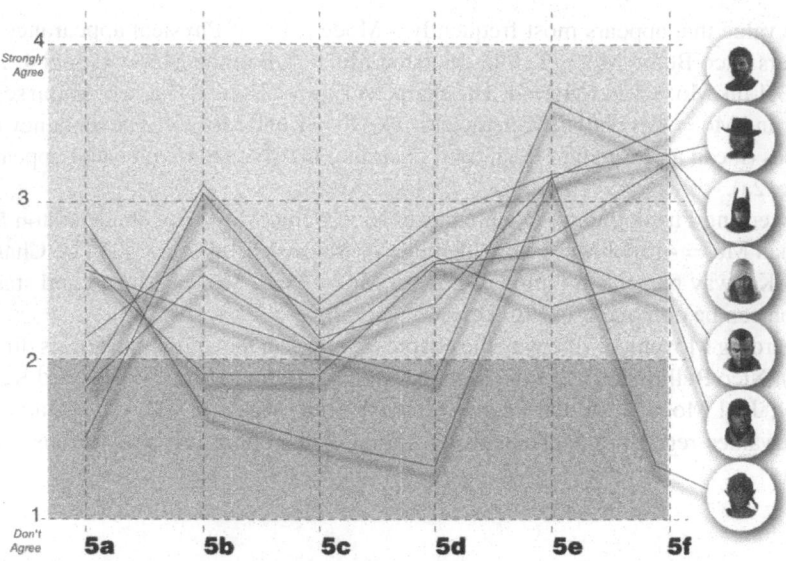

Fig. 3. Character dimensionality fifth survey section questions answers: Mean.

4.3 Characters Perception: Non-played Characters

Regarding the respondents' universe, the number of valid responses of the survey question to survey Sect. 6 varies depending on whether or not the player had played the games under review: Niko Bellic N = 37; John Marston N = 66; Batman N = 60; Edward Kenway N = 47; Joel N = 61; Aiden Pearce N = 61; Link N = 64 (Fig. 1).

Respecting the Physical Robustness perception of the characters, the character batman presented a Mo = 4, Aiden Pearce and Link Mo = 2, and the rest of the characters Mo = Query3, (mean and standard deviation can be consulted in Fig. 4a). Regarding Psychological robustness, all the characters showed Mo = 3 except Nico Bellic (Mo = 2), (Mean and standard deviation can be consulted in Fig. 4b). Regarding charisma, based on Mo, the most charismatic Character is Batman Mo = 4. The less charismatic Characters are Niko Bellic and Aiden Pearce Mo = 2. The rest of the characters present Mo = 3. The mean and standard deviation of the variables, Physical, Psychological Robustness, and Charisma, are shown in Fig. 4c).

Based only on the visual perception regarding Intelligence, Nico Bellic is the character who presents the lowest value, Mo = 2. The highest value, Mo = 4, is related to Batman and Aiden Pearce. The rest of the characters show Mo = 3; the same happens with mean values, as is shown in Fig. 5a).

Regarding Kindness, Link presented a bimodal score (Mo = 3 and 4). Then Joel Mo = 3. Nico Bellic is the one who presents a low Kindness Mo (Mo = 1). The remaining characters show Mo = 2 regarding Kindness (Fig. 5b).

Respecting sympathy towards the Character (Fig. 5c), Joel and Link show Mo = 3, John Marston presents a bimodal score of Mo = 2 and Mo = 3, and the rest of the characters Mo = 2.

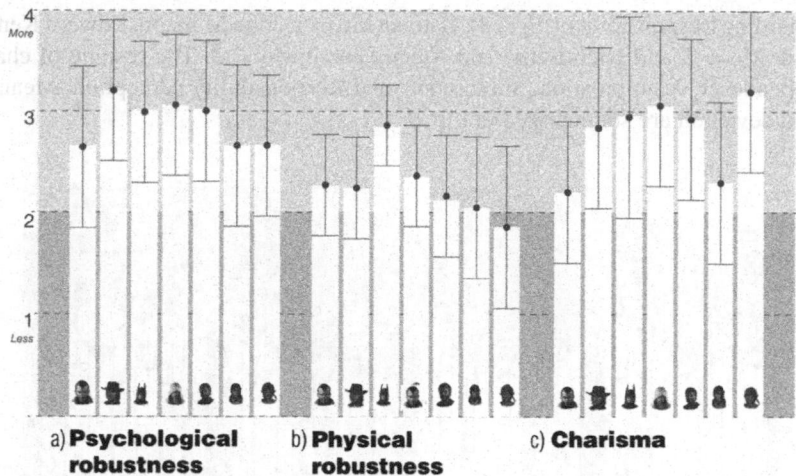

a) **Psychological robustness**   b) **Physical robustness**   c) **Charisma**

Fig. 4. Psychological, Physical robustness, and charisma perception of the respondents who did not play with the characters in analysis: Mean and standard deviation.

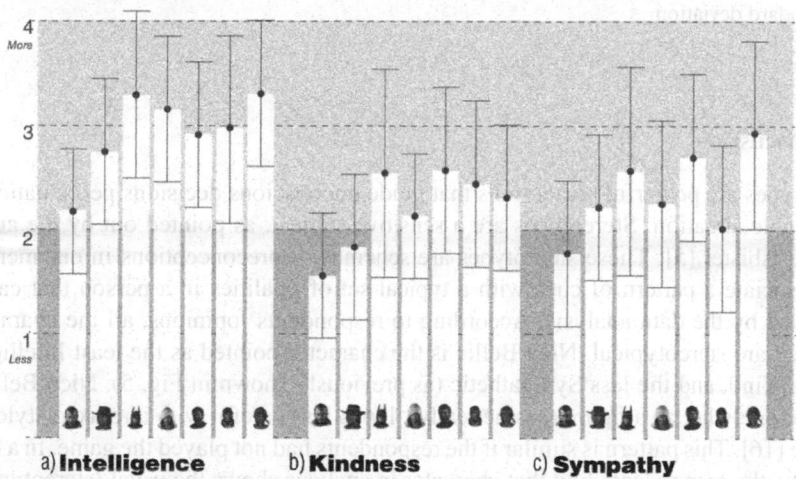

a) **Intelligence**   b) **Kindness**   c) **Sympathy**

Fig. 5. Intelligence, Kindness, and Sympathy towards the characters: Mean and standard deviation.

The variable Dependence (Fig. 6a) for the other characters, the Mo = 1, happens in all the characters except Joel Miller, Aiden Pearce, and Link show Mo = 2. Regarding Manipulation, John Marston and Edward Kenway present the low Mo score (Mo = 1) Nico Bellic and Batman bivariate score of Mo = 1 and Mo = 2. The rest of the characters have Mo = 2. Respect the Submission (Fig. 6c); all the characters present the lowest possible Mo score (Mo = 1) except Aiden Pearce and Link (Mo = 2).

Regarding Responsibility (Fig. 6d): Batman Mo = 1; John Marston, Edward Kenway and Link Mo = 2 and Nico Bellic and Aiden Pearce Mo = 3. The resume of characters Dependence, Manipulation, Submission, and Responsibility perception, Mean and standard deviation are summarized in Fig. 6.

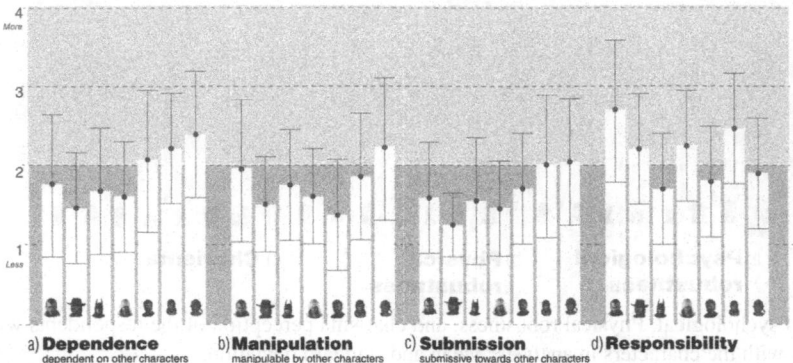

a) **Dependence**
dependent on other characters

b) **Manipulation**
manipulable by other characters

c) **Submission**
submissive towards other characters

d) **Responsibility**

Fig. 6. Characters Dependence, Manipulation, Submission, and Responsibility perception: Mean and standard deviation.

4.4 Discussion

Stereotypes are powerful social tools that guide unconscious decisions perpetuating an inequitable situation. Stereotypes are a sensitive subject, as pointed out by the author Katrine Isbister [5]. These stereotypes are schemas or preconceptions in our memory that associate a pattern of cues with a typical set of qualities in a person that can be perceived by the data analysis. According to respondents' opinions, all the characters analyzed are stereotypical. Nico Bellic is the character pointed as the least Intelligent, the less Kind, and the less Sympathetic (as previously shown in Fig. 5). Nico Bellic is also the one who, as a figure (aesthetically), looks less careful with a relaxed style and posture [16]. This pattern is similar if the respondents had not played the game. In a large majority, the respondents find that character in analysis shows the usual (stereotypical) behavior (Fig. 2).

The hero of the game *Read Dead Redemption*, John Marston, is seen as a stereotyped character regarding Physical Appearance, Physiognomy, and Movement. He is generally perceived as an Intelligent character for most of the respondents and psychologically complex (considering respondents' replies). From the respondents that have not played with him, he is also seen as a Physically and Psychologically Robust, Intelligent, and Charismatic character but less Kind and Sympathetic (Fig. 5). This outcome can be explained by his super masculine aesthetic [17].

According to the data collected from the respondents who had played the game *Batman: Arkham City*, Batman is the most stereotypical character (Fig. 2). He is seen as Charismatic, Intelligent, Kind, Sympathetic, Responsible (Fig. 5). He is also viewed as Independent, not manipulable nor submissive (Fig. 6). Batman is the only cross-media character in analysis, so the data collected must have influenced other media, like movies [18].

Edward Kenway also presents a super masculine aesthetic with big muscles and scars on his face. For this reason, the respondents who have played the game Assassin's Creed IV: Black Flag pointed as a stereotypical character (Fig. 2). Regarding the respondents who did not play the game, their opinion matches those who played (as is it possible to check Figs. 5 and 6). Edward Kenway is seen as physical and psychologically robust, with Charisma, Intelligence, and Sympathy (with mixed feelings about their Kindness).

Joel Miller is globally seen as stereotypical. Unlike others, regarding the psychological perception of the character (character dimensionality), the respondents' answers show some tendency. It is possible to conclude that most respondents find that Joel distinguishes moral values and is psychologically complex, matching with the three-dimensional (3d) definition proposed by Adams [6]. This tendency (finding Joel Psychological robust) fits the respondents' perception that they did not play the Game Last of Us.

Regarding the character Aiden Pearce, he is also seen as a stereotyped character with Psychological and Physical Robustness and Charisma below average compared to the rest of the characters in the research (Fig. 2). The respondents who did not play the game see him as Intelligent and Kind but not so Sympathetic (Fig. 5).

According to the respondents' opinion, the least psychologically complex character is Link (Fig. 3 – 5f); Link is also the character pointed as more dependent (Fig. 6a). Simultaneously, Link is pointed out as the least stereotypical and the only one with babyface features [22].

Regarding the specific attributes, Physical appearance; Physiognomy/Countenance, Movement, all the characters present a mean and Mo above 2 (Table 2 and Fig. 2) regarding respondents' perception of these characters. The Characters Dependence, Manipulation, Submission values are globally less than 2, as shown in Fig. 6 (perception of respondents who did not play the game).

All the characters analyzed are the heroes of their games, so they are designed to show some heroism regarding their appearance, as Isbister [5] pointed out. The characters in the analysis are from digital games produced by major publishers whose characters and games beneficiate from global publicity and marketing actions. In that sense, this could be a factor that influences the respondents' perception.

Regarding Adams' dimensionality, except for Joel, none of the other characters in the analysis show any tendency regarding their psychological depth. The direction of the line in the graph should be a straight line: proportionality positive if the character were more complex and proportionality positive if the character had a low dimensionality. This tendency cannot be seen (Fig. 3).

4.5 Conclusions, Limitations, and Future Work

The study shows a discrepancy concerning the representation between biological sex: The respondents' biological sex was distributed almost equally between the two (Female N = 107 and Male N = 110) in the original sample. Compared with the final selection, after eliminating the respondents who had not played 3 digital games in their lives, 34 were female respondents, and 76 were male respondents. This finding matches with common sense that female gamers are commonly regarded as a minority [28].

Besides the small sample, regarding the gamers perception analysis (as shown in Fig. 1), this research validates that stereotypes are accurate in digital games, as Isbister suggest [29], especially in the most played games reported in ESA reports [2, 8, 11, 13, 14, 30–32].

These characters were designed with stereotypes, enhancing attractiveness to communicate attributes like Intelligence, Kindness, and Charisma (Table 1); the same is true even in gamers who do not play the digital game or experience the game narrative (Fig. 4).

The sample nationality is mainly from Portugal. It is impossible to predict if other cultures have a different perception of these characters, especially regarding the character Link – the only character who presents babyface features. Link comes from an Asian publisher (Nintendo), and the rest of the characters show Caucasian features.

The results of this study should be seen as exploratory and a starting point so that more questions can be asked about the aesthetics of the Playable Characters. Playable Characters are the center of playability in several digital games. Besides, as stated by Isbister [5] and confirmed by the respondents in this research, stereotypes may indicate visual cues about what the character type may be. It should be asked if stereotypical characters are pleasant and necessary for the narrative or character development. As examples of the other entertainment products, like the stories pointed out at the beginning of the article, "the ugly" does not need to be "the bad". The one who has the big muscles does not need to be the least dependent, and so on. These major digital game publishers perpetuate stereotypes that enhance masculinity as a synonym for heroism and power. This preconception does not place in a plural society, especially when approximately 21% of the gamers are in their teenage years [33].

Regarding future work, we suggest expanding the sample by implementing the survey in other countries and continents to test if the perception of these characters is the same between different cultures and ethnic groups.

The games analyzed correspond to a convenience sampling based on sales reports. They must be considered to open the scope to other characters. As said in the previous section, the character in the analysis came from major publishers, so it was not certain that it was the first time respondents saw the character. We suggest testing other characters from other minor and major publishers. And, of course, a deep understanding of the character depth must be made since it was impossible to categorize the study's characters, as shown in Fig. 3.

Acknowledgments. The study reported in this publication was supported by FCT – Foundation for Science and Technology (Fundação para a Ciência e Tecnologia), I.P. nr. SFRH/BD/143863/2019 and DigiMedia Research Center, under the project UIDB/05460/2020.

References

1. Farber, M., Schrier, K.: The Limits and Strengths of Using Digital Games as "Empathy Machines." India (2017)

2. ESA.: Entertainment Software Association (2020)
3. Hefner, D., Klimmt, C., Vorderer, P.: Identification with the player character as determinant of video game enjoyment. In: Ma, L., Rauterberg, M., Nakatsu, R. (eds.) ICEC 2007. LNCS, vol. 4740, pp. 39–48. Springer, Heidelberg (2007). https://doi.org/10.1007/978-3-540-74873-1_6
4. Salen, K., Zimmerman, E.: Salen, Zimmerman_rules of play: game design fundamentals. Int. J. Artif. Intell. Tools. **9**. MIT Press (2004)
5. Isbister, K.: Better Game Characters by Design : A Psychological Approach. CRC Press (2006). https://doi.org/10.1201/9780367807641
6. Adams, E.: Fundamentals of Game Design. Design, 2nd edn. New Riders (2013)
7. Nisbett, R.E., Wilson, T.D.: The halo effect: evidence for unconscious alteration of judgments. J Pers. Soc. Psychol. **35**, 250–256 (1977). American Psychological Association (APA). https://doi.org/10.1037/0022-3514.35.4.250
8. ESA.: 2009 Sales, Demographic and Usage Data Essential Facts about the Computer and Video Game Industry (2009)
9. ESA.: 2010 Sales, Demographic and Usage Data Essential Facts about the Computer and Video Game Industry (2010)
10. ESA.: 2011 Sales, Demographic and Usage Data Essential Facts about the Computer and Video Game Industry (2011)
11. ESA.: 2012 Sales, Demographic and Usage Data Essential Facts about the Computer and Video Game Industry (2012)
12. ESA, and Entertainment Software Association.: 2013 Essential Facts about the Computer and Video Game Industry. Entertainment Software Association, Massachusetts (2018)
13. ESA.: 2015 Sales, Demographic and Usage Data Essential Facts about the Computer and Video Game Industry (2014)
14. ESA.: 2016 Essential Facts about the Computer and Video Game Industry (2016)
15. Bartle, R. (MUSE Ltd).: Hearts, clubs, diamonds, spades: players who suit MUDs. J MUD Res. **6**, 39 (1996). https://doi.org/10.1007/s00256-004-0875-6
16. Rockstar North.: Grand Theft Auto IV. Rockstar Games (2008)
17. Rockstar North, Rockstar San Diego.: Red Dead Redemption. Rockstar Games (2010)
18. Rocksteady Studios, WB Games Montreal.: Batman: Arkham City. Warner Bros, Interactive Entertainment (2011)
19. Baptizat, E., Ubisoft.: Assassin's Creed IV: Black Flag. Ubisoft (2013)
20. Minkoff, J., Naughty Dog.: The Last of Us. Sony Interactive Entertainment (2013)
21. Ubisoft.: Watch Dogs. Ubisoft, AK Tronic (2014)
22. Aonuma, E., Nintendo Entertainment Planning & Development.: The Legend of Zelda: Breath of the Wild. Nintendo (2017)
23. Katz, S.D.: Film Directing: Shot by Shot. Edited by Michael Wiese Productions. Michael Wiese Productions (1991)
24. Shaw, A.: On not becoming gamers: moving beyond the constructed audience. ADA: J. Gend. New Media Technol **1**, 1–25 (2013). https://doi.org/10.7264/N33N21B3
25. Shaw, A.: Do you identify as a gamer? Gender, race, sexuality, and gamer identity. New Media & Soc. **14**, 28–44. SAGE Publications Sage UK, London, England (2012). https://doi.org/10.1177/1461444811410394
26. De Grove, F., Courtois, C., Van Looy, J.: How to be a gamer! Exploring personal and social indicators of gamer identity. J. Comput.-Mediat. Commun. **20**, 346–361 (2015). https://doi.org/10.1111/jcc4.12114
27. Juul, J.: A Casual Revolution: Video Games and Their Players. A Casual Revolution (2010)
28. Lien, T.: No girls allowed | Polygon. Dec. 2 (2013)
29. Isbister, K.: Better Game Characters by Design: A Psychological Approach (The Morgan Kaufmann Series in Interactive 3D Technology). Education. Elsevier/Morgan Kaufmann (2006). https://doi.org/10.1016/B978-1-55860-921-1.50012-0

30. ESA.: 2019 Essential Facts about the Computer and Video Game Industry (2019)
31. ESA.: 2013 Sales, Demographic and Usage Data Essential facts about the Computer and Video Game Industry (2013)
32. ESA.: 2018 Sales, Demographic, and Usage Data Essential Facts about the computer and Video Game Industry (2018)
33. ESA.: 2020 Essential Facts About the Video Game Industry (2021)

Guidance is Good: Controlled Experiment Shows the Impact of Navigational Guidance on Digital Game Enjoyment and Flow

Uday Sai Reddy Ambati, Gregory Brandt, and Owen Schaffer[✉]

Computer Science and Information Systems, Bradley University, 1501 W Bradley Avenue, Peoria, IL 61625, USA
OSchaffer@Bradley.edu

Abstract. There is a notion popular among game designers that it is better to avoid too much hand-holding, and to allow players to figure out what to do and where to go themselves rather than guiding them each step of the way. Flow is the psychological state of "getting in the zone", of enjoying overcoming a series of optimally challenging goals for the sake of the enjoyment they provide. Flow theory suggests that knowing what to do and where to go next throughout an activity is a flow condition, or a factor that leads to that enjoyable flow state. Is guidance hand-holding that decreases enjoyment or a flow condition that increases enjoyment? Does more guidance increase or decrease enjoyment? Humor and Laughter was identified in a previous card sorting study as a source of enjoyment, but to the best of our knowledge there has yet to be a controlled experiment testing if humor increases enjoyment in games. To address these questions, a controlled experiment with a 2 × 2 × 2 factorial design was conducted to test the impact of a Navigational Pointer, a Quest Log, and Humorous NPC Dialog on player Flow and Enjoyment. 314 participants played one of eight versions of a 2D action-adventure RPG custom game and filled out a survey. The Navigational Pointer, an arrow pointing where to go next throughout each step of the game, significantly increased player flow and enjoyment. The Quest Log and Humorous NPC Dialog did not have a significant impact on enjoyment or flow, but were more text-based and less effective than the Navigational Pointer. Implications for designing for enjoyment and flow are discussed.

Keywords: Enjoyment · Navigational guidance · Humor · Clear proximal goals · Controlled experiment · Flow · Intrinsic motivation · Game design · Gamification · Serious games · Computer games · Digital games

1 Introduction and Related Work

Is it better to avoid too much hand-holding, and to allow game players to figure out what to do and where to go themselves rather than guiding them each step of the way? Or is it better that the game communicates player goals clearly to ensure players know what to do next throughout the game, and uses navigational guidance to make it clear where

X. Fang (Ed.): HCII 2022, LNCS 13334, pp. 101–118, 2022.
https://doi.org/10.1007/978-3-031-05637-6_7

to go next in the game world? Also, does humor in digital games really increase player enjoyment? These are the central research questions driving the present research.

Popular games like *Elder Scrolls V: Skyrim* [1] and *World of Warcraft* [2] use text prompts to communicate the next step in the player's current task, quest, or mission and navigational aids like on-screen marks on a compass or map or on-screen arrows or paths indicating the direction the player needs to go to get to their next step. On the other hand, some games like the *Dark Souls* [3] series do not use these game design elements to communicate this information to players, instead leaving players to figure out what to do and where to go without this guidance. Directly comparing these commercial off-the-shelf games would introduce too many confounding variables. But by manipulating game design elements in a controlled experiment, game design elements can be isolated and their effects on player enjoyment and flow can be tested.

Flow is the experience of overcoming optimal challenges for the enjoyment they provide while continuously adjusting performance based on feedback. Unlike Self-Determination Theory which focuses on satisfying needs for autonomy, competence, and belonging [4, 5], flow theory focuses directly on the autotelic experience or the experience of intrinsic motivation, enjoyment of an activity as the primary motivation for that same activity. Flow theory begins with the idea that this enjoyment is a desirable end result rather than a means to any other end, even if flow may have other benefits.

Much of the research on flow has attempted to measure how much people are in flow. For example, several flow measures consist of 9 dimensions from Csikszentmihalyi's [6, 7] popular books on flow (e.g. [8–10]). However, treating all of these factors as measures of how much a person is in flow may not be accurate because some of these factors are conditions that lead to flow, while others indicate how much the person is in flow. It would be better in our view to measure flow with the flow indicators and to test the impact of the flow conditions by designing controlled experiments to test them.

Nakamura and Csikszentmihalyi [11] separated flow into two sets of factors: flow conditions, which are the factors that lead to flow, and the characteristics of flow or flow indicators, which are the factors that indicate how much a person is in flow. Most previous research that has measured flow has failed to separate flow conditions and indicators [8, 10, 12]. The flow conditions identified by Nakamura and Csikszentmihalyi were clear proximal goals, immediate progress feedback, and optimal challenge. The flow indicators they identified were effortless concentration, sense of control, merging of action and awareness, loss of reflective self-consciousness, altered perception of time, and autotelic experience.

For those who wish to design for flow, the logical focus would be on the flow conditions. Optimal challenge is extent to which a person perceives the task they are doing has a level of task difficulty that is high enough to stretch their perceived skills without overwhelming them. Immediate progress feedback is how much the person feels they know how well they are performing the activity or how well they are making progress through the activity. Clear proximal goals is how much the person feels they know what to do next throughout an activity. The word "proximal" emphasizes continuously receiving information about the goal of the next step rather than simply the overall goal, facilitating task engagement by providing step-by-step information about how to complete each task. As Csikszentmihalyi and Nakamura [13] explained, "What counts is not that the overall goal of the activity be clear but rather that the activity present a clear goal for the next step in the action sequence, and then the next, on and on, until the final goal is reached" (p. 187).

These three flow conditions were identified by Nakamura and Csikszentmihalyi [11] with descriptive research using interviews and the Experience Sampling Method [14, 15], not with controlled experiments. Evidence from controlled experiments with random assignment is needed to test the causal relationship between these flow conditions and increased flow, and to test if other factors increase flow and enjoyment. Controlled experiments with random assignment need to be conducted to test what specific design differences actually increase flow and enjoyment among users or players.

If practitioners know what conditions lead to flow, designs can be engineered to meet the flow conditions. Controlled experiments have shown that optimal challenges lead to flow [16] and that immediate progress feedback leads to flow [17, 18]. However, the causal relationship between clear proximal goals and flow has yet to be demonstrated with a controlled experiment. This paper aims to fill this research gap. In addition, two other factors of interest were explored, Clear Navigation and Humor. Applying and extending the concept of Clear Proximal Goals to the task of navigating a game world, we define Clear Navigation here as knowing where to go next throughout each step of an activity. It has been theorized that knowing where to go may be a flow condition when navigation is involved with a task [19], but to the best of our knowledge prior research has yet to test the impact of Clear Navigation on flow and enjoyment with a controlled experiment.

In a previous card sorting study, Humor and Laughter was identified as a potential source of enjoyment in digital games [20]. Much of the empirical research that has been done on Humor has focused on it as an individual trait, with measures focusing on an individual's sense of humor [21–23] or humor styles [24–28]. Perry [29] conducted an experiment and found that humor in commercials made TV programs more enjoyable, but to the best of our knowledge there has yet to be an experiment testing the impact of humor on enjoyment in games. Dormann and Biddle [30–32] discussed theories and functions of humor and asserted that humor seems to be an important source of pleasure for game players. However, their research was qualitative and did not test the connection between humor and enjoyment with a controlled experiment. The causal link between the experience of Humor and Enjoyment of digital games has yet to be tested with a controlled experiment.

We define enjoyment as the extent to which people positively evaluate their experience. But there is little to no consensus about what leads to that positive experience of enjoyment when people play digital games. Existing theories of game enjoyment are incomplete or not comprehensive enough as Lazarro's Four Keys to Fun [33, 34], Self-Determination Theory [4], Player Experience of Needs Satisfaction (PENS) [35], Flow Theory [11], the Game Engagement Questionnaire [36], Yee's model of motivations to play online games [37, 38], Malone's model of intrinsically motivating educational games [39, 40], the taxonomy of gameplay enjoyment from Quick et al. [41], and the Player Experience (PLEX) Framework [42]. An extensive review of the literature on what makes games enjoyable has been conducted, which summarizes 61 relevant peer-reviewed research articles and papers and categorizes them into 12 topic areas [43]. An iterative card sorting study with game players reduced 167 sources of enjoyment drawn from the literature to 34 sources of enjoyment in digital games [20], but the causal links between these sources of enjoyment and enjoyment need to be tested with controlled experiments. The present research is one step forward towards this larger goal of identifying and testing what causes enjoyment with a series of controlled experiments.

Knowing what makes digital games enjoyable is important not only for video and computer game designers, but also for Gamification and Serious Games as well. Gamification is "the use of game design elements in non-game contexts" [44], such as to make non-game systems more game-like and enjoyable. Serious games are "full-fledged games for non-entertainment purposes" [44], such as education, exercise, research or persuasion. Design for enjoyment is the common aim of Game Design, Gamification, and Serious Games. To reliably engineer enjoyable systems, practitioners need empirical research using controlled experiments to test what makes digital games enjoyable.

There is a popular notion among game designers and developers that it is better to avoid too much hand-holding, and to allow game players to figure out what to do and where to go themselves rather than guiding them each step of the way. This is incompatible with flow theory's notion of clear proximal goals, which suggests that it is best to ensure players know what to do next throughout the game. So, when it comes to conveying what the player is supposed to do next throughout a game, is guidance good or is it better to avoid too much hand-holding? Which leads to more flow and enjoyment among players?

The research questions that drove this research were: 1) Does having a Navigational Pointer that guides players where to go next lead to more player enjoyment and flow than not having one? 2) Does having a Quest Log with text prompts that communicate what to do next lead to more enjoyment and flow among players? 3) Does having NPC dialog text that is humorous lead to more player enjoyment and flow than non-humorous NPC dialog? This study will contribute both to the theory and practice of designing interactive systems for enjoyment. This is an important aim for practitioners and researchers in Game Design and Development and Human-Computer Interaction.

2 Method

2.1 Participants

Three-hundred and fourteen participants were recruited with Amazon Mechanical Turk. Participants were 18 years or older, US-only, and had an approval rate of at least 97% on at least 1000 HITs. Participants were screened to ensure they were accessing the survey with a laptop or desktop computer to be sure they could play the research game. Participants were excluded from analysis if they responded incorrectly to attention-checking questions using the Conscientious Responders Scale [24], if they spent less than 15 min on the survey, or if their responses to the open-ended qualitative questions were incomplete or did not answer the questions that were asked. The minimum time to complete the survey was determined from the pilot testing, and the median time taken to complete the survey after playing the game was 37.41 min. Participant demographics and gameplay habits are summarized in Table 1 below.

Table 1. Participant demographics

Total N	314 participants
Females	188 (59.87%)
Males	125 (39.81%)
Non-binary	1
Mean average age	42.03 years
Age range	20–78 years
Range of years played digital games	0–51 years
Mean average years playing digital games	18.72 years
Range of hours played per week	0–70 h
Mean average hours played per week	8.72 h
Range of hours played per day	0–10 h
Mean average hours played per day	1.97 h

2.2 Procedure

Participants were recruited using Amazon Mechanical Turk (MTurk) to participate in an online study. MTurk has been found to be a reliable tool for recruiting participants for Human-Computer Interaction Research [45] as long as sufficient precautions are taken to ensure data quality, such as using attention checks and excluding respondents who are not paying attention [46, 47]. Participants were given information about informed consent played a custom research game for 30 min and then responded to a survey questionnaire about their experience playing the game. The study took approximately one hour to complete. Participants were given $3.25 USD as an incentive to participate. The study was approved by the Bradley University Internal Review Board, the Committee on the Use of Human Subjects in Research.

2.3 Measures

Participants responded to a survey about their experience playing the game that included psychometric measures of player Enjoyment, the dimensions of Flow, and Humor. These measures consisted of 7-point Likert scales of agreement ranging from Strongly Disagree to Strongly Agree.

Enjoyment was measured with an Enjoyment Questionnaire (Cronbach's $\alpha = 0.979$). One of the flow indicators, Autotelic Experience, contained items such as "I really enjoyed the experience", and in previous studies [17, 18, 48] this Autotelic Experience factor merged with Enjoyment, specifically with the Enjoyment-Interest subscale of the Intrinsic Motivation Inventory [49], so Autotelic Experience and Enjoyment were measured as one Enjoyment factor in this study as well.

The remaining flow indicators were measured with the Flow Indicator Questionnaire, which assesses the factors that indicate how much a person is in a flow state [17, 18] with the subscales Sense of Control (Cronbach's $\alpha = 0.898$), Full Focusing of Attention (Cronbach's $\alpha = 0.898$), Merging of Action and Awareness (Cronbach's $\alpha = 0.871$), Loss of Self-Consciousness (Cronbach's $\alpha = 0.809$), and Altered Perception of Time (Cronbach's $\alpha = 0.939$).

The Flow Condition Questionnaire was used to measure the factors that flow theory suggests lead to flow. It had the subscales Optimal Challenge (Cronbach's $\alpha = 0.904$), Continuous Feedback (Cronbach's $\alpha = 0.925$), and Clear Goals and Navigation (Cronbach's $\alpha = 0.977$). Each subscale had at least 4 items. To assess Clear Navigation, or how well players knew where to go next, original items were generated based on the items for the flow condition Clear Proximal Goals. However, in preliminary factor analysis, these Clear Navigation items merged with Clear Proximal Goals. These items loaded strongly onto the same factor and fit well together conceptually, so this factor was labeled Clear Goals and Navigation.

The Enjoyment Questionnaire, Flow Indicator Questionnaire, and Flow Condition Questionnaire have been used in previous research on flow in games, and they were found to have sufficient construct validity and reliability [17, 18]. These measures were adapted to the context of digital games, and drew items primarily from the more general Activity Flow Scale [50], which was itself adapted from the Flow State Scale [9], a measure of flow in the context of sports.

A seven-item Humor Questionnaire was used to measure how much participants experienced humor and laughter while playing the game (Cronbach's $\alpha = 0.949$). Example items include, "This game made me laugh," and "This game was really funny." Existing measures of humor focused on a sense of humor as an individual trait [21–23], but the measure used in this study instead focused on measuring the extent to which people experience humor and laughter while playing the game. Because an existing measure of the experience of humor could not be easily found, an original measure was developed and used in this study. Preliminary factor analysis showed all of the Humor items loaded onto their own factor with factor loadings above 0.7 and no cross-loadings within 0.2 of that main factor loading, providing preliminary evidence that Humor has construct validity as well [51, 52].

This study was part of a larger survey. Open-ended qualitative questions were asked, for example about what they enjoyed most and least about the game, and participants were asked to type in their answers. At the end of the study, participants filled out a demographics and gaming habits questionnaire.

2.4 Experimental System and Design

A between-subjects controlled experiment with a $2 \times 2 \times 2$ factorial design was conducted with random assignment of participants into eight experimental conditions. Eight versions of a custom research game were developed for this study with the Unity game engine and C#. The games were built with WebGL and embedded on Qualtrics, an online survey platform. The randomizer feature of Qualtrics was used to randomly assign participants to play only one of the versions of the game. The research game was a 2D top-down action-adventure RPG with an open world and towns with Non-Player Character (NPC) villagers separated by wilderness occupied by monsters. The game had dynamic difficulty adjustment to maintain optimal challenge across different levels of player skill and control for individual differences in skill and changes in skill over time. The speed that enemies moved and attacked would increase gradually over time, would increase when enemies took damage, and would decrease when the player took damage or died; minimum and maximum enemy speeds were set based on internal playtesting. There were respawn checkpoints throughout the game world. The game ended automatically after 30 min; the timer paused when the game was paused and the game automatically paused after 15 s without player input.

A between-subjects controlled experiment with a $2 \times 2 \times 2$ factorial design was conducted with random assignment of participants into eight conditions. The conditions consisted of playing different versions of the same game, with the different versions designed to be identical except for specific design differences intended to manipulate Clear Navigation, which we define here as how much participants knew where to go next throughout each step of the game, Clear Proximal Goals, which is how much participants knew what to do next through each step of the game, and Humor, which is how much the humorous content in the game made participants laugh. To manipulate these internal player perceptions about their experience, specific design differences were implemented across the different versions of the custom research game.

The first independent variable and design difference was the presence or absence of an on screen Navigational Pointer, an on-screen arrow indicating the direction the player needed to move their character in the game to reach their current proximal goal, or the next step of the game. The Navigational Pointer was close to the player near the middle of the screen, offset from the player's position enough that the arrow did not overlap with the player character. As the player moves, the arrow rotates around the player to point at the player's next destination in the game world. This design difference was intended to increase the experience of Clear Navigation.

The second independent variable or design difference was the presence or absence of an on screen Quest Log consisting of a box at the top right of the screen with a text prompt indicating the current proximal goal, meaning the goal of the next step in the sequence of actions the game requires players to do to complete the game. In the conditions where this Quest Log was present, each time the player completed the current step they are on, the text prompt in the Quest Log was be updated to show the next step that needed to be completed to continue making progress in the game.

Preliminary factor analysis results found that player perceptions of Clear Proximal Goals and Clear Navigation merged into a single factor, Clear Goals and Clear Navigation, but the Quest Log and Navigational Pointer operationalized these design differences separately. They can be thought of as two different ways to operationalize increasing the player's experience of Clear Goals and Clear Navigation through design differences. The Quest Log was intended to convey information about what to do next, while the Navigational Pointer was intended to convey information about where to go next in the game world.

The third design difference and independent variable was whether the text for the Non-Player Character (NPC) dialog was written to be humorous or not. In the Humorous Dialog condition, the NPC dialog is written to be humorous using fourth-wall-breaking satire of roleplaying game conventions, while in the No Humorous Dialog condition, the NPC dialog was written to be about the same length of text but without humor. For

Fig. 1. Screenshot of the research game showing the Navigational Pointer to the right of the player, the Quest Log at the upper right of the screen, and an NPC dialog text box.

example, in the Humor condition, Sebastian says, "I'd like to help you find one, but I can't walk. Because I'm an NPC, I wasn't given the ability to walk." In the No Humor condition he says, "I'd like to help you but I must look after Gallagher." In the Humor condition, the old man who gives you the sword says about giving you a stronger sword, "Look I know the fate of the world hangs in the balance and what not. But the game would be too short if I just gave it to you here and now. Ah, I know! You can get my dry cleaning!" In the No Humor condition, the old man instead says, "In order for you to prove that you are the chosen one, I propose a trial. Go now to the cave where the king's soul resides, defeat it and return to me."

Using a $2 \times 2 \times 2$ factorial design, this study tested the impact of these three design differences on enjoyment and flow. Table 2 below shows the participant demographics and gameplay habits of those in each of those eight experimental groups.

2.5 Hypotheses

The following hypotheses were made:

H1. Players in the Navigational Pointer condition will report greater Enjoyment (H1A) and Flow (H1B) than players in the No Navigational Pointer condition.
H2. Players in the Quest Log condition will report greater Enjoyment (H2A) and Flow (H2B) than players in the No Quest Log condition.
H3. Players in the Humorous Dialog condition will report greater Enjoyment (H3A) and Flow (H3B) than players in the No Humorous Dialog condition.

Table 2. Participant demographics in each experimental condition

	No Pointer, No Quest, No Humor	No Pointer, No Quest, Humor	No Pointer, Quest, No Humor	No Pointer, Quest, Humor	Pointer, No Quest, No Humor	Pointer, No Quest, Humor	Pointer, Quest, No Humor	Pointer, Quest, Humor
N	33	39	37	39	40	44	41	41
Females	17	30	22	18	22	25	33	21
Males	15	9	15	21	18	19	8	20
Other	1	0	0	0	0	0	0	0
Mean Average Age	41.33	43.00	44.27	42.13	41.22	43.79	40.22	40.24
Age Range	28-78 years	21-76 years	23-69 years	22-69 years	21-71 years	20-68 years	21-71 years	25-69 years
Mean average years playing digital games	18.48 years	15.79 years	20.75 years	17.08 years	16.22 years	19.27 years	21.34 years	20.66 years
Range of years played digital games	0-40 years	0-41 years	0-51 years	1-41 years	0-38 years	1-49 years	0-42 years	3-40 years
Mean average hours played per week	11.18 hours	7.89 hours	6.49 hours	9.61 hours	10.90 hours	7.03 hours	7.46 hours	9.63 hours
Range of hours played per week	0-70 hours	0-30 hours	0-25 hours	0-40 hours	0-70 hours	0-30 hours	0-21 hours	0-50 hours
Mean average hours played per day	2.57 hours	1.79 hours	1.78 hours	1.94 hours	2.15 hours	1.78 hours	1.85 hours	1.53 hours
Range of hours played per day	0-10 hours	0-5 hours	0-5 hours	0-6 hours	0-8 hours	0.5-6 hours	0-7 hours	0-7 hours

2.6 Efforts Made to Ensure Data Quality

Several measures were taken to ensure data quality. The protocol developed by Winter et al. [53] was used to screen out those using Virtual Private Networks to hide their country of origin and to help screen out duplicate responses. The Conscientious Responders Scale [47] was used as an attention check, with items such as "Choose the first option – "strongly agree" – in answering this question." mixed into the questionnaire. These items were randomly mixed into the sources of enjoyment questionnaire questions. Participants were excluded from analysis if they responded incorrectly to attention-checking questions using the Conscientious Responders Scale [47], if they spent less than 15 min on the survey, or if their responses to the open-ended qualitative questions were incomplete or did not answer the questions that were asked.

The game automatically paused after 15 s without player input and the game's count-down timer paused when the game was paused to make it more likely that participants had enough experience playing the game to respond to the survey. Player location in the game was logged every second and at the end of the game it was sent from Unity to a PHP server. Heatmaps were created with the location data and manually examined by the researchers to ensure participants were actually playing the game, and respondents who appeared to be staying in one place for much of the game were excluded.

3 Results

A 2 × 2 × 2 factorial MANOVA was conducted with IBM SPSS 27 to compare the mean scores on all of the measures across the experimental groups. Tables 3, 4 and 5 show the means, standard deviations, F values, p values, and *partial* η^2 effect size for the main effects of each independent variable on all measures.

A statistically significant MANOVA effect was found for playing the game with the Navigational Pointer, indicating there was an effect on one or more of the measures

(*Pillai's Trace* = 0.477; $F_{10,297}$ = 27.078; $p < 0.001$, *partial η^2* = 0.477). Participants who had a Navigational Pointer experienced significantly more Enjoyment (F_1 = 38.124; $p < 0.001$, *partial η^2* = 0.111). This was evidence supporting hypothesis H1A.

Player perceptions of each of the flow conditions, the player perceptions that flow theory suggests lead to flow, were higher for those in the Navigational Pointer conditions as well. Having a Navigational Pointer increased player perceptions of Clear Goals and Navigation (F_1 = 218.4; $p < 0.001$, *partial η^2* = 0.416), Continuous Feedback (F_1 = 49.715; $p < 0.001$, *partial η^2* = 0.140), and Optimal Challenge (F_1 = 32.423; $p < 0.001$, *partial η^2* = 0.096). The greatest effect size was found for Clear Goals and Navigation (*partial η^2* = 0.416), indicating this experimental manipulation had the intended effect of increasing this factor. The Navigational Pointer made it more clear to players where to go and what to do next and increased enjoyment. The positive effect on the other flow conditions may mean the flow conditions are interconnected in a way that makes it difficult to separately manipulate perceptions of the flow conditions, as was found in a previous study of flow in games [18].

Participants with a Navigational Pointer experienced more flow than those without it, as measured by the flow indicators. The Navigational Pointer led to increased player Sense of Control (F_1 = 25.140; $p < 0.001$, *partial η^2* = 0.076), Merging of Action and Awareness (F_1 = 12.494; $p < 0.001$, *partial η^2* = 0.039), Altered Perception of Time (F_1 = 10.992; $p < 0.001$, *partial η^2* = 0.035), and Focusing of Full Attention (F_1 = 4.082; $p < 0.001$, *partial η^2* = 0.013). This means having a Navigational Pointer increased players' perception that they had the situation under control, they could act automatically without having to think, they lost their normal awareness of time passing, and they had their attention focused entirely on what they were doing. The greatest effect on the flow indicators by effect size was found on Sense of Control (*partial η^2* = 0.076), meaning the pointer helped make players feel like they had everything under control. These results support H1B. The flow indicator Loss of Self-Consciousness was not significantly different.

Having the Navigational Pointer led participant to rate their experience higher on Humor (F_1 = 5.634; $p < 0.001$, *partial η^2* = 0.018). Humor was the only dependent variable to show a significant Levene's test of unequal variances ($p < 0.001$), so this difference was followed up with *Welch's F* test, which is robust for unequal variances. *Welch's F* test confirmed that having the Navigational Pointer led to increased ratings of Humor while playing the game (*Welch's* $F_{1,311.551}$ = 5.257; $p = 0.023$). Perhaps the experience of not having the Navigational Pointer made the experience of playing the game less humorous, but the effect size was relatively small (*partial η^2* = 0.018). Table 3 shows the results of having a Navigational Pointer on each measure.

The MANOVA showed playing the game with a Quest Log had a marginal but non-significant effect on the measures (*Pillai's Trace* = 0.058; $F_{10,297}$ = 1.82; $p < 0.057$, *partial η^2* = 0.058). Quest Log had a marginal but non-significant effect on two of the flow conditions, Clear Goals and Navigation (F_1 = 3.848; $p = 0.051$, *partial η^2* = 0.012) and Continuous Feedback (F_1 = 3.773; $p = 0.053$, *partial η^2* = 0.012). The effect size was also small (*partial η^2* = 0.012). The lack of a significant effect on the factor this experimental manipulation was intended to vary, Clear Goals and Navigation, means that the design difference of having the Quest Log as it was implemented in this study

Table 3. MANOVA results for main effect of navigational pointer

Measure	Navigational Pointer		No Navigational Pointer		F	p	Partial η^2
	M	SD	M	SD			
Enjoyment	4.547	1.658	3.391	1.625	38.124	<0.001	0.111
Clear goals and navigation	5.034	1.581	2.600	1.323	218.400	<0.001	0.416
Continuous feedback	4.183	1.528	2.963	1.573	49.715	<0.001	0.140
Optimal challenge	4.821	1.549	3.811	1.567	32.423	<0.001	0.096
Sense of control	4.386	1.481	3.529	1.557	25.140	< 0.001	0.076
Merging of action and awareness	4.196	1.284	3.693	1.312	12.494	<0.001	0.039
Altered perception of time	4.315	1.732	3.696	1.649	10.992	0.001	0.035
Focusing of full attention	5.972	1.056	5.696	1.250	4.082	0.044	0.013
Loss of self consciousness	5.538	1.079	5.341	1.295	2.047	0.154	0.007
Humor	2.412	1.506	2.050	1.292	5.634	0.018	0.018

did not significantly increase players' perception that they knew where to go or what to do next through each step of the game. The Quest Log also did not have a significant impact on Enjoyment or the flow indicators, the dependent variables of interest. These results did not support Hypotheses H2A or H2B. Table 4 shows the results of having a Quest Log on each measure.

The MANOVA showed playing the game with Humorous NPC Dialog had a significant effect on one or more of the measures (*Pillai's Trace* = 0.085; $F_{10,297}$ = 1.82; p = 0.003, *partial* η^2 = 0.085). The Humorous NPC Dialog had a significant positive effect on Humor (F_1 = 14.953; p < 0.001, *partial* η^2 = 0.047). Since Humor showed a significant Levene's test of unequal variances (p < 0.001), this difference was followed up with *Welch's F* test, which is robust for unequal variances. *Welch's F* test confirmed that Humorous NPC Dialog led to increased player ratings of Humor and laughter while playing the game (*Welch's* $F_{1,302.351}$ = 15.036; p < 0.001). However, the Humorous NPC Dialog did not have a significant effect on Enjoyment or flow. These results did not support Hypotheses H3A or H3B. Table 5 shows the results of Humorous NPC Dialog on each measure.

The MANOVA did not show statistically significant interaction effects between the three independent variables manipulated in this experiment. This did not support hypotheses H4A or H4B.

Table 4. MANOVA results for main effect of quest log

Measure	Quest Log		No Quest Log		F	p	Partial η^2
	M	SD	M	SD			
Enjoyment	3.981	1.744	4.023	1.739	0.038	0.845	0.000
Clear goals and navigation	4.027	1.849	3.745	1.951	3.848	0.051	0.012
Continuous feedback	3.769	1.679	3.444	1.636	3.773	0.053	0.012
Optimal challenge	4.361	1.552	4.329	1.720	0.066	0.798	0.000
Focusing of full attention	5.748	1.185	5.937	1.127	2.009	0.157	0.007
Merging of action and awareness	4.013	1.255	3.904	1.384	0.722	0.396	0.002
Loss of self consciousness	5.418	1.304	5.473	1.062	0.140	0.708	0.000
Sense of control	3.964	1.475	4.000	1.674	0.016	0.899	0.000
Altered perception of time	4.142	1.672	3.903	1.762	1.633	0.202	0.005
Humor	2.289	1.495	2.193	1.339	0.557	0.456	0.002

Table 5. MANOVA results for main effect of humor dialog

Measure	Humorous NPC dialog		No humorous NPC dialog		F	p	Partial η^2
	M	SD	M	SD			
Enjoyment	3.935	1.703	4.075	1.780	0.411	0.522	0.001
Clear goals and navigation	3.874	1.896	3.900	1.916	0.015	0.901	0.000
Continuous feedback	3.545	1.666	3.677	1.662	0.375	0.541	0.001
Optimal challenge	4.321	1.590	4.371	1.687	0.029	0.864	0.000
Focusing of full attention	5.825	1.088	5.861	1.234	0.137	0.712	0.000
Merging of action and awareness	3.933	1.325	3.988	1.317	0.033	0.857	0.000
Loss of self consciousness	5.421	1.215	5.471	1.163	0.150	0.699	0.000
Sense of control	3.923	1.573	4.045	1.578	0.311	0.577	0.001
Altered perception of time	3.964	1.663	4.087	1.781	0.210	0.647	0.001
Humor	2.531	1.546	1.929	1.194	14.953	<0.001	0.047

4 Discussion

This study investigated the impact of having a Navigational Pointer, a Quest Log, and Humorous Dialog on player flow and enjoyment with a between-subjects $2 \times 2 \times 2$ factorial controlled experiment using different versions of a custom-built research game. The Navigational Pointer had a significant impact on player enjoyment and flow, while the Quest Log and Humorous NPC Dialog did not have a significant impact on enjoyment or flow in this study. The significant impact of the Navigational Pointer will be discussed, and then the lack of a significant finding for the other two will be discussed.

Players experienced significantly more enjoyment and flow if they played the game with a Navigational Pointer, an arrow on screen pointing players to their next destination in the game world. Players who had a Navigational Pointer had significantly higher ratings of enjoyment, all three of the flow conditions, and all but one of the flow indicators. The highest effect size was on Clear Goals and Navigation, showing the pointer had the intended effect of making it more clear what to do and where to go next throughout the game compared to the control group. The Navigational Pointer continuously provided information about where to go to players in a way that was easy to see and understand without needing to read text, while players who did not have the pointer may have gotten lost or not known where to go without that information.

The other two flow conditions were also greater for those with the Navigational Pointer, Continuous Feedback and Optimal Challenge. Knowing where to go may have made it easier for players to tell how well they were playing the game, perhaps because those with the Navigational Pointer made more progress in the game than those without it and making progress made players feel they were getting more clear feedback. Feeling lost or unsure where to go may have made the level of challenge feel too high because they could not find their way or too low because they did not feel challenged when they could not easily find their way rather than having just the right amount of challenge.

All but one of the flow indicators, the factors that indicate how much a person is in a flow state [11, 17, 18], were significantly higher for players with the Navigational Pointer. Players with the pointer felt a greater Sense of Control, meaning the pointer made them feel more in control of their situation than those without it. They also felt more Merging of Action and Awareness, meaning they were playing the game automatically without having to think about it. This make sense because they were able to follow the Navigational Pointer without having to think about which way to go. Players with the pointer experienced more Altered Perception of Time, perhaps because time was flying when they were having fun, or because their attention was focused more on their task or quest in the game rather than finding their way. Players with the pointer also experienced more Focusing of Full Attention or concentration on the task at hand, again perhaps because they were not distracted from their current task in the game by the additional task of finding their way. The remaining flow indicator, Loss of Reflective Self-Consciousness, refers to not worrying about how one is presenting oneself or what others may be thinking of oneself. This factor was not significantly impacted by having a Navigational Pointer. Loss of Self-Consciousness may be less relevant than other flow indicators in the domain of flow in games than in studies of flow in other domains such as sports [9], but this will only become clear by conducting many studies like the present one and comparing results across them.

Since having the Navigational Pointer significantly increased player enjoyment and flow, this evidence supports the notion that guidance is good. To design for enjoyment and flow, it is better to provide navigational guidance rather than avoiding too much hand-holding. It is best to provide that navigational guidance in a way that makes it immediately clear which way to go, such as an arrow or path showing the way to go rather than a text description.

The Quest Log with the text-based prompts did not have a significant impact on player enjoyment or flow. This may have been because the text information displayed in the quest log was not required in order to make progress in the game, and much of that information about what to do next could also be found by locating NPCs and reading the NPC dialog text. It may have been because the information was displayed as text and players did not read it, or that the Quest Log was displayed at the top right of the screen and players did not look at that part of the screen. However, there were efforts made to mitigate the possibility of the Quest Log being overlooked or not read by using very short text in the Quest Log, using a graphic design for the Quest Log intended to draw the player's attention (see Fig. 1), and updating the Quest Log with each new quest or task given to the player throughout the game.

The Humorous NPC Dialog Text also did not have a significant impact on player enjoyment or flow. It appears it did lead players to report experiencing significantly more humor and laughter, but that did not increase player ratings of enjoyment or any of the flow indicators. This could be because the effect on humor was not large enough to impact flow or their overall enjoyment of the game, or this could be because humor does not actually have an impact on enjoyment or flow in games. In the present study, no link was found between making NPC dialog text humorous and player enjoyment or flow in games. Future research is needed to further test the link between humor and enjoyment in games by designing an experiment that will have a larger effect on players' experience of humor and laughter. Like the Quest Log, the Humorous NPC Dialog was delivered through text. It is possible that humor delivered with visuals or audible voice acting that does not depend on players reading text may be more effective at increasing player enjoyment or flow. It is also possible that humorous text that is simply more humorous than that used in this study, or a study designed with a control group that is more clearly non-humorous may be more effective at finding an impact of humor on player enjoyment or flow. Future research on the effect of humor in games would be advised to take into account these lessons learned.

Regarding the limitations of this study, controlled experiments benefit from greater internal validity, meaning the ability to make causal inferences, but tend to have less external validity, meaning the results of this study may not generalize to all complex tasks, games, or contexts. Future studies wishing to explore the external validity of these findings could study commercial off-the-shelf games rather than custom research games. Another possible limitation of the study was that the Quest Log and the Humorous NPC Dialog were both text based, and users may skim over or simply not read text. The NPC dialog was revealed one letter at a time to make it more likely that players would read it, but players were able to increase the speed that the text was revealed by holding the spacebar. The text of the quest log was kept very brief and persisted on the screen, but its position at the upper right may have made it less likely that participants noticed and read it. Future studies could test the effectiveness of presenting information about clear proximal goals and humorous content in a non-text format, such as by accompanying the text with audible voice acting or presenting the information using visible objects on the screen rather than text. Future research could also present the clear proximal goals information and humor in a more salient or easy-to-notice way.

More broadly, future research could explore the effectiveness of other potential sources of enjoyment and flow on players' experience. More controlled experiments are needed to test the effectiveness of the 34 sources of enjoyment identified by Schaffer and Fang's card sorting study [20], and to operationalize and test these sources of enjoyment by testing how well specific game design features increase player enjoyment and flow.

5 Conclusion

This study showed that having an arrow pointing players towards their destination increased player enjoyment and flow in 2D action-adventure RPG game custom-built for this research. For those who wish to design for player enjoyment and flow, this study gives some evidence that guidance is good, that it is better to make it clear to players where to go throughout each step of the game rather than avoiding hand-holding. Providing players with navigational guidance showing where to go next increased player flow and enjoyment. Specifically, the navigational guidance in this study used on-screen arrow showing the direction to go, so the navigational guidance was visual and did not rely on players reading text on the screen. If we want to design for player flow and enjoyment, it is better to avoid players getting lost in the game world by providing navigational guidance. Rather than navigational guidance making the game feel boring as the concept of avoiding too much hand-holding seems to suggest, a persistent on-screen navigational arrow pointing the way to go actually led to more optimal challenge, flow, and enjoyment.

No effects were found on player enjoyment or flow for adding a Quest Log with text-based information about what to do next or for adding humor to the NPC Dialog text. This may have been because the Quest Log and Humorous NPC Dialog were text-based and players simply did not read the text, or it may mean that these design differences simply did not have a significant impact on player enjoyment and flow. The Humorous NPC Dialog did have a significant effect on players' experience of humor and laughter, but this did not significantly increase their enjoyment or flow. Perhaps the text was not funny enough, or the control group was not sufficiently un-funny, or perhaps humor and laughter does not significantly increase enjoyment or flow when people play digital games.

Controlled experiments with random assignment like the present study need to be conducted to test what specific design differences actually increase flow and enjoyment among users or players. Well-designed controlled experiments can provide actionable recommendations to design for enjoyment and flow. Operationalizing design differences for controlled experiments also makes it more concrete how to design for the factors that lead to flow and enjoyment.

More controlled experiments with random assignment like the present study must be done to operationalize potential sources of enjoyment as specific design differences and test how effective they really are at causing increased flow and enjoyment among players. Building this evidence base through controlled experiments is important for practitioners and researchers who wish to reliably design games and other interactive systems for flow and enjoyment. There is more research to be done to engineer evidence-based interactive systems that reliably provide users with flow and enjoyment. The hope is that this research can be used to make games and other interactive systems more fun, and maybe even make life a little bit more fun.

Acknowledgements. This work was supported by a grant from the Caterpillar Fellowship Award.

References

1. Bethesda Game Studios: The Elder Scrolls V: Skyrim. Bethesda Game Studios (2015)
2. Blizzard Entertainment: World of Warcraft. Blizzard Entertainment (2004)
3. FromSoftware: Dark Souls. Namco Bandai Games (2011)
4. Ryan, R.M., Deci, E.L.: Self-determination theory and the facilitation of intrinsic motivation, social development, and well-being. Am. Psychol. **55**, 68–78 (2000). https://doi.org/10.1037// 0003-066X.55.1.68
5. Deci, E., Ryan, R.M.: Intrinsic Motivation and Self-Determination in Human Behavior. Plenum Press, New York (1985)
6. Csikszentmihalyi, M.: Finding Flow: The Psychology of Engagement with Everyday Life. Basic Books, New York, NY (1998)
7. Csikszentmihalyi, M.: The Evolving Self: A Psychology for the Third Millennium. Harper-Collins (1993)
8. Fang, X., Zhang, J., Chan, S.S.: Development of an instrument for studying flow in computer game play. Int. J. Hum.-Comput. Interact. **29**, 456–470 (2013). https://doi.org/10.1080/104 47318.2012.715991
9. Jackson, S.A., Marsh, H.W.: Development and validation of a scale to measure optimal experience: the flow state scale. J. Sport Exerc. Psychol. **18**, 17–35 (1996)
10. Jackson, S.A., Eklund, R.C.: The Flow Scales Manual. Fitness Information Technology (2004)
11. Nakamura, J., Csikszentmihalyi, M.: The concept of flow. In: Flow and the foundations of positive psychology, pp. 239–263. Springer, Dordrecht (2014). https://doi.org/10.1007/978-94-017-9088-8_16
12. Sweetser, P., Wyeth, P.: GameFlow: a model for evaluating player enjoyment in games. Comput. Entertain. (CIE) **3**, 3–3 (2005)
13. Csikszentmihalyi, M., Nakamura, J.: Effortless attention in everyday life: a systematic phenomenology. In: Bruya, B. (ed.) Effortless Attention: A New Perspective in the Cognitive Science of Attention and Action, pp. 179–190. The MIT Press (2010). https://doi.org/10. 7551/mitpress/9780262013840.003.0009
14. Csikszentmihalyi, M., Csikszentmihalyi, I.S. (eds.): Optimal Experience: Psychological Studies of Flow in Consciousness. Cambridge University Press, Cambridge; New York (1988)
15. Hektner, J., Schmidt, J., Csikszentmihalyi, M.: Experience sampling method. SAGE Publications, Inc., 2455 Teller Road, Thousand Oaks California 91320 United States of America (2007)
16. Keller, J., Bless, H.: Flow and regulatory compatibility: an experimental approach to the flow model of intrinsic motivation. Pers. Soc. Psychol. Bull. **34**, 196–209 (2008). https://doi.org/ 10.1177/0146167207310026

17. Schaffer, O., Fang, X.: Finding flow with games: does immediate progress feedback cause flow? Presented at the Americas conference on information systems (AMCIS), Puerto Rico (2015). https://doi.org/10.13140/RG.2.1.4236.8725
18. Schaffer, O., Fang, X.: Impact of task and interface design on flow. Presented at the HCI research in MIS workshop (SIGHCI) at the International Conference on Information Systems (ICIS), Dublin, Ireland (2016)
19. Schaffer, O.: Crafting Fun user Experiences: A Method to Facilitate Flow. Human Factors International (2013)
20. Schaffer, O., Fang, X.: What makes games fun? card sort reveals 34 sources of computer game enjoyment. Presented at the americas conference on information systems (AMCIS) 2018, New Orleans (2018)
21. Svebak, S.: The development of the sense of humor questionnaire: from SHQ to SHQ-6. Humor – Int. J. Humor Res. **9**, 341–362 (1996). https://doi.org/10.1515/humr.1996.9.3-4.341
22. Thorson, J.A., Powell, F.C.: Development and validation of a multidimensional sense of humor scale. J. Clin. Psychol. **49**, 13–23 (1993). https://doi.org/10.1002/1097-4679(199301)49:1%3c13::AID-JCLP2270490103%3e3.0.CO;2-S
23. Martin, R.A.: The situational humor response questionnaire (SHRQ) and coping humor scale (CHS): a decade of research findings. Humor – Int. J. Humor Res. **9**, 251–272 (1996). https://doi.org/10.1515/humr.1996.9.3-4.251
24. Chen, G.-H., Martin, R.A.: A comparison of humor styles, coping humor, and mental health between Chinese and Canadian university students. Humor – Int J. Humor Res. **20**(3), 215–234 (2007)
25. Dyck, K.T., Holtzman, S.: Understanding humor styles and well-being: the importance of social relationships and gender. Personality Individ. Differ. **55**, 53–58 (2013)
26. Hampes, W.P.: The relation between humor styles and empathy. Europe's J. Psychol. **6**, 34–45 (2010)
27. Martin, R.A., Puhlik-Doris, P., Larsen, G., Gray, J., Weir, K.: Individual differences in uses of humor and their relation to psychological well-being: development of the humor styles questionnaire. J. Res. Pers. **37**, 48–75 (2003)
28. Navarro-Carrillo, G., Torres-Marín, J., Corbacho-Lobato, J.M., Carretero-Dios, H.: The effect of humour on nursing professionals' psychological well-being goes beyond the influence of empathy: a cross-sectional study. Scand. J. Caring Sci. **34**, 474–483 (2020). https://doi.org/10.1111/scs.12751
29. Perry, S.D.: Commercial humor enhancement of program enjoyment: gender and program appeal as mitigating factors. Mass Commun. Soc. **4**, 103–116 (2001)
30. Dormann, C., Biddle, R.: A review of humor for computer games: play, laugh and more. Simul. Gaming **40**, 802 (2009)
31. Dormann, C., Biddle, R.: Making players laugh: the value of humour in computer games. In: Proceedings of the 2007 Conference on Future Play, pp. 249–250. ACM, New York, NY, USA (2007). https://doi.org/10.1145/1328202.1328254
32. Dormann, C., Biddle, R.: Humour in game-based learning. Learn. Media Technol. **31**, 411–424 (2006). https://doi.org/10.1080/17439880601022023
33. Lazzaro, N.: Why we play games: four keys to more emotion without story. In: Game Dev. Conf. (2004)
34. Lazzaro, N.: Why we play: affect and the fun of games: designing emotions for games, entertainment interfaces, and interactive products. In: Sears, A., Jacko, J. (eds.) Human-Computer Interaction: Designing for Diverse Users and Domains, pp. 155–176. CRC Press (2009). https://doi.org/10.1201/9781420088885.ch10
35. Ryan, R.M., Rigby, S.C., Przybylski, A.: The motivational pull of video games: a self-determination theory approach. Motiv. Emot. **30**, 344–360 (2006). https://doi.org/10.1007/s11031-006-9051-8

36. Brockmyer, J.H., Fox, C.M., Curtiss, K.A., McBroom, E., Burkhart, K.M., Pidruzny, J.N.: The development of the game engagement questionnaire: a measure of engagement in video game-playing. J. Exp. Soc. Psychol. **45**, 624–634 (2009). https://doi.org/10.1016/j.jesp.2009.02.016
37. Yee, N.: Motivations for play in online games. Cyberpsychol. Behav. **9**, 772–775 (2006)
38. Yee, N., Ducheneaut, N., Nelson, L.: Online gaming motivations scale: development and validation. In: Proceedings of the SIGCHI Conference on Human Factors in Computing Systems, pp. 2803–2806. ACM (2012)
39. Malone, T.W.: What makes things fun to learn? Heuristics for designing instructional computer games. In: Proceedings of the 3rd ACM SIGSMALL Symposium and the First SIGPC Symposium on Small Systems, pp. 162–169. ACM, New York, NY, USA (1980). https://doi.org/10.1145/800088.802839
40. Malone, T.W.: Toward a theory of intrinsically motivating instruction. Cogn. Sci. **5**, 333–369 (1981)
41. Quick, J.M., Atkinson, R.K., Lin, L.: Empirical taxonomies of gameplay enjoyment: personality and video game preference. Int. J. Game-Based Learn. **2**, 11–31 (2012)
42. Korhonen, H., Montola, M., Arrasvuori, J.: Understanding playful user experience through digital games. In: International Conference on Designing Pleasurable Products and Interfaces. Citeseer (2009)
43. Schaffer, O., Fang, X.: Digital game enjoyment: a literature review. In: Fang, X. (ed.) HCII 2019. LNCS, vol. 11595, pp. 191–214. Springer, Cham (2019). https://doi.org/10.1007/978-3-030-22602-2_16
44. Deterding, S., Dixon, D., Khaled, R., Nacke, L.: From game design elements to gamefulness: defining gamification. In: Proceedings of the 15th international academic MindTrek Conference: Envisioning Future Media Environments, pp. 9–15. ACM (2011)
45. Mason, W., Suri, S.: Conducting behavioral research on Amazon's mechanical turk. Behav. Res. **44**, 1–23 (2012). https://doi.org/10.3758/s13428-011-0124-6
46. Thomas, K.A., Clifford, S.: Validity and mechanical turk: an assessment of exclusion methods and interactive experiments. Comput. Hum. Behav. **77**, 184–197 (2017). https://doi.org/10.1016/j.chb.2017.08.038
47. Marjanovic, Z., Struthers, C.W., Cribbie, R., Greenglass, E.R.: The conscientious responders scale: a new tool for discriminating between conscientious and random responders. SAGE Open 4(3), 1–10 (2014). https://doi.org/10.1177/2158244014545964
48. Schaffer, O.: A desire fulfillment theory of digital game enjoyment. https://via.library.depaul.edu/cdm_etd/18. (2019)
49. McAuley, E., Duncan, T., Tammen, V.V.: Psychometric properties of the intrinsic motivation inventory in a competitive sport setting: a confirmatory factor analysis. Res. Q. Exerc. Sport **60**, 48–58 (1989). https://doi.org/10.1080/02701367.1989.10607413
50. Payne, B.R., Jackson, J.J., Noh, S.R., Stine-Morrow, E.A.L.: In the zone: flow state and cognition in older adults. Psychol. Aging. **26**, 738–743 (2011). https://doi.org/10.1037/a0022359
51. Hair, J.F., Black, W.C., Babin, B.J., Anderson, R.E.: Multivariate Data Analysis. Cengage Learning, Hampshire, UK (2019)
52. Pett, M.A., Lackey, N.R., Sullivan, J.: Making Sense of Factor Analysis: The Use of Factor Analysis for Instrument Development in Health Care Research. SAGE Publications Inc, Thousand Oaks, Calif (2003)
53. Winter, N., Burleigh, T., Kennedy, R., Clifford, S.: A Simplified Protocol to Screen Out VPS and International Respondents Using Qualtrics. Social Science Research Network, Rochester, NY (2019). https://doi.org/10.2139/ssrn.3327274

Slow, Repeat, Voice Guidance: Automatic Generation of Practice Charts to Improve Rhythm Action Games

Shio Takidaira, Yoshiyuki Shoji(✉) ⓘ, and Martin J. Dürst ⓘ

Aoyama Gakuin University, Sagamihara, Kanagawa 252-5258, Japan
takidaira@sw.it.aoyama.ac.jp, {shoji,duerst}@it.aoyama.ac.jp

Abstract. This paper proposes a method to automatically generate personalized charts (music scores in rhythm action games) for improving music game skills by analyzing the play logs of music games. When learning a song, dance, or musical instrument, it is common to slowly repeat only the part the learner has difficulty with, or for the instructor to say "one, two, step, turn" in rhythm. This paper aims to confirm whether this kind of practice method can be applied to learning music games. For this purpose, we have added a function to collect logs for an existing music game, and a function to automatically generate a new practice chart from the logs. The generated chart slows down according to the failure rate of the previous play, and the section with the most mistakes is repeated. In addition, voice guides are inserted, such as "Tan Ta Ta Tan" when the player needs to tap the notes, and "from the right!" or "alternating!" for specific patterns in the chart. A comparative experiment with 12 participants showed that the learning efficiency tended to increase when all the methods were combined, and to decrease when they were used individually.

Keywords: Rhythm action game · Chart · Play log analysis · Memory

1 Introduction

Music games have become deeply ingrained in our daily lives nowadays. Rhythm action games, born in the 1990s, grew in variety and exploded in video arcades. Since then, many players have played them on home game consoles and in entertainment facilities. In recent years, these games have become more and more popular and influential in society; many world championships have been held, and the games are used in the medical field to rehabilitate the elderly[1]. Music games are also attracting attention for their educational aspects; some music

---

[1] BANDAI NAMCO CSR Rreport 2007, p. 13: "Rehabilitainment", https://www.bandainamco.co.jp/cgi-bin/releases/index.cgi/file/view/8239?entry_id=5836.

© The Author(s), under exclusive license to Springer Nature Switzerland AG 2022
X. Fang (Ed.): HCII 2022, LNCS 13334, pp. 119–138, 2022.
https://doi.org/10.1007/978-3-031-05637-6_8

games have been adopted as part of the elementary school curriculum to develop the body and the sense of rhythm[2].

However, even with such widespread use, the best way to practice a music game has not yet been found, unlike for other music-based expressive activities such as playing musical instruments, singing and dancing. Music games often have training modes, but their functionality is limited. Functions include not quitting a song midway even if a player made some mistakes, choosing the same song continuously, and changing the play speed. In such a situation, to become more proficient in a music game, a player has to start with an easy song and repeat that song from beginning to end continuously. When they play that song well enough, they can move on to the next, slightly more complex, song, repeating the same process.

One of the main reasons people start playing music games is that the player's favorite songs were added to the game. The newcomer wants to play the song, so they start playing the music game. However, if this song is complicated, the player will have to play unrelated songs over and over again to practice their skills. If they start out wanting to play a particular favorite song, but they have to practice with an unrelated song, it can cause frustration.

Therefore, we propose a method for automatically generating the **chart** (music score in rhythm action game). The goal is to help learners improve their musical game skills by playing the same song, using techniques from traditional music education. We focused on rhythm action games in which players have to react to the notes of a scrolling chart at the correct timing (see Fig. 1 and Fig. 2 for examples of a screen and a chart). Our method incorporates learning methods used in playing musical instruments, singing, and dancing into the practice of a such kind of game. In the field of learning music, it is common for trainers to watch the learners' behavior and give advice. The trainer may ask the learner to repeat the same part or give verbal instruction on rhythm as the learner plays. The proposed system logs the learner's behavior while playing to enable this kind of learning in music game practice. By analyzing the learner's log, the system can estimate the learner's proficiency level and areas of weakness. Then, at the end of playing a song, the system automatically generates a personalized practice chart based on the analysis results.

When practicing singing or instruments, it is common to divide the song into phrases, repeat them frequently, or practice phrases that the learner is not good at with a slower tempo. In fact, in an extensive survey of musicians, it was pointed out that repetition is often used in the practice of advanced musicians [15].

It is also common to teach music performance by putting the movements into words and rhythm. Classically, when learning a dance choreography, trainers often attach tentative lyrics to the songs, such as "One, two, step, turn!" and so on. In the same way, when learning a musical instrument, giving tentative

---

[2] Konami Official Website: "American Public Schools Use KONAMI's Game for Physical Education Programs - Dance Dance Revolution -" https://www.konami.com/sustainability/en/culture/ddr.html.

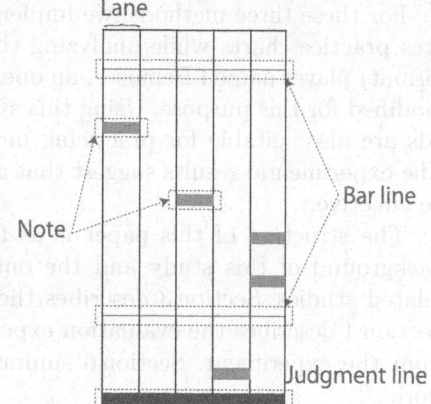

Fig. 1. Play screen of Bemuse, the open-source rhythm action game, used in the experiment

Fig. 2. An example of a chart in a typical rhythm action game

lyrics related to fingering is a common technique. These phenomena are often discussed in connection with dual coding theory [1].

When people remember non-verbal information, they can associate it with verbal information to make it easier to recall. For example, the phenomenon of skilled jazz dancers memorizing choreography by verbalizing it has been reported [19]. Some studies have shown that learning choreography is more efficient when both visual and auditory cues are used [20].

We focus on three common techniques used in such kind of musical practice:

1. **Slow:** The Slow function changes the playback speed so that the player can practice slowly. Specifically, the charts of the music game consist of background music and sound effects that are played when the buttons are tapped correctly, so that these can be played slowly without changing their pitch.
2. **Repeat:** The repeat function allows the learners to practice only their weak parts over and over again. The proposed method estimates the learner's weak parts from the play log. The method rewrites the chart so that the weak parts are repeated an arbitrary number of times. Blank bars are inserted before and after each repeat.
3. **Voice Guidance:** According to the pattern of notes in the score, the voice guide function gives tentative lyrics that make it easier to remember the action. In other words, to make it easier for the learners to grasp the rhythm, the method gives them a "Tan, Ta Ta Tan" voice to go with the notes. Also, for specific patterns, such as when the player needs to tap the left and right notes one after the other with two fingers, the system will say "Alternating!", and when the player has to tap from one note to the next in succession, the system will say "From the right!"

For these three methods, we implemented a system that dynamically generates practice charts while analyzing the logs. A BMS (Be-Music Source, a file format) player named Bemuse[3], an open-source rhythm action game engine, was modified for this purpose. Using this system, we confirmed whether these methods are also suitable for practicing music games through subject experiments. The experimental results suggest that a combination of these three methods can be effective.

The structure of this paper is as follows. This section describes the social background of this study and the outline of our method. Section 2 describes related studies. Section 3 describes the details of our actual proposed method. Section 4 describes the evaluation experiment, and Sect. 5 discusses the findings from the experiment. Section 6 summarizes our research and discusses future work.

2   Related Work

This research aims to improve music game skills by automatically generating personalized practice charts for each player. This is related to existing research on improving music games and effective practice methods for improving music based on music learning theory. Therefore, we will explain the existing studies from these perspectives and show the position of this research.

2.1   Music Games

In recent years, research on music games has been very active. A typical example is developing serious games for learning music. Other research includes the automatic generation of music game charts, analysis of music games themselves, and various other research.

Many studies have been done on music games using games as a method of gamification and learning. As an example, Denis et al. [4,5] propose a music game that can be used for music education by applying the theory of gamification.

As an example of the broader use of music games, Dannenberg et al. [13] proposed a music game for the elderly to improve dual tasks in motor cognition. Through an experiment with older adults over 65 years, the authors point out that music games can improve cognitive abilities. The music game, combined with exercises, shows the possibility of practical use for cognitive training of the elderly.

Charlotte et al. [18] investigate how a serious music game can encourage independent learning behavior in players. They propose three models: The feedback model, the incentive and achievement model, and the progression model. In these studies, serious games still need to be improved for practical learning management, even though they have already been used in education in some cases.

---

[3] Bemuse: "Bemuse - Beat Music Sequence" https://dt.in.th/Bemuse.html#etymology.

Many studies automatically generate music game charts for various applications. Liang et al. [11] use fuzzy labels and C-BLSTM models to generate music scores for music games automatically. Lin et al. [14] also propose generating charts for a real rhythm action game using deep neural networks. Their system estimates the timing of the note's placement from arbitrary music files, and generates appropriate charts for each player based on their skills. Halina et al. [8] have proposed TaikoNation, a method for automatically generating more natural charts by focusing on humans' patterns. Similarly, Donahue et al. [6] proposed a method to generate a dance game score from a song using a convolutional neural network. In these studies, the goal is to automatically generate charts for new songs. On the other hand, we do not generate charts from songs in this study, but edit and adjust existing charts for learning.

Regarding the social demand for music games, Johanna et al. [9] have conducted a large-scale user survey from the perspective of the social and physical impact of the game series Dance Dance Revolution on players' lives. The environment surrounding the music games themselves, which are becoming popular, is also a research topic. For example, research has been conducted to detect bots in online music games [12].

2.2 Music Training Support by Using Information Technology

There has been a lot of research on the use of information technology to create practice content that meets the needs of learners [2,3]. Roger et al. [21] proposed an electronic tutoring system for piano learning in the early days of computer use. This tutoring system is a classical expert system with piano input and multimedia output. The system reads the learner's input from the piano keyboard and presents followup material according to the level through multimedia. Similarly, some research aimed to support piano practice with computers comprehensively [7].

Another example of music learning support, Nakamura et al. [16] have conducted research on motion capture and rich information presentation interfaces to help learners train dance. For this kind of computer-based music learning, technologies have been proposed that use sensors to detect performance errors in more detail, and technologies that present information such as visualizing finger movements during practice [5,10,17].

Our research also refers to these methodologies, but as an objective, our proposed method aims to improve the skills of music games themselves through playing music games.

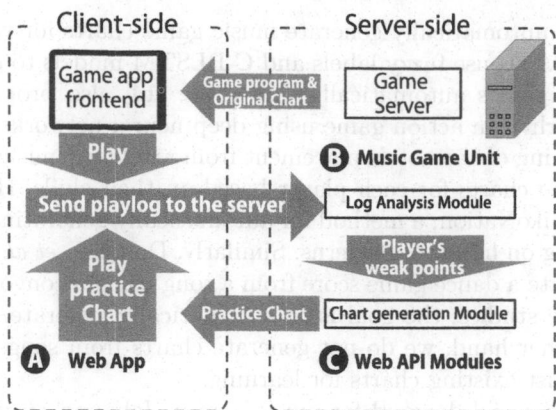

Fig. 3. Overview of the system. It consist of three parts; Client (A), Game Unit (B), and Web API Modules (C).

3 Automatic Generation of Practice Chart

This section describes our method for generating personalized practice charts containing slow, repeat, and voice guidance, by analyzing players' operation logs.

Since such a method for automatic chart generation is inseparable from the system, it was necessary to implement a working system. Therefore, this section explains the method with a description of the working system. The proposed system first collects logs, then identifies the player's weak part, and finally generates a personalized chart.

Because we used Bemuse, an open-source BMS (Be-Music Source) player, in the experiment, the rules of the game, the chart's specifications, and the system's outline will be described using this player as an example.

3.1 System Overview

In order to actually create such a practice score automatically, it is necessary to add a function to the front-end of the game that collects and sends logs. It also requires a program to analyze the logs and generate the score from the analysis results. Figure 3 shows the overview of the entire system.

When a player plays the chart of a song, a log is generated of the results of that play. The server-side application automatically generates a score for the practice based on the log. By playing the generated chart, the player can practice in a personalized way.

The proposed system is a Web application that consists of a client and a server. The client consists of a music game front-end and a log collection/sending module. The server consists of a music game server, a log receiving/analyzing module, and a personalized chart generation module. The log collection/sending module collects the logs of the chart played on the music game front-end, and sends them to the server side. The server receives the logs from the log receiving/analyzing module, and analyzes each player's weak points in the chart. The analysis results are passed to the chart generation module, which automatically generates a chart for practice. This chart is for one song that a player can play through, including slow, repeat, and voice guidance.

In the experimental implementation in this paper, we needed to prepare variant methods for comparison, such as voice guidance only, repeat only, and so on. Thus, each module is implemented as a Web API, and can be played under different conditions by simply switching the API.

3.2 Collecting and Formatting Play Logs

First, gameplay logs are collected to identify the weak points of each player. Since this music game is a web application, it is divided into a front-end that runs on the client and a server that delivers the program and charts. The front-end program runs in the browser. When users access the Web application, the program (written in HTML and Javascript) is downloaded and executed. Then the player can choose the chart to be played and download it from the server. Next the player can actually play the chart. Logging is performed by modifying the front-end program to record what is tapped at what timing sequentially (A in Fig. 3). Formatting and cleansing of the logs is performed by the API that receives the logs (B in Fig. 3).

The play screen in this game is shown in Fig. 1 (this screenshot is the same as the original Bemuse screen, because we did not modify it except for the log collection function and the guiding voice). A schematic diagram of the chart is shown in Fig. 2. A song chart consists of bars, and a bar contains several notes. Each song has a BPM (Beats Per Minute) and a time signature (*e.g.*, four-quarter time). In this game, the notes fall from the top of the screen to the bottom in time with the music. If the player taps the corresponding lane on the screen just when the note touches the judgment line, a sound effect will be played, and the player will get a score. The player will be given a grade of "Excellent", "Good", or "Bad", depending on how well they tap the screen with the right timing.

Results of the gameplay are logged in units of play. In this log, when and where the player tapped is recorded. By checking this against the chart, this is formatted into note units. Specifically, the format is generalized to the form of *(note ID, bar number, grade)*. For example, if a player got a Good evaluation by tapping the 20th note in bar 12, the result would be *(20, 12, GOOD)*. In this way, the system can handle the player's play log in an uniform way.

3.3 Estimating Player's Weak Part

Next, from the collected logs, the method estimates the player's proficiency level and the parts they are not good at (C in the Fig. 3). As shown in Fig. 2, a song consists of many bars, and each bar contains several notes. It is then judged for each note whether the player was able to tap the screen correctly or not. Based on the percentage of correct taps, the player's weak bars can be determined. The weakness score $weak(i)$, the degree to which a player is not good at playing the i-th bar of a song, can be defined as

$$weak(i) = \begin{cases} 0 & (O_i = \phi), \\ \dfrac{\sum_{note \in O_i} loss(v_{note})}{|O_i|} & (otherwise), \end{cases} \quad (1)$$

where notes in the i-th bar are defined as O_i. The function $loss(v)$ normalizes the gap v between the time the note is actually tapped and the ideal timing. Here, the note $note_j$ can be expressed from the bar i it belongs to and the evaluation value v as

$$note_j = (i, v). \quad (2)$$

Using the above definition, the total degree of weakness $pro(s, e)$ from the s-th bar to the e-th bar can be expressed as

$$pro(s, e) = \sum_{i=s}^{e} weak(i). \quad (3)$$

Here, the sequential parts where $pro(s, e)$ is the maximum among all pairs of s and e, where $e = s + n$ for the arbitrary number of n, were defined as the player's weak parts. The method automatically generates practice chart data for these extracted weak parts.

3.4 Automatic Generation of Charts with Slow and Repeat

Next, the method generates practice chart data for the extracted weak parts by cutting out parts of the score and modifying them. The method applies slow and repeats to the chart as a simple change. The Fig. 4 shows an overview of the application of slow and repeat to the chart in the system.

Slow is a modification that reduces the playback speed of a song, just as a learner slows down the playing tempo when practicing an instrument. In order to actually reduce the playback speed of music games, some implementation techniques are necessary. The output sounds during music gameplay can be categorized into two main types:

- **BGM (background music):** sounds that are generated regardless of the player's input, and
- **Operation sound:** Sounds made in response to player actions.

Furthermore, operation sounds in music game charts are classified into

- **Keypad tone:** sound that is a component of a song, played when the player correctly taps a note, and
- **Sound effect:** sound played by the player's input that is unrelated to the completion of the music.

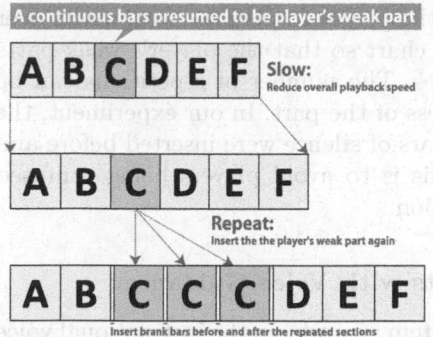

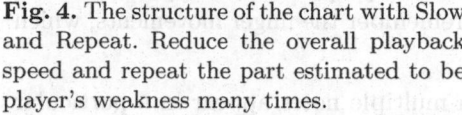

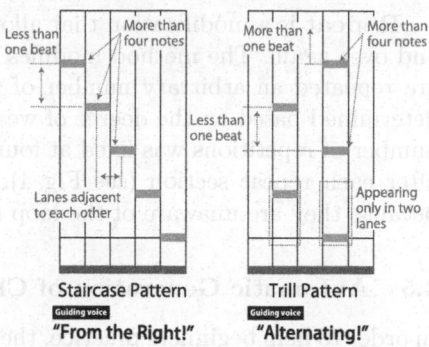

Fig. 4. The structure of the chart with Slow and Repeat. Reduce the overall playback speed and repeat the part estimated to be player's weakness many times.

Fig. 5. Examples of a voice guide for multiple note sequences. In the case of a staircase or alternating (called drumrolls), the corresponding voice is played.

In games that adopt a keypad tone, a missed tap will cause the song's melody to be choppy. Whether a keypad tone or a sound effect is played when a player taps notes depends on the game and the song. For example, in Beatmania and "pop'n music", pressing a button will play the composition sound of the song. On the other hand, in games such as Dance Dance Revolution and Taiko no Tatsujin (Drum Master), when the player operates in time with the background music, sounds unrelated to the music are played.

When slowing down a song in a game that adopts the keypad tones, it is necessary to reduce the playback speed of both the background music and the operation sounds. In this case, only the playback speed must be reduced without changing the pitch of the sound. On the other hand, in the case of a game where sound effects are played when the player taps a note, reducing the playback speed of the sound effects would be unnatural. Since the sound effects are sounds that do not originally exist and are independent of the music, the playback speed should be reduced only for the background music.

The system used in this experiment can have both patterns depending on the song. Since it is difficult to estimate this automatically, we limited the songs used for the evaluation to songs that adopted keypad tones. Therefore, the tempo of both the background music and the operation sounds was slowed down in our system.

In addition, the tempo was not slowed down only for the weak parts that the player had difficulty with, but for the entire song. In a preliminary experiment, it was observed that beginners tended to be unable to respond quickly to sudden changes of speed during play. Since this research aims to support first-time learners, the slow method's personalization was limited for evaluation with novice participants.

Repeat is a modification that allows the player to play the weak parts over and over again. The method modifies the chart so that the player's weak parts are repeated an arbitrary number of times. The number of repetitions can be determined based on the degree of weakness of the part. In our experiment, the number of repetitions was fixed at four. Bars of silence were inserted before and after each repeat section (see Fig. 4). This is to avoid players being confused because they are unaware of the loop section.

3.5   Automatic Generation of Charts with Voice Guidance

In order to help beginners practice, the system reproduces the instructional voice guide commonly used when studying music. We prepared three types of guiding voice suitable for beginners to help them remember the finger movements, which are physical actions:

- **form of note sequence:** voice when multiple notes appear in a particular sequence, such as a staircase,
- **number of notes:** voice when a series of notes appears together in a series or in parallel, and
- **rhythm:** voice simply to learn the rhythm of the notes.

The **form of note sequence** verbalizes the appearance of the group of notes and plays the guiding voice according to the form of the sequence. Figure 5 shows an example of notes flowing from the upper direction. The system discovers staircase and trill patterns based on the temporal difference and the number of lanes between one note and the next.

If all the time differences are less than one beat and subsequent notes are shifted in a specific direction, a group of notes is considered a staircase. This only applies to cases where the gap is one or two lanes. A guiding voice was created to help the user remember that the notes appear as a staircase, intuitively matching the finger movements. Since the staircase notes have a direction, we give them a specific voice: "from the right" or "from the left".

The left part of Fig. 5 shows an example of a staircase. The time difference between each subsequent note is less than one beat. In addition, each note is placed one lane to the left to the previous note. So, when the first note (*i.e.*, the one displayed at the bottom) should be tapped, the voice guidance "From the right!" will be played.

If a group of four or more notes, all with a time gap of one beat or less, are alternately located in two specific lanes, then the note group is considered a trill-like pattern. This pattern of alternately tapping two lanes is typical in music games in general, and is often called drumrolls. The right part in Fig. 5 shows an example of a trill pattern. The five notes shown have a time difference of less than a beat each. The five notes are placed alternately in the second and fourth lanes. Therefore, the system considers this group of notes as a trill pattern. The guiding voice will say "Alternating!" when the lowest note touches the line.

The **number of notes** guiding voice tells the player the number of notes that need to be tapped, when notes appear in succession at equal intervals, or when multiple notes need to be tapped simultaneously. Figure 6 shows an example of two types of the number of note guiding voices. In the left part, there are three or more notes in a row, evenly spaced on the same lane. The system recognizes this group of notes as a Serial Pattern. It announces the number of notes that need to be tapped in succession. In this example, the voice "5 notes" is played when the first note touches the judgment line.

Similarly, if two or more notes are horizontally lined up simultaneously, a similar guiding voice will be played. This is considered a Parallel Pattern. The right part of Fig. 6 shows an example of a Parallel Pattern.

Finally, as **rhythm guide**, we assigned a simple guiding voice to notes that did not fit into the two patterns described above. The purpose of this voice is simply to make the user remember the timing of tapping. Specifically, as shown in Fig. 7, the guiding voice is like "Tan Ta Ta Tan". If the number of beats between a note and the next note is more than one, the phrase "Tan" is played, and if it is less than one beat, the phrase "Ta" is played. The form pattern and the number pattern don't apply to many parts of a song's chart. Therefore, in many parts of the song, a voice like "Tan Ta Ta Tan" is constantly played.

These guiding voices can be generated by combining only a few dozen phrases. In this implementation, each phrase was created using female voices from a commercially available synthetic voice library, and the guiding voice was realized by combining them on time during play.

These guiding voices are automatically assigned in decreasing frequency of appearance (*i.e.*, the order of form, number, and rhythm). However, in actual music game charts, it is common for multiple notes to appear at the same time at all times, especially in songs of high difficulty. The scope of this rule-based implementation is limited to simple songs with not more than a single melody line.

Note that the system was implemented in Japanese, and the experiments were also conducted in Japanese. Therefore, the guiding voice is also implemented in Japanese, and translated into English in this paper.

Through this series of processes, the system becomes able to estimate the weak part of the player for the song from the play log. Then, it is possible to support the learning of music games with slow, repeat, and voice guidance.

4   Evaluation

In order to confirm whether the system we created is effective in improving players' music game skills, we conducted a subject experiment. Twelve experimental participants were each assigned two of four learning methods, including the proposed method, and played the game seven times with each method. The increase in gaming score between the seven games and the correct tap rate for each game were then measured.

The contributions in our method can be broadly divided into changing the structure of the chart by **slow and repeat** and changing the sound of the song

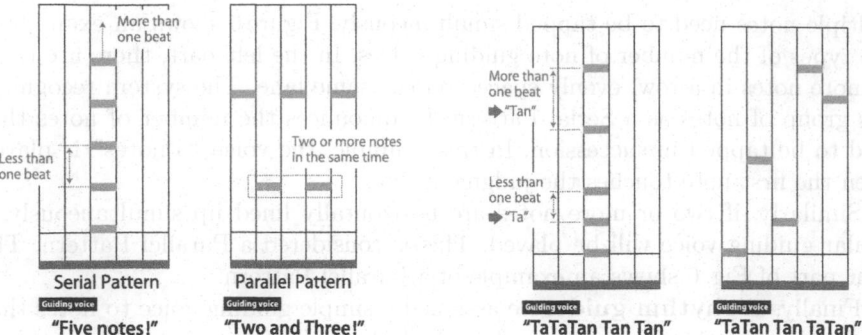

Fig. 6. Examples of a guiding voice when multiple notes appear in series or parallel. When multiple notes appear in the same lane at equal intervals (called jackhammers), the number of notes is announced. When multiple keys need to be pressed simultaneously (called chords), the number of notes is announced in the same way.

Fig. 7. Example of voice guidance in the case the notes do not correspond to either the form pattern or the number pattern. Simply, the sounds of "Ta" and "Tan" are played at the correct timing.

by **voice guidance**. Therefore, to discuss how effective each of these is, we created comparative methods in combination with them.

The subject experiments were conducted in the years 2020 and 2021. A browser on an iPad was used to access our system and play the game. The experiment took about an hour per participant, and the participants received a gratuity of about ten US dollars.

4.1   Implementation

The system was implemented as shown in Fig. 3. We modified Bemuse, an open-source online BMS player. The front-end of Bemuse is developed in Javascript, and the server-side is developed in node.js. We modified the front-end to send a detailed log in the JSON format to the server when the player finishes playing a song and transitions to the result screen. The server side has been modified to deliver a new chart at any time.

As a set of APIs in the server, we created a module that receives logs, cleanses and reshapes them, and analyzes them. We also created a module that actually generates a BMS chart file based on the log analysis result. This module outputs a new chart for practice when receiving an arbitrary BMS file and the log analysis results. To implement these APIs, we used flask, a python web framework. One limitation of the implementation is that the current rule-based guiding voice assignment function is incomplete. Therefore, it only works correctly for songs with simple melody lines and not so many notes appearing at the same time.

Table 1. Four comparison methods used in the subject experiment

Method	Description
Both	Proposed method. The chart was modified with both voice guidance, and slow and repeat
Voice Only	A comparative method for testing the effectiveness of voice guidance. The chart structure remains the same as the original one; only voice guidance was added
Slow+Repeat	A comparative method to test the effectiveness of changing the chart structure. Slow down the entire song and repeat the weak part four times
Baseline	Play the original score without any modifications

Table 2. Assignment of methods and songs for each task. All participants played the proposed method, and the songs were assigned without bias.

Task ID	1st play		2nd play	
	Song	Method	Song	Method
1	A	Baseline	B	Both
2	A	Voice Only	B	Both
3	A	Slow+Repeat	B	Both
4	A	Both	B	Baseline
5	A	Both	B	Voice Only
6	A	Both	B	Slow+Repeat
7	B	Baseline	A	Both
8	B	Voice Only	A	Both
9	B	Slow+Repeat	A	Both
10	B	Both	A	Baseline
11	B	Both	A	Voice Only
12	B	Both	A	Slow+Repeat

4.2 Comparison Methods

We prepared four comparative methods to evaluate the effectiveness of changing the chart structure and the voice guidance. Table 1 shows the list of methods, including our proposed method. The method **Both** includes both modifications to the chart structure and voice guidance. The methods **Slow+Repeat** and **Voice Only** only change one of them, respectively. Note that **Voice Only** is not personalized, as the guiding voice is given throughout the entire song.

We imposed several restrictions on each method to fit the experimental setup of this study. For methods containing personalization, the number of repetitions was fixed at four. In addition, we fixed the number of week parts to one place of four bars. This is to avoid significant differences in playing time between personalized and non-personalized methods. Such practice time differences would have a more substantial effect than the method differences we are investigating. For the same reason, we set the slow methods' playback speed to be uniformly 0.8 times the speed of the original song.

4.3 Experimental Settings

We chose two songs for the task and adjusted the game for the experiment. In choosing the songs, we considered the following conditions:

- The song's tempo is not changed in the middle of the song,
- The length of the song is around 100 s (or the first part of the song is around 100 s and can be cut),
- The number of notes to be tapped at the same time does not exceed four, and
- The density of the notes is less than four notes per second throughout the entire song.

We eventually used the following two songs for our experiment:

- **Song A**: Dream Map and Our Journey[4]
  (Original title: Yume no Chizu to Bokura no Tabi.), and
- **Song B**: My Own Affairs[5]
  (Original title: Jibun Goto).

These two songs were used in a famous BMS event. In our experiments, we removed the prelude of the songs and used only the first half of the songs. The player needs to tap about 3.5 notes per second in these songs.

We also assigned each participant songs and methods, taking into account order to avoid bias. Table 2 shows the actual method and song assignment for each task. For each method, the song is used the same number of times. In this experimental setting, the order effect in the experiment is expected to be strong because participants are beginners. Therefore, we ensured that the number of times each method was used was equal in the first play and second play. Since we wanted to focus mainly on the difference between the proposed method and the others in the analysis, the proposed method was set to be played by all subjects. In this experiment, each task was assigned to a single participant.

As in other detailed experimental settings, the time to determine if a note was tapped correctly was set to 120 ms. This is the standard value for combo (a rule that gives a player bonus points when they tap notes in succession) in BMS. The Lead Time, which determines the speed throughout the game, was set to 1,800 ms. For the experiment, we used an iPad with a 10.2-in. display. During the experiment, the 3D mode was used, as shown in Fig. 1, and participants tapped directly on the lanes on the screen. Participants used earphones during the experiment.

4.4 Experimental Task

The participants in the experiment were asked to play a rhythm action game to measure their playing skill improvement. First, the participants were given iPads and were explained the rules of the rhythm action game and the basic operation of the system. Next, each subject played each song seven times. Figure 8 shows an overview of the sequence of steps performed by the participants during the experiment. Except for the baseline, participants played three different charts. They played the original chart the first time. Then, the next two times, they played a practice chart generated based on the first play. The fourth time, they played the original chart again. Then they played the practice chart generated from the fourth play log twice. Finally, they played the original chart again.

There are two reasons why we choose such task settings. One is that if the system created practice charts from the play logs of the practice charts, there

---

[4] G2R 2018 Climax Song Information: "Dream Map and Our Journey" (in Japanese) http://manbow.nothing.sh/event/event.cgi?action=More_def&num=287&event =123.

[5] The BMS Fighters XVI Song Information: "My Own Affairs" (in Japanese) http:// manbow.nothing.sh/event/event.cgi?action=More_def&num=181&event=133.

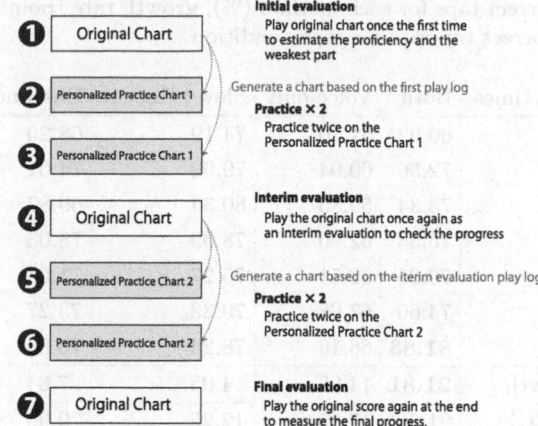

Fig. 8. Participants' tasks during the experiment. Participants played the game a total of seven times. To fix the experimental setup, all participants played the original chart three times and two generated training charts two times each.

would be a difference in playing time depending on the participants' initial skill. For example, if an awkward player makes a mistake in a repeated part again and again, the chart gets longer with each turn. The other reason is that we wanted to compare methods on the same chart.

The participants performed two sets of the task, with each set consisting of seven such plays. They played different songs and methods in the first and second sets. There was a break in between the two sets.

4.5   Experimental Results

To see how much the participants actually improved, we calculated the correct tap rate during each play, and the amount of progress throughout the seven plays. The correct tap rate was calculated by dividing the number of correct taps (*i.e.*, the number of times the participant tapped the lane within 60 ms before or after the note touched the judgment line) by the total number of notes that appeared in the chart. If all notes are tapped within this interval, the rate is 100%; if none are tapped, the rate is 0%.

Table 3 and Fig. 9 show the correct tap rate for each play time, and the degree of growth from the first time to the seventh time for each method. The degree of growth is the difference of rates between the seventh time and the first time. The method using both voice and slow and repeat had the highest final correct tap rate (81.83%) and the highest growth (21.81 points). Participants who practiced with the proposed method became able to tap more than 80% of the notes correctly after seven practice sessions. On the other hand, the method with the smallest difference was the slow-repeat method, with a difference of only 4.05 points, which resulted in less improvement than simply playing the regular chart repeatedly.

Table 3. Rate of correct taps for each method (%), growth rate (points) and standard deviation (SD) of correct tap rate for each condition.

Play times	Both	Voice only	Slow+Repeat	Baseline
1	60.02	51.20	74.19	68.20
2	72.56	60.04	79.92	74.01
3	73.34	59.85	80.34	69.87
4	76.53	62.90	78.09	78.03
5	70.95	62.51	75.27	71.03
6	74.66	67.08	79.33	73.27
7	**81.83**	66.16	78.24	75.84
Growth	**21.81**	14.95	4.05	7.64
SD @ 1	21.60	17.95	12.25	9.99
SD @ total	18.86	15.83	12.25	13.17

5   Discussion

This section discusses the characteristics of the proposed method and its usefulness based on the experimental results obtained. First, the usefulness of method **Both** was significantly higher in terms of growth rate. From Table 3, we can see that the degree of increase in the correct tap rate of method **Both** is 21.81 points, which is higher than the other methods. This result suggests that the proposed method may actually be effective in improving rhythm action game skills.

Focusing on the possibility that some participants improved faster than others in the music game, from the first row in Table 3 we can see that even though all the participants played the same chart on the first play, there was a difference in the scores for each method. This trend can also be seen in the standard deviation of the first play and the average. It indicates that people have different suitability for rhythm action games. However, all participants had played the proposed method once, which was effective for them. Therefore, we can assume that this result does not depend on the potential of the participants.

Next, we consider the cause of the decrease in progress efficiency in the **Slow+Repeat** method. Compared with the other methods and the baseline method, the increase in the correct tap rate of the **Slow+Repeat** method was relatively low, at 4.05 points. One reason could be that the change in speed was too burdensome for the novices. As described in Sect. 3, beginners may not be able to respond quickly to speed changes or sudden changes in their gameplay. In the experiment, the speed changes during the fourth and seventh task in the set, which may have hindered the beginner's progress.

These results suggest a synergistic effect between the voice guidance and **Slow+Repeat** methods. The proposed method, which includes slow-repeat,

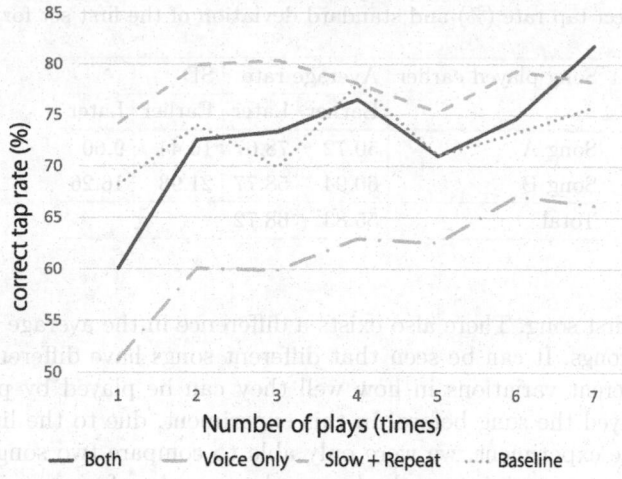

Fig. 9. Number of plays vs. correct tap rate of notes for each method.

may also have inhibited the improvement due to playback speed changes. However, the participants who practiced with the **Both** method improved faster.

Considering this result, it is possible that the voice guidance accelerated the memorization of phrases. It is important to remember and internalize which notes to tap when learning to play. It is difficult to feel the beat if the tempo is too slow when trying to internalize the rhythm without audio guidance. It can be assumed that the phrase was learned quickly by practicing the weak part slowly and repeatedly, with the tap timing and fingering indicated by the voice guide.

Intuitively, it is similar to the behavior when learning a song; once a song is learned perfectly, it can be sung at different tempos. Once the player has internalized the rhythm, performance may become more resistant to tempo variations. One of the reasons why the **Voice Only** method did not promote growth could be that the original tempo was too fast and only be practiced once, thus failing to promote the internalization of phrases.

In addition, order effects should be discussed. We focused on which of the methods and songs was tried first during the evaluation experiment. The participants played different songs in the first and second sets in the experiment. Table 4 shows the correct tap rate and its standard deviation for each song and position. Overall, it can be seen that the participants improved more in the second set than in the first set. This may be because their skill to play music games improved while playing the first set of songs, and they were able to demonstrate the skill even when they saw the score for the first time in the second set of songs.

We discuss the difficulty and quality of the songs themselves. Comparing the standard deviation, we can see that when Song A was played as the first song, the standard deviation was lower in the second song than when Song B was

Table 4. Correct tap rate (%) and standard deviation of the first set for each song

Song played earlier	Average rate		SD	
	Earlier	Later	Earlier	Later
Song A	50.72	78.67	16.44	9.60
Song B	60.94	58.77	21.93	16.26
Total	55.83	68.72		

played as the first song. There also exists a difference in the average correct tap rate between songs. It can be seen that different songs have different difficulty levels and different variations in how well they can be played by players who have never played the song before. In this experiment, due to the limitation of the scale of the experiment, we were only able to compare two songs. In order to actually compare training methods on a large scale, of course, it would be necessary to conduct experiments using a more significant number of songs.

In the end, the proposed method showed a tendency to be useful, but the details are not precise. It will be necessary to evaluate in detail what kind of support contributes to the improvement of rhythm action games through a large-scale evaluation experiment with a larger number of songs.

6   Conclusion

We proposed an automatic generation of rhythm action game charts for practice by analyzing the game's operation logs to match each player's weak parts. We modified Bemuse, an open-source game engine, to implement a system that can receive logs and play practice scores. The music practice methods of slow, repeat, and voice guidance were applied to a music game and evaluated in a subject experiment. The experimental results showed that the combination of all these methods can help novice players improve their game skills faster. The experiment suggested that voice guidance and slow+repeat may synergize and help players internalize phrases.

On the other hand, the results of this experiment are limited. Some issues for future research were found. One of the issues is to improve the accuracy of extracting the parts that players are not good at. We simply used consecutive bars with a low correct tap rate as the weakest sections; however, we did not consider the difficulty of the bar itself or the number of notes it contains. The scale of the experiment is also an important issue. This paper conducted a small-scale experiment using two songs for 12 participants. Subjects practiced the prescribed song seven times, interspersed with the original charts. However, this task is unnatural compared to a real player trying to improve their skills while playing a music game. We hope to conduct a larger-scale evaluation in the future.

Acknowledgements. This work was supported by JSPS KAKENHI Grants Number 18K18161 and 21H03775.

References

1. Clark, J.M., Paivio, A.: Dual coding theory and education. Educ. Psychol. Rev. **3**(3), 149–210 (1991)
2. Dannenberg, R.B., Sanchez, M., Joseph, A., Capell, P., Joseph, R., Saul, R.: A computer-based multi-media tutor for beginning piano students. J. New Music Res. **19**(2–3), 155–173 (1990)
3. Dannenberg, R.B., Sanchez, M., Joseph, A., Joseph, R., Saul, R., Capell, P.: Results from the piano tutor project. In: Proceedings of the Fourth Biennial Arts and Technology Symposium, pp. 143–150 (1993)
4. Denis, G., Jouvelot, P.: Building the case for video games in music education. In: Second International Computer Game and Technology Workshop, pp. 156–161 (2004)
5. Denis, G., Jouvelot, P.: Motivation-driven educational game design: applying best practices to music education. In: Proceedings of the 2005 ACM SIGCHI International Conference on Advances in Computer Entertainment Technology, ACE 2005, pp. 462–465. ACM, New York (2005)
6. Donahue, C., Lipton, Z.C., McAuley, J.: Dance dance convolution. In: Precup, D., Teh, Y.W. (eds.) Proceedings of the 34th International Conference on Machine Learning, vol. 70, pp. 1039–1048. PMLR, International Convention Centre, Sydney, 06–11 August 2017
7. Gower, L., McDowall, J.: Interactive music video games and children's musical development. Br. J. Music Educ. **29**(1), 91–105 (2012)
8. Halina, E., Guzdial, M.: TaikoNation: patterning-focused chart generation for rhythm action games. In: The 16th International Conference on the Foundations of Digital Games (FDG), FDG 2021. ACM, New York (2021)
9. Höysniemi, J.: International survey on the dance dance revolution game. Comput. Entertain. **4**(2), 8-es (2006)
10. Inoue, N., et al.: Effect of display location on finger motor skill training with music-based gamification. In: Gao, Q., Zhou, J. (eds.) HCII 2020. LNCS, vol. 12208, pp. 78–90. Springer, Cham (2020). https://doi.org/10.1007/978-3-030-50249-2_6
11. Liang, Y., Li, W., Ikeda, K.: Procedural content generation of rhythm games using deep learning methods. In: ICEC-JCSG (2019)
12. Lin, R.M., Ho, H.C., Chen, K.T.: Bot detection in rhythm games: a physiological approach. In: Proceedings of the 8th International Conference on Advances in Computer Entertainment Technology, pp. 1–8 (2011)
13. Lin, Y.H., Mao, H.F., Lin, K.N., Tang, Y.L., Yang, C.L., Chou, J.J.: Development and evaluation of a computer game combining physical and cognitive activities for the elderly. IEEE Access **8**, 216822–216834 (2020)
14. Lin, Z., Xiao, K., Riedl, M.: GenerationMania: learning to semantically choreograph. In: Proceedings of the Fifteenth AAAI Conference on Artificial Intelligence and Interactive Digital Entertainment, AIIDE 2019. AAAI Press (2019)
15. Maynard, L.M.: The role of repetition in the practice sessions of artist teachers and their students. Bull. Council Res. Music Educ. 61–72 (2006)
16. Nakamura, A., Tabata, S., Ueda, T., Kiyofuji, S., Kuno, Y.: Multimodal presentation method for a dance training system. In: CHI 2005 Extended Abstracts on Human Factors in Computing Systems, CHI EA 2005, pp. 1685–1688. Association for Computing Machinery, New York (2005)
17. Nakamura, T., Nakamura, E., Sagayama, S.: Real-time audio-to-score alignment of music performances containing errors and arbitrary repeats and skips. IEEE/ACM Trans. Audio Speech Lang. Process. **24**(2), 329–339 (2016)

18. Pierce, C., J. Woodward, C., Bartel, A.: Learning management models in serious mobile music games. In: Proceedings of the Australasian Computer Science Week Multiconference, ACSW 2020. ACM, New York (2020)
19. Poon, P.P.L., Rodgers, W.M.: Learning and remembering strategies of novice and advanced jazz dancers for skill level appropriate dance routines. Res. Q. Exerc. Sport **71**(2), 135–144 (2000)
20. Shehan, P.K.: Effects of rote versus note presentations on rhythm learning and retention. J. Res. Music Educ. **35**(2), 117–126 (1987)
21. Smoliar, S.W., Waterworth, J.A., Kellock, P.R.: pianoFORTE: a system for piano education beyond notation literacy. In: Proceedings of the Third ACM International Conference on Multimedia, pp. 457–465 (1995)

User Experience in Games and Gamified Interactions

Conveyance of Narrative Through Digital Game Environments

Michael Brandse[✉]

Digital Hollywood University, Ochanomizu Sola City Academia 3F, 4-6 Kandasurugadai,
Chiyoda-ku, Tokyo 101-0062, Japan
michaelbrandse@dhw.co.jp

Abstract. Generally, when discussion narrative in games, designers and researchers alike tend to refer to more traditional narrative devices. While some attempts have been made to include the game world itself into the narrative as well, research on this front is still relatively lacking. In this research, we focus on how much narrative players can learn from the game world and how this affects their experience with the game. By conducting an experiment where the participants explored a number of game environments and then explained the environments they think they saw, we found a number of elements within game environments that were responsible for conveying narrative and how much narrative these could convey. Additionally, we found that users used narrative to directly inform themselves of game-flow and found that a subset of participants also described the environments using emotive keywords rather than direct descriptions. Finally, we found that participants showed higher immersion rates in narrative environments, leading us to conclude that game environments are not only capable of conveying narrative, but can have a significant impact on user experience and can even influence how a user interacts with the game.

Keywords: Kansei engineering · Storytelling · User experience design · Video game design · Interaction design

1 Introduction

While the concept of narrative may not seem like an important part of interaction design, narrative in games plays an important role in the user experience as it has been used as a reward mechanic to entice players to keep playing the game, even if opinions seem divided on how well narrative and gameplay can mix [1, 2]. Older games, such as Final Fantasy [3] but also newer games such as Horizon Zero Dawn [4] all use narrative as "bait" to drive players forward in the game. In these games, players will explore environments, complete any fixed events and encounters found within the environment and be subsequently rewarded with narrative exposition necessary to understand the game world at large. Narrative can also conveyed through collectibles in games, as can be seen by the audio logs in Bioshock [5] or the books that can be read in Wild

© The Author(s), under exclusive license to Springer Nature Switzerland AG 2022
X. Fang (Ed.): HCII 2022, LNCS 13334, pp. 141–159, 2022.
https://doi.org/10.1007/978-3-031-05637-6_9

Arms 3 [6]. Some game genres even completely revolve around narrative discovery, with for instance visual novels like Stein's Gate [7] and Phoenix Wright: Ace Attorney [8] being very limited in interactivity, instead focusing more on exploring the game's characters and narrative. Finally, in certain game genres, narrative is even used directly for interactive purposes, as can be seen in Mass Effect [31] and Dues Ex: Human Revolutions [32]. In these games, there are instances where the player needs to interact with NPCs and guide conversations to endings that benefit the player. In some instances, guiding conversations will also directly affect the character the player is roleplaying as, such as in the aforementioned Mass Effect. In this game, the player can collect "paragon" and "renegade" points through conversations, the former being associated with being a virtuous character and the latter being associated with a more villainous disposition. The effectiveness of game narrative on user experience can especially be seen in the game Final Fantasy 7 [9], where the hero and his companions spend the game chasing after the antagonist Sephiroth, a villain considered to be one of the more iconic villains in video game narratives [10, 11]. This fame would not have been possible had the game not properly established Sephiroth as the antagonist in its narrative.

Due to this, it's no wonder that when game designers and academics alike discuss narrative in games, they tend to refer to traditional narrative elements or interactive elements that can perform the role of a narrator [1, 12]. However, we argue that narrative in games is not just limited to the more traditional narrative elements, but that game environments can function as carriers for narrative as well. For instance, Doug Church argues that the game story does not necessarily mean "expository prewritten text," but rather that it refers to "any narrative thread, whether design-driven or player-driven, that binds the events together and drives the player forward to the completion of the game." [12, 13]. Additionally, Phil Co [14] mentions the concept of a "level narrative," a narrative that is unique to that particular game environment, further suggesting that game environments can potentially convey narrative. Finally, Salen and Zimmerman [15] defined two components, namely the narrative spaces and narrative descriptor, which defines the world as a narrative component.

1.1   Narrative World Design Model

In prior research [16], we have argued that the game world is able to function as a narrative component and defined a number of narrative elements that were commonly present within game environments (see Fig. 1), building on the aforementioned basic definitions established by Salen and Zimmerman [15].

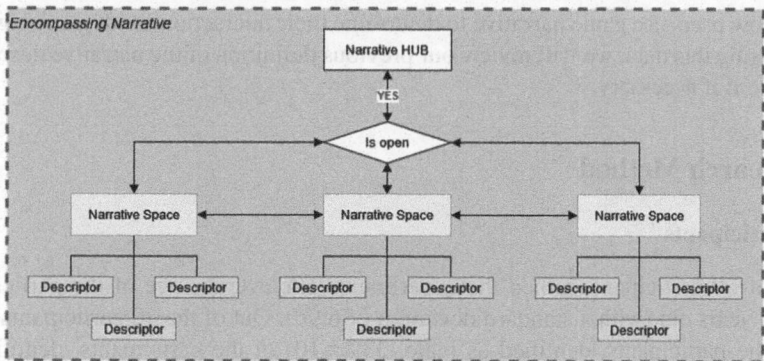

Fig. 1. Narrative world design model.

Within this model, we defined a number of key concepts.

- The encompassing narrative is the collection of all the information required to build all the locales within the game. This information is not necessarily communicated to the player in its entirety.
- Narrative spaces are the containers that hold all the descriptors and can be considered as the game's locales. If the game is open, in the sense that players can return to previously visited environments, one or more narrative spaces may take the role of a HUB, which is a narrative space that can contain other narrative spaces.
- Narrative descriptors are the smallest quantifiable part of the visual design of the game world and communicate their role and the role of the narrative space within which they are contained to the player. On top of this basic descriptor, two additional types of descriptors were created; the functional descriptor and the narrating descriptor. The functional descriptor serves to communicate game-play opportunities to the player and does not necessarily always make sense from a narrative standpoint. An example of this would be a visual target specifically designed to be activated through a player skill, which generally share the same design throughout the entire game, disregarding the environment they are in. The narrating descriptor directly supplies exposition to the player when the player chooses to interact with it.

To validate these findings, we investigated the effects of narrative descriptors on players. While the research showed a positive effect on immersion rates of players the more narrative descriptors were present within the environment, the research was not able to establish to what extent narrative could be conveyed purely through the use of the environment without relying on narrators or narrating descriptors of any kind, nor did it compare differences between environments with a robust narrative design and environments without. Furthermore, we felt that the definition of the basic narrative descriptor in our model was still too broad and would benefit from further investigation. Therefore, in this paper we investigate the ability of the game environment to convey narrative, as well as how users use game narrative to determine their interactions with game environments. Using this data, we will review our previous definition of the narrative descriptor and revise it if necessary.

2 Research Method

2.1 Participants

A total of 30 participants joined the experiment. The average age of the participants was 22.0 years old (with a standard deviation of 6.96). Out of the 30 participants, 63% (19) of the participants identified as male, 33% (10) of the participants identified as female and 3% (1) of the participants identified as non-binary. Game experience was determined by having participants fill in the years they have been playing games as well as the hours per week they play them, focusing primarily on so-called triple A games, games produced and distributed by mid to large sized game publishers. We found that on average, participants either had around 11.3 years of experience playing games or played games for 11.3 h per week. Only 20% of all participants had less years of experience and played games for less hours per week than the average. Most of the participants were Japanese (19) with other participants being primarily from other East Asian countries like Korea or Indonesia (9). 2 participants were of Dutch origin.

2.2 Equipment

Due to the influence of the COVID-19 virus, experiments were conducted both on-site as well as remote. On-site experiments were conducted using a computer with an Intel Core i9–10900 2.81 GHz, with 64.0GB RAM and a NVIDIA Geforce RTX 2080 Super (8192MB GDDR6). The operating system used was Windows 10 Pro. The prototype used for the experiment was developed using Unreal Engine 4.25. For the remote experiments, additional software (TeamViewer and Zoom) were used. TeamViewer was used to have the participant log in to the experiment supervisor's computer to conduct the experiment remotely. Zoom was used for feedback and problem solving for the duration of the experiment.

2.3 Preparations

To simplify the controls of the game as much as possible, a side scrolling game was developed for the experiment. In a side-scrolling game, the camera is fixed to the side of the avatar, limiting movement to either moving left, moving right or jumping. No difficult jumps were required and no other obstacles were introduced in the environments so that we could have the participant focus on the environment in particular. This would guarantee participants without game experience could complete the experiment without issues as well. It also allowed us for control in what the participant could see since players have very little control over the camera in side-scrolling games. For movement, two control sets were made using different keys. This was done for remote experiments using TeamViewer, as TeamViewer did not allow real-time replication of any number or letter key. This meant that for remote sessions we had to use keys that were generally not considered favorable as game input keys.

In addition to movement, we allowed for zooming the camera in and out. Since we couldn't guarantee colors would be the same across all monitors in case of remote experiments, we also added basic input options for altering the brightness of the game.

Game Environment Design

To measure the ability for environments to convey narrative, we developed 6 environments, divided into 2 types; 3 generic and 3 narrative environments. This was done to measure whether game environments with specifically designed narrative elements were able to better convey narrative than areas that had no specifically designed narrative elements. Of each environment 3 versions were made, and in each version we doubled the number of narrative descriptors (see Fig. 2). Generic environments simply resembled the basic narrative space, where the descriptor count just contributed to the basic theme, without adding any additional narrative elements. The narrative environments were designed to have narrative descriptors to convey specific bits of narrative, where increased descriptor count also meant additional unique narrative descriptors (see Table 1).

To speed up the development of the prototype, premade graphic assets were used [17–28].

Table 1. The narrative keywords that each of the environments and their derived sets were designed after. Environment 1 through 3 are generic environments, whereas environment 4 through 6 are narrative environments.

Environment/set	Set A keyword	Set B keyword	Set C keyword
Environment 1	Cave	Cave	Cave
Environment 2	Plain	Plain	Plain
Environment 3	Beach	Beach	Beach
Environment 4	Ghost town	Ghost town	Ghost town
	Northern area	Northern area	Northern area
		Mine	Mine
			Bandit attack
Environment 5	Ship	Ship	Ship
	Captain's cabin	Captain's cabin	Captain's cabin
		Storm	Storm
			Haunted
Environment 6	Cave	Cave	Cave
	Abandoned	Abandoned	Abandoned
		Mine	Mine
			Pirates hideout

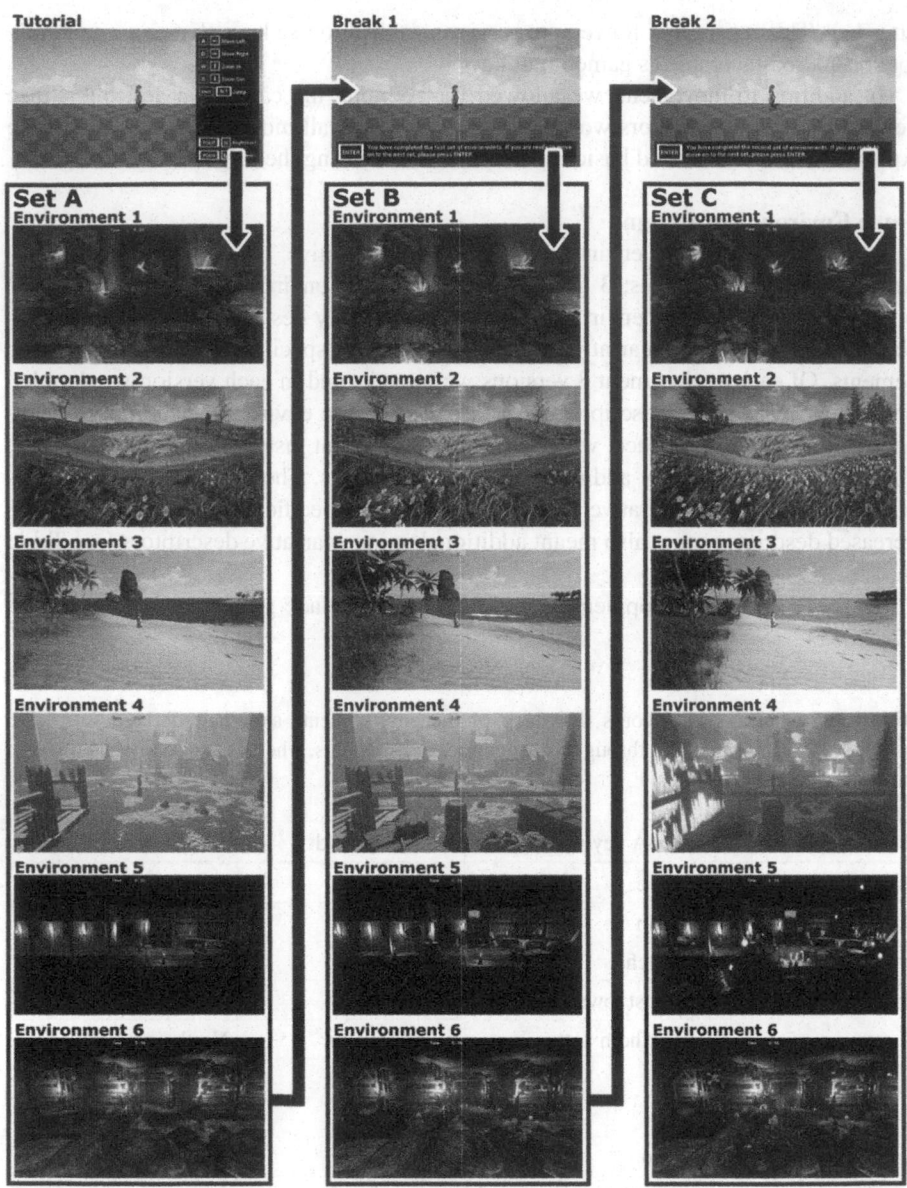

Fig. 2. Experiment flow, including screenshots of the developed environments and their derived sets.

2.4 Data Analysis

After each environment, participants were required to describe the environment they just observed with 3 keywords, as well as a short explanation of why they chose those 3 keywords. Afterwards, to measure their user experience in regards to the environment, we also conducted the game experience questionnaire [29].

The game experience questionnaire (GEQ) is specifically optimized and tested to measure user experience in games from a number of angles depending on the type of module being used and is unique in the sense that it also measures a user's experience with the narrative, making it perfect for this research. We primarily used the in-game and core module, particularly using the sensory and imaginative immersion, flow, negative and positive affect components. The other components, namely competence, tension, as well as challenge dealt with experiences the experimental prototype was not specifically designed for (like the difficulty of the game) and were therefore not relevant for the data analysis.

The social presence module of the GEQ was not used in the experiment, as the game developed for the experiment had no social or on-line elements. The post-game module was not used either, since our experiment was heavily guided in terms of game-flow as well as the time spent within each environment. To determine user experience, the game experience questionnaire uses Likert scale questions, with values ranging from 0.0 to 4.0.

2.5 Protocol Design

Participants were first explained the goal of the experiment, after which they were required to fill out basic data, such as gender. Before starting the experiment, participants could practice the game controls using a tutorial stage, a stage which visual design was purposefully kept simple to prevent any bias in subsequent observations. In the tutorial stage, we also added an interface showing all the possible controls of the game.

Starting the experiment, participants would complete a set of 3 generic and 3 narrative environments of one particular level of density starting at the lowest. For each environment the participant was given 1 min of observation time. The countdown would start on the first movement, to prevent participants from being unable to properly observe the environment due to lag in case of remote experiments. To deal with lag during the observation, a pause option was created to temporarily stop the countdown; this pause option could only be invoked by the experiment supervisor. After 1 min of observation time, participants gave their description of the environment using the 3 keywords and the explanation. After this description, the participants were required to fill out the in-game module of the GEQ. After having completed an entire set of environments, the participants were required to fill out the core module of the GEQ, to give their impression of the set as a whole. Following that, participants would continue with the next set with a higher level of detail density. Between each set there was a break environment, using the same environment as the tutorial environment, but without the interface explaining the possible game controls. A complete visual representation of the experiment flow can be seen in Fig. 2.

To reduce the chance of noise in the data, it was decided that the environment order would not be randomized. We feared that the risk of a participant being exposed to a high detail density environment could have a significant effect on their impressions of subsequent low detail density environments, risking the validity of the data.

3 Results

To determine how much narrative participants could derive from an environment, we looked at the number of words they wrote in their explanation of the environments (see Tables 2 and 3) as well as whether the words participants used in the keywords and the explanation corresponded to the keywords we had set per environment (see Table 1). Since participants were from various countries and not necessarily familiar with the English language, we also had non-English submissions. These submissions were translated into English using DeepL [33] in order to maintain consistency and properly compare the explanation word count to one another.

To see whether participant keywords corresponded to our own, we did two analyses; one comparing each set separately and another one comparing the environment as a whole, ticking off the keyword if it appeared in at least one set (See Figs. 3, 4, 5 and 6). Finally, we compared how the users experienced the worlds, in particular the generic environments compared to the narrative environments, to see whether there was a difference in user experience (See Figs. 10, 11, 12 and 13).

Table 2. Average explanation word count for the generic environments (with standard deviation between parentheses)

Environment	1A	1B	1C	2A	2B	2C	3A	3B	3C
Average	35.6	34.2	35.7	40.7	37.2	30.5	45.2	40.4	33.0
	(18.4)	(18.3)	(20.2)	(18.0)	(16.4)	(14.5)	(21.6)	(24.2)	(16.3)
Set average	35.2 (18.8)			36.1 (16.7)			39.5 (21.3)		
Total average	36.9 (19.1)								

Table 3. Average explanation word count for the narrative environments (with standard deviation between parentheses)

Environment	4A	4B	4C	5A	5B	5C	6A	6B	6C
Average	48.7	46.5	35.4	52.9	45.6	38.3	41.1	43.3	40.1
	(26.2)	(23.3)	(16.2)	(29.4)	(25.4)	(19.0)	(20.7)	(25.3)	(18.0)
Set average	43.5 (22.8)			45.6 (25.4)			41.5 (21.3)		
Total average	43.4 (23.2)								

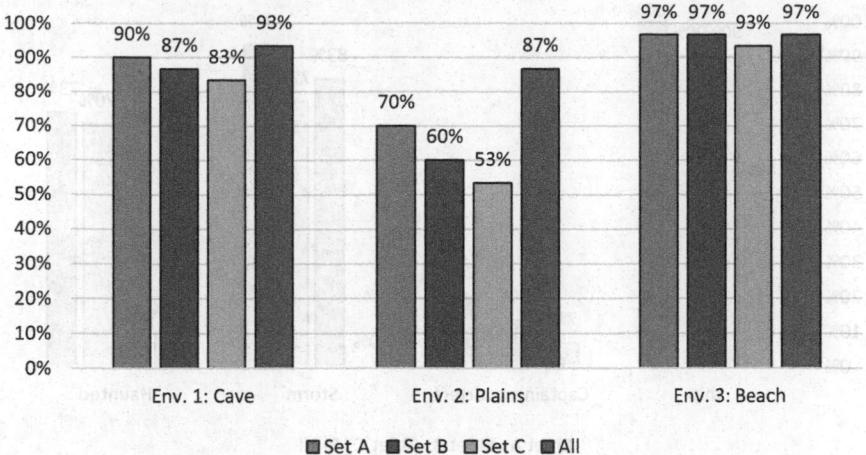

Fig. 3. Narrative comprehension percentages for all generic environments, comparing each set separately and all sets as a whole.

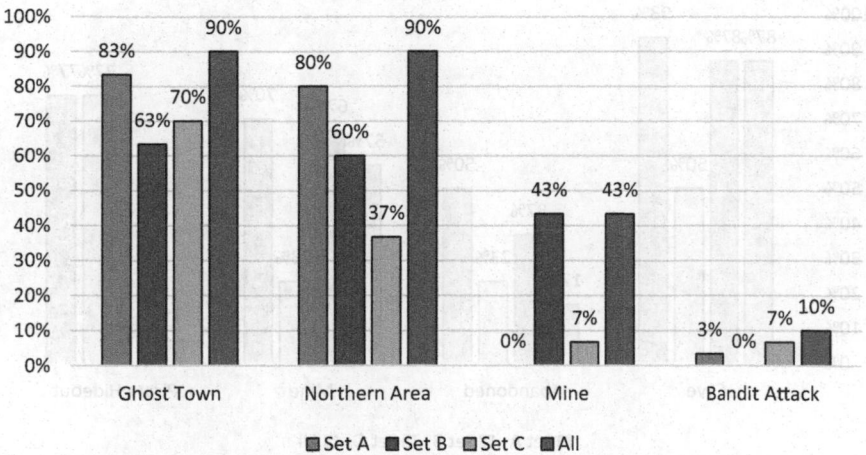

Fig. 4. Narrative comprehension for narrative environment 1 (northern mine village), comparing each set separately and all sets as a whole.

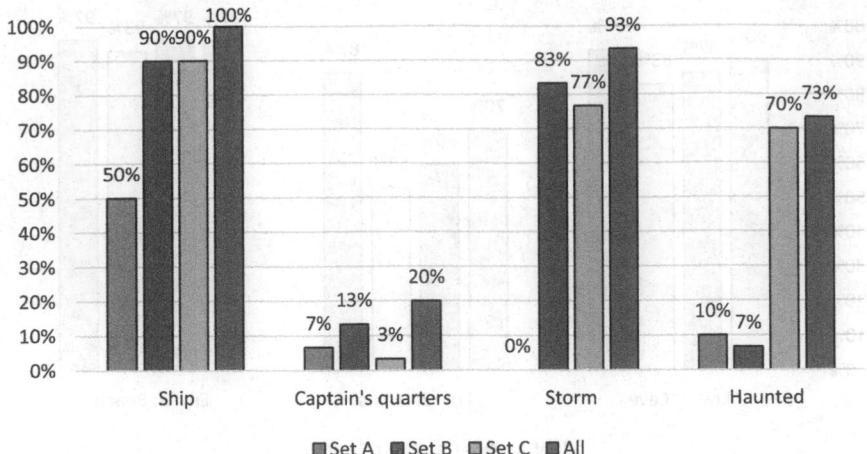

Fig. 5. Narrative comprehension for narrative environment 2 (haunted ship), comparing each set separately and all sets as a whole.

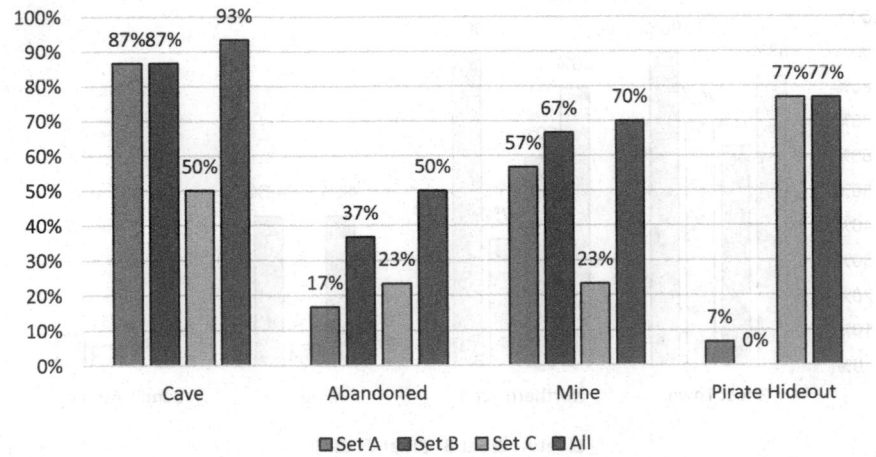

Fig. 6. Narrative comprehension for narrative environment 3 (pirate's hideout), comparing each set separately and all sets as a whole.

3.1 Narrative Comprehension Through the Game World

We identified 3 new descriptors in our research, as well as narrative properties that can be assigned to the descriptors, and updated our previously defined model accordingly (see Fig. 7).

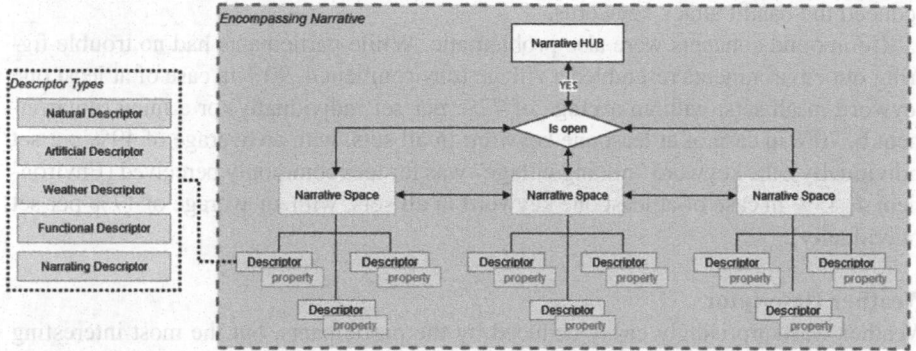

Fig. 7. Modified narrative world design model.

Natural Descriptor

Natural descriptors are descriptors that further establish the basic identity of the narrative space within which they are contained. For instance, if the narrative space is a cave, examples of natural descriptors would be the rocks, stalactites or other objects commonly associated with caves. We found through the keywords that the participants used especially in the generic environments, that these narrative descriptors don't contribute to the perceived narrative of the environment no matter their number. In this sense, they could also be perceived as filler descriptors. It should be noted that a number of participants expressed dislike when natural descriptors were too numerous.

Artificial Descriptor

The most narrative was perceived in environments that had some form of man-made objects, primarily in the narrative environments (see Tables 2 and 3), with participants writing on average 6.6 more words in the narrative environments (43.5 words) compared to the generic natural environments (36.9 words). Participants were also more likely to write bigger explanations for narrative environments, leading to the standard deviation being higher in narrative environments (23.2 versus 19.1). Most of those words were in relation to the man-made structures and objects that were present within those environments, leading us to conclude that the descriptor primarily responsible for indirectly conveying narrative to the player is man-made, or artificial.

However, while these artificial descriptors can convey narrative, their ability to do so is limited. We found that specific concepts, such as a captain's quarters in a ship or a bandit attack on a village, were very hard to convey. In the fifth environment, only 20% of all users deduced the keyword captain's quarters in at least one set (see Fig. 5), a number that dropped to an average of 8% if we compared it per set individually. This is despite the fact that the vast majority of participants figured out that the fifth environment resembled a ship (100% in case of at least one keyword in all sets, with an average of 77% per set individually). In the fourth environment, only 10% of the participants were able to deduce the bandit attack keywords in at least one of the sets, with the average dropping to 3% if we compared it per set individually. Even in set C of environment 4 (see Fig. 4), where the most narrative descriptors were present, only 7% of all participants deduced the bandit attack keywords.

Compound concepts were also problematic. While participants had no trouble figuring out environments resembled a village (environment 4, 90% in case of at least one keyword in all sets, with an average of 72% per set individually) or a mine (environment 6, 70% in case of at least one keyword in all sets, with an average of 49% per set individually), the keyword "mining village" was far less commonly perceived (Environment 4, 43% in case of at least one keyword in all sets, with an average of 17% per set individually).

Weather Descriptor
Weather was surprisingly easily deduced by the participants, but the most interesting thing we found was that this weather was also used to explain how participants saw the environment. In environment 5, in set B and C descriptors were present to visualize a "storm." Not only was this readily perceived by participants, participants also used these storm descriptors to deduce the environment was a ship (leading to a 40% increase in participants deducing the ship keyword, from set A to B). Participants also used the snow in environment 4 to deduce the location of the mining village, with 90% of all participants deducing the location of the village in at least one set. However, it should also be noted that in environment 4, the total number of participants deducing the location of the village per set dropped with each subsequent set, leading us to believe that weather may not be the primary descriptor players use to interpret the narrative in an environment.

Interestingly, while participants used weather descriptors to deduce the narrative in environments, the same cannot be said for descriptors depicting time of day. While there were a few participants that defined the specific time of an environment using the present descriptors, this did not affect their opinion on what the environment represented.

Narrative Descriptor Property
While we did observe that compound keywords were very rarely interpreted correctly by the participants in our findings with the artificial descriptor, we found that participants did often assign an additional property to certain keywords. For instance, while participants were not able to deduce the mining village compound keywords, participants did often describe the environment as abandoned or ruined. In environment 5, participants had no problem deducing the ship was "haunted" (particularly in set C, where we introduced ghost descriptors). These properties were even assigned in the generic environments, with environment 1 often being described as "magical." This leads us to believe that a narrative descriptor property can be assigned to any narrative descriptor, not just the artificial descriptor.

3.2 Narrative to Inform Gameplay

We found that a fair amount of participants relied on past game experiences to help them understand the environment they were in (see Fig. 8), in particular to help them understand the flow of the game. A common thread here was that of "danger." Especially in set C of environment 4 (see Fig. 2) participants would anticipate danger in the form of a "boss," the final monster of a level that is generally more powerful than normal enemies, meant as the final obstacle before the player can clear the level. Environment 6 also gave this impression until the treasure narrative descriptors were introduced, due to the skeletons scattered about. However, danger was not the only thing participants were on the lookout for. Environment 2, the "plains," was often interpreted as the "first level" of the game, the environment a player would start in. In this environment, participants anticipated they would arrive at a village that would form the start of their journey. This kind of starting stage is common in role playing games, especially those of Japanese origin like Dragon Quest XI [30]. While less common, a number of participants also directly referenced past game works as a means to interpret the environment they were in.

This leads us to believe that when designing the narrative of an environment, designers should also take into account similar works, as that may make it easier to establish a narrative within a game environment without directly having to convey this narrative to the player. Furthermore, with participants anticipating game flow, the narrative design of an environment may directly serve to inform the player of certain interactive events, such as monster encounters.

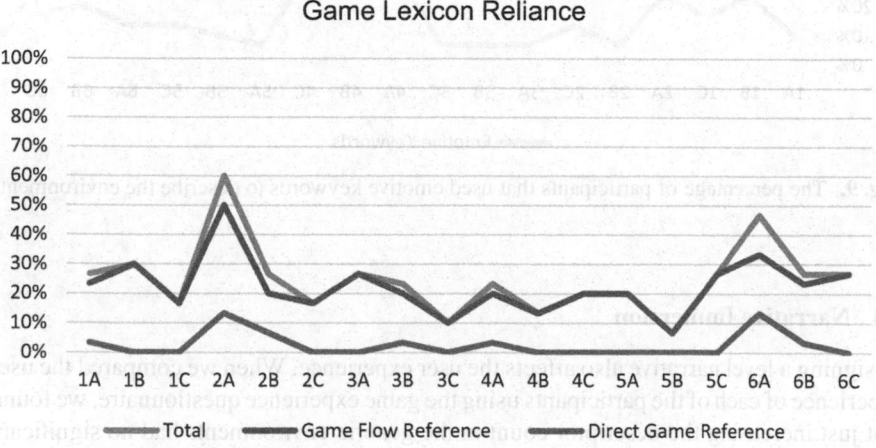

Fig. 8. The percentage of participants that relied on previously established game knowledge to interpret the environment. Total indicates the total number of participants that used at least 1 direct game reference, 1 reference to game flow, or both.

3.3   Emotive Interpretation of Narrative in Game Worlds

Rather than using keywords to directly describe the environment, a number of participants also used emotive keywords to describe it instead, leading us to believe that the atmosphere of an environment is also important. Emotive keywords were also important for anticipating game-flow, with environments where participants expected some kind of monster encounter oftentimes described as eerie, dangerous or something similar. This can be seen in environment 4 (see Fig. 9), an environment resembling a ruined mining village, where a spike in emotive keyword usage can be seen in the entirety of environment 4. When comparing for gender differences, we found that female participants (32%) are more likely to use emotive keywords than their male counterparts (8%), though it should be noted that male participants outnumbered female participants 2 to 1. As such, we feel it is too early to conclude whether gender differences have an impact on the amount of emotive keywords being used.

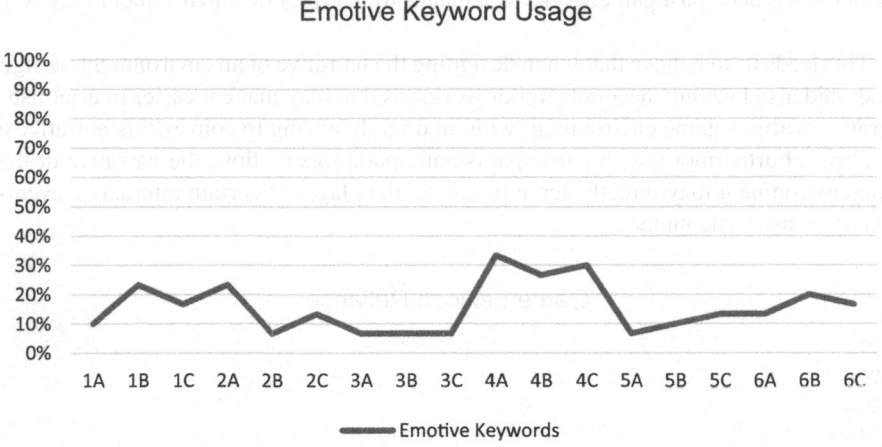

Fig. 9. The percentage of participants that used emotive keywords to describe the environment.

3.4   Narrative Immersion

Designing a level narrative also affects the user experience. When we compared the user experience of each of the participants using the game experience questionnaire, we found that just increasing the descriptor count in the generic environments had no significant impact on the user experience (see Table 4), even when users used their past experience with games to make up their own perceived narratives. However, when we increased the count and simultaneously introduced new narrative information to the environments (in the narrative environments), we found a significant increase in user experience in sensory and imaginative immersion and flow, particularly comparing set B to set C (see Table 5). Furthermore, when comparing the differences in experience between the generic environments and narrative environments, not only did we find that narrative environments scored higher in all sets in at least sensory and imaginative immersion (see Fig. 10), flow (see Fig. 11) and positive affect (see Fig. 13), we also found that the differences in the experience between the generic and narrative environments were significant as well for sensory and imaginative immersion as well as flow (see Table 5). This suggests that even if players cannot identify the narrative of the environment in great detail, the user experience still significantly improves (Fig. 12) (Table 6).

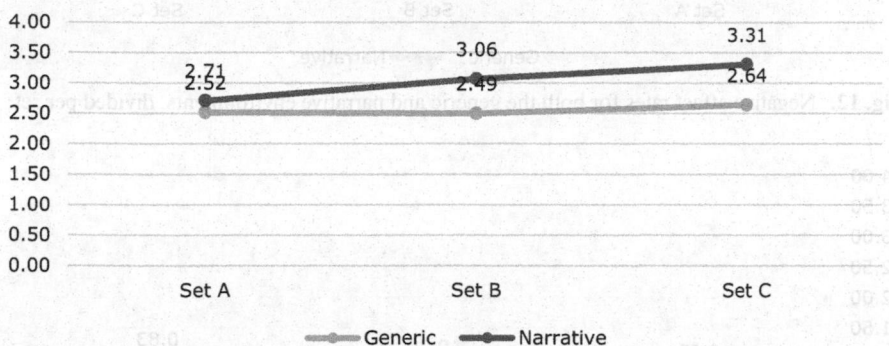

Fig. 10. Sensory and Imaginative Immersion rates for both the generic and narrative environments, divided per set.

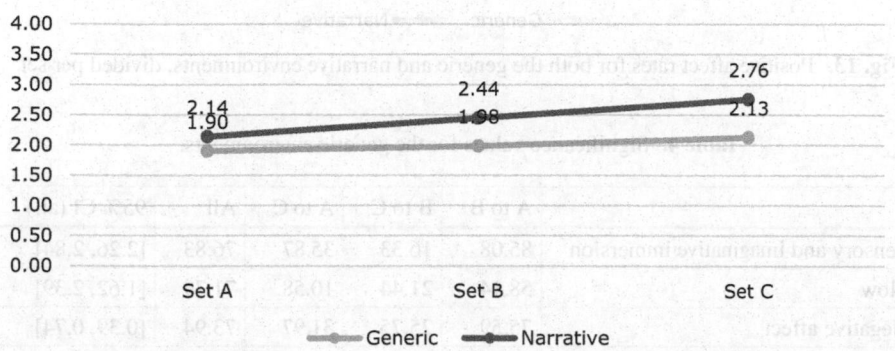

Fig. 11. Flow rates for both the generic and narrative environments, divided per set.

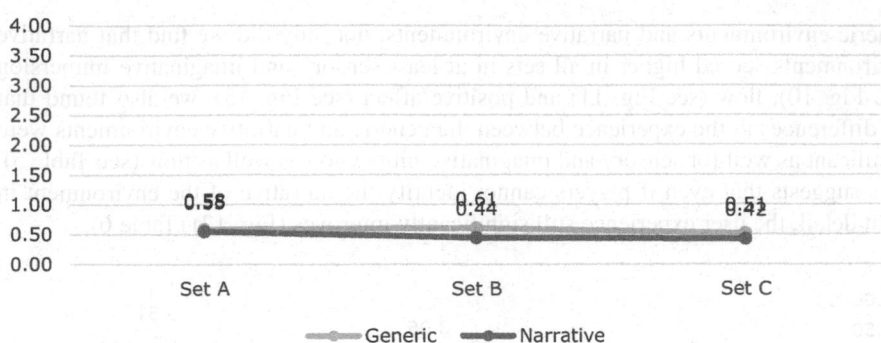

Fig. 12. Negative affect rates for both the generic and narrative environments, divided per set.

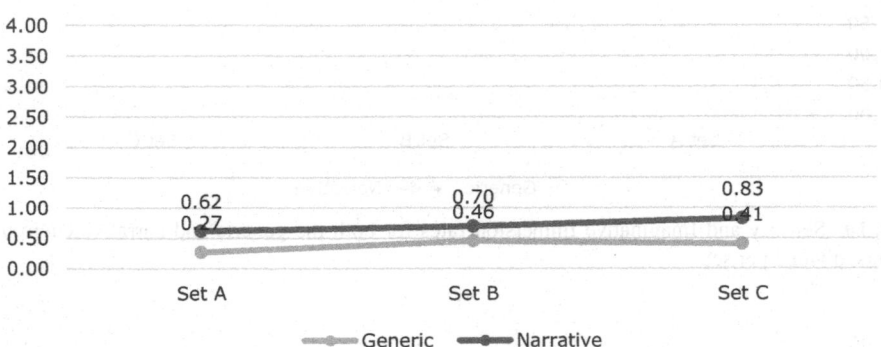

Fig. 13. Positive affect rates for both the generic and narrative environments, divided per set.

Table 4. Significance values for the generic environments.

	A to B	B to C	A to C	All	95% CI (all)
Sensory and imaginative immersion	85.08	16.33	35.87	76.83	[2.26, 2.84]
Flow	58.14	21.44	10.58	71.79	[1.62, 2.39]
Negative affect	75.59	25.75	31.97	73.94	[0.39, 0.74]
Positive affect	78.12	30.94	22.11	76.64	[2.21, 2.81]

Table 5. Significance values for the narrative environments.

	A to B	B to C	A to C	All	95% CI (all)
Sensory and imaginative immersion	0.15	1.63	0.00	0.43	[2.77, 3.28]
Flow	6.20	3.53	0.00	7.87	[2.07, 2.83]
Negative affect	11.34	73.79	15.13	57.02	[0.30, 0.65]
Positive affect	1.44	10.06	0.02	14.14	[2.26, 2.88]

Table 6. Significance values for the differences in user experience between generic and narrative environments.

	Set A difference	Set B difference	Set C difference
Sensory and imaginative immersion	6.49	0.00	0.00
Flow	3.73	0.15	0.00
Negative affect	66.24	4.49	38.31
Positive affect	34.79	32.78	16.37

4 Conclusion

In summary, this paper argued that the game environment itself is a potent device for conveying narrative to the player. While in prior research we defined a basic narrative world design model, this model was lacking as the research by which it was defined never accurately measured how much narrative could be conveyed. This problem was remedied in this paper, and using the findings we were able to improve the narrative world design model by defining 3 new types of narrative descriptors.

The first newly defined descriptor is the natural descriptor, a descriptor that primarily serves as filler for natural environments and are not very capable at expressing narrative (an example would be rocks in a cave or palm trees on a beach). The second defined descriptor is the artificial descriptor, a descriptor that is primarily used to express man-made objects or constructs and are relatively capable at expressing narrative, though there are limitations. Finally, there is the weather descriptor, a descriptor that can serve as a support to the artificial descriptors or can even convey information regarding the placement of the narrative space to the player. We also defined the narrative property, which serves to further describe the narrative descriptor and can be applied to any descriptor (for example, a ship becomes a "haunted" ship).

We also found that narrative in environments can have applications for interaction design as well, as players use the narrative their perceive in an environment to determine game-flow; what environment they can expect next, what dangers they can anticipate and even wether or not they think an environment may contain items or skills necessary for progression. Finally, players do not just perceive concrete narrative, but they may also perceive the feel of the environment as important. This links back to how players anticipate game-flow, as one way of perceiving the feel is to perceive danger.

References

1. Silva, I., Cardoso, P., Oliveira, E.: Narrative and gameplay: the balanced and imbalanced relationship between dramatic tension and gameplay tension. In: Proceedings of the 9th International Conference on Digital and Interactive Arts (ARTECH 2019), Article 30, pp. 1–8. ACM, New York, NY, USA (2019)
2. Hocking, C.: Ludonarrative dissonance in Bioshock: the problem of what the game is about. https://clicknothing.typepad.com/click_nothing/2007/10/ludonarrative-d.html (2007). Accessed 20 Sep 2021

3. Square: Final Fantasy (Software). Square, Japan (1987)
4. Guerilla Games: Horizon Zero Dawn (Software). Sony Interactive Entertainment, Japan (2017)
5. 2K Boston: Bioshock (Software). 2K Games, United States (2007)
6. Media Vision: Wild Arms 3 (Software). Sony Computer Entertainment, Japan (2002)
7. 5pb., Nitroplus: Steins; Gate (Software). 5pb, Japan (2009)
8. Capcom Production Studio 4: Phoenix Wright: Ace Attorney (Software). Capcom, Japan (2005)
9. Square: Final Fantasy VII (Software). Square, Japan (1997)
10. Nonato Braid, N.: Final Fantasy 7: 10 reasons why Sephiroth is scarier in the original game than the remake. https://www.thegamer.com/final-fantasy-7-sephiroth-original-remake/ (2021). Accessed 20 Sep 2021
11. Sterling, J.: The rise and fall of Sephiroth. https://www.destructoid.com/the-rise-and-fall-of-sephiroth/ (2007) . Accessed 20 Sep 2021
12. Huaxin, W.: Embedded narrative in game design. In: Proceedings of the International Academic Conference on the Future of Game Design and Technology (Futureplay '10), pp. 247–250. ACM, New York, NY, USA (2010)
13. Church, D.: Formal abstract design tools. In: Salen, K., Zimmerman, E. (eds.) The Game Design Reader: A Rules of Play Anthology. MIT press, Cambridge (2006)
14. Phil, C.: Level Design for Games: Creating Compelling Game Experiences. New Riders Games, USA (2006)
15. Salén, K., Zimmerman, E.: Rules of Play. MIT press, Cambridge (2004)
16. Brandse, M., Tomimatsu, K.: Immersion levels in digital interactive environments. In: Proceedings of the 5th Kansei Engineering and Emotion Research (Linkoping Electronic Conference Proceedings), pp. 897–905. Linkoping University Electronic Press, Linkoping, Sweden (2014)
17. JoeGarth: Brushify - tropical pack (Software). https://www.unrealengine.com/marketplace/en-US/product/brushify-tropical-pack (2019). Accessed 30 July 2021
18. JoeGarth: Brushify - arctic pack (Software). https://www.unrealengine.com/marketplace/en-US/product/brushify-arctic-pack (2019). Accessed 30 July 2021
19. Kligan: Crystal mines - scene and assets (Software). https://www.unrealengine.com/marketplace/en-US/product/crystal-mines-scene-and-assets (2019). Accessed 30 July 2021
20. NatureManufacture: Environment set (Software). https://www.unrealengine.com/marketplace/en-US/product/environment-set (2017). Accessed 30 July 2021
21. Dragon Motion: Flowers and plants nature pack (Software). https://www.unrealengine.com/marketplace/en-US/product/flowers-and-plants-nature-pack (2018). Accessed 30 July 2021
22. Epic Games: Infinity blade: grass lands (Software). https://www.unrealengine.com/marketplace/en-US/product/infinity-blade-plain-lands (2015). Accessed 30 July 2021
23. Dokyo: Low poly snow forest (Software). https://www.unrealengine.com/marketplace/en-US/product/low-poly-snow-forest (2016). Accessed 30 July 2021
24. NatureManufacture: Meadow - environment set (Software). https://www.unrealengine.com/marketplace/en-US/product/meadow-environment-set (2019). Accessed 30 July 2021
25. KK Design: Old mine tunnel & caves (Software). https://www.unrealengine.com/marketplace/en-US/product/old-mine-tunnel-caves (2020). Accessed 30 July 2021
26. Vertex Interactive: Spring landscape (Software). https://www.unrealengine.com/marketplace/en-US/product/spring-landscape (2016). Accessed 30 July 2021
27. Dzen Games: Stone boulders (Software). https://www.unrealengine.com/marketplace/en-US/product/stone-boulders (2018). Accessed 30 July 2021
28. James Stone: SHADERSOURCE - tropical ocean tool (Software). https://www.unrealengine.com/marketplace/en-US/product/beach-wave-water (2017). Accessed 30 July 2021

29. IJsselsteijn, W.A., de Kort, Y.A.W., Poels, K.: The Game Experience Questionnaire. Technische Universiteit Eindhoven (2013)
30. Square Enix: Dragon quest XI: echoes of an elusive age (Software). Square Enix, Japan (2017)
31. Bioware: Mass effect (Software). Microsoft Game Studios, USA (2007)
32. Eidos Montreal: Deus Ex: human revolution (Software). Square Enix, Japan (2011)
33. DeepL, S.E.: DeepL Translate: the world's most accurate translator (2017). https://www.deepl.com/translator. Accessed 30 July 2021

Design of Emotion-Driven Game Interaction Using Biosignals

Yann Frachi[✉], Takuya Takahashi, Feiqi Wang, and Mathieu Barthet

Queen Mary University of London, London, UK
{y.n.frachi,t.takahashi,f.wang,m.barthet}@qmul.ac.uk

Abstract. Video games can evoke a wide range of emotions in players through multiple modalities. However, on a broader scale, human emotions are probably an important missing part of the current generation of Human Computer Interaction (HCI). The main goal of this project is to start investigating how to design video games where the game mechanics and interactions are based on the player's emotions. We designed a two-dimensional (2D) storytelling game prototype with Unity. Game designers and creators manage the user's experience and emotions along the play through visual effects, sound effects, controls and narration. In particular for this project, we have chosen to create emotionally-driven interactions for two specific aspects: sound (audio effects, music), and narration (storytelling). Our prototype makes use of the Ovomind smart band and biosignals analysis technology developed by the first author. By wearing the smart band, human body physiological information are extracted and classified using signal processing method into groups of emotions mapped to the arousal & valence (AV) plane. The 2D AV emotion representation is directly used as an interactive input into the game interaction system. Regarding music, we propose a system that automatically arranges background music by inputting emotions analysed by the smart band into an AI model. We evaluated the results using video recordings of the experience and collected feedback from a total of 30 participants. The results show that participants are favorable to narrative and music game adaptations based on real-time player emotion analysis. Some issues were also highlighted e.g. around the coherence of game progression. Participants also felt that the background music arrangements matched the player's emotions well. Further experiments are required and planned to assess whether the prospects expressed by participants match their personal experience when playing the emotion-driven game.

Keywords: UX · Biosignals · Emotions · HMI · HCI · Affective computing · User research · Video games · Automatic music arrangement

1 Problem

Emotions contribute to what defines us, the way we emotionally react to events form part of who we are. In current gaming experience the only way to express our individuality and interact with the game is to use a keyboard with a mouse or game controllers. This study addresses the potential limitation in interactivity with classic game controllers. Since their creation and democratisation the number of ways to interact has increased from one button in the 70s to a full keyboard or more than 15 buttons with analog sticks nowadays. We suggest that the more a player can input her/his intentions and feelings into a game, the richer and more personalised the experience would be. The underlying question is how much of our self get transmitted to the game and is it beneficial?

As Frome [11] mentioned, game creators have the intent to generate a specific range of emotions at specific moments during the experience. Callele et al. [5] specified two parts for the emotional requirements in video games: the game designer's selected group of emotions and the chosen means to induce the target emotional state using audiovisual modalities. One important aspect regarding emotions is the impact of the story events and particularly the relationship between causes and consequences on the emotional engagement: the narration. We designed a video game prototype based on real-time (RT) analysis of a player's emotions and where emotional features influence gameplay. Regarding the RT emotional classification from biosignals in video games, a similar work was achieved by Granato et al. [13], however the authors focus on emotion recognition rather than using emotional features as inputs into the game.

"The will to overcome an emotion, is ultimately only the will of another, or of several other, emotions."—Friedrich Nietzsche.

2   Related Work

Regarding storytelling and game design, Widen, Pochedly and Russell [36] explored the development of emotions in children and adolescents. Contrary to traditional assumptions, children better interpret/label someone's emotion from a story than from the person's facial expression. The assumption was that there is a *story superiority effect* compare to face expressions for children and adolescents (N= 90, 8–20 years) for the following emotions: fear, disgust, shame, embarrassment, and pride. The experimental protocol was to freely label the emotion the participant inferred from the description of a cause and consequence and separately from the corresponding facial expression. The article's conclusion is that story is a better cue to emotion than facial expression on all age group(except for pride): *"The story superiority effect is strong from childhood to early adulthood and opens the door to new accounts of how emotion concepts develop."*(Widen, Pochedly and Russell, 2015). Wellman et al. [35] proposed the hypothesis that children organize emotion concepts around their perception of the other's beliefs and desires. Also for children, the understanding of a situation happening in mind versus that happening in real world occurs around the age of 4. Video games put the player as the main actor of the action and narration. A very particular link is created between the player and her avatar [31]. The experiment in [6] involved 306 participants, who completed a series of self-report questionnaires online. The results showed that if the avatar has player's similarities, there is a stronger feeling of identification. This identification concept was studied by Klimmt, Hefner and Vorderer [6] and it is based on socio-psychological models of self-perception. Video game experiences bring an alteration of the player's self-perception. The gaming experience can be described with two distinct phases: when the player is aware of her shift of self-perception and when the player doesn't even realise that she is playing (automatic cognition). Thus, evidence shows that storytelling (narrative) and emotions are deeply connected. We suggest that emotional interaction of the player into the narrative part could further improve the affinity between avatar and player.

Koelsch [16] stated that music is an universal feature of human societies and in all cultures. Music has the power to evoke strong emotions and has a direct impact on people's moods. Thanks to recent neuroimaging techniques, we now know that music activates the brain's part involved in the emotion's generation [27] such amygdala, nucleus accumbens, hypothalamus, hippocampus, insula, cingulate cortex and orbitofrontal cortex. Koelsch [16] concludes that music can provoke changes in activity in the core structures underlying emotion *"music can trigger changes in the major reaction components of emotion, indicating that music can evoke real emotions"*. Also autonomic and endocrine responses as well as facial expression can be provoked by music.

Emotions have been shown to be closely linked to music (Barthet et al. [2]), for example, Makris et al. [19] proposed a method for automatically generating music based on emotions. They firstly proposed a method that associate emotional qualities to chord qualities. Then, using a sequence-to-sequence model, they attempted to learn the relationship between musical emotions (A/V score) and symbolic music, and to generate lead sheet data (melodies and chords) based on emotions. The results of subjective evaluation with 42 participants proved that the system is able to generate music that can convey the specified emotions. However, their method cannot automatically produce music in RT.

The most utilised and adopted technologies for affective computing are computer vision (CV) for face geometry tracking and electroencephalogram (EEG) which tracks brain waves [14]. In a casual gaming situation at home, with potentially low light levels and tricky camera angles requirements, facial coding cannot be effectively used and camera have a strong intrusive aspect: a constant use of a video camera to track a player's facial expressions during gameplay may raise concerns regarding privacy and security in networked environments, self-awareness disrupting immersion in the game, etc. EEG systems require the player to wear a headband and signals are noisy [15]. For our research instead of facial coding, we have chosen a technology which is already used on a daily basis by a wide range of people, wearable sensors which measure physiological activity and from which emotion classification can be conducted using biosignal computing.

3   Emotions and Biosignals

The principle used for emotional analysis in our study is to estimate arousal and valence scores yielding a 2D representation of emotions as proposed by Scherer and Klaus [29]. Prior to this research, the first author developed a technology (Ovomind[1]) enabling signal processing and feature estimation for emotional classification using a smart band based on Shu et al. [30]. For the setup using electrocardiogram (ECG), electromyography (EMG), respiration (RSP) and galvanic skin response (GSR), Shu et al. [30] obtained a 92% of recognition rate of joy, anger, sadness and pleasure (music stimulation). The following part describes each sensor and the linked emotional features. These sensors are available on the Ovomind smart wristband but also on other similar research wristbands developed for affective computing and biosignals such as Empatica's E4. McCarthy et al. [20] studied and compared E4 smart band with clinical devices showing positive results for the smart band.

- GSR which falls under the umbrella term of electrodermal activity or EDA) refers to changes in sweat gland activity that are reflective of the intensity of our emotional state [26]. Posada-Quintero et al. [26], state that indicators of autonomic nervous system (ANS) reactions can be used as reliable stress indicators and found out that GSR can be considered as a promising alternative for the non-invasive assessment of sympathetic control of the ANS. Using time frequency domain and power spectral analysis, GSR or EDA can potentially be used to detect cognitive stresses.

  The GSR can yield the following emotional features:
  1. GSR Phasic and Tonic representing the conductance moving baseline [4, 10]
  2. GSR Peaks representing the detection of rapid variation of the conductance baseline value [8,10].
- Body Temperature and Skin temperature features: the system uses slope temperature monitoring. Nummenmaa et al. [24] states in his article that emotions trigger topographic human-body temperature modifications. Over 701 participants participated and confirmed an independence of topographies across emotions. The smart band device that we will use, has an accurate body-temperature sensor.
- PPG or Heart rate features: a photoplethysmogram (PPG) is an optically obtained plethysmogram that can be used to detect blood volume changes in the microvascular bed of tissue [12]. Gil et al. [12] analysed Heart Rate Variability(HRV) using PPG and Pulse Rate Variability (PRV) this sensor is often available on smart bands or smartwatches devices. They used time frequency (TF) analysis and extracted HRV from PRV and obtained a 99% correlation % [28]. Some interesting results were found in the PPG signal frequency analysis on Low frequencies (LF), High frequencies (HF) and the ratio LF/HF.

  Bolanos et al. [3] compared the estimation of HRV from PPG and electrocardiography (ECG) also known as the gold standard for HRV analysis especially for R-R intervals (accurate time between two heart beats) estimation. Schäfer

---

[1] www.ovomind.com.

and Vagedes [28] concluded that PRV can be used for HRV estimation in low-noise (rest position) situations. Video game activity where the player position remains in a fairly static position with little arm movement should be a suitable context for such HRV analysis.

As McCraty and Zayas [21] stated there exists interactions among physiological, cognitive and emotional systems. The authors measured how much each organ is involved in the emotional function and the self-regulatory ability. They concluded that cardiac coherence which is a particular pattern of the heart rate signal, is strongly linked with positive emotions.

The heart rate in that case adopts very specific waveforms for coherent (Appreciation or positive valence) and incoherent (Anger or negative valence) [9] behavior. De Jonckheere et al. [9] led a similar study around breathing exercises and using a smartphone PPG sensor and had close results. Another important element to focus on to be able to characterise a player's emotions is the respiration and breathing patterns.

The method to estimate the arousal score presented in this research is based on a rolling time calculation window of 15 to 25 s from the power spectral density (PSD) and an EMD (Empirical Modal Decomposition) of the GSR signal similarly proposed by Posada-Quinter et al. [25].

Regarding valence the system calculates the R-R interval by applying a bandwidth filtering on frequencies (0.04 to 0.26 Hz) on the PPG signal to calculate the Heart Rate Variability (HRV). When a person is under stress or experiencing negative emotions, the heart rate variability tend to be lower due to the endocrine system [17]. On the other hand when the person is relaxed the heart rate starts to trace a sinusoidal shape (cardiac coherence). By estimating the coherence level of the heartbeat from the PPG signal, it becomes possible to obtain a robust indicator of the level of emotional valence and calculate dynamic thresholds beyond which this valence level changes significantly. HRV is an important piece of information for cognitive RT analysis like was studied by Shang and Wang [33]. Once the valence level has been estimated, it is then possible to check the arousal level by controlling the spectral range of the level of physiological activation from the GSR signal. This is used to deduce in RT the emotional state of the individual and communicate it to the multimedia system. The emotion can be classified with a single unit timestamped array of data in the 2D emotion space like presented in this particular subject [38].

During stress, the sympathetic nervous system predominates and leads to increased level of physiological arousal. Increased heart rate or an acceleration of the inter-beat interval (IBI) is characteristic of this state. At rest, on the contrary, the parasympathetic nervous system is activated, reflecting a decrease in physiological wakefulness and cardiac frequency. In addition, the alternation of accelerations and deceleration of the heart rate becomes regular and consistent (state of cardiac coherence) in states of well-being, calm, control (positive valence) while in states of stress, anxiety, anger (negative valence), the tachograph corresponding to the couple arousal and valence becomes irregular, its layout chaotic and its magnitude will decrease. By estimating the coherence level of the heartbeat from the PPG signal, it becomes possible to obtain a robust indicator of the level of valence.

4 Emotion-Driven Game Design

The main goal of this study was to create a realistic prototype of a video game experience reacting with the player's emotions. The player should become aware of the direct impact of her emotion, on the story, music and overall progression.

4.1 Story

To create an engaging story, we designed a script using the Hero's journey[2] proposed in 2007 by Christopher Vogler, a famous screenwriter. This mythology can be use for any purpose from a simple presentation to a real hollywood movie script. There are several structures possible for the Hero's Journey, we selected the most recent version including 12 steps and we designed and developed a prototype featuring 6 out of the 12 (half of the experience).

The story in our prototypical game is about a caveman scavenging a cave who meets a magical orb of energy representing his inner soul and emotions. The cave is a reference to the subconscious mind, the player will explore his/her personal emotional potential through the experience, a direct reference to the *"Allegory Of The Cave"* from Plato.

"Let me show in a figure how far our nature is enlightened or unenlightened"—Plato.

4.2 What Kind of Video Game Experience?

Our most important inspiration was a game named LIMBO with simple graphic black and white style but really immersive story.[3] JOURNEY also inspired us for its aesthetically impressive design and remarkable soundscape.[4] The game experience we have developed is a 2D game, where the player controls an avatar and goes to a destination. Along the way, events occur based on a number of emotional interactions.

We developed all the game interactions (from control to animations) using the development software Unity[5]. We created the aesthetic assets and designed 3 main levels for the progression. The levels have progressive darker tones illustrating the fact that the character is going deeper into the cave. We also implemented the sound design for basic controls (jumping, steps, orb etc.) using Creative Commons audio from the Freesound platform[6].

---

[2] https://www.youtube.com/watch?v=V4iARp0OZIo.
[3] https://playdead.com/games/limbo/.
[4] https://www.youtube.com/watch?v=61DZC-60x20.
[5] https://unity.com/.
[6] https://www.freesound.org/.

The initial work was to set-up the camera properties and its behavior. 2D games have the advantage to propose a linear progression regarding the narratives for example like LIMBO. We follow the same scheme for our prototype with a right to left progression. In general the 2D games have a left to right progression (e.g. Super Mario bros games). The fact to propose the player to go in opposite way is a choice to help to illustrate the introspective process. However, we chose to have a 3D game in 2D camera configuration because the design of animations and interactions could be implemented in a simple way.

We used the helpful resources and user-friendly animation engine for humanoid characters called Mixamo[7] including an auto rigging system for humanoid character. We have uploaded the 3D asset characters and downloaded from the website all the animations (in total 9) and a new version of the 3D asset main character in T-pose shape.

To get the A/V scores estimated from the band's biosignals available on the Unity console and allowing game interactions, we used a Microsoft Windows library developed by Ovomind. The A/V scores are available in RT as well as heart rate available in the game User Interface (UI) on the top left of the screen as shown in Fig. 2. For the demonstration used in the user evaluation, we are using only the A/V scores and beats per minute (BPM) information.

4.3   Emotional Interactions

In this section, we are presenting the emotional interactions we designed around A/V scores. We decided to implement the three main emotional interactions.

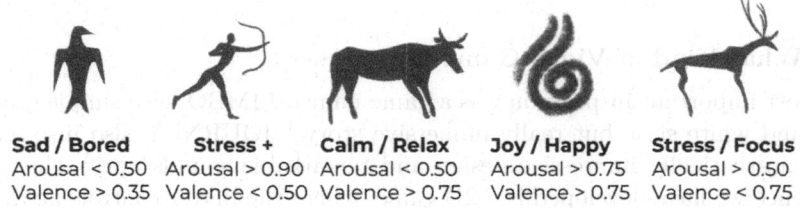

Sad / Bored	Stress +	Calm / Relax	Joy / Happy	Stress / Focus
Arousal < 0.50	Arousal > 0.90	Arousal < 0.50	Arousal > 0.75	Arousal > 0.50
Valence > 0.35	Valence < 0.50	Valence > 0.75	Valence > 0.75	Valence < 0.75

Fig. 1. Primitive drawings images.

The Primitive Drawings. Depending on the combination of A/V scores we varied the nature of drawings made by the game character in the cave (see Fig. 1). Each drawing represents one emotion. Sad/Bored is represented by birds in the sky that the caveman looks up to when he is bored. Stress is represented by the hunter (the caveman himself when he is hunting), alluding to the tension of hunting. Cattle are depicted when the caveman is Calm/Relax, in allusion to the

---

[7] https://www.mixamo.com/.

stability of pastoralism and the gentle nature of the cattle being kept. Furthermore, we have used a campfire symbol as Joy/Happy, as it is used for cooking and keeping warm. Finally, the deer represents the tension and concentration of the hunters (Stress/Focus). In this way, each primitive drawing is linked to the caveman's emotions (i.e. the player's emotions) based on the game narrative. During gameplay, the caveman draws the drawing based on based on the player's emotions as estimated by the smart band. Therefore, the linking between avatar and player emotions is one of the characteristic emotional interactions that aims to improve the affinity between avatar and player.

Avatar Behaviour. In the game narrative, the main character is able to meet the an energy orb (Symbol of the inner soul) flying in the cave. This orb is connected to the player's emotional states and it represents the state of the power of the avatar. All of these powers will be used for the player progression in the story. For example, when the player is relaxed, the orb can heal the character (see Fig. 2). The player's avatar powers (orb colours) are linked with the A/V scores as follows:

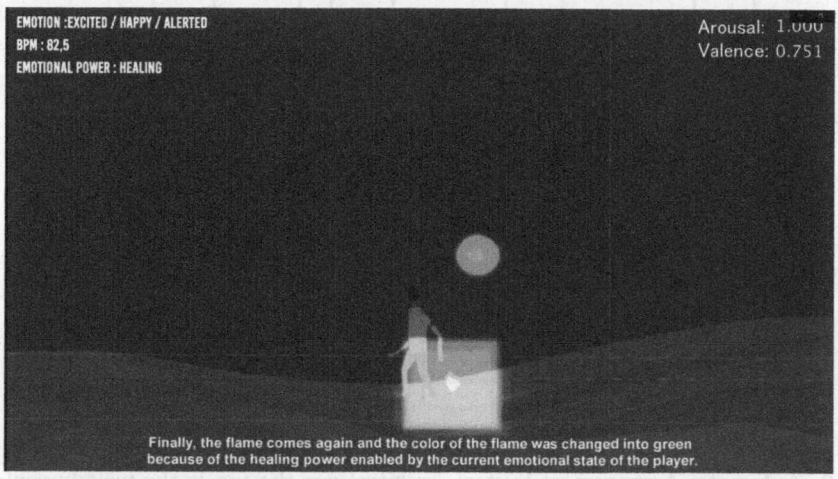

Finally, the flame comes again and the color of the flame was changed into green because of the healing power enabled by the current emotional state of the player.

Fig. 2. Healing power: *main color is green* (Color figure online)

- Joy/relax or High arousal (>0.75) and positive valence (>0.75) Flame/Magic orb color: Green, new power = Healing. (See Fig. 2)
- Fear/stress or High arousal(>0.50) and negative valence (<0.75) Flame/-Magic orb color: Red, new power = Burning.

Music Arrangements. We developed a specific interactive audio system to produce adaptive music following the A/V scores. The goal of this system is to automatically arrange a loop melody to express emotions felt by the player. The outputs were chord progression and tempo, which have been shown to relate to music emotions [7,18].

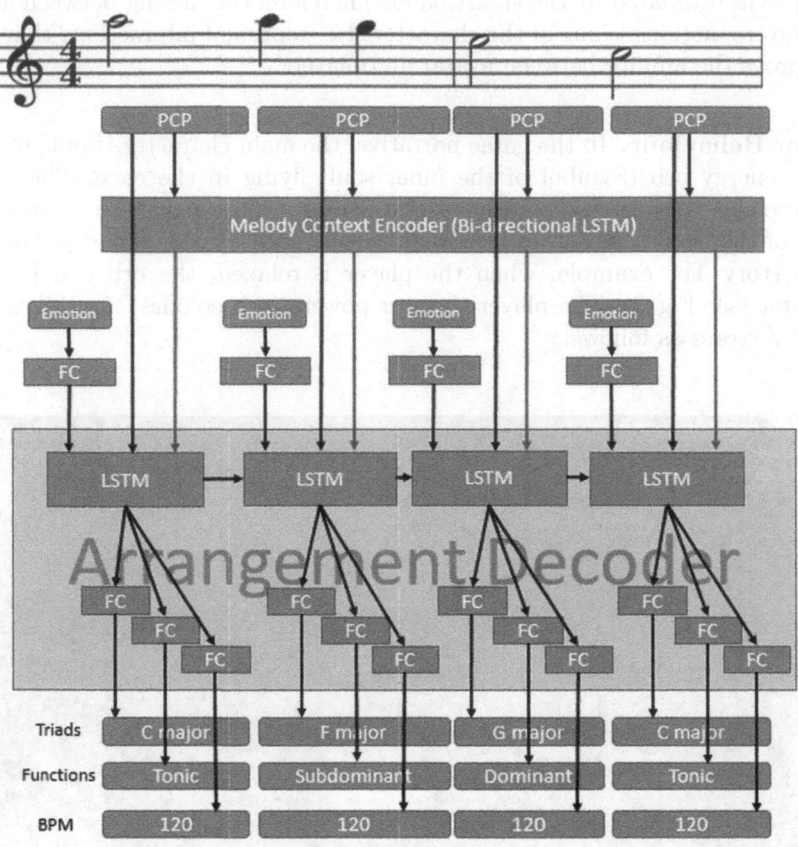

Fig. 3. Automatic Arrangement System Architecture: the top is the melody context encoder and the bottom is the arrangement decoder. The green LSTM block represents the standard long short-term memory network, and FC represents the fully connected layer. Eventually, chords, chord functions and tempo are output. (Color figure online)

Deep learning was used to learn the relationship between emotions and symbolic music. Figure 3 shows the network architecture used for learning and inference. The melodies were encoded by a Bi-directional Long short-term memory (LSTM) [37], which can take into account time series information. An arrangement decoder was also designed to decode the arrangement information (chords, harmony functions and tempo) based on the encoded melodic context and emotions. For this arrangement decoder, we used a forward-only LSTM so that it can be processed in RT during inference. However, it is assumed that the melody context has been calculated in advance at the time of inference for real-time applications.

To train the networks, the HTPD3 [37] symbolic music dataset was used. However, since emotion labels are not provided in that dataset, we obtained mood labels for each song from last.fm[8] and allmusic.com[9] based on the song title and artist name, and quantified the labels based on the experimental results of Warriner et al. [34]. If a song had more than one label, we converted those labels into emotional values and then averaged them. This is because the output of the Ovomind smart band is an A/V score. Ultimately, the resulting dataset contained about 4000 songs. This model was trained by a transfer learning strategy that pre-trains a melody context encoder for about 7000 songs in HTPD3 that could not be assigned an emotional value. The performance of the proposed model in reflecting emotions to arranged music has been evaluated in Takahashi et al. [32].

We integrated this system so that it could generate music for each game scene time unit, as shown in Fig. 4. By measuring the player's emotional state during the gameplay with the Ovomind smart band and inputting the measured values A/V scores to the proposed system, we realized an interaction system that changes the arrangement of the background music in RT. However, each decoder receives the A/V scores every two beats and arranges the background music, so there is a delay of two beats (e.g. 1 s duration at 120 BPM).

5 Evaluation

5.1 Stimuli and Procedure

Given the pandemic context, the user evaluation was based on a demonstration video showcasing the emotional interactive system.[10] The video recording shows a gameplay session of the first author wearing the Ovomind smart band for RT A/V estimation. The video lasts around 5 min and features the three main levels including emotion-driven events and music.

Participants had to first watch the video and then answer a questionnaire. The study took approximately 15 min to complete. The study received ethics approval from our institution (ref: QMERC20.455).

---

[8] https://www.last.fm/.
[9] https://www.allmusic.com/.
[10] https://bit.ly/3sziY41.

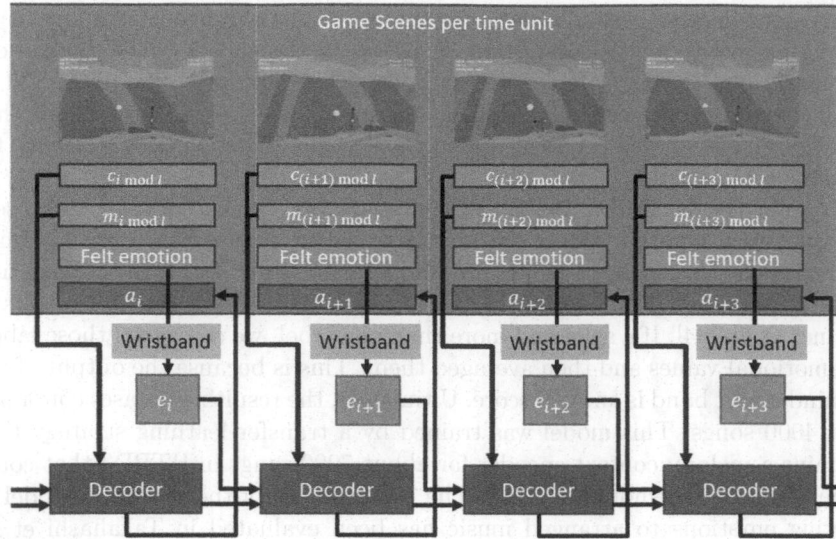

Fig. 4. An architecture for RT arrangement with games. For each unit of time, the system takes the felt emotions by the player in the previous unit of time as input. c represents the context embedding of the melody, m represents the PCPs of the melody, e represents the emotional value and a represents the generated arrangement. Decoder represents the arrangement decoder at the bottom of this appendix.

The questionnaire included 31 Likert items to be rated on a 7-point scale, with a single choice possible from "completely disagree" to "completely agree" including a neutral point which provides a reference and more granularity along the scale.

We aimed to assess the relevance of emotion-driven narrative and background music, and general interests in affective gaming. The questionnaire is organised into five categories: UI, emotion prediction, visual effect and narrative, music, affective gaming interest and prospect, and participants' experiences. The question numbers indicates the actual order in which they were presented to the participants.

UI

- Q1: Information about the player's emotions and physiological response could be clearly seen in the game interface.
- Q9: The player's emotional response was well integrated into the game design.

Emotion Prediction

- Q10: The emotions predicted with the wristband seem to follow well the player's emotional response.

Visual Effect and Narrative

- Q2: The player's emotional response influenced the narrative of the game.
- Q6: The player's emotional response influenced the visual components of the game.

Music

- Q3: The player's emotional response influenced the background music over time.
- Q4: The musical accompaniment matched the melody.
- Q5: The background music matched the atmosphere of the game scene.

Affective Gaming Interest and Prospect

- Q7: I would be keen to play such a game.
- Q8: I am interested in playing video games that adapt to my emotions.

Participants' Experience. We also used parts of the Goldsmiths Musical Sophistication Index (Gold-MSI) questionnaire [23] to assess the musical experience of participants:

- Q20: I spend a lot of my free time doing music-related activities.
- Q21: I don't spend much of my disposable income on music.
- Q22: Pieces of music rarely evoke emotions for me.
- Q23: I often pick certain music to motivate or excite me.
- Q24: I am able to identify what is special about a given musical piece.
- Q25: I am able to talk about the emotions that a piece of music evokes for me.
- Q26: I listen attentively to music for x per day.
- Q27: I engaged in regular, daily practice of a musical instrument (including voice) for x years.
- Q28: At the peak of my interest, I practised my primary instrument for x hours per day.
- Q29: I have had formal training in music theory for x years.
- Q30: I have had x years of formal training on a musical instrument (including voice) during my lifetime.
- Q31: Do you have absolute pitch? Absolute or perfect pitch is the ability to recognise and name an isolated musical tone without a reference tone, e.g. being able to say 'F#' if someone plays that note on the piano.

Moreover, we have developed a questionnaire on gaming experience, based on the music experience questionnaire.

- Q11: I spend a lot of my free time playing video games.
- Q12: I'd like to spend some of my disposable income on video game.

- Q13: I often play video games to excite and release myself.
- Q14: My emotion will be affected by game narrative, e.g., I will get nervous when being attacked.
- Q15: My emotion will be affected by game narrative, e.g., I will get nervous when being attacked.
- Q16: I will let my emotions flow naturally along with the story, and I won't deliberately control them.
- Q17: I've heard about affective games and would love to have more such games in the market.
- Q18: I have had formal experiences in playing video games for x years.
- Q19: I play video game attentively x per week.

5.2   Participants

30 participants were recruited online. They were mostly under 30 years old and can be considered digital natives (young person who has grown up in the digital age, in close contact with computers, the Internet, and video game consoles). The mean was 29.1 years old (83% under 30) and there were 26% of students.

The participants were well balanced in terms of gender representation with 56% of males and 44% of females.

Most of the participants were Japanese residents (66%) and 16% were from the UK. Regarding nationality 63% were Japanese. The other nationalities were German, Italian and Chinese.

5.3   Analysis and Results for Likert Items

5.4   Narratives/Gameplay Related Questions

In general, the gameplay and narrative tend to have been positively received as it is shown on the Fig. 5. A notable information, the highest mean value was attributed to the Q8 (M: 4.96, SE: 0.24). The statement was about the interest for playing emotion-driven games. This corroborates results from Q7 (M: 4.56, SE: 0.26) asking the participant if they would be keen to play the actual game recorded in the video. Video game experience was homogeneous across participants (Q18), the majority had more than 8 years of video game experience. The panel was significantly mixed (largest Interquartile range and STD: 2.42) in term of time playing video games spent per week (Q19). The mean indicates that the average amount of time spent playing video games is between 2–3 h a week. This is in line with Q11 statistic about the fact that the participants spent a lot of their free time playing video games (M: 3.43, SE: 0.33). The interface tends to provide good clues regarding player's emotion information for the participants (Q1) (M: 3.43, SE: 0.21). The participants reported that the perception of the emotional influence in the narrative was noticeable (M: 3.90, SE: 0.18) (Q2). The smallest standard deviation (0.92) is attributed to the Question 10 with a mean of 3.66. This question is related to the predicted emotions and it seems that the participants perceived a match with the player's felt emotions and the predicted emotions detected by the wristband. The panel of participants mostly agreed about the fact that the narration may impact their emotions on the Q15 (M: 3.73, SE: 0.25).

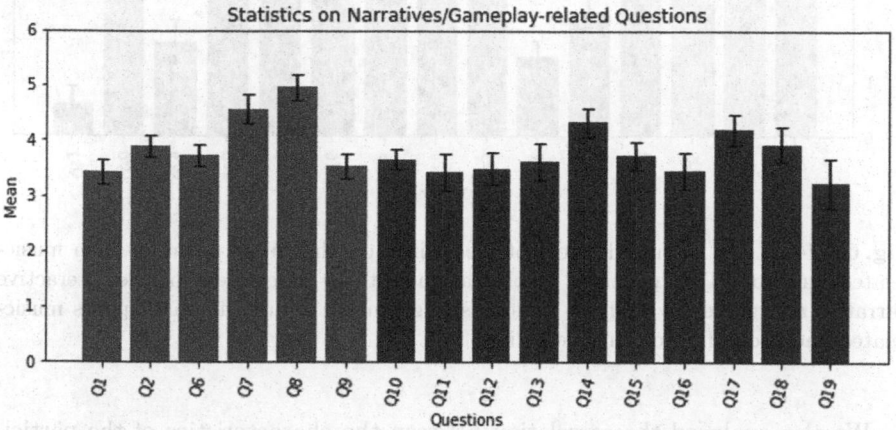

Fig. 5. Means and standard errors of the ratings on the Likert scale for each gameplay/narrative-related question. The questions in blue are about the assessment of the interactive narrative and gameplay and the questions in green are about the participants background and interests in video games. (Color figure online)

Finally an important information is reported from Q16: the participants replied with diversity on the statement that they will let their emotions flow naturally along the game. Indeed to be truly ecologic the players need to have the less awareness of the emotional tracking. Otherwise some bias [22] will be added in the detection.

5.5 Music Related Questions

The statistics for each question relating to music are summarised in the Fig. 6. According to Q3 to Q5 which are related to game experience, the background music generated by the proposed arrangement system was rated as being able to reflect the player's emotions (M: 4.27, SE: 0.17) without losing musical coherence (M: 4.97, SE: 0.16), and matched with the atmosphere of the game (M: 4.73, SE: 0.19). Thus, those results tend to show that proposed model can learn relationships between music and emotions.

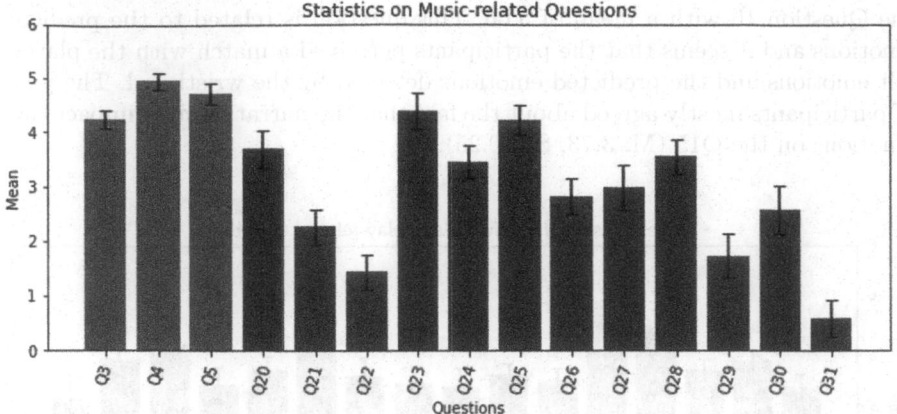

Fig. 6. Means and standard errors of the ratings on the Likert scale for each music-related question. The questions in blue are about the assessment of the interactive narrative and gameplay and the questions in green are about the participants music-related background. (Color figure online)

We also analysed the correlation between the characteristics of the participants (Fig. 6 green part and Fig. 5 green part) and their answers to the questions of game experience (Fig. 6 blue part) using Pearson's correlation coefficient. Those who said they were interested in emotion-based games were more likely to say that the background music was able to reflect the player's emotions ($r = 0.52$, $p < .0001$).

The more time participants spent on music, the more they said the emotions were reflected in the background music ($r = 0.35$, $p = 0.002$). Participants who spent more time playing video games are more likely to say that the background music matches the atmosphere of the game ($r = 0.44$, $p < .0001$). This indicates that the more knowledgeable participants are about the game or music, the more they rate the game background music highly. In other words, this result lends credibility to the fact that the system was able to output a plausible arrangement result. However, it also suggests that without musical experience, it may not have be possible to understand the differences between the generated arrangements.

5.6   Analysis and Results for Open Questions

In addition to Likert items, the evaluation comprised the three following open questions and we summarize the replies below.

What Were the Positive Aspects in the Video Game? The most recurrent positive aspect is the fact that the technology seems to help the participants to acknowledge emotions. The background music was also favourably seen. Another positive aspect is that the game's interactions were simple and the narration followed a linear progression and it was easy to keep the player's attention. Some participants reported to think that this technology makes possible to train their emotional reactions. The graphic design of the game was also reported as being good. The most reported positive feedback is the new possibilities around emotions and game design meaning that a game could be played repeatedly while keeping to be different (*"By using the unique input of one's own emotions, which cannot be easily manipulated by oneself, the game has the potential to become a one-off, or rather, a game that changes each time it is played, making it special in its own way. Therefore, if developed from the current content, it could become a game that is interesting to play repeatedly"*). The game brought up an overall peaceful feeling.

What Were the Negative Aspects in the Video Game? Regarding the negative aspects, participants reported that the purpose of the game was not clear which may lose a player's interest in a short amount of time. The difficulty to follow the emotional changes with the UI (User Interface) was also reported. The UI contained too much text. Some report the fact that emotional tracking can become stressful if the game-design requires one emotion and the user cannot feel it. Some users were confused with the events and didn't get the link between the player's emotions and game progression. The aspect of a technology in too early stage for demonstration was reported: *"The goal isn't clear. The game seems to be more of a tech demo, which would be interesting to test for a few minutes (i.e. check how well one's emotions are detected and processed), but from what I can tell one doesn't really feel like "playing" a game."*. The fact that the emotions are changing slowly may not suit fast-paced games, as mentioned by one participant. It was also pointed out that the music should change more boldly when an emotion change occurs to show the interaction more clearly. Some participants reported the lack of narrative aspects. Also some participants reported the necessity of a really accurate emotional measurement if the game progression relies on it.

How Would You Improve the Link Between the Player's Emotions and the Video Game? The participants proposed a lot of ideas in order to improve the experience. For example by adding more interactions with negative emotions. The focus could be put more on calming state as progress condition because excitement outweights often the calming emotions during a play. Some proposed to add haptic feedback like vibrations. A participant suggested to deal with emotional impact at different levels within the game: *"The first thing that comes to mind, since visuals and environment will likely affect a player's emotions, the music and the environment should be a key factor guiding those emotions. You can still have the player's emotions make changes to the environment but being more of a complementary addition rather than the only thing driving the change: for example, a cave is going always to be a cave, should be dark and oppressing to elicit different emotions."* One participant proposes idea of making narrative and game mechanics in order to generate emotion: for example when the player needs to be calm to unlock a progress. The game can propose rain or nature sounds or relaxing background music to help the player to reach the particular emotional state.

With regard to music, we received feedback emphasised that more pronounced changes should be activated in the music for clearer links with player's emotions. It was suggested that the generated arrangements from the proposed system should be more exaggerated as an element of an interactive game since the changes to convey the specific emotions are difficult to notice for non-musical experts. However, even non-music experts have answered that the system can actually reflect the player's emotions to some extent in the accompaniment. Therefore, we believe that more obvious arrangements (e.g. sudden changes of tempo, modulations, etc.) would lead to a stronger agreement.

6 Summary and Conclusion

By initiating a new paradigm around affective gaming interactions using AI interactions, this research project and this first integration into a prototype act as an initial proof of concept. The technical feasibility of emotional interaction and audio-visual effects based on player's emotion was demonstrated with the prototype. Moreover some the potential benefits like the possibility for the player to train his/her emotional reactions during specific situations.

Some of the negative feedback (e.g. purpose of the game unclear) may be due to the fact that participants were not playing themselves but watching a video of a gameplay. Having participants actively playing the game should mitigate these feelings. Another interesting outcome are reflections on the fact that the game design can become difficult if the game designers expect the player to feel specific emotions at a certain point but the player cannot feel them, the progression would be impossible. Those points need to be addressed and considered in the initial game design. Another constraint to consider for the game designer is time for emotions to manifest themselves at the physiological level, which can induce time lapses of several seconds in the responsiveness of the interactive system.

Characterising a player's emotions during gameplay should provide a better understanding of the player's reactions and personality [1] along the play. In the experience we developed, the game is now able to "feel" the player's emotions using arousal and valence classification and to propose new story plots according to player's feelings. This project represents a first step, as a first gaming experience including interactive narrative and audio-visual effects to the player's emotions.

In future work, we will expand the prototype and integrate additional mechanics on the initial script and storyboard.

The second step of our research and evaluation will include physiological data collections and self-reports of felt emotions. Participants will be invited to play the game with a controller and wear a smart band for biosignal collection and processing.

Acknowledgments. This work was partly supported by Ovomind and the EPSRC and AHRC Centre for Doctoral Training in Media and Arts Technology (EP/L01632X/1). We would also like to thank the user evaluation participants.

References

1. Amaresha, A.C., Venkatasubramanian, G.: Expressed emotion in schizophrenia: an overview. Indian J. Psychol. Med. **34**, 12–20 (2012). https://doi.org/10.4103/0253-7176.96149
2. Barthet, M., Fazekas, G., Sandler, M.: Music emotion recognition: from content-to context-based models. In: Aramaki, M., Barthet, M., Kronland-Martinet, R., Ystad, S. (eds.) CMMR 2012. LNCS, vol. 7900, pp. 228–252. Springer, Heidelberg (2013). https://doi.org/10.1007/978-3-642-41248-6_13
3. Bolanos, M., Nazeran, H., Haltiwanger, E.: Comparison of heart rate variability signal features derived from electrocardiography and photoplethysmography in healthy individuals. In: Annual International Conference of the IEEE Engineering in Medicine and Biology - Proceedings, pp. 4289–4294 (2006). https://doi.org/10.1109/IEMBS.2006.260607
4. Boucsein, W., et al.: Publication recommendations for electrodermal measurements. Psychophysiology **49**, 1017–1034 (2012). https://doi.org/10.1111/j.1469-8986.2012.01384.x
5. Callele, D., Neufeld, E., Schneider, K.: Emotional requirements in video games. In: Proceedings of the IEEE International Conference on Requirements Engineering, pp. 299–302 (2006). https://doi.org/10.1109/RE.2006.19
6. Christoph, K., Hefner, D., Peter, V.: The video game experience as "true" identification: a theory of enjoyable alterations of players' self-perception. Commun. Theory **19**, 351–373 (2009). https://doi.org/10.1111/j.1468-2885.2009.01347.x
7. Coutinho, E., Cangelosi, A.: Musical emotions: predicting second-by-second subjective feelings of emotion from low-level psychoacoustic features and physiological measurements. Emotion **11**(4), 921 (2011)
8. Critchley, H.D.: Electrodermal responses: what happens in the brain. Neuroscientist **8**, 132–142 (2002). https://doi.org/10.1177/107385840200800209
9. De Jonckheere, J., Ibarissene, I., Flocteil, M., Logier, R.: A smartphone based cardiac coherence biofeedback system. In: 2014 36th Annual International Conference of the IEEE Engineering in Medicine and Biology Society, EMBC 2014, pp. 4791–4794 (2014). https://doi.org/10.1109/EMBC.2014.6944695
10. Dehzangi, O., Rajendra, V., Taherisadr, M.: Wearable driver distraction identification on-the-road via continuous decomposition of galvanic skin responses. Sensors (Switzerland) **18**, 1–16 (2018). https://doi.org/10.3390/s18020503
11. Frome, J.: Eight ways videogames generate emotion. In: 3rd Digital Games Research Association International Conference: "Situated Play", DiGRA 2007, pp. 831–835 (2007)
12. Gil, E., Orini, M., Bailón, R., Vergara, J.M., Mainardi, L., Laguna, P.: Photoplethysmography pulse rate variability as a surrogate measurement of heart rate variability during non-stationary conditions. Physiol. Meas. **31**, 1271–1290 (2010). https://doi.org/10.1088/0967-3334/31/9/015

13. Granato, M., Gadia, D., Maggiorini, D., Ripamonti, L.A.: Feature extraction and selection for real-time emotion recognition in video games players. In: Proceedings - 14th International Conference on Signal Image Technology and Internet Based Systems, SITIS 2018, pp. 717–724 (2018). https://doi.org/10.1109/SITIS.2018.00115

14. Huang, X., et al.: Multi-modal emotion analysis from facial expressions and electroencephalogram. Comput. Vis. Image Underst. **147**, 114–124 (2016). https://doi.org/10.1016/j.cviu.2015.09.015

15. Jovanovic, N., Popovic, N.B., Miljkovic, N.: Empirical mode decomposition for automatic artifact elimination in electrogastrogram. In: 2021 20th International Symposium INFOTEH-JAHORINA, INFOTEH 2021 - Proceedings, pp. 17–19 (2021). https://doi.org/10.1109/INFOTEH51037.2021.9400683

16. Koelsch, S.: Brain correlates of music-evoked emotions. Nat. Rev. Neurosci. **15**, 170–180 (2014). https://doi.org/10.1038/nrn3666

17. Krkovic, K., Clamor, A., Lincoln, T.M.: Emotion regulation as a predictor of the endocrine, autonomic, affective, and symptomatic stress response and recovery. Psychoneuroendocrinology **94**, 112–120 (2018). https://doi.org/10.1016/j.psyneuen.2018.04.028

18. Lerdahl, F., et al.: Tonal Pitch Space. Oxford University Press, USA (2001)

19. Makris, D., Agres, K.R., Herremans, D.: Generating lead sheets with affect: a novel conditional seq2seq framework. arXiv preprint arXiv:2104.13056 (2021)

20. McCarthy, C., Pradhan, N., Redpath, C., Adler, A.: Validation of the Empatica E4 wristband. In: 2016 IEEE EMBS International Student Conference: Expanding the Boundaries of Biomedical Engineering and Healthcare, ISC 2016 - Proceedings, pp. 4–7 (2016). https://doi.org/10.1109/EMBSISC.2016.7508621

21. McCraty, R., Zayas, M.A.: Cardiac coherence, self-regulation, autonomic stability and psychosocial well-being. Front. Psychol. **1090**, 1–13 (2014). https://doi.org/10.3389/fpsyg.2014.01090

22. Mühlenbeck, C., Pritsch, C., Wartenburger, I., Telkemeyer, S., Liebal, K.: Attentional bias to facial expressions of different emotions - a cross-cultural comparison of Akhoe Hai—om and German children and adolescents. Front. Psychol. **11**, 1–9 (2020). https://doi.org/10.3389/fpsyg.2020.00795

23. Müllensiefen, D., Gingras, B., Musil, J., Stewart, L.: Measuring the facets of musicality: the Goldsmiths Musical Sophistication Index (Gold-MSI). Pers. Individ. Differ. **60**, S35 (2014)

24. Nummenmaa, L., Glerean, E., Hari, R., Hietanen, J.K.: Bodily maps of emotions. Proc. Natl. Acad. Sci. U.S.A. **111**, 646–651 (2014). https://doi.org/10.1073/pnas.1321664111

25. Posada-Quintero, H.F., Florian, J.P., Orjuela-Cañón, A.D., Aljama-Corrales, T., Charleston-Villalobos, S., Chon, K.H.: Power spectral density analysis of electrodermal activity for sympathetic function assessment. Ann. Biomed. Eng. **44**, 3124–3135 (2016)

26. Posada-Quintero, H.F., Florian, J.P., Orjuela-Cañón, A.D., Chon, K.H.: Electrodermal activity is sensitive to cognitive stress under water. Front. Physiol. **8**, 1–8 (2018). https://doi.org/10.3389/fphys.2017.01128

27. Ribeiro, F.S., Santos, F.H., Albuquerque, P.B., Oliveira-Silva, P.: Emotional induction through music: measuring cardiac and electrodermal responses of emotional states and their persistence. Front. Psychol. **10**, 1–13 (2019). https://doi.org/10.3389/fpsyg.2019.00451

28. Schäfer, A., Vagedes, J.: How accurate is pulse rate variability as an estimate of heart rate variability?: a review on studies comparing photoplethysmographic technology with an electrocardiogram. Int. J. Cardiol. **166**, 15–29 (2013). https://doi.org/10.1016/j.ijcard.2012.03.119

29. Scherer, K.R.: What are emotions? And how can they be measured? Soc. Sci. Inf. **44**, 695–729 (2005). https://doi.org/10.1177/0539018405058216

30. Shu, L., et al.: A review of emotion recognition using physiological signals. Sensors (Switzerland) **18**, 2074 (2018). https://doi.org/10.3390/s18072074

31. Soutter, A.R.B., Hitchens, M.: The relationship between character identification and flow state within video games. Comput. Hum. Behav. **55**, 1030–1038 (2016). https://doi.org/10.1016/j.chb.2015.11.012

32. Takahashi, T., Mathieu, B.: Automatic arrangement system for melodies based on felt emotions (2022). Submitted

33. Wang, C., Wang, F.: An emotional analysis method based on heart rate variability. In: Proceedings - IEEE-EMBS International Conference on Biomedical and Health Informatics: Global Grand Challenge of Health Informatics, BHI 2012, pp. 104–107 (2012). https://doi.org/10.1109/BHI.2012.6211518

34. Warriner, A.B., Kuperman, V., Brysbaert, M.: Norms of valence, arousal, and dominance for 13,915 English lemmas. Behav. Res. Methods **45**(4), 1191–1207 (2013)

35. Wellman, H.M., Cross, D., Watson, J.: Meta-analysis of theory-of-mind development: the truth about false belief. Child Dev. **72**, 655–684 (2001). Published by: Wiley on behalf of the Society for Research in Child Development Stable. http://www.jstor.org/s

36. Widen, S.C., Pochedly, J.T., Russell, J.A.: The development of emotion concepts: a story superiority effect in older children and adolescents. J. Exp. Child Psychol. **131**, 186–192 (2015). https://doi.org/10.1016/j.jecp.2014.10.009

37. Yeh, Y.C., et al.: Automatic melody harmonization with triad chords: a comparative study. J. New Music Res. **50**, 37–51 (2021)

38. Yu, L.C., et al.: Building Chinese affective resources in valence-arousal dimensions. In: 2016 Conference of the North American Chapter of the Association for Computational Linguistics: Human Language Technologies, NAACL HLT 2016 - Proceedings of the Conference, pp. 540–545 (2016). https://doi.org/10.18653/v1/n16-1066

Frankenhead - Exploring Participatory Engagement and Play as a Cultural Event

Andreas Kratky(✉), Joanna Shen, Hesiquio Mendez Alejo, Rong Deng, and Fabian Bock

University of Southern California, Los Angeles, CA 90089, USA
akratky@cinema.usc.edu, fbock@usc.edu

Abstract. *Frankenhead* is a playable sculpture inspired by Mary Shelley's 1818 novel "Frankenstein; or, the Modern Prometheus." It explores the idea of constructing an artificial creature from the bits and pieces of existing beings. Just as the imaginary Dr. Frankenstein, in the 19th century, used electricity to build a creature and bring it to live, players use digital media to puzzle together body parts drawn from a database containing a large collection of representations of Frankenstein's monster, ranging from the first illustrations of the novel to contemporary depictions of the Frankenstein myth. The public installation allows multiple players to collaboratively piece together the monster. Players can use a face detection software that takes their own picture, decomposes it into its parts, and inserts it into the *Frankenhead* database to become part of the monster-puzzle. Players insert internally coded, blank modules into sockets in the sculpture; once inserted, the modules appear as the body parts they are. Players can move them around to piece together a monster of their liking. The project realizes a contemporary take on the topic of the novel and remaps aspects of the techno- and gender-criticism of Shelley's writing to today's techno-social landscape. The paper presents the design decisions and implementation of the installation and discusses the findings made observing players during the event.

Keywords: Collaborative play · Public interactive · Playable sculpture · Projection mapping · Emergent play

1 Introduction

At the occasion of the anniversary of Mary Shelley's novel "Frankenstein; or, the Modern Prometheus.", which was first published in 1818 anonymously, and in 1821 under her real name in the second edition, the *Frankenhead* project was conceived as a hybrid of a public interactive and a playable sculpture. It was part of a larger event to commemorate the 200th anniversary of the novel, consisting of animated short films projection-mapped on the building of Doheny Library at the University of Southern California and several other public activations. The event was hosted by the libraries of the University.

© The Author(s), under exclusive license to Springer Nature Switzerland AG 2022
X. Fang (Ed.): HCII 2022, LNCS 13334, pp. 180–195, 2022.
https://doi.org/10.1007/978-3-031-05637-6_11

Frankenhead is a large interactive sculpture in the form of an oversized head, presented in an outdoor space after sunset. It explores a staged design of public engagement to accommodate as many players as possible during this one-evening event of several hours of extension. The design is meant to make it easy for passers-by to engage and begin playing. We paid special attention to solutions that present a minimal barrier to entry, to make engaging with the sculpture easy and smooth, while also allowing for additional, deeper, levels of engagement, connecting to the conceptual topics of the Frankenstein novel. The goal for the *Frankenhead* installation was to serve as a portal to the larger event. It was situated at the perimeter of the event location, visible to passers-by on campus, to attract attention and invite people to come closer and explore the full event. To appropriately fulfill this function, the realization of an effective staging of audience approach and engagement in the gameplay of the piece was central. Our intention for the conceptual design was to introduce the context of the Frankenstein novel and make a point, why this narrative is relevant still today; and finally, we also wanted to make a critical comment with the experience itself, communicated through the gameplay, and provide a pleasurable and fun experience. The following will describe our design strategies to accomplish these goals.

1.1   Historical Context

To explain the concept of how the *Frankenhead* project metaphorically transfers the tenets of the original novel to today's moment, we will give a brief summary of the role the novel played in its days and continues to play in the history of literature. In the often-cited history of science fiction by the English writer and scholar Brian Aldiss, the Frankenstein novel is characterized as the first true science fiction novel. For our purpose, rather than engaging in a discussion of literary history, it is relevant to understand, why Aldiss made this classification, rejecting countless other stories that deal with cosmic travel and other motifs that we might consider characteristic for science fiction. We can see the Frankenstein novel as a new version of the Faustian dream of unlimited knowledge, but instead of making a pact with the devil, Dr. Frankenstein of Shelley's novel conducts laboratory research and uses rational, scientific methods to bring about new knowledge. What Aldiss sees here as a turning point is the departure from mythical, pre-scientific, and fantastical thinking to a methodical questioning of the role of the human in the world [1]. This notion becomes a central tenet in Aldiss' definition of science fiction, which he considers as "the search for a definition of mankind and his status in the universe which will stand in our advanced but confused state of knowledge (science)" [1].

This focus on the methodical questioning of assumed truths, of myths, and dominant narratives weaves across both the criticism (and celebration) of rationality and the critical feminist positions formulated in the novel and is the central tenet of its criticism. This focus is also the central element we are leveraging in the *Frankenhead* experience.

1.2   Critical Tenets of the Novel

The Frankenstein novel has been the subject of regular scholarly study, elaborating several areas of critical analysis, which are tightly interwoven in the novel and hard to separate as individual lines of argument. Without discussing the complex critical positions inherent to the novel, we will look predominantly at the position toward science and technology, as well as the position toward social structure and identity. The somewhat ambiguous relationship of Shelley to science and technology is expressed in the creation of the monster by Dr. Frankenstein: The monster turns out to be a horrific creature in conflict with humans and uncontrollable in its actions. Nevertheless, it is a tremendous achievement of the scientist Frankenstein to have created and awoken to life this creature. We see both a fascination with the new possibilities opened by science and technology and a skepticism and concern about their possible results. At the time the novel was written, the results of the scientific revolution were becoming a tangible part of every-day life in the form of steam engines, power looms, electricity, galvanism, and other applied phenomena of rational, scientific inquiry. The promise of these new technologies clearly inspired the young author, not only from a fascination with technologies of which the possibilities still needed to be understood, but also in respect to her role as a woman and a mother. In the introduction to her 1813 edition of the novel, Mary Shelley speculates that galvanism could be a solution to artificially give life: "Perhaps a corpse would be re-animated; galvanism had given token of such things: perhaps the component parts of a creature might be manufactured, brought together, and endued with vital warmth" [2]. The proximity of life and death that appears in the connection of corpse-parts, assembled to Frankenstein's creature, which then, is given new life, is characterized as an autobiographically inspired reflection of Mary Shelley. Ellen Moers analyzes the feeling of guilt that Mary seemed to have, feeling responsible for the premature death of her mother, who died from complications of giving birth to Mary, as one of the inspirations for pondering alternative ways of conception [2]. Mary also lost her own daughter soon after her birth and experienced several cases of death and birth among her close friends and family [2]. While this proximity of life and death can be understood from her biography, a particularly revealing motif of the hopeful but conflicted relationship to science is expressed in the account of one dream of Mary Shelley: "dream that my little baby had come back to life again, that it had only been cold, and that we rubbed it before the fire, and it lived. [...] I thought, that if I could bestow animation upon lifeless matter, I might in process of time renew life where death had apparently devoted the body to corruption" [2]. This double-edged relationship to science and technology is rooted in Mary Shelley's biography. Daughter of the philosopher, feminist thinker, and activist Mary Wollstonecraft and political philosopher William Godwin, Mary Shelley was an avid reader and very attuned to rational thinking and criticism. At the same time, as Paul Youngquist writes, Mary felt unease with her parents' leaning toward rationalism, criticizing "that her mother's feminism reduces the human to a rational corpse" [3]. Uneasy with the situation that is imposed on her, Shelley formulates a criticism of the dominant role models of her society, in which women live under the oppressiveness of a concept of feminine domesticity that fundamentally prescribes different roles to women and men [4].

2 Game Design Concept

In our game design concept, we decided to integrate the double-edged stance toward technology. If making a statement with technology, in our case the use of an interactive installation, a basic affirmative stance inheres to such a statement. Technology is not rejected outright, instead we explore its possibilities to make an argument that is critical about technology. Akin to Shelley's position, who did not reject science and technology, but had hopes for a potential improvement of society – and in particular of the role of women, we are translating the criticism in Shelley's account to a critique of contemporary data collection methods for the training of artificial intelligence and personality modeling. Across its history of reception, the novel has been read in numerous ways as a parallel to contemporary phenomena, such as cloning or the notion of the responsibility of scientists for their actions. For our purpose, building on the topic of data-collection and -assembly made sense and allowed us to engage the topic of privacy, data-harvesting and computational modeling for purposes like targeted advertisement. As the creature of the novel was created out of a collage of parts of different bodies, we set up a growing database of body parts, beginning with early depictions of Frankenstein's creature in the first illustrations of the novel to contemporary depictions of the Frankenstein myth. While the initial content of the database is a historical reference to the various incarnations and readings of the Frankenstein novel, players also can use a face detection software that takes their picture, decomposes it into its parts, and inserts it into the *Frankenhead* database. With this possibility to become part of the data-puzzle constituting the monster, we are making the connection from the historic to today's moment and the issue of the collection of personal data.

Using a game to make this point on one hand allows us to use the simulative aspect of a game to "play through" what is means to feed personal data into a database that creates uncontrollable creatures – or even monsters – from them, and it suggests, at the same time, how lightly we tend to take this issue, as if it were just play, taking place in a sphere separate from the "real world."

Another aspect of the original Frankenstein novel is the criticism of the notion that every individual has to conform to pre-defined and fixed roles in the society context. What Shelley hints at in her writing, we take as a rather literal inspiration for the mechanic of our installation: players can put their creature together by plugging modules that correspond to body-parts into the sculpture. The way the modules are coded, suggests that each part can only function "correctly" in its designated slot - for example, a module representing an eye can only "correctly" be placed where an eye belongs in the face of the creature. But as players engage into playing with the modules and where they might belong in the sculpture, they increasingly get accustomed to the idea that the modules can be placed anywhere, and by taking the notion of a *creature* seriously, we can challenge the concept of what is considered as "normal" or as deformed or "monstrous", and what we consider possible or not. We see this as a parallel to the fact that a lot of the data modeling operating with "personality parts" does not create a comprehensive rendering of the personality of the modeled individual, but only, so to speak, distorted and abbreviated truncations of the actual individuals, and how stereotypes and assumptions are used to categorize these models.

A third aspect we decided to integrate into our game design is the notion that our actions can have unexpected consequences. As Dr. Frankenstein, in the novel, did not anticipate that his creation will turn into a monster, instill horror and eventually kill several of his family members, we wanted to integrate a surprise effect where players realize that their creation takes on unexpected power and becomes larger than they expected: The creature they are composing, in the end, appears in a giant facade projection on the nearby library building. Amplified to an oversized monster, the creation of the players takes on its own life and provides a kind of endpoint to the experience, while guiding them to the rest of the event.

2.1 Playable Sculpture vs. Public Interactive

To realize our conceptual goals and harmonize them with the requirement for short-form gameplay and the role as a portal to the rest of the event, we settled on a large physical sculpture that allows for tangible interaction. The interaction takes place as a layered experience, of which players can either spend more time and go through several of the experience layers or move on as they please, without missing too much of the experience goal. We refer to the installation as a hybrid of a public interactive and a playable sculpture, because it combines the approachability and playful invitation of playable sculptures, a genre we know from playground installations for children, with the more complex rhetoric of public interactive experiences we know, for example, from science museums or similar contexts. These two categories serve as models of two ends of a spectrum of interactive engagement: The playable sculpture has a low barrier of entry and tends to be a simple and hands-on set-up that immediately invites players to climb on it, step into it, interact with it in simple and straightforward actions. This is the design notion we use for the first phase of players' approach to *Frankenhead* and their first steps of entering the game play of the experience. The design elements based on the concept of public interactives are coming to bear post-approach and are intended to draw players into deeper levels of engagement. Our use of the term "public interactive" is inspired by Anne Balsamo's classification of it as a set-up "for the active reproduction of technocultural understandings, mythologies, values, and the circulation of new knowledges" [5]. Public interactives, in this sense, are designed for audience members to spend a certain amount of time with, interact with the apparatus and learn from the interaction with it. Balsamo characterizes these apparatuses as using "innovative technologies" and are situated in public space, so that a wide range of public audiences can engage with them. She sees urban screens as part of this category, as well as touch-screen based kiosk systems etc. [5].

The narrative design of the *Frankenhead* sculpture is inspired by a form of poetic sculpture, as instantiated by the Surrealist giraffe sculpture described and partially realized by Luis Buñuel and Alberto Giacometti. Film theorist Marsha Kinder describes the sculpture as an interactive piece, designed to deliver a "powerful surrealistic jolt" [6]. The giraffe was a temporary sculpture created by Buñuel and Giacometti in 1932, which was placed in the garden of the villa of Marie-Laure and Charles de Noailles in Hyères, in the South of France. The sculpture had hidden compartments that contained, upon further examination, various conceptual surprises and, as Buñuel wrote, "it should be noted that this giraffe doesn't make complete sense until its full potential is realized, that is to say, until each of its spots performs the function for which it was intended" [7]. The concept of the giraffe with its seemingly ordinary slots, which invite players to manipulate them and explore what they have to offer, is very close to the design approach we settled on. The *Frankenhead* sculpture similarly has nine slots in which seemingly undifferentiated play pieces can be inserted. Once the player engages in this activity, both slots and play pieces reveal their hidden functions and possible meanings.

2.2   Problem of Approachability

Users who are encountering an interactive experience somewhat accidentally and without an already existing decision to engage with the experience are often hesitant to engage with it. Despite the growing popularity of large format screens as well as touch screens in the public realm, the use and adoption of these screens is limited [8]. Intended users are frequently hesitant to approach and interact with the systems; confusion as to the purpose of the system or what the right actions might be to operate the system is a common obstacle among those users. Various solutions have been proposed to mitigate this lack of engagement among intended users with these screens. One of the solutions is an interaction model that is structured in various phases that build on each other. Cheung proposes a phase model that proceeds from a "passing-by" phase to a phase of "notice and approach" and ends with user interaction determined to "explore and discover" [9].

This problem of discovering how we can operate something that we have never seen before is a common phenomenon. Don Norman has provided a comprehensive reflection on the processes involved in this discoverability problem in his book "The Design of Everyday Things." Norman suggests that, normally, people resort to concepts they know already that are based on prior experience with the world; they interpret the affordances of the system they see in front of them and try to match what they know with what they see and from this devise a strategy how to operate the system [10]. Taking recourse to pre-existing experience of operating different systems relies on similarity - if a system is very similar to one that was experienced earlier, users will find it easier to determine how to use the system in front of them. This experience transfer becomes increasingly difficult with growing degrees of difference. For an experience like 'the creation of a monster from different body-parts,' it is likely that very little pre-existing experience can be assumed. Therefore, the design of *Frankenhead* made use of very explicit affordances and simple shapes that can easily be read, interpreted and translated into potential actions. Our inspiration is something like logical blocks, using simple geometric shapes. We also found that it is easier to use rotationally symmetric shapes, so users do not have to pay attention to orientation. They can be solely focused on a simple shape matching task. We will describe the design a little further down in detail. In terms of readability as well as general attraction, the use of tangible forms of interaction is useful to encourage players to engage [11]. Using multiple modalities, such as visual and haptic affordances supports players to quickly grasp what the interaction possibilities are and how to use them effectively. This is the reason why, for *Frankenhead*, we decided to implement a form of interaction with multiple expressive tangible objects.

The design challenge for the geometric appearance is not only limited to the affordances of the objects users interact with directly, also the overall shape of the sculpture plays a role in attracting players. The physical appearance of the display (and sculpture, for that matter) has an effect on how potential players engage with it. In a study on the effect of the physical layout of multiple connected screens, ten Koppel et al. have discovered that a flat versus a concave versus a hexagonal arrangement of the screens has effects on user engagement. They found, for example, a concave display arrangement suppresses collaborative interaction and the most active social interaction patterns occur in screen settings where multiple users can see each other, their actions, and their results [12].

This finding corresponds with the interactions we saw occurring around the *Frankenhead* installation, which led us to adopt a collaboration-inducing display arrangement. In our particular case, collaboration is intended and encouraged. A compounding effect that makes user interaction in public displays difficult is the number of people surrounding, and potentially observing, the person who is interacting. As we found with numerous interactive museum display settings, audience members are afraid of revealing themselves as lacking sophistication or knowledge in operating devices in front of a large group of bystanders. As for the *Frankenhead* experience, it is important to encourage collaboration, as this is the best way to avoid the feeling of isolated performance anxiety of individual players. The entire game play is designed to be collaborative, fast, and accessible.

2.3 Design for Staged Interaction

The large luminous sculpture of *Frankenhead* functions as a landmark that is visible from a distance and attracts people as they approach the event site. As they come closer, they encounter the sculpture and it's smaller, moving parts, which are conceived such that potential players "stumble onto them" and easily understand those parts as puzzle pieces that they can manipulate. Once they work with the puzzle pieces, which can be operated by several players collaboratively, as they piece together new faces for the "*Frankenhead*-Creature," they encounter a face-scanning station that allows them to scan their face and become part of a growing database of body-part images with which players can create new *Frankenhead*-Creatures. As the installation is evocative of the creation myth of the monster in the Frankenstein novel, we designed a mechanic that allows players to puzzle different body-parts together and create different faces for the giant head. A large switch allowed them to turn their creation "on" and bring it to life. The assemblage in *Frankenhead* is facilitated by a growing database of different face-parts, comprising a range of different artistic styles and faces from players. Once players have engaged in the face-scanning component and become part of the installation, we observed that the level of engagement significantly changes and an expectation of seeing and manipulating their own, contributed elements to the installation emerges. As players progress through the experience, the final pay-off happens when they realize that their play is part of a giant façade projection on the nearby library building. This sense of amplification has a strong effect on players, both as a surprise and as an enlargement of their activity. From this point, players get oriented toward other activations of the event and have a sense of closure with the *Frankenhead* sculpture. Depending on wait-time at the face-scanning station, the length of stay in the installation tends to be somewhere between 5 to 10 min (Figs. 1, 2, 3, 5, 6 and 7).

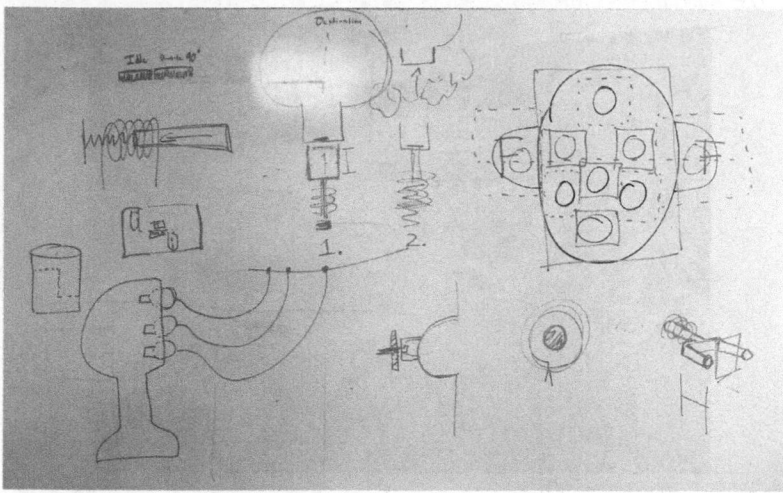

Fig. 1. Whiteboard with design elements from one of our many brainstorm sessions.

Stage One: Landmark as Attraction

The first stage was meant to attract potential players and ease them into the game play. Since the premises of the event were rather large, we decided to build a large sculpture of a head (which we fondly nicknamed "Frankenhead"). Since the event was going to take place after sunset, the sculpture had to be luminous and large enough to stand out. We designed an over-life-size sculpture that was massive head with a height of circa seven feet. The front of the head was conceived as a projection surface on which the visual feedback for the game play, the facial pieces and expressions from our database, would be projection-mapped. The front served as the "game board" and was made of a flat wooden panel with seven openings cut into it with sockets to hold seven spherical game pieces.

Due to the size of our sculpture, we had to take portability, weight, and volume of materials into account. To tackle this, we used lightweight materials such as Paper-mâché and newspaper to cover and form the basic shape of *Frankenhead*. An interior wooden scaffolding supported the structure and had weights to make sure it could resist wind. We used starch glue, as an economical alternative to regular glue, to glue the paper together. Since we utilized lightweight materials wherever possible, we were able to use slightly heavier materials like wood and wire mesh to create a stable base for the sculpture. A logic system to support the game play was installed in the interior of the head.

The size of the head sculpture provided a space for several players to collaborate piecing together their creation. In order to do that, the main game loop began with an empty head, showing a white surface with some veins going across it. The seven sockets are empty and the interactive game pieces are lying on the floor in front of the head. The interactive game pieces were easily noticeable and accessible for players to approach the sculpture and collaborate with others, inserting the pieces into the sockets in the head. As players pick up the pieces, they do not know what part of the face a piece represents; in order to find out, they have to insert the piece into a slot in the head, upon which the

Fig. 2. Construction of the head-sculpture made of paper-mâché.

Fig. 3. *Frankenhead* sculpture, showing its interior scaffolding. The front plate is placed on the ground in front of it, showing the control electronics and mechanics.

presence of the piece is recognized by the system and an animation of the respective face part is displayed on the surface of the page piece. Now players can decide to change the socket and where on the head they want to position the face part. As they insert more game pieces, the face becomes more formulated. When game pieces are inserted, they trigger an animation that cycles through different versions of the same face part. For example, the game piece, that represents the nose, cycles through all the versions of noses that exist in the database. Once players decided that they are satisfied with their creation, they can pull a large switch to breathe life into their creation. This ends the animation cycles and locks in the face part that is visible in that moment and starts an animation of that part, e.g. an eye blinking etc.

Fig. 4. The *game loop begins with an empty face; players collaborate to insert the game pieces into the head sockets; and finally, they activate their creation with a large switch.*

We created seven spherical game pieces, each piece representing a different facial feature on *Frankenhead*. We constructed them using large styrofoam balls, plastic cup containers, newspaper, and starch glue. After prototyping and experimenting with various shapes prior to making the final game piece, we decided to carve them in a mushroom shape with a slightly tapered stem. This is to allow the pieces to fit into the cylinder-shaped sockets of the Frankenhead face and stay in place. And it would allow the players to easily recognize how the game pieces fit into the sockets.

Each game piece had an RFID (Radio Frequency Identification) tag attached that was specific to a facial feature. In the face sockets we had RFID readers that correlated to each RFID tag. There were seven features, and the sculpture could have multiple combinations of eyes, noses, and mouths. For this structure to be re-playable we had to design a mechanism that would reset the parts of the head. We added seven solenoids to each face socket and placed them in the middle of RFID readers. So once players inserted the pieces into the sockets, their RFID tag was recognized, and the corresponding animation was displayed. Once the players activated the switch the face part gets locked in and plays its individual animation. When the game needed to reset, the player would turn the switch off, and the face parts were ejected by the solenoids and fell to the ground for people to start over with the game. All these components were attached to an Arduino microcontroller which would control and send the needed information to a computer that controlled the projection onto the head sculpture.

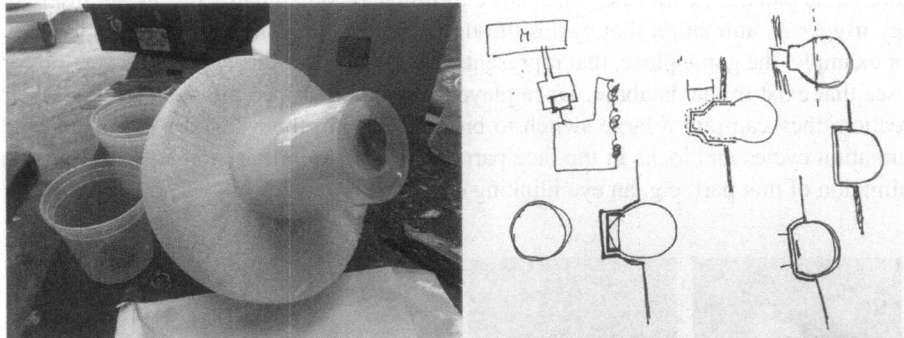

Fig. 5. Right: diagrams of ideas we had for the shape of the game piece. Left: one of the seven final game pieces shaped like a mushroom that fits snugly into the face socket.

Stage Two: Personal Involvement

To realize a second stage of deeper game play, we added a face scanning station. Players could go to the station to scan their face and add it to the *Frankenhead* database of facial parts. Once the scanner detects a face, it scans it and decomposes it into seven components, the nose, the eyes, the mouth, the cheeks, and the forehead. These face parts get inserted into the loops of body parts that cycle through when a face piece gets inserted into a socket. At this stage, players have the eagerness to see their own face parts appearing on the *Frankenhead*. Since they are not shown in the full facial context, it is sometime difficult to clearly say whose face part is shown, so multiple players start guessing and arguing about whose parts are shown. Now, the challenge becomes to turn the switch in the right moment to lock in the desired face parts from the animation cycles.

Fig. 6. The face scanner and its facial recognition algorithm that decomposes the scanned faces into their component parts.

The addition of the face scanner added a stage of intensified game play and player engagement. Players have something personal at stake; and they also see, as they observe other players, how their facial features become the playball of other players. This second stage is central to making the argument about data collection, ethics and privacy we discussed earlier.

Stage Three: Amplification

The third stage of engagement is the one where the unexpected amplification of the player's actions takes place. The sculpture is set up in such a way that the nearby library building is somewhat covered. Players get a view on the building when they go to the activation switch, which they do toward the end of their interaction with the sculpture. At this point they realize that the creature they have been working on is projected onto the façade of the library building and it is watched by a large crowd of people who is looking at projection mapped animations created in response to the novel. The façade projection shows an alternating program of animations and the creature of the *Frankenhead* sculpture. Players realize that, what they thought they were doing with their friends, is actually presented in a giant scale and watched by many people. At this point, players tend to turn off the switch, eject the game pieces from the head and start the game loop anew for the next group of players. They move on to watch other activations of the event.

Fig. 7. The *facade projection on the Doheny library building and the Frankenhead creature on the facade.*

3 Observations and Evaluation

To assess the effectiveness of the *Frankenhead* installation, we did observations of player interactions, video recordings, and did open form conversations in situ, asking questions about players' impressions and interpretations of what they experienced. Player interactions were recorded on video to allow us to study different players, demographics and age groups in their interactions with the installation after the actual event. Since the event was of short duration and a single evening, video recording was intended to take off a some of the pressure of the present facilitators to conduct conversations and observe all at the same time.

To establish evaluation criteria for the installation, we turn first toward the stated goals and assess, to which degree the installation fulfilled these. The stated goals were a) the installation was supposed to serve as a portal and landmark to attract people to the larger event; b) it was meant to introduce audience members to the context of the Frankenstein novel and make a point for its continued relevance communicating a critical thought by translating some of the novel's aspects into a contemporary context; and c) the installation should engage players into a pleasurable and fun experience. We follow [13] as a way to structure our assessment and provide comparability to other public interactive installations. [13] is a meta-study, evaluating 34 different installations and their assessment methods to formulate a consistent and general evaluation framework. According to the distinctions made in [13], *Frankenhead* is an experimental study, which is based on the actual tangible deployment of a public interactive installation. The authors suggest a two-part approach, developing certain metrics for the direct assessment of the installation and a characterization of the site, where the installation was deployed.

3.1 Site

The site where the *Frankenhead* installation was installed combines several characteristics that impact the user behavior and the expectable audience. As it was deployed on a university campus, the site is a semi-public space. The event itself was advertised broadly to both a campus and a general audience. It is expectable, though, that the players come predominantly from a university-related audience. The exact place, where *Frankenhead* was set up was in a park, i.e. a leisure environment, in which passers-by tend to not pursue a direct goal and have some time to spare to engage in an interactive experience. This behavior was supported by the time of day of the deployment. The main event was to begin at 8 pm, to allow for sufficient darkness for the large façade-projection of the main event to be of appropriate quality. The *Frankenhead* installation started earlier, and even though it also used projection-mapping, the mapping was on a smaller surface and therefore a powerful projector was able to deliver enough contrast. The installation was intended to serve both as a spatial portal to draw passers-by to the main event, taking place on the other end of the park, as well as temporal portal, to attract people who had business on campus and were about to leave, to capture their interest to stay for the main event. While being set up in a park, the installation was adjacent to one of the main thoroughfares and main squares of the campus and therefore functioning as a landmark for passers-by to turn toward the park and come closer to the site of the main event. Thus, according to the categorization proposed by [13], the *Frankenhead* site combines characteristics of a controlled, semi-public environment, with the traffic flow of a transit-location and the leisure possibility of the park. The particular qualities of the site have an influence on how the installation fulfills its goals: We can expect an audience that is more inclined to engage, potentially attuned to the historical background of the Frankenstein novel and potentially more open-minded toward technology and interaction with technology than an average audience in a non-semi-public space.

3.2 Evaluation Criteria

The main areas of analysis of general applicability informing our assessment are three-fold; we look at user behavior, use instances and spatial influence and flow impact. In addition to these aspects we are adding case specific abstract measures, which we derive from our specific goals for the *Frankenhead* public interactive.

In terms of user behavior, we are looking at two main aspects, of which the first is how users interact with the installation and the second is how they engage with other players to synchronously interact with the installation. User behavior in conjunction with the spatial influence parameter gives us the best clues to respond to our first evaluation criterion, the landmark and portal function. From the fact that a lot of people crossing the campus square or walking down the thoroughfare, came straight to the *Frankenhead* installation to investigate what it is, tells us that the landmark-function was well achieved. As we did not do exact flow measurements on both the square and the thoroughfare, we can only estimate that attention of approximately 80% of the passers-by was sparked (looking over to the installation and coming closer), and about 65% of those passers-by going out of their intended way to come over to the sculpture. Of the people who came over to the sculpture only a subset could actively play because only a limited number of slots and play-pieces was available. The sweet spot for collaborative play was three players interacting at the same time (c.f. Fig. 4). The majority of use instances was with a concurrent interaction of two to three players. Approximately 20% of the use instances were single users.

Use instances were predominantly short, mostly in the range of 3 to 6 min. This gives us some information about how deep players got engaged into the staged structure of the interaction, one of the case specific abstract measures for the *Frankenhead* installation. We wanted to find out how well the staged design worked, with an easily approachable main game-loop, an intensified engagement including the interaction with the face scanner and the exit to the main event as the last stage. We can clearly say that the overwhelming majority of players (ca. 95%) completed the main game-loop of inserting the play pieces with facial features into their slots and turning them active. Approximately 30% of the players also went on to use the face scanner; the interaction including the face scanner tended to be longer, covering a duration of 7 to 10 min. Even though the actual scanning process was quite fast, the increase in interaction time was caused by the fact that it is not a given that the newly scanned face will immediately appear in the animation cycles of the projection. As these cycles are chosen at random from the entire database, it can take some time for new images to appear. In order to prioritize new facial features to a certain degree, we added an algorithm to pull in the new images within the next 5 to 10 cycles of the animation, which corresponds to a timeframe of 1 to 2 min. Finally, 90% of the players moved on to the main façade projection, once they had turned active the creature they had puzzled together and saw the result appear on the façade nearby.

Another case specific abstract measure was our attempt to find out whether players indeed felt that they had a better understanding of the Frankenstein context and whether they felt that there is still relevance and critical potential in the story. This measure we could only determine through open form conversations that we had with players and others who did not actively play but observed players in their actions. We found that most players where reasonably familiar with the novel's overall premise. Most of those we engaged in conversation felt that there was still relevance to it and that it was such an important piece of literature that it continued to wield influence. The critical note about data collection, privacy and the ethics related to it, was less clearly communicated to audience members, even though we found that some players had a second though about scanning their face into the *Frankenhead* database once they left and were not there anymore to observe play "with their face".

4 Discussion

We found that, upon its debut, *Frankenhead* was a success in capturing the attendees' attention and drawing them into the play space with its size and presentation. The rotating facial features projected onto the sculpture and game pieces spread out on the ground in front of *Frankenhead* intrigued attendees to approach and speculate what was happening. Attendees quickly grasped the goal of the game and proceeded to place the game pieces into the face sockets. Because they don't know beforehand which facial feature a particular game piece represents until they place it into one of the face sockets, they are surprised and delighted upon discovering the facial feature and where they've placed it on *Frankenhead*. The attendees experience a sense of satisfaction when they pull the switch that plays the animation for each facial feature, and accomplishment upon seeing the final, unique *Frankenhead* face they created as a result of their actions.

Many of our attendees expressed joy, surprise, and when they interacted with *Frankenhead*. Our design allowed for many layers of rewarding experiences that encouraged attendees to keep playing to see all the possible outcomes. The more time players spend with the experience, the more layers of engagement they discover: As their first action they discover the different facial features represented by the game pieces; once they decide to pull the switch, they see the final face in action; if players proceed to the face-scanning station, they discover yet another layer of inserting their own faces; and finally, they see it all in a giant projection on the library building. At this moment, players expressed a feeling of surprise, revelation and satisfaction, which gave a sense of closure with the experience.

Though there were some attendees who did not approach the sculpture, there were many who joined in on the game when they saw other people interacting with the game pieces. Other attendees chose to participate in an alternative way by interacting with the facial-recognition station that allowed us to capture their facial features and display them on *Frankenhead*. Offering attendees different ways of interaction allowed a wider range of attendees to participate in the installation.

Creating a landmark installation came with challenges with encouraging attendees to participate in the experience and designing an intuitive gameplay loop for a larger audience. By choosing to build a large-scale puzzle head with projection mapping elements, we created a multi-layer rewarding experience with different interaction methods for players to enter the experience at their own comfort level.

The short duration of the event limits the possibilities of assessment. In the timeframe of one evening only a certain amount of people could interact, which means the results do not allow for a comprehensive statistical evaluation. What we were able to find, though, was a general confirmation of our original design assumptions in terms of approachability and sculpture design. Communicating critical messages with a comparable setting is difficult to do in respect to a precisely testable message. But we found it encouraging to see that people tended to formulate complex thoughts about the Frankenstein novel and its critical potential.

References

1. Aldiss, B.W., Wingrove, D.: Trillion Year Spree: The History of Science Fiction. Paladin Grafton, London (1988)
2. Shelley, M.W.: Frankenstein, or, The Modern Prometheus. In: Colburn, H., Bentley, R. (eds.) London, Bell and Bradfute, Edinburgh (1831)
3. Youngquist, P.: Frankenstein: the mother, the daughter, and the monster. Philol. Q. **70**, 339–359 (1991)
4. Levine, G., Knoepflmacher, U.C.: The Endurance of Frankenstein: Essays on Mary Shelley's Novel. University of California Press (1982)
5. Balsamo, A.: Designing Culture: The Technological Imagination at Work. Duke University Press Books, Durham NC (2011)
6. Kinder, M.: Hot spots, avatars, and narrative fields forever: buñuel's legacy for new digital media and interactive database narrative. Film Q. **55**, 2–15 (2002). https://doi.org/10.1525/fq.2002.55.4.2
7. Buñuel, L.: An Unspeakable Betrayal: Selected Writings of Luis Buñuel. University of California Press (2002)
8. Michelis, D., Müller, J.: The audience funnel: observations of gesture based interaction with multiple large displays in a city center. Int. J. Hum. Comput. Interact. **27**, 562–579 (2011). https://doi.org/10.1080/10447318.2011.555299
9. Cheung, V.: Improving interaction discoverability in large public interactive displays. In: Proceedings of the Ninth ACM International Conference on Interactive Tabletops and Surfaces, pp. 467–472. Association for Computing Machinery, New York, NY, USA (2014). https://doi.org/10.1145/2669485.2669489
10. Norman, D.A.: The Design of Everyday Things. MIT Press, Cambridge, MA, USA (1998)
11. Claes, S., Moere, A.V.: The role of tangible interaction in exploring information on public visualization displays. In: Proceedings of the 4th International Symposium on Pervasive Displays. pp. 201–207. Association for Computing Machinery, New York, NY, USA (2015). https://doi.org/10.1145/2757710.2757733
12. Ten Koppel, M., Bailly, G., Müller, J., Walter, R.: Chained displays: configurations of public displays can be used to influence actor-, audience-, and passer-by behavior. In: Proceedings of the SIGCHI Conference on Human Factors in Computing Systems, pp. 317–326. Association for Computing Machinery, New York, NY, USA (2012). https://doi.org/10.1145/2207676.2207720
13. Kjær Søgaard, A., Jacobsen, B., Utne Kærholm Svendsen, M., Lundegaard Uggerhøj, R., Löchtefeld, M.: Evaluation framework for public interactive installations. In: Media Architecture Biennale 20, pp. 79–86. Association for Computing Machinery, New York, NY, USA (2021). https://doi.org/10.1145/3469410.3469418

Targeting IMPACT: A New Psychological Model of User Experience

Leah Kurta[✉] and Jonathan Freeman

Goldsmiths University of London, 8 Lewisham Way, London SE14 6NW, UK
Leah.kurta@i2mediaresearch.com, j.freeman@gold.ac.uk

Abstract. User experience (UX) models present, in broad terms, the domains of influence affecting users' experience of a given technology. Since the number of variables that could affect a user's experience are manifold and context specific, UX models tend to specify broad categories of influence. Prominent models highlight technology form, content, context, business goals and individual differences as key domains which all affect how a user will experience a technology product or service. These high-level conceptualisations often miss identification of key psychological variables affecting UX. Identifying psychological factors could support user-centred design by designing for user goals, critiquing why different design choices are effective and for guiding evaluation choices. To address this gap, this paper presents a new psychological model of UX, The IMPACT model, meaning Interesting, Meaningful, Personalised, Affective, Collective and Transportive dimensions of experience. The model was developed by reconceptualising an evaluation framework of technology impact and undertaking a literature review. In this paper, we apply the model to a user journey of gameplay, demonstrating the model's use for assessing which strategies build interest, enjoyment and engagement throughout the user journey. Whilst it is not a fully comprehensive psychological model of UX, we suggest hypotheses to empirically test the model for different user types. We offer these next steps as a framework to support gaining new knowledge about gamers and gaming.

Keywords: User experience · Psychological model of UX · Design tool · Affective design

1 Introduction

1.1 The User Journey

The Nielsen-Norman Group defines user experience (UX) as 'all aspects of the end-user's interaction with the company, its services, and its products' [34]. Important in the definition is the recognition of the user journey, from first hearing about a product, to engaging with it, to potentially recommending it to others. Defining the range of factors affecting user experience across the user journey is challenging due to individual, temporal, and contextual dependencies [19, 22].

1.2 Practical Issues: UX Models

In the last two decades, UX research has moved away from a purely functional representation of technology effectiveness and is increasingly interested in the psychological domains of experience, both antecedents and outcomes. In their 2006 review Hassenzalh and Tractinsky chart this rising importance. They state that psychological elements fall into three major domains: addressing human needs beyond the instrumental, affective, and emotional aspects of experience and the combined, temporal influence of contextual and individual differences [19].

Designing for Psychological Outcomes. UX models, which serve as 'thinking tools' to understand these key domains of influence are subsequently high-level, macro conceptualisations of both pragmatic and psychological domains. By remaining high-level they account for the ephemeral nature of UX. However, from an applied perspective these models may not adequately help practitioners critique and evaluate their design choices, where the aim is to design for the psychological outcomes of an experience. Hassenzahl [18, 19] asks whether it is possible to design for psychological outcomes and questions whether emotional and psychological states are too ephemeral and too context dependent to design for. He suggests there may not be a way to guarantee psychological outcomes through product design. We propose the intention of psychological UX models is not to guarantee the psychological outcomes of the design, rather an attempt to clarify what the designer is aiming for and to better assess the intended psychological effectiveness. Without a psychological UX model to inform design, practitioners may not select appropriate evaluation metrics to assess the effectiveness of their products. Indeed there is evidence of this issue; upon examining the UX literature regarding individual product evaluation, the multitude of psychological outcome variables evaluated in relation to experience of technology products (e.g., games, utilitarian products, and immersive technologies) is vast. Variables such as motivation, personalisation, cognition, affect, satisfaction, beauty, presence, immersion, and attention are frequently measured in relation to UX [2, 18, 38, 45, 56]. This suggests two things; there may be common states which are important markers of product success, and that without a model to guide their evaluation choices, practitioners may be overwhelmed by the range of evaluation measures available. Currently, it appears there is limited published research modelling the common factors which denote preferable psychological outcomes of an experience, developed specifically to aid product design. Our model seeks to address this gap.

A review of current UX models demonstrates practical issues for informing design choices. Lessiter et al. [30] suggest the technology form, the content, the context of use, and individual differences are the key domains of influence. This model's psychological component concerns antecedents rather than outcomes of experience. For example, an individual's technology literacy may affect perception of a product. Using this model, a designer may gain knowledge of the contextual and individual temporality of experience, but they would not necessarily determine important psychological outcomes to design for. Simple models of UX highlight that user and business goals shape experience [24, 48]. The CUBI model [48] includes content, user goals, business goals and interaction as its core elements. It then breaks these down further into sub-factors, for example, user goals are a combination of user needs, motivations and behaviours which are said to inform intended psychological outcomes. Using this model, a designer may begin to consider psychological outcomes, but again would not determine key states. These models highlight antecedents of product usability, namely individual differences and user goals, yet they do not identify common psychological outcome domains predictive of a good user experience. We suggest that understanding the important user outcome states is necessary for optimal design and guiding evaluation choices. Many UX models, whilst useful for understanding key domains of UX, are not appropriate for linking design choices to user states due to the breadth of their scope and focus on psychological antecedents rather than outcomes of experience.

Player Types in Games. The tendency to focus on antecedents of experience is also prevalent in gaming research. Much attention is paid to player motivation and how differences in these domains affect game enjoyment. Identification of 'player types' helps the industry consider different user goals and how individuals differently perceive enjoyment. The Hexad player types builds on Bartle's classic typology (Achievers, Explorers, Killers and Socialisers) to help designers personalise gameplay to suit a range of needs and motivations. Researchers correlated 32 common games design elements with each Hexad user type to help map common player traits with design features [15]. Using player typologies does provide some insight into how the nuances of game enjoyment may depend in part on player motivation and personality domains.

Enjoyment of Games. Enjoyment of gaming can be categorised as part of the players emotional response. Multiple evaluation measures for game enjoyment exist which indicate different emotional outcomes. Yet there are concerns around the limited scope of these measures [44] and the lack of validation using empirical research [25] which may decrease confidence in their utility. Furthermore, in practical terms, without a process for hypothesis development to aid design, insights from measurement tools may not easily be interpreted into design decisions [29]. Therefore, linking evaluation methods to design features is necessary for a joined up iterative design process. There are measurement tools which seek to do this, for example Johnson et al. [25] measure both emotional outcomes and the success of controls and Abeele et al. [1] developed a measure of both player action and psychosocial experience to enable designers to link specific player action to response. Whilst these are helpful for linking some common features of games design to intended outcomes of an experience, they do not allow for all design elements to be mapped to corresponding psychological states. As such some design features could be misinterpreted as being more important than others simply due to the absence of an evaluation process for features not listed in current metrics.

A more flexible but less specific approach could use a games UX model to link designs to intended outcomes. Lazzaro's Four Keys to Fun model [17] suggests that enjoyment via fun is the primary psychological outcome to design for. In contrast Eyal [11] suggests that all human behaviour is motivated by reducing emotionally uncomfortable states (e.g., boredom or jealousy). In his Hooked Model he suggests prioritising design choices based on how well they satisfy what the user is psychologically 'missing'. These approaches are two sides of the same coin, they encourage designs which either reduce uncomfortable emotions, or optimise positive ones.

In the domain of emotion, there appears to be linkage of tools and research, from player typologies which help determine key antecedents of games enjoyment, to measurement tools for evaluation of enjoyment and design models to define and articulate the emotional states of interest. We propose that whilst this provides practitioners with a range of tools to design and assess gameplay, it is still limited. Firstly, it prioritises the emotional response, over and above other psychological outcome states, which may miss elements of user satisfaction. Secondly, it focusses all design effort on engagement during gameplay rather than addressing the full spectrum of the user journey. This may lead to a piecemeal design approach which does not fully allow for designs which build user interest, engagement, and investment in the game long term.

A New Psychological Model of UX. Considering these limitations we propose that a the a more comprehensive, yet broadly applicable, psychological model of UX would aid technology design across the user journey, having application for games and many other industries. Whilst there is academic and applied interest in psychological outcomes of experience, to our knowledge models which organise and conceptualises these elements are limited. The IMPACT model helps to address this imbalance by providing a model which practitioners can use whilst developing their designs and to inform evaluation criteria. The IMPACT model is conceptual in approach, and it highlights key psychological states which, if optimised through design choices, should lead to enhanced user satisfaction and loyalty. Future empirical research to test the model's effectiveness in different domains may result in adaptations. While we acknowledge that no model will be fully comprehensive, we propose these states offer a good starting point for designers. Moreover, the model is helpful for developing hypotheses to test which in turn will generate new knowledge about gamers and gaming. The remainder of this paper discusses the model's application to games during all phases of the user journey, to help illuminate how game enjoyment can be optimised.

2 Method: Developing the IMPACT Model

To develop our conceptual model, we evaluated how i2 media research's proprietary measure of audience experience, the Audience Impact Metric (AIM), could be reconceptualised as a design canvas. The AIM is an evaluation measure which was developed in 2017 through sector research and a literature review [32]. The AIM measures 5 key domains of experience; general quality, engagement, emotional intensity, cultural value, and willingness to pay. It has been used extensively to measure audience experience across a range of immersive media productions from theatrical, gaming and arts/experiential content. The AIM also incorporates items from the Sense of Presence Inventory (SOPI) i2 media research's measure of presence developed in 2001 for the Independent Television Commission [30]. The SOPI has been cited in academic literature 1292 times and is used to assess presence across a range of media outputs (e.g., TV, games, immersive media).

Once the initial target states had been defined, we reviewed a selection of relevant literature from several perspectives and disciplines, for example user experience literature, psychology, and audience/cultural literature. The literature reviewed was both scientific and applied since we wanted to capture both how UX is measured and assessed academically and how creative and design practitioners operationalise user experience. Taking this broad view was important for specifying the theoretical components of the model, as well as ensuring accessibility and resonance to the industries we seek to engage in its practical application. Relevant literature was selected based on its contribution to answering our guiding research questions:

- What psychological qualities of user experience are measured in technology evaluation research?
- Which of these qualities conceptually align with the IMPACT model?
- What models of user experience exist?
- What are the similarities and differences in these models?
- What theories support the psychological elements of experience which are measured?

A bibliographic search was conducted on PsychINFO and Google Scholar using a range of search terms ('User experience', 'UX model', presence + UX, psychology of UX.) A total of 74 papers were reviewed to further evidence the domains of experience included in the IMPACT model and align with relevant psychological theory (see Table 1). Theories relating to our conceptual model were selected based on their relative support for the conceptual factors generated in the model.

Six psychological states were defined from our reconceptualisation of the AIM and the literature review; these were:

- **Interesting**: Capturing initial interest through automatic and personalised attentional cues.
- **Meaningful**: Connecting to user values and cultural or universal goals. Meaning goes beyond initial interest.
- **Personalised**: Personalising design features. Personalisation focusses on individual relevance, e.g., achieves personal 'to be goals' [20].
- **Affective:** Emotionally arousing. The affective dimension acknowledges how changes in arousal level are important for maintaining interest and engagement.
- **Collective:** Enabling social experience or ability to connect and share with others. Features may connect individually or demonstrate collective action or community.
- **Transportive:** Feeling presence, sustained attentional engagement. The transportive dimension guides design which resolves user friction and minimises disengagement via distraction.

Each element of the model can be thought of as a 'lens' to apply to iterative design, allowing teams of designers, researchers and engineers to query features and align them with their intended psychological purpose. It is anticipated this will help design teams adopt a human-centred design approach.

3   Applying the IMPACT Model Across the User Journey

The following sections of the paper illustrate the model's application for informing design choices across the full spectrum of the user journey. We firstly apply to model

Table 1. Showing theories which support the IMPACT model dimensions

Theory	IMPACT model dimensions
Attenuation theory of attention [50]	Sensory and semantic processing of stimuli happens concurrently. Individuals attend to stimuli which is personally relevant and meaningful (Interesting, Meaningful, Personalised)
Habituation [13]	Interest in novel stimuli decreases over time as familiarity increases (Interesting)
Self-determination theory [40]	Motivation stems from the need to be fulfilled in competence, autonomy and relatedness (Interesting, Personalised, Meaningful, Collective)
Theory of aesthetic response [4]	Emotional arousal facilitates interest. Theory suggests there is an optimal level of emotional arousal (Interesting, Affective)
Variable reward [14]	Variable reward compels individuals to attend to the stimuli which generates rewards. Dopamine release at variable intervals builds anticipation and arousal (Interesting, Affective)
Biased-competition theory of attention [9]	Processing of stimuli will be biased to personal relevance or that which is within current visual field (Interesting)
The drive theory of social facilitation [58, 59]	An audience helps facilitate performance by increasing emotional arousal (Interesting)
Locus focus sensus model of presence [54]	Proposes that presence is achieved a combination of attention to a stimulus as well as minimising distractions through supported design (Transportive)

to demonstrate the effectiveness of different marketing strategies for initially engaging users; secondly, we show how design choices in games optimise engagement, and finally we show which post-experience user engagement strategies are likely to be most effective for gaining loyalty. The user journey model described is based on The Engagement Arc [6] which identifies three phases of experience, a preparation phase where awareness of the product is generated, an engagement phase where the user is experiencing the product directly and a post-experience processing phase where the user engages in meaning-making, to hopefully build satisfaction and loyalty. The Engagement Arc model was chosen for its simplicity and overall alignment with more complex user journey models [10].

3.1 Awareness

Adopting successful marketing approaches is critical to enticing users into gameplay. Central to deploying a successful strategy is knowledge of the intended audience. This is often achieved through identifying industry trends, applying segmentations, and creating customer personas to identify and describe customer characteristics. Here we discuss how the interesting, personalised, meaningful, and affective dimensions of our model are central psychological states to target within a marketing strategy.

Design Choices Which Maximise Interest. Underpinned by attention theory, the interesting, meaningful and personalised dimensions of our model suggest it is important to make design choices which maximise interest in games by tailoring marketing to user goals and motivations. Targeting these psychological states can help marketing practitioners improve their customer portraits by considering the core psychological components which may motivate or demotivate users to engage with their product. The Attenuation theory of attention [50] suggests attentional allocation to given stimuli is processed visually, linguistically and for semantic relevance concurrently, before short-term memory processing. It suggests that whilst visual and auditory cues are important for capturing attention, users will be assessing stimuli for its personal, semantic relevance at the same time.

This shows that whilst visual design is important, marketing materials which resonate with the personal needs and goals of the user are likely to be more attentionally captivating. Adding personal relevance to visual and auditory cues in any design will optimise meaning making when users are scanning their environment for personally relevant stimuli. Bright visuals and loud sounds may serve as an external trigger to capture attention initially, whereas personalised and meaningful gaming adverts will sustain user engagement and more likely lead to gaming uptake and to enjoyable interactions within gameplay.

So important is initial interest and meaning that the Nielsen-Norman Group argue the overall utility of a product or service *is* its ability to meet a user need and if it cannot meet the need then the other elements of the experience are superfluous. In other words, capture interest in a personalised, meaningful way or risk losing prospective users before gameplay even begins. Establishing interest at the earliest moment in the user journey is important for sustained engagement. When users know why they are interested in a product, internal distraction (such as, users querying "what's in it for me") should be diminished.

Lazzero's gaming model Four Keys to Fun [17] posits that emotion, specifically fun, is key to capturing attention. Serious fun, hard fun, easy fun and social fun are posed as key mechanics to utilise in game design. Yet, Sander and Nummenmaa [42] show that stimuli must be personally salient and relevant to user needs to elicit an emotional response. Therefore, without personally relevant, interesting stimuli incorporated into marketing campaigns, the four elements of fun highlighted in Lazzaro's model would not necessarily be achieved through designs which consider these features alone.

To support longer term engagement and increase the likelihood of experiencing game enjoyment then, we advocate incorporating personally relevant material within marketing content. For example, users could be shown a personalised avatar or personalised trailers of a game focussing on emotionally arousing moments. This design approach could be effective for generating initial interest and an emotional connection between the user and the game before purchase and support on-boarding to the emotional design features present during gameplay.

3.2 Engagement in Gameplay

Once initial awareness and interest is established and prompts purchase or download, users move into direct engagement with the game. Successful game design approaches often focus on creating captivating visuals, developing fun game dynamics (e.g., challenge and reward), designing compelling storylines and characterisation which is then supported by frictionless, easy to grasp controls. We will consider why these design features are successful at the psychological level relating to the IMPACT model.

Optimising Interest via Novelty and Contrast. As with attracting initial attention to a game through successful marketing techniques, an initial trigger to captivate interest is necessary when users first engage in gameplay. Games designers often use contrast and novelty in their visual designs [23]. From a psychological perspective these design features are effective because they capture attention via automatic attentional responses.

Consistent with the Biased-Competition theory of attention [9], high contrast designs are easy to attend to, hard to ignore, and lead to a higher firing rate in neurons in the visual cortex [36]. As such, use of this design feature gains user interest through automatic attentional processes which have evolved to help us effectively detect important stimuli within our environment. Considering Tetris's classic layout, the use of high contrast colours between the background and the shapes moving in the display is key to capturing and sustaining our attention during gameplay. Since reconfiguration of the shapes is critical to the success of the player, high contrast between the shapes and the background is an important design choice. If instead Tetris shapes had blurred edges or were less defined from their background users could become frustrated and potentially disengage since it would be challenging to fulfil the game objective. The visual simplicity of the design allows the player to focus attention on the game dynamics. By helping the user to focus their attention on the critical object, they can better fulfill their goal and optimise their enjoyment.

Regarding novelty, infant research shows that babies attend less to familiar items and more to those which are novel. Over time they attend less to the novel item as it increases in familiarity. This process, known as habituation, is the mechanism by which we understand what is safe in any given environment [8, 13]. A well-established theory, habituation explains why novel stimuli capture our attention. More recent research on novelty suggests that the automatic response is implicated via our orienting attentional mechanism. Johnston et al. [26] explored the ability to distinguish the location of familiar and novel stimuli in a mixed array and showed that localisation accuracy was better for novel stimuli than for familiar. This implies an evolutionary advantage in attending to novel stimuli and that our orienting system is key to this process.

Again, considering Tetris, novelty plays a key role for aiding pattern matching at speed. The design offers multiple combinations of how different shapes might fit together in different permutations of their own format. There are a recognisable number of shapes which the user can easily hold in memory to support building skill, yet there is novelty in how they appear in the display window which serves to capture interest and helps users re-engage with the game over time. Given the aim of Tetris is to reorient shapes as fast as possible so that they fit together, the link to the Johnston et al. [26] study is of note. The novelty of the shapes is likely implicated in our ability to orient our attention to the appropriate area of the screen with the speed needed to succeed in the game. If instead Tetris shapes were always the same colour or appeared on screen in their same configuration, it may be more difficult to orient attention quickly enough. This could lead to frustration, making gameplay less enjoyable and the game purpose less effective. Therefore, knowledge of automatic attentional processes to garner interest can inform the design of visuals and support player goals.

The Role of Novelty in Sound Design. Automatic attentional cues are not just present in visual designs. Auditory cues are also important, particularly given the needs of gamers with sight impairments for whom auditory features serve to make games more accessible and enjoyable [37]. Like visual design, novelty is important to consider in sound design. Research exploring patterns in music indicates that music which establishes repetition at least once and then changes (known as the AAB pattern), serves to violate our expectations and provide novelty. These patterns are said to capture attention due to an innate response of needing to pay attention to that which is novel [39]. *Assassins Creed*, successfully employs this technique, composing a simple refrain in an AAB pattern. The refrain is used throughout the game to highlight emotionally salient elements of narrative and foster greater attention from the player to these emotive moments.

Use of this technique more broadly could serve to better engage audiences and help to capture attention of gamers who may not be able to access visual designs. Making games interesting by exploiting these automatic attentional processes within visual and sound design is one effective mechanism for facilitating user goals and exemplifying emotional aspects of games.

Affective Mechanisms. Whilst visual and auditory design will help establish initial attention and focus, alone it is unlikely to sustain interest in gameplay. Self-determination theory (SDT) suggests ongoing motivation is driven by an intrinsic need for growth which is achieved through developing, autonomy, competence and relatedness [40]. In line with SDT game play may satisfy our need to develop in these domains and research shows the association with game enjoyment [41]. Regarding competence game players improve skills via challenge, competition and reward and as Hunike, LeBlanc and Zubek [21] advocate, this helps *sustain* the interest of the player and is also key to the emotional response. Where intrinsic motivation may help players sustain their interest, the emotional response must provide some form of reward to build engagement over the long term.

Challenge and reward are related to how we enjoy aesthetic experiences generally. Berlyne [4] proposed that experiencing moderate arousal and its resolution is key to enjoyment of any aesthetic experience. Although within gaming we would expect challenge and reward to be interactive mechanisms of gameplay, Berlyne's analysis helps illuminate how novelty and complexity in any design feature can also serve to challenge an audience. Berlyne's theory proposes that the process of resolving challenges, whether that be establishing meaning in an artwork, or resolving ambiguity in a narrative, serves to pique interest and arousal and sustain our engagement until such resolution or reward comes. In practice this translates into feeling optimally challenged by the game so that winning seems possible but is not immediately achievable. Lazzaro [17] describes this as 'hard fun', when players develop skills and thereby resolve complexity and frustration. Games which offer more complex controls and reward users for successful mastery of these skills serve to evoke a strong emotional response through building initial frustration, piquing arousal which then resolves upon mastery and reward.

Easier games still tap into this 'frustration – resolve' mechanic however, they are more likely to achieve this by employing variable reward schedules first discovered by Ferster and Skinner in 1957 [14] and popularised by Eyal [11] in the Hooked Model. Rewarding users for behaviour on a variable schedule sustains interest via reward anticipation and variable dopamine release in the brain [12]. Variable reward has been found to be highly addictive and is the mechanism employed by slot machines to keep users pulling the lever to see what rewards might be released. It is also now widely deployed across digital products (e.g., social media) and the gaming and technology sectors [11]. Whilst it offers short term gains for retaining users, critics of deploying variable reward schedules suggest there are ethical implications such as gaming addiction and manipulation of users [47].

Whilst there is more to be done to ensure user safety, affective designs which capitalise on variable arousal and its resolve via easy or hard mechanics are critical for sustaining engagement and a players return through the gaming loop. When assessing design choices using the affective dimension of the IMPACT model, we recommend identifying the emotional range within the game and opportunities to create and resolve arousal.

Using Personalised, Meaningful Content to Align with User Values. Emotional arousal alone, however, does not necessitate player enjoyment and satisfaction. When compelled purely by emotional arousal (e.g., relief from boredom), users can experience disengagement due to regret. Research on binge-watching illustrates that whilst binging is pleasurable, after a threshold (4 h continuous watching) users experience regret [53]. Regret was experienced when the user perceived they had wasted their time or been prevented from achieving other more meaningful goals. As with binge-watching, hours spent gaming could also lead to regret should the activity be perceived as lacking personal meaning. This leads to our inclusion of the personalised and meaningful dimensions within our model to support successful design. The 'Enabling the Good Life' study in 2017 showed that consumers were moving away from consumption for its own sake to a more meaningful use of technology products. People stated they wanted balanced simplicity and for tech products and services to support them in their values and goals [43].

Serious games such as *Pick your Plate* (a game to help children understand nutrition) and *Breaking Harmony Square* (a game to help people stop disinformation) offer users meaning by helping users achieve life goals [33]. Whilst these games are created primarily with the intent of helping users achieve a goal other than gameplay, this is a key feature of their success. Hassenzahl [20] describes this as helping users achieve 'to be goals' (e.g., those which support aspirations, learning and self-development) which similarly aligns with the core premise of SDT, that development of competence is meaningful for individuals.

Design which supports these personal and meaningful user needs is therefore worth incorporating into non 'serious' games. In 2020 the video games industry in collaboration with the United Nations Environment Programme incorporated environmental missions and messages within popular games like *Angry Birds 2, Golf Clash* and *Subway Surfers* [51]. The companies were responding to gamers' interest in raising money for environmental campaigns through in-app purchases. These moves by the industry in response to consumers echo the 'Enabling the Good Life' findings in 2017 that users are interested in games becoming a medium by which to tap into broader values and aspirations. Using the personalised and meaningful lenses in the model it is possible to separate out features which will optimise general enjoyment and those which will offer users greater meaning and sense of personal achievement.

Collective Design Features for Increased Performance and Emotional Arousal. We have discussed how the meaningful dimension encourages designers to connect their content with wider social causes, yet personal social meaning is also relevant to explore. As Bartle [3] and Yee [57] attest, one of the key motivations to game is to socialise by spending quality time with others in the pursuit of fun. There are several gaming mechanisms which enable social bonding and a collective experience. Cooperation and competitive features allow players to interact with one another or with characters in the game, thus prompting a collective experience, which is shown to increase affect [52].

Social interaction at the individual or group level via competition or cooperation is arguably a defining characteristic of games. However, the larger-scale gaming audience is also important. The recent rise in popularity of platforms like Twitch allow players to be performers, demonstrating their gaming technique and ability to audiences via live streaming. Audiences can use the Twitch platform to chat to players. Commenting on gameplay establishes dialogue, connecting players with their audience. The drive theory of social facilitation [58, 59] is helpful for understanding why platforms like Twitch have gained traction in recent years. The theory suggests that for those skilled in their domain, an audience helps to increase arousal, and this facilitates performance [5]. For the skilled player then, having an audience present via Twitch may increase their performance and enjoyment of the game.

Sustained Engagement via Transportive Experiences. Once we have garnered interest, built affective response, and achieved meaningful and collective engagement, how do we get users to experience transportive states of presence, and why is this dimension important to consider as a separate lens? As we move towards widespread adoption of the 'metaverse' and to a more integrated method of experiencing entertainment, it will be important to re-evaluate how to keep users interested and engaged in games. Although a fully integrated metaverse is still many years away, early releases by Meta are expected in 2022 [46]. Indeed, users can already engage in games across a range of immersive platforms from fully immersive VR to MR and AR applications. Even non-immersive games still incorporate elements of the metaverse, for example Fortnite's inclusion of music concerts with real-world artists Travis Scott and Ariana Grande or the ability to buy designer clothing for Fortnite characters [46]. The way we experience gaming is changing and with it, user expectations. Whilst the IMPACT model is technology agnostic, the transportive dimension of the model is particularly relevant for future-proofing game designs given the expected rise in popularity of immersive technology.

Central to the XR (extended reality; including VR, AR and MR) is the user's experience of presence [49]. Presence is defined as the experience of 'perceptual illusion of non-mediation yielding a subjective sensation of being there in a mediated environment' [16]. Whilst presence is distinct from interest, users do need to be interested to be present [7]. Whereas the interesting dimension of our model encourages designers to think about initially capturing attention, the transportive dimension encourages consideration of design features which prolong engagement. The Focus, Locus, Sensus model of presence [54] highlights the importance of minimising distraction as well as captivating initial attention. This requires a subtle balance of design features to support maintained engagement.

Easy to use controls are one feature which support users to feel transported by gameplay [40]. Controls which are learnable, give users feedback and match their conceptual map should reduce user frustration [35]. Distraction through clunky and difficult to master controls is a common source of user friction, this inability to behave naturally in the environment leads to users feeling disengaged and less present during an experience [31].

One challenge for immersive game designers is creating interaction mechanisms which are simple enough for users to achieve when viewing representations of their controllers in a virtual world. In a study of a mixed reality gaming researchers found that simple gestures such as a thumbs-up or swiping motion supported feelings of presence [28]. The simple design, using interactions already familiar to users, was quickly learnable and did not detract from engagement in gameplay or the narrative. Immersive technology offers designers the chance to blur the boundaries of traditional games and blend them with experiences and complex narratives. While a compelling narrative can help to draw a player in, designers will need to consider the complexity of the narrative with the need for interaction. As attentional literature shows, during task management, (e.g., game interaction tasks) users engage in attentional switching to best achieve aims and monitor for potentially salient distractions [55]. In immersive gaming if users need to interact, and simultaneously focus on the narrative, it will likely lead to switching attention to the salient task at hand. This task-switching where the user goal is undefined is likely to diminish presence and increase friction, since users may feel they are missing something important in the game. We propose therefore, that designs which optimise presence, are those which successfully guide the user to engage in narrative *or* interactive elements with effective signals and signifiers.

3.3 Post Experience

The final phase of the Engagement Arc concerns what happens after gameplay. It describes the player evaluation of the experience where loyalty can be established. A challenge for any product designer is keeping users engaged after an experience has ended. What are the best methods to use to encourage users to recommend a game or to re-engage with a game at another point in time? Whilst the interesting and transportive dimensions of the IMPACT model can be applied to post-experience features, we advise the emphasis of design features should be on the collective dimension which in turn makes experiences more meaningful, personalised and affective.

Collective Design Supports Loyalty. The collective dimension helps designers consider how they leverage social influence and social approval behaviours. Social commerce studies suggest that there are two principal ways to incorporate collective features, either through social features which are embedded into the (gaming) platform, or by connecting with users' social media platforms [60].

Games which connect users to their network are likely to extend competitive and cooperative behaviours and thereby encourage re-engagement, sharing and loyalty. For example, *Candy Crush* allows users to reach out to their network on Facebook to request lives, rather than pay for extra lives. This social component is an effective way of extending the gaming experience via cooperative behaviour. By asking your network for a favour it leverages cooperative and more altruistic behaviour whilst building reputation and awareness of the game via the social network of contacts. *Candy Crush* also extends competitive elements of play by incorporating their brand within Facebook to increase the likelihood of sustained use. For example, users can live stream their gameplay on Facebook and post about their achievements. For the collective network of users, seeing an individual's skilled gameplay triggers what Kim [27] refers to as 'aspirational neighbours', a form of social influence where players see what they could achieve in the game before they have personally achieved it. It stimulates competition and motivation, encouraging users back to gameplay, entering another 'gaming loop'. This prompts the user back into the Engagement Arc or 'hook' [11] where users need to engage with the game again to resolve frustration and gain rewards, prompting dopamine release. As we can see, social design features help to build the gaming habit, increasing loyalty to the game and associated brand.

4 Future Directions

Through this exploration we have shown how design features link to the IMPACT model of psychological outcomes. This should help practitioners design for and better describe their target users. It is also a tool for generating hypotheses and empirically testing elements of the design. For example, one could test the relative importance of different design features for different user groups. We specify several hypotheses of interest to inspire practitioners and researchers to use the IMPACT model as a framework for generating new knowledge of gamers and games.

There are several individual and cultural differences which suggest different responses to the importance of the IMPACT dimensions. Firstly, individualistic, western cultures may require higher levels of game personalisation to appeal to individualistic goals and values, whereas collectivist cultures may prefer games which are personalised at the group level and are more focussed on collective elements of gameplay. Secondly, personality dimensions are important to consider. Extroversion may affect the degree to which the collective design features are preferred, with extroverts preferring more social features compared to introverts. Conscientiousness levels may also affect the degree to which meaningful elements are important with those high in conscientiousness enjoying more meaningful experiences compared to those lower in this trait. Finally, gaming experience may affect the degree to which novel design features can capture attention. Experienced gamers may need a greater degree of novelty in designs compared to novice or younger gamers who will have less familiarity with 'typical' games features. We expect that through testing these hypotheses we could offer guidance on how the IMPACT states interact and affect one another, and how these interactions may change in different contexts and with different user types.

4.1 Limits to the Model

These hypotheses indicate there is much scope for further development and empirical assessment of the IMPACT model. Whilst we propose its use for ideation and hypothesis building, it is not a tool for evaluation. Rather it should guide the selection of evaluation methods and metrics to those which best measure the target IMPACT states once defined in detail by a design team. In line with other models of UX, we assert that high-level categories are helpful thinking aids to stimulate conversation and deliberation during design sprints, whilst allowing designers to own and specify the project goals. Each game will serve different purposes, for example some may target a joyful emotion, whereas others may target fear and jeopardy. The model is not designed to provide this level of detail, since this may constrain the design process, which is not our intention. Although the model does not seek to offer this granular detail, we acknowledge that as a high-level model, it is not comprehensive. It is expected that as new knowledge emerges from future research, the model will be developed either to include other psychological outcomes, or to provide more nuanced guidance in the use of the model as it is applied practically. The model is not intended to create a strict hierarchy of design, rather it should help designers view their ideas in a layered and dynamic fashion and prompt discussion around which features offer most value in different contexts.

5 Conclusions

Through an exploration of the user journey, we can see that using psychological lenses can illuminate why certain game design choices form impactful user experiences. Whether using automatic cues to orient and guide attention, using emotion to build habit, or using social design to increase loyalty, the IMPACT model is a tool which can be applied to any human-centred design process. The model can be used for ideation, to critique designs, and to guide evaluation. Whilst there is much scope for empirical assessment of the model, we hope that this initial view of key psychological states will support practitioners to effectively communicate the value of their designs from a user perspective.

References

1. Abeele, V.V., Spiel, K., Nacke, L., Johnson, D., Gerling, K.: Development and validation of the player experience inventory: a scale to measure player experiences at the level of functional and psychosocial consequences. Int. J. Hum Comput Stud. **135**, 102370 (2020)
2. Battarbee, K.: Co-experience: Understanding User Experiences in Interaction. Aalto University (2004)
3. Bartle, R.: Hearts, clubs, diamonds, spades: players who suit MUDs. J. MUD Res. **1**(1), 19 (1996)
4. Berlyne, D.E.: Aesthetics and psychobiology. J. Aesthetics Art Criticism **31**(4) (1973)
5. Bowman, N.D., Weber, R., Tamborini, R., Sherry, J.: Facilitating game play: how others affect performance at and enjoyment of video games. Media Psychol. **16**(1), 39–64 (2013)
6. Brown, A., Ratzkin, R.: Making sense of audience engagement. San Francisco Foundation **1**, 78 (2011)
7. Coelho, C., Tichon, J.G., Hine, T.J., Wallis, G.M., Riva, G.: Media presence and inner presence: the sense of presence in virtual reality technologies. In: From Communication to Presence: Cognition, Emotions and Culture Towards the Ultimate Communicative Experience, pp. 25–45. IOS Press, Amsterdam (2006)
8. Cohen, L.B., Gelber, E.R.: Infant visual memory. In: Cohen, L.B., Salapatek, P. (eds.) Infant Perception: From Sensation to Cognition, vol. 1, pp. 347–403. Academic Press, London (1975)
9. Desimone, R., Duncan, J.: Neural mechanisms of selective visual attention. Annu. Rev. Neurosci. **18**(1), 193–222 (1995)
10. Digital Catapult: The Immersive Audience Journey. https://assets.ctfassets.net/nubxhjiwc 091/339MNWGlE2nYvzi6oQdBpb/76a0a32be23a0c4278af993895850704/20200715_DC_ 142_AOTFReport_Digital.pdf (2020)
11. Eyal, N.: Hooked: How to Build Habit-forming Products. Penguin (2014)
12. Eshel, N., Tian, J., Bukwich, M., Uchida, N.: Dopamine neurons share common response function for reward prediction error. Nat. Neurosci. **19**(3), 479–486 (2016)
13. Fantz, R.L.: Visual experience in infants: decreased attention to familiar patterns relative to novel ones. Science **146**, 668–670 (1964). https://doi.org/10.1126/science.146.3644.668
14. Ferster, C.B., Skinner, B.F.: Schedules of reinforcement. Appleton-Century-Crofts (1957). https://doi.org/10.1037/10627-000
15. Fortes Tondello, G., Wehbe, R.R., Diamond, L., Busch, M., Marczewski, A., Nacke, L.: The gamification user types Hexad scale. In: Proceedings of the 2016 Annual Symposium on Computer-Human Interaction in Play, pp. 229–243 (2016)
16. Freeman, J.: Implications for the measurement of presence from convergent evidence on the structure of presence. In: Presence at ICA 2004 – Proceedings. https://ispr.info/presence-con ferences/previous-conferences/presence-at-ica-2004-proceedings/ (2004)
17. Games, W.W.P.: Four Keys to More Emotion Without Story (2004)
18. Hassenzahl, M.: The interplay of beauty, goodness, and usability in interactive products. Hum.-Comput. Interaction **19**(4), 319–349 (2004)
19. Hassenzahl, M., Tractinsky, N.: User experience – a research agenda. Behav. Inform. Technol. **25**(2), 91–97 (2006)
20. Hassenzahl, M.: The hedonic/pragmatic model of user experience. Towards a UX Manifesto, p. 10 (2007)
21. Hunicke, R., LeBlanc, M., Zubek, R.: MDA: A formal approach to game design and game research. In: Proceedings of the AAAI Workshop on Challenges in Game AI, vol. 4, no. 1, p. 1722 (July 2004)

22. IJsselsteijn, W., De Kort, Y., Poels, K., Jurgelionis, A., Bellotti, F.: Characterising and measuring user experiences in digital games. In: International Conference on Advances in Computer Entertainment Technology, vol. 2, p. 27 (June 2007)

23. Impey, S.: 7 Incredible Game Design Examples and why they Work. Game Analytics. https://gameanalytics.com/blog/incredible-game-design-examples/ (13 Nov 2018)

24. Jetter, C., Gerken, J.: A simplified model of user experience for practical application. In: The 2nd COST294-MAUSE International Open Workshop "User Experience-Towards a Unified View", NordiCHI 2006, Oslo, pp. 106–111 (2007)

25. Johnson, D., Gardner, M.J., Perry, R.: Validation of two game experience scales: the player experience of need satisfaction (PENS) and game experience questionnaire (GEQ). Int. J. Hum. Comput. Stud. **118**, 38–46 (2018)

26. Johnston, W.A., Hawley, K.J., Plewe, S.H., Elliott, J.M., DeWitt, M.J.: Attention capture by novel stimuli. J. Exp. Psychol. Gen. **119**(4), 397 (1990)

27. Kim, J.: The Compulsion Loop Explained. Game Developer https://www.gamedeveloper.com/business/the-compulsion-loop-explained (23 March 2014)

28. Kurta, L., Freeman, J., Turner-Brown, B., Edwards, H.: The Interaction Paradox; developing mechanics which support presence in mixed reality (2022) (in preparation)

29. Law, E.L.C., Van Schaik, P., Roto, V.: Attitudes towards user experience (UX) measurement. Int. J. Hum. Comput. Stud. **72**(6), 526–541 (2014)

30. Lessiter, J., Freeman, J., Keogh, E., Davidoff, J.: A cross-media presence questionnaire: the ITC-Sense of Presence Inventory. Presence: Teleoperators Virtual Environ. **10**(3), 282–297 (2001)

31. Lorenz, M., et al.: Presence and user experience in a virtual environment under the influence of ethanol: an explorative study. Sci. Rep. **8**(1), 1–16 (2018)

32. Nesta and i2 Media Research: Evaluating Immersive User experience and Audience Impact. Digital Catapult. https://assets.ctfassets.net/nubxhjiwc091/4NRgMh7xiMmK8IIyYqQkuE/1cb04c272a49c96af1b945fdbee0dbdf/Evaluating_Immersive_User_Experience_and_Audience_Impact.pdf (2018)

33. Newbury, E.M.H.: Games Round Up: Serious Games in 2020. Wilson Centre. https://www.wilsoncenter.org/blog-post/games-round-serious-games-2020 (15 Dec 2020)

34. Nielsen. J., Norman. D.: The definition of User Experience (UX). Nielson Norman Group. https://www.nngroup.com/articles/definition-user-experience/ (n.d.)

35. Norman, D. (2013). *The design of everyday things: Revised and expanded edition.* Basic books

36. Pashler, H., Dobkins, K., Huang, L.: Is contrast just another feature for visual selective attention? Vis. Res. **44**(12), 1403–1410 (2004)

37. Rai, S., Ravenscroft, J., Miller, S., Turner-Brown, L., Kurta, L., Freeman, J.: Blind and partially sighted people's experience of the accessibility of digital games (2022) (in preparation)

38. Rousi, R., Sariluoma, P., Leikas, J.: Unpacking the contents – a conceptual model for understanding user experience in user psychology. In: Proceedings of ACHI 2011: The Fourth International Conference on Advances in Computer-Human Interactions. Guadeloupe, FR, 23–28 Feb. 2011, pp. 28–34 (2011)

39. Rozin, P., Rozin, A., Appel, B., Wachtel, C.: Documenting and explaining the common AAB pattern in music and humor: establishing and breaking expectations. Emotion **6**(3), 349 (2006)

40. Ryan, R.M., Deci, E.L.: Self-determination theory and the facilitation of intrinsic motivation, social development, and well-being. Am. Psychol. **55**(1), 68 (2000)

41. Ryan, R.M., Rigby, C.S., Przybylski, A.: The motivational pull of video games: a self-determination theory approach. Motiv. Emot. **30**(4), 344–360 (2006)

42. Sander, D., Nummenmaa, L.: Reward and emotion: an affective neuroscience approach. Curr. Opin. Behav. Sci. **39**, 161–167 (2021)

43. SB Insights. Harris Poll: Enabling the Good Life. https://s3.amazonaws.com/sbweb/docs/SB-Report-The-Good-Life.pdf (2017)
44. Schaffer, O., Fang, X.: What makes games fun? Card sort reveals 34 sources of computer game enjoyment (2018)
45. Shin, D.: How do users experience the interaction with an immersive screen? Comput. Hum. Behav. **98**, 302–310 (2019). https://doi.org/10.1016/j.chb.2018.11.010
46. Snider, M., Molina, B.: Everyone wants to own the metaverse including Facebook and Microsoft. But what exactly is it? USA Today Tech. https://eu.usatoday.com/story/tech/2021/11/10/metaverse-what-is-it-explained-facebook-microsoft-meta-vr/6337635001/ (n.d.)
47. Søraker, J.H.: Gaming the gamer? The ethics of exploiting psychological research in video games. J. Inform. Commun. Ethics Soc. (2016)
48. Stern, C.: CUBI A User Experience Model for Project Success. UX Magazine. https://uxmag.com/articles/cubi-a-user-experience-model-for-project-success (25 Sept 2014)
49. Steuer, J.: Defining virtual reality: dimensions determining telepresence. J. Commun. **42**(4), 73–93 (1992)
50. Treisman, A.M.: Selective attention in man. Br. Med. Bull. **20**(1), 12–16 (1964)
51. United Nations Environment Programme: How video games are joining the fight to save the planet. https://www.unep.org/news-and-stories/story/how-video-games-are-joining-fight-save-planet (18 August 2020)
52. Vorderer, P., Hartmann, T., Klimmt, C. Explaining the enjoyment of playing video games: the role of competition. In: Proceedings of the Second International Conference on Entertainment Computing, pp. 1–9 (May 2003)
53. Walton-Pattison, E., Dombrowski, S.U., Presseau, J.: 'Just one more episode': Frequency and theoretical correlates of television binge watching. J. Health Psychol. **23**(1), 17–24 (2018)
54. Waterworth, E.L., Waterworth, J.A.: Focus, locus, and sensus: the three dimensions of virtual experience. Cyberpsychol. Behav. **4**(2), 203–213 (2001)
55. Wickens, C.D., McCarley, J.S.: Applied Attention Theory. CRC Press (2019)
56. Wu, H., Cai, T., Luo, D., Liu, Y., Zhang, Z.: Immersive virtual reality news: a study of user experience and media effects. Int. J. Hum.-Comput. Stud. **147** (2021). https://doi.org/10.1016/j.ijhcs.2020.102576
57. Yee, N.: Motivations for play in online games. Cyberpsychol. Behav. **9**, 772–775 (2006). https://doi.org/10.1089/cpb.2006.9.772
58. Zajonc, R.B.: Social facilitation. Science **149**, 269–275 (1965)
59. Zajonc, R.B.: Compresence. In: Paulus, P.B. (eds.) Psychology of Group Influence, pp. 35–60. Erlbaum, Hillsdale, NJ (1980)
60. Zhang, K.Z., Benyoucef, M.: Consumer behavior in social commerce: a literature review. Decis. Support Syst. **86**, 95–108 (2016)

Practical Considerations on Applications of the Popularity of Games: The Case of Location-Based Games and Disaster

Nicolas LaLone[1]([✉])(iD), Phoebe O. Toups Dugas[2](iD),
and Konstantinos Papangelis[3](iD)

[1] University of Nebraska at Omaha, Omaha, NE 68182, USA
nlalone@unomaha.edu
[2] New Mexico State University, Las Cruces, NM 88003, USA
phoebe.toups.dugas@acm.org
[3] Rochester Institute of Technology, Rochester, NY 14623, USA
kxpigm@rit.edu

Abstract. In the midst of a disaster event like a hurricane, all electrical, connected objects are typically rendered useless. A lack of connectivity, electricity, and potential mobility issues render devices (and sometimes users) unable to perform their basic functions. The potential for the sheer volume of these devices, of the apps installed on them, are as such that they are an unused canvas of design. We present extensible design, the activity of designing new uses for existing applications that may possess functionality that is useful outside of its intended function. We present a description of extensible design and provide a fictional example of what that approach may provide. In so doing, we help address existing gaps between emergency management and consumer-based communication behaviors during disaster. The "Decentralized Layer," an extension of location-based games like *Pokémon Go, Pikmin Bloom*, and *Harry Potter: Wizard's Unite*, is meant to provoke discussion about the potential use of apps and the app ecosystem past its current, limited expression. We conclude by offering next steps, road blocks, and additional considerations for extensible design that will need to be in order for it to be realized.

Keywords: Game studies · Design fiction · Extensible · Play · Location-based games

1 Introduction

Game studies has been in a perpetual defensive stance by simultaneously attempting to show that games were worthy of academic inquiry and that game studies was a field worthy of academia [1,20]. Having accomplished the task of showing its worth, academia has seen the study of games spread to a variety of disciplines [20] and stabilize in the form of journals, grant funding, college departments, conferences, and special interest groups. The need to move past

© The Author(s), under exclusive license to Springer Nature Switzerland AG 2022
X. Fang (Ed.): HCII 2022, LNCS 13334, pp. 213–233, 2022.
https://doi.org/10.1007/978-3-031-05637-6_13

proving its worth to using the knowledge game studies has generated is becoming more pressing. Small attempts at this have been successful through applications like gamification or serious games, which call back to Huizinga's original debate with Carl Schmitt on the seriousness or lack of seriousness of play [40].

Others have used the tenets of play in an effort to foster games-based learning or actively use the making of games to teach programming through fantasy consoles like PICO-8 [66]; game engines like Twine [8]; programming languages like Processing [59]; and projects like Handmade Hero [47]. Yet, there remains an ever-increasing potential in games that extends past their internal components. The popularity of games and the sheer number of app downloads, physical consoles, and other crowd-based efforts remains a vast, untapped resource. Often in the 10s of millions, the use of these computational resources for contexts other than the various ways we play them could foster new, innovative ways to reconsider games, play, people, non-human objects, and culture in concert.

The contribution of the present research is to present a theoretical realm of design we call "extensible design": the application of new capabilities to existing products. More than modding, hacking, or writing addons, "extensible design" is a way of seeing other products as spaces of play through which other types of development can occur. For example, popular location-based games (LBGs) like *Pokémon Go*, *Pikmin Bloom*, and *Harry Potter: Wizards Unite* afford the player location-based services, a routinized map interface, and certain types of communication tools [55,56].

Each of the affordances of these tools can be used in other ways, for other reasons, and in ways that can benefit not only the player, but other players, places, and contexts [55]. For example, when disaster strikes, the affordances these games possess can be useful to emergency management, disaster response, and first responders whose job it is to understand where survivors might be and what their needs are – and they are available on an astounding scale. With extensible design, we envision ways that users can note their locations even if connectivity to the centralized network is severed. We display this vision through a design fiction [5,15,28,36,51,61].

1.1   A Design Fiction for Extensible Design

Design fiction is the use of speculation to outline, display, criticize, and explore potential futures as a way to facilitate debate and discussion around current modes of design [5,15,28,36,51,61]. Through this concept we outline the creation of an "extensible design" meant to harness the popularity of location-based games as a safety tool given devastation, destruction, and even connectivity loss.

We use "extensible" languages in computer science like lua or, at least, extensible grammars like Perl6, Lisp, Red, and Racket [70] to inform this definition. By extensible, we mean that, within these languages, it is possible to move beyond the limitations of a controlled environment. Programmers can instead create emergent types of structures or syntax that extend the operation of these products to places that the creators and maintainers of the languages did not expect. This metaphor is appropriate as we envision this concept as an extension of what already exists as understood through the task-artifact cycle [11].

Extensible design is additionally tool design using existing tools. It could also be referred to as appropriation [23] or a "design for hackability" [29], though we prefer to think of it as an extension of the task-artifact cycle [11]. The basis of this tool is the standard array of affordances that location-based games possess: friend lists, map-based play, location-based services, and the use of that location on an accurate map. And through this tool, our design fiction begins with a prompt that asks, "what would it take to make a mobile device or internet-enabled device useful in the circumstance of no power, no connectivity, and no ability to communicate?" This prompt is one central to current issues in the domain of crisis informatics [53].

Crisis informatics, or the study of information flow during disaster, has been attempting to harness the sheer number of mobile devices in the midst of crisis for over 15 years [53,63,65]. There are multiple bottlenecks to this research, including a lack of computer science presence in emergency management in any meaningful capacity. The most prevalent bottleneck is that, in the midst of crisis, data lines do not function, electricity does not function, and, without these things, all those mobile devices, tablets, and computers are functionally worthless. This does not have to be. Instead, we develop a design fiction around a fictional, but buildable and relatively inexpensive, Bluetooth transponder. This hardware can be used to create and extend a decentralized mesh network. Through that decentralized network, extensible applications can created that work only on that type of network. These applications are the focus of this work as these apps can be created to work without electricity or connectivity in mind.

To outline this fictional product, we begin by discussing the act of design with specific attention to the task-artifact cycle [11]. The task-artifact cycle, in this case, is the push and pull of designers creating an artifact to perform a task and users engaging with that product in ways designers did not intend, thus forcing the designers to change the artifact and restarting the cycle. After discussing the task-artifact cycle, we begin to provide the foundation for our design fiction, "The Decentralized Layer" by focusing on its needs, its audience, and its intended use. So founded, we then move on to the components, its parameters, and its potential affordances given what it is extensing.

"The Decentralized Layer" is a new use for LBGs manifested by a push and pull between a lack of connectivity and the affordances of LBGs. We offer that transponders can create a battery-powered mesh network that mobile devices can log onto as long as those mobile devices have additional capabilities to harness that local network. These transponders would be inserted into disaster-proof boxes around populated areas that will activate given a lack of electrical current. Upon detecting this potential signal, the extensible applications that exist within popular apps like LBGs, will activate. Using low-energy mode, users might share low resource messages that are geo-coded (e.g., they are trapped and need help, they are assisting others, they are on the move) in order to provide useful information to responders as they enter ground zero.

While this network is active, drones and other equipment that can reach populated regions faster than responders can pull on the meta-data of these applications [45] and feed it to the search and rescue (SAR) teams that will be among the first to arrive to begin to treat others. In offering location and brief descriptions of where survivors are, SAR team members can have an understanding of where humans are and what their needs might be, focusing effort and reducing the need for wide search patterns [38]. In offering this fictional account of a product at the beginning stages of development, we provide a way to not only extend game studies to a practical space, but offer different ways to think about the data generated during a disaster.

2   Background: The Task-Artifact Cycle

This section outlines the design process as it relates to the task-artifact cycle in human-computer interaction (HCI). We begin by discussing a series of decisions made in the foundation of modern computer science. After this, we will discuss scenario-based design and various iterations of user-centered design. Finally, we will connect play to the act of design and move toward extending the task-artifact cycle or "extensible design."

2.1   Whence Does the Task-Artifact Cycle Come?

In order to understand the task-artifact cycle, it is important to situate it in the history of computer science and the design of software. Much of the task-artifact cycle can be followed back to the creation of ALGOL60 [4]. The creation of this computer language was significant for 3 reasons. First, through the work of Peter Naur, Edsger Dijkstra, and Jaap A. Zonneveld, this was the first language that allowed for recursion [16,21]. Second, this language was the first to be compiled and run as software [37]. Third, this was a language that moved the creation of software to be generalized whereas most languages and machines at that time were specialized [16]. The creation of ALGOL60 [4] and the events surrounding Peter Naur and Edsger Dijkstra [49] after its creation help us understand the origin of the task-artifact cycle [11].

Naur, who had played a part in the creation of some of the earliest computer programming languages, believed that individual perception of human-based issues that computers could solve were important. "Programming as Theory Building" was a treatise to this effect [48]. In this article, Naur outlines a concept of design wherein a group of programmers create a program to mediate human activity and stick with that program as it represents the end result of building a theory of human activity [48].

Dijkstra, on the other hand, believed that science, that objective reality was a requisite factor in the creation of software [22]. To Dijkstra, "short is beautiful" was a way to show that only elegant, easily replicable programs should be sought [18]. What this provided was not an understanding of human activity, but of a problem that could be solved mathematically [18].

What this essentially builds toward is a representation of the goals of programming that has expanded to the current day. Naur, on one side, sees a computer program as essentially a theory of human activity that must be continually adjusted [49]. Dijkstra, on the other side, sees a computer program as the shortest answer to a question [17,18]. This binary is not simply one between Naur and Dijkstra, but is often seen within the tensions between qualitative research and quantitative research, natural science and social science, or human factors and HCI.

The consequences of this clash and the subsequent victor can be seen in the various paradigms of HCI [24]. As HCI separated from human factors engineering, HCI inherited the search for simplicity in programming as well as its initial drive to represent humanity through the "elegance" of mathematics [10]. This was translated by early designers as it developed into user-experience engineering, user studies, and user-interface design [24]. Its codification and stabilization was the creation of the task-artifact cycle [11,14].

2.2   The Task-Artifact Cycle

To wit, software is typically the briefest answer to creating an artifact for a task. For example, *Microsoft Word* revolves around the idea of writing. *Microsoft Excel* is a spreadsheet program that allows users to organize data in rows and columns. Whereas answers to questions like, "how can software replicate writing?" the answers themselves, once deployed as software, encounter the pluralism of humanity [17]. Tasks are rarely static and computer programs themselves cannot adjust to meet how a task changes unless re-deployed, patched, or replaced. As a result, programs like *Microsoft Excel* and *Microsoft Word* evolve, the task changes and in turn, the program changes.

Users will appropriate [23,25] *Microsoft Word* as a photo editing program and so attention is paid to affordances that allow users to edit photos in some way. *Microsoft Excel's* task has extended to charts, graphics, and statistical measures. And so, Microsoft's designers have had to adjust *Microsoft Excel*, affording users more and more of an ability to use *Microsoft Excel* as one would use *SPSS*, *R*, or *SAS*. This is the task artifact cycle, a piece of software is created for a task and this locks a company or designer into a consistent pattern of design and re-design as the task changes due to users understanding a program [11]. We can see this process at work through patches, versions, and relaunches.

Yet, within the constant barrage of change, there is an inherent weakness in the task-artifact cycle. While tasks evolve, we must always have a set task that we can afford users to perform. This is a bounded space, a magic circle [32] that must always exist as its current version does. Each new version re-situates the circle, reboots the space for a new version of that task. Regardless of the task or the artifact, its interpretation, context, or the way users use the artifact, the space inside the magic circle stays there.

Another way to consider this is that all of the tasks that have artifacts devoted to them have essentially bounded an area, seeded it, and will keep reinforcing the boundaries. The number of tasks has ever-increased and within the operating environment we now have boundless, single-task-devoted applications. While there are an infinity of tasks that can be performed, these artifacts cannot communicate with one another save for occasional handshakes or token exchanges.

And what's more interesting is that all of these applications are created for tasks that require data connections, electricity, and infrastructure. Artifacts exist in reference to tasks and the underlying assumption of both is that there is a stable environment to perform that task in.

Carroll and Rosen [13] outlined a way to extend this task-artifact cycle through "scenario-based design." This action-oriented method allows for designers to escape the task and make cases for certain kinds of use that go beyond the task itself. While useful for extending tasks and artifacts to potentially overlap one another, there are 3 issues with this.

First, the claims of these scenarios unfortunately often only focus on what is good or what will minimize controversy and increase user-retention. For example, "the mulching of the elderly" outlines the issues surrounding this approach in that fairness, accountability, and transparency are not inherently good [35]. Second, the dissonance of what a designer intends and what a user demands is almost always out-of-balance [11,71]. Therefore, attempting to guess what users want through scenarios is a double-edged sword and both edges could cut users off from their prior knowledge and the task itself.

Finally, the task-artifact cycle has fostered a new type of issue given the growing dissonance between designers and users. There is now a vast ecosystem of applications that cannot communicate with each other or be used for anything but what they are intended to be used for [39]. As such, the dissonance of the sum of all artifacts and their tasks are a tightly compacted, exhaustible list of tasks for stable environments. Use when an environment is not stable means that the space of use for that artifact cannot form at all, use cannot occur. While future attempts would be made to overcome these issues, approaches like adaptive design did not achieve their intended effect [23,46]. We suggest that play is a more useful heuristic for re-considering design.

2.3   Making the Task-Artifact Cycle Extensible

To make the task-artifact cycle [11] extensible, we suggest that we need to think about design through the lens of play. With regard to play; however, it is important to first fully define what play has and currently meant. In the past, play has been defined by Huizinga as freedom independent of real life that contains its own source of order and goals [32]. While useful, Huizinga wrote this definition as modernity and empiricism swept throughout Europe and the United States just before World War 2 [32]. Later, Callois [9] added to Huizinga that play always began with uncertainty and was guided by rules and contained imaginaries that may or may not be set against the real world. More recently, Salen and Zimmerman [64] condensed these definitions to a more simplistic but direct call for play as freedom within constraint.

For the purposes of the present research, we define *play* as an act that does not explicitly identify its affordances (or the potential abilities of an object [52]) before the act begins [7]. Within that act, expression is limited by the focus of the player and limitations of the space in which the act is performed. Play is not a diversion, but a name for the act of *getting something to work* and observing the results [7]. This definition of play allows researchers to identify a number of aspects around which to design research.

Within this definition of play, space and place are still created, it is where the action is [26]. This space, sometimes called a magic circle [32] or playground [7] is impermanent which is why it fits the task-artifact cycle so well. It is constantly reified, dissolved, reformed, and is recursive in that one could go to work and within work, do something new but all circles will dissolve in roughly similar orders. Within those circles, an order exists that is dependent on the people and things inside of it. That order is the task-artifact cycle. The drift between a task and an artifact speaks to the power of constraints embedded in affordances but also to the impermanence of tasks.

By assigning and defining play in this way, the task becomes both focal and extended. Focal in that affordances are still the primary point of design but extended in that affordances are not designed for the task in mind, but their potential for other things in the same space. Disagreement, workarounds, and appropriating affordances for other means are all potentialities within both this definition and the spaces of getting something to work. Play loosens tasks by essentially affording for appropriation potential by allowing the imaginary to exist in the design process. Through this, the task-artifact becomes extensible, we can add tasks to an artifact that are tangential to its central task. To demonstrate this approach, we describe a fictional product we will refer to as "The Decentralized Layer."

3   The Decentralized Layer

This section describes the product in general. Our approach, described above, presumes that the sheer number of devices and apps provides an interesting way to think about safety, accessibility, danger, and destruction of local environments. In essence, we can design software using software already designed and installed. Each city, municipality, neighborhood, or area is connected to a centralized network. That layer of connectivity can be disrupted by everything from car accidents to hurricanes. When this occurs, that area ceases to be able to communicate with any other portion of the centralized network. Yet, while inter-connectivity may be missing, residents of the city will still have objects like phones, tablets, laptops, and portable gaming devices. We envision a decentralized layer, one that allows residents in an area suddenly unable to access the internet, to use their devices to chat with each other and alert first responders to their location and their situation.

In order for this type of system to work, it must be able to exist outside of the centralized web and without connection to the power grid. At the user level, basic functionality must be in place, basic in a sense that it uses little battery power. The functionality needed for this design should have the following parameters.

The system needs a way:

1. to connect devices (hardware);
2. for devices to communicate within that connection (software);

3. to locate the device (and, by proxy, the owner) and provide location data;
4. to provide some context about the user's situation at their location;
5. to note if the user is with others;
6. to note if the user is injured or impaired;
7. to communicate with those around them;
8. to remain private from others but not emergency management; and
9. to call those nearby due to an emergency.

This system encapsulates a number of needs within emergency situations. It also allows for devices that cannot connect to anything to gain functionality as a device that can be used within the current vicinity. All that is required is a Bluetooth-based connectivity hub that can host a mesh network. The software required is an application that can capture location-based data in order to feed to search and rescue (SAR) team members. The final portion is a way for that data to get to emergency management.

3.1 The Hardware

The hardware required for this service must be installed and maintained by local or city government. Private contractors often require terms of service that can be aimed at data sharing or data gathering. So by installing and maintaining these themselves, it can remain open and limited to local use much like tornado sirens or other kinds of emergency infrastructure. But much like tornado sirens, the device must be straightforward, incorporate existing infrastructure, and be invisible, but regularly visible.

To this then, the objects must:

1. have their own rechargeable battery power that is triggered by grid failure;
2. be able to survive catastrophic conditions (e.g., earthquake, hurricane, fire, gun shots, grenades, flooding);
3. be able to last on battery power for up to 24 h;
4. be robust to operating system, hardware, and standard changes;
5. be able to broadcast their signals up to a mile and mesh with other objects of the same type; and
6. (where absolutely necessary) be able to be accessed by a variety of private industry partners by an open-source add-on.

Physically, the box is perhaps the easiest part. The box can be made of cast iron or a similar metal. This would allow the box itself to sustain heavy damage and remain intact. Additionally, these boxes could be placed on the sides of buildings like parking garages, placed on the sides of cell phone towers, and used as park bench infrastructure if they were made longer. Embedded within these boxes could be filaments or wiring that would use the metal as an antennae or signal booster. What is inside the box is more important as while the box itself may be able to sustain heavy damage, the equipment within must be able to survive as well and that is far more delicate.

At their core, the box contains a Bluetooth transceiver connected to a hard drive though more work is needed to explore requirements in terms of potential additional hazards related to batteries. This additional work is needed because Bluetooth transceivers are delicate devices that cannot sustain things like water, impact, or surges. Therefore, the box must be filled with some sort of foam or non-conductive rubber-like material that can allow the objects to survive destructive events. For additional survivability, the transceiver and hard drive can be stored inside of a small enclosure like an Arduino or 3D-printed open-source enclosure. Each device has minimal software on it and has enough space to store the text-based data that will be generated during its use.

Each Bluetooth transceiver is part of a wide-scale mesh network that can be accessed by a variety of applications using an open-source product [2,60]. Functionality is also included at the administrator side for drone operators to connect to the Bluetooth network in order to download and send the data from the hard-drives on the network. The network can be activated for testing using a routine created during its installation. Our example application focuses heavily on play and the mode of exploration that is situated between the two: the map and its interface.

3.2   The App in Specific

In this section, we outline the type of software that will be used to access that network. LBGs have been pushing players out into the city since their creation [44,50,55]. Games like *Pokèmon GO*, *Harry Potter: Wizard's Unite*, and *Ingress*, allow play to be mixed with exploration [27,55,56]. The use of maps as a source of play is well-documented [67,68] and, while LBGs provide a rich stream of research for those interested in maps (e.g. [3,27,31,33,57]), they could potentially serve another use [58].

As a game situated with a map, it is constantly downloading user locations for the local client and storing that data server side. Users who have these types of games on their phone are used to the type of affordances and scenarios that encompass use of these games. The combination of play-based exploration via a map provides an ample affordance space to players whose locations may suddenly become of supreme importance post-catastrophe.

Therefore, we propose that it is possible to use the structure of these games as a beacon (e.g. [42]) or as a client on a mesh network. When the phone cannot locate a cell phone signal, users can instead search for Bluetooth-based access points. Once on that Bluetooth access point, users can load one of these games that have installed the crisis client on it in order to load the crisis interface. See Fig. 1 for a graphic representation of this system in action.

Overall, the app can be deployed on any software that a) has allowed the decentralized layer to tie-in to portions of its environment and b) has a dedicated number of developers maintaining its compatibility with different versions of that software. And that software that ties in to existing software is stripped down to maximize battery time. The application operates from end-to-end in the following three ways.

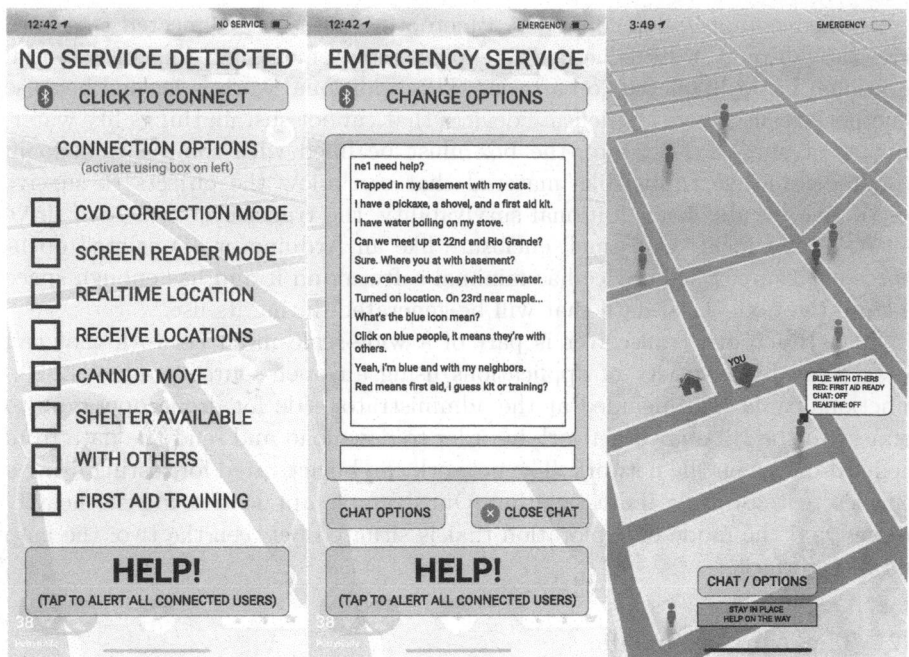

Fig. 1. In this series of illustrations, we can see a user (left) being prompted with the discovery that no service is detected on the device and that airplane mode is not activated. The user is offered a series of options to connect with as well as a button to press that will begin a search for Bluetooth-based connections. In the next illustration (center), the user has connected to the service via Bluetooth. The user can see a chat room and has basic functionality like send to chat, send a ping out broadcasting their location, and to close the chat. Finally, on the right, the user can see the current (last known) position of users on the map itself as represented by the *Pokèmon GO* user-interface. On this screen, different colors on different body parts represent those users having selected different options. Below the button to re-open chat is a status indicator that will allow users to know if a drone has connected to the signal and downloaded location data or not. Once it has, the drone will send that data back to base camp to communicate to Search and Rescue (SAR) personnel. (Color figure online)

First, when users are in a crisis situation, the applications that can access the decentralized layer can be launched and, once they detect no signal, be prompted to connect. The connection between the mesh network and the devices will first, store location data inside of the hard drive foe each node active on the network. By storing locations, with time stamps and additional options selected by the users, drones flying to take initial images of the impacted area will connect to the network and download a delimited data file. There is little need to store images or anything more than basic data that can be sent and evaluated quickly in order to understand where survivors may be. While this focuses on the parameters of the initial connection, there are a number of additional options for that connection before it begins.

Next, as users engage the decentralized layer, they are prompted with the following list of options.

- **CVD (Colorblind) Correction Mode** - This ensures that the colors used by the device will be corrected to maximize the color scheme for other options.
- **Screen Reader Mode** - The data for this option will download a packet from the mesh network that will allow the device to read map-based data.
- **Realtime Location** - This will allow the app to maintain a realtime location triangulated by the nearest Bluetooth Nodes. While this will additionally maintain location data for this device, it will constantly delete and replace the line associated with the device in the delimited data.
- **Receive Locations** - This option will activate realtime location and will download data from the mesh network in order to populate a realtime map on top of the existing interface of whatever app is used to access the decentralized layer.
- **Cannot Move** - When this option is marked, it shows the search and rescue team that is evaluating the data that this person is potentially pinned down or otherwise trapped in rubble. If this item is selected, it will automatically populate a location for other people on the mesh network.
- **Shelter Available** - This option notes on the map that you have room to accept people who might have lost their shelter. This option can be turned off any time in order to show that no more shelter space is available.
- **With Others** - So many people are often surrounded by co-workers, family members, or other members of the public. Marking this option will activate realtime location but show a crowd on screen.
- **First Aid Training** - This option allows members of the mesh network to designate themselves as having received some sort of first-aid training.

Each of these options, can – as with most things – be abused by spoil sports [19,32]. Abuse related to knowing the location of survivors is not without a need for caution. This abuse potential includes marking one's self as having room to shelter others, being around others, and marking one's self as trapped or unable to move. None of these options have to be checked. Simply accessing the network allows the SAR team to know that you are there. Additionally, connecting to the network in any way will allow you to connect to chat.

The chat function is a replica of a localized internet-relay chat (IRC) server wherein chat requires few centralized resources. Everything about this app – save use of Bluetooth power (though this is changing thanks to Bluetooth Low Power [6,75] – is meant to keep phones using as little charge as possible. Chat though, is available for those who need it though it too can be abused. However, given that these applications are not meant to be used unless the area around the user is damaged or otherwise in crisis, this level of risk is reasonable. Training and other forms of help-based text can help users understand risk though we would expect most users to be more concerned with their survival at the time of need. How to overcome this issue requires the paradox of the active user to be confronted [12].

Third and finally, the map interface itself allows users to witness who is near them. Each device is shown as a low-poly figure that is color-coded according to the options that they picked. While viewing the map, each individual that is nearby can be touched to see what options they have selected. When the option for having shelter available is marked, it will be shown as a small house on the map. By showing who is where and what options have been selected, users can congregate, or avoid, others. Or, if users are trapped and unable to move, they may be able to be located and helped before SAR teams arrive.

This aspect of the map will be draining on batteries. As such, it will be updated every 30 s. At the bottom of the map where users can go back to options and the chat box will be a color-coded box that marks 3 different options:

- **Red** - This color means that that device's data has not been downloaded by a drone yet. This color will include the message, "location not delivered."
- **Yellow** - This color means that the device's data has been downloaded but that nothing has been dispatched to the field quite yet. This color will include the message, "location delivered, awaiting dispatch."
- **Green** - This color notes that the users in that area should stay in place and that help is on the way. This color will include the message, "Stay in place. Help on the way."
- Each of these colors can be altered for color blindness.

The way that this data is updated is first by a drone accessing the data and transmitting it to base camp. The data is then analyzed and a special package is sent to another drone that is monitoring traffic. People in a geographic location that has been assigned to a SAR team will be sent a special ping that changes the color and message on that specific bar.

4   Author's Statement and Discussion

Within the current mode of design, production, and deployment, the task-artifact cycle stands as the standard mode of operations. While this mode has been useful and productive, the likelihood that software devoted to a task will include tie-ins for additional tasks or potentials is extremely low. However, there is an opportunity (and potentially a requirement) for extensible design to afford these software far more uses than they currently possess and these can be pursued with, or without the original creators. We have presented a play-centric interpretation of the task-artifact cycle we call extensible design. Within this paradigm, we presented a fictional approach to design, one that takes existing products and blends portions of the artifact in a way as to allow them to be re-purposed when needed.

The application we outlined in the previous design fiction presents what we refer to as the "decentralized layer," a bounded space that will appear and connect internet-enabled devices temporarily given the eventuality of a disaster-level event. We outlined this layer and an application to show what the extended task-artifact cycle would perceive of existing tasks, potential needs within the city, and how to begin to design around them. While disruptive in its own right in terms of intellectual property, private or closed source software, and issues involving permissions and rights on operating systems, what this design provides is a fictional account of a way that designers could maintain their normal mode of operation while fostering a more ingredient-based aspect of design.

An important aspect of this design is not so much the basics of how it could work should it exist, but in the infrastructure and additional work needed for the application to work at all. The assumptions made by the authors allows us to re-contextualize and explain some aspects of the design that have to either be answered elsewhere or worked around. Next, because of the way that software has been created over time it is important to note that there is a supreme amount of labor, hardware, and materials that need to be paid for by someone. Finally, there are the users themselves. How do users 1) learn that these systems exist 2) download them before a disaster event and 3) use them under potentially life-threatening conditions?

4.1 The Assumptions Made by the Authors

The assumptions of this design are set by the authors in order to highlight the needs of a product that is designed to support disruption in addition to its normal functions. In this case, the design is focused on large-scale disasters and incorporate software, especially software that use maps. It should be this way because this type of design will provide essential services according to the author's previous work in non-GIS-based maps and mapping technologies [38, 67,68]. Further, in the interest of keeping this design fiction as non-fiction as possible, we needed to use products that exist and materials that exist.

Since we are designing for a municipal government and are partnering with private industry (in this case, Niantic, makers of *Pokèmon GO*), there are additional aspects specific to what we have in mind. First, while private industry will have the capacity to absorb certain kinds of expenses at the behest of government entities, local governments will have to pay for hardware themselves. As a result, there are three specific assumptions that center on hardware and the city's perspective.

1. From material to components, everything must be off-the-shelf, easily installed, inexpensive, and physically hearty.
2. Everything must be decentralized but use existing technologies that will remain compatible for a time of 10 years or more.
3. Everything must be testable (like tornado sirens), public, and open.

By keeping hardware to easily used and configured off-the-shelf components, these can be purchased in bulk and assembled quickly. Alternatively, an open-source community could offer municipalities access to their systems at cost [30].

An aspect of designs like these will be in keeping up with operating system patches, application patches, and other ways that hardware and software lose compatibility. As a result, these products must be selected on the basis of their continual use. Finally, testing is incredibly important for any safety-oriented tool. Much like tornado sirens, software like this needs to have a test mode that activates the network. This can be a tremendous source of city participation with mesh-network-based messages to all participants on the network for password protected deals and brief sales.

In following these parameters, we can appropriately ground any hardware design that comes out of this extended version of the task-artifact cycle. Next, in order to ground this even further, we needed another metaphor to help situate this product in terminology that designers are used to. This will help us move from describing this work through play, a somewhat opaque and loaded term, to something more useful for designers. The use of a metaphor will guide us toward the intent behind the product we will describe. In doing this, not only can we deploy extensible design, but provide new tools for consumers to use in the midst of disaster that emergency management can use easily, thus meeting the suggestions of crisis informatics about technology adoption [54,62].

We used the concept of "extensible" languages in computer science like lua or, at least, extensible grammars like Perl6, Lisp, Red, and Racket to achieve this end [70]. By extensible, we mean that, within these languages, it is possible to move beyond the limitations of a controlled environment. Programmers can instead create new types of structures or syntax that extend the operation of these products to places that the creators and maintainers of the languages did not expect. This metaphor is appropriate as the previous sections outlined a design paradigm centered on play and disruption. Design would – by default – be outside the intended limits of the environment.

By extending the design of products like that of extensible languages, we can conceptualize hardware that can be accessed by many different programs with specific, open and pre-installed software. With software, the competitive, profit-driven aspect of the apps aimed at extending is as such that there needs to be a set of limits for extension in order to minimize their diversity. And so, within the existing three assumptions that center on the environment that the hardware will exist in, we then see three additional assumptions for the software portion of this design, or the private industry's involvement. These assumptions are:

1. Installed with existing applications.
2. Easily applied to any design or language, open source, and well-commented.
3. Applications that use these hardware will be advertised for free throughout the city.

With this in mind, the components of this design are hardware and software in the form of an application that is installed on the side of existing applications. Since this product would exist within the city and is safety-oriented, the type and severity of the emergency being used as a design inspiration is important. This would allow cities to offer posters and training to use these products. Publicity can also be performed through private partners who open up their products to those interested in the initiative.

In this capacity, we will designed around total failure states. For example, a flood, widespread destruction due to an earthquake, or failure of the electrical grid of a particular area of a city due to some sort of event. While this type of event is rare, it allows us to highlight certain kinds of potential for extensible design. Through these assumptions, we are able to 1) reach designers using terminology that they can understand, 2) grounded design in the nearest future possible, and 3) set up a context for use and design. In the next section, we further discuss the maintenance and installation of those systems.

4.2 Software Creation, Maintenance, and Change

Extensible design is perhaps a thought manifested by a pollyanna, those who see things only as positive and ignore all negatives. Extensible design, as outlined, may potentially neglect the incredibly complicated politics and history of software production, city management, civil engineering, disaster science, and innumerable other domains. Yet, we believe that extensible design affords each of those domains a new approach to consider, one that may potentially get us away from the stalemates and stopping points of those domains. By maneuvering focus away from artifacts created in the current task-artifact cycle, extensible design can foster more consideration for the social life of apps after their creation and those outside of the task-artifact cycle.

Cities and municipalities do not often have the capacity to maintain, produce, or install this type of product. Civic software has often been seen as a useless gesture or at best, one meant to provide support from a company that is then given to a municipality and summarily abandoned due to its lack of support [69]. By fostering cooperation among different actors within the creation process, maintenance, change, and creation is distributed to the effect that one would expect the Pareto principle, or power laws, to carry the creation, maintenance, and change forward by removing a single driver from the project [74].

The software created for this applications is created and maintained by open source allies. This space has recently begun to maneuver itself into becoming more welcome when new contributors engage a product [43]. Additionally, through concepts like the software carpentry movement [72,73], participation in highly technical aspects of programming is becoming more widespread. By fostering these aspects of design, of democratizing design, this method of mutually dependent development can foster further cooperation among disparate actors. Open source work with corporate contributors has become a far more pronounced aspect of open source work and should provide much needed lubricant for acceleration in this space [34].

4.3   User Training and Knowledge Building

The last aspect of this product is one of the paradox of the active user [12]. Within this concept, users will bring their knowledge of how other tasks have worked in the past through artifacts and attempt to deploy that knowledge on the product before them. The crux of this paradox is situated within the task-artifact cycle. The potential to misinterpret a task when it is translated by a design team and embedded in an artifact results constantly rises. The likelihood of disagreement between various interpretations of that task and because software design is hierarchically situated, designers will always have power of that artifact and, by and large, the task itself. By extending the cycle through play, by understanding that a product should be situated not in an experience, not in a task, but as an ingredient that can be used in multiple ways, we expect that the paradox of the active user could not only be ignored, but overcome.

This is perhaps the most difficult aspect of this design fiction to accept as suspension of disbelief can only be pushed so far. Users using products how they want, or how they need to independent of user experience design, user interface design, or a product's overall afforded intent is simply removed in favor of use independent of design. Yet, much like *Robinson Crusoe* in *Friday, the Other Island*, detonating all of those concepts may irrevocably free us [41] from the task-artifact cycle completely. As such, there is little to say here but to "wait and see."

5   Conclusion

In this design fiction, we outlined "extensible design" or the use of existing software in special circumstances. We defined extensible design by situating play, the constant formation of self-contained, self-defining spaces, as a lens through which to see design as ingredient-focused rather than task-artifact-focused. We then provided a fictional description of a potential system that could be built with this lens. The system, the "decentralized layer" is a 2-part system that places Bluetooth transceivers throughout a city that will activate given the catastrophic loss of power.

Once the system activates, users can access a decentralized network that additionally uses existing software to connect users to chat, location-based affordances, and brief signaling options that can be easily downloaded and sent back to a SAR basecamp so that personnel can be dispatched to areas where help is needed most. While waiting for help, users within the decentralized layer can find each other, self-organize, and triage each other's harm as best they can before trained help arrives. While this application requires a moderate amount of work dissolving barriers of access, barriers of resources, and barriers of computational knowledge, this lens provides a way through which to 1) view those barriers, 2) understand how they are created, and 3) distribute responsibility to enough partners to allow the project to succeed.

More design fiction, more world building, is needed to realize the potential of extensible design. The sheer number of mobile devices and applications installed in the centralized network that connects us all to each other has other uses and this concept of extensible design affords those objects more uses than they currently contain. Play, though it may seem antithetical, is an essential lens for that confrontation. Through the lens of play, we see apps and devices not as a magic circle in and of themselves, but as another ingredient, another tool through which to consider design. And in so doing, our obscenely complex ecosystem of apps, devices, and users can find new avenues of growth.

References

1. Aarseth, E.: Computer game studies, year one. Game studies **1**(1), 1–15 (2001)
2. Aggelou, G.: Wireless Mesh Networking. McGraw-Hill Professional, New York (2008)
3. Alha, K., Koskinen, E., Paavilainen, J., Hamari, J.: Why do people play location-based augmented reality games: a study on Pokémon GO. Comput. Hum. Behav. **93**, 114–122 (2019)
4. Backus, J.W., et al.: Report on the algorithmic language ALGOL 60. Commun. ACM **3**(5), 299–314 (1960)
5. Baumer, E.P., Blythe, M., Tanenbaum, T.J.: Evaluating design fiction: the right tool for the job. In: Proceedings of the 2020 ACM Designing Interactive Systems Conference, pp. 1901–1913 (2020)
6. Bernardos, A.M., Bergesio, L., Metola, E., Ortiz, D., Casar, J.R.: Deploying a BTLE positioning system: practical issues on calibration. In: 2017 IEEE 28th Annual International Symposium on Personal, Indoor, and Mobile Radio Communications (PIMRC), pp. 1–6. IEEE (2017)
7. Bogost, I.: Play Anything: The Pleasure of Limits, the Uses of Boredom, & the Secret of Games. Basic Books, New York (2016)
8. Boom, K.H., Ariese, C.E., van den Hout, B., Mol, A.A., Politopoulos, A.: Teaching through play: using video games as a platform to teach about the past. In: Communicating the Past, vol. 27 (2020)
9. Caillois, R.: Man, Play, and Games. University of Illinois Press, Champaign (2001)
10. Card, S.K., Moran, T.P., Newell, A.: The model human processor - an engineering model of human performance. Handb. Percept. Hum. Perform. **2**(45-1) (1986)
11. Carroll, J.M., Kellogg, W.A., Rosson, M.B.: The task-artifact cycle. In: Designing Interaction: Psychology at the Human-Computer Interface, pp. 74–102. Cambridge University Press (1991)
12. Carroll, J.M., Rosson, M.B.: Paradox of the active user. In: Interfacing Thought: Cognitive Aspects of Human-Computer Interaction, pp. 80–111. MIT Press (1987)
13. Carroll, J.M., Rosson, M.B.: Getting around the task-artifact cycle: how to make claims and design by scenario. ACM Trans. Inf. Syst. (TOIS) **10**(2), 181–212 (1992)
14. Corsar, D., Edwards, P., Baillie, C., Markovic, M., Papangelis, K., Nelson, J.: GetThere: a rural passenger information system utilising linked data & citizen sensing. In: Proceedings of the 12th International Semantic Web Conference (Posters & Demonstrations Track), ISWC-PD 2013, vol. 1035, pp. 85–88. CEUR-WS.org, Aachen, DEU (2013)
15. Coulton, P., Lindley, J., Sturdee, M., Stead, M.: Design fiction as world building. In: Proceedings of the 3rd Biennial Research Through Design Conference, pp. 163–179 (2017)

16. Daylight, E.G.: Dijkstra's rallying cry for generalization: the advent of the recursive procedure, late 1950s-early 1960s. Comput. J. **54**(11), 1756–1772 (2011)
17. Daylight, E.G., Grave, K.D.: Pluralism in Software Engineering: Turing Award Winner Peter Naur Explains. Lonely Scholar, Zurich (2011)
18. Daylight, E.G., Wirth, N., Hoare, T., Liskov, B., Naur, P., Grave, K.D.: The Dawn of Software Engineering: From Turing to Dijkstra. Lonely Scholar, Zurich (2012)
19. DeKoven, B.: The Well-Played Game: A Player's Philosophy. MIT Press, Cambridge (2013)
20. Deterding, S.: The pyrrhic victory of game studies: assessing the past, present, and future of interdisciplinary game research. Games Culture **12**(6), 521–543 (2017)
21. Dijkstra, E.W.: Recursive programming. Numer. Math. **2**(1), 312–318 (1960)
22. Dijkstra, E.W., et al.: Notes on structured programming (1970)
23. Dix, A.: Designing for appropriation. In: Proceedings of HCI 2007 The 21st British HCI Group Annual Conference University of Lancaster, UK, vol. 21, pp. 1–4 (2007)
24. Dix, A.: Human-computer interaction, foundations and new paradigms. J. Vis. Lang. Comput. **42**, 122–134 (2017)
25. Dourish, P.: The appropriation of interactive technologies: some lessons from placeless documents. Comput. Supported Cooper. Work (CSCW) **12**(4), 465–490 (2003)
26. Dourish, P.: Where the Action Is: The Foundations of Embodied Interaction. MIT Press, Cambridge (2004)
27. Dunham, J., Papangelis, K., LaLone, N., Wang, Y.: Casual and hardcore player traits and gratifications of Pokémon GO, Harry Potter: Wizards Unite, Ingress. arXiv preprint arXiv:2103.00037 (2021)
28. Dunne, A., Raby, F.: Speculative Everything: Design, Fiction, and Social Dreaming. MIT Press, Cambridge (2013)
29. Galloway, A., Brucker-Cohen, J., Gaye, L., Goodman, E., Hill, D.: Design for hackability. In: DIS 2004: Proceedings of the 5th Conference on Designing Interactive Systems, pp. 363–366. ACM Press (2004)
30. Germonprez, M., Hovorka, D.S.: Member engagement within digitally enabled social network communities: new methodological considerations. Inf. Syst. J. **23**(6), 525–549 (2013)
31. Hamari, J., Malik, A., Koski, J., Johri, A.: Uses and gratifications of Pokémon GO: why do people play mobile location-based augmented reality games? Int. J. Hum.-Comput. Interact. **35**(9), 804–819 (2019)
32. Huizinga, J.: Homo Ludens: A Study of the Play-Element in Culture. Martino Fine Books, Eastford (2014)
33. Jones, C., Papangelis, K.: Reflective practice: lessons learnt by using board games as a design tool for location-based games. In: Kyriakidis, P., Hadjimitsis, D., Skarlatos, D., Mansourian, A. (eds.) AGILE 2019. LNGC, pp. 291–307. Springer, Cham (2020). https://doi.org/10.1007/978-3-030-14745-7_16
34. Kendall, K.E., Kendall, J.E., Germonprez, M., Mathiassen, L.: The third design space: a postcolonial perspective on corporate engagement with open source software communities. Inf. Syst. J. **30**(2), 369–402 (2020)
35. Keyes, O., Hutson, J., Durbin, M.: A mulching proposal: analysing and improving an algorithmic system for turning the elderly into high-nutrient slurry. In: Extended Abstracts of the 2019 CHI Conference on Human Factors in Computing Systems, pp. 1–11 (2019)
36. Knutz, E., Markussen, T.: The role of fiction in experiments within design, art & architecture-towards a new typology of design fiction. Artifact: J. Des. Pract. **3**(2), 8–1 (2014)

37. Kruseman Aretz, F.: The Dijkstra-Zonneveld ALGOL 60 compiler for the electro-logica X1 (2003)
38. LaLone, N., Alharthi, S., Toups Dugas, P.O.: A vision of augmented reality for urban search and rescue. In: Proceedings of the 1st Halfway to the Future Symposium, pp. 1–5. ACM, Nottingham, UK (2019)
39. LaLone, N.J.: Association mapping: social network analysis with humans and non-humans. Ph.D. thesis, The Pennsylvania State University (2018)
40. Lambrow, A.: The seriousness of play: Johan Huizinga and Carl Schmitt on play and the political. Games Culture 16(7), 820–834 (2021)
41. Latour, B.: The Pasteurization of France. Harvard University Press, Cambridge (1993)
42. Lin, X.Y., Ho, T.W., Fang, C.C., Yen, Z.S., Yang, B.J., Lai, F.: A mobile indoor positioning system based on iBeacon technology. In: 2015 37th Annual International Conference of the IEEE Engineering in Medicine and Biology Society (EMBC), pp. 4970–4973. IEEE (2015)
43. Lumbard, K., Buhman, A., Wethor, G.E., Hale, M., Goggins, S., Germonprez, M.: Welcome? Investigating the reception of new contributors to organizational-communal open source software projects. In: AMCIS 2020 Proceedings. AMCIS (2020)
44. Matyas, S., Matyas, C., Schlieder, C., Kiefer, P., Mitarai, H., Kamata, M.: Designing location-based mobile games with a purpose: collecting geospatial data with CityExplorer. In: Proceedings of the 2008 International Conference on Advances in Computer Entertainment Technology, pp. 244–247 (2008)
45. Meo, R., Roglia, E., Bottino, A.: The exploitation of data from remote and human sensors for environment monitoring in the SMAT project. Sensors 12(12), 17504–17535 (2012)
46. Moran, T.P.: Everyday adaptive design. In: Proceedings of the 4th Conference on Designing Interactive Systems: Processes, Practices, Methods, and Techniques, pp. 13–14 (2002)
47. Muratori, C.: Handmade hero (2021). https://handmadehero.org/
48. Naur, P.: Programming as theory building. Microprocess. Microprogram. 15(5), 253–261 (1985)
49. Naur, P.: Computing: a human activity. ACM (1992)
50. Nicklas, D., Pfisterer, C., Mitschang, B.: Towards location-based games. In: Proceedings of the International Conference on Applications and Development of Computer Games in the 21st Century: ADCOG, vol. 21, pp. 61–67 (2001)
51. Noortman, R., Schulte, B.F., Marshall, P., Bakker, S., Cox, A.L.: HawkEye - deploying a design fiction probe. In: Proceedings of the 2019 CHI Conference on Human Factors in Computing Systems, CHI 2019, pp. 422:1–422:14. ACM, New York (2019). https://doi.org/10.1145/3290605.3300652
52. Norman, D.: The Design of Everyday Things: Revised and Expanded Edition. Basic Books, New York (2013)
53. Palen, L., et al.: Crisis informatics: human-centered research on tech & crises (2020)
54. Palen, L., Anderson, K.M.: Crisis informatics-new data for extraordinary times. Science 353(6296), 224–225 (2016)
55. Papangelis, K., Chamberlain, A., LaLone, N., Cao, T.: Insights and lessons learned from the design, development and deployment of pervasive location-based mobile systems "in the wild". In: Soares, M.M., Rosenzweig, E., Marcus, A. (eds.) HCII 2021. LNCS, vol. 12781, pp. 79–89. Springer, Cham (2021). https://doi.org/10.1007/978-3-030-78227-6_7

56. Papangelis, K., et al.: Locating identities in time: an examination of the formation and impact of temporality on presentations of the self through location-based social networks. ACM Trans. Soc. Comput. (TSC) **4**(3), 1–23 (2021)
57. Papangelis, K., Metzger, M., Sheng, Y., Liang, H.N., Chamberlain, A., Khan, V.J.: "Get off my lawn!": starting to understand territoriality in location based mobile games. In: CHI EA 2017 Proceedings of the 2017 CHI Conference Extended Abstracts on Human Factors in Computing Systems, pp. 1955–1961. ACM Press (2017). http://dl.acm.org/citation.cfm?doid=3027063.3053154
58. Papangelis, K., Sheng, Y., Liang, H.N., Chamberlain, A., Khan, V.J., Cao, T.: Unfolding the interplay of self-identity and expressions of territoriality in location-based social networks. In: Proceedings of the 2017 ACM International Joint Conference on Pervasive and Ubiquitous Computing and Proceedings of the 2017 ACM International Symposium on Wearable Computers. ACM (2017). https://doi.org/10.1145/3123024.3123081
59. Pellicer, J.L., Blanes, J.S., Tormos, P.M., Frau, D.C.: Using processing.org in an introductory computer graphics course. In: Eurographics 2009-Education Papers, pp. 23–28 (2009)
60. Raniwala, A., Chiueh, T.C.: Architecture and algorithms for an IEEE 802.11-based multi-channel wireless mesh network. In: Proceedings IEEE 24th Annual Joint Conference of the IEEE Computer and Communications Societies, vol. 3, pp. 2223–2234. IEEE (2005)
61. Reeves, S., Goulden, M., Dingwall, R.: The future as a design problem. Des. Issues **32**(3), 6–17 (2016)
62. Reuter, C., Hughes, A.L., Kaufhold, M.A.: Social media in crisis management: an evaluation and analysis of crisis informatics research. Int. J. Hum.-Comput. Interact. **34**(4), 280–294 (2018)
63. Reuter, C., Kaufhold, M.A.: Fifteen years of social media in emergencies: a retrospective review and future directions for crisis informatics. J. Contingencies Crisis Manag. **26**(1), 41–57 (2018)
64. Salen, K., Zimmerman, E.: Rules of Play: Game Design Fundamentals. MIT Press, Cambridge (2004)
65. Tan, M.L., Prasanna, R., Stock, K., Hudson-Doyle, E., Leonard, G., Johnston, D.: Mobile applications in crisis informatics literature: a systematic review. Int. J. Disaster Risk Reduction **24**, 297–311 (2017)
66. Toftedahl, M., Engström, H.: A taxonomy of game engines and the tools that drive the industry. In: DiGRA 2019, The 12th Digital Games Research Association Conference, Kyoto, Japan, 6–10 August 2019. Digital Games Research Association (DiGRA) (2019)
67. Toups Dugas, P.O., Lalone, N., Alharthi, S.A., Sharma, H.N., Webb, A.M.: Making maps available for play: analyzing the design of game cartography interfaces. ACM Trans. Comput.-Hum. Interact. **26**(5), 30:1-30:43 (2019). https://doi.org/10.1145/3336144
68. Toups Dugas, P.O., LaLone, N., Spiel, K., Hamilton, B.: Paper to pixels: a chronicle of map interfaces in games. In: Proceedings of the 2020 ACM Designing Interactive Systems Conference, DIS 2020, pp. 1433–1451. Association for Computing Machinery, New York, NY, USA (2020). https://doi.org/10.1145/3357236.3395502
69. Townsend, A.M.: Smart Cities: Big Data, Civic Hackers, and the Quest for a New Utopia. WW Norton & Company, New York (2013)

70. Tsai, W.T., Tu, Y., Shao, W., Ebner, E.: Testing extensible design patterns in object-oriented frameworks through scenario templates. In: Proceedings of the Twenty-Third Annual International Computer Software and Applications Conference (Cat. No. 99CB37032), pp. 166–171. IEEE (1999)

71. Vermeulen, J., Luyten, K., van den Hoven, E., Coninx, K.: Crossing the bridge over Norman's Gulf of Execution: revealing feedforward's true identity. In: Proceedings of the SIGCHI Conference on Human Factors in Computing Systems, pp. 1931–1940 (2013)

72. Wilson, G.: Software carpentry: getting scientists to write better code by making them more productive. Comput. Sci. Eng. 8(6), 66–69 (2006)

73. Wilson, G.: Software carpentry: lessons learned. F1000Research 3 (2014)

74. Yamashita, K., McIntosh, S., Kamei, Y., Hassan, A.E., Ubayashi, N.: Revisiting the applicability of the pareto principle to core development teams in open source software projects. In: Proceedings of the 14th International Workshop on Principles of Software Evolution, pp. 46–55 (2015)

75. Zhao, X., Xiao, Z., Markham, A., Trigoni, N., Ren, Y.: Does BTLE measure up against WiFi? A comparison of indoor location performance. In: European Wireless 2014; 20th European Wireless Conference, pp. 1–6. VDE (2014)

Research on the User Experience of Affordance of the Cube Game Interface Design

Hongyu Li[1,2](✉) and Chien-Hsiung Chen[2]

[1] Ningbo Childhood of Educations College, Ningbo 315336, Zhejiang, China
hongyuli521@gmail.com
[2] Department of Design, National Taiwan University of Science and Technology,
Taipei 106335, Taiwan

Abstract. Revisiting the classic, the Tetris game was once a leader in handheld games and a well-known. The advancement of digitization has changed the way people entertain and live, and the wide application of mobile terminal devices has enriched and diversified game content and forms. This study focuses on affordance visual perception to explore the user experience of Tetris game iterative development in new media communication. A 2×3 mixed factorial experimental design was applied to help comprehend whether different Gender (i.e., Male and Female) and Operation Mode (i.e., Single, Double, and Multiple) may influence users' task performance and subjective evaluation. Using the convenience sampling method, a total of 12 participants were recruited to take part in the experiment. The results show that: (1) There is a significant difference in task performance among the three operation modes, the participants spent time the least with the "Single" and "Double" types, especially the "Single" type. (2) There is a significant difference in subjective evaluation among the three operating modes, the total score result shows that participants think the "Single" type and "Double" are easy to use and has the highest evaluation, especially the "Double" type. (3) Participants of different genders have different perceptions of casual puzzle games, and female players prefer games that are simple and easy to operate and have beautiful graphics.

Keywords: Relieve · Perception · Mobile game · Affordance · User experience

1 Introduction

Mobile devices provide multiple possibilities for the development of media technology. Smart touch screens provide multiple possibilities for user interaction and product presentation [1]. Users can take advantage of the fragmented time to participate in interactive entertainment anytime and anywhere. Among them, the mobile game market accounts for a significant proportion, and it has increasingly become a part of people's leisure life [2]. At the same time, mobile games can not only delight the mood but also serve as a window to convey cultural features, with the effect of "edutainment". The use of gamification in education can help increase student motivation, engagement, and community building [3] and promote student engagement in the curriculum [4]. Puzzle games help

© The Author(s), under exclusive license to Springer Nature Switzerland AG 2022
X. Fang (Ed.): HCII 2022, LNCS 13334, pp. 234–244, 2022.
https://doi.org/10.1007/978-3-031-05637-6_14

inspire students' thinking and stimulate their creativity. The classic Tetris game that was once popular all over the world continues to be new with time. It has become a cultural symbol. In the digital age, the unlimited possibilities brought by mobile devices have promoted the diversification of the game market and fierce competition. The refurbishment of classics and integration into mobile games is inevitable. The mobile phone is an active device and its user interface design affects user perception of operation. Therefore, it will be a significant challenge to attract players to pay attention to whether the traditional game media can return to the classics. In the HCI field, affordance emphasizes intuitive interaction [5]. The four factors of affordance include cognition, objects, functions, and senses [6], which have a significant impact on the design of mobile equipment and user interface. With the development of intelligent digitalization, affordance design has gradually penetrated into various fields, such as the medical field [7, 8]. Based on the intuitive interaction of interface design to help understand the influencing factors of affordance perception on the user interface design of mobile games. It will contribute to the development of classic new forms and future games. Game entertainment can provide users with rich social interaction and establish the bonding between people and products, and between people [9].

Games are engaging primarily through "action, feedback, and emotion" to create human-computer interaction [10]. The dynamic icons of the interface design can provide players with high affordance, clarify the design intent of the game content, reduce perceived uncertainty, and help players interact smoothly and effectively [11, 12]. At the same time, game interface visual cues affect player perception [13]. Different players have different requirements for gameplay. According to the statistical report of Newzoo, a data research agency, there are more than 1 billion female game lovers in the world, accounting for about 46% of all audiences [14]. Among them, the largest group tends to use games to fill their free time or social activities, and prefer mobile games on devices, accounting for about 36% of the total population; and among men, the largest group will enjoy high-quality games [14]. For example, female players are more inclined to develop games, pursue beautiful pictures, and be easy, pleasant, and easy to operate. Male players prefer fighting and competitive games, which require games to be logical and challenging. But this division is not absolute. With the increasing variety of games, players have more choices, and players' preferences are also diversified. Therefore, this study takes Tetris puzzle games as an example to understand the perception experience of male players and female players on puzzle casual games, hoping to help designers develop games and provide suggestions and opinions.

2   The Purpose and Research Questions

The purpose of this study is to investigate the impact of affordance perception on the user experience of the Tetris mobile game. The purpose of this paper is to investigate the impact of affordability design on the user experience of Tetris mobile game and to explore the visual perception of puzzle game interface design by different gender players. We asked the following four questions:

Q1: Do the three different modes of Tetris game interface design significantly affect user visual perception?

Q2: Is there a significant effect of gender in Tetris game interface design?

Q3: Do the three different operating modes and gender significantly affect participants' task performance and subjective assessments?

Q4: Participants in the Single type spent the shortest task time and were most satisfied with the subjective assessment?

3 Method

The experimental research includes two phases, i.e., experiment 1 and experiment 2. Experiment 1 includes three mobile cube games already on the market. The game is a type of one-directional control game. Experiment 2 is a new type of 3D battle cube game created based on Experiment 1. The research study focuses on the design of the cube game interface, with the influencing factors of visual perception as the principal axis, which explores the main influencing factor of a classic block game interface design. Based on the research, we will explore the feasibility of the new game, change the game strategy, and help improve the user experience through the transition from one-directional control to battle function.

3.1 The Experiment 1

The experiment used a 2 × 3 mixed factorial design. The two independent variables were Gender and Operation Mode. The experimental data collection includes qualitative and quantitative. Before the experiment begins, we will read the experiment content and information to the participants. They would need to perform four tasks and each of their task time would be recorded. Moreover, after an experiment was completed, the participants would require to fills out the questionnaire of system usability scale (SUS) and questionnaire of subjective evaluations to help investigate their subjective evaluations. Finally, semi-structured interviews would be conducted with participants on specific issues pertinent to Tetris cube games' user interface design. The total experiment time was fewer than 40 min.

Participants. The convenience sampling method was used in this study. A total of 12 participants (i.e., 6 males, 6 females) took part in the experiment. The age is between 21–43 years old, 45% of the participants are students of the Design Institute, who have experience in playing games. 85% of the participants had block game experience and were able to complete the experimental tasks independently.

Experiment Design and Procedure. The experiment was executed on a HUAWEI P10 with a 5-inch screen and fixed in the designated field to ensure uniform network speed. The experimental design adopted representative cube game applications (App) on the market. Each participant experienced three operation modes, i.e., the "Single", "Double", and "Multiple" types, and completes the corresponding game tasks. The three games are all puzzle Tetris mobile games. The main differences between them are the operation mode and the visual aesthetics of the interface. The "Single" type is the application of the original Tetris handheld game on the mobile phone carrier, with a single, simple and intuitive interface. The "Double" type is iterative innovation based on the traditional Tetris game, retaining the original game concept, enhancing the visual beauty of the screen, the operation method can be double implemented, and the content is richer. The "Multiple" types are novel and unique, combining science fiction elements, multi-modal integration of operation forms, rich content, and good picture quality.

3.2 The Experiment 2

Based on Experiment 1, a newly researched three-dimensional battle cube game will be evaluated. That is, participants will subjectively evaluate its user interface design and gameplay, and put forward opinions and suggestions. The experiment 2 is still in the investigation process.

4 Results and Analyses

This study used the two-way analysis of variance (ANOVA) to assist analyze the collected data from the experiment 1. By using the statistical software of SPSS, the participant's task performance, SUS, and Subject Evaluation were analyzed. Significant main effects were further analyzed by post hoc comparison of LSD.

4.1 Task Analyses

The generated results of each task pertinent to participants' task finish time were revealed in Table 1.

Table 1. The results of mixed two-way ANOVA regarding task completion time

	Source	SS	df	MS	F	P	LSD
Task 1	Gender	1493.565	1	1493.565	1.733	.217	
	Operation mode	7551.540	2	3775.770	2.452	.112	
	Gender × operation mode	682.744	2	341.226	0.222	.148	
Task 2	Gender	4098.347	1	4098.347	3.086	.109	
	Operation mode	8699.891	2	4349.946	4.194	.030*	Double < multiple
	Gender × operation mode	1311.610	2	655.673	0.632	.542	
Task 3	Gender	601.230	1	601.230	0.747	.408	

(continued)

Table 1. (*continued*)

Source	SS	df	MS	F	P	LSD
Operation mode	8502.936	2	4251.468	9.983	.001*	Single < double = multiple
Gender × operation mode	126.618	2	63.309	0.149	.863	
Task4 Gender	1173.748	1	1173.748	6.151	.033*	Female < male
Operation mode	6019.301	2	3009.651	16.894	.000*	Single < double < multiple
Gender × operation mode	2887.257	2	1443.629	8.103	.003*	

* Significantly different at $\alpha = 0.05$ level (*P < 0.05).

The first task: Please participants to initiate a game state, then close and exit the game. There existed no significant difference in the main effect of Gender (F (1, 10) = 1.733, P = 0.217 > 0.05). There existed no significant difference in the main effect of the Operation Mode (F (2, 20) = 2.452, P = 0.112 > 0.05). There also existed no significant interaction effect between Gender and Operation Mode (F (2, 20) = 0.222, P = 0. 733 > 0.05).

The second task: Please participants to activate the game state, turn off and on the music, then continue to enter the game, and finally exit the game. There existed no significant difference in the main effect of Gender (F (1, 10) = 1.952, P = 0.193 > 0.05). There also existed no significant interaction effect between gender and Operation Mode (F (2, 20) = 0.632, P = 0.542 > 0.05).

Nonetheless, there existed a significant difference in the main effect of the Operation Mode (F (2, 20) = 4.194, P = 0.030 < 0.05) in the second task. The post hoc comparison showed that the "Multiple" (M = 79.18, SD = 55.20) and "Single" types (M = 50.88, SD = 17.32) showed no significant difference (P = 0.136 > 0.05). The "Multiple" and "Double" types (M = 42.96, SD = 24.66) revealed a significant difference (P = 0.010 < 0.05). The "Single" and "Double" types showed no significant difference (P = 0.411 > 0.05). The results showed that participants' task performance regarding the "Double" type was faster than the "Multiple" type.

The third task: Please participants to start the game state, operate the block game for four rounds, and then exit the game. There existed no significant difference in the main effect of Gender (F (1, 10) = 0.747, P = 0.408 > 0.05). There also existed no significant interaction effect between Gender and Operation Mode (F (2, 20) = 1.149, P = 0.759 > 0.05).

Nevertheless, there existed a significant difference in the main effect of the Operation Mode (F (2, 20) = 9.983, P = 0.001 < 0.05). The post hoc comparison showed that the "Multiple" (M = 71.13, SD = 35.53) and "Single" types (M = 33.53, SD = 5.65) showed a significant difference (P = 0.003 < 0.05). The "Multiple" and "Double" types

(M = 50.66, SD = 16.68) revealed no significant difference (P = 0.068 > 0.05). The "Single" and "Double" types showed a significant difference (P = 0.001 < 0.05). The results showed that participants' task performance regarding the "Single" type was faster than the "Double" and "Multiple" types.

The fourth task: Please the participants to start the game state, operate the block game to the left and quickly fall, and quickly fall to the right to exit the game. It can be seen that there was a significant difference in the main effect of Gender (F (1, 10) = 6.151, P = 0.033 < 0.05).

The main effects of Operation Mode also showed significantly difference (F (2, 20) = 18.508, P = 0.000 < 0.05). The post hoc comparison showed that the "Multiple" (M = 51.21, SD = 27.22) and "Single" types (M = 20.34, SD = 6.60) showed a significant difference (P = 0.001 < 0.05). The "Single" and "Double" types (M = 29.64, SD = 9.06) also revealed a significant difference (P = 0.010 < 0.05). The "Single" and "Double" types showed a significant difference (P = 0.003 < 0.05). The results showed that participants' task performance regarding the " Single" type was faster than the "Double" type and the "Double" type was faster than the "Multiple" type.

There also existed a significant interaction effect between Gender and Operation Mode (F (2, 20) = 8.103, P = 0.003 > 0.05). According to the interaction diagram in Fig. 1, on the Single type, the time spent by the participants to complete the task was slightly lower for women than for men. On the "Multiple" type, the time taken by the participants to complete the task was significantly less for men than for women. On the "Double" type, women and men took the same amount of time to complete the task, with no significant difference. In other words, when choosing a Tetris game, female players are more suitable for the "Single" type, and male players are more suitable for the "Multiple" type. The "Double" type is suitable for both male and female players.

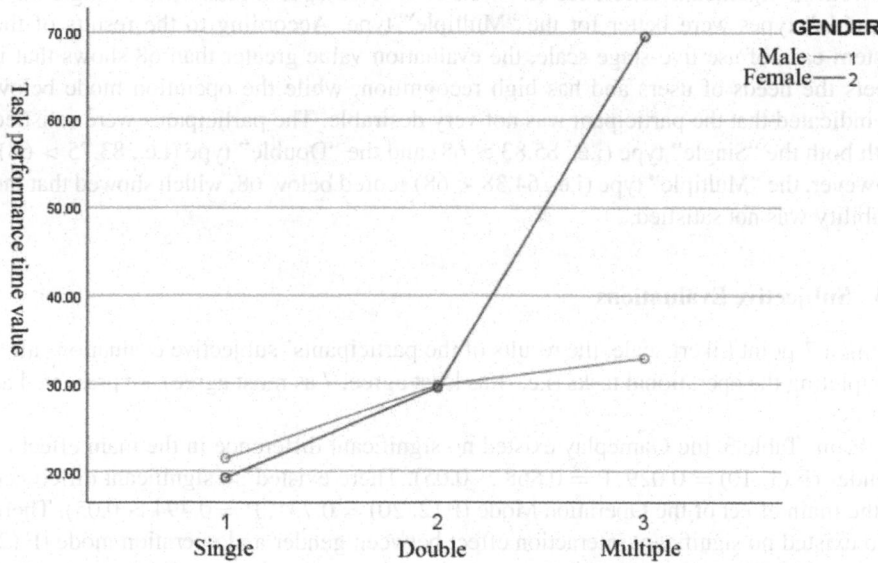

Fig. 1. Task 4: The interaction diagram between gender and operation mode.

4.2 System Usability Scale (SUS)

After the experiment, the participants were asked to fill out the SUS questionnaire after completing the assigned tasks. The generated results from the mixed two-way ANOVA are illustrated in Table 2.

Table 2. The results of mixed two-way ANOVA regarding SUS

	Source	SS	df	MS	F	P	LSD
SUS	Gender	264.063	1	264.063	0.426	.529	
	Operation mode	3360.764	2	1680.382	10.964	.001*	Single = double > multiple
	Gender × operation mode	132.292	2	66.146	0.432	.655	

* Significantly different at $\alpha = 0.05$ level (* P < 0.05).

The result shown that there was no significant difference in the main effect of Gender (F (1, 10) = 0.426, P = 0.529 > 0.05). As there were no interaction effects between Gender and Operation Mode (F (2, 20) = 0.432, P = 0.655 > 0.05).

Nevertheless, there was a significant difference in the main effect of Operation Mode (F (2, 20) = 10.964, P = 0.001 < 0.05). The post hoc comparison showed that the "Multiple" (M = 64.38, SD = 21.46) and "Single" types (M = 85.83, SD = 18.75) showed a significant difference (P = 0.005 < 0.05), as did the "Multiple" and "Double" types (M = 83.75, SD = 14.71) (P = 0.005 < 0.05), the "Double" and "Single" types showed no significant difference (P = 0.567 > 0.05). As a result, the "Single" and "Double" types were better for the "Multiple" type. According to the results of the system ease of use five-stage scale, the evaluation value greater than 68 shows that it meets the needs of users and has high recognition, while the operation mode below 68 indicated that the participant was not very desirable. The participants were satisfied with both the "Single" type (i.e., 85.83 > 68) and the "Double" type (i.e., 83.75 > 68). However, the "Multiple" type (i.e., 64.38 < 68) scored below 68, which showed that the usability was not satisfied.

4.3 Subjective Evaluations

Using a 7-point Likert scale, the results of the participants' subjective evaluations after completing the operational tasks (i.e., 1 as least agree; 7 as most agree) are presented as follows.

From Table 3, the Gameplay existed no significant difference in the main effect of Gender (F (1, 10) = 0.029, P = 0.868 > 0.05). There existed no significant difference in the main effect of the Operation Mode (F (2, 20) = 0.731, P = 0.494 > 0.05). There also existed no significant interaction effect between gender and operation mode (F (2, 20) = 1.439, P = 0. 261 > 0.05). Comparing the averages shows that the three operation

Table 3. The results of mixed two-way ANOVA regarding subjective evaluations

	Source	SS	df	MS	F	P	LSD
Gameplay	Gender	0.111	1	0.111	0.029	.868	
	Operation mode	1.722	2	0.861	0.731	.494	
	Gender × operation mode	3.056	2	1.694	1.439	.261	
Affordance	Gender	0.444	1	0.444	0.141	.715	
	Operation mode	7.167	2	3.583	2.710	.091	
	Gender × operation mode	0.389	2	0.194	0.147	.864	
Aesthetic	Gender	1.000	1	1.000	0.180	.680	
	Operation mode	6.222	2	3.111	3.636	.045*	Single = multiple < double
	Gender × operation mode	0.667	2	0.333	0.390	.682	
Identifiability	Gender	2.250	1	2.250	0.971	.348	
	Operation mode	12.500	2	6.250	8.523	.002*	Multiple < single = double
	Gender × operation mode	2.167	2	1.083	1.477	.252	

*Significantly different at $\alpha = 0.05$ level (*P < 0.05).

modes are all high than 4. According to the evaluation requirements of the 7-point Likert scale, the participants are all very satisfied with the three operating modes.

The Affordance existed no significant difference in the main effect of Gender (F (1, 10) = 0.141, P = 0.715 > 0.05). There existed no significant difference in the main effect of the Operation Mode (F (2, 20) = 2.710, P = 0.091 > 0.05). There was also existed no significant interaction effect between Gender and Operation Mode (F (2, 20) = 0.147, P = 0.864 > 0.05). Comparing the averages shows that the three operating modes are all high than 4. According to the evaluation requirement of the 7-point Likert scale, the participants are all very satisfied with the three operating modes.

The Aesthetic existed no significant difference in the main effect of Gender (F (1, 10) = 0.180, P = 0.680 > 0.05). There also existed no significant interaction effect between Gender and Operation Mode (F (2, 20) = 0.390, P = 0.682 > 0.05).

However, there existed a significant difference in the main effect of Operation Mode to the Aesthetic level (F = 3.636, P = 0.045 < 0.05). The post hoc comparison showed that the "Multiple" type (M = 5.17, SD = 1.95) and the "Single" type (M = 5.50, SD = 1.45) had no significant difference (P = 0.467 > 0.05). The "Multiple" type and the "Double" type (M = 6.17, SD = 0.94) showed a significant difference (P = 0.026 < 0.05). The "Single" type and the "Double" type also showed a significant difference (P = 0.046 < 0.05). The results indicated that in terms of Aesthetic level, participants preferred to use the "Double" type most and it was better to the "Single" and "Multiple" type. Comparing the averages shows that the three operating modes are all high than 4. According to the evaluation requirement of the 7-point Likert scale, the participants are all very satisfied with the three operating modes.

The Identifiability existed no significant difference in the main effect of Gender (F $(1, 10) = 0.971$, P $= 0.348 > 0.05$). There also existed no significant interaction effect between Gender and Operation Mode (F $(2, 20) = 1.477$, P $= 0.252 > 0.05$).

However, there existed a significant difference in the main effect of Operation Mode to Aesthetic level (F $= 8.523$, P $= 0.002 < 0.05$). The post hoc comparison showed that the "Multiple" type (M $= 4.75$, SD $= 1.36$) and the "Single" type (M $= 5.67$, SD $= 1.03$) had a significant difference (P $= 0.016 < 0.05$). The "Multiple" type and the "Double" type (M $= 6.00$, SD $= 1.04$) showed also a significant difference (P $= 0.012 < 0.05$). The "Single" type and the "Double" type showed no significant difference (P $= 1.000 > 0.05$). The results indicated that in terms of Identifiability level, participants preferred to use the "Single" and "Double" types most, and they were better to the "Multiple" type. Comparing the averages shows that the three operating modes are all high than 4. According to the evaluation requirement of the 7-point Likert scale, the participants are all very satisfied with the three operating modes.

5   Discussion

The results generated from the experiment 1 consistently show that participants believe that the "Double" type system is the easiest to use, and the overall satisfaction rating is better except for the "functional operation." Participants also tend to believe that functional visibility affects operational perception. The performance of the three operation modes in this content is not very optimistic. They all had a low satisfaction rate, especially the "Double" type. Four factors of affordance affect user perception of mobile game interface design. The visual cues influence the accuracy of the participant's judgment of the interface information, and the cognitive affordance helps the users recognize and understand the operation task. However, among the three operating modes, the average score shows that the participants were most satisfied with the "Double," but are not satisfied with the "Single" and "Multiple" types, especially the "Single" type have very weak clues.

The screen size of the mobile phone and the touch screen affect the user's perception of operation. Interface design should be handled appropriately with the change of the active device. Object affordance can help users implement assigned tasks. The sensory affordance design feature refers to the user's visual perception of the interface content and smooth interaction with it. Visual information elements such as icons, buttons, and colors help users clearly and intuitively perceive the feasibility of task goals. It also affects cognitive affordance and objects affordance. It can be seen that the four affordance factors of cognition, object, function, and senses affect the playability of participants' perception of game interface design.

To sum up, changing the way of one-directional control of the cube game and adopting a battle-type three-dimensional game may help break through the traditional gameplay style and enhance the user experience in terms of visual form and strategy.

6 Conclusion

Firstly, there are significant differences among the three operating modes in task performance. The time it took for participants to complete the task was the shortest on the "Single" type and the longest on the "Multiple" type. The reason may be that the "Single" type interface is simple and intuitive, retaining the characteristics of the traditional handheld game of Tetris. However, the "Multiple" type enriches the content and level of information on the operation interface during the iterative concept innovation and development, allowing players to experience different visual senses.

Secondly, in terms of subjective evaluations, there are significant differences in the system usability among the three operating modes. Participants believed that the "Single" and "Double" types were easier to use, while the "Multiple" type was more difficult to use. Through further analysis, we found that there were also significant differences among the three operating modes in terms of subjective satisfaction evaluation. Participants were relatively satisfied with all three products, especially the "Double" type.

In addition, after semi-structured interviews, we also found that participants still have a sense of nostalgia for traditional classic cube games, and revisiting the classics can help recall the good memories of the past. At the same time, the participants are also very interested in the new form of Tetris game developed by us and look forward to seeing unique and innovative block game products.

It can be seen that new media technologies have provided favorable opportunities for people's leisure activities and enriched people's lives and entertainment. The combination of traditional culture and digital new media technology not only enriches innovative products but also plays a role in inheriting and promoting traditional culture, allowing audiences to review the classics and feel the cultural meaning behind game entertainment. By studying the transformation of classic Tetris game media application, it will help to further optimize the product presentation form and broaden the application orientation. This provides reference opinions and suggestions for the subsequent development of new products and inspires us to develop new game product concepts. Making full use of digitalization to promote the development of traditional cultural industries also provides a new way to open up regional cultural heritage preservation and promote the development of the ecological chain of cultural and creative industries. Culture and traditions are inseparable parts of the development of human civilization [15]. It is of great significance and value to face up to development and modern entertainment on the road of an intelligent digital economy.

Acknowledgments. This paper is supported by Zhejiang Provincial Philosophy and Social Sciences Planning Project (No. 22NDJC303YBM), Zhejiang Provincial Educational Science Planning Project (No. 2022SCG132), and Ningbo Childhood of Educations College Reform Teaching and Research Project in 2021 (No. NSJG202110).

References

1. Orphanides, A.K., Nam, C.S.: Touchscreen interfaces in context: a systematic review of research into touchscreens across settings, populations, and implementations. Appl. Ergon. **61**, 116–143 (2017)
2. Molyneux, L., Vasudevan, K., Gil de Zúñiga, H.: Gaming social capital: exploring civic value in multiplayer video games. J. Comput. Mediated Commun. **20**(4), 381–399 (2015)
3. Moccozet, L., Tardy, C., Opprecht, W., Léonard, M.: Gamification-based assessment of group work. In interactive collaborative learning (ICL). In: 2013 International Conference on IEEE (2013)
4. Denny, P.: The effect of virtual achievements on student engagement. In: Proceedings of the SIGCHI Conference on Human Factors in Computing Systems. ACM (2013)
5. Norman, D.A.: The Psychology of Everyday Things. Basic Books, New York, NY (1988)
6. Hartson, H.R.: Cognitive, physical, sensory and functional affordances in interaction design. Behav. Inform. Technol. **2003**(22), 315–338 (2015)
7. Wang, Q., Zhang, Y., Chen, G., Chen, Z., Hee, H.I.: Assessment of heart rate and respiratory rate for perioperative infants based on ELC model. IEEE Sens. J. **21**(12), 13685–13694 (2021). https://doi.org/10.1109/JSEN.2021.3071882
8. Wang, Q., Liu, W., Chen, X., Wang, X., Chen, G., Zhu, X.: Quantification of scar collagen texture and prediction of scar development via second harmonic generation images and a generative adversarial network. Biomed. Opt. Express **12**(8), 5305–5319 (2021)
9. Li, H., Chen, C.H.: Effect of the affordances of the FM new media communication interface design for smartphones. Sensors **21**(2), 384 (2021). https://doi.org/10.3390/s21020384
10. Werbach, K., Hunter, D.: For the win: how game thinking can revolutionize your business. https://fliphtml5.com/ndhs/wtqf/basic (2012). Accessed 5 Jan 2020
11. Li, H., Chen, C.H.: Effects of affordance state and operation mode on a smart washing machine touch sensitive user interface design. IEEE Sens. J. (2021). https://doi.org/10.1109/JSEN.2021.3101666
12. Zikmund-Fisher, B.J., Witteman, H.O., Fuhrel-Forbis, A., Exe, N.L., Kahn, V.C., Dickson, M.: Animated graphics for comparing two risks: a cautionary tale. J. Med. Internet Res. **14**(4), e2030 (2012)
13. Li, H., Chen, C.H.: Research on the classic block interface design of mobile games. In: 2021 IEEE International Conference on Consumer Electronics and Computer Engineering (ICCECE), pp. 626–629. IEEE (2021)
14. Newzoo: Games Market Data. https://Newzoo.com (2022)
15. Roy, S., Singh, P.P., Padun, A.: Game-Based Learning for the Awareness of Culture & Tradition: An Exploratory Case Study on the Indigenous Naga Tribe. In: Chakrabarti, A., Poovaiah, R., Bokil, P., Kant, V. (eds.) Design for Tomorrow—Volume 2. SIST, vol. 222, pp. 293–304. Springer, Singapore (2021). https://doi.org/10.1007/978-981-16-0119-4_24

Online Social Games in the Eyes of Children and Teens: A Systematic Review

Sean Li[1(✉)], Erin Li[1], and Xiaojun Yuan[2]

[1] Cherry Hill High School East, Cherry Hill, NJ 08003, USA
sean.h.haoranli@gmail.com
[2] University at Albany, State University of New York, Albany, NY 12222, USA
xyuan@albany.edu

Abstract. During the pandemic, online learning has become the main learning format for children and teens. For some students, social games have become an important communication channel to stay connected with their friends. Research has shown the positive and negative sides of playing social games. It is important to discover if social games can benefit children and teens. This systematic review surveyed the literature by exploring how social games have been adopted and perceived by children and teens. Using the PRISMA review framework, we carried out three rounds of systematic selection in five databases: PsycINFO, Education Source, Web of Science, ACM Digital Library, and IEEE Xplore Digital Library. The final sample includes 8 articles. The types of social games involved in these studies include location-based games, language play games, educational games, affective social games, health games, and intelligent tutoring games. Results indicated that it is important to research the use and perception of social games by children and teens and that there is a research gap that should be addressed in this field.

Keywords: Social game · Group game · Children · Teens · User perception

1 Introduction

The COVID-19 Global Pandemic has exposed many issues. Because of the lockdown in March 2020, public schools transferred to fully online for some time. Students had to fully rely on technical devices, such as computers, chrome books, laptops, tablets, cell phones, and virtual conferencing and training software (e.g., Google Classroom, Zoom) to learn from teachers, complete their assigned homework, and socialize with their friends. Social games have become one of the most important channels for students to communicate with their friends. According to [23], social game refers to games that "allow or require social interaction between players as opposed to games played in solitude." Social interaction among players is the key here. There are many types of social games, including board games, online games, as well as indoor and outdoor social games. [18] mentioned that the definition of online games has been expanded from network games played on a PC to include mobile online games because of the development of mobile devices. Research has shown that children and teens spend more time interacting with online communities than their surrounding communities [14, 19]. Many students have become addicted to online social games (e.g., League of Legends). Research has shown that this addiction has had a significant impact on their school performance, daily routines, and sometimes even mental health [10]. This observation triggers our interest in exploring the impact of social games on children and teens. We hope to discover whether social games can benefit children and teens and feel that it is important to first learn from children and teens about their perception of social games. There is a great deal of research on topics related to social games, but few focus on children and teens, especially how they perceive and adopt social games.

This systematic review examines the adoption and perception of social games on children and teens. Specifically, the review revolves around two research questions (RQs):

RQ1: How do children and teens use online social games?
RQ2: What is the perception of online social games by children and teens?

This review raises awareness of the importance of this topic, and providing guidelines and suggestions for designers and developers of social games. We will present previous work, describe the review methodology and results in detail, discuss the findings, and then conclude with future research directions.

2   Previous Work

As aforementioned, social interaction among players is crucial to social games. It is also important to note that mobile social games are supported by online services and that their contents change according to how many times the game is played and which choices have been made by the players [18].

Researchers have discovered that social interaction in online games can improve social relationships among players [2, 5], because online social games enabled many players to interact and complete shared goals together. With the goal of understanding how playing social networking games affects intergenerational family relationships, [2] studied sixteen pairs of Chinese parents and their adult children and found that game-based communication offers a relaxed environment for multi-intergenerational family members to stay connected with each other.

Children need to play. Playing games is important for the development of children and adolescents [10]. With the fast development of advanced technologies, children and teens can play games on computers with virtual people in the online communities [6, 10]. As Wiederhold [22] mentioned, children and teens of today have been "raised on technology" and are "digital natives, used to, and most comfortable with, socializing via their devices." Research has shown that playing social games has a positive impact on children and teens, including re-creating socialization chances available in the real world [22], offering entertainment and distraction [9], and providing children and adolescents a chance to practice their social skills [9]. Due to the pandemic, social games have become even more important because they offer children and teens the opportunity to practice their social and emotional skills at a time when there were very few chances to do so in the real world. [12] found that video game usage was not related to an increased risk of mental health problems, and video gaming can have a positive impact on young children in terms of cognitive functioning, academic achievement, and some aspects of mental health.

However, concerns about game addiction have arisen. First, multiplayer computer games are easy to get addicted to. Cole and Hooley [3] claimed that multiplayer computer-based games could lead to internet addiction in that such kind of games are more motivating than other games due to the rapid gratification they offer. Second, children and adolescents who have an internet addiction prefer to use the computer for games rather than for other tasks [10]. Third, online games have a negative impact on children's language behavior. In a study on online game and children's language behavior, [19] found that one third of teens play online games every day and 7% of children play online games for at least 30 h a week. Munawir [14] further reported that playing online games gives children an opportunity to absorb a lot of abusive or negative language that led to distorted language, and provided suggestions to parents, teachers, and policy makers to recommend children against playing online games that are violent and have a verbal interaction menu. Last, game addiction may cause social anxiety for children. [10] examined the risk factors involved in online game addiction (OGA) among middle school students. Results indicate that "having a mother who is employed, having parents who completed high school or a higher level of education, and the time spent on the computer are risk factors for OGA" (p. 830). This study recommended that health workers should develop programs to prevent addictions related to the use of the internet and the computer for children and adolescents, and that scientific studies should be performed to test the effectiveness of those programs.

3   Methodology

Based on the PRISMA review framework (PRISMA Review), we performed three rounds of systematic selection in five databases: PsycINFO, Education Source, Web of Science, ACM Digital Library, and IEEE Xplore Digital Library. These five databases were selected because they include articles in psychology, education, science, social science, and technology.

We performed three rounds of systematic selection in the selected databases. First, we searched predetermined keywords. Next, we screened the titles and abstracts using predetermined inclusion/exclusion criteria. Finally, we screened the full-text of selected articles to ensure that they met the same inclusion/exclusion criteria. In general, we chose English-written articles from journals and conferences, and excluded reviews, commentaries, dissertations, and columns, etc. Studies about the perception and adoption of social games by children and teens, and about the factors that may affect their use of online social games are included.

3.1   Keyword Search

First, we searched predetermined keywords. On February 21, 2022, we searched the PsycINFO database in the title and abstract fields for articles using the following three sets of keywords ("social game" OR "group game") AND (children OR child OR teenager OR kids OR teens), and produced 26 results. We also searched the title and abstract fields in the Education Source, Web of Science, and the ACM databases using the same keywords and produced 18, 27, and 6 articles respectively. We searched the All metadata in the IEEE Xplore database and generated 6 results. In total, 83 records were retrieved. After excluding 29 duplicates, a total of 54 non-duplicate results remained for round two screening.

3.2 Screening the Titles and Abstracts

Next, we screened the titles and abstracts of these 54 articles independently. The authors each independently screened approximately 1/3 of the titles and abstracts of the 54 articles. This round of screening was based on the rationale that the focus of our systematic literature review is about the perception and use of online social games by children and teens. Other topics are outside of the scope of this review. Specifically, we removed an article if it met at least one of the following exclusion criteria:

- Not an empirical study (e.g., literature review, summary, dissertation, thesis; $n = 5$).
- Not online social game related ($n = 11$).
- Not social game related (n = 3).
- Not children or teens related ($n = 5$).
- Not a social game used by children or teens (e.g., algorithms, approaches; $n = 5$).

After removing 29 articles, a total of 25 articles remained in the sample.

3.3 Screening the Full Text

We then screened the full text of all 25 remaining articles. During this round, we eliminated 17 more articles from our sample because they met at least one of the aforementioned exclusion criteria:

- Not an empirical study (e.g., dissertation, review; $n = 2$).
- Not online social game related ($n = 11$).
- Not a social game used by children or teens (e.g., prototype; algorithms, approaches; $n = 4$).

A total of 8 articles remained in the final sample.

Following the PRISMA guidelines for reporting systematic reviews, we summarize the selection process in Fig. 1. During the first-round review of abstracts and titles, the articles were selected for inclusion based on the research focus. A total of 54 articles were included. During the second-round review, the articles were reviewed in their entirety and mapped by the research question, methodology, and type of social game studied. Finally, 8 articles were selected for inclusion. Figure 1 shows the PRISMA review.

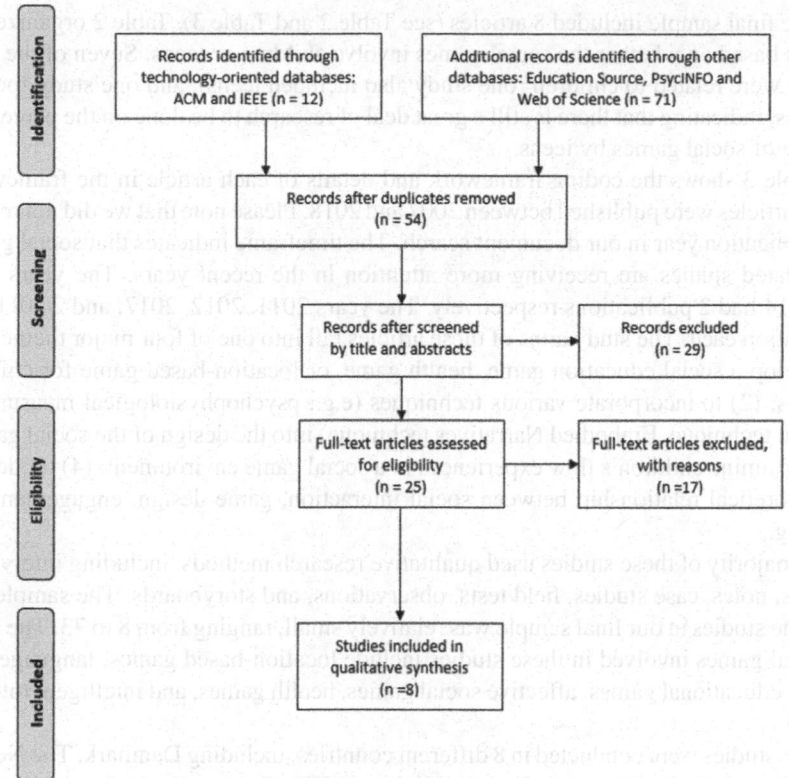

Fig. 1. PRISMA review

4 Results

Our initial searches found 54 articles. Through multiple rounds of screening, we removed 46 of them from our final sample. The reasons for excluding these 46 articles are summarized in Table 1.

Table 1. Summary of reasons for the excluded articles

Reason for exclusion	No.
Not an empirical study (e.g., literature review, summary, dissertation, thesis)	7
Not online social game related	22
Not social game related	3
Not children or teens related	5
Not a social game used by children or teens (e.g., prototype, algorithms, approaches)	9
Total	46

The final sample included 8 articles (see Table 2 and Table 3). Table 2 organizes the articles based on whether the social games involve children or teens. Seven of the eight studies were related to children (one study also included teens), and one study focused on teens, indicating that there is still a great deal of research to be done on the perception and use of social games by teens.

Table 3 shows the coding framework and details of each article in the framework. These articles were published between 2007 and 2018. Please note that we did not restrict the publication year in our document search. The timeframe indicates that social games and related studies are receiving more attention in the recent years. The years 2007 and 2014 had 2 publications respectively. The years 2011, 2012, 2017, and 2018 had 1 publication each. The study aims of these articles fall into one of four major themes: (1) to develop a social education game, health game, or location-based game for children or teens; (2) to incorporate various techniques (e.g., psychophysiological measures as an input technique, Embodied Narratives technique) into the design of the social games; (3) to examine children's flow experiences in a social game environment; (4) to identify the theoretical relationship between social interaction, game design, engagement and learning.

A majority of these studies used qualitative research methods, including interviews, surveys, notes, case studies, field tests, observations, and storyboards. The sample size of all the studies in our final sample was relatively small, ranging from 8 to 73. The types of social games involved in these studies include location-based games, language play games, educational games, affective social games, health games, and intelligent tutoring games.

The studies were conducted in 8 different countries, including Denmark, The Netherlands, Japan, Spain, Germany, Turkey, USA, and UK. Two studies were conducted in a lab or classroom setting, and three studies were performed in a public park, hospital, and primary school respectively. One study was conducted in both home and school. The settings of the rest two studies were not reported. Many studies reported positive outcomes in favor of the social games or potential benefits for the children and teens.

Table 2. Summary of the articles in the final sample

Social games	Children	Teens
Location-based mobile social game	[17]	
Affective social game	[1]	
Language Play Group game	[15]	
Educational social game	[4]	
Health social game		[7]
Interactive social game	[8]	
Educational social game	[13]	[13]
Intelligent tutoring game	[20]	

Table 3. Coding framework

Paper/Year	Study aim	Country	Method	Social game	Participant	Setting	Key finding
[17] 2018	To give the family location specific game experiences via physical play	Denmark	Field test	MeteorQuest, Location-based mobile social game	3 families, 12 participants (10–57 years old)	Public park	The families had fun playing the game and enjoyed the game experience
[1] 2007	To integrate psychophysiological measures as an input technique for social gaming applications for children	The Netherlands	Observation; interviews	aMAZEd, Affective social game	8 children	Not reported	Children felt that the psychophysiological input was fun; It supports social interaction among players
[15] 2014	To propose a system supporting the Shotoku Taishi game, a language play game that uses the voice of children	Japan	Notes; interviews	Language Play group Game	36 elementary school students, (grade 6, 11 to 12 years of age)	Lab/classroom	The participants enjoyed the Shotoku Taishi game; The group activity was creative and deepened their understanding of the Japanese language
[4] 2012	To incorporate Embodied Narratives technique to examine how children develop non formal learning when playing games, to co-design motivating and playful social games with children	Spain	Combination of storyboards, video recordings, photos taken by experimenters	Educational social game	73 children from ages 10 to 12	Home, school	Children talked about previous experiences to make their groupmates understand why something was dangerous; Children tended to group the risks they found while interacting with the environment
[7] 2011	To introduce a health game prototype that can facilitate the intercommunication of teenagers in cancer treatment	Germany	Questionnaires, Interviews. Between-subjects design	"Adventures in Sophoria", health social game	26 patients with cancer; 10 parents; 5 medical staff;	The Essen and Hannover hospitals	The implicit game version received higher enjoyment and acceptance in comparison to the explicit version; Most patients wanted to have more contact with their friends, instead of playing with other hospitalized children

(continued)

Table 3. (*continued*)

Paper/Year	Study aim	Country	Method	Social game	Participant	Setting	Key finding
[8] 2007	To examine children's flow experiences in a social game environment	Turkey	Observations, interviews	Interactive social game	33 children aged from 7 to 9 years	Computer lab	Flow experiences happen more often among boys than girls in the social games; Girls were more inclined than boys to play educational games; Complexity elements of games had more impact on the flow experiences of the children than clear feedback
[13] 2014	To teach computational thinking skills by building on children's current game playing interest and skills	USA	Interviews, within-subjects design	"CTArcade", teaching computational thinking skills, educational social game	18 children and teens	Not reported	A majority of the participants preferred CTArcade to paper; They liked the teaching aspect and novelty of the system
[20] 2017	To identify the theoretical relationship between social interaction, game design, engagement and learning	UK	Qualitative exploratory case study approach, instrumental case study	"Words Matter", intelligent tutoring game targeting children's word decoding, spelling and fluency	8 children with dyslexia (aged 11–12 years old)	A primary school in North London	Children keep talking about both game state failures and successes within their group; Children tend to engage in "game talk" about game performance, content, actions and experiences

5 Discussion

This paper conducted a systematic review of the perception of social games by children and teens and the possible factors that may affect their perception of social games. Five databases (Education Source, ERIC, ACM digital library, Web of Science, and IEEE Xplore Digital Library) were selected for literature search and 54 non-duplicated articles came out. After title/abstract full paper screening, 8 articles were included in the final review sample.

This review suggests that it is critical to consider the perception and usage of social games by children and teens amid the COVID-19 pandemic. Our review indicates a huge research gap in this field. This is evident in that a large number of the articles in our initial searches either focused on the design of the prototype, or using traditional social or group games as the method to perform experiments. The lack of user studies and user evaluation of the online social games for children and teens could be because of that the design and development of online social games, the IRB (Institutional Review Board) application and evaluation of user studies require a significant amount of investment of time and effort.

A majority of these articles in the final sample showed positive results with the use of social games by children and teens. The eight studies were conducted in eight different countries, indicating an increasing interest in this research area outside of USA. It also calls for research in this area in USA. The authors of these articles are familiar with the areas of science, technology, education, computer science, educational technology, applied cognitive science, and human-computer interaction, showing the multidisciplinary nature of the research.

Social interaction happened "in the form of cooperation and competition within and between the teams respectively" ([1], p. 55). It was interesting to note that children loved playing with each other and cooperating despite the fact that a team may lose a turn due to their partner's wrong decision or judgment. They supported each other and worked as a team to achieve the shared goal [1]. This result coincides with findings of Knorr [11]; that is, social games provide a platform for children to socialize with each other, and that the shared experiences are beneficial for young people because they become more willing to help each another in both online and offline settings.

This systematic review has its limitations. The selection of our initial search terms was not exhaustive. We used only "social game" or "group game" as our social game-related search terms and may have missed systems or technologies that did not use these terms but instead used "computer game" or "mobile game." The children and teen-related search terms may not have been comprehensive either. There is a potential for selection bias, whereby articles were unintentionally chosen to support the belief of the authors. We used three coders to reduce the potential for this bias. Despite these limitations, our systematic review is valuable, as it has identified existing work on social games with children and teens.

6 Conclusions

The findings of this systematic review indicate the existing research gap on how children and teens adopt and perceive social games. One advantage of social games is to increase the interaction of children and teens and thus in turn improve their social ability. However, addiction to social games can cause serious issues for children and teens in every aspect of their daily lives. In the future, we would like to examine how social games can be used in a way that can benefit high school students in both their studies and social lives.

Social anxiety, "a condition that typically begins in childhood and adolescence and leads to a noticeable decay in social functions and quality of life" ([10], p. 831), is a topic that we want to further explore. The study of [10] indicated that improving the social skills of students has a significant impact on reducing related health problems. We are interested in investigating the factors that cause social anxiety for high school students, how high school students can be educated to balance their school work and social lives, and, more importantly, whether social games can play a positive role in reducing the social anxiety of high school students. We believe that this kind of research will help improve not only the learning outcome of high school students but also the relationship between teachers/parents and students. An online survey is under preparation.

Acknowledgements. We thank all the reviewers for their constructive comments.

References

1. Al Mahmud, A., et al.: aMAZEd: designing an affective social game for children. In: Proceedings of the 6th International Conference on Interaction Design and Children, pp. 53–56 (2007)
2. Chen, Y., Wen, J., Xie, B.: "I communicate with my children in the game": Mediated Intergenerational Family Relationships through a Social Networking Game. J. Community Inform. **8**(1) (2012)
3. Cole, S.H., Hooley, J.M.: Clinical and personality correlates of MMO gaming: anxiety and absorption in problematic internet use. Soc. Sci. Comput. Rev. **31**(4), 424–436 (2013). https://doi.org/10.1177/0894439312475280
4. Díaz, P., Paredes, P., Alvarado, D., Giaccardi, E.: Co-designing social games with children to support non formal learning. In: 2012 IEEE 12th International Conference on Advanced Learning Technologies, pp. 682–683 (2012)
5. Ducheneaut, N., Yee, N., Nickell, E., Moore, R.J.: "Alone together?" Exploring the social dynamics of massively multiplayer online games. In: CHI 2006: Proceedings of the ACM Conference on Human-Factors in Computing Systems. ACM Press, NY (2006)
6. Fadhil, A., Villafiorita, A.: An adaptive learning with gamification & conversational UIs: the rise of CiboPoliBot. In: Adjunct Publication of the 25th Conference on User Modeling, Adaptation and Personalization, pp. 408–412 (2017)
7. Fuchslocher, A., Gerling, K., Masuch, M., Krämer, N.: Evaluating social games for kids and teenagers diagnosed with cancer. In: 2011 IEEE 1st International Conference on Serious Games and Applications for Health (SeGAH), pp. 1–4. IEEE (2011)
8. Inal, Y., Cagiltay, K.: Flow experiences of children in an interactive social game environment. Br. J. Educ. Technol. **38**(3), 455–464 (2007)
9. Johannes, N., Vuorre, M., Przybylski, A.K.: Video game play is positively correlated with well-being. Roy. Soc. Open Sci. **8**(2), 202049 (2021)
10. Karaca, S., Karakoc, A., Can Gurkan, O., Onan, N., Unsal Barlas, G.: Investigation of the online game addiction level, sociodemographic characteristics and social anxiety as risk factors for online game addiction in middle school students. Community Mental Health J. **56**(5), 830–838 (2020)
11. Knorr, C.: How video games can help kids socialize during this isolated time (2020). https://www.nationalgeographic.com/family/article/video-games-might-be-good-for-kids-now-coronavirus
12. Kovess-Masfety, V., et al.: Is time spent playing video games associated with mental health, cognitive and social skills in young children? Soc. Psychiatry Psychiatr. Epidemiol. **51**(3), 349–357 (2016). https://doi.org/10.1007/s00127-016-1179-6
13. Lee, T.Y., Mauriello, M.L., Ahn, J., Bederson, B.B.: CTArcade: computational thinking with games in school age children. Int. J. Child-Comput. Interact. **2**(1), 26–33 (2014)
14. Munawir, A.: Online game and childrens's language behavior. IDEAS: J. Engl. Lang. Teach. Learn. Linguist. Lit. **7**(2) (2019)
15. Nakadai, T., et al.: KIKIWAKE: participatory design of language play game for children to promote creative activity based on recognition of Japanese phonology. In: Proceedings of the 2014 Conference on Interaction Design and Children, pp. 265–268 (2014)
16. PRISMA Review: PRISMA (prisma-statement.org)
17. Rosenqvist, R., Boldsen, J., Papachristos, E., Merritt, T.: MeteorQuest-bringing families together through proxemics play in a mobile social game. In: Proceedings of the 2018 Annual Symposium on Computer-Human Interaction in Play, pp. 439–450 (2018)
18. Shibuya, A., Teramoto, M., Shoun, A.: Systematic analysis of in-game purchases and social features of mobile social games in Japan. In: DiGRA Conference (2015)

19. Syahran, R.: Ketergantungan online game dan penangananya. Jurnal Psikologi Pendidikan dan Konseling **1**(1), 84–92 (2015). 2443–2202
20. Vasalou, A., Khaled, R., Holmes, W., Gooch, D.: Digital games-based learning for children with dyslexia: a social constructivist perspective on engagement and learning during group game-play. Comput. Educ. **114**, 175–192 (2017)
21. Wen, J., Kow, Y.M., Chen, Y.: Online games and family ties: influences of social networking game on family relationship. In: Campos, P., Graham, N., Jorge, J., Nunes, N., Palanque, P., Winckler, M. (eds.) INTERACT 2011. LNCS, vol. 6948, pp. 250–264. Springer, Heidelberg (2011). https://doi.org/10.1007/978-3-642-23765-2_18
22. Wiederhold, B.K.: Kids will find a way: the benefits of social video games. Cyberpsychol. Behav. Soc. Network. **24**(4), 213–214 (2021)
23. Wikipedia: Social game (2022). https://en.wikipedia.org/wiki/Social_game

Artistic and Communication Strategies of Creating Playful Experiences in New Media Arts

A Reconnaissance

Anna Maj(✉) ⒾⒹ

Department of Humanities, University of Silesia, Katowice, Poland
anna.maj@us.edu.pl

Abstract. New media art (or cyberarts) can be treated as an experimental field or laboratory for testing various interactions between man and technology, discovering new dependencies and boundary conditions of communication, and expanding the limitations of interfaces. VR & AR technology and animation are core areas of these artistic activities. They are the subject of experiments related not only to the image (simulation, visualization, reproduction), but also to the problems of narrative and interaction (especially in the area of testing new interfaces, indicating the conditions of user identification with narrative and embodiment). Experiences of artists specializing in interactive art, often related to social activities (cyberactivism) and subversive (counter-systemic) activities, are of particular interest in this regard. The artists often create works that cross the generic limits between games, public intervention and spectacle. The presented analysis is devoted to selected artistic practices and works in the field of cyberarts, which can be perceived as innovative in relation to consumer games. Artistic and communicative strategies which lead to the creation of an experience of playfulness and receivers' pleasures that contribute to the communicative success of both a work and an artist – will be discussed.

Keywords: Cyberarts · Interaction design · Interface limitations

1 Introduction - Strategies and Tactics in Cyberarts

New media art is a space of creation that can be regarded as a particular laboratory of cultural practices focused on inventing, designing and testing new communication technologies and channels, new interfaces and manners of interaction. New media artists function at the intersection of art, science, design and creative industries. The purpose of this article is to show artistic and communication strategies that have been developed and tested in the field of cyberarts and to indicate specific pleasures offered by artists to receivers in this type of communication. It is a laboratory of social practices also in terms of approaching the playfulness category of new interfaces, technologies and new media narratives.

Creating aesthetic experience, once described by Roman Ingarden and widely taken for granted by aesthetics and critics of traditional art (I mean non-media art, also the

X. Fang (Ed.): HCII 2022, LNCS 13334, pp. 256–268, 2022.
https://doi.org/10.1007/978-3-031-05637-6_16

contemporary and avant-garde ones), in cyberarts means *de facto* creating a category of pleasure and playfulness (although differently understood by senders-media artists and receivers-vusers). We will look at examples of applying specific strategies proposed by cyberartists, as well as examples of receiving tactics associated with them. I will try to indicate art-specific new media examples of activities beyond the standard usage of existing technologies (VR, AR) and narrative manners. I will present in detail some works that are (or were) intended to develop new technologies and interfaces, shifting the boundaries of possible interactions at different levels.

New media art theory uses different typologies describing possible artistic activities and approaches. An interesting ordering attempt in this field was made by Ryszard W. Kluszczyński who in doing so referred to Michel de Certeau's concept of cultural practices [1]. Kluszczyński described characteristics of the most important artistic strategies (used in opposition to receiving tactics) in contemporary media art. He distinguished several strategies that can be reconstructed on the basis of the concept of artwork: 1) instrument; 2) game; 3) archive; 4) labyrinth; 5) rhizome; 6) system; 7) network; 9) performance [2]. I have analyzed the strategies elsewhere in detail, reflecting on the ideological and communication meaning of artists' approach to media artwork [3], here I would like to indicate the ordering value of the mentioned typology for understanding the test potential of media art for the HCI area. And while the strategy of the game most clearly addresses issues related to the potential of playfulness and interaction, it is undoubtedly worth looking closely at other strategies highlighted here from this perspective. All of them thematize the tension between playfulness and communication, in different ways inviting the receiver to discover the meaning potential of the artwork. It must also be added that these artworks are not necessarily purely aesthetic, they often balance on the border of activist actions, media education, scientific project and product intended for the mass market of audiovisual narratives receivers.

In another publication I described three basic attitudes characterizing media artists, namely cyberbricolers, cyber activists and cyborgs [4]. I pointed to different approaches to technology as a matter of creative activities, different distance and potential of such practices. In the first approach, technology is a medium in which the artist delves, giving it new meanings, functionality, forms and interfaces, often playing with it, "digging" in it as a child dismantling a toy or a cyberculture folk artist drawing from the repertoire of past practices. The second approach assumes the desire to establish dialogue with the receivers through technology, the desire to negotiate meanings of technology, to build reflection on its role in the life of modern societies and individuals. It is within this area that the subversive art and hacktivism are located. The third attitude is the most radical: the artist often transforms their body through technology, becoming both a creator and a material. The biotechnological body of the man-cyborg is an artifact in itself. The artist becomes a medium as a matter of their own artwork, and the process frequently occurs in an irreversible way and with the risk of endangering health or life. The body thus becomes a discursive object, it acquires attesting power. The limits of technological interference in the biological object, namely in the human body, are pushed and the body becomes an interface to techno everyday life. Lev Manovich [5] also discusses the changing role of the media artist being under the influence of artificial intelligence. The researcher indicates that it is still more difficult and perhaps also less reasonable to distinguish between machine (non-human) creativity, AI based creativity and human-artists one, most of the latter using computer tools based on AI algorithms anyway. The distinction between human and machine within creation therefore becomes a dubious distinction.

With this in mind, it is worth returning to the previously mentioned concept of Kluszczyński who writes about interactive art (and the methodology of its research) and sees its key element in strategies, not simply in artistic attitudes or artifacts as it was characteristic of classical art explored by classical aesthetics. Referring to de Certeau's concept, distinguishing between cultural strategies and tactics within everyday practices, Kluszczyński states that the strategy in interactive art is a kind of musical score prepared by the artist for the audience, and tactics are ways of reading it – they often fall within its area, but they can also reinterpret it creatively [6]. This means that although the receiver has potential freedom to follow their paths, they are in most cases predetermined or even designed by an artist who determines both the degree of openness of their artwork, a way, or ways, of action of the artwork as well as potential movements of the receiver. Moreover, the operations of hacktivists and cyberactivists suggest to receivers-participants certain activity scenarios and interpretive paths by proposing specific patterns of action and anticipating ways of thinking of the emotionally engaged audience [7]. The category of subversiveness thus becomes a refutable, or perhaps even ideological, category.

Artistic strategies vary in terms of openness: for example, the strategy of labyrinth provides fewer opportunities than the strategy of rhizome, the strategy of instrument launches potentially different (more diverse) competencies than the fairly formalized strategies of game or archive. Building engagement in interaction may also appear at different levels: motor or sensory interaction, full immersion (involving the whole body and perceptual apparatus), intellectual or emotional engagement. All artistic strategies foresee certain forms of behavior, but the receiver-interactor may also go beyond the scheme, refusing to interact with the artist or negotiating meanings with the artist, the receiver may finally co-create the performance which becomes the act of reception of the artwork. The artwork often acquires a processual rather than artifactual (material) character nowadays.

2   Creating Playful Experiences: A Reconnaissance

Based on several decades of observation of the development of cyberarts, I concluded that a certain typology of pleasures offered to its audience (interactors, vusers) could be suggested. I would like to highlight the following pleasures: 1) visualization and simulation, 2) interaction (low and high degree of engagement, casual and long-term interaction) and full immersion, 3) game and participation, 4) interactive performance and 5) encounter (confrontation and recognition). In this article, I would like to discuss the first three categories.

2.1   Pleasures of Visualisations and Pleasures of Simulations

Exhibiting Media Art and Problems of the User. Ars Electronica Center is one of the first interactive museums in Europe which has presented media art and interactive art for educational and popularization purposes since the mid-1990s. It is worth recalling the historical installation from the exhibition functioning here in the years 1996–2008. In retrospect, it is apparent how much an exhibition presented at a given time reflects evolving beliefs about what media and media art are. The *Humphrey* flight simulator was the main installation, together with *The CAVE*, which was intended to intrigue and encourage visitors to experience VR. It was presented in a specially separated circular balcony space encircled by a vertical balustrade, visible already from the entrance to the museum. At first glance, it gave the promise of full immersion: the user put on a suit and goggles, and was suspended in a horizontal position in front of several large LCD screens. In the course of the experiment, however, it turned out that the suit was simply a piece of clothing with a wire (data suit), goggles did not work properly, simulations designed to give a sense of flying over a city were only an imperfect visualization – a rather schematic image of urban architecture.

Relatively quickly, the user also reached the limit of the digital map, due to the fact that it was difficult to relate the movements of the suspended body with unnatural gestures required by the controller. When designing interaction with VR space, it was not taken into account that users would want to make gestures known from pop cultural patterns, such as Superman's gestures, for example. The installation users' required a different repertoire of motions, difficult to quickly implement in a situation of relatively large inertia of the suspended body. The simulation therefore had basic drawbacks: a lack of coupling between gestures and image, difficulty of combining gestures with motions enabling full-body balance, imperfect mapping of the city from a bird's eye view, the imperfection of 3D graphics, a long time interval between a gesture controlling the image and a simulated movement of the image. After a while, instead of attracting, the installation became a place which was avoided or which caused frustration among its few brave users. The new exhibition at Ars Electronica Center, opened in 2009, no longer includes this type of installations owing to popularization of VR games. It seems to be the right decision. The example of *Humphrey* shows the lack of adjusting the interface to users' expectations, a problem often arising during media art exhibitions. Perhaps the installation promised too much regardless the capabilities of the technology used. Moreover, the strategy of instrument used here could not be fully applied due to the project drawbacks (not enough hooking points to assure stability) which made exploration of the installation contents difficult. In this situation, it is hard to talk about building a sense of contentment, and pleasure was replaced by frustration.

However, the most famous early exposition showing VR technology to wide audience was the installation called *The CAVE*, a reconstructed concept by Dan Sandin, an artist and scientist, and Thomas A. DeFanti, a computer graphics pioneer from the USA [8]. It offered a possibility to interact with a digital image projected on three walls and the floor (approximately 3 m high and wide). In the 1980s and 1990s the possibility to interact in real time with a stereoscopic digital image creating a virtual environment seemed promising and fascinating.

However, this technology became outdated unusually quickly because of the dynamic development of 3D graphics. Replacing the software for a more appealing one proved too slow. Additionally, the possibility to interact with the image by means of an interactive helmet in *The CAVE* was given only to one user, and this was usually a guide explaining the principle of operation of the technology to the audience. Thus, the receivers had the opportunity to test the interaction with the installation only potentially. In exceptional cases, after justification of the request, the testing was possible, but only for a short while and only in the case when the rest of the group gave their consent. At Ars Electronica Center *The CAVE* was exhibited until 2008. The simulations and visualizations shown then seemed extremely primitive compared to the games present on the consumer market at the time, the latter offering a higher degree of real time interaction and better 3D graphics. *The CAVE* thus became an installation depicting the development of VR, or rather showing its outdated image.

In 2005 when I first tested it, the installations presented within its frame consisted of abstract images placed chaotically in 3D space or visualizations of actual tourist spaces. Yet, it is difficult to talk about real time interaction here because the delay in interaction was noticeable and the movements of the interactor were limited. *The CAVE* technology did not offer full immersion, it included only (or as many as) three walls of screens and the floor, with a stereoscopic data helmet attached on a cable in the center of the installation that prevented free interaction and greater mobility. The installation was too small to really feel virtual space.

Despite this confinement, artists made various attempts to adapt the installation. *World Skin* by Maurice Benayoun [9] is a good example. This work combined a serious topic of war images with interactive experience associated with looking and taking photos. The receiver could watch visualizations based on documentary photographs depicting various war conflicts; however, it was also possible to interact with them by photographing scenes of one's choice. Then the selected shots disappeared from the visualization and gave way to images of the characters. Interactors could therefore erase images of war from the screens by means of preserving them in a photographic form, which gained the dimension of recorded individual memories but at the same time disappeared from the audience's view. This work combined the experience of media audience with the one of a tourist, and created a new interactive experience based on the paradox of visualization and disappearance of images, which simulated memory processes. Benayoun processed the available technology, giving it the nature of a cultural experience in which technology was only one element of reality. The artist applied the strategy of instrument, but also the strategy of labyrinth. The receivers themselves must detect patterns and solve a kind of puzzle by following a non-obvious path paved by the creator. Unfortunately, such valuable and cognitively creative approaches to *The CAVE* technology were rare.

From this perspective, it may seem interesting that the promise not fulfilled by *The CAVE* or *Humphrey* was met at another exhibition in the new Ars Electronica Center building equipped with a special cinema space of a new type: *Deep Space*. VR space is simulated here owing to two 9×16 m screens, one of which is a wall and the other a floor, as well as to projectors displaying 8K images and laser tracking. This enables observing or interacting with graphic, photographic and film objects of different characteristics, displaying spatial images, creating and playing interactive games dedicated to this space, as well as presenting documentary projects, displaying and explaining scientific models or educational narratives. Compared to previously described projects, the technology used here gives its developers more application capabilities, at the same time allowing individual or group audience interaction. Drawbacks of *Humphrey* and *The CAVE* are avoided - users are no longer immobilized by the interface, their movement is tracked with a laser, light 3D glasses are sufficient for full interaction in the space, giving not only a perfect delusion of spatiality of the viewed forms but also enabling interaction with forms larger than the user, which undoubtedly stimulates the perceptual apparatus far more than interaction with home 3D cinema.

Scientific projects are particularly worth mentioning, for example the one in cooperation with NASA presenting a model of the universe and stories about images taken by the Hubble Telescope [10]. It fosters astronomical education of a new type where the receiver virtually traverses the Cosmos, begins to understand cosmic distances, is able to understand spatial relations between the Solar System and the rest of the Milky Way or other currently observed astronomical bodies, and, at the same time, can approach a selected astronomical object, such as the Sun, the Moon or a planet. "To approach" literally means the possibility of approaching a several-meter large spatial model that seems to hang in the middle of a dark room. It is more than a cinematic "window to the world." *Deep Space* becomes the window of a rushing rocket showing (rather than: simulating) the Cosmos. It can also be a window showing a completely different reality or a board of an interactive gameplay.

Deep Space does not offer more than modern technology is able to assure. Adaptation of the receiver's expectations to the technical capabilities of the presentation space, as well as focusing the program on different types of imaging are of main importance here. The VR cinema space appeals to the traditional cinema space, but transforms it. Thus certain expectations are suggested to the audience. Then the expectations are positively verified (the receiver gets the impression that they are in a new, better cinema or in the game space). The art of media is only one of many possibilities that can make use of this space, the others include games, educational, scientific, cognitive narratives and virtual travels. *Deep Space* implements more than just the strategy of instrument, it rather uses a bundle of strategies: of instrument, game, labyrinth, archive. Perhaps this is the reason why the new exhibition is so successful. It can, of course, be expanded and improved, but thanks to its size, it enables immersing into the image much better than in the case of *The CAVE* which quickly revealed its limits. Significantly, in the new project one can share their experience with others - the pleasure of the gameplay or even the projection itself is thus much bigger.

2.2 Pleasures of Interaction and Pleasures of Immersion

Low Level-Engagement Interactions. Many examples of media art focus on a different type of imaging, based on the boundary between looking and interacting. Christa Sommerer & Laurent Minnogneau are artists who have been exploring this field since the early 1990s. They program digital objects and virtual environments resembling artificial life or artificial ecosystems. They do not require complicated interactions but rather invite interactors to explore the capabilities of the interfaces. The artists do not set the boundaries of interaction, nor enforce one specific path of action – they give freedom while proposing an aesthetically intriguing visualization or virtual space that can be slowly explored. The works of Sommerer and Minnogneau [11] make it possible to penetrate into the essence of interactions and to understand the history or idea hidden in them. Even the oldest deeds by these artists, such as *Interactive Plant Growing* (1992) and *A-Volve* (1994–1995), invite to creative activities, yet even the mere presence of an interactor in a given space co-creates a virtual space of the artwork. *Interactive Plant Growing* is basically a visualization of plant growth processes by means of user tracking in space. *A-Volve*, on the other hand, is a work showing an ecosystem in which, owing to a touch screen, the user can create imaginary aquatic animals which are animated and displayed on the water of the swimming-pool located nearby. The user can interact with them and affect their actions, making some of them survive and others not. Animals evolve owing to the interaction with other digital creatures and with the installation users. A later artwork, *Electronic Typewriter* (2006), is in turn a multimedia installation whose central interface is a typewriter. The effect of the user's operation is a text which appears on a paper roll, however, after a while it comes to life as paper functions as a screen. The letters turn into digital insects which are actually a digital projection based on a special algorithm inspired by a genetic code. The insects take different forms, depending on how quickly the text was typed. They feed on the text, grow and even multiply, they can also be killed by dragging the paper roll towards the machine. The user interacts and at the same time creates unique individuals which enter into relations with their creator and other insects. The principles of the evolution process, predetermined code and users' aleatoric behavior are intertwined here. *Corona Diary* (2020), a peculiar video journal of pandemic times, visualizing the coronavirus circling around the artists during their one-day quarantine, corresponds with the above mentioned approach. In the works of Sommerer & Minnogneau, the strategy of game prevails: its rules are determined by the genetic code of a given digital organism and the processes of evolution contained in the operation of the algorithm. This is, at the same time, the strategy of system because digital entities designed or programmed by the artists form a specific digital ecosystem, reminiscent of biological life.

High Level Long Time Engagement Interactions and Full Immersion. It is very difficult to distinguish works requiring a high level of engagement in interaction from works that allow for full immersion. It seems that engagement can turn into immersion under certain conditions, depending on the user themselves, the time spent on interacting and emotional and perceptual engagement. For example, *FEED* (2005–2006) by Kurt Hentschlager is a virtual environment using digital fog. It is designed to make the viewer-interactor immerse in it completely, but it does not affect every receiver in the same way (some receivers leave the installation space due to the feeling of uneasiness, others try to only observe and oppose the process of sensory immersion). In general, however, the user-receiver enters the installation space with their whole body and absorbs it with all senses while not being connected to any interface. The user-receiver is subjected to intense visual, audial and tactile stimuli by means of pulsating stroboscopes, visualizations of "unreal human characters", intense soundscaping (composed of sounds, infrasounds and sub-low bass) and artificial fog [12]. All these elements locate the receiver at the limits of their perceptual apparatus' capabilities, the receiver loses spatial orientation and requires assistance in order to leave the installation safely. It is the strategy of performance, a kind of interactive spectacle, but also the strategy of labyrinth as the receiver discovers a designed path that evokes the feeling of being lost, a pleasure *a rebours*.

In turn, the work *Inferno* by Louis-Philippe Demers and Bill Vorn, a robotic inter-active performance visualizing the circles of hell, allows for immersion on a different level. Receivers are invited to actively participate in the performance, sometimes they can only watch, too. Interactors put on robotic exoskeletons consisting of several sepa-rate machines (a total of 25 were built) [13] acting on the interactors' body in a specific way variable in time or inducing specific physical reactions in the interactors' body. The performance lasts an hour and is accompanied by electronic music evoking hellish sensations. Initially, the interactors seem to have fun, they can steer machines to some extent, in the course of time, however, it turns out that the movements they program will become their curse: in successive circles of hell the moves will be repeated, intensified and eventually they will cause pain. The original playfulness and techno-dance turn into fatigue which results from the movement, fighting with the machines, and, eventually, surrendering to the exoskeleton and its motions. Playfulness and dance turn into parox-ysm and monotonous, tiresome movements independent of muscle pain and general discomfort. The pleasure of the interaction becomes a nightmare. The strategy adopted by the artists in this case is the strategy of performance and game. It is undoubtedly intended to evoke negative feelings among the audience. Physical pain, stimuli exceed-ing the limits of pleasure, and, above all, the lack of control over the machine enveloping the whole body, the inability to stop movement, the impossibility of escape – are the means by which the artists wanted to show the idea of hell. They portrayed a techno-logical hell where man has no possibility of movement, nor power over themselves and over the incomprehensible controlling technology. It is again a pleasure *a rebour,* but this is exactly what the public wants. We are to regret putting ourselves into the power of machines. It is a *dance macabre* of our epoch.

The installation *Flow of Qi* (2007) by ITRI Creativity Lab exhibited at the National Museum of Taiwan is a very subtle but immersive work designed to present history of culture, ancient Chinese manuscripts, the role of writing, the art of calligraphy and the meaning of the *chi* energy flow in nature. An interesting thread of this installation is the usage of the interactor's breath and heart rhythm as a signal that processes the input and co-creates the output visualized through the projection of calligraphy on the sand. Chest movements of the users sitting on two seats, located directly opposite a big sandbox, are measured every few milliseconds by means of the UWB technology (non-contact ultra-wideband radar technology based on microwave impulses to detect motion) [14]. Once interactor's heart rhythm and another's breathing are measured here, so that one of them affects the speed of writing and the other the density of the recording visible in the projec-tion. Thus, the meaning of the artwork is felt by interactors and controlled through their body, as well as a certain emotional and intellectual effort. The perception of the ancient art of calligraphy, accompanied by the read text of manuscripts, helps to relax, to unwind the body and mind, and finally results in easing the reactions, and thus creates a com-munication loop, a reflexive system, calming the visualized image of script. However, achieving a state conducive to the correct flow of *chi* energy and beautiful "writing with breath" and heartbeat rhythm is not easy and, unlike a calligraphy master, the interactor does not use a brush on paper but controls the interface with their body, in an invisible and subtle way, eluding the perception of bystanders and difficult to intellectually pro-cess. Moreover, the interaction of two people complicates the situation as it makes them adapt or "tune in" to each other. It needs to be added that such control of the installation system is manifested by a light ray which writes virtual characters (ideograms) on glossy sand. Breath is turned into light and it seems to be extreme sublimation of the idea of energy flow being at the same time a visualization understandable at the level of intercultural and intercivilization communication, resembling the divine breath. Thus, the artwork - in an aesthetically appealing and intellectually moving manner - pursues the educational goals of its creators. It also draws attention to the interrelationality of entities in nature and culture, to the interactions between elements, human body and various entities. Human thought, as well as its record, emerge as further elements in this natural sequence. The technical record seems to be another link in the great cycle of *chi* energy flow. This symbolic interpretative trait is communicated through the artistic strategy of instrument, with the instrument being both the interface of the artwork and the body of the interactor, and the space surrounding them. The interactor experiences full immersion in the virtual world of the artwork and the narrative proposed by it.

2.3 Pleasures of Game and Pleasures of Participation

Games for the Body. Games represent an element often used in media art in various ways. They happen to be the object of subversive processing, they also constitute a structural principle, represent a certain logic of the artist's work. Creators allow their receivers to go through different levels of the game, have them solve certain tasks and overcome difficulties, usually for purposes referred to as discursive rather than entertaining (but they can coexist in a media artwork).

Intimate Transactions (2005–2008) by Transmute Collective (Keith Armstrong, Guy Webster and Lisa O'Neill) is an interactive installation with game features that uses a novel haptic interface – affecting the users' whole bodies – as well as animation and sound [15]. The installation is networked but it requires specially prepared rooms – it functions in parallel in two independent locations (galleries in remote cities or two adjacent rooms in one museum). The artists' intention is to create sensations of intimate interactions despite the physical remoteness of player-interactors. The sensations are possible to appear through the process of discovering hidden principles of interactions designed in the installation. This is fostered by highly abstract animation, referring to unexpected quasi-biological forms, oneiric electronic music using infrasounds, as well as the interface itself consisting of several elements defined as "smart furniture" by the creators: "bodyshelf", "haptic pendant" and specially prepared acoustics of the hall. Bodyshelf is a specific support for the body that allows the interactor to adopt a stable, albeit inclined backward, position. It enables interaction with the back, buttocks (the interface transmits vibrations) and feet (a moving platform), which triggers the body to operate in an unexpected, surprising way for the interactor. Placed on the neck and abdomen, the haptic interface in the form of a large circular pendant enhances physical sensations. Vibrating in different ways, it becomes a source of pleasant or unpleasant stimuli. The very location of the interface close to the intimate sphere of the body, and at the same time at the center of balance, energy and digestion, may provoke associations with sports, gastric or erotic sensations. The interactors interact with the other players they cannot see or hear (but whose existence they are aware of) via abstract luminous avatars, visible on the screen. They establish their own ways of action and interaction, though the game encourages them to cooperate, to come into contact with the other avatar. The haptic interface, oneiric sounds and abstract animations, however, create a virtual environment that allows for sensory immersion, yet not necessarily a full or a pleasant one. Vibrations can cause, for example, a kind of nausea, and visualizations can be associated with both the encounter with ghosts and the act of fertilization, by creating a sense of intimacy at completely different (also physiologically impossible) levels. The interactor is invited here to experience the virtual world in all possible ways, however preference is given to those that promote interaction with the other man/avatar. It means that the emphasis is put on the very experience of interaction. Not so much on the interface (although it is also interesting) but on the very experience of the virtual presence of the other person, the co-interactor. The virtual encounter proves possible only when both individuals connected to the installation act in the same way – together performing certain tasks and being bodily and kinaesthetically harmonized in isolated physical spaces. The avatars, however, share virtual space and intimate transactions, symbolic encounters between two (disembodied) representations of the interactors' bodies take place. The strategy of game, as well as of instrument and labyrinth, are used here. The aim of the artists is to create precisely a relationship of intimacy based on network and distance, and at the same time to create an "ecological awareness" (connective and ecological understanding of space and of media space) [16], "co-affect" and "'intimate', bodily 'energy transfer' between participants" [17].

Games for the Mind. It is also necessary to mention the works of the group Blast Theory (led by three artists: Matt Adams, Ju Row Farr and Nick Tandavanitj) that became famous for innovative activities at the intersection of games, audiovisual media and performative actions, implemented since the early 1990s. The recent work of the collective, *A Cluster of 17 Cases: Online* [18] is a creative rework of the project implemented for WHO and results from the group's artistic residency in Geneva in 2018. Based on observations of the agency's work and interviews with experts from the Strategic Health Operation Centre (SHOC), artists from Blast Theory created a game which enables understanding how the SARS epidemic was spread on February 21, 2003. The interactor impersonates real 17 people who became communication hubs in the global transmission of the coronavirus. By selecting a room number, the player follows the stories of individual people who got infected with a mysterious illness during one night spent on the 9th floor at The Metropole Hotel in Hong Kong. The subject of the narrative is the mysterious transmission of the disease, which long remained unexplained. This narrative fits into horror scripts about cursed hotels, mysterious illnesses and murders. The "cursed 9th Floor" became the source of global transmission of SARS. How could the infection be transmitted between people who had no contact with each other and only spent the night in the same hotel? Experts had investigated the case like detectives until finally smoke tests solved the mystery. Smoke is a visual element present in the Blast Theory game which was initially prepared in the form of an installation for several museums (Laiden, New York, Hong Kong), and then – already during the SARS-CoV2 pandemic – in the form of an online game. The strategy of game helps us memorize details about people who became first victims of the virus. The game is therefore both an educational tool and a form of commemoration. At the very beginning the player is warned that the gameplay offers mostly dramatic scenarios, and part of the characters, depending on the choice of the room number, will lose their lives. So, the player consciously incarnates people who died. It is difficult to talk about pleasure of the game, unless it is the pleasure of exploring a difficult, traumatic history, identifying with the victims of the epidemic and deepening one's knowledge of it.

Blast Theory is known for many previous developments in the form of urban games, in which it linked reality and virtuality in very different shapes and scenarios, but always creating works that are excellent entertainment and at the same time an experience forcing players to move in urban (and virtual) space, and to reflect – e.g. *Can You See Me Now?* [19]. Nowadays, with the *Bloodyminded* project, it enters the sector associated with interactive life streamed feature film [20]. It should be added that contemporary urban gaming, interactive tracking and related social mapping and city hacking with game elements are often used as methods of action by artistic groups (e.g. Mongrel, GRL, Blast Theory, Senseable City Lab MIT, etc.). Their common denominator is the desire to develop social or political discussion related to the scope of privacy, civil liberties, as well as reflection on technology and social relationships. Subversive activities and social activism are important elements of the discursive role played by media art, but it cannot be forgotten that the media art's success is assured by pleasure stemming from the game and from participation. Participation (most often a group one) in a narrative structure organized in a certain way, whose distinction from everyday reality is evident, gives interactors the promise of entertainment and evokes in them the desire to play, even if the topic is unpleasant and difficult. Balancing these elements is the task that artists face.

3   Conclusion - Interaction Design and Interface Limitations

The reconnaissance presented here should be summarized. Receiver-interactor's engagement is built in the new media art in various ways. Among them one can find techniques of imaging, narrative building, creating attractive interfaces and a promise of experiencing pleasure. "Promise" is an extremely important category - it must be revealed shortly after the beginning of the interaction. It should clearly relate to the receiver's experience and competence, should give a sense of novelty and at the same time offer some cognitive values. Artists suggest its existence through intriguing interfaces, multi-sensory installations, constructing the artwork as a specific invitation to play. The principles of constructing aesthetic experience, present in art for centuries, interact here with the principles characterizing the art of narrative, storytelling and gamification. The pleasure of consumption is important both in the area of mass entertainment and of quite elitist experience shared by the user of an interactive art installation or media artwork of another type.

Moreover, art often triggers not necessarily positive emotions and sensations, however even a certain discomfort of the receiver is treated as a form of "playing in engagement". The media art receivers accept unpleasant sensations which they understand *a rebours* as a specific pleasure of communing with an aesthetic and technical object. This attitude is undoubtedly a consequence of modern audiences' experience with avant-garde art, as the new media art is its successor. We looked at selected artistic strategies and examples of works and practices from this area, as well as the types of pleasures they offer. Owing to this reconnaissance one can see that the new media art includes various approaches to creating pleasure and playful experiences, but it is far from programming the user and their actions, it rather designs a general path of user experience along with its different variants and options. It is rather a co-creation process in which the user plays a vital role and thus builds their pleasure of experiencing the artwork.

New media art may be seen as a laboratory of cultural and communication practices, but also as an area of testing the limits of interfaces and expanding the repertoire of possible interactions. Engaging the interactor becomes not only a challenge in terms of the verifiability of the artist's concept and vision, but also a specific test of operation of existing technology in a new reconfiguration or a type of test for an original prototype proposal from this area. A common way of social popularization of such projects is to present works at well-known festivals of new media and new technologies that gather an international audience of experts and amateurs. Hence, invitations to participate in a particular spectacle, performance or experiment are sometimes accompanied by legal disclaimers and necessity of giving a formal consent in order to experience a "novelty". Being a vuser has its strengths (ennobling contact with elitist technology and art), but also weaknesses (physiological or psychological threats). In other words, experiencing a media artwork may be challenging as it may cause specific discomfort or even potential health repercussions. However, a substantial part of the audience see nothing puzzling in a situation where an artist, in the name of their own fame, suggests potential bodily harm to the user of a given interface and at the same time does not want to bear legal consequences for it. This is undoubtedly due to the high appraisal of artistic activity in culture and the trust placed in the show or festival organizers.

It need to be added, the artworks are often destroyed during festivals as they are tested too heavily by interactors, used incongruously or are simply subjected to testing by too many people in a relatively short time. This often means a failure to adapt the interface of an interactive work to a situation of increased interaction. Thus, continuous service and protection of artifacts of a very diverse nature pose the challenge for organizers of interactive art exhibitions. Another challenge emerges from artistic projects whose interaction is designed for urban space, by definition open to randomness and unpredictability of usage conditions. A different problem is created by artworks that can only be shown through their documentation (e.g. bio art), as well as illegal art, implying illegal practices for the purpose of discussing important new social problems arising from technology. They all fall within new media art.

References

1. de Certeau, M.: The Practice of Everyday Life. University of California Press, Berkeley (1984)
2. Kluszczyński, R.W.: Sztuka interaktywna [Interactive Art]. WAIP, Warsaw (2010)
3. Maj, A.: From cyberbricoleurs through cyberleaders to cyborgs: emerging artistic strategies and possible tactics of reception. Transformations. Interdisc. J. 3–4(90–91), 147–164 (2016)
4. Ibidem
5. Manovich, L., Arielli, E.: Artificial aesthetics: a critical guide to AI, media and design. [ongoing online project], Chap. 2, pp. 1–24 (2022). http://manovich.net/index.php/projects/artificial-aesthetics. Accessed 9 Feb 2022
6. Kluszczyński, op. cit., p. 220

7. Maj, A.: Noosphere reframed: communication and cybersociety in the times of sentient city, blogjects and ubicomp paradigm. In: Maj, A. (ed.) Cyberculture Now. Social and Communication Behaviours on the Web. Inter-Disciplinary Press Literature & Cultural Studies Special E-Book Collection, 2009–2016. Brill, Leiden—Boston, pp. 15–26 (2019)
8. The CAVE. https://ars.electronica.art/futurelab/en/projects-cave/
9. World Skin by Maurice Benayoun. https://ars.electronica.art/futurelab/en/projects-world-skin/
10. Deep Space. Hubble Space Telescope by NASA. https://ars.electronica.art/center/en/hubble-space-telescope/
11. Sommerer, C., Minnogneau, L.: Works. http://www.interface.ufg.ac.at/christa-laurent/WORKS/FRAMES/FrameSet.html
12. Hentschlager, K.: FEED. http://www.kurthentschlager.com/portfolio/feed/feed.html
13. Demers, J.-P., Vorn, B.: Inferno. https://billvorn.concordia.ca/robography/Inferno.html
14. Flow of Qi. ITRI Creativity Lab. https://www.nextroom.at/event.php?id=9932
15. Transmute Collective (Keith Armstrong, Guy Webster and Lisa O'Neill): Intimate Transactions. http://embodiedmedia.com/homeartworks/intimate-transactions
16. Armstrong, K.: Towards an ecosophical praxis of new media space design. Ph.D. thesis. http://embodiedmedia.com/Resources/KMAPHDTHESIS.pdf?phpMyAdmin=b6PkCEYZ%2CteP6XdDyTa6wOnF%2C61
17. Bertelsen, L.: Affect and care in intimate transactions. Fibreculture J. 21, 24 (2012). http://twentyone.fibreculturejournal.org/fcj-149-affect-and-care-in-intimate-transactions/#sthash.YBGXjzRu.dpbs
18. Blast Theory: A Cluster of 17 Cases: Online. https://www.blasttheory.co.uk/projects/a-cluster-of-17-cases-online/
19. Blast Theory: Can You See Me Now? https://www.blasttheory.co.uk/projects/can-you-see-me-now/
20. Blast Theory: Bloodyminded. https://www.blasttheory.co.uk/projects/bloodyminded/

Apples and Oranges: A Study of "Tend & Befriend" as a Phenomenon in Digital Games

Zoë O'Shea[1]([⊠])[ID], Richard Bartle[2][ID], Xueni Pan[1][ID], and Jonathan Freeman[1]

[1] Goldsmiths, University of London, London, England, UK
z.oshea@gold.ac.uk
[2] University of Essex, Colchester, England, UK
https://www.gold.ac.uk/computing/

Abstract. This paper describes the process of developing and collecting data for analysis via a Qualtrics survey on "Tend & Befriend Theory" and the Acute Stress Response, *i.e.* "Fight or Flight Response". We discuss the constraints and implications of current thinking around "Tend & Befriend", the descriptive results of our initial study, present a methodology for categorising Tend & Befriend games, frame our results in the context of gaming experience, and outline our next research steps in addition to areas of future interest. Our study suggests that Tend & Befriend can be considered as a concrete phenomenon in games, supported by data. Our findings show some games can be considered as "archetypal" titles, making them useful references for research and discourse.

Keywords: Tend and Befriend · Fight or Flight · Stress response · Video game design

1 Introduction

Digital games are increasingly acknowledged as being the most profitable sector in the entertainment industry – regularly out-performing film, TV and music combined [11]. Designers and developers note the rapid expansion of the "gaming" population in which players are no longer limited to public perceptions of teenage youth in basements, or casual cookie-clicking commuters on trains [1]. In recent years, the potential of alternative theories and frameworks [10] as tools for developers to better understand the evolving player-market, as well as the culture of gaming has been demonstrated by the inclusion of psychology and user-research tracks at conferences (e.g. GDC, Develop Brighton).

One such theory that is gaining popularity is "Tend & Befriend" theory (TB) – an alternative theory of physiological stress-response proposed by Shelly Taylor [14]. Taylor suggested that in addition to an adrenal response (commonly thought of as "Fight or Flight") (FF), women may have developed behavioural systems that engage activities of mutual care ("tend") and social connectivity ("befriend") to increase odds of evolutionary survival and self-regulation [13].

© The Author(s), under exclusive license to Springer Nature Switzerland AG 2022
X. Fang (Ed.): HCII 2022, LNCS 13334, pp. 269–288, 2022.
https://doi.org/10.1007/978-3-031-05637-6_17

Within the space of digital games, TB has been introduced to developers by companies such as TRU LUV, and leaders such as Brie Code [7], who advocate the potential in developing experiences that are accessible for players whom previous design systems have typically excluded (e.g. Flow theory and conflict-based mechanics) [3,4].

However, to date there has been no empirical study on the phenomenon of TB as a design construct in digital games. Although anecdotally compelling, most work in this area has been based on supposition or borrowed from research in other fields [12]. This can be explained by a number of factors, most likely that it is a relatively new and unknown concept; any active research of TB may be within the confines of propriety development.

We present this paper which outlines the development of a survey and early TB research methodology. We describe our process in creating the survey, the descriptive results, further methods of analysis and our findings. Finally, we present our conclusions, outline our next intent for the research and areas of future interest.

2   Study Aims

When designing the study, we decided on three central questions (aims) to help develop our understanding of TB in relation to digital games.

The first was to establish whether or not TB/FF theory was as robust as it was anecdotally accepted to be. Does it represent a meaningful construct in games and when asked, could players agree with reasonable consistency what constitutes a TB game, or not?

The second aim for the study arose when we decided to assess games for the survey itself. Knowing that we would likely have data on an individual "game-by-game" basis, we wanted to highlight games (if any existed), that researchers could use as evidence-based case studies or "archetypes" when engaging in TB/FF discussion.

The final goal was to develop a method of operationalising TB for study, in order explore its application and context in games and design. TB games are often put into juxtaposition with FF games – however, this is not necessarily accurate. Shelly proposed TB theory as an additional system that builds on FF response, not in direct opposition to it [14]. Using FF as counter-examples when discussing TB conversationally affords a quick and easy way to highlight the distinctions between a so-called "TB game" and other titles which can be misleading. In developing this study, we found that this could imply a false dichotomy, where TB and FF were placed as opposites on a continuum rather than two distinct (but connected) processes. The range of games, players and experiences that exist highlight the limitations to such over-simplifications of this phenomena in digital games. As an example, there are games with features that suggest strongly that they engage both TB and FF responses in players. Take the popular *Pokémon* series published by Nintendo. In these games you are encouraged to form bonds and raise your creatures diligently and kindly - but also engage with regular "battles" involving harm and domination over opponents, and "wild" pokémon. As a player, you have some agency in how much or how little energy you invest into these mechanics. This level of complexity led us to structure the survey to account for what we hypothesised as "TB-ness" and "FF-ness" (or lack thereof) in order to limit conflation of TB/FF as much as possible.

Although the theory of TB is presented as a gendered difference, there is limited research available on the validity of making such a distinction, particularly for the purpose of games design. As such, we chose to exclude such questions for study at this time and emphasise the important cultural and contextual caveats that would make such a claim for this study of this level inappropriate. Examples include the marketing of games, public perception, social and cultural factors as well as the limitations of the population sample.

3 Survey Development

When developing the survey, we found there is no definition for TB/FF to which participants could refer. TB is relatively niche, so a "common understanding" of it in games, much less other areas of expertise would be unlikely with survey participants. Similarly, it would be difficult to say the extent that respondents might categorise or otherwise conceptualise TB/FF, even if aware of the theories. In order to address these concerns we felt it necessary to present an outline of TB/FF features for participants' use when completing the survey measures. The outline would serve as a loose definition for respondents to use when making their own judgements. It would need to be broad enough to capture the potential range of TB/FF phenomena, but not so wide that anything could fit within the outlines, rendering them unhelpful. We acknowledge the risks in developing our own definitions for TB/FF, and attempted to limit bias from the researchers or the creation of leading/self-fulfilling results in the process. This was done by codifying available literature on TB/FF in digital games and constructing it into the following terms:

"The definition of **Tend and Befriend** *includes: The experience of playing a game that affords nurturing behaviour, loving feelings, close relationships and friend-groups, support, the development and maintenance of a network, characters, care, and/or safe spaces.*

The definition of **Fight or Flight** *includes: The experience of playing a game that affords combat, threat, violence, escape, fear or danger - as well as featuring patterns of aggression and dominance over another, or confrontation."*

We emphasise that the outlines are not presented as complete definitions of TB/FF in games – but only intended for such use in the survey.

With the basis (outlines) for respondents to refer to while completing the survey decided, presenting a sample of games for users to rate was the next logical step. A total of 45 games (or game series) were selected for the survey and respondents would rate them along a set of 7-point Likert scales (ranging from "1 Strongly disagree" to "7 Strongly agree"), asking them to indicate the extent to which they felt the game in question was: (1) TB (2) FF and (3) enjoyable.

15 titles were chosen for three separate categories; the categories were pre-coded as potential TB, FF or Other. Games selected for Other were those which featured elements of TB and FF features, or seemly lacked both, such as *World of Warcraft* or *Tetris*. They were selected according to: researcher familiarity with their features; games that are regularly associated with each other or had market-shares; relative popularity or fame in games culture; as well as any reviews or articles commonly associating those games with features of TB/FF consistent with the study aims. The titles and their categories are presented in Table 1.

As it was highly unlikely that participants will have played all 45 games in our survey, we asked respondents to confirm their familiarity with titles prior to rating them. All games (or series) were presented in random order to each participant in the survey. Participants were asked to confirm if they had played (or felt they had adequate experience with the title via other means, such as watching streamers) before continuing. If participants said they did not know the title, it was skipped for the next random game in the queue until all remaining titles were offered. Participants were not presented with the same game more than once, but it was possible to skip "back" to previous answers if they felt they made had made an error at any point.

Although it would be easier to suggest that any game within a particular franchise share similar features, mechanics, aesthetics, etc. this is not the case. The diversity of a franchise can range dramatically with some games only sharing names in common. An example of this would be early survival-horror *Resident Evil* titles versus the more co-op action-orientated *Resident Evil 5*. To account for this, when a franchise had released multiple instalments, respondents were also requested to select a title from a list of options from which they would base their evaluation. This was designed specifically to filter any "outlier" titles considered too removed from others in its series for accurate comparison. Additionally, if there were notable Expansions, Content Modes or DLC (e.g. *Fortnite*) that might drastically skew results - these were also presented as options for survey respondents.

As part of a larger research project, it was decided early on that it would be useful to include measures of individual differences for the survey, in addition to standard demographic data, to complement any TB/FF results for later analysis. Although outside the scope of this paper, participants were asked to complete three measures of individual differences: the Interpersonal Reactivity Index (IRI) [5,6], the Gaming Attitudes, Motives and Experiences Scale (GAMES) [9] and the Ten-Item Personality Inventory (TIPI) [8]. The IRI was selected as a method of quantifying empathy between respondents, while GAMES was selected due to its potential in capturing nuance between game genres and experiences. As the survey was of significant length, the final addition of the TIPI was included for its succinct nature (10 items) in measuring personality.

Table 1. Table with pre-coded games by category.

	Tend/Befriend	Fight/Flight	Other
1	Shelter	Call of Duty	Tetris
2	Monument Valley 2	Gears of War	Prof. Layton
3	Animal Crossing	Resident Evil	Super Hexagon
4	Abzû	Metal Gear Solid	Temple Run
5	Pikmin	Destiny	Mario Kart
6	Neko Atsume	Halo	SimCity
7	Harvest Moon	Tekken	Candy Crush Saga
8	Pokémon	Fortnite	Mass Effect
9	Minecraft	Shadow of the Colossus	World of Warcraft
10	Florence	DOOM	Final Fantasy
11	Journey	Tomb Raider	Final Fantasy XIV Online
12	Flower	Silent Hill	Euro Truck Simulator
13	ICO	Souls Series	flOw
14	The Sims	X-COM	FIFA
15	FarmVille	Civilization	Surgeon Simulator

4   Data Collection and Results

We conducted an online survey of the "Tend & Befriend Response" in games, positioning it in relation to the Acute Stress Response (commonly known as "Fight or Flight"). The survey was hosted on Qualtrics and available in English (UK). It was largely distributed through social media platforms (Twitter, Instagram and Facebook), as well as Reddit, Discord and word-of-mouth.

The survey received 510 respondents: 64.9% male, 30% female and a remaining 5.1% which included individuals who identified by specific gender, chose to omit their response or selected "Other". Half of the participants indicated that they fit into the (25–34) age bracket, and a further 26.7% and 16.5% in (18–24) and (35–44) respectively. A majority reported playing games regularly, with a cumulative 87% describing their activity as, "Several times a week" to "Everyday", and 72.4% playing for over an hour per session.

The results were downloaded from the Qualtrics platform server and IBM SPSS Statistics software (ver.27) was used to process the responses. As we had 45 games in the study, it would not be possible to present all of them here. We present a selection that met our criteria as TB/FF archetypes during later analysis (See: Archetype Classification). It is important to note that the results for the games revealed a range of scores, as well as marked difference in opinion between players themselves at times (e.g. the mode for Abzû was split between 5 and 7). Games pre-coded as "Other" had less definitive results in some cases, and more complex outputs in others – attributable to a number of factors which we explore further in Discussion.

At the end of this section we also present a summary of our descriptive data and the results per game and category.

4.1 Pre-coded: Tend & Befriend

Animal Crossing Series

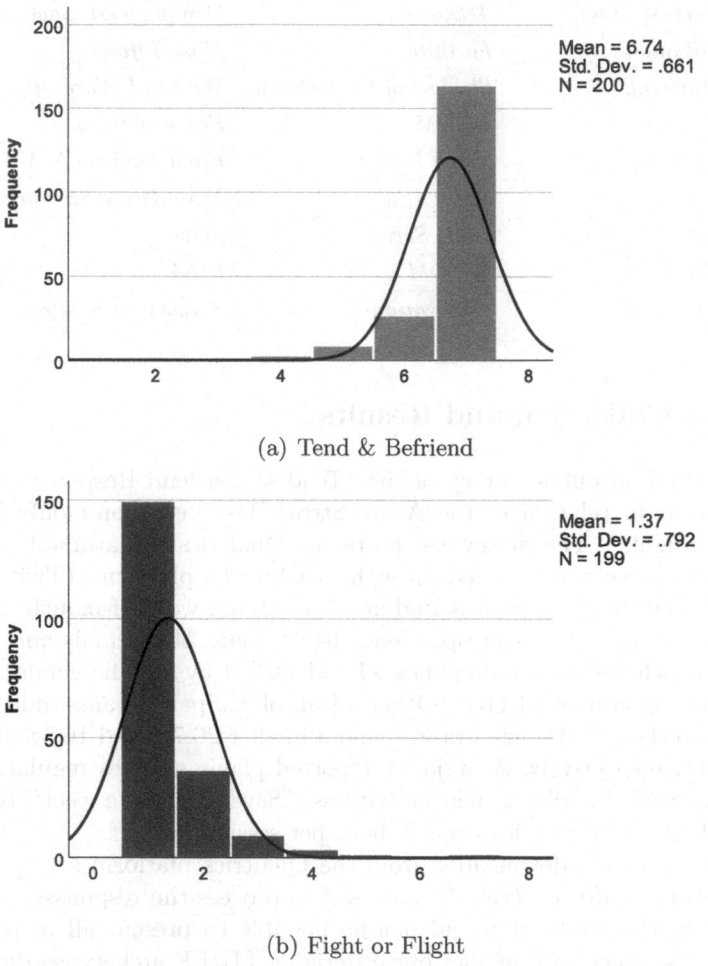

(a) Tend & Befriend

(b) Fight or Flight

Fig. 1. Histogram for *Animal Crossing* Series TB/FF Ratings, demonstrating high TB ratings in green, and low FF ratings in red. (Color figure online)

Neko Atsume (Kitty Collector) (Fig. 2).

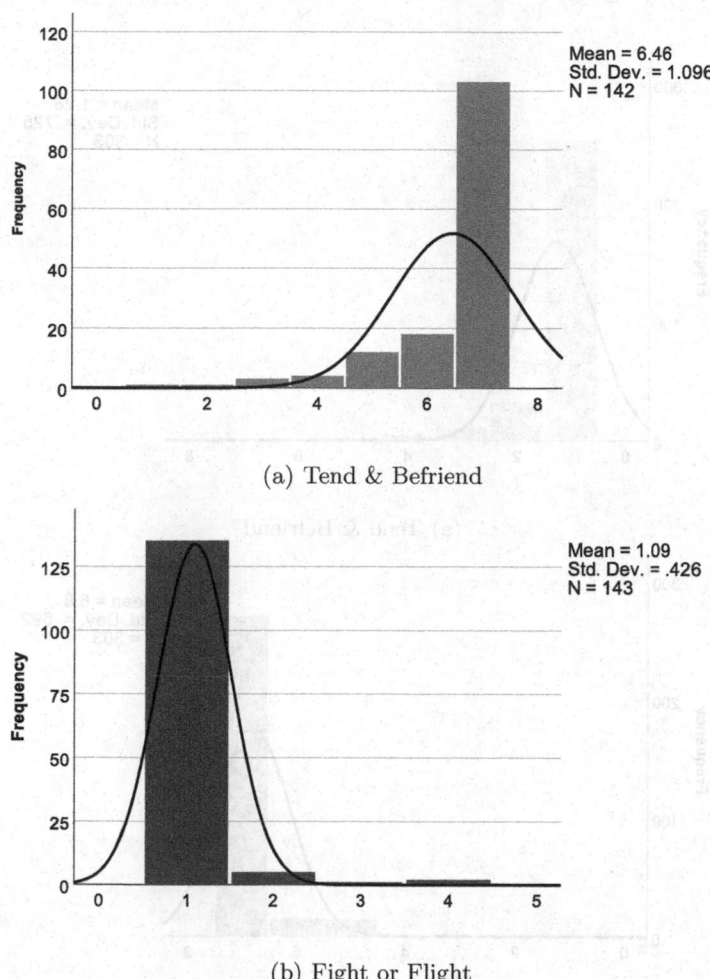

(a) Tend & Befriend

(b) Fight or Flight

Fig. 2. *Neko Atsume* TB/FF Ratings, demonstrating the pattern of TB-archetype titles, as seen in Fig. 1 *Animal Crossing*.

4.2   Pre-coded: Fight or Flight

DOOM Series (Fig. 3).

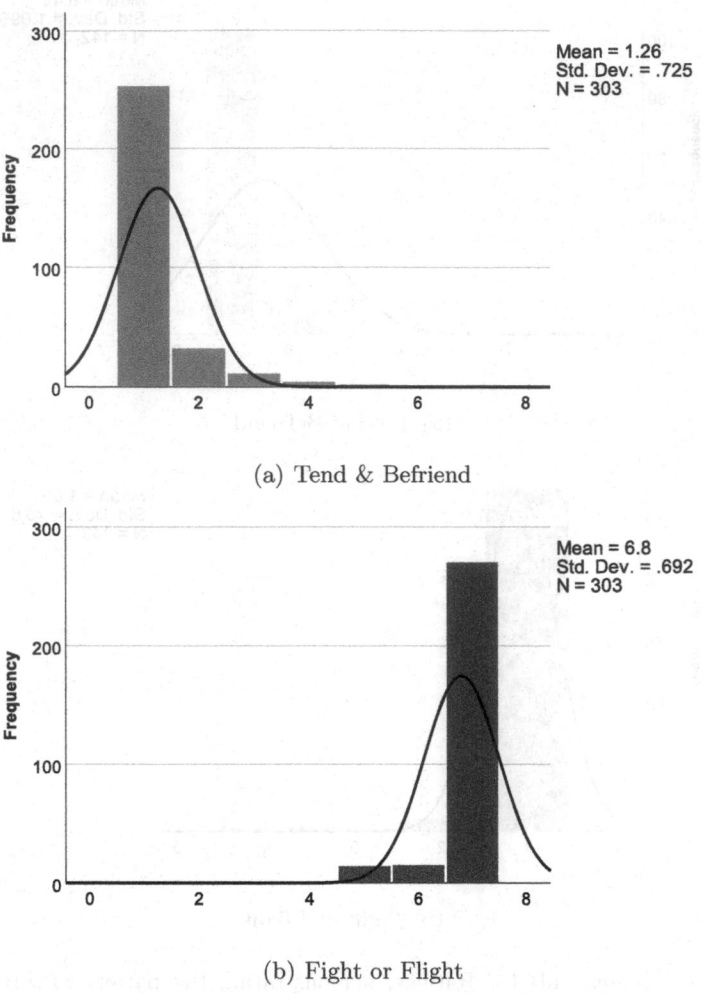

(a) Tend & Befriend

(b) Fight or Flight

Fig. 3. Histogram for FF archetype *DOOM* Series. TB/FF Ratings demonstrating a reverse pattern from TB-archetype titles such as *Animal Crossing* and *Neko Atsume*.

Souls Series (Fig. 4).

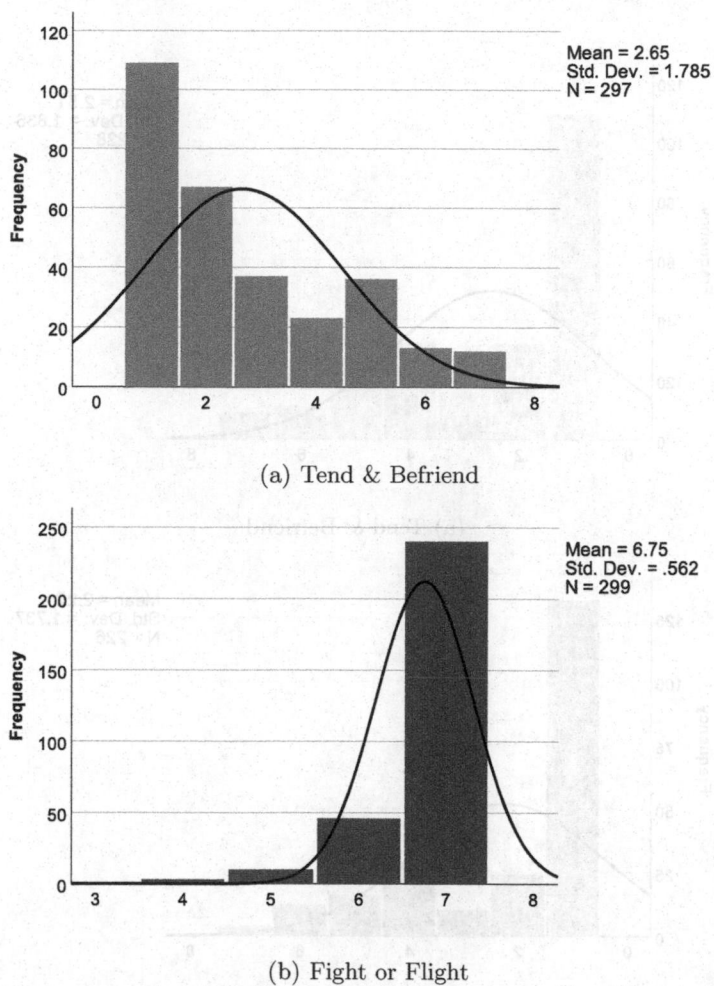

(a) Tend & Befriend

(b) Fight or Flight

Fig. 4. Histogram for *Souls* Series TB/FF Ratings. TB ratings are still skewed towards the lower end of the scale but with a more gentle distribution. However, FF ratings are still heavily weighted towards to upper end of the scale.

4.3   Pre-coded: Other

Candy Crush Saga (Fig. 5).

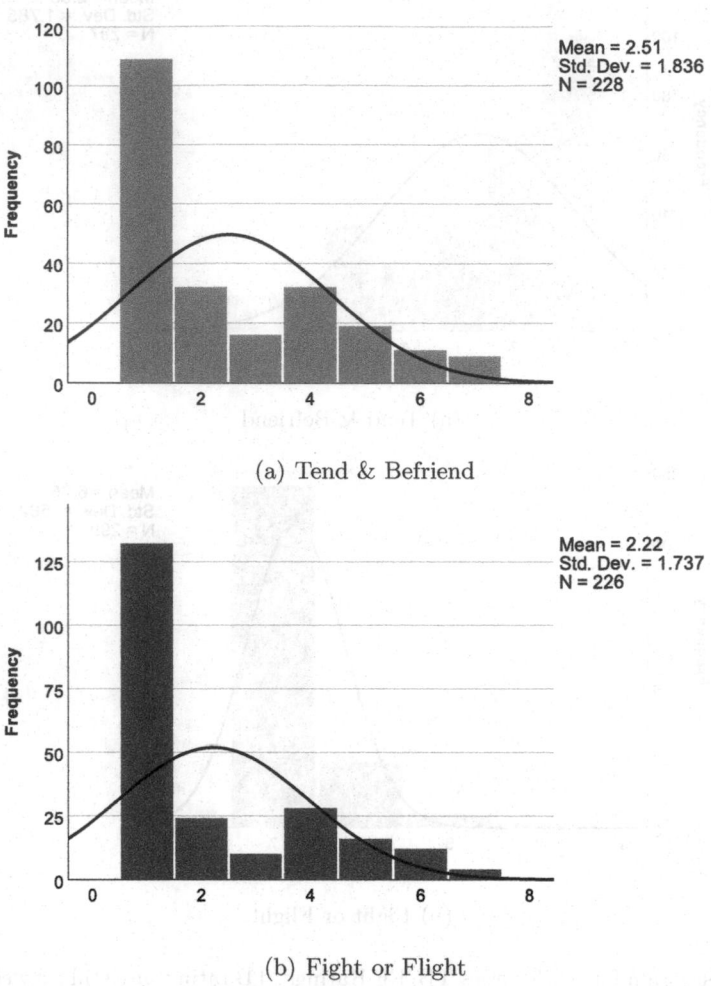

(a) Tend & Befriend

(b) Fight or Flight

Fig. 5. Histogram for *Candy Crush Saga* showing low ratings across both TB/FF scales.

Mass Effect Series (Fig. 6).

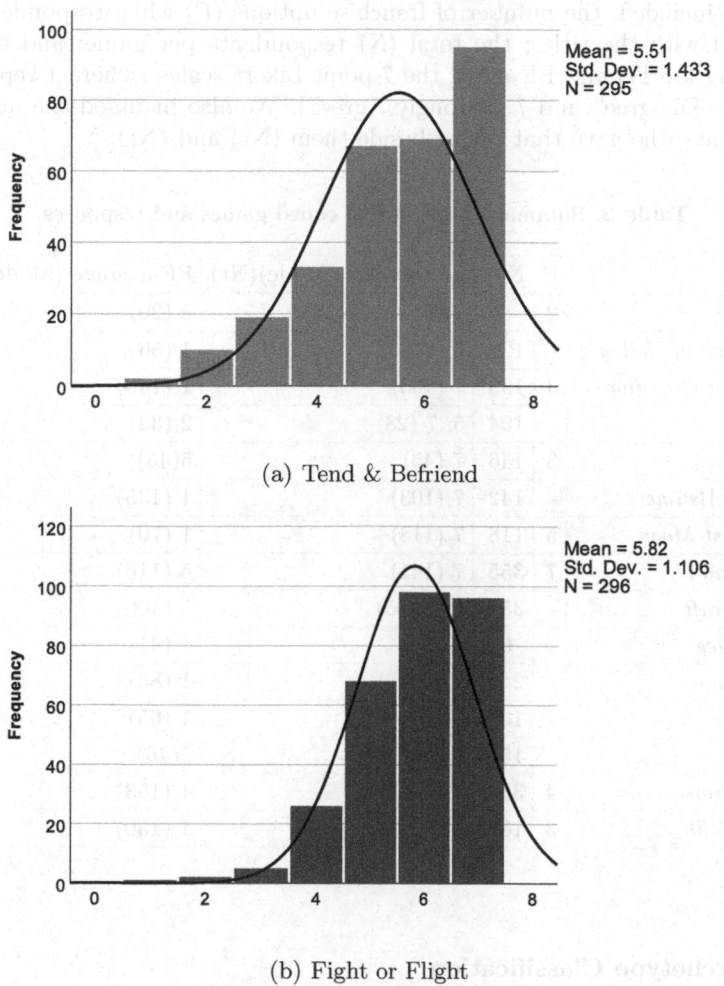

(a) Tend & Befriend

(b) Fight or Flight

Fig. 6. Histogram for *Mass Effect* Series demonstrates mid-high ratings across both TB/FF scales suggesting that the game features elements of both.

4.4 Summary

Tables 2, 3 and 4 show summaries of the data, separated by pre-coding category. We have included: the number of franchise options (F) when respondents were presented with the titles; the total (N) respondents per game; and the average rating for TB and FF along the 7-point Likert scales (where 1 represented "Strongly Disagree" and 7 "Strongly Agree"). We also included the number of respondents who gave that rating beside them (Nt) and (Nf).

Table 2. Summary table of **TB** coded games and responses.

Title	F	N	TB average (Mode)(Nt)	FF average (Mode)(Nf)
Shelter	2	56	7 (24)	5 (20)
Monument Valley 2	-	122	5 (31)	1 (56)
Animal Crossing	3	199	7 (163)	1 (149)
Abzŭ	-	104	5; 7 (28)	2 (32)
Pikmin	3	146	7 (45)	5(45)
Neko Atsume	-	142	7 (103)	1 (135)
Harvest Moon	5	118	7 (118)	1 (70)
Pokémon	7	355	7 (141)	5 (110)
Minecraft	-	351	6; 7 (95)	5 (106)
Florence	-	61	7 (35)	1 (41)
Journey	-	245	7 (114)	1 (86)
Flower	-	133	7 (40)	1 (65)
ICO	-	157	7 (56)	5(46)
The Sims	4	358	7 (195)	1 (153)
FarmVille	3	163	7 (62)	1 (130)

4.5 Archetype Classification

A criterion for establishing titles as being TB or FF was developed for use in further analysis. This methodology involved taking the percentage of responses which rated a title on the two most extreme ends of the Likert scale (1–2 and 6–7) compared to the its total responses received. We considered games as categorised TB or FF if 80%+ of respondents N for that title rated the game as 6 or 7 ("Strongly Agree") on its relative scale. The three highest-rated games per category are presented in Table 5.

These titles are regularly referenced in media and games discourse (e.g. *Animal Crossing*) as examples of TB-centric experiences, which positively suggests our methodology captures the necessary data [15]. Our methodology was less robust when trying to categorise games that we pre-coded as Other, with results demonstrating reasonably high variability across TB/FF scales.

Table 3. Summary table of **FF** coded games and responses.

Title	F	N	TB average (Mode)(Nt)	FF average (Mode)(Nf)
Call of Duty	9	317	1 (133)	7 (235)
Gears of War	4	214	1 (60)	7 (152)
Resident Evil	5	266	2 (79)	7 (178)
Metal Gear Solid	6	256	3 (52)	7 (112)
Destiny	4	218	5 (51)	7 (104)
Halo	4	316	1 (86)	7 (179)
Tekken	7	273	1 (146)	7 (181)
Fortnite	2	235	1 (48)	7 (131)
Shadow of the Colossus	-	258	5 (62)	6 (83)
DOOM	3	303	1 (253)	7 (270)
Tomb Raider	7	312	1 (82)	7 (133)
Silent Hill	6	205	1 (63)	7 (138)
Souls Series	4	297	1 (109)	7 (240)
X-COM	4	229	5 (63)	7 (116)
Civilization	5	295	5 (86)	5 (86)

Table 4. Summary table of **Other** coded games and responses.

Title	F	N	TB average (Mode)(Nt)	FF average (Mode)(Nf)
Tetris	-	464	1 (276)	1 (196)
Prof. Layton	6	150	5 (33)	1 (75)
Super Hexagon	-	156	1 (122)	7 (34)
Temple Run	5	216	1 (160)	7 (60)
Mario Kart	6	405	1 (90)	5 (119)
SimCity	3	242	5 (56)	1 (89)
Candy Crush Saga	3	226	1 (109)	1 (132)
Mass Effect	3	295	7 (95)	6 (98)
World of Warcraft	-	312	7 (91)	7 (99)
Final Fantasy	6	280	5 (82)	6 (95)
Final Fantasy XIV Online	-	96	6 (30)	5 (26)
Euro Truck Simulator	2	100	1 (30)	1 (59)
flOw	-	117	1 (22)	1 (29)
FIFA	4	125	1 (29)	5 (34)
Surgeon Simulator	-	213	1 (83)	1 (66)

Table 5. TB/FF archetype games and %-age respondent agreement

Tend & Befriend	%	Fight or Flight	%
Animal Crossing	94.97	*Call of Duty*	90.85
Neko Atsume	85.21	*DOOM*	94.06
Harvest Moon	93.22	*Souls*	96.30

5   Discussion

Of the 15 games pre-coded as TB-centric, 3 titles qualified using our method. Of the proposed 15 FF titles, 11 qualified under the same criteria.

Of the 15 titles classified as Other, none met our expectations for categorisation. We had hypothesised that some games would be rated "low" (1–2) across both TB/FF measures, suggesting that the game in question was "Neither" TB or FF, or that some would be rated "high" (6–7) across the scales, implying that those games featured "Both" TB/FF elements. This area of "Neither/Both" (NB) is of great interest, and will be useful when discussing the limitations of TB/FF. NB supports the increasing need for nuance when utilising a theory such as TB to describe digital games.

For the purposes of the study, we asked players to score games in their entirety as being TB/FF, however it is our intention to continue this research with greater specificity. That is to say, rather than investigate titles as a whole, perhaps it would be informative to explore them from a mechanic-based lens, aesthetic-lens, motivational-lens, *etc*.

Some games may have a majority of TB features but perhaps an individual level will act as a "surprise" for players or be used to narrative-mechanical effect (e.g. a scenario where a player will suddenly have to flee something). Our survey did not account for such a change in the player journey, and this might explain some variability in the histogram results.

Aside from the potential for TB/FF games and mechanics, it can be noted (e.g. in the case of *World of Warcraft*) that games scored highly along the two scales, but were not Archetypes. This demonstrates a limitation of the current classification method: while we can see that *WoW* leans heavily towards both extremes of the TB/FF histograms, only 54.59% (TB) and 60.26% (FF) is accounted for in the process and therefore it did not meet our benchmark. Interestingly, MMOs (such as *WoW*, *FFXIV*) and games with strong social/multiplayer features (such as *Destiny*, *Fortnite*, and *FIFA*) scored relatively high as TB experiences, though they might not seem as such at first glance. In our study, *FIFA* was pre-coded as Other, while *Destiny* and *Fortnite* were FF. This suggests that games with strong social features are able to engage TB experiences to some degree. Additionally, games that provide players with a broad range of mechanics (such as MMOs) can provide simultaneous TB/FF experiences for individual players and player-groups. In other words, if the game offers a range of TB/FF features, players can engage with which features they most enjoy or desire, and potentially ignore those that they do not.

This implies that not only are there TB/FF games and TB/FF mechanics, but potentially TB/FF players too. By this, we mean there are players that may intrinsically enjoy or navigate towards experiences that allow them to engage with their preferred play-style regardless (or even in spite of) the intended game mechanics. An example of this would be a player who primarily uses *Grand Theft Auto* games as a driving simulator. This echoes Bartle's Player Taxonomy, in which he proposes that players would be willing to switch or engage with activities that are less satisfying, provided that it meets their primary goal in the end [2] Such an example might be a player who regularly plays a First-Person Shooter (FPS) not because they enjoy shooting targets, but supporting and socialising with their team or clan (Fig. 7).

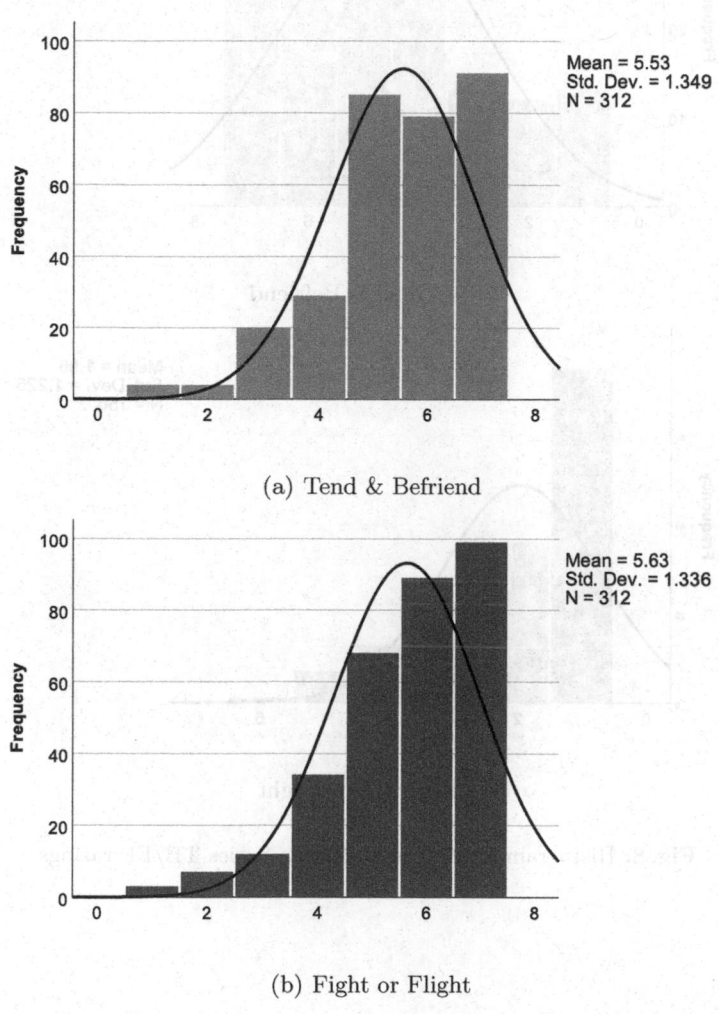

(a) Tend & Befriend

(b) Fight or Flight

Fig. 7. Histogram for *World of Warcraft* TB/FF ratings

Professor Layton and *Super Hexagon* demonstrate games that scored very low (1–2) along one TB/FF scale, but middling along the other. One potential explanation of this might be that while the games have a average consistency in one factor (e.g. FF in *Super Hexagon*), they could be described as specifically "un-TB" in the other (Figs. 8 and 9).

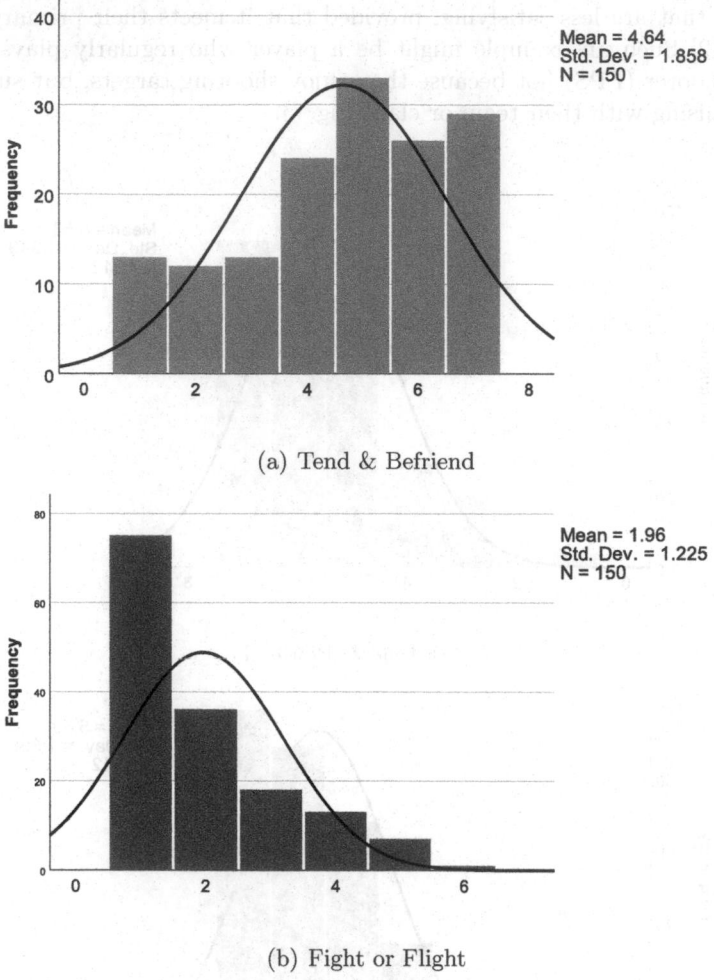

(a) Tend & Befriend

(b) Fight or Flight

Fig. 8. Histogram for *Professor Layton* Series TB/FF ratings

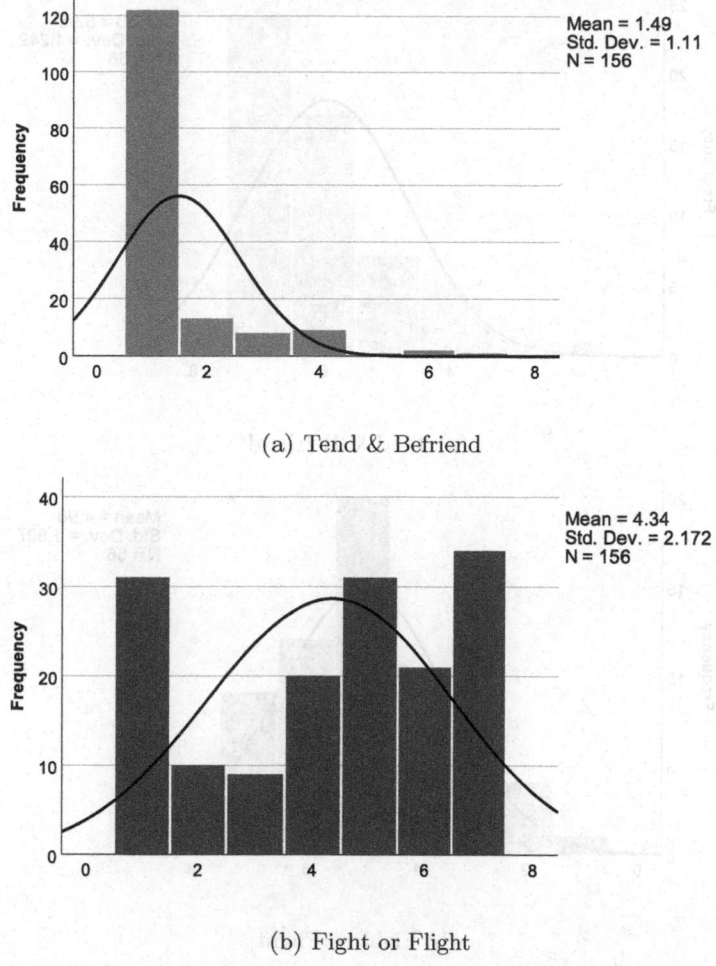

(a) Tend & Befriend

(b) Fight or Flight

Fig. 9. Histogram for *Super Hexagon* TB/FF ratings

Shelter is an example in which TB is skewed positively, yet it features FF highly in the middle range - not the extreme. This implies that the difference between (for example) an FF archetype game and a game that has elements of FF, could be significant when discussing them (Fig. 10).

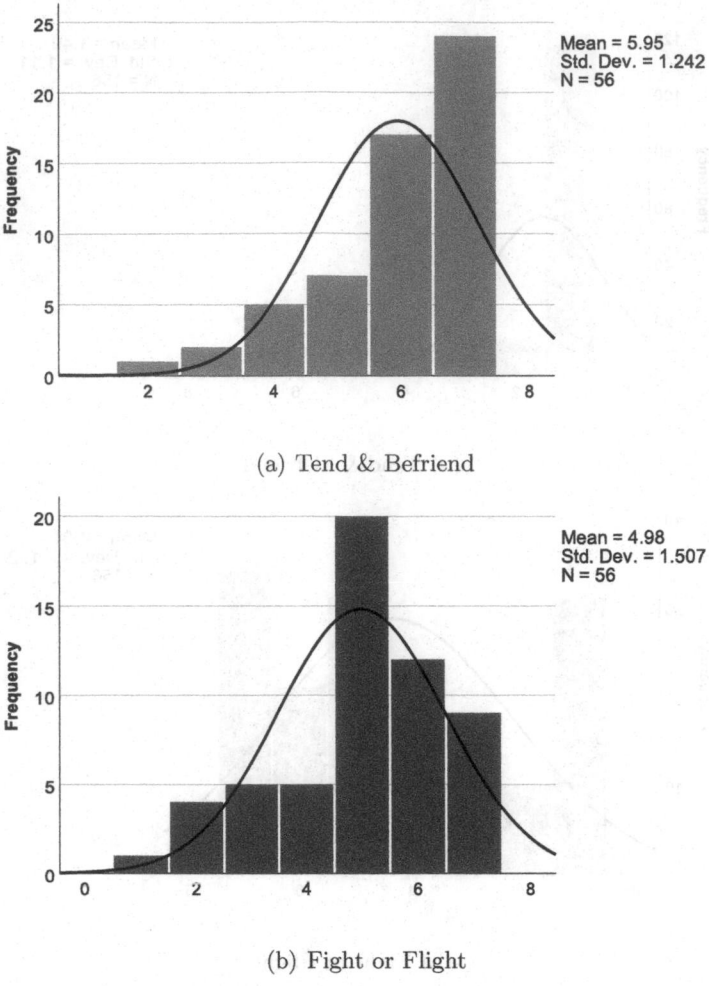

(a) Tend & Befriend

(b) Fight or Flight

Fig. 10. Histogram for *Shelter* Series TB/FF ratings

As TB is a gender-based theory, we highlight that the responses to our survey were mostly male (64.9%), but hesitate to comment on the impact this might have on the data. This is because categorisation was made on a game-by-game basis (as not every survey respondent will have familiarity with the complete set of 45 titles), and so the gender distribution of respondents vary accordingly. Looking at the demographic data per game is an area for potential investigation, as well as one possible approach to engaging with the topic.

6   Conclusion

Our data-driven study suggests that TB can be considered as a concrete phenomenon in games; there are archetypal titles which may serve as useful references for research and discourse based on this and other stress-response design theories. These games are presented in Table 5.

We propose that TB/FF are best investigated in relation to one another, and that treating such phenomena as working in tandem (rather than as a dichotomy) will be more productive and representative for future discourse. In addition to this, we encourage the view of TB/FF-ness as two distinct spectrums, and pay particular attention to note that rating of the phenomena may need measurement in both range (*intensity of*) and volume (*amount of*) present in a game.

Some games demonstrated low scores on both the TB/FF scales, which lends support to our hypothesis that TB/FF is not an all-encompassing theory, and some games could be considered "Neither", "Both" – or a new method of classification entirely. Regardless, variability in the results and the limits of this study mean that further investigation is necessary to develop these claims.

As part of our own research, we will continue to analyse our data beyond the descriptive level presented here, and follow up the questions raised by the data thus far.

TB is an nascent area of research in digital games, and the methodology and approaches we present here provide informative starting points. We encourage greater exploration into the way researchers, developers and designers choose to define TB/FF titles; what the shared features or mechanics might be of such titles; how the public may frame or position themselves in relation to these titles; and what the value Tend & Befriend response might bring (or limit) in the evolution of game design.

References

1. Entertainment software association. https://www.theesa.com/wp-content/uploads/2021/03/Final-Edited-2020-ESA_Essential_facts.pdf. Accessed 10 Nov 2021
2. Bartle, R.: Virtual Worlds: Why People Play. https://mud.co.uk/richard/VWWPP.pdf. Accessed 28 Jan 2022. Chapter. In: Massively Multiplayer Game Development 2, Alexander, T. (2005)
3. Brie Code: Slouching toward relevant video games. https://www.gamesindustry.biz/articles/2017-03-08-slouching-toward-relevant-video-games. Accessed 10 Nov 2021
4. Csikszentmihalyi, M.: Flow: The Psychology of Optimal Experience. Harper & Row. https://www.researchgate.net/publication/224927532_Flow_The_Psychology_of_Optimal_Experience. Accessed 10 Nov 2021
5. Davis, M.: Measuring individual differences in empathy: evidence for a multidimensional approach. J. Pers. Soc. Psychol. **44**, 113–126. https://www.eckerd.edu/psychology/iri/
6. Davis, M.: A multidimensional approach to individual differences in empathy. In: JSAS Catalog of Selected Documents in Psychology, vol. 10, p. 85. https://www.eckerd.edu/psychology/iri/

7. Glendinning, M.: How Canadian programmer brie code is changing the way we interact with our phones. https://fashionmagazine.com/wellness/brie-code-interview/. Accessed 10 Nov 2021

8. Gosling, S., Rentfrow, P., Swann, W., Jr.: A very brief measure of the big five personality domains. J. Res. Pers. **37**, 504–528. http://gosling.psy.utexas.edu/scales-weve-developed/ten-item-personality-measure-tipi/. Accessed 10 Nov 2021

9. Hilgard, J., Engelhardt, C.R., Bartholow, B.: Individual differences in motives, preferences, and pathology in video games: the gaming attitudes, motives, and experiences scales (games). Front. Psychol **4**(608). https://doi.org/10.3389/fpsyg.2013.00608

10. O'Shea, Z., Freeman, J.: Game design frameworks: where do we start? Article 25, pp. 1–10. Association for Computing Machinery. https://doi.org/10.1145/3337722.3337753

11. Richter, F.: Gaming: the most lucrative entertainment industry by far. https://www.statista.com/chart/22392/global-revenue-of-selected-entertainment-industry-sectors/. Accessed 10 Nov 2021

12. Ruberg, B., Scully-Blaker, R.: Making players care: the ambivalent cultural politics of care and video games. Int. J. Cultural Stud. **24**(4), 655–672. https://doi.org/10.1177/1367877920950323

13. Taylor, S.: Tend and befriend: biobehavioral bases of affiliation under stress. Curr. Directions Psychol. Sci. **15**(6), 273–277. https://doi.org/10.1111/j.1467-8721.2006.00451.x

14. Taylor, S., Klein, L., Lewis, B., Gruenewald, T., Gurung, R., Updegraff, J.: Biobehavioral responses to stress in females: tend-and-befriend, not fight-or-flight. Psychol. Rev. **107**(3), 411–429. https://doi.org/10.1037/0033-295X.107.3.411

15. Wilson, C.: Animal crossing and beyond: why people are falling in love with 'wholesome' video games. https://www.abc.net.au/news/science/2020-06-05/wholesome-games-animal-crossing/12318570. Accessed 10 Nov 2021

Design Implications for a Gamified Recycling House

Adam Palmquist[1](✉) [iD], Ole Goethe[2] [iD], Jeanine Krath[3] [iD], Joacim Rosenlund[4] [iD], and Miralem Helmefalk[5] [iD]

[1] Department of Applied IT, University of Gothenburg, Forskningsgången 6,
417 56 Gothenburg, Sweden
adam.palmquist@ait.gu.se
[2] Nord University, Universitetsalléen 11, 8026 Bodø, Norway
[3] University of Koblenz-Landau, Universitaetsstrasse 1, 56070 Koblenz, Germany
[4] Department of Biology and Environmental Science, Linnaeus University,
Universitetsplatsen 1, 392 31 Kalmar, Sweden
[5] Department of Marketing, Linnaeus University, Universitetsplatsen 1, 392 31 Kalmar, Sweden

Abstract. This paper encircles explorative design research in a multiple stakeholder triple helix project concerning circular economy and household recycling. Design ethnography was employed to find implications for outlining a gamification artifact that would facilitate recycling behaviors. We collected our data during 27 weeks by attending two field sites: *Site A*, project stakeholder meetings and a participatory design workshop, and *Site B*, semi-structured interviews in the household stakeholders' residences. Our thematic analysis of the sites' collected ethnographic record extrapolated two specific categories: Stakeholder requirements and Gamification ruleset, together enfolding five key-themes and various sub-themes that could be used to inform the design of a gamification artifact aimed at recycling. Also, based on our research, we propose two research propositions regarding storytelling and understanding for further gamification design researchers to investigate.

Keywords: Gamification · Design ethnography · Informing design · Recycling · Circular economy · Participatory design · Thematic analysis · Interviews · Stakeholder

1 Introduction

In the 2010s, an increasing number of communities from various domains concerted that our planet had finite resources [1], and it also became clearer which domains in society in various parts of the world, e.g., America, Europe, and part of Asia, were contributing seriously to the risk that we will not achieve the goal to limit global warming to 2 degrees Celsius by the year 2100 [2].

One important aspect in fighting climate change are various behavioral patterns regarding sustainable day-to-day living [3]. A track towards more sustainable societies, in general, is the circular economy [4]. The circular economy, which involves sharing, leasing, reusing, repairing, refurbishing and recycling existing materials and products as long as possible [5], has been suggested as a transition to a more well-organized society that pays more attention to the earth's limited resources and stresses resource efficiency, waste prevention and recycling in all areas of society [4]. The circular economy paradigm has been foreseen to have a vast potential for developing a more sustainable society, e.g., by decreasing greenhouse gas emissions and/or countering the planet's resource scarcity. However, while the circular economy is predicted as feasible and, together with several transnational policies [6] as well as progressive grassroots initiatives [7] intending to redirect parts of society from a linear towards a more circular one, the transformation is taking too long. In the 2020s, globally produced waste is anticipated to increase due to economic growth and social development [8].

While preventing waste is a priority, recycling systems often serve as the most visible and prominent circular economy systems in a society. Their potential is also enhanced by their role in mobilizing entire communities with an "everyone can make a differ-ence" approach. However, waste recycling in households, as is the case in Sweden, is likewise one of the circular economy liabilities, making it reliant on individual house-holds' environmental interests and opinions. Appropriate recycling thus depends on occurring behavioral patterns, influenced by household demographics like age, gen-der, employment, income, standard of living and educational background [9], and the afforded recycling condition in the imminent area.

As the household's resolution to participate and contribute to the transformation to an eco-friendlier society largely cruxes around habitual and behavioral patterns, there have been propositions as well as diminutive experimental investigations suggesting that techniques from the field of behavioral economics [10, 11] and gamification [12] may be proficient in influencing the choice architecture of individual households. These motivational techniques are designed to facilitate the change that various households must accomplish for the sake of the future of our planet and its prospective inhabitants.

While there have existed suggestions in the literature concerning gamified recycling [13, 14], there is a deficiency in designing gamified artifacts that afford and sustain behavioral patterns for sustainable household recycling. Additionally, even if there is a multitude of gamification design frameworks, several approaches lack independent ver-ification [15]. Human-computer interaction and Interaction design [16] utilize ethnogra-phy approaches to inform untried artifact designs [17–19]. Accordingly, the goal of this study is by employment of ethnographic design lenses to find design implication for a gamification artifact addressing recycling behavior in the context of an onsite physical recycling house.

1.1   Related Work: Nudging and Gamification in Sustainability

When it comes to influencing individuals' behaviors, such as recycling, nudging - that is, changing people's decision-making patterns without prohibiting options or substantially altering economic incentives [20] - is a promising approach [21, 22]. Nudges can be con-ceptualized as self-image nudges (focusing on people's desire to maintain an attractive self-image, e.g., by facilitating behavior change through the provision of information about different choices), social nudges (targeting people's desire to mimic the behavior of peers), or default nudges (targeting default values to guide behavior in the absence of active decision making) in the context of sustainable behavior [23]. For effective nudging, the use of game elements that lead to gameful experiences, i.e., gamification [24], can be a valuable approach. For example, achievements awarded for certain choices can provide a form of self-image nudges to improve self-monitoring [25], while rankings or status ranks can allow for social comparison [25] and thus constitute a form of social nudges.

Gamification has been shown to be effective in influencing various sustainable behaviors, most notably energy conservation and sustainable commuting [26]. For example, gamification positively impacts awareness, learning, and behavioral outcomes related to energy efficiency [27–29]; encourages walking, biking, and public transportation use [29, 30]; persuades drivers to adopt fuel-efficient driving habits [31]; and supports environmentally friendly dietary choices [32]. In addition, gamification has been used to promote water conservation [33] and heating cost reduction [34].

Specifically, regarding behaviors related to the circular economy, previous studies have shown that gamification can serve to reduce waste production [34] and promote recycling behaviors both among tourists [35] and in individual households [13, 14, 36]. In addition, serious games have recently been developed to teach knowledge about the circular economy and corresponding individual behaviors [37, 38]. However, apart from these individual studies, the use of gamification to promote waste recycling is still largely unexplored.

1.2 The Gamified Recycling House Project

The two year triple helix project resides in the city of Kalmar, which is situated by the Baltic Sea and has approximately 40 000 inhabitants. Linnaeus University is the project coordinator in a consortium of various regional partners from public and private sectors, as well as the University of Gothenburg. The project investigates the probability affecting communities' habitual and behavioral patterns by constructing a novel gamified recycling house.

The innovative recycling house which is intended to be enhanced by a gamified approach has a purposeful futuristic form, resembling a snowflake, with its entire exterior composed of a mirrored glass facade (Fig. 1); the progressive recycling house design intends to proclaim the significance of acting (like recycling) for the sake of our planet's future.

One of the aims of the project is that by integrating a gamification artifact in the process of the domestic garbage disposal, creating a gameful experience to incentivize recycling, the household resident(s) will increase overall recycling rates in the household. If successful, the project can advance the idea of the circular economy onwards by providing a critical piece of the puzzle for sustainability on our planet.

Planning and constructing the house lasted from January until November 2021. In December 2021, 15 selected households began to recycle six waste fractions in the house (Fig. 2). Interviews with the fifteen households were performed before the recycling started and will be repeated afterwards. The current research presents the results of the first interview round and aims to answer the following research question (RQ):

What co-existing stakeholder themes should the gamification artefact consider?

Fig. 1. The recycling house onsite. Photo by Anders Olsson

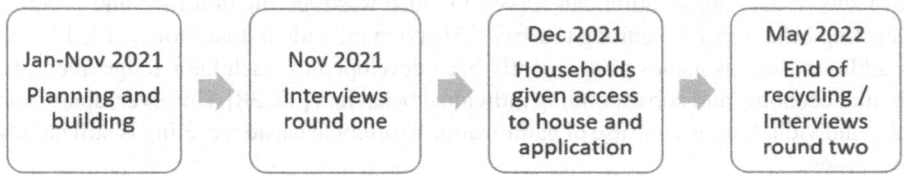

| Jan-Nov 2021 Planning and building | Nov 2021 Interviews round one | Dec 2021 Households given access to house and application | May 2022 End of recycling / Interviews round two |

Fig. 2. Project audit trail

2 Methodology

As our review of the literature implies that the domain of gamified waste recycling is unexplored. Therefore, the presented research employs an exploratory design ethnographic approach [39–41] to mutually inform our forthcoming gamification design for recycling and contribute to the body of knowledge of how to outline gamification in the rapidly emerging fields of sustainability and environmental studies.

In design ethnography research, interventions and design bleed into each other. It is an iterative process that requires the designer/researcher to move swiftly between various tactics. Therefore, the designer/researcher should adhere to methodological rules, but can adapt and transcend them. Salvador et al. plead for using methods creatively by continuously developing them specifically for a particular field context [42]. Another way of saying it is: "Design ethnography is therefore a "dirty" practice that tends toward anarchy" [40 p. 91]. Undertaking design ethnography, the designer/researcher needs to constantly adapt to various stakeholder perspectives [40] because s/he functions as an ambassador and cultural interpreter for the design project stakeholders [43].

The data collected through the ethnographic techniques are used to give 'implications for design'. It is a type of design knowledge employed to create novel technologies or enhance existing ones [44]. In Human-Computer Interaction, this design discourse has commonly been used to investigate a social context, hence, generating design implications for such context [45]. Design ethnography is employed habitually in the initial stages of the design process when grounded design research is needed to understand individuals in specific settings to inform novel artifacts designs.

A design ethnographic approach has been employed in this study with techniques such as participatory design [46] semi-structured interviews [47], and a thematic analysis [48, 49]. Thus, we achieved rich ethnographic records with interconnected conclusions informing the design [42] of the forthcoming gamification artifact.

2.1 Thematic Analysis Approach

Two field sites were visited conducting the presented research: a participatory design workshop session with the project stakeholders, and semi-structured interviews with project participating households, shaping the study's ethnographic records [41]. The ethnographic record was transcribed by authors 1 and 5 and uploaded in the MAXQDA software - an analysis tool that we used to overview the rich dataset and increase the speed of the analysis. In the MAXQDA software, the field sites' ethnographic records were structured and analyzed separately and afterward related with a thematic approach.

Thematic analysis is one of the most frequently used analysis approaches when examining a qualitative ethnographic record [48], clustering the collected data into groups which each are given individual labels; it can depend on various social, cultural, and environmental phenomena depending on the research question and purpose of the ethnographic study [48, 49]. We conducted a six-phase thematic analysis on our collected ethnographic records [50]. As we conducted an explorative study, our analysis can be categorized as an inductive (bottom-up) analysis approach that scans the collected data after pieces with symbolic similarities and then attempts to generalize from these data pieces.

For the project stakeholder from Site A, the majority of the thematic analysis was completed in June 2021, and for the participating households from Site B in December 2021. Both underwent a similar process, as described in the following paragraphs. During the entire process, but mostly during Stage III and IV, several models were divided, merged, transformed, and omitted due to various reasons.

As always it is imperative to socialize with collected data quickly [50]. Therefore authors 1 and 4 promptly transcribed the field notes from the participatory design workshop and simultaneously performed a descriptive coding (Stage I) to ensure the retention of valuable insights from the conversations [see 50]. Digital post-it notes from the stakeholder design workshop using Miro were re-clustered and transcribed into a spreadsheet. Then the Miro board data underwent a descriptive coding (Stage I); subsequently, all the collected data were uploaded in the data analyzing software MAXQDA for the remaining analysis, which was done both synchronously and asynchronously in MAXQDA's cloud service due to the geographical distance between the authors. A similar procedure was conducted with the semi-structured interviews six months later.

We scrutinized ethnographic records for initial patterns (Stage II), signifying preferences, needs, requirements, affordance, and engagement related to the project, which could be enveloped in the artifact design. The following process implied an inductive and iterative focused coding approach (Stage III) in which authors 1 and 2 were "moving back and forth" amongst novel and previously coded data probing for matching arrangements. When the concentrated and focused clusters had been outlined, they became platforms for the following stages of the thematic analysis.

Subsequently began a data connotation to identify clusters' relationship patterns (Stage IV). Authors 1 and 2 scrutinized the emerging patterns through a systematic breakdown that generated various categories that comprised agreed-upon enablers and barriers for the gamification artifact design discovered in the records.

Afterward, authors 1 and 2 engaged in a componental analysis (Stage V), uniting the most evident comparable patterns in the site's ethnographic record, creating the essential themes, followed by a final and thorough mapping of the remaining data patterns creating the sub-themes. Then, we dubbed themes with decisive thematic names.

At the final stage (Stage VI) in January 2022, author 1 concluded both sites' ethnographic records regarding their relations, groupings, patterns, and themes. Inspired by Crabtree et al. [41], two overarching categories were created: Stakeholder requirements and Gamification ruleset. The related themes from both sites were placed in each category to serve as design implications for the upcoming gamification artifact (see Fig. 3).

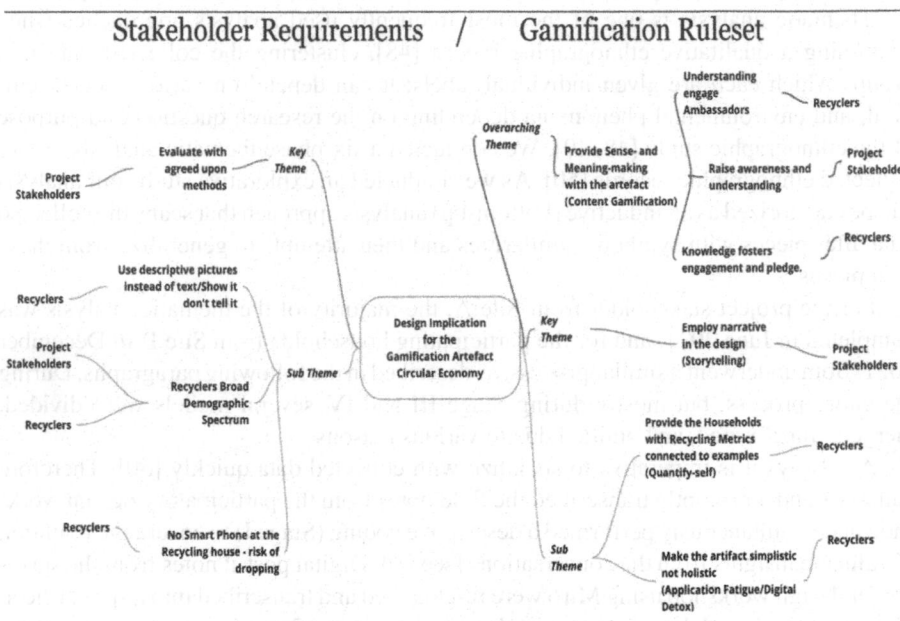

Fig. 3. Thematic findings

2.2 Field Sites and Stakeholders

Two field sites constituted our ethnographic record: a participatory design workshop, Site A, and various interview situations with the households regarding the gamification artifact, Site B. These two sites should be viewed as limited 'micro-cultures' [51] - making our findings less generalizable - visited to assemble ethnographic records for informing the gamification artifact design.

Crabtree et al. [41] prescribes that it is crucial to provide a 'thick' description of what is 'going on' in a setting in employing design ethnography. The thick and rich descriptions are one of the trademarks of ethnographic methodology [see 52], and an abundant depicted analytic account is a strategy for qualitative methods to achieve a type of external validity [53] but also ensuring the qualitative concept of trustworthiness [54]. Therefore, the two field sites are given thick descriptions regarding their thematic key-themes, while their sub-theme is presented in the online appendix.

Site A's description focuses on the stakeholders' interactions in the design workshop and what they added to the Miro board. Site B's description gives scope to the given quotes due to their centrality in this setting. The implications for the design for the gamification artifact are depicted in the discussion session.

Site A was an idea-generating, and knowledge-sharing half-day participatory design workshop with the industrial stakeholders. The workshop included 12 individuals from 8 organizations. A participatory design workshop and observations from the workshop and several meetings were used to collect the site's ethnographic record.

Site B is the household stakeholders (Recyclers) using the current recycling house, which will later be using the gamified recycling house. The community consists of 15 households, including one informant each. Connected semi-structured interviews were used to collect the site's ethnographic record. The ethnographic records from both sites are categorized in Table 1 and the interviewees in Table 2.

Table 1. The ethnographic records

Field sites	Context	Method/Data	Informants	Date
Site A	Meetings and participatory design workshop with project stakeholders	Participatory design workshop, participant observation/Workshop artifacts: Miro-board, Field notes, Informal talks	12 participants from 8 organizations	May 2021
Site B	Visited households in the project	Semi-structured interviews	15 households	December 2021

Table 2. Household recyclers (Site B)

Recycler	Gender	Education	Household inhabitants
1	Male	Upper secondary education	1
2	Female	Other	2
3	Female	Upper secondary education	2
4	Male	Upper secondary education	1

(continued)

Table 2. (*continued*)

Recycler	Gender	Education	Household inhabitants
5	Female	Other	1
6	Male	Other	2
7	Female	Other	2
8	Male	Other	1
9	Male	Upper secondary education	1
10	Female	Upper secondary education	1
11	Male	Upper secondary education	1
12	Male	Upper secondary education	2
13	Female	Elementary school	2
14	Male	Elementary school	3
15	Male	Upper secondary education	1

3 Results

The study period spanned 27 weeks, starting with the participatory design workshop and ending when the results had been compared and thematically analyzed. We are writing the five key-themes as prompts in a design recipe [46, 51].

Gamification ruleset includes four key-themes: *Employ the narrative in the design, Raise awareness and understanding, Foster engagement with knowledge* and *Form ambassadors through understanding.*

Stakeholder Requirements contain one key-theme: *Assess with agreed-upon method.*

3.1 Site A: Participatory Design Workshop with Project Stakeholders

The design workshop exercises undertaken, and the topics discussed had a clear connection to the recycling project, which considered household residents and their behaviors and responses in the gamified recycling context that had not yet been designed at that time. The stakeholder groups represented at the workshop were regional property owners, residential-construction companies, a local federation with a sustainability assignment, a provincial government agency, a recycling company, and one regional business association. The three-hour workshop was held by author 1 using the software applications Zoom and Miro (Fig. 4) due to the Covid-19 situation. The workshop had an exploratory purpose and was organized as a mixed-group-sessions with exercises such as project-problem-setting, envisioning, and sketching [46] regarding the anticipated gamification artifact. These exercises were planned by author 1 drawing inspiration from recognized workshop-techniques from Interaction Design and Human-Computer Interaction such as Affinity diagramming, Heat maps and Collaborative brainstorming [18].

Their primary purpose was to afford the stakeholders to share their (tacit) knowledge within their areas of expertise. The secondary purpose was to incorporate mutual learning [see 46] among the project's stakeholders.

The exercises were constructed in a similar pattern: author 1 explained the objective of the exercise, then followed a quiet ideation and post-it note writing phase for 10–15 min; thereafter, author 1, together with participants, did a superficial clustering which was followed by a group discussion on the contemporary co-constructed themes. Each exercise addressed a hypothetical yet possible situation for the project.

The workshop started with a presentation about gamification, given by author 1. It explained the gamification concept, previous gamification projects focusing on sustainability and gamification design ethics. In the workshop, authors 4 and 5 acted as attendants; their primary objective was to conduct participant observation and take field notes.

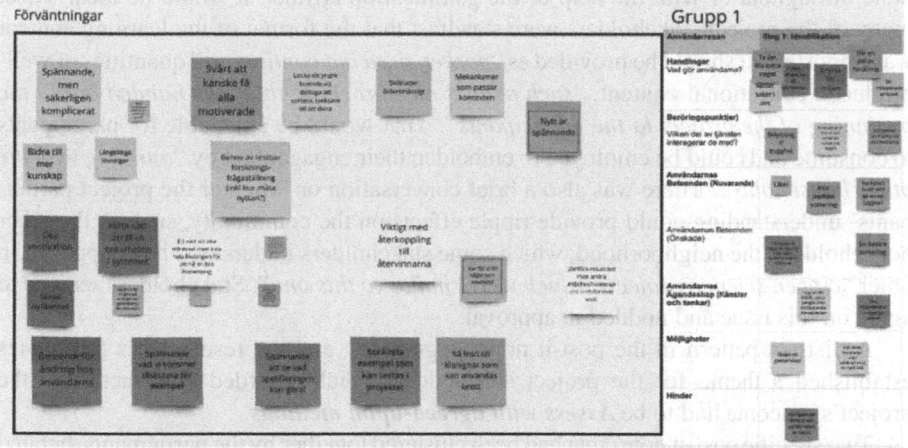

Fig. 4. Miro board screenshot from the participatory design workshop

The participatory design workshop with the project stakeholders provided several general insights for the research project. Three key-themes and various sub-themes (see online appendix) were identified when analyzing the design workshop material.

The first identified theme was *Employ the narrative in the design.* The stakeholders that took part in the workshop saw a necessity of incorporating the project narrative in the forthcoming artifact. The reasons for applying a narrative were expressed in several digital post-it notes with text such as *"using narrative is always engaging"* and *"storytelling is everything"* and *"narrative helps us learn to connect to 'these things'"*.

In particular, one workshop participant uttered her thoughts on this during one of the workshop exercises, which was regarded as significant and captivating by the other stakeholders: *"...when humans starting to walk on a struggling path where s/he must make own sacrifices there is a need of a clearly stated why"*.

When the participant was asked to elaborate further on this by another participant, she replied: *"I mean, this (circular economy) effort is going to be life-long for some of us. And for many coming generations. Today, we are trying to fix the earlier generations' mistakes. This is something we clearly didn't ask for. If we are going to stay committed over such a long time, we, at least I, need to be reminded of the purpose now and again. I need 'hooks' to hang the storyline on".*

The household's knowledge acquisition regarding the circular economy in general and recycling in particular, was also interesting for the stakeholders. They reasoned that the artifact should **Raise awareness and understanding**, a prompt dubbed the second theme. It was crucial for executing the project's prime concept: increased awareness that everybody can do something and that everyone needs to contribute for a large-scale circular economic process to transpire. Digital post-it notes displayed *"Plant a solution-seed that can spread and be used widely"* and *"Contribute to further knowledge, it will deliver long-term results".*

When these and digital post-it notes with similar messages were discussed more in-depth, the stakeholders settled that if knowledge-sharing on sustainability could be done throughout or with the help of the gamification artifact, it would be ideal. Also, many of the project stakeholders were steadfast that the format of the learning content was important. It should be provided as *"pocket-sized but continuous"* quantities of well-produced educational content, *"such as that nice brochure that was handed out at the beginning of the project to the participants".* That would be amenable for participants to consume and could be employed to embolden their engagement by *"quizzing with the other households".* There was also a brief conversation on whether the project participants' understanding could provide ripple effects on the community, such as the other households in the neighborhood, which some stakeholders understood had happened in other *"citizen science projects, which were similar to this one".* Stakeholders seemed to agree on this issue and nodded in approval.

A distinct pattern in the post-it notes, arguments, and the researcher's field notes established a theme for the project stakeholder, which regarded "the fact" that the project's outcome had to be **Assess with agreed-upon methods**.

Two specific post-it notes that had been clustered together by the participants dictated *"Decrease costs for waste disposal with 20%"* and *"Measure the project results with the mean of other recycling stations in the country".* Also, project stakeholders opted for utilizing quantifiable performance indicators, and relating methods to these indicators, as such methods were *"more trustworthy".* Another stakeholder expressed that the concrete result had to be tangible, depending on *"improved"* waste sorting and overall recycling process of the participating households, otherwise, there would be no point for the project.

In summary, categorizing Site A's themes emphasizes that the gamified intervention should be **Assess with agreed-upon method** in Stakeholder Requirements while also **Employ the narrative in the design** and **Raise awareness and understanding** to the Gamification ruleset.

3.2 Site B: Interviews with Household Stakeholders About the Recycling House

We employed an exploratory semi-structured interview approach to provide flexibility and more deeply inquire complex issues of the participants' expressed perceptions of engagement, recycling, and waste sorting. Before the interview, the recyclers received educational material about recycling, giving all the households an equal knowledge base about the Swedish recycling system focusing on six waste fractions.

The interviewees participated in one semi-structured interview session. The interview session encircled waste sorting, recycling, conceptions, motivations, meaning- and sensemaking regarding recycling as well as notions regarding the upcoming recycling house. The interviews were conducted onsite in each Recycler's household and recorded after getting verbal consent. The goal of the interviews was to retain knowledge about their recycling behavior in their day-to-day activities—specific questions regarding their notions, opinions, and overall perception of the upcoming artifact ensued.

Site B gave two key-themes and several sub-themes informing the gamification artifact design (See online appendix). The first key-theme that emerged was *Foster engagement with knowledge.* The participants expressed that having gained an understanding regarding circular economy supported the participant towards more substantial commitment and more engagement in terms of doing waste sorting and recycling. Recycler 6 expressed:

> *"If I had less insight, I might not have been as committed. But now I have got a little blowtorch under my feet, which I think many more people actually would need. Though most people do what is the most convenient, and it is not always the most convenient to sort your waste and then head to the recycling room when you can just throw it in a garbage can, that is just 'around the corner'."* Recycler 6

Notions related to knowledge as a catalyst for increasing households' commitment and engagement were expressed, to a various degree, by all the interviewees. For example, Recycler 7 and 13 expressed similar opinions as Recycler 6:

> *"I think that having an understanding affects a lot, yes. The more you know, the more you can contribute - and you get a clean conscience too."* Recycler 7

> *"The knowledge of what happens to the waste affects the commitment, yes. For instance, all the plastic trash is dumped outdoors; it will take forever to disappear. But if it is recycled, it doesn't."* Recycler 13

The above excerpts indicate that having knowledge about the concept of a circular economy and understanding of why the households also must do their part seems to nurture the Recyclers' overall engagement and willingness to commit and participate. Furthermore, the participants also expressed that developing a profound knowledge about the circular economy contributed to the households overall meaning-making considering recycling.

Expressing that they had a profound conception of the circular economy, the recyclers indicated a notion of sharing their understandings, leading to the site's second key-theme. The *Form ambassadors through understanding* theme illustrates Recyclers' contemporary awareness regarding recycling as an essential part of solving the sustainability puzzle. This made them adopt specific behavior patterns that were not just visible to themselves but also affected their peers towards changing their household waste sorting and recycling behaviors:

"I think I give little pieces of advice about different things, all the time. Take dishcloths, for example, you know: Wettex (a longstanding Swedish dishcloths brand). In my days, everybody used them just once or twice then just threw them away. Because that's how we had always done. A lot of people still act like that. Though now I have started to use textile dishcloths, those that you can wash, and I say to everyone I meet, that it is great. You affect others by doing so [...] Yes, I have to say that. If others tell me that they do not recycle, I tell them that I recycle." Recycler 2

"When my friends are at my house, they know that I can be very meticulous nowadays. That all waste must be sorted correctly, and if they sort inaccurately, I correct and inform them. When I do that I may not be so pedagogically about it." Recycler 7

"Yes, when my live-apart is at home with me. I usually manage him a bit about what to throw where. I am trying to make him realize that you might actually be able to contribute in the long run." Recycler 10

A distinct pattern that also emerged in this theme during the interview's thematic analysis was that some Recyclers had started to share and inform their peers about the effects as well as the significance of having a fundamental garbage sorting in a Swedish household and to be thorough at a recycling site:

"Good question. I do it mostly to inspire and motivate. For example, "how do you do it in your household? How do I?". For instance, we have had that dialogue a lot at my work, and after that, you have gained more insight into the whole thing (waste sorting). If you just talk about it, I think you can find many answers. I do not actively communicate and share; no. Though, is it a discussion? If it shows up? I'll share it with you. It can be at work or at home. Yea, it is just as important to share the knowledge you have as it is to acquire knowledge that you don't have. If you do not know something but still want to, you can try to find it in some way. Either if you talk to others about how they do, or stuff like that." Recycler 12

"I am only sharing with my friends. Sometimes it's actually important. Electronics are pretty dangerous to just throw away like that, and they must be thrown in environmental rooms, so I think it is important to point it out." Recycler 9

"I try to do it (sharing the awareness) at my university; I study to be a middle school teacher, so I have to try to take it further because it is such an important thing!" Recycler 4

The Recyclers expressed that they wanted to distribute their awareness hoping to provide a positive influence on peers in the short run, but the environment in the long run. The opinions expressed imply that if more households employed a structure for their waste sorting and recycling, it would have an impact.

Summarizing Site B's key-themes gives that the gamification artifact should ***Foster engagement with knowledge*** as well as ***Form ambassadors through understanding*** - both themes included in the Gamification ruleset category.

4 Discussion

The design ethnography methodology employed in this work gave design implications for gamification artifacts in triple-helix sustainability projects with multiple stakeholders in general and house recycling in particular. From our ethnographic record, we extrapolated two thematic categories, and their themes will now be discussed.

Stakeholder Requirements are recognized in information technology development [41, 43] and due to different and misaligned expectations, projects with various stakeholders from other domains have been depicted as problematic [46]. The *Assess with agreed-upon method* key-theme indicated that some stakeholders at Site A expected a direct result of the artifact's employment, which gave quite complex design implications for the artifact. In elaborating on how this requirement could be involved in the artifact outline, we saw a possible solution inspired by already employed gamified technology for energy conservation [55, 56]. The implication would enclose connecting the gamification artifact to the recycling containers using tracking technology (e.g., Near Field Communication sensors and Internet of things (IoT)) to measure recycling behavior and calculate agreed-upon critical performance outcomes.

However, this would imply that the gamification artifact would need to be accompanied by a more complex hardware and software infrastructure. In this regard, some of our findings indicate that some of the project stakeholders saw a necessity towards more business-oriented values which could be translated as the return of investment, that could hamper the implementation of an IoT infrastructure. Misaligned expectations and project misconceptions have previously been observed when gamification transfers into a business-to-business context [57, 58]. Therefore, we interpret this finding as a potential issue that could further down the project road cause frustration and potential problems, which is not unique for gamification [59]. We propose that a due diligence based on compatibility between stakeholders should be conducted before the project starts or perhaps in the early collaboration phase, especially in projects with multiple stakeholder groups. The notion of adding various stakeholders to provide multiple lenses on a layered problem such as sustainability appears intriguing, but a multitude of stakeholders also brings a multitude of requirements that has to be addressed.

Designing and implementing a gamification artifact is not just an issue of whether it should be implemented or how it should be outlined for the end-users in the context, but also what various stakeholders are required to view the artifact as attractive.

Additional industrial research and practical cases demonstrate gamification project nuance on how gamification is implemented, the involvement of different stakeholders, and issues that can arise.

Gamification Ruleset: schemas focusing on the essential gamification logic rules are described in several gamification frameworks [15] but are rarely prevalent in empirical gamification design research. In neighboring fields such as Interaction design or Human-computer interaction, designers are interested in solutions that can be shared across a community of practice; with such a mindset, we constructed this category.

The design ethnography key-themes of *Foster engagement with knowledge* and *Form ambassadors through understanding* gave design implications that engagement for circular economy in general and recycling in particular could be fostered by providing a better understanding of the process. This was implicit at both sites.

It was expressed by the household stakeholders their newfound knowledge provided them with agency and standing among their peers. Understanding also seemed to affect their engagement to recycle. This needs, of course, to be validated through other approaches.

Thus, we can presume that a gamification artifact with multiple uses, providing learning content in addition to regular motivational incentives, would have an engaging effect in the context studied. This presumption forms the first design proposition of our explorative research.

Second as depicted in the *Employ the narrative in the design* theme, the project stakeholders also considered the use of *storytelling* as a critical design rule for the gamification artifact, an argument devised from the idea that the project has a compelling narrative within it – saving the planet. Correspondingly, to some extent, the Recyclers communicated similar notions addressing that their contemporary knowledge on recycling gave them a sort of calling, a mission, to edify their peers and thus save the planet. Therefore, we assume that employing a recycle-to-save-the-world narrative integrated into the gamification design could influence the users' mindset, which, in turn, could affect their behavioral outcome [see 60, 61]. This assumption constructs the second design proposition of our explorative research.

4.1 Conclusion, Future Research, and Limitations

Our study aimed to comprehend the requirements and expectations of different project stakeholders involved in a research project concerning a gamified recycling house. In addition, it gave insights into the opinions and daily practices of the everyday recyclers and forthcoming users of the prospective recycling house. In the ethnographic intersection between two groups and field sites, we extrapolated an understanding of the Stakeholder requirements and a rudimentary Gamification ruleset to be used as design implications in the growing application context of sustainability in general and recycling in particular. Our presented work is intended to function as a tentative set of prescriptive statements, a reasonable first step for designing specific gamification artifacts for household recycling. Through our explorative work, we present the following two research propositions (RP):

- RP 1: Integrating a compelling narrative based on the current state of the world's ecosystem into gamification design for sustainability affects the users' recycling behavior.
- RP 2: A gamification artifact in a recycling context that provides appropriate learning content besides regular motivational incentives affects the users' influencing their recycling behavior.

Future research on gamification design for recycling context may find value in exploring whether the research propositions formulated in this study are correct or incorrect, referring to an observable phenomenon in a gamified recycling context.

The study's limitations are that we did not have the chance to formally observe the Recyclers use the gamified recycling house, which had been valuable to draw other conclusions that could have been beneficial design implications. Participant observation will be conducted in the coming project stages. Another is that the household stakeholders were not present at the project stakeholder meetings or participatory design. Their voice in these forums might have been valuable for either strengthening or weakening the design implications presented here and perhaps also have given more refined ones.

Acknowledgements. Recognition goes to Sofie Stenfelt for aiding with data collection at Site B. This project was funded by the Kamprad Family Foundation for Entrepreneurship, Research & Charity.

Online Appendix

https://miro.com/app/board/uXjVOSS1aXU=/?invite_link_id=349769055901.

References

1. Lenton, T.M., Rockström, J., Gaffney, O., et al.: Climate tipping points. Nature **575**, 592–595 (2019)
2. Raftery, A.E., Zimmer, A., Frierson, D.M.W., et al.: Less than 2 °C warming by 2100 unlikely. Nat. Clim. Change **7**, 637–641 (2017)
3. Beasy, K.: Interpretations of sustainability beyond the middle class. Aust. J. Environ. Educ. **36**, 246–263 (2020)
4. Geissdoerfer, M., Savaget, P., Bocken, N.M.P., Hultink, E.J.: The circular economy – a new sustainability paradigm? J. Clean. Prod. **143**, 757–768 (2017)
5. Stahel, W.R.: The circular economy. Nature **531**, 435–438 (2016)
6. Hartley, K., van Santen, R., Kirchherr, J.: Policies for transitioning towards a circular economy: expectations from the European Union (EU). Resour. Conserv. Recycl. **155**, 104634 (2020)
7. Rosenlund, J.: The environmental concerns of food ecopreneurs. Sustainability **13**, 6 (2021)
8. Kopnina, H.: The victims of unsustainability: a challenge to sustainable development goals. Int. J. Sustain. Dev. World Ecol. **23**, 113–121 (2015)
9. Knickmeyer, D.: Social factors influencing household waste separation: a literature review on good practices to improve the recycling performance of urban areas. J. Clean. Prod. **245**, 118605 (2019)
10. Elaine, R., Noreen, S., Catherine, C., Caledonia, G.: Exploring the motivations to nudge consumer engagement with alternative circular economy consumption models (2021)
11. Annelien, S., Bram, L.: Nudging sustainable behaviour: the use of data-driven nudges to support a circular economy in smart cities. **151** (2018)
12. Helmefalk, M., Rosenlund, J.: Interactivity, game creation, design, learning, and innovation. In: 8th EAI International Conference, ArtsIT 2019, and 4th EAI International Conference, DLI 2019, Aalborg, Denmark, 6–8 November 2019, Proceedings. Lecture Notes of the Institute for Computer Sciences, Social Informatics and Telecommunications Engineering, pp. 415–426 (2020)
13. Magista, M., Dorra, B.L., Pean, T.Y.: A review of the applicability of gamification and game-based learning to improve household-level waste management practices among schoolchildren. Int. J. Technol. **9**, 1439–1449 (2018)

14. Marcucci, E., Gatta, V., Pira, M.L.: Gamification design to foster stakeholder engagement and behavior change: an application to urban freight transport. Transp. Res. Part Policy Pract. **118**, 119–132 (2018)
15. Mora, A., Riera, D., González, C., Arnedo-Moreno, J.: Gamification: a systematic review of design frameworks. J. Comput. High. Educ. **29**(3), 516–548 (2017). https://doi.org/10.1007/s12528-017-9150-4
16. Deterding, S.: The lens of intrinsic skill atoms: a method for gameful design. Hum. Comput. Interact. **30**, 294–335 (2015)
17. Hughes, J., King, V., Rodden, T., Andersen, H.: The role of ethnography in interactive systems design. Interactions **2**, 56–65 (1995)
18. Preece, J., Sharp, H., Rogers, Y.: Interaction design: beyond human-computer interaction (2015)
19. Rapp, A.: In search for design elements: a new perspective for employing ethnography in human-computer interaction design research. Int. J. Hum. Comput. Interact. **37**, 1–20 (2020)
20. Thaler, R.H., Sunstein, C.R.: Nudge: Improving decisions about health, wealth, and happiness. Nudge: Improv. Decis. About Health Wealth Happiness **6**, 1–293 (2008)
21. Ferrari, L., Cavaliere, A., Marchi, E.D., Banterle, A.: Can nudging improve the environmental impact of food supply chain? A systematic review. Trends Food Sci. Tech. **91**, 184–192 (2019)
22. Byerly, H., Balmford, A., Ferraro, P.J., et al.: Nudging pro-environmental behavior: evidence and opportunities. Front. Ecol. Environ. **16**, 159–168 (2018)
23. Schubert, C.: Green nudges: do they work? Are they ethical? Ecol. Econ. **132**, 329–342 (2017)
24. Seaborn, K., Fels, D.I.: Gamification in theory and action: a survey. Int. J. Hum.-Comput. Stud. **74**, 14–31 (2015)
25. Orji, R., Vassileva, J., Mandryk, R.L.: Modeling the efficacy of persuasive strategies for different gamer types in serious games for health. User Model. User-Adap. Inter. **24**(5), 453–498 (2014). https://doi.org/10.1007/s11257-014-9149-8
26. Krath, J.: Gamification for sustainable employee behavior: extended abstract for the CHI PLAY 2021 doctoral consortium. In: Extended Abstracts of the 2021 Annual Symposium on Computer-Human Interaction in Play, pp. 411–414. ACM, New York (2021)
27. Johnson, D., Horton, E., Mulcahy, R., Foth, M.: Gamification and serious games within the domain of domestic energy consumption: a systematic review. Renew. Sustain. Energy Rev. **73**, 249–264 (2017)
28. Morganti, L., Pallavicini, F., Cadel, E., et al.: Gaming for Earth: Serious games and gamification to engage consumers in pro-environmental behaviours for energy efficiency. Energy Res. Soc. Sci. **29**, 95–102 (2017)
29. Lieberoth, A., Jensen, N.H., Bredahl, T.: Selective psychological effects of nudging, gamification and rational information in converting commuters from cars to buses: a controlled field experiment. Transp. Res. Part F Traffic Psychol. Behav. **55**, 246–261 (2018)
30. Ferron, M., Loria, E., Marconi, A., Massa, P.: Play & go, an urban game promoting behaviour change for sustainable mobility. Interact. Design Archit. **40**, 24–45 (2019)
31. Günther, M., Kacperski, C., Krems, J.F.: Can electric vehicle drivers be persuaded to eco-drive? A field study of feedback, gamification and financial rewards in Germany. Energy Res. Soc. Sci. **63**, 101407 (2020)
32. Berger, V.: Social norm-based gamification to promote eco-friendly food choice. J. Consum. Mark. **36**, 666–676 (2019)
33. Koroleva, K., Novak, J.: How to engage with sustainability issues we rarely experience? A gamification model for collective awareness platforms in water-related sustainability. Sustain.-Basel **12**, 712 (2020)
34. Ro, M., Brauer, M., Kuntz, K., et al.: Making cool choices for sustainability: testing the effectiveness of a game-based approach to promoting pro-environmental behaviors. J. Environ. Psychol. **53**, 20–30 (2017)

35. Aguiar-Castillo, L., Clavijo-Rodriguez, A., Saa-Perez, P.D., Perez-Jimenez, R.: Gamification as an approach to promote tourist recycling behavior. Sustain.-Basel **11**, 2201 (2019)
36. Gibovic, D., Bikfalvi, A.: Incentives for plastic recycling: how to engage citizens in active collection. Empirical evidence from Spain. Recycling **6**, 29 (2021)
37. Manshoven, S., Gillabel, J.: Learning through play: a serious game as a tool to support circular economy education and business model innovation. Sustain.-Basel **13**, 13277 (2021)
38. Keivanpour, S.: Work-in-progress-digital twin and gamification for designing an educational lab for circular economy. In: 2021 7th International Conference of the Immersive Learning Research Network, ILRN, pp. 1–3 (2021)
39. Baskerville, R.L., Myers, M.D.: Design ethnography in information systems. Inform. Syst. J. **25**, 23–46 (2015)
40. Müller, F.: Design Ethnography, Epistemology and Methodology. SpringerBriefs in Anthropology, Springer, Cham (2021). https://doi.org/10.1007/978-3-030-60396-0
41. Crabtree, A., Rouncefield, M., Tolmie, P.: Doing Design Ethnography. Human Computer Interaction (2012)
42. Salvador, T., Bell, G., Anderson, K.: Design ethnography. Des. Manage. Rev. **10**, 35 (1999)
43. Nova, N.: Beyond Design Ethnography. SHS Publishing (2014)
44. Sas, C., Whittaker, S., Dow, S.: Generating implications for design through design research (2014)
45. Shin, J., Odom, W.: Collective wisdom. In: Proceedings of 2019 CHI Conference on Human Factors in Computing Systems, pp. 1–14 (2019)
46. Bannon, L., Ehn, P.: Routledge International Handbook of Participatory Design (2012)
47. Lazar, J., Feng, J.H., Hochheiser, H.: Research Methods in Human Computer Interaction (2017)
48. Aronson, J.: A pragmatic view of thematic analysis. Qual. Rep. **2**, 1–3 (1995)
49. Atkinson, P.: Handbook of Ethnography. Sage, London (2007)
50. Braun, V., Clarke, V.: Using thematic analysis in psychology. Qual. Res. Psychol. **3**, 77–101 (2006)
51. Cranz, G.: Ethnography for Designers. Routledge, London (2016)
52. Clifford, G.: The Interpretation of Cultures. Basic Books (1973)
53. Lincoln, Y.S., Guba, E.G.: Naturalistic inquiry. Int. J. Intercult. Rel. **9**, 438–439 (1985)
54. Shenton, A.K.: Strategies for ensuring trustworthiness in qualitative research projects. Educ. Inform. **22**, 63–75 (2004)
55. Papaioannou, T.G., Dimitriou, N., Vasilakis, K., et al.: An IoT-based gamified approach for reducing occupants' energy wastage in public buildings. Sens. Basel Switz. **18**, 537 (2018)
56. Lu, C.-H.: IoT-enabled adaptive context-aware and playful cyber-physical system for everyday energy savings. IEEE Trans. Hum.-Mach. Syst. **48**, 380–391 (2018)
57. Jedel, I., Palmquist, A., Gillberg, D.: A practical view of gamifying information systems for the future. Int. J. Gaming Comput. Simul. **13**, 1–13 (2021)
58. Palmquist, A.: Lost in translation: a study of (mis)conceptions, (mis)communication and concerns when implementing gamification in corporate (re)training. In: Proceedings of the 54th Hawaii International Conference on System Sciences (2021)
59. Mohedas, I., Daly, S.R., Sienko, K.H.: Requirements development: approaches and behaviors of novice designers. J. Mech. Design **137**, 071407 (2015)
60. Hamari, J., Koivisto, J.: Why do people use gamification services? Int. J. Inform. Manage. **35**, 419–431 (2015)
61. Landers, R.N., Auer, E.M., Collmus, A.B., Armstrong, M.B.: Gamification science, its history and future: definitions and a research agenda. Simulat. Gaming **49**, 315–337 (2018)

Player Behavior and Games Impact

Social Anxiety Strategies Through Gaming

Matthew Copeman[1,2(✉)] and Jonathan Freeman[2]

[1] Arden University, Middlemarch Park, Coventry CV3 4FJ, UK
mcopeman@arden.ac.uk
[2] Goldsmiths, University of London, New Cross, London SE14 6NW, UK

Abstract. Anxiety and depression cases have trebled within the last decade [1], with diagnoses of social anxiety disorder increasing the most. With such an escalation in care needed, and the ever-struggling mental health service, a new approach to affective mental health options is imperative. The aim of this research was to highlight common, mainstream video games as potential strategies for those struggling with social anxiety disorder, and to understand how these games help sufferers. This was displayed by demonstrating themes in games that those with social anxiety disorder played. The study used a participation selection model mixed method approach utilising the Leibowitz social anxiety scale to invite participants with high social anxiety scores back to interview. Firstly, quantitative results showed that the Leibowitz Social Anxiety Scale maintains reliability in detecting those at risk of clinical diagnoses, being able to significantly predict a clinical diagnosis from a higher score, with younger age groups showing more risk, though this latter finding was a statistically non-significant trend. Qualitative findings showed four main themes were identified when carrying out thematic analysis: the day has been hard for mental health, short solo breaks of play, helping with mental health and growing as a person with game genres including colony or role-playing games. Future research suggests a move to a transdiagnostic approach to anxiety disorders with an early-stage intervention model utilising video games with the themes uncovered. This would aim to improve access to young adolescents and increase uptake of clinical mental health provisions while offering self-directed care in the first instance.

Keywords: Video games · Social anxiety · Transdiagnostic

1 Social Anxiety Strategies Through Gaming

Mental health diagnoses, have seen a marked increase in the past 10 years with one in six young people being diagnosed with a mental health disorder [2]. Social Anxiety Disorder (SAD), defined as a debilitating condition causing extreme bouts of anxiety for those confronting social situations [3–5]. With the workload of the NHS increasing, new ways of providing mental health services are needed.

© The Author(s), under exclusive license to Springer Nature Switzerland AG 2022
X. Fang (Ed.): HCII 2022, LNCS 13334, pp. 309–326, 2022.
https://doi.org/10.1007/978-3-031-05637-6_19

Video games offer a unique solution: training basic social interaction that cover a plethora of social situations [6–8]. Fleming et al. [8] suggested that stories, character interactions and worlds offer an immersive learning experience for patients. Objective measures like play time has also shown improved well-being [9]. This has already been successful in the treatment of various phobias as well [10, 11] by showing significant reductions in symptoms. A recent meta-analysis showed improvements for depressive and comorbid anxiety symptoms [12, 13]. With videogames already demonstrating promise, approaching social anxiety in such a manner is a logical next step to take.

1.1 Social Anxiety

The Liebowitz Social Anxiety Scale (LSAS) [14] was developed for highlighting people at risk of developing it. Common symptoms include shunning social situations, discomfort around others and, in the extreme, removing social connections entirely. Interventions for SAD often take a pharmaceutical approach, such as the use of selective serotine re-uptake inhibitors, or therapeutic approaches like cognitive behavioural theory (CBT), or a combination of both [15, 16].

Recent reviews suggest however, this approach is unsustainable and unable to be deployed to all those at risk [4]. This is highlighted for younger children and adolescents, as CBT has been shown to be less effective as an intervention, and the use of drugs might cause adverse effects to developing brain chemistry [17, 18]. Research also suggests SAD is an early developmental disorder. Neuroimaging evidence supports this, showing during early years and adolescence, that neural activity has a role in the onset of SAD [19]. The use of drugs and neural activity could see potential negative side effects in young people. In fact, research suggests that CBT was almost ineffective for young adolescents and young adults, defined as those up to age 24 [20]. Support after a CBT course has been shown to hamper the use of techniques learnt in therapy [12] highlighted by Hudson et al. [21], that after a typical 10-week CBT course, 50% of outpatients sought readmission after three months. Further to this, Catanzano et al. [22] suggested that uptake rates for younger people is lower compared to older people for therapy, and once mental health problems start, these younger people are often left with no help. Hofmann et al. [23] suggested that individualistic cultures have seen increasing young SAD diagnoses due to demands of social media to maintain a positive look on life.

However, smaller forms of aftercare and positive reinforcement showed a significant reduction in SAD symptoms and readmission [24] showing that providing feedback to a sufferer helps them [18, 25]. Video games could be utilized here, being able to give interactions, teachable experiences, positive feedback, reward reinforcement, and opportunities for continuous learning reinforcement. Globally, as of 2020, 74% of six to 24 year olds played video games for an average of eight and a half hours a week [26]. Knowledge acquisition using video games has been shown to have positive effects on behavioural, cognitive and physiological aspects [27] with real impacts on memory and social improvements [28, 29]. This feedback could deliver a bespoke, narrative experience to help those with SAD. Games such as "Sym" [30] have already been produced. However, this type of game is limited: targeting sufferers who are already open to help.

To use video games as an intervention for SAD, they need to teach, not just enlighten. This requires studying mainstream games to understand the systems that offer benefits, and why SAD gamers play them.

1.2   Learning Through Virtual Interactions

Research has investigated learning through a virtual interface for a specific experience, bringing a participant into a virtual space. Presence and belonging are shown to aid in learning tasks [31]. Virtual experience could provide SAD sufferers the ability to learn in an immersive virtual environment, taking ownership of their mental health and raising their self-esteem. Research on Self-Determination Theory (SDT) [32] supports this, showing intrinsic and extrinsic motivations having positive changes to well-being and self-esteem [9, 33, 34]. By gamifying learning SAD sufferers can also improve autonomy, competency, and relatedness, the three principal components of SDT.

By structuring the research around SDT, the building of theory can suggest how video games can work for SAD sufferers to alleviate their symptoms. Independent gamified learning links directly to SDT with improvements in motivation and self-esteem, suggesting people aim to better themselves, and in the absence of knowing how, video games could offer learning and autonomy. Gamifying treatment has the potential to generalise wellbeing and motivations, with Fleming et al. [35] calling for a paradigm shift in the treatment of many psychological disorders to one that promotes gamifying of learning and coping with problems [36].

1.3   Aims of the Current Study

The aims of the current study are to identify which games are played by people with SAD, and the systems that help them with their disorder. The hypotheses will enable future research, interventions, and resources to be targeted, by understanding which populations suffer with SAD. The themes that are reported will be analysed to build a new theoretical framework for what a game built to help those with SAD could consist of in the future.

The study asked two main research questions for qualitative analysis and had two hypotheses for quantitative analysis:

RQ_1: What type of video games are being played by people with SAD and why?
RQ_2: How do these games help SAD sufferers?
For quantitative analysis, the research study had two hypotheses.
H_1: The Liebowitz Social Anxiety Scale will significantly predict a clinical diagnosis of SAD.
H_2: Age will significantly predict a clinical diagnosis of SAD.

2 Method

2.1 Design

For the current study, a participation selection model mixed method was used, where quantitative results informed participant selection for the qualitative element [37]. The quantitative data was also used to add to research on the LSAS [14]. The research questions were assessed based on those diagnosed with SAD and how they responded to the questions. Ethical approval was obtained prior to the study commencing.

2.2 Participants

Data was collected from 82 participants responding to an internet survey distributed via social media. Ages ranged from 18 – 72 ($M = 27.40$ $SD = 8.56$). Participants ranged in education, with 26.8% having completed a bachelor's degree. There were 44 males, 36 females and two others. Five participants were selected for the qualitative stage of the study based on their answer's prior being diagnosed with SAD and accepting the interview. Five of 11 eligible participants agreed to participate in further interviews and ranged in age from 22–35 ($M = 28$ $SD = 5.70$), with three males and two females. Of these, three had completed a bachelor's degree, whilst the others master's degrees.

2.3 Measures

Qualtrics was used to build and distribute the survey. Demographic information such as age, gender and educational achievement was obtained. The LSAS assessed participant's social anxiety, with questions designed to ascertain how fearful or avoidant of various social situations they may be. Example situations are "telephoning in public" or "going to a party" with participants answering on two four-point Likert scales for each question ranging from "Never" to "Usually" [14]. There was a further question asking if participants had been clinically diagnosed with SAD. The qualitative interview was based on questions asked by Elliot et al. [38], studying gameplayers with post-traumatic stress disorder, modified to fit SAD. This semi-structured interview was not overtly enquiring about a participant's social anxiety, but so they would feel comfortable talking about their mental health and provide valuable insight into how video games help them with their SAD.

2.4 Procedure

Data was collected through anonymous distribution of the questionnaire via social media. Participants gave consent and completed basic demographic questions, the LSAS and gave a brief outline of their experience of video games. They submitted their email address if they wished to be considered for interview. Those that had previously been diagnosed with SAD, and scoring above 65 on the LSAS, the threshold for being high risk, were invited back to a video and audio recorded semi-structured interview lasting on average one hour conducted via Skype. Central questions were "How do you perceive video gaming relating to your own mental health and wellbeing?", "Have you ever thought of playing a video game as a potential help tool for your own wellbeing?" and "What aspects of the game do you feel are important and positively affect your wellbeing?". Where appropriate, participants were asked further questions to gain more insight on answers they gave to expand on relevant and interesting responses.

2.5   Data Analysis

Thematic analysis was employed [39] following transcription of recorded interviews with participants being coded. This involved reading and re-reading each interview with the goal of identifying potential themes. This led to producing overarching higher themes that would encompass what the participants were discussing, informed by the video games being played and discussed, and the research questions set out. Lastly, quotes were identified that were congruent with the identified themes and naming of the themes took place to outline the processes described by participants.

3   Results

3.1   Quantitative Analysis

To analyse the predictive ability of the LSAS, scores and a categorical diagnosis of SAD were entered into a logistic regression. LSAS scores ranged from 0 to 112 ($M = 53.24$ $SD = 28.02$), with a score of 65 or higher indicating risk of clinical diagnosis [14, 40]. In total, 18 people, or 22% of participants had a clinical diagnosis of SAD. Due to missing data, the total sample size fell to 63, with 11 being clinically diagnosed. A power analysis concluded for a logistic regression with one predictor variable, suggested the sample size should be 75 or greater [41]. However, given the effects found, this was deemed acceptable with 6 less than the power analysis. For the first hypothesis, the model was significantly worse at predicting if a clinical diagnosis was present, $\chi2(1) = 7.53, p = 0.06$. As such, the LSAS Score was entered into the logistic regression, and was found to be a significant predictor of a clinical diagnosis, with a Wald test indicating its level of significance, $Z(1) = 6.46, p = .011$. The odds of being diagnosed with an increasing LSAS score was almost 1:1, $e^B = 1.04$. For the second hypothesis, the model was deemed significantly worse without the addition of age, $\chi2(1) = 4.89, p = 0.027$. However, age was not a significant predictor of being diagnosed with SAD, $Z(1) = 3.74$, $p = .053$, with the odds of being diagnosed being less than 1:1, $e^B = .91$.

3.2   Qualitative Analysis

For the qualitative analysis, four main themes were identified: a) day has been hard for mental health, b) short solo breaks of play, c) helping with mental health and d) growing as a person. Each theme has smaller sub-themes which trended across participants in their feedback.

Day Has Been Hard for Mental Health

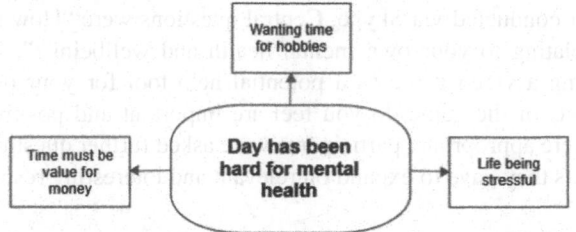

Fig. 1. Theme map for "Day has been hard for mental health"

Most interviewees responded that everyday life was stressful and this impacted their wellbeing. They discussed seeking downtime, and reported wanting to alleviate these stressors. Participant one, a 22-year-old female teaching assistant spoke of this:

"I can't really leave my work at work because you know, they're kids and I know how much they... especially my one that I work with looks up to me. You do come home at the end of the day kind of still thinking about work and did I do this right did I handle that right".

Participant two, a 34-year-old male student also commented on the stressors faced in his life:

"At the moment it's just getting through the master's frankly... making sure I'm managing my money effectively and so I can get through the degree without going completely broke"

Participant three, a 24-year-old male researcher, also spoke of bringing work stress home with him:

"there's your kind of perception of everything which is like an added like level that can be stressful but nothing specific if you know what I mean... So maybe that's like a different type of stress I'm experiencing I'm not sure".

This theme was characterised by wanting to leave work behind and spend time on hobbies. Value was placed on time and money spent on gaming, as participant four, a 36-year-old male primary teacher, commented on the importance of finding time for himself at the end of the day:

"Stayed with them for a couple of minutes had a look thought right okay, they're busy, they won't mind me going off to play now for a little bit".

Participant 3 echoed this, stating game choice depended on relative value for time and money:

"But yeah, once you've kind of bought into their kind of battle pass progression thing you definitely feel compelled to get to the end of it because otherwise, you're not going to get your money back... Yes to defend my, you know to get my value for money. I'm almost compelled to yeah play".

Participant 4 also commented value for money defining his hobby, noting that advertising played a particular role in the purchase of one game that he felt let down by,

"I've got suckered in by the ad campaign. I thought oh yeah got that and it weren't half as good as I was led to believe it was".

Clearly there is importance in daily downtime, but the importance of both time and money should not be overlooked, as modelled in Fig. 1.

Short Solo Breaks of Play

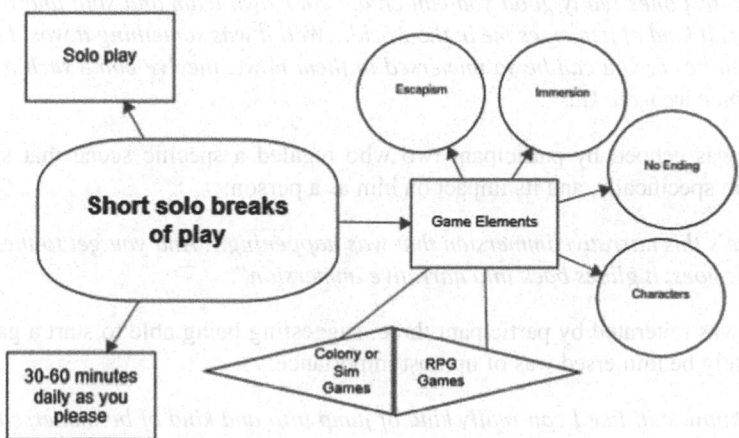

Fig. 2. Theme map for "Short solo of breaks"

The second theme was short solo breaks of play. All participants suggested that 30 to 60 min of playtime most days helped with stress or mental health. Key game elements were mentioned, emphasising the type of game that was played. Participant four said:

"I need that half an hour just mind numbingly doing something"

Participant five, a 26-year-old female student said:

"I want to play something in the afternoon"

Participant two elaborated why shorter sessions were useful, that investment into long stories was not feasible given his life now:

"So, I try to stick with light games, games you get on for like an hour and get back off not a game that you have to invest 10 hours to, to get to the tutorial".

This approach to gaming sessions was also echoed by participant four stating:

"I haven't got to remember what happened three hours ago and have the right item to get into that next bit".

This style of gameplay makes sense, wanting quick access to the hobby to relax. This supports existing research that short sessions of gameplay can be beneficial [33]. When questioned what types of games they enjoyed playing, four main elements were highlighted. Immersion within the game, escaping reality, little to no story, and the characters within the game. Immersion within games was the most common theme that emerged with participant four commenting:

"The latest ones really good you can create your own team and stuff and it kind of helps it kind of immerses me in the world...Well it was something it was, I think you can be so, you can be so immersed in them now...they've come such a long way since we were kids".

This was echoed by participant two who regaled a specific scene that spoke of immersion specifically, and its impact on him as a person:

"There's this narrative immersion that was happening... And you get to the boss fight, it goes, it glides back into narrative immersion".

This was reiterated by participant three, suggesting being able to start a game and immediately be immersed was of upmost importance:

"You know stuff like I can really kind of jump into and kind of be immersed into my thing".

These interviews indicate immersion is a key factor for SAD sufferers. A further element was games allowing the player to escape their reality. Participant four spoke of his insight into this:

"I think now it's a bit different because of lockdown and the way it's gone people have kind of had to retreat online, almost just to get a bit of normality. Hmm yeah... I think you hit the nail on the head really, it's just a way of escaping and having a bit of down time and a bit of me time. Yeah definitely, definitely. You know, definitely parts of my life for where like escapisms were needed".

This was highlighted by participants two and one also:

"So yeah, it was a good way for me to distract myself and like I'm gonna work on this in Minecraft and I think focus on this"

"I obviously wasn't going out to work at all and being inside my own four walls was feeling quite claustrophobic... And again, I get all that you know, I get all that same escapism".

These excerpts suggest that transportive ability of a game to another reality was key for SAD sufferers, seemingly to escape stressors in their lives and being immersed instantly. Linked to these are the last two sub-themes, a need for no specific story and the characters that are in the game. Participant four spoke of this:

"Yeah, that kind of game that you continuously get something out of, get something out of... with the likes of FIFA and formula one, you know, there's no end in sight so you can just have a play".

These elements were also spoken about by participant two:

"And like there's no story...and I start having ideas about different builds and I want to start again so I think I can get a bit bored and like, oh yeah keep doing new things rather than finishing old things as I try and make myself persevere".

Participant two formed a family-like bond, commenting on this impact of a virtual character within a game he had played:

"The character was kind of like a big sister, sister like she you know, there wasn't a romantic interest, it was just this person that was helping you",

These elements working together are important to those suffering with SAD. They add to research suggesting that a virtual world to escape to and become immersed in, with characters to have meaningful relationships with, could be of great benefit to others with SAD as modelled by Fig. 2.

Helping with Mental Health

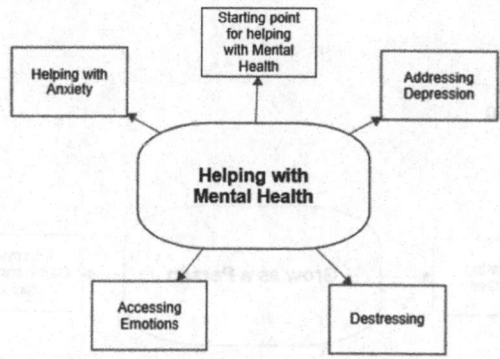

Fig. 3. Theme map for "Helping with mental health"

The third evident theme was, games help with mental health. This theme was seen in all participants, that games have helped them with anxiety and depression. Participant four spoke of this (Fig. 3):

"Ha it's that it's that down time really hmm, my job is quite kind of high mental load, it's like a lot of decisions every day and it's a bit of downtime you can escape".

Participant two spoke further, offering how games have helped him with his mental health and wellbeing:

"I've had some pretty profound experiences with gaming that has left an emotional impact so to say... I mean I could go on on about like games as therapy... So yeah, I'm definitely on I I definitely think games could be a new form of therapy".

Participant three also spoke of games helping him with his mental health:

"I feel like they can be applicable, and they can be beneficial so... yeah no its definitely helped me yeah in detaching from day-to-day problems, especially the ones I can't do anything about".

These experiences were echoed by participant one:

"I think like I think to myself like oh, you know, I can unwind today after playing a game... and like shutting off the thoughts when I read as when I play games... you know, get these little sense of affirmation from if you you play little games or you're winning that gives you like a little adrenaline kick".

Clearly, gaming can benefit mental health. These experiences suggest games could offer an option to SAD sufferers, by allowing them to explore and challenge their own mental health. Participant five offered additional thoughts, commenting that games cannot replace traditional therapy but could be a useful starting point for sufferers:

"Be a good tool I think it can be a really good tool in moderation as like a starting point".

Growing as a Person

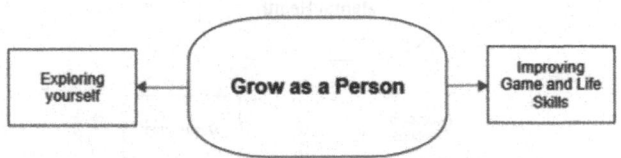

Fig. 4. Theme map for "Grow as a person"

Theme four was: games foster growing as a person, by improving skills both in and out of games. Games highlighted new ways of exploring your sense of self. Participant four spoke of his experience applying games in problem solving in teaching (Fig. 4):

"I did a lot of stuff with Apple, got some Apple accreditations and it was the gaming and it was the problem-solving approach and the kind of a gaming aspect of it"

Furthermore, he spoke of gaming growing within his family and the development of his young son, mentioning:

"Oh, I love that in particular because he's really confident when he does that and he's not unconfident, but he knows what he's doing he's in that environment, he's really, really confident he can, he can kind of order me about a little bit and I love to hear him".

Discussing this revealed he regularly played with his eight-year-old son watching him develop confidence and leadership skills from sessions. Participant five gave personal accounts on working towards goals in games to achieve and learn:

"So, you are working with them towards a goal and probably a sense of achievement".

Participant two spoke of expanding social skills within video games:

"Applaud MMORPGs for helping the socially awkward individuals come out".

Participant three commented on learning about themselves from the games they have played and the interview itself:

"I mean after talking with you I think it's made me realise how much erm, yeah how, how, how your kind of play style and your kind of and your kind of how you act in real life how you are in real life can intercept... like something to push someone to develop their social skills".

The last sub-theme was being able to explore your sense of self. Participants discussed how video games had informed life choices. Participant four mentioned that game play had helped with the direction of his life and choices he faced:

"It inspired me, why inspired that's a strong word? I'd like to think that it helped me later on in life"

Participant two's emotional experience let him notice that other people perceived him differently and that this was a direct consequence of its impact on him:

"Definitely like after the after like those tears came out people said 'man, you feel this, you seem softer or what happened', you know, you you and 'he cares' it's funny having an experience like that",

Participant three also explored this. He spoke about the many choices and paths he would take in games, first playing as what he would do, then on further playthroughs, playing as though he were his ideal self, enabling him to explore both game and self:

"Love the kind of choices and how many different things there to do in it... to an extent the the range of choices and roots you can take through the game...which I love and and yeah kind of crafting a character to reflect yourself...or to reflect parts of yourself that you want to explore".

Finishing up with a very introspective view of his own life:

"I think those kinds of games in a very basic kind of obvious way they kind of they're good for reminding you that you do have choices and and that they do have consequences and that you need to be ok with that and maybe risk negative consequences to make a correct or right decisions yeah".

The ability to experience more aspects of life from games is vast and evident. From simple exploration within games, improving game skills, to exploring their own sense of self. Games can clearly offer freedom of choice and expression, unjudged by other people. This freedom to explore oneself and the game is key for SAD sufferers and could help in the future to tackle their condition.

4 Discussion

The aim of this mixed methods study was two-fold. Firstly, the quantitative element tested the reliability of the LSAS, and if age was a significant predictor of SAD. Secondly, the qualitative aims were to ascertain themes in gameplay that would aid SAD sufferers.

Firstly, this study added to research, showing the validity claimed by the LSAS was accurate. The measure predicted being clinically diagnosed with SAD. This supports previous research and shows the LSAS is still a valuable tool for assessing SAD, showing it can highlight those who are at risk of a clinical diagnosis of SAD [40].

The study also suggested the usefulness of age in predicting SAD, expanding on links between early age and the onset of SAD [22, 42]. While this study did not show age significantly predicted a clinical diagnosis, the trend suggests that age could be an important factor. Limited results here could be due to the average age of a participant being over 27, older than the range defined as adolescence of 24 years, [43]. This trending result could be examined by future studies with younger populations.

The qualitative element was to understand themes in games SAD sufferers played to help them, producing four themes. The first was short breaks of play, by themselves, almost every day. This is consistent with previous research, reporting than an hour of video games a day can be beneficial [9, 27]. Games were played as a self-constructed coping mechanism to handle everyday stress. While there was some emphasis on this investment being good value for money, the theme suggested that games were used to get back to a hobby, and to alleviate stress. There has been a strong link in recent years for the need to unwind after work, and the benefits this can have, from reducing the risk of cardio-vascular disease [44] to increasing work productivity and general life satisfaction [45].

Another theme was using games to grow, including gaining skills in real life and in games, using both to explore yourself. This aligns with previous research that video games help realise what people envisage as their 'ideal' self [46]. Using character avatars to realise an 'ideal' version of oneself has been shown to help improve intrinsic motivation [47]. Furthermore, the theme shows real life skills can be learnt through gameplay supporting previous research [28], however, the skills learnt in this study go further by using sophisticated games with complicated input systems.

The final theme was games helping with mental health. This is expected given the numerous studies highlighting their possible benefits. Some examples would be the works of Lau et al. [48] showing a positive trend in reported mental health scores after playing games. Mandryk and Birk [7] suggested that video games could be used as a complimentary tool to classical therapeutic applications, as well as many other studies highlighting benefits to mental health and well-being [49–51]. The current study adds to this area by highlighting mainstream video games helping with common mental health problems. Importantly, video games are not suggested as an alternative therapy, but that video games can support mental health, providing positivity and well-being. Furthermore, improvements to stress and accessing emotions are an important factor in today's world. This supports new clinical methods and builds evidence for using the transdiagnostic approach in mental health diagnoses [42, 52].

The themes identified help to answer the games played by SAD sufferers are short, immersive, with little story, playable in small sessions with strong characters to escape the hardships of the day. The research shows games allow SAD sufferers new opportunities to address their own mental health and grow as a person, both in and out of game.

4.1 Limitations and Improvements

The transdiagnostic approach to mental health presents limitations of the current research. Importantly, questions asked in the semi-structured interviews were not explicitly about SAD: participants were not asked how games benefitted their SAD, rather how games helped their mental health. No participant spoke about their SAD, either positively or negatively. More than one type of generalised mental health disorder was discussed, including anxiety with depression, lack of emotionality, stress, and low mood. Recent research discusses that many mental health disorders are in fact comorbid, especially anxiety and depression [53, 54]. By asking a wider range of questions to tackle the most common mental health disorders, the research could be improved. Whilst specific enquiries into SAD are beneficial, the framework of the transdiagnostic approach helps to address mental health as general symptoms [52]. This approach might allow for a wider and more accurate understanding of how games can positively affect mental health.

Whilst the qualitative research here is necessary, drawing conclusions from a small population must carry careful interpretation. The findings are indeed promising and suggest interesting ways for both mental health and digital interventions to move forward. However, further research is needed with a wider range of participants with varied mental health disorders. This is supported by the themes extracted from this research. Immersion and escapism have been common themes throughout gaming research history, but there are still conflicting definitions for both [55]. A solution here would be to compare gameplay and application-based immersion [47]. By applying quantitative analysis to a qualitative conundrum, more insight into both topics could be gained.

Participant's motivation to game is also due consideration [34, 56]. Research in recent years has sought to understand how video gameplay, especially violent video gameplay, interacts with aggressive tendencies [46]. Substantial evidence has shown that people play games for specific motivations, especially improving self-esteem, as well just enjoying the hobby [57]. Therefore, this could potentially affect the results found as the participants already played video games. Findings might be different for those who do not play video games. However, with the number of people playing video games being vast [26] it would seem likely that most people have encountered a video game in some form [58]. This makes the approach plausible to consider as an alternative approach to tackling mental health. This could take the form of multiple games being needed for different diagnoses or symptoms, or a transdiagnostic approach, as suggested by Chronis-Tuscano et al. [59].

The age of the participants in the current study could also be a limitation. An important point of research was the young age at which SAD can be predicted. The quantitative analysis found a trending result that suggested younger populations would be more likely to be clinically diagnosed with SAD. This supports recent research suggesting that the onset of mental health problems is most prominent in early adolescent years, defined as the ages of 10–24 [20]). By limiting future studies to a maximum age of 24, there could be a more direct link between video games and their effects of participant's overall perceptions of their own mental health. This would also allow questions to be asked of the younger populations, who are traditionally less likely to seek more traditional therapeutic methods [22].

Future research could also approach the use of video games and mental health by adapting a transdiagnostic approach. Video games can offer a broad spectrum of tools, as presented. To assess games for their transdiagnostic abilities would be a reasonable next step. By first categorising symptom clusters for the most common mental health disorders, video games could be used as an early intervention into mental health. Similar research has already focused on video games improving well-being [9, 60]. However, more research is still needed to identify games that can be used for an intervention-like use-case. Given that these symptom clusters often account for sign of multiple disorders such as anxiety, depression and obsessive compulsions [61], future research could identify which types of games could address the underlying symptoms of these common mental health disorders.

Linked to research on age, if future research were to develop a way for young adolescents to take ownership of their mental health, this could offer an exciting new way to tackle large scale mental health problems. Adolescent uptake of mental health prevention strategies has been traditionally low [49] and video games could offer an intrinsic way to provide mental health help to adolescents. The transdiagnostic approach with targeted video games presents an exciting new area of future research. This could benefit groups at risk, where explicit help might not be the first thing they look to engage with.

4.2 Conclusion

To conclude, the current research aimed to identify key themes in video games that could be used help those with SAD. The study also contributed to the validity of the LSAS and suggested that more research could emphasize the importance of age predicting SAD. The LSAS is still valid in modern day diagnoses of SAD. This suggests the tool is suitable for continued use in the research and applied settings. Regarding age, while not significant, more research surrounding SAD being particularly more worrisome for younger people could prove beneficial. Qualitative analysis yielded four main themes elicited from thematic analysis of semi-structured interviews. These four themes were: the day has been hard for mental health, short solo breaks of play, helping with mental health and growing as a person. The themes discovered from this research offer an interesting way to approach video games in mental health. Games can be used as first entry into mental health help, as a means of self-directed help. There were limitations to this approach. Qualitative research struggles to be generalised. However, these initial findings suggest that underlying game mechanisms could be useful for self-directed help, particularly among younger people. Furthermore, research could investigate transdiagnostic approaches to tackling mental health through video games. Broader approaches might be more beneficial for wider populations. Those suffering with mental health would then have the agency to 'level up' their abilities to tackle their own life. In doing so, they would be more equipped to combat their biggest enemy: overcoming their mental health and take their first step towards freedom.

References

1. Slee, A., Nazareth, I., Freemantle, N., Background, L.H.: Trends in generalised anxiety disorders and symptoms in primary care: UK population-based cohort study. Br. J. Psychiatry 1–7 (2020). https://doi.org/10.1192/bjp.2020.159
2. NHS ENGLAND: Mental health of children and young people in England, 2020: wave 1 follow up to the 2017 survey - NHS Digital. Mental Health of Children and Young People in England, 2020: Wave 1 follow up to the 2017 survey (2020). https://digital.nhs.uk/data-and-information/publications/statistical/mental-health-of-children-and-young-people-in-england/2020-wave-1-follow-up. Accessed 28 May 2021
3. American Psychiatric Association: Diagnostic and Statistical Manual for Mental Disorders, 5th edition (DSM-5), 5th edn. American Psychiatric Publishing, Arlington (2013)
4. Spence, S.H., Rapee, R.M.: The etiology of social anxiety disorder: an evidence-based model. Behav. Res. Ther. **86**, 50–67 (2016). https://doi.org/10.1016/J.BRAT.2016.06.007
5. Stein, M.B., Stein, D.J.: Social anxiety disorder (2008). https://doi.org/10.1016/S0140-6736(08)60488-2
6. Johnson, D., Deterding, S., Kuhn, K.A., Staneva, A., Stoyanov, S., Hides, L.: Gamification for health and wellbeing: a systematic review of the literature. Internet Intervent. **6**, 89–106 (2016). https://doi.org/10.1016/j.invent.2016.10.002
7. Mandryk, R.L., Birk, M.V.: Toward game-based digital mental health interventions: player habits and preferences. J. Med. Internet Res. **19**(4), e128 (2017). https://doi.org/10.2196/jmir.6906
8. Fleming, T.M., et al.: Maximizing the impact of E-therapy and serious gaming: time for a paradigm shift. Front. Psychiatry **7**(APR), 65 (2016). https://doi.org/10.3389/fpsyt.2016.00065
9. Johannes, N., Vuorre, M., Przybylski, A.K.: Video game play is positively correlated with well-being. R. Soc. Open Sci. **8**(2), 202049 (2021). https://doi.org/10.1098/rsos.202049
10. Botella, C., Baños, R.M., Perpiñá, C., Villa, H., Alcañiz, M., Rey, A.: Virtual reality treatment of claustrophobia: a case report. Behav. Res. Ther. **36**(2), 239–246 (1998). https://doi.org/10.1016/S0005-7967(97)10006-7

11. Botella, C., Fernández-Álvarez, J., Guillén, V., García-Palacios, A., Baños, R.: Recent progress in virtual reality exposure therapy for phobias: a systematic review. Curr. Psychiatry Rep. **19**(7), 1–13 (2017). https://doi.org/10.1007/s11920-017-0788-4

12. Karyotaki, E., et al.: Efficacy of self-guided internet-based cognitive behavioral therapy in the treatment of depressive symptoms : a meta-analysis of individual participant data. JAMA Psychiatry **74**, 351–359 (2017). https://doi.org/10.1001/jamapsychiatry.2017.0044

13. Opriş, D., Pintea, S., García-Palacios, A., Botella, C., Szamosközi, Ş, David, D.: Virtual reality exposure therapy in anxiety disorders: a quantitative meta-analysis. Depress. Anxiety **29**, 85–93 (2012). https://doi.org/10.1002/da.20910

14. Liebowitz, M.R.: Social phobia. Mod. Probl. Pharmacopsychiatry **22**, 141–173 (1987). https://doi.org/10.1159/000414022

15. Leigh, E., Clark, D.M.: Understanding social anxiety disorder in adolescents and improving treatment outcomes: applying the cognitive model of clark and wells (1995). Clin. Child. Fam. Psychol. Rev. **21**(3), 388–414 (2018). https://doi.org/10.1007/s10567-018-0258-5

16. Mayo-Wilson, E., et al.: Psychological and pharmacological interventions for social anxiety disorder in adults: a systematic review and network meta-analysis. Lancet Psychiatry **1**(5), 368–376 (2014). https://doi.org/10.1016/S2215-0366(14)70329-3

17. Hudson, J.L., et al.: Clinical predictors of response to cognitive-behavioral therapy in pediatric anxiety disorders: the genes for treatment (GxT) study. J. Am. Acad. Child Adolesc. Psychiatry **54**(6), 454–463 (2015). https://doi.org/10.1016/j.jaac.2015.03.018

18. Klein, A.M., et al.: Interpretation modification training reduces social anxiety in clinically anxious children. Behav. Res. Ther. **75**, 78–84 (2015). https://doi.org/10.1016/j.brat.2015.10.006

19. Beesdo, K., Knappe, S., Pine, D.S.: Anxiety and anxiety disorders in children and adolescents: developmental issues and implications for DSM-V. Psychiatr. Clin. North Am. **32**(3), 483–524 (2009). https://doi.org/10.1016/j.psc.2009.06.002

20. Sawyer, S.M., Azzopardi, P.S., Wickremarathne, D., Patton, G.C.: The age of adolescence. Lancet Child Adolesc. Health **2**(3), 223–228 (2018). https://doi.org/10.1016/S2352-4642(18)30022-1

21. Hudson, J.L., Rapee, R.M., Lyneham, H.J., McLellan, L.F., Wuthrich, V.M., Schniering, C.A.: Comparing outcomes for children with different anxiety disorders following cognitive behavioural therapy. Behav. Res. Ther. **72**, 30–37 (2015). https://doi.org/10.1016/j.brat.2015.06.007

22. Catanzano, M., et al.: Evaluation of a mental health drop-in centre offering brief transdiagnostic psychological assessment and treatment for children and adolescents with long-term physical conditions and their families: a single-arm, open, non-randomised trial. Evid. Based. Ment. Health **24**(1), 25–32 (2021). https://doi.org/10.1136/ebmental-2020-300197

23. Hofmann, S.G., Anu Asnaani, M.A., Hinton, D.E.: Cultural aspects in social anxiety and social anxiety disorder. Depress. Anxiety **27**(12), 1117–1127 (2010). https://doi.org/10.1002/da.20759

24. Spence, S.H.: Preventative strategies suicide and sudden death bereavement view project. Int. Handb. Phobic Anxiety Disord. Child. Adolsecents (1994). https://doi.org/10.1007/978-1-4899-1498-9_24

25. Rapee, R.M., Gaston, J.E., Abbott, M.J.: Testing the efficacy of theoretically derived improvements in the treatment of social phobia (2009). https://doi.org/10.1037/a0014800

26. ISFE: Key Facts 2020 Europe's Video Games Industry (2020). https://www.isfe.eu/wp-content/uploads/2020/08/ISFE-final-1.pdf. Accessed 18 July 2021

27. Boyle, E., et al.: An update to the systematic literature review of empirical evidence of the impacts and outcomes of computer games and serious games. Comput. Educ. **94**, 178–192 (2016). https://doi.org/10.1016/j.compedu.2015.11.003

28. Hewett, K.J.E., Zeng, G., Pletcher, B.C.: The acquisition of 21st-century skills through video games: minecraft design process models and their web of class roles. Simul. Gaming **51**(3), 336–364 (2020). https://doi.org/10.1177/1046878120904976

29. Granic, I., Lobel, A., Engels, R.C.M.E.: The benefits of playing video games. Am. Psychol. **69**(1), 66–78 (2014). https://doi.org/10.1037/a0034857

30. Atrax Games: "Sym." Mastertronic (2015). https://store.steampowered.com/app/342100/Sym/. Accessed 06 Oct 2020

31. Lessiter, J. Freeman, J., Keogh, E., Davidoff, J.: A cross-media presence questionnaire: the ITC-sense of presence inventory (2001). https://eprints.gold.ac.uk/483/1/PSY_Freeman_2001a.pdf. Accessed 11 Apr 2019

32. Deci, E.L., Ryan, R.M.: Self-determination theory. In: Handbook of Theories of Social Psychology, vol. 1, pp. 416–437. SAGE Publications Inc. (2012)

33. Przybylski, A.K., Rigby, C.S., Ryan, R.M.: A Motivational model of video game engagement. Rev. Gen. Psychol. **14**(2), 154–166 (2010). https://doi.org/10.1037/a0019440

34. Ryan, R.M., Rigby, C.S., Przybylski, A.: The motivational pull of video games: a self-determination theory approach. Motiv. Emot. **30**(4), 347–363 (2006). https://doi.org/10.1007/s11031-006-9051-8

35. Fleming, T.M., et al.: Serious games and gamification for mental health: Current status and promising directions. Front. Psychiatry **7**(JAN), 1 (2017). https://doi.org/10.3389/fpsyt.2016.00215

36. Tolks, D., Horstmann, D., Dadaczynski, K., Paulus, P.: The wellbeing game. How to promote wellbeing using gamification. Adaptation of a gamified web application in German context 69 PUBLICATIONS 108 CITATIONS SEE PROFILE The Wellbeing Game. How to promote wellbeing using gamification Adaptation of a gamified. In: 6th International Conference on Serious Games Applications for Health (IEEE SeGAH 2018), no. May, pp. 2–4, May 2018. https://www.researchgate.net/publication/325320089_The_Wellbeing_Game_How_to_promote_wellbeing_using_gamification_Adaptation_of_a_gamified_web_application_in_German_context. Accessed 04 Mar 2020

37. Creswell, J., Clark, J., Gutmann, V.: An expanded typology for classifying mixed methods research into designs (2008). http://www.corwin.com/upm-data/19291_Chapter_7.pdf. Accessed 04 July 2021

38. Elliott, L., Golub, A., Price, M., Bennett, A.: More than just a game? Combat-themed gaming among recent veterans with posttraumatic stress disorder. Games Health J. **4**(4), 271–277 (2015). https://doi.org/10.1089/g4h.2014.0104

39. Braun, V., Clarke, V.: Using thematic analysis in psychology. Qual. Res. Psychol. **3**(2), 77–101 (2006). https://doi.org/10.1191/1478088706qp063oa

40. Heimberg, R.G., et al.: Social anxiety disorder in DSM-5. Depress. Anxiety **31**, 472–479 (2014). https://doi.org/10.1002/da.22231

41. Newsom: Sample Size and Power for Regression (2019). https://davidakenny.shinyapps.io/MedPower/. Accessed 04 July 2021

42. Gillan, C.M., Seow, T.X.F.: Carving out new transdiagnostic dimensions for research in mental health. Biol. Psychiatry Cogn. Neurosci. Neuroimaging **5**(10), 932–934 (2020). https://doi.org/10.1016/j.bpsc.2020.04.013

43. Pine, R., Fleming, T., McCallum, S., Sutcliffe, K.: The effects of casual videogames on anxiety, depression, stress, and low mood: a systematic review. Games Health J. **9**(4), 255–264 (2020). https://doi.org/10.1089/g4h.2019.0132

44. Van Amelsvoort, L.G.P.M., Kant, I.J., Bültmann, U., Swaen, G.M.H.: Need for recovery after work and the subsequent risk of cardiovascular disease in a working population. Occup. Environ. Med. **60**(SUPPL. 1) (2003). https://doi.org/10.1136/oem.60.suppl_1.i83

45. De Bloom, J., Kinnunen, U., Korpela, K.: Recovery processes during and after work: associations with health, work engagement, and job performance. J. Occup. Environ. Med. **57**(7), 732–742 (2015). https://doi.org/10.1097/JOM.0000000000000475

46. Sailer, M., Hense, J.U., Mayr, S.K., Mandl, H.: How gamification motivates: an experimental study of the effects of specific game design elements on psychological need satisfaction. Comput. Hum. Behav. **69**, 371–380 (2017). https://doi.org/10.1016/j.chb.2016.12.033

47. Birk, M.V., Atkins, C., Bowey, J.T., Mandryk, R.L.: Fostering intrinsic motivation through avatar identification in digital games (2016). https://doi.org/10.1145/2858036.2858062

48. Lau, H.M., Smit, J.H., Fleming, T.M., Riper, H.: Serious games for mental health: are they accessible, feasible, and effective? A systematic review and meta-analysis. Front. Psychiatry **7**(JAN), 1 (2017). https://doi.org/10.3389/fpsyt.2016.00209

49. Poppelaars, M., Lichtwarck-Aschoff, A., Otten, R., Granic, I.: Can a commercial video game prevent depression? Null results and whole sample action mechanisms in a randomized controlled trial. Front. Psychol. **11**, 3674 (2021). https://doi.org/10.3389/fpsyg.2020.575962

50. Tinker, J.: Statistics relating to Social Anxiety and related Mental Health Conditions (2019). https://www.ncbi.nlm.nih.gov/pubmed/15297904. Accessed 04 Mar 2020

51. Wols, A., Hollenstein, T., Lichtwarck-Aschoff, A., Granic, I.: The effect of expectations on experiences and engagement with an applied game for mental health. Games Health J. (2021). https://doi.org/10.1089/g4h.2020.0115

52. Dalgleish, T., Black, M., Johnston, D., Bevan, A.: Transdiagnostic approaches to mental health problems: current status and future directions. J. Consult. Clin. Psychol. **88**(3), 179–195 (2020). https://doi.org/10.1037/ccp0000482

53. Garber, J., Weersing, V.R.: Comorbidity of anxiety and depression in youth: implications for treatment and prevention. Clin. Psychol. Sci. Pract. **17**(4), 293–306 (2010). https://doi.org/10.1111/j.1468-2850.2010.01221.x

54. Mineka, S., Watson, D., Clark, L.A.: Comorbidity of anxiety and unipolar mood disorders. Annu. Rev. Psychol. **49**, 377–412 (1998). https://doi.org/10.1146/annurev.psych.49.1.377

55. Sanders, T., Cairns, P.: Time perception, immersion and music in videogames (2010). www.falstad.com/maze. Accessed 01 Nov 2018

56. Yee, N.: Motivations for play in online games. CyberPsychol. Behav. **9**(6), 772–775 (2006). https://doi.org/10.1089/cpb.2006.9.772

57. Przybylski, A.K., Weinstein, N., Ryan, R.M., Rigby, C.S.: Having to versus wanting to play: background and consequences of harmonious versus obsessive engagement in video games (2009). https://doi.org/10.1089/cpb.2009.0083

58. Richter, F.: Gaming: the most lucrative entertainment industry by far. Statista, 22 September 2020. https://www.statista.com/chart/22392/global-revenue-of-selected-entertainment-industry-sectors/. Accessed 18 July 2021

59. Chronis-Tuscano, A., Danko, C.M., Rubin, K.H., Coplan, R.J., Novick, D.R.: Future directions for research on early intervention for young children at risk for social anxiety. J. Clin. Child Adolesc. Psychol. **47**(4), 655–667 (2018). https://doi.org/10.1080/15374416.2018.142 6006

60. Przybylski, A.K., Mishkin, A.F.: How the quantity and quality of electronic gaming relates to adolescents' academic engagement and psychosocial adjustment. Psychol. Pop. Media Cult. **5**(2), 145–156 (2016). https://doi.org/10.1037/ppm0000070

61. Lewandowski, K.E., Barrantes-Vidal, N., Nelson-Gray, R.O., Clancy, C., Kepley, H.O., Kwapil, T.R.: Anxiety and depression symptoms in psychometrically identified schizotypy. Schizophr. Res. **83**(2–3), 225–235 (2006). https://doi.org/10.1016/j.schres.2005.11.024

Does Gamification Increase Purchase Intention? A Systematic Review

Yichen Gao(✉) and Zhanwei Wu

Shanghai Jiao Tong University, 800 Dongchuan RD. Minhang District, Shanghai, China
ethangaok@163.com

Abstract. In recent years, application of gamification methods in e-business activities has become an increasingly common phenomenon. Based on the assumption that gamification can promote purchase intention, the use of gamification design in commercial activities has become more and more common. This study attempts to address some questions that are fundamental yet have not been clearly answered through systematic review, such as (1) whether there is empirical evidence showing that gamification has an impact on purchase intention; (2) whether there is research evidence showing which mediator/moderator variables used by gamification affect purchase intention; and (3) which gamification features are used in existing researches and whether there is empirical evidence showing that they have direct or indirect impacts on purchase intention. The literature search hits 164 results, and 25 articles were finally included in the full paper review. The results show that there is adequate evidence to support the existing hypothesis, which is gamification can influence purchase intention through perceived value. Further details of results and discussion were concluded in the article. Recommendations for future research of gamification and purchase intention in e-business context were provided as well.

Keywords: Gamification · Games · Purchase intention · Perceived value

1 Introduction

In recent years, application of gamification methods in e-business activities has become an increasingly common phenomenon, especially in the context of emerging multi-channel and omni-channel retailing. Large companies such as Amazon, eBay, Nike, Samsung Nation, Teleflora and Gilt Groupe has already used gamification extensively on their e-commerce platforms. Gamification is usually defined as "the strategic attempt to enhance systems, services, organizations, and activities in order to create similar experiences to those experienced when playing games in order to motivate and engage users" [1].

On the other hand, previous research in business domain has already confirmed that perceived value has positive impacts on purchase intention. Recent research showed that the perceived value can arouse consumers' willingness to purchase value-added services in various free games [2]. A common definition used in e-business study is "customer's perceived preference for and evaluation of those product attributes, attribute performances, and consequences arising from use that facilitate achieving the customer's goals and purposes in use situations" [3]. The above finding may not necessarily be limited to games. Hsu and Lin (2015) found that in mobile application environment, emotional value and price have a direct and significant impact on the purchase intention of non-free applications. Gaming/gamification is widely considered as an effective method to promote perceived value, either economically or non-economically. However, it is still unclear whether gamification can actually affect perceived value, especially in making purchase decisions.

Since gamification can bring enhanced customer experience [4], it is not surprising that the research community has shown great interest in whether gamification promotes purchase intention through perceived value. From a practical point of view, the answers to these questions will also help to better design innovative retail services, promote business activities and customer-brand interaction. However, researches are scattered in different research fields, such as: human-computer interaction, psychology, business, etc. At present, there still lacks a comprehensive overview of existing research conclusions and related knowledge, so as to provide references for researchers to carry out further research work, and to provide retail practitioners guidelines to better design service experiences.

Therefore, this article aims to answer some basic questions through a systematic literature review:

RQ1 Whether there are empirical evidences showing that gamification has direct or indirect impacts on purchase intention.
RQ2 Whether there is research evidence showing which mediator/moderator variables used by gamification affect purchase intention.
RQ3 Which gamification features are used in existing researches and whether there is empirical evidence showing that they have direct or indirect impacts on purchase intention.

Considering that statistically significant evidence is needed to draw more credible conclusions, this article mainly extracts evidence and conclusions from empirical research. In addition, because related papers are distributed in various disciplines, their research objects, experimental methods, and data reports are often quite different, which makes it impossible to use meta-analysis for secondary data analysis.

2 Method

The literature search was conducted in the Scopus database on June 2021, using the following search strings for Scopus search: TITLE-ABS-KEY ("purchase intention" or "intention of purchase") and TITLE-ABS-KEY ("game" or "gamif*"). In this article we use Scopus as the search engine because it contains all other databases with potentially relevant content, e.g. ACM, IEEE, Springer, and the DBLP Computer Science Bibliography. Also, using only one database instead of several was considered a preferable method in order to increase the rigor, clarity and replicability of the literature search process [5].

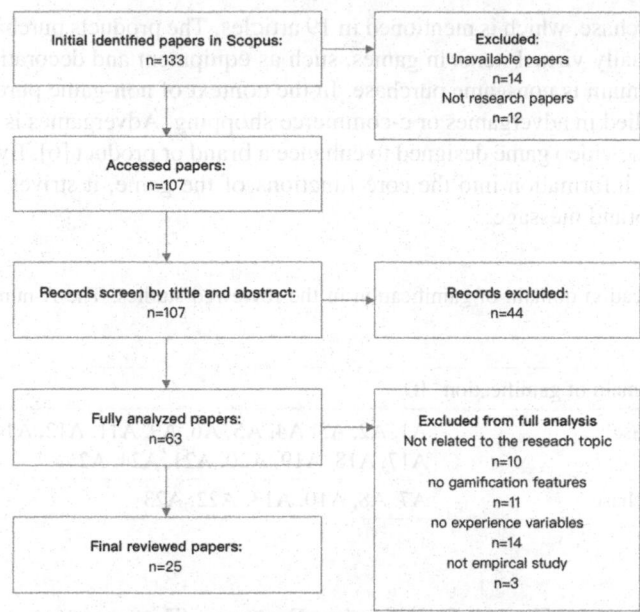

Fig. 1. Literature search process and outcomes.

Figure 1 demonstrates the literature search procedure. The literature search produced 164 results, and some studies were included or excluded during further examination according to the following criteria:

1) studies are excluded if they are neither journal article, conference paper nor book chapters.
2) studies are excluded if they are not written in English.
3) studies are excluded if they are not related to gamification and purchase intention.
4) studies are excluded if they are not related to perceived value.
5) studies are excluded if they contain no empirical research (To draw credible conclusions, we argue that empirical evidences are needed).

After examining the search results according to the above-mentioned criteria, 25 articles were finally determined as the main body of the literature review. A full list of the 25 studies (A1–A25) is provided in Appendix 1 and this review uses the IDs to refer to the corresponding articles.

3 Result

3.1 Descriptive Information

Application Domain. The application domains of gamification that related to purchase intention can be divided into two categories (see Table 1). The main application domain is In-game purchase, which is mentioned in 19 articles. The products purchased by consumers are usually virtual items in games, such as equipment and decoration. Another application domain is non-game purchase. In the context of non-game purchase, gamification is applied in advergames or e-commerce shopping. Advergames is defined as a specific purpose video game designed to enhance a brand or product [6]. By embedding brand-specific information into the core functions of the game, it strives to make the game itself a brand message.

Table 1. Application domain of gamification in the reviewed studies. The A-numbers refer to Appendix IDs

Application domain of gamification	ID
In-game purchase	A1, A2, A3, A4, A5, A6, A9, A11, A12, A14, A15, A16, A17, A18, A19, A20, A21, A24, A25
Non-game purchase	A7, A8, A10, A13, A22, A23

Perceived Value and Typical Gamification Features. The previous researches have given substantially similar definitions to perceived value, while different researches describe the value in different ways. For the convenience of reading, all the value and related gamification features are summarized and classified in Table 2. Those value and gamification features that are proved to have effects on purchase intention through experiments are displayed. According to the previous theoretical research that summarized in previous section [7], the exact terminology to describe customer experience in each paper is clustered into four categories of perceived value: emotional value, social value, functional value and other. Emotional value refers to the value that motivates people to do something in game for its own satisfaction rather than to obtain extrinsic rewards, which is highly personalized (e.g. enjoyment, challenge). For example, competition between players will increase players' willingness to buy items in order to improve their performance in games (Study A23). Social value refers to the value derived from the ability of the service or product to enhance the social self-concept of the customer [7]. For example, peers' opinions on purchasing virtual goods will affect consumers' purchase intention, etc. Functional value is decomposed into quality and economic value. Quality value refers to the utility derived from the perceived quality and expected performance of the product. While economic value means the value which motivates people to do something for expected outcome (e.g. rewards) (Study A23). For example, players may be motivated to be more engaged in games if they can earn real money from it. Variables that do not fall into the above three categories are classified as other.

Participants. Among 25 articles, the maximum number of participants in the experiment was 4556, and the minimum was 43. There were 5 articles with more than 1,000 people involved in the experiment and 1 with less than 100 people. The participants of the experiments were mostly consumers with gaming experience, or people with previous experience in in-game purchases.

Table 2. Summary of perceived value which have effects on purchase intention and related gamification features presented in the reviewed studies. The A-numbers refer to Appendix IDs

Categories of perceived value		Description of the value in articles	Game/Gamification features
Emotional value		Hedonic value (A3, A13, A19), playfulness (A4), enjoyment value (A5, A17, A18, A25), flow (A7, A8, A16, A24), addiction (A3, A12, A20), engagement (A14, A15, A22), hedonic gratification (A15), affective involvement (A16)	Interactivity (A7), challenge (A7, A18), flexibility (A15), skill-challenge balance (A17), achievement (A18), aesthetic design (A24), character competency (A25)
Social value		Social value (A1, A17), subjective norm (A2, A19), social motivation (A3), socializing (A5), character identification (A9, A22, A25), social interaction (A10, A18, A20), social presence (A14), social gratification (A15), social identity (A16), community involvement(A18), perceived uniqueness (A23), connectedness (A24)	Avatar (A9), interactivity (A14)
Functional value	Economic value	Economic value (A1), value for money (A4, A24), monetary value (A17), perceived uniqueness (A21)	Reward (A24)
	Quality value	Ease of use (A5), perceived usefulness (A10, A23), perceived quality (A1, A21, A24), satisfaction (A24, A25)	
Other		Loyalty (A4, A12), nostalgia (A5, A18), telepresence (A7), perceived authenticity (A9), perceived fairness (17), novelty-seeking (A13)	Flexibility (A4), reward (A4), scarcity (A21), aesthetic design (A9)

Game/Gamification Types. Games for entertainment purposes (e.g. RPG, FPS games, etc.) account for the largest number of game/gamification types in experiments.

Purchased Items. Most purchased items mentioned (19 articles) are virtual products and subscription services in or out of games, which refer to items that related to consumers' game experience, such as game props that enhance consumers' ability in games. The items mentioned in the remaining 6 articles are physical products and services, such as game peripheral products, food, sports products etc.

Measurements. All studies measure consumers' purchase intentions through questionnaires. The scales used in the studies are usually self-defined or adapted from other similar studies to measure variables and to examine the results. Experiments in 4 articles use self-developed prototypes for evaluation before filling out the questionnaires.

3.2 Empirical Analysis and Answer of Questions

Answer for RQ1. Outcomes of all researches included in this literature review support the idea that gamification has statistically significant impact on purchase intention, though the relationship is complicated. Most researches focus on the indirect relation between gamification and purchase intention, namely how perceived value generated through game/gamification affects purchase intention. The reason may exist in the fact that as summarized in introduction section, previous researches have already identified perceived value that have impacts on purchase intention. Hence, for gamification researchers, it seems more promising to follow the existing direction and evaluate those perceived value first.

Answer for RQ2. In the literature review, mediator/moderator variables used by gamification are divided into 5 categories (see Table 2). In conclusion, 25 articles in this literature review provided empirical evidences that value gained from game or gamification application have statistically significant impact on purchase intention. 12 of them conclude that emotional value is positively related to purchase intention, while 2 articles (Study A1, A2) show that the enjoyment value has a negative impact on players' willingness to purchase virtual goods in free games. The most commonly mentioned perceived value that affects purchase intention is social value, which has been mentioned in 18 articles in total. 5 studies proved that economic value can affect purchase intention. The experimental results of 7 studies proved that the perceived quality will affect purchase intention. Among them, Study A10, A23 and A28 studied the quality of physical products, while Study A1, A5, A21, and A24 focused on the quality and ease of use of games or virtual products in games. It is worth mentioning that a few researches argued that the gamification method may have compound effects on purchase intention, which means that even if perceived value induced by gamification affect purchase intention positively, the gamification as a whole may not necessarily have the same effect. For example, Study A13 found in a user experiment of the gamified omnichannel retailing that while perceived hedonic value of gamification application are proved to influence repurchase intention positively, the gamification as a whole has significantly negative effect on repurchase intention in some consumer groups. The reason, according to the researcher's analysis, may come from the complicated relationship among consumers' perceived hedonic value, gamification, repurchase intention, and consumers' novelty-seeking traits in the context of omnichannel retailing.

Answer for RQ3. In the existing researches, the game/gamification features mentioned mainly include: reward (6 articles), challenge (5 articles), avatar (5 articles), competition (3 articles), interactivity (3 articles), achievement (2 articles), badges (2 articles), goals (2 articles), stage/rank (2 articles), flexibility (2 articles) and aesthetic design (2 articles). A total of 10 articles verify that game features can affect the experience. The gamification features that have been verified to be able to affect the perceived value are: interactivity (A7), challenge (A7, A18), avatar (A9, A25), interactivity (A14), flexibility (A15), skill-challenge balance (A17), achievement (A18, A28), reward (A24, A29), aesthetic (A24), competition (A28). In conclusion, statistically verified correlation between gamification features and perceived value in existing researches are summarized as follows.

4   Findings and Discussions

4.1   Key Findings and Lessons Learned

The results of this literature review show that gamification can produce a compound effect on purchase intention through a series of perceived value (see Fig. 1). Among the articles in this literature review, except for 1 article (Study A13) which proved the direct impact of gamification on purchase intention, other articles found that gamification features influence perceived value, and therefore further indirectly affect purchase intention. Further findings are provided as follows (Fig. 2).

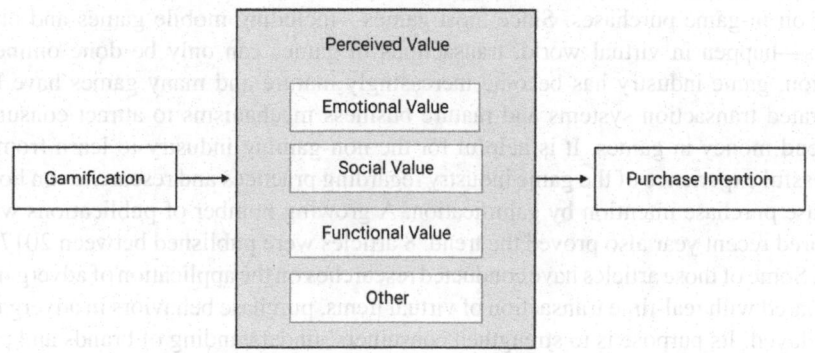

Fig. 2. Results of literature review.

Influence of Consumers' Characteristics on Gamification's Effects on Purchase Intention. Although the games or gamified applications used in each study are quite different, certain patterns can still be summarized from the conclusions.

First, there are more male consumers than female ones in games/gamified applications and the two groups act quite differently. One possible explanation is that current mainstream games on the market are more popular among male players. One research has also pointed out that men are more inclined to play more competitive games, while women are more willing to play "pink games", such as dressing and cooking games (Study A4). It can be assumed that men and women may have different purchasing preferences. However, most experiments in existing studies did not include gender as a control variable.

Secondly, most of experimental participants are aged under 30. Some studies believe that elderly people are less willing to do shopping (Study A4) in game/gamified applications. On the one hand, mainstream games are more attractive to young people. On the other hand, there may be a lack of appropriate strategies targeting the elderly in current games or gamification designs. In addition, consumers with or without game experience act differently when making purchase decisions in game/gamified applications. For example, Study A22 and A23 have found that in non-gaming environment, consumers with game experience are more willing to buy gamified products. Even among game players, gamification design has different effects on different types of players. For example, the paying players' purchase intention is determined by both intrinsic value and extrinsic value (e.g. playfulness, good price, and reward), while nonpaying players' intention is determined only by extrinsic value (e.g. good price) (Study A4). It has also been proved that the rewarded virtual products have more attraction to non-paying players (Study A24). Compared with hardcore players, casual players need more tutorial guidance to increase their retention rate and purchase intention (Study A11). These abovementioned differences are more or less discussed in various existing studies, but the relation between different consumer groups and their purchase intention still needs to be further studied in the future (Study A15, A17).

Upward Trend in Research of Non-game Purchase Intention. Most of the research focus on in-game purchases. Since most games—including mobile games and online games—happen in virtual world, transactions in games can only be done online. In addition, game industry has become increasingly mature and many games have built integrated transaction systems and mature business mechanisms to attract consumers to spend money in games. It is helpful for the non-gaming industry to learn from the successful experience of the game industry regarding practices and researches on how to increase purchase intention by gamification. A growing number of publications which appeared recent year also proved the trend. 8 articles were published between 2017 and 2021. Some of those articles have conducted researches on the application of advergames. Compared with real-time transaction of virtual items, purchase behaviors in advergames are delayed. Its purpose is to strengthen consumers' understanding of brands and products, so that consumers are more likely to buy these products in the future. Other studies have also mentioned the application of gamification in e-commerce shopping, which is an emerging hot topic both in theory and practice. However, it has not been thoroughly studied and still needs further research.

Methods which Used Most Frequently in Experiment. Most studies use questionnaire to measure related variables, and some of the studies also conducted survey interviews to better understand consumers' intuitive feelings. The scales used in the studies are usually self-defined or adapted from other similar studies to measure variables and to examine the results. Items were mostly measured on a seven-point Likert scale (strongly disagree–strongly agree). Some studies also pointed out that future studies need to further examine physiological data, such as eye tracking data (Study A11). The advantage of using physiological data is that the data obtained will be more objective and accurate. In addition, most experiments currently use existing gamified applications or game interfaces for testing, and seldom design prototypes by themselves. Only in a few studies, for example Study A13, self-designed interface was used to simulate a shopping system, and experiments were conducted on the influence of gamification features such as badge levels on consumers' repurchase intentions. Although existing games have a more complete business model and purchase system, the fact that too many features have already been integrated in the interface makes it harder to measure the effects of some specific game features. Some researches argue that self-built prototypes can be used to conduct controlled experiments with a few target variables, and thus allow more precise evaluation on specific gamification features.

Gamification Design Strategies that Enhance Purchase Intention. Firstly, the inability to continue enjoying the game may become an incentive for players to purchase. Game developers attempt to increase the desirability of in-game items by intentionally increasing the frustration experienced with the free-core game (Study A5). Free games do not directly stimulate consumers to consume at the early stage. Instead, designers gradually limit consumers' gaming experience when they have already spent much time playing, and thereby tempting them to purchase corresponding services. In business, some companies have also used this strategy. For example, Dropbox initially provided limited free storage space for consumers and consumers can "get" more storage space by completing some small challenges (Study A1). Similar to the strategy of free games, it is increasingly difficult to obtain free storage space, but consumers' need for storage space remains unchanged. In order to unlock more space, consumers gradually feel inclined to purchase advanced services.

Secondly, it should be noted that when using gamification, designers should choose an appropriate way to improve user experience, rather than hastily applying classic and popular methods. For example, games with more social features emphasize gamification features related to social value, such as competition and virtual images, with which the games can effectively increase consumers' social value. In the case of M-SNGs, Study A15 suggests to establish more interactive modes and create an "asynchronous cooperative game mode" in which consumers can cooperate to finish a game mission at different times, since the interactivity and competition in this mode can to some extent increase consumers' social value.

Finally, design for non-game products should pay more attention to enhancing consumers' perception of usefulness, quality and economic value of products. Though research on gamification design for non-game products are rare in the body of literature review. There still be some experience can be learned from the design methods and purposes of online advertising games, namely to enhance consumers' understanding of products through games and thereby increase their purchase intention. Advertising games usually use commodities as key props (Study A7, A8) in games, so that consumers can have a deeper understanding of certain products and brands during such games. Compared with in-game products, the advantage of non-game products is that consumers can physically touch and feel the products. Therefore, promotion of non-game products should make use of such advantage. In addition, economic value has a strong influence on first-time consumers (Study A4). In general, shopping design strategy for non-game products should pay more attention to enhancing consumers' perception of usefulness and quality, and economic value of products and providing a sense of satisfaction through interaction and other methods by integrating products into the game process, so as to further stimulate purchase intention.

4.2 Recommendation for Future Research

The following suggestions are made for future research in this field:

Future researches can further explore the effects of applying gamification to offline shopping scenarios. The existing researches largely focus on the influence of gamification on purchase intention regarding online virtual goods. As Study A13 mentioned, creating an offline version of the gamified concept would help to give a more hands-on experience, i.e., in-store events that would have some of the gamified components included. This could be a gamified points system for a specific purchase as one example.

It is recommended to use purposefully designed prototype as a stimulus for higher quality experiments in future researches so as to learn the effect of each game features to purchase intention. Since it should be noted that when using gamification, designers should choose an appropriate way to improve user experience, rather than hastily applying classic and popular methods such as points and badges [8]. For example, to enhance purchase intention by effectively increasing consumers' social value, it may be better to use games with more social features or emphasize gamification features related to social value, such as competition and virtual images. Currently, there have been few researches that verified the effects of specific gamification features on purchase intention. Through prototypes, the effects of different gamification features can be measured more accurately with the help of controlled experiments. In addition, it is possible to combine questionnaires with instruments to collect psychophysiological data to reduce the cognitive bias caused by questionnaire measurement. For example, researchers can use eye trackers to measure objective data and at the meantime use questionnaire to measure consumers' subjective feelings.

Future researches can evaluate the effects of gamification on people who never or seldom play games. Participants in experiments of existing researches are mostly game players. Consumers can be classified according to their occupation, income, education level, etc., to further analyze whether and how the effects of gamification on different groups may differ.

In follow-up researches, it is also necessary to study improper design strategies of gamification and evaluate corresponding adverse effects. Existing researches in this field mostly focus on the positive side of gamification, such as its functions in improving user experience, increasing purchase intention and activating market. However, gamification mechanism may also have some negative effects, such as generating extra cognitive burden or wasting consumers' time, leading to unwanted consumption, or causing privacy and security problems. The negative impact on young consumers may be even greater.

Appendix A. Full List of the Reviewed Publications

ID	Full citation
A1	Hamari, Juho, Hanner, N., & Koivisto, J. (2020). "Why pay premium in freemium services?" A study on perceived value, continued use and purchase intentions in free-to-play games. International Journal of Information Management, 51(November 2018), 102040
A2	Hamari, J. (2015). Why do people buy virtual goods? Attitude toward virtual good purchases versus game enjoyment. International Journal of Information Management, 35(3), 299–308
A3	Jimenez, N., San-Martin, S., Camarero, C., & San Jose Cabezudo, R. (2019). What kind of video gamer are you? Journal of Consumer Marketing, 36(1), 218–227
A4	Hsiao, K. L., & Chen, C. C. (2016). What drives in-app purchase intention for mobile games? An examination of perceived values and loyalty. Electronic Commerce Research and Applications, 16, 18–29
A5	Hamari, J, Malik, A., Koski, J., & Johri, A. (2019). Uses and Gratifications of Pokémon Go: Why do People Play Mobile Location-Based Augmented Reality Games? International Journal of Human-Computer Interaction, 35(9), 804–819
A6	Chen, H., & Chen, H. (2020). Understanding the relationship between online self-image expression and purchase intention in SNS games: A moderated mediation investigation. Computers in Human Behavior, 112
A7	Catalán, Sara, Martínez, E., & Wallace, E. (2019). The role of flow for mobile advergaming effectiveness. Online Information Review, 43(7), 1228–1244
A8	Catalán, S, Martínez, E., & Wallace, E. (2019). Analysing mobile advergaming effectiveness: the role of flow, game repetition and brand familiarity. Journal of Product and Brand Management, 28(4), 502–514
A9	Wu, S.-L., & Hsu, C.-P. (2018). Role of authenticity in massively multiplayer online role playing games (MMORPGs): Determinants of virtual item purchase intention. Journal of Business Research, 92, 242–249
A10	Zhu, D. H., & Chang, Y. P. (2015). Effects of interactions and product information on initial purchase intention in product placement in social games: The moderating role of product familiarity. Journal of Electronic Commerce Research, 16(1), 22–33
A11	Moirn, R., Léger, P. M., Senecal, S., Roberge, M. C. B., Lefebvre, M., & Fredette, M. (2016). The effect of game tutorial: A comparison between casual and hardcore gamers. CHI PLAY 2016 - Proceedings of the Annual Symposium on Computer-Human Interaction in Play Companion, 229–237
A12	Balakrishnan, J., & Griffiths, M. D. (2018). Loyalty towards online games, gaming addiction, and purchase intention towards online mobile in-game features. Computers in Human Behavior, 87(June), 238–246
A13	Kim, C., Costello, F. J., & Lee, K. C. (2020). The Unobserved Heterogeneneous Influence of Gamification and Novelty-Seeking Traits on Consumers' Repurchase Intention in the Omnichannel Retailing. Frontiers in Psychology, 11

(continued)

(continued)

ID	Full citation
A14	Jin, W., Sun, Y., Wang, N., & Zhang, X. (2017). Why users purchase virtual products in MMORPG? An integrative perspective of social presence and user engagement. Internet Research, 27(2), 408–427
A15	Huang, T., Bao, Z., & Li, Y. (2017). Why do players purchase in mobile social network games? An examination of customer engagement and of uses and gratifications theory. Program, 51(3), 259–277
A16	Huang, E. (2012). Online experiences and virtual goods purchase intention. Internet Research, 22(3), 252–274
A17	Wang, L., Gao, Y., Yan, J., & Qin, J. (2020). From freemium to premium: the roles of consumption values and game affordance. Information Technology and People
A18	Ghazali, E., Mutum, D. S., & Woon, M. Y. (2019). Exploring player behavior and motivations to continue playing Pokémon GO. Information Technology and People, 32(3), 646–667
A19	Hsieh, J.-K., & Tseng, C.-Y. (2018). Exploring social influence on hedonic buying of digital goods - Online games' virtual items. Journal of Electronic Commerce Research, 19(2), 164–185
A20	Jang, M., Lee, R., & Yoo, B. (2019). Does fun or freebie increase in-app purchase?: Analyzing effects of enjoyment and item experience intention to purchase mobile game contents. Information Systems and E-Business Management
A21	Chen, H. J., & Sun, T. H. (2014). Clarifying the impact of product scarcity and perceived uniqueness in buyers' purchase behavior of games of limited-amount version. Asia Pacific Journal of Marketing and Logistics, 26(2), 232–249
A22	Shelton, J., & Chiliya, N. (2014). Brand endorsements: An exploratory study into the effectiveness of using video game characters as brand endorsers. Mediterranean Journal of Social Sciences, 5(14), 260–275
A23	Bittner, J. V, & Shipper, J. (2014). Motivational effects and age differences of gamification in product advertising. Journal of Consumer Marketing, 31(5), 391–400
A24	Hsiao, K. L., Lytras, M. D., & Chen, C. C. (2019). An in-app purchase framework for location-based AR games: the case of Pokémon Go. Library Hi Tech, 38(3), 638–653
A25	Lee, K. C., & Park, B. W. (2010). A general Bayesian network approach to analyzing online game item values and its influence on consumer satisfaction and purchase intention. Communications in Computer and Information Science, 114 CCIS, 53–62

References

1. Hamari, J.: Gamification. The Blackwell Encyclopedia of Sociology, pp. 1–3 (2007)
2. Hamari, J., Hanner, N., Koivisto, J.: "Why pay premium in freemium services?" A study on perceived value, continued use and purchase intentions in free-to-play games. Int. J. Inf. Manage. 51, 102040 (2020)
3. Woodruff, R.B.: Marketing in the 21st century customer value: the next source for competitive advantage. J. Acad. Mark. Sci. 25(3), 256 (1997)

4. Insley, V., Nunan, D.: Gamification and the online retail experience. Int. J. Retail Distrib. Manage. (2014)
5. Paré, G., et al.: Synthesizing information systems knowledge: a typology of literature reviews. Inf. Manage. **52**(2), 183–199 (2015)
6. Tina, W., Buckner, K.: Receptiveness of gamers to embedded brand messages in advergames: attitudes towards product placement. J. Interact. Advert. **7**(1), 3–32 (2006)
7. Sweeney, J.C., Soutar, G.N.: Consumer perceived value: the development of a multiple item scale. J. Retail. **77**(2), 203–220 (2001)
8. Hassan, L., Hamari, J.: Gameful civic engagement: a review of the literature on gamification of e-participation. Gov. Inf. Q. **37**(3), 101461 (2020)

How is Video Game Playing Time Linked to Parent-Child Communication Frequency? A Longitudinal Cross-Lagged Analysis

Jiawen Gou(✉) ⓘ, Lihanjing Wu ⓘ, and Hui Li ⓘ

Central China Normal University, Wuhan 430070, Hubei, People's Republic of China
{JiawenGou,Lihanjing}@mails.ccnu.edu.cn,
huilipsy@mail.ccnu.edu.cn

Abstract. With the development of computer technology, more and more teenagers devote abundant time and effort to video games. Previous cross-sectional studies have found a negative relationship between video game playing time and parent-child communication frequency, but the causal direction between the two is still unclear. Therefore, the current study aimed to explore the direction of the relationship between video game playing time and parent-child communication frequency among Chinese junior high school students. We analyzed the longitudinal data from the China Education Panel Survey (CEPS). A total of 7340 junior high school students were analyzed across an academic year using cross-lagged analysis. The study results showed that the relationship between video game playing time and parent-child communication frequency is bidirectional. Our research helps to prevent and intervene in junior high school students' excessive video game playing from a family perspective. Given the bidirectional influence between these two variables, families should focus on increasing parent-child communication with children to prevent junior high school students from excessive video game playing time.

Keywords: Parent-child communication · Video game playing · Cross-lagged analysis

1 Introduction

During the past two decades, computer technology has remarkably changed people's leisure activities. Playing video games has unarguably become an essential form of electric entertainment for young people [1]. Late childhood and early adolescence are the age that spends the most time playing video game [2, 3]. According to a recent study from the USA, 8- to 10-year-olds spend 8 h a day, and adolescents spend more than 11 h per day with various electronic media [2, 4]. Data from China Internet Network Information Center (CNNIC) suggests that playing video games is one of the main online entertainment activities for Chinese netizens aged 6- to 18-year-old, and 62.5% of them used to play video games [5]. Video games constantly incentivize children with gaming points, "lives", new weapons, and so on to get new gaming skills, which attracts children

X. Fang (Ed.): HCII 2022, LNCS 13334, pp. 340–353, 2022.
https://doi.org/10.1007/978-3-031-05637-6_21

to devote ample time and effort [6]. Previous studies found that video game playing time is closely associated with obesity [7], sleep disturbances [8], depressive symptoms [9], problem behavior [3] and problematic Internet use [10]. However, Hartanto, Toh and Yang [11] argued that the impact of video game playing time on adolescents depends on contextual conditions. The time spent on video games on weekends was positively related to academic performance, while the time spent in playing video games on weekdays was negatively related to academic performance [11, 12]. The importance of video game playing to children's development has attracted a host of researchers to explore the possible influencing factors of video game playing time [13–17], and parent-child communication has been proven to be an important one [18].

Communication is the assertive and inoffensive expression of ideas and feelings and the attentive and accurate receiving of ideas expressed by others [19, 20]. Parent-child communication is a dynamic procedure where parents and their children can exchange information and emotions [21]. From the bio-ecological perspective, communication processes are the enduring interactions to express warmth, attachment, concern, and interest between and among parents and children [20, 22]. Good parent-child communication is important to children's development [23], and it is a key method to attaining and enhancing cohesion and intimacy between parents and their children [24, 25]. Previous research has indicated that good parent-child communication could prevent health-risk behaviors [20], such as risky sexual behavior [26], maladaptive eating behaviors [27] and Internet addiction [28]. Nevertheless, lack or low quality of parent-child communication is related to negative consequences, such as depression [29, 30], anxiety [31], as well as pathological Internet use [32]. Therefore, it is imperative for researchers to understand parent-child communication further. Recently, several cross-sectional studies found that parent-child communication is negatively correlated with video game playing time [32, 33]. However, the direction of the causal association between video game playing time and parent-child communication frequency is ambiguous, and existing studies are unable to confirm it. So far, there are three different perspectives to explain the causal relationship between them.

Specifically, some studies illustrated that video game playing time is a predictor of parent-child communication frequency. According to Displacement Hypothesis [34], excessive use of the Internet may replace interpersonal communication in real life. An empirical study found that the more time spent on the Internet, the less time spent with family [35]. Inordinate use of the Internet may decrease social involvement, especially in face-to-face interaction, and increase loneliness and isolation [36]. Hermawati et al. [37] found that 66.6% of children aged 44–78 months have no parent-child interaction during electronic screen exposure. Through the longitudinal data analysis across 73 households, Kraut et al. [34] found that using the Internet causes declines in participants' communication with family members in the household, but the amount of family communication does not predict further Internet use. Various research found that playing video games is the most common purpose of using the Internet [38]. Blais et al. found that playing video games predicts decreases in adolescents' close relationships [39]. An empirical study of Korean children aged 10–12 years found that playing video games decreases the time spent communicating with family members [40]. Another interesting finding of this study is that the impact of Internet use time on family communication depends on the type of online activities that children engage in, implying that family communication is displaced by functionally equivalent online activities rather than total Internet time. For example, playing video games could reduce time spent with family, while searching for educational information on the Internet might not affect family communication.

Conversely, some researchers argue that it's not the amount of time spent playing video games that leads to less parent-child communication, but that individuals with less parent-child communication are more dependent on video games. According to Family Systems Theory [41], the structure and organization of a family could predict and influence the behaviors of junior high school students intensively. Parent-child communication is a crucial aspect of the family life [24], and positive parent-child communication fulfills children's psychological needs for belonging and affection [42]. Based on Psychological Need Satisfaction Theory, the Internet can compensate for the unmet psychological needs of individuals in real life [43]. According to certain studies, video games attraction stems from its ability to satisfy people's basic psychological requirements [44]. Papacharissi and Rubin [45] found that those who feel less valued in their social interactions turn to serve the Internet as a substitute and interpersonal tool for face-to-face communication, and individuals who use the Internet to fulfill needs of affection, expression and social interaction tend to use it the most. Video games provide ways for junior high school students to interact and communicate [46]. When the needs of children to communicate with their parents can not be met, they will seek comfort through video game playing [47]. Sioni, Burleson, and Bekerian [48] discovered that video games might fulfill the needs for social interaction and approval for those who struggle with face-to-face interaction. Similarly, a longitudinal study investigating 1591 Canadian adolescents found that less positive parent-child relationships in early high school could predict a higher frequency of Internet use in late high school [49]. On the other hand, the more frequent parent-child communication, the more opportunities parents will have to regulate their children's video game playing time. An empirical study indicated that inadequate parental restrictions are a risk factor that affects children's video game playing time [50]. Warren [51] found that parents who frequently communicate with their children have more mediation on their children's four media use (television, video game, Internet and cellphone).

Besides, there is a third viewpoint that there may be a bidirectional association between parent-child communication frequency and video game playing time. This view can be thought of as a combination of the first two. That is, the amount of time spent playing video games can be seen as both a cause and a result of how often parents communicate with their children. Bronfenbrenner's Ecological Systems Theory emphasizes that individual development results from the interaction between an individual and the environment [52]. Children's extended video game playing time may have a negative impact on their parent-child communication frequency, and less parent-child communication may also lead to children's longer video game playing duration, which in turn affects the children's parent-child communication frequency. Although there is no empirical research exploring the bidirectional relationship between parent-child communication frequency and video game playing time, some comparable findings support this view. A previous study of the relationship between loneliness and social uses of the Internet has found that lonely children are more likely to develop Internet addiction, which further isolates them from peer relations [53]. That means there is a vicious circle in which lonely individuals go online to fill voids and emptiness, and in turn, their online time creates voids in their non-Internet social life [53]. Hygen [54] found that the children who have greater social competence at 8 and 10 have less game playing time two years later, and more age-10 gaming time predicts less social competence at age 12. Consequently, it can be speculated that the causality between video game playing time and parent-child communication frequency might go in both directions. However, no longitudinal research has empirically explored the reciprocal relationship between parent-child communication frequency and video game playing time. Therefore, an in-depth investigation of the potential bidirectional relationship between parent-child communication frequency and video game playing time is required.

Given the adverse repercussions of enormous time spent on video games and a lack of parent-child communication, it is crucial to elucidate the relationship between video game playing time and parent-child communication frequency. However, the majority of prior research is cross-sectional, which has limitations in explaining the direction of the relationship between parent-child communication frequency and video game playing time [55, 56]. As a result, more longitudinal studies are needed to address this issue.

The purpose of the present study was to explore the direction of the causal relationship between video game playing time and parent-child communication frequency based on longitudinal data by cross-lagged analysis. The findings might serve as a theoretical foundation for preventing and intervening with excessive video game playing. Based on the perspectives mentioned above, we hypothesize that parent-child communication frequency and video game playing time have a bidirectional relationship, that is, video game playing time predicts future parent-child communication frequency, and parent-child communication frequency also predicts future video game playing time.

2 Methods

2.1 Participants

The data analyzed in this study were sourced from the China Education Panel Survey (CEPS) conducted by the National Survey Research Center (NSRC) at the Renmin University of China. The CEPS is a large-scale, nationally representative, longitudinal survey for junior high school students that aims to explain the association between individuals' educational outcomes and multiple contexts of families, school processes, communities and social structure, and further investigate the effects of educational outcomes during people's life course. Starting with two cohorts (the 7th and 9th graders) in the 2013–2014 academic year, the CEPS randomly selected a school-based, nationally representative sample of approximately 20,000 students in 438 classrooms of 112 schools in 28 county-level units in mainland China with a multi-stage stratified probability proportional to size (PPS) sampling design. The baseline survey of CEPS was completed in the 2013–2014 academic year. The follow-up surveys are annual as the sample students enroll throughout the junior-high stage and in the 1st, 3rd, 7th, 8th, 17th and 27th years after they graduate from junior high school.

We used the available data from the CEPS's first two waves (2013–2014 and 2014–2015). This study was conducted according to the following sample selection criteria.

This study excluded the 9th graders in the 2013–2014 academic year for starters. By the 2014–2015 academic year, the 9th graders who took part in the baseline survey had graduated from junior high school. As they progress to high school, the stricter management system may have a huge constraint on their video game playing, and the boarding system will reduce the amount of time they have to interact with their families numbers, so the data of 9th graders in the baseline survey was deleted. In the CEPS, there were 10,279 7th students at the time of the baseline survey, and they were tracked in grade 8. Second, participants were successfully followed in the 2014–2015 academic year. 830 students were lost to follow up for transferring to other schools, dropping out and other reasons, so a total of 9,449 students were successfully followed. Third, this study further restricted the sample with defects and extreme values. Based on the above criteria, a total sample of 7340 cases who were 7th graders in the 2013–2014 academic year (Time1) and 8th graders in the 2014–2015 academic year (Time2) was included for data analysis. Among all the samples, 3610 of them were male (49.2%), 3609 were female (49.2%) and 121 were unknown (1.6%); 3432 were one-only children (46.8%) and 3908 were children with siblings (53.2%).

2.2 Measures

Video Game Playing Time. Video game playing time was measured using the two items in the CEPS: "How much time on average did you spend on surfing on the Internet or playing video games from Monday to Friday last week?", "How much time on average did you spend on surfing on the Internet or playing video games last weekend?" After we unified the data formats of the baseline survey and the follow-up survey, the items of weekday (weekend) video game playing time were rated on a scale of $1 = 0$ h, $2 =$ Less than 1 h (Less than 2 h), $3 =$ About 1–2 h (About 2–4 h), $4 =$ About 2–3 h (About 4–6 h), $5 =$ About 3–4 h (About 6–8 h), $6 =$ More than 4 h (More than 8 h). Higher scores on this scale indicate more video game playing time on weekdays and weekends respectively.

Parent-Child Communication Frequency. We measured parent-child communication frequency using the four items of the CEPS: "How often do your parents (your mother/your father) discuss the following with you (the specific issues discussed include: things that happened at school; the relationship between you and your teachers; the relationship between you and your teachers; your worries and troubles)?" The items were rated on a 3-point scale, $1 =$ never, $2 =$ sometimes, $3 =$ often. The sum of the four items was computed, with a higher score representing a higher frequency of parent-child communication. In this study, the Cronbach's alpha coefficients of these items were 0.830 at Time1, 0.872 at Time2.

2.3 Statistical Analysis

SPSS 22.0 and AMOS 23.0 were used to conduct the statistical analysis. First, calculate descriptive values for all measures in SPSS. Second, use Pearson Correlation analyses to test the bivariate correlations among the variables in SPSS. Third, test the data for cross-lagged models in AMOS.

3 Results

3.1 Preliminary Analyses

The descriptive statistics of both video game playing time and parent-child communication frequency are presented in Table 1. The results showed that the parent-child communication frequency (CF), weekday video game playing time (Weekday_VGPT) and weekend video game playing time (Weekend_VGPT) increased over time.

Table 2 displays the correlations among variables at both measurement points. The results of Pearson Correlation analyses showed that VGPT T1 and VGPT T2 are significantly and positively related ($r_{weekday} = 0.279$; $r_{weeekend} = 0.406$, ps < 0.01), and there was also a significant positive correlation between CF T1 and CF T2 ($r = 0.494$, p < 0.01). It illustrated that VGPT and CF of junior high school students show some level of stability within an academic year. Furthermore, VGPT T1 was significantly negatively correlated with CF T1 ($r_{weekday} = -0.048$; $r_{weekend} = -0.055$, ps < 0.01) and CF T2 ($r_{weekday} = -0.048$; $r_{weekend} = -0.052$, ps < 0.01); VGPT T2 was also significantly negatively correlated with CF T1 ($r_{weekday} = -0.051$; $r_{weekend} = -0.059$, ps < 0.01) and CF T2 ($r_{weekday} = -0.089$; $r_{weekend} = -0.116$, ps < 0.01). It showed that VGPT T2 and CF T2 are not only related to their initial levels, but also to the other's initial levels.

Table 1. Means, standard deviations and the results of Paired-Samples T Test of CF, Weekday_CGPT and Weekend_VGPT

Variables	Mean	SD	t	p
CF T1	16.631	3.932	−2.883	0.004
CF T2	16.765	3.996		
Weekday_VGPT T1	1.739	1.193	−23.346	0.000
Weekday_VGPT T2	2.160	1.365		
Weekend_VGPT T1	1.998	0.986	−38.379	0.000
Weekebd_VGPT T2	2.570	1.295		

Note, CF = parent-child communication frequency; Weekday_VGPT = weekday video game playing time; Weekend_VGPT = weekend video game playing time; T1 = Time1; T2 = Time2

3.2 Cross-Lagged Analysis

On the basis of correlation analysis, the causal relationships between CF and Weekday_VGPT (Model 1) or Weekend_VGPT (Model 2) were explored through two cross-lagged models. The detailed results are shown in Fig. 1 and Fig. 2. The two-way arrows in the figures represent the results of correlation analysis, and the data are correlation coefficients; the one-way arrows represent the results of path analysis, and the data are standardized regression coefficients (β). Since it is a saturated model, there is no model fit index. From the regression coefficients, the results of cross-lagged analyses indicated

Table 2. Correlations between CF, Weekday_CGPT and Weemend_VGPT for both measurement points

Variables	CF T1	CF T2	Weekday_ VGPT T1	Weekday_ VGPT T2	Weekend_ VGPT T1	Weekend_ VGPT T2
CF T1	1					
CF T2	0.494**	1				
Weekday_ VGPT T1	−0.048**	−0.048**	1			
Weekday_ VGPT T2	−0.051**	−0.089**	0.279**	1		
Weekend_ VGPT T1	−0.055**	−0.052**	0.467**	0.244**	1	
Weekend_ VGPT T2	−0.059**	−0.116**	0.244**	0.541**	0.406**	1

Note, ** *p < 0.01; CF = parent-child communication frequency; Weekday_VGPT = weekday video game playing time; Weekend_VGPT = weekend video game playing time; T1 = Time1; T2 = Time2*

that CF T1 could negatively predict Weekday_VGPT T2 (β = −0.038, p < 0.001) and Weekend_VGPT T2 (β = −0.037, p < 0.001); Weekdays_VGPT T1 (β = −0.024, p = 0.017 < 0.05) and Weekend_VGPT T1 (β = −0.025, p = 0.016 < 0.05) could also predict CF T2.

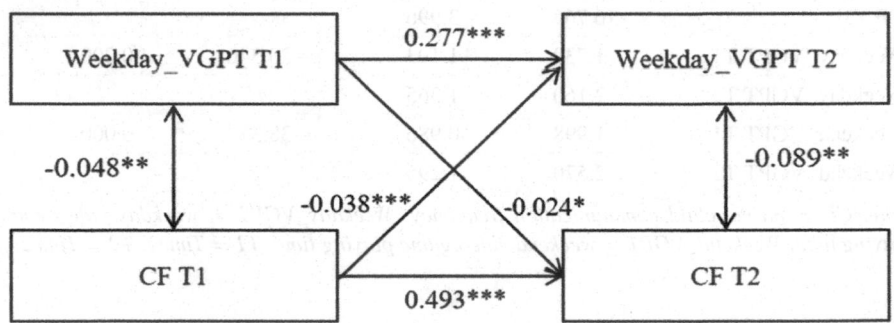

Fig. 1. Cross-lagged model for Weekday_VGPT and CF. *Note, the residuals are not shown; ***p < 0.001, **p < 0.01, *p < 0.05*

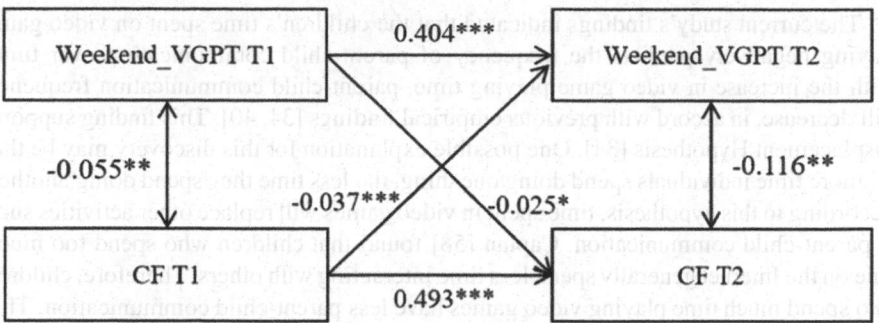

Fig. 2. Cross-lagged model for Weekend_VGPT and CF. *Note, the residuals are not shown;* ***p < 0.001, **p < 0.01, *p < 0.05*

4 Discussion

This study used the longitudinal tracking method to explore the direction of the link between video game playing time and parent-child communication frequency. The study found a significant positive correlation between the levels of video game playing time and parent-child communication frequency at the two measurement points. It revealed that they all have a certain degree of stability. This finding is consistent with the previous studies [34, 57]. In addition, on the auto-regressive path, both the video game playing time and the parent-child communication frequency at Time1 significantly and positively predicted their levels an academic year later. This demonstrated that if junior high school students' adverse video game playing and negative parent-child communication are not intervened, they may gradually deteriorate, posing a risk to their further development. This is consistent with the finding of Willoughby [49]. Willoughby [49] found computer game playing time in early high school is the strongest predictor of that in late high school.

Consistent with the existing cross-sectional studies [32, 33], our findings showed a significant negative relationship between the amount of video game playing time and the frequency of parent-child communication in each of the measurement time points. The present study used the cross-lagged analysis to clarify the causal relationship between the two variables. This finding indicated that parent-child communication frequency and video game playing time would have a reciprocal relationship, that is, junior high school students' time spent on video games could predict the parent-child communication frequency one academic year later, and vice versa, supporting the hypothesis of this study. In addition, this study found that the bidirectional predictive effects between video game playing time on parent-child communication frequency is significant for both weekday and weekend video game playing time. This is inconsistent with several findings that the impact of weekday video gaming time on children (e.g., academic performance) differs from that of weekend video gaming time [11, 12]. The explanation may be that the two activities, playing video games and communicating with parents, are similar in weekday and weekend contexts because Chinese junior high school students usually complete both of them in extracurricular free time at home whether on weekends or weekdays.

The current study's findings indicated that the children's time spent on video game playing negatively predicts the frequency of parent-child communication over time. With the increase in video game playing time, parent-child communication frequency will decrease, in accord with previous empirical findings [34, 40]. This finding supports Displacement Hypothesis [34]. One possible explanation for this discovery may be that the more time individuals spend doing one thing, the less time they spend doing another. According to this hypothesis, time spent in video games will replace other activities such as parent-child communication. Caplan [58] found that children who spend too much time on the Internet generally spend less time interacting with others. Therefore, children who spend much time playing video games have less parent-child communication. This result also corroborates the viewpoint of Lee and Chae [40]. In addition, another possible explanation is that excessive playing of video games may deteriorate the parent-child relationship [33, 46] and parent-child attachment [59] or cause parent-child conflict [56, 60], which in turn reduces parent-child communication. Good family relationships facilitate parent-child communication [61]. Edwards et al. [62] found that Child-Parent Relationship Training effectively enhances parent-child communication. Last but not least, according to Social Cognitive Theory [63], children's behavior of playing video games may result from observing behaviors from their parents' video game playing [64]. More video game playing time in children may reveal more playtime of parents, research found that parents' playing of video games may also reduce interaction and communication with their children [65].

Besides, the present study found that parent-child communication frequency could predict children's video game playing time negatively, revealing that individuals with less parent-child communication have more video game playing time. This result is consistent with previous results of empirical studies [49] and supports Family Systems Theory [41] and Psychological Need Satisfaction Theory [43] mentioned above. One possible explanation is that the lack of parent-child communication cannot meet children's psychological needs for belonging and emotions, so children choose games to meet their social interaction and recognition needs [43, 48]. Another explanation might be that more parent-child communication enables junior high school students to establish a positive self-concept, leading to less video game playing. According to Attachment Theory, children form an internal mental representation of self and others by drawing upon experiences with their parents [66]. Frequent parent-child communication makes junior high school students have a positive self-concept [67]. Referring to the Cognitive-Behavioral Model [68], dysfunctional self-related cognitions are central factors in the development and maintenance of excessive Internet use, so junior high school students with negative self-concept might spend more time playing video games [68, 69]. Furthermore, in families lacking parent-child communication, it is difficult for parents to regulate and mediate children's video game playing, so that children have more video game playing time [50].

Although previous researchers hypothesized the bidirectional predictive relationship between parent-child communication frequency and video game playing time [33, 46], they have not verified the hypothesis empirically. This study examined the bidirectional relationship between parent-child communication frequency and online gaming time by longitudinal tracking data, and the results showed that: there is a bidirectional predictive relationship between parent-child communication frequency and video game playing time. Specifically, children who spent more time playing video games had less communication with their parents, and children who lack parent-child communication are more likely to spend more time on video games. The finding differs from the viewpoint of Kraut et al. [34] who discovered family Internet usage causes the decrease of family communication, but not family communication predicts time on the Internet. On one hand, Kraut's study was conducted with 73 households (including parents, children, and other family members), while the current study only focused on middle school students who have a great psychological need for parent-child communication. On the other hand, the variable of Kraut's research was the total amount of time using the Internet, while there are two types of Internet use: instrumental Internet use and ritualized Internet use, which reflects people's different psychological needs [45].

There are some limitations in this study, which need to be further improved in future research. First, the results of parent-child communication and video game playing time relied on junior high school students' self-report, which could lead to socially desirable answers or biased outcomes. In order to guarantee a reliable measure of variables, future studies could validate this result by using multi-method assessments such as parents' reports or observational data. Second, limited by the amount of data exposed by CEPS, the data used in the study was only obtained from two measurement points. The number of waves of data is an important factor in the design of longitudinal studies [70]. Future research should further explore the dynamic relationship between video game playing time and parent-child communication frequency through multi-wave measurement data analysis. Third, the present study examined the reciprocal relation between parent-child communication and video game playing time without exploration of its underlying mechanism. Therefore, it is worthwhile to introduce the longitudinal mediation and moderation models to improve our understanding of the mechanisms involved. Last but not least, our findings were based on a sample of Chinese junior high school students belonging to a collectivist culture, which may show the effect of cultural differences [71]. Future studies should examine whether these findings apply to children in other age groups and cultures.

Despite these limitations, the present study contributes to understanding the reciprocal nature of the relation between video game playing time and parent-child communication frequency by a large sample of longitudinal data. This pioneering study has tested the bidirectional relations between parent-child communication frequency and video game playing time across time. Therefore, considering the bidirectional relationship between these two variables, parents should pay attention to increasing parent-child communication with junior high school students to prevent them from playing video games for too long. Studies have found that interventions to improve parent-child communication can effectively reduce adolescents' sedentary behaviors (e.g., watching TV and playing video games) [72]. In addition, parents should also limit their children's video game playing time reasonably to ensure adequate parent-child communication between them. From the perspective of junior high school students, they should also be aware of the risk of falling into a vicious cycle of video game playing time and parent-child communication.

References

1. Paulus, F.W., Ohmann, S., Von Gontard, A., Popow, C.: Internet gaming disorder in children and adolescents: a systematic review. Dev. Med. Child Neurol. **60**(7), 645–659 (2018)
2. Rideout, V.J., Foehr, U.G., Roberts, D.F.: Generation M^2: media in the lives of 8-to 18-year-olds. Henry J. Kaiser Family Foundation (2010)
3. Holtz, P., Appel, M.: Internet use and video gaming predict problem behavior in early adolescence. J. Adolesc. **34**(1), 49–58 (2011)
4. Strasburger, V.C., et al.: Children, adolescents, and the media. Pediatrics **132**(5), 958–961 (2013)
5. China Internet Network Information Center. http://www.cnnic.net.cn/
6. Skoric, M.M., Teo, L.L.C., Neo, R.L.: Children and video games: addiction, engagement, and scholastic achievement. Cyberpsychol. Behav. **12**(5), 567–572 (2009)
7. Stettler, N., Signer, T.M., Suter, P.M.: Electronic games and environmental factors associated with childhood obesity in Switzerland. Obes. Res. **12**(6), 896–903 (2004)
8. Lam, L.T.: Internet gaming addiction, problematic use of the Internet, and sleep problems: a systematic review. Curr. Psychiatry Rep. **16**(4), 1–9 (2014)
9. Lemola, S., Brand, S., Vogler, N., Perkinson-Gloor, N., Allemand, M., Grob, A.: Habitual computer game playing at night is related to depressive symptoms. Pers. Individ. Differ. **51**(2), 117–122 (2011)
10. Caselli, G., Marino, C., Spada, M.M.: Modelling online gaming metacognitions: the role of time spent gaming in predicting problematic Internet use. J. Rational-Emot. Cogn.-Behav. Ther. **39**(2), 172–182 (2021)
11. Hartanto, A., Toh, W.X., Yang, H.J.: Context counts: The different implications of weekday and weekend video gaming for academic performance in mathematics, reading, and science. Comput. Educ. **120**, 51–63 (2018)
12. Gomez-Gonzalvo, F., Devis-Devis, J., Molina-Alventosa, P.: Video game usage time in adolescents' academic performance. Comunicar. **28**(65), 87–96 (2020)
13. Liu, C.Y., Kuo, F.Y.: A study of Internet addiction through the lens of the interpersonal theory. Cyberpsychol. Behav. **10**(6), 799–804 (2007)
14. Molina, J.A., Campana, J.C., Ortega, R.: Children's interaction with the Internet: time dedicated to communications and games. Appl. Econ. Lett. **24**(6), 359–364 (2017)
15. Nikken, P., Jansz, J.: Parental mediation of children's videogame playing: a comparison of the reports by parents and children. Learn. Media Technol. **31**(2), 181–202 (2006)
16. Richard, J., Temcheff, C.E., Derevensky, J.L.: Gaming disorder across the lifespan: a scoping review of longitudinal studies. Curr. Addict. Rep. **7**(4), 561–587 (2020)
17. Winn, J.L., Heeter, C.: Gaming, gender, and time: who makes time to play? Sex Roles **61**(1–2), 1–13 (2009)
18. Wallenius, M., Rimpela, A., Punamaki, R.L., Lintonen, T.: Digital game playing motives among adolescents: Relations to parent-child communication, school performance, sleeping habits, and perceived health. J. Appl. Dev. Psychol. **30**(4), 463–474 (2009)
19. Robin, A.L.: Problem-solving communication training: a behavioral approach to the treatment of parent-adolescent conflict. Am. J. Fam. Ther. **7**(2), 69–82 (1979)
20. Riesch, S.K., Anderson, L.S., Krueger, H.A.: Parent-child communication processes: preventing children's health-risk behavior. J. Spec. Pediatr. Nurs. **11**(1), 41–56 (2006)
21. Chen, Y.J., Li, L., Hu, Y.H., Guo, X.P.: Relationship between parent–child communication and Internet addiction among college students (in Chinese). Chin J School Health. **37**(02), 221–223 (2016)
22. Bronfenbrenner, U., Morris, P.A.: The ecology of developmental processes, 5th edn. In: Lerner, R.M. (eds.) Handbook of Child Psychology, Vol. 1: Theoretical Models of Human Development, pp. 993–1028. Wiley, New York (1998)

23. Barker, D.H., et al.: Predicting behavior problems in deaf and hearing children: the influences of language, attention, and parent-child communication. Dev. Psychopathol. **21**(2), 373–392 (2009)
24. Barnes, H.L., Olson, D.H.: Parent-adolescent communication and the circumplex model. Child Dev. **56**(2), 438–447 (1985)
25. Kerr, M., Stattin, H., Trost, K.: To know you is to trust you: parents' trust is rooted in child disclosure of information. J. Adolesc. **22**(6), 737–752 (1999)
26. Sutton, M.Y., Lasswell, S.M., Lanier, Y., Miller, K.S.: Impact of parent-child communication interventions on sex behaviors and cognitive outcomes for Black/African-American and Hispanic/Latino youth: a systematic review, 1988–2012. J. Adolesc. Health **54**(4), 369–384 (2014)
27. Mogul, A., Irby, M.B., Skelton, J.A.: A systematic review of pediatric obesity and family communication through the lens of addiction literature. Child. Obes. **10**(3), 197–206 (2014)
28. Cai, J.J., Wang, Y., Wang, F., Lu, J.J., Li, L., Zhou, X.D.: The association of parent-child communication with Internet addiction in left-behind children in China: a cross-sectional study. Int. J. Public Health **66**, 1–7 (2021)
29. Chapman, R., Parkinson, M., Halligan, S.: How do parent-child interactions predict and maintain depression in childhood and adolescence? A critical review of the literature. Adolesc. Psychiatry **6**(2), 100–115 (2016)
30. Kushalnagar, P., Bruce, S., Sutton, T., Leigh, I.W.: Retrospective basic parent-child communication difficulties and risk of depression in deaf adults. J. Dev. Phys. Disabil. **29**(1), 25–34 (2017)
31. Berryhill, M.B., Smith, J.: College student chaotically-disengaged family functioning, depression, and anxiety: the indirect effects of positive family communication and self-compassion. Marriage Fam. Rev. **57**(1), 1–23 (2021)
32. Liu, Q.X., Fang, X.Y., Deng, L.Y., Zhang, J.T.: Parent-adolescent communication, parental Internet use and Internet-specific norms and pathological Internet use among Chinese adolescents. Comput. Hum. Behav. **28**(4), 1269–1275 (2012)
33. Hood, R., Zabatiero, J., Zubrick, S.R., Silva, D., Straker, L.: The association of mobile touch screen device use with parent-child attachment: a systematic review. Ergonomics **64**(12), 1606–1622 (2021)
34. Kraut, R., Patterson, M., Lundmark, V., Kiesler, S., Mukopadhyay, T., Scherlis, W.: Internet paradox - a social technology that reduces social involvement and psychological well-being? Am. Psychol. **53**(9), 1017–1031 (1998)
35. Nie, N.H., Hillygus, D.S., Erbring, L.: Internet use, interpersonal relations, and sociability. In: Wellman, B., Haythornthwaite, C., (eds.) Internet Everyday Life 215–243 (2002). https://doi.org/10.1002/9780470774298
36. Arnd-Caddigan, M.: Sherry Turkle: alone together: why we expect more from technology and less from each other. Clin. Soc. Work J. **43**(2), 247–248 (2015)
37. Hermawati, D., Rahmadi, F.A., Sumekar, T.A., Winarni, T.I.: Early electronic screen exposure and autistic-like symptoms. Intractable Rare Dis. Res. **7**(1), 69–71 (2018)
38. Yang, C.K.: Sociopsychiatric characteristics of adolescents who use computers to excess. Acta Psychiatr. Scand. **104**(3), 217–222 (2001)
39. Blais, J.J., Craig, W.M., Pepler, D., Connolly, J.: Adolescents online: the importance of Internet activity choices to salient relationships. J. Youth Adolesc. **37**(5), 522–536 (2008)
40. Lee, S.J., Chae, Y.G.: Children's Internet use in a family context: Influence on family relationships and parental mediation. Cyberpsychol. Behav. **10**(5), 640–644 (2007)
41. Bowen, M.: Use of family theory in clinical practice. Compr. Psychiatry **7**(5), 345–374 (1996)
42. Li, J.J., Yu, C.F., Zhen, S.J., Zhang, W.: Parent-adolescent communication, school engagement, and Internet addiction among Chinese adolescents: the moderating effect of rejection sensitivity. Int. J. Environ. Res. Public Health **18**(7), 1–12 (2021)

43. Deng, L.Y., Fang, X.Y., Wan, J.J., Zhang, J.T., Xia, C.C.: The relationship of psychological needs and need gratification with Internet addiction among college students(in Chinese). J. Psychol. Sci. **35**(01), 123–128 (2012)
44. Przybylski, A.K., Rigby, C.S., Ryan, R.M.: A motivational model of video game engagement. Rev. Gen. Psychol. **14**(2), 154–166 (2010)
45. Papacharissi, Z., Rubin, A.M.: Predictors of Internet use. J. Broadcast. Electron. Media **44**(2), 175–196 (2000)
46. Lo, S.K., Wang, C.C., Fang, W.C.: Physical interpersonal relationships and social anxiety among online game players. Cyberpsychol. Behav. **8**(1), 15–20 (2005)
47. Lin, Y., Liu, Q.X., Yu, S., Zhou, Z.K.: The relationship between parents neglect and online gaming addiction among adolescents: the mediating role of hope and gender difference (in Chinese). Psychol. Dev. Educ. **37**(01), 109–119 (2021)
48. Sioni, S.R., Burleson, M.H., Bekerian, D.A.: Internet gaming disorder: social phobia and identifying with your virtual self. Comput. Hum. Behav. **71**, 11–15 (2017)
49. Willoughby, T.: A short-term longitudinal study of Internet and computer game use by adolescent boys and girls: prevalence, frequency of use, and psychosocial predictors. Dev. Psychol. **44**(1), 195–204 (2008)
50. Chang, F.C., et al.: Urban–rural differences in parental Internet mediation and adolescents' Internet risks in Taiwan. Health, Risk Soc. **18**(3-4), 188–204 (2016)
51. Warren, R.: Multi-platform mediation: U.S. mothers' and fathers' mediation of teens' media use. J. Children Media. **11**(4), 485–500 (2017)
52. Bronfenbrenner, U.: Contexts of child rearing: problems and prospects. Am. Psychol. **34**(10), 844–850 (1979)
53. Morahan-Martin, J., Schumacher, P.: Loneliness and social uses of the Internet. Comput. Hum. Behav. **19**(6), 659–671 (2003)
54. Hygen, B.W., et al.: Time spent gaming and social competence in children: reciprocal effects across childhood. Child Dev. **91**(3), 861–875 (2020)
55. Bjelland, M., et al.: Associations between parental rules, style of communication and children's screen time. BMC Public Health **15**, 1–13 (2015)
56. Punamaki, R.L., Wallenius, M., Holtto, H., Nygard, C.H., Rimpela, A.: The associations between information and communication technology (ICT) and peer and parent relations in early adolescence. Int. J. Behav. Dev. **33**(6), 556–564 (2009)
57. Mazzer, K., Bauducco, S., Linton, S.J., Boersma, K.: Longitudinal associations between time spent using technology and sleep duration among adolescents. J. Adolesc. **66**, 112–119 (2018)
58. Caplan, S.E.: Preference for online social interaction - a theory of problematic Internet use and psychosocial well-being. Commun. Res. **30**(6), 625–648 (2003)
59. Kim, K., Kim, K.: Internet game addiction, parental attachment, and parenting of adolescents in South Korea. J. Child Adolesc. Subst. Abuse **24**(6), 366–371 (2015)
60. Bonnaire, C., Phan, O.: Relationships between parental attitudes, family functioning and Internet gaming disorder in adolescents attending school. Psychiatry Res. **255**, 104–110 (2017)
61. Liu, T., Fuller, J., Hutton, A., Grant, J.: Factors shaping parent-adolescent communication about sexuality in urban China. Sex Educ.-Sex. Soc. Learn. **17**(2), 180–194 (2017)
62. Edwards, N.A., Sullivan, J.M., Meany-Walen, K., Kantor, K.R.: Child parent relationship training: parents' perceptions of process and outcome. Int. J. Play Ther. **19**(3), 159–173 (2010)
63. Bandura, A.: Social Learning Theory. Prentice Hall, Englewood Cliffs (1977)
64. Lauricella, A.R., Wartella, E., Rideout, V.J.: Young children's screen time: the complex role of parent and child factors. J. Appl. Dev. Psychol. **36**, 11–17 (2015)
65. Lemish, D., Elias, N., Floegel, D.: "Look at me!" Parental use of mobile phones at the playground. Mob. Media Commun. **8**(2), 170–187 (2020)

66. Bowlby, J.: Attachment and Loss: Vol. 3. Loss: Sadness and Depression. Basic Books, New York (1980)
67. Razali, A., Razali, N.A.: Parent-child communication and self-concept among Malays adolescence. Asian Soc. Sci. **9**(11), 189–200 (2013)
68. Huang, S.M., Hu, Y.Q., Ni, Q., Qin, Y., Lu, W.: Parent-children relationship and Internet addiction of adolescents: the mediating role of self-concept. Curr. Psychol. **40**(5), 2510–2517 (2021)
69. Marcia, J.E.: Identity in Adolescence. Wiley, New York (1980)
70. Willett, J.B., Singer, J.D., Martin, N.C.: The design and analysis of longitudinal studies of development and psychopathology in context: statistical models and methodological recommendations. Dev. Psychopathol. **10**(2), 395–426 (1998)
71. Lansford, J.E., et al.: Longitudinal associations between parenting and youth adjustment in twelve cultural groups: cultural normativeness of parenting as a moderator. Dev. Psychol. **54**(2), 362–377 (2018)
72. StGeorge, S.M., Wilson, D.K., Schneider, E.M., Alia, K.A.: Project SHINE: effects of parent–adolescent communication on sedentary behavior in African American adolescents. J. Pediatr. Psychol. **38**(9), 997–1009 (2013)

A Study on Player Experience in Real-Time Strategy Games Combined with Eye-Tracking and Subjective Evaluation

Jiawei Jiao, Jinchun Wu, and Chengqi Xue(⊠)

School of Mechanical Engineering, Southeast University, Nanjing 211189, China
ipd_xcq@seu.edu.cn

Abstract. Video games have been a novel type of entertainment with the rapid development of computer technology in the information era. Real-time strategy games (RTSGs) have obtained great popularity among players for a mass of classics among various genres. Based on previous studies, there are two aims in this study. The first aim is to investigate whether a discrepancy exists between expert and casual players in various HUD layout and Player experience (PX) in RTSGs by eye-tracking and key-mouse interaction records. The other one is to investigate whether a strategic difference exists between different levels of players in completing the same type of mission under various time pressure by eye-tracking, key-mouse interaction records, and subjective evaluation. In experiment 1, there is a significant difference in HUD layout choice among players with different expertise from the perspective of the duration of mission accomplished, eye-tracking data, but there is no significant difference in key-mouse interaction between different expertise of players. In experiment 2, there is a significant difference in strategy shift between different levels of players under various time pressure from the perspective of eye tracking data and subjective evaluation. This study provided the research idea for PX study in RTSGs and HCI scenario involving monitor mission, and it could be a reference for the improvement of RTSGs design, including the interaction mode, UI design, and the mechanism of RTSGs, et al.

Keywords: Player experience (PX) · Real-time strategy games (RTSGs) · Eye-tracking · Key-mouse interaction

1 Instruction

With the rapid development of the computer and internet technology in the information era, electronic products, including PC and smartphones, have gradually become one of the most popular forms of entertainment. E-sports emerged as a novel sports competition form with the trend of industrialization development. The income of the video games industry in 2018 ($134.9 billion) and the record-breaking audience rating of the League of Legends World Championships in 2019 [1] indicated that the e-sports industry is booming around the world. The reason for this situation is not only for the successful market operation but also for the Award-winning game experience.

There are two characteristics of video games: interaction and imitativeness [2]. Interaction means that players need to complete the game in the interaction with different characters or players. imitativeness means that the game player plays always possesses objects existing in real life or objects abstracted from real life. Therefore, video games are still an extension of real life. Some video games have been applied in education. As a result, a favorable PX study could improve the design of video games thus the experience of players could be improved. what's more, it could teach through lively activities to supplement the classroom teaching.

There is a great variety in video games, many of them originate from RTSGs and are ameliorated and recreated based on RTSGs. As a consequence, the video game genre concentrated on in this study is RTSG.

1.1 The Overview of the RTSGs and Their Mechanism

There are two characters in RTSGs, including real-time and strategy. On the one hand, "real-time" means that players can perceive and analyze the game state in real-time, and make corresponding decisions in real-time according to the real-time changes of the situation in the game scene visible domain. On the other hand, "strategy" means that players could control all units they possess instead of only one character.

There are three basic tasks in RTSGs: detection, development and defeat.

At the beginning of the game, all players are distributed in different locations around the game world with a certain number of settlers, soldiers, and some resources to develop for them. The rest of the areas are unknown and covered with the shadow in the scenario and minimap of the game. Players need to manipulate units to move to the unknown areas to detect/discover so that they can understand the geography, resource distribution and situation of the game. If the detected areas are out of the sight of units, the light of units would decrease and the change of the situation could not display.

At the same time, players also need to concentrate on the development of themselves. The development part contains the collection of resources, the construction of buildings, the improvement of technology, as well as the training of military units. After knowing the location of opponents, the task of players is increased: guarantee the development of them and prevent the development of opponents. In this stage, there could be sporadic conflicts among players.

After finishing the discovery, the tasks of game change from the discovery, development and defeat to the detection, development and combat. Development includes resources gathering and the construction of the base. The development of the economic lays a good foundation for combat, efficient economic development mechanism helps quickly replenish military units, so that players have a stable and powerful combat effectiveness; Powerful military units helped players lay a good foundation for economic development. The expert players could combine the development and the combat so that they could complete the terminal target of the game: defeat opponents. The connection between development and combat is shown in Fig. 1.

There are two parts: the macro management and the micromanagement in the whole RTSG play. Generally speaking, the corresponding interaction devices are keyboard and mouse. The wide variety of resources with different functions, as well as different functions from unit to unit, makes it necessary to balance the allocation of attention resources between macro management and micromanagement for a better PX.

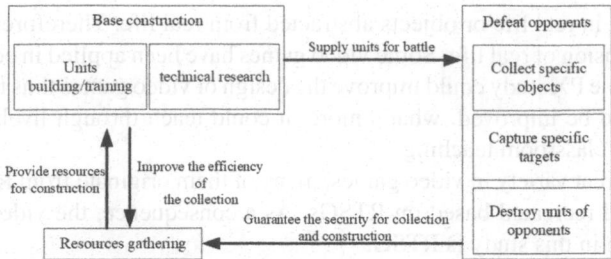

Fig. 1. The connection between development and combat.

1.2 The Layout of RTSGs

In general, the interface of RTSGs is conducted in two parts: the scenario and the head-up display (HUD) of the game (see Fig. 2). The scenario displays in the third person perspective, players manipulate their units to move in it, carry out a variety of tasks and perceive the real-time change in the whole scenario.

There are several elements in HUD, including control button areas, unit information areas, a minimap, a message box, the duration of game, and Training queue. Players are able to be aware of the current number of resources, the duration of the game, the information of chosen units, as well as the function players control which could increase the situation awareness of them so that they could manipulate units and make decisions better.

Fig. 2. The interface of RTSGs (the age of empires 3: the definitive edition)

1.3 Related Works

For the study of the PX in video games, there are two parts: the definition and indexes of the PX. Several studies explored the impact of video games on players' cognitive activities through the detection of the physical signal.

Hou et al. [3] discussed the concept of human-computer interaction (HCI) and RTSGs and the connection between them, and proposed the five-grade entertainment quality of the PX: utility, usability, ease of use, the joy of use, and "FLOW". What's more, she classified the HUD layout according to different functions and proposed a theoretical guidance for the study of PX in RTSGs.

In the study of the subjective evaluation in PX, Qin et al. [4] studied the method of immersion measurement of RTSGs from the view of the game narrative. Jennett et al. [5] defined the immersion of video games through experiments and found that in a high immersion environment, the fixation duration of players' area of interest would gradually decrease over time through eye tracking, providing a physiological basis for the study of PX from the perspective of immersion. Fang et al. [6, 7] developed a questionnaire for immersion experience in video games, verified its validity and reliability, and developed a questionnaire to measure the FLOW of game players. Gross and Sanchez et al. [13] proposed "playability" based on the target of user experience and "usability", and divided it into 7 parts, 29 specific indexes. Phan et al. [8] developed the game user experience satisfaction scale (GUESS) and verified its validity and reliability.

Caroux et al. [9] classified elements of HUD according to whether they display fixedly, sorted the elements of HUD according to the importance for players through the method combined with the physical index and the subjective evaluation, and explored the effect of different HUD layouts for players with different expertise in subjective evaluation. The result indicated that the conduction and layout of HUD could influence the PX, this influence is related to the expertise of players. When players have higher expertise, the impact of the HUD layout is larger for the PX of them. Besides, the study introduced the SEEV model, which is related to situation awareness, to guide the design and evaluation of the HUD of video games in theory. Kalar et al. [10] revealed the achievement in the principle of multi-agent monitor, command and control design, and also provided the method of the design and evaluation of user interface in other missions through the eye-tracking and action per minute (APM) of RTSG players.

Furthermore, Gong et al. [11] studied brain activities of participants in peaceful state, watching movies, and playing Action Real-time Strategy Games (ARSG) by EEG, found that the attention resources of participants were paid more on controlling the attention, and the activity in frontal lobe was more active and performed stronger information process ability in game play. Kim et al. [12] compared the diffusion tensor by fMRI between players and non-players and found that the performance of players was better than that of non-players. It also revealed that RTSGs are related with the change of higher-order cognition and the connection between visual and cognitive areas in the brain, as well as contribute the early stage of visual perception learning, supported the hypothesis that the visual perception learning could occur without the participation of the visual areas in the brain.

1.4 The Present Research

The aim of this study is to research PX of RTSGs based on the current achievements and the mechanism and interaction characteristics of RTSGs. There are two parts in this study: first of all, the study aims to explore whether different HUD layouts make various effects on players with different expertise, and require players to choose the HUD layout which they prefer. After that, the second experiment is conducted: participants should complete the same kind of mission without and within time limitation, fill in the modified GUESS so that they could evaluate their experience in subjective perspective. Finally, the data and subjective evaluation are analyzed to explore the difference in the preference of HUD layouts between various players and the difference in the same mission accomplishment between various time pressures.

2 Method

In this paper, the research methods mainly adopted include objective methods, such as behavioral data, eye tracking, and subjective evaluation such as GUESS. The difference in PX between various players and the strategy to accomplish the mission under different time pressures will be explored from behavioral data, eye-tracking data and subjective evaluation perspectives.

In this study, APM, including keystrokes and mouse clicks, are applied on behalf of the behavioral data. APM means keystrokes and mouse clicks per minute. Generally speaking, the higher the APM value, the more manipulation in gameplay, which means the level of players are higher in some cases.

Eye tracking data, i.e. the glance times and the average duration of areas of interest (AOI), which could reflect the concentration of players, are collected to record in the experiment. These indexes are always related to the specific situation players faced.

The subjective evaluation is conducted by the GUESS filled after players finish their experience missions. Except questions of the social part in the GUESS that have no connection with the study, the questionnaire combined with modified GUESS-18 and Likert 5-point scale are used to be subjective evaluation questionnaire in this study.

3 Material and Location

3.1 Material

In this study, the latest edition of the classical RTSG: "The Age of Empires III: The Definitive Edition" is applied to the research material in the study. The five frequently-used HUD elements are chosen to be AOIs, including the control button area, unit information areas, the minimap, the home city button, and the resource bar. The functions of AOIs are depicted in Table 1.

This study was held in the ergonomic laboratory with good light and two computers, one was used to record the Eye tracking data in the study, and another was used for participants to play games and record the key-mouse interaction data in the study. The Dell P2418D 24-in. monitor was used as the display device. The Dikablis eye tracker with a 60-Hz sampling rate was used as the eye tracking data recorder. The experiment environment is shown in Fig. 3.

4 Participants

There were 12 participants with reward in this study, all male students of the Southeast University (mean age: 23.4, variance: 8.27). After pretreatment, the data of eleven persons were valid. Combined with the result of the study of Sanchez et al. (2012) [13] (see Table 2) and the result of participants' practice before formal experiments, participants were classified into 5 casual players and 6 expert players.

Before formal experiments, participants were required to fill in the questionnaire of their basic personal information, and carried out the tutorial exercises experiments under the guidance of the default HUD layout (see Fig. 4), to roughly understand the interaction and mechanism of the game, avoid the negative impact on the performance of participants caused by immature manipulation. When finishing the practice, experiment 1 was carried out.

Table 1. The functions of AOIs

Name of the AOI	Picture	Function
Control buttons area		Show orders players could manipulate to the unit chosen in icon form
Unit information area		Show the name, hp, and other information of the unit chosen
Minimap		Show the geographical information, resources distribution and the current situation of the game.
Home city button		Show the number of current reinforcements available from the home city and the Countdown next reinforcement available
Resources bar		Show the number, gathering speed, and gatherers' number of all resources and population player have currently

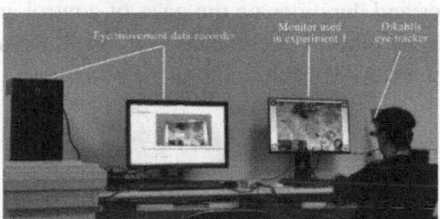

Fig. 3. The environment of the experiment

Table 2. The characters of various type of players

	Experienced players	Casual players
Duration per week	≥5 h/week	<5 h/week
Genre of games	Real-time strategy games/(RTSGs) Turn-based strategy games	Less experience or even no experience in RTS/strategy games
Gameplay platform	Use PC primarily	Less PC use

Fig. 4. The interface in practice experiment

5 Experiment 1

5.1 Goal

The aim of experiment 1 is to explore whether PX in RTSGs is different in various HUD layouts with diverse expertise.

5.2 Hypothesis

H1: The more experienced players are, the more different experiences in various HUD layouts from a physiological perspective are, and experienced players are more professional in the HUD layout they are adept at.

H2: There are few times and durations on the gaze of control areas of interest (AOIs) existing among experienced players, accompanied by high average APM values and a high percentage of keyboard APM values in total APM values.

5.3 Procedure

After understanding the interaction and mechanism of the game, experiment 1 was carried out. In experiment 1, participants completed the same mission-resource collection, units training, building construction, and make their "civilization" upgrade to the second age: "the Colonial age"- with two types of HUD layouts (see Fig. 5) randomly in the "simple" level of the game. The duration participants played, keyboard and mouse APM values, as well as Eye tracking data, were recorded. Finally, participants should choose their appropriate HUD layout as the HUD layout used in experiment 2.

5.4 Results

Duration
Durations of all participants in two HUD layouts is shown in Table 3.

The expertise of players and the type of HUD layout are set as factors, the duration is set as response. The multi-factors ANOVA is carried out, and the result is depicted in Table 4.

(a) DE HUD layout   (b) CLASSICAL HUD layout

Fig. 5. Two types of HUD spatial layouts in experiment 2.

Table 3. The duration in two HUD layouts

Expertise	DE HUD (s)	CLASSICAL HUD (s)	Expertise	DE HUD (s)	CLASSICAL HUD (s)
Expert	345*	313	Casual	313	270*
	369	478*		661*	282
	485	280*		328*	415
	372	314*		385*	291
	332*	371		401	501*
	351	236*			

* means the HUD layout participants chose.

Table 4. The multi-factors ANOVA of duration in experiment 1

Response: Duration

Source	SS	Dof	MS	F-value	P-value
Modified Model	12541904.12[a]	3	4180634.70	423.247	.000
Intercept	1231327369.53	1	1231327369.53	124659.326	.000
HUD Layout	6105755.87	1	6105755.87	618.145	.000
Expertise	5152630.08	1	5152630.08	521.651	.000
HUD Layout*Expertise	1019305.32	1	1019305.32	103.194	.000
Error	79968556.57	8096	9877.53		
Total	1338886783.67	8100			
Revised total	92510460.69	8099			

a. $R^2 = 0.201$ (Adjusted R^2 =0.068)

According to Table 4 and Fig. 6, the HUD layout, the expertise, and interactive effect between them are significant and their F value was decreased in order. In the DE HUD layout, the duration of participants is obviously higher than it is in the CLASSICAL layout. This is more obvious in expert players than in casual players. what's more, the

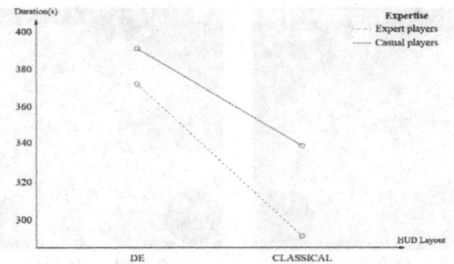

Fig. 6. The estimated marginal mean of the duration in experiment 1

duration of casual players is generally longer than expert players. In terms of duration, the H1 is proved.

Keyboard and Mouse Interaction Data
The keyboard and mouse interaction data include total keystrokes, mouse clicks (MCs), APM values and the percentage of the duration that keyboard APM (KAPM) value $\geq$ 0.5 total actions (MPK, the sum of MCs and keystrokes) value ($p_{(KAPM \geq 0.5MPK)}$).

$$APM = \frac{MPK}{duration\ (min)} \tag{1}$$

The expertise of players and HUD layouts are set as factors, the MCs value, MPK value, APM value, as well as $p_{(KAPM \geq 0.5MPK)}$ value are set as responses, a multi-factor ANOVA is carried out and the result of it is shown in Table 5.

As is shown in Table 5, only the response "$p_{(KAPM \geq 0.5MPK)}$" has a significant variation with factors. However, the expert players' Estimated marginal mean of the $p_{(KAPM \geq 0.5MPK)}$ in experiment 1 is obviously lower than that of casual players (see Fig. 7). The H2 is not proved.

Eye-Tracking Data
The number of glace and glance duration of AOIs of participants are recorded and processed, the represent index-AOI Attention ratio(AOI AR), Glance Location Probability(GLP)-are calculated. The equations of AOI AR and GLP are shown as follows:

$$AOI\ AR = \frac{\sum_{X=1}^{n} glance\ duration\ X}{duration\ of\ the\ selected\ time\ interval} \times 100\% \tag{2}$$

$$GLP = \frac{number\ of\ glances\ at\ an\ AOI\ during\ a\ particular\ time\ interval}{number\ of\ all\ of\ the\ glances\ in\ a\ time\ interval} \times 100\% \tag{3}$$

The AOI AR and GLP are set as responses, the HUD layout, AOIs and the expertise of players are set as factors. A multi-factor ANOVA is carried out (see Table 6). There are significant differences in p value between AOIs and responses, there are significant differences in p value between the interactive effect and response "GLP", too. There is no significant difference in others.

Table 5. The ANOVA of the key-mouse interaction data in experiment 1

Response: MCs, MPK, APM, $p_{(KAPM \geq 0.5MPK)}$

Source	Response	SS	Dof	MS	F	P-value
Modified Model	MCs	30983.558[a]	3	10327.853	0.839	.490
	MPK	27431.639[b]	3	9143.880	0.526	.670
	APM	406.093[c]	3	135.364	0.402	.753
	$p_{(KAPM \geq 0.5MPK)}$	288.846[d]	3	96.282	2.285	.114
Intercept	MCs	779504.733	1	779504.733	63.330	.000
	MPK	1116770.002	1	1116770.002	64.253	.000
	APM	28545.232	1	28545.232	84.867	.000
	$p_{(KAPM \geq 0.5MPK)}$	656.205	1	656.205	15.572	.001
Expertise	MCs	18117.824	1	18117.824	1.472	.241
	MPK	877.456	1	877.456	0.050	.825
	APM	374.271	1	374.271	1.113	.305
	$p_{(KAPM \geq 0.5MPK)}$	286.836	1	286.836	6.807	.018
HUD Layout	MCs	856.824	1	856.824	0.070	.795
	MPK	2596.183	1	2596.183	0.149	.704
	APM	10.141	1	10.141	0.030	.864
	$p_{(KAPM \geq 0.5MPK)}$	1.048	1	1.048	0.025	.876
Expertise * HUD Layout	MCs	12497.552	1	12497.552	1.015	.327
	MPK	25209.456	1	25209.456	1.450	.244
	APM	18.901	1	18.901	0.056	.815
	$p_{(KAPM \geq 0.5MPK)}$	.781	1	.781	0.019	.893
Error	MCs	221553.533	18	12308.530		
	MPK	312853.633	18	17380.757		
	APM	6054.332	18	336.352		
	$p_{(KAPM \geq 0.5MPK)}$	758.508	18	42.139		
Total	MCs	1060476.000	22			
	MPK	1472108.000	22			
	APM	35845.894	22			
	$p_{(KAPM \geq 0.5MPK)}$	1631.880	22			
Revised total	MCs	252537.091	21			
	MPK	340285.273	21			
	APM	6460.425	21			
	$p_{(KAPM \geq 0.5MPK)}$	1047.355	21			

a. R^2 =0.123 (Adjusted R^2 =-0.024); b. R^2 =0.081 (Adjusted R^2=-0.073);
c. R^2 =0.063 (Adjusted R^2 =-0.093); d. R^2 =0.276 (Adjusted R^2=0.155)

In various AOIs, the AOI AR and GLP value of all participants' control buttons area and unit information are highest, the next highest are resource bar's and minimap's. the lowest AOI AR and GLP value of all participants' AOI is the home city button.

For casual plyers, the GLP values of their resource bar in the DE layout is significantly higher than it in the CLASSICAL layout. The GLP values of other AOIs show no significant difference between DE layout and CLASSICAL layout (see Fig. 8(a)). For expert players, the GLP values of the Unit Information area, resource bar and home city

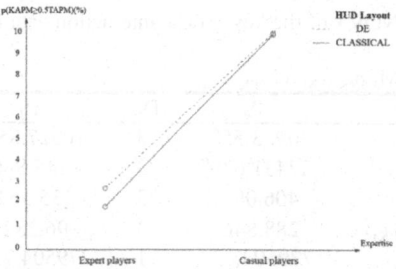

Fig. 7. The estimated marginal mean of the $p_{(KAPM \geq 0.5MPK)}$ in experiment 1

button in the CLASSICAL layout are significantly higher than those in the DE layout, but the GLP values of control buttons in the CLASSICAL layout are significantly lower than it in the DE layout. What's more, there is no significant difference in GLP values between different layouts of the minimap (see Fig. 8(b)).

The GLP values of resource bar and unit information of casual players in DE layout are significantly higher than those of expert players, but the GLP values of control buttons area of expert players are significantly higher than those of the casual. There was no significant difference in GLP values of other AOIs (see Fig. 8(c)). In the CLASSICAL layout, only the GLP values of the control buttons area and the resource bar are in different between casual players and expert players, with the higher GLP values of the control button for casual players and the lower GLP values of the resource bar for expert players (see Fig. 8 (d)).

Discussion

Combined with the mission completion duration and the HUD layout selected by participants at the end of experiment 1, it can be considered that players with different expertise have significant differences in their choice of HUD layout. Finally, two-thirds of the expert players chose the CLASSICAL layout, and there was a significant difference in their task completion time between the two types of HUD layouts, while the casual players had little difference in their final choice and mission completion time, which to some extent verified hypothesis 1. However, the key-mouse interaction data showed that hypothesis 2 was not true in experiment 1. Eye tracking data shows that there are significant differences in AOI AR and GLP values among different AOIs, and the interactive effect of the three factors also leads to a significant difference in GLP values, indicating that the area, shape, and information displayed in AOIs have a more significant impact on players' eye-tracking data. However, the expertise of players and HUD layout did not significantly affect the eye-tracking data.

6 Experiment 2

6.1 Goal

To explore whether there are differences in players performing the same type of mission under different time pressure levels.

Table 6. The ANOVA of the eye tracking data in experiment 1

Source	Response	SS	Dof	MS	F	P-value
Modified model	AOI AR	318.963[a]	19	16.788	3.619	0.000
	GLP	19988.799[b]	19	1052.042	8.780	0.000
Intercept	AOI AR	434.111	1	434.111	93.596	0.000
	GLP	43636.276	1	43636.276	364.181	0.000
Expertise	AOI AR	3.541	1	3.541	0.763	0.385
	GLP	4.364×10^{-8}	1	4.364×10^{-8}	0.000	1.000
HUD layout	AOI AR	1.056	1	1.056	0.228	0.634
	GLP	3.030×10^{-8}	1	3.030×10^{-8}	0.000	1.000
AOIs	AOI AR	262.931	4	65.733	14.172	0.000*
	GLP	17275.006	4	4318.752	36.044	0.000*
Expertise * HUD layout	AOI AR	1.677	1	1.677	0.362	0.549
	GLP	3.030×10^{-8}	1	3.030×10^{-8}	0.000	1.000
Expertise * AOIs	AOI AR	2.371	4	.593	0.128	0.972
	GLP	425.742	4	106.436	0.888	0.474
HUD layout * AOIs	AOI AR	21.271	4	5.318	1.147	0.340
	GLP	464.693	4	116.173	0.970	0.428
HUD layout * Expertise * AOIs	AOI AR	22.523	4	5.631	1.214	0.310
	GLP	1519.115	4	379.779	3.170	0.017*
Error	AOI AR	417.434	90	4.638		
	GLP	10783.823	90	119.820		
Total	AOI AR	1181.342	110			
	GLP	74772.542	110			
Revised total	AOI AR	736.396	109			
	GLP	30772.622	109			

a. $R^2 = 0.433$ (Adjusted $R^2 = 0.313$); b. $R^2 = 0.650$ (Adjusted $R^2 = 0.576$); * $P < 0.05$

6.2 Hypothesis

Military strategies will be paid more attention to than strategies of resources gathering so that players are able to achieve their goals as fast as possible, rather than general "resources collection, building or training, and enemy defeating". This hypothesis is significant in players spending less time finishing the task.

6.3 Procedure

Based on experiment 1, all participants are required to complete the same type of mission with no time limitation (see Fig. 8(a)) and with a time limitation (20 min) (see Fig. 8(b))

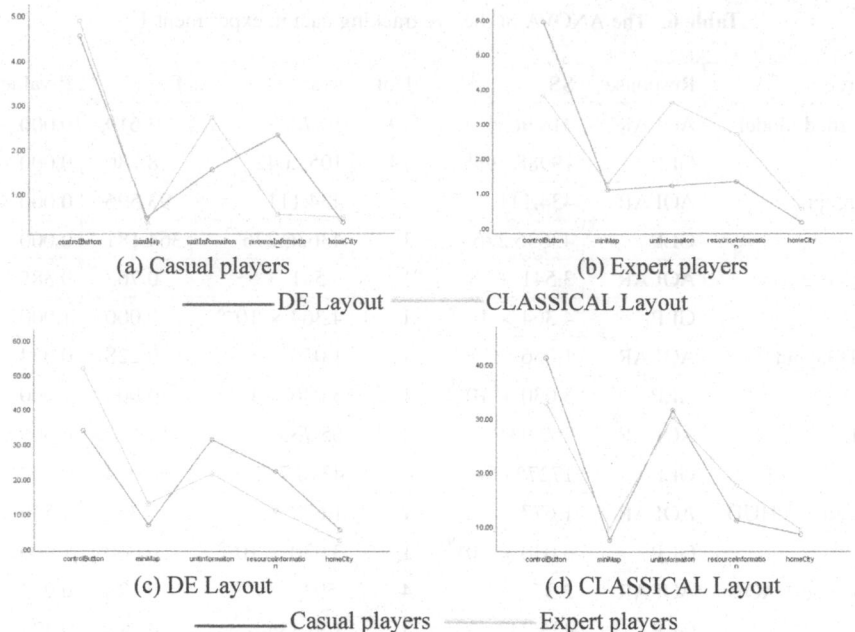

(a) Casual players   (b) Expert players

————— DE Layout ————— CLASSICAL Layout

(c) DE Layout   (d) CLASSICAL Layout

————— Casual players ————— Expert players

Fig. 8. The AOI AR & GLP distributions of players in experiment 1

successively using the HUD layout chosen in experiment 1: search for the target building of the opponent and destroy it. If participants did not finish the mission or not finish the mission in time limitation, the mission could be seen as failed. The key-mouse interaction data and eye-tracking data would be recorded by devices. Whereafter, participants are needed to fill in a modeled GUESS questionnaire. The scenario of the mission in experiment 2 is shown in Fig. 9.

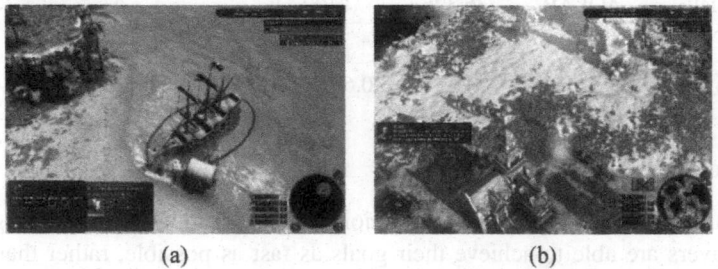

(a)   (b)

Fig. 9. The scenarios of the tasks without/with time limitation in experience 2

6.4   Results

Duration

The duration of participants in experiment 2 is shown in Table 7.

Table 7. The duration of participants in experiment 2

Expertise	No time-limited (s)	Time limited (s)	Expertise	No time-limited (s)	Time limited (s)
Casual	3690	964	Expert	1385	494
Casual	1817	557	Expert	1772	1200
Casual	2400	928	Expert	1650	545
Casual	943	927	Expert	967	700
Casual	1240	1200*	Expert	1353	564
			Expert	1560	752

* The participant failed to finish the task

According to Table 8, There are significant differences in the mission completion time under different time pressures, while there are no significant differences in the mission completion time under different expertise, which is also confirmed by the one-way variance test of the two groups of players with different expertise. The difference between the two types of mission completion duration for expert players is significantly greater than that for casual players ($F(22.125) > F(4.909)$, see Table 9 and Table 10). It indicated:

Time pressure has a certain negative impact on the mission completion of casual players. That's because it is difficult for them to change the game strategy and reduce the time spent on resources collection and units training. As a result, it takes a long time to complete the mission, some participants even failed to accomplish the mission time limited.

Under time pressure, expert players change their strategy, spend less time on resources collection and units training, and more time on military units training to destroy target buildings faster.

Table 8. The ANOVA of all participants' duration in experiment 2

Response: Duration

Source	SS	Dof	MS	F	P-value
Modified Model	6093912.458[a]	3	2031304.153	7.070	0.002
Intercept	37979020.042	1	37979020.042	132.186	0.000
Expertise	772927.042	1	772927.042	2.690	0.117
Time pressure	5116190.042	1	5116190.042	17.807	0.000
expertise * Time Pressure	204795.375	1	204795.375	0.713	0.409
Error	5746288.500	20	287314.425		
Total	49819221.000	24			
Revised total	11840200.958	23			

a. $R^2 = 0.515$ (Adjusted $R^2 = 0.442$)

Table 9. The single-factor ANOVA of casual players' duration in experiment 2

Response: Duration

	SS	Dof	MS	F	P-value
Interblock	3040419.600	1	3040419.600	4.909	0.058
Intrablock	4954920.800	8	619365.100		
Total	7995340.400	9			

Table 10. The single-factor ANOVA of expert players' duration in experiment 2

Response: Duration

	SS	Dof	MS	F	P-value
Interblock	1636885.333	1	1636885.333	22.125	0.001
Intrablock	739835.667	10	73983.567		
Total	2376721.000	11			

Key-Mouse Interaction Data

The expertise of players and time pressure are set as factors, the MCs value, MPK value, APM value, as well as $p_{(KAPM \geq 0.5MPK)}$ value are set as responses, a multi-factor ANOVA is carried out and the result of it is shown in Table 11: there is no significant difference among factors groups except the Extremely weak difference between time pressure and the interactive effect of expertise and MPK.

Table 11. The ANOVA of the key-mouse interaction data in experiment 2

Source	Response	SS	Dof	MS	F	P-value
Modified models	MCs	534385.139[a]	3	178128.380	0.858	0.481
	MPK	1582677.252[b]	3	527559.084	1.129	0.364
	APM	1440.636[c]	3	480.212	0.935	0.444
	$P_{(KAPM \geq 0.5MPK)}$ (%)	0.006[d]	3	0.002	0.118	0.949
Intercept	MCs	12458607.638	1	12458607.638	59.992	0.000
	MPK	20820758.523	1	20820758.523	44.575	0.000
	APM	45537.575	1	45537.575	88.629	0.000
	$P_{(KAPM \geq 0.5MPK)}$ (%)	0.150	1	0.150	8.909	0.008
Expertise	MCs	41745.456	1	41745.456	0.201	0.659
	MPK	121503.068	1	121503.068	0.260	0.616
	APM	554.739	1	554.739	1.080	0.313
	$P_{(KAPM \geq 0.5MPK)}$ (%)	0.004	1	0.004	0.218	0.646
Time pressure	MCs	492601.456	1	492601.456	2.372	0.141
	MPK	1458974.183	1	1458974.183	3.123	0.094
	APM	755.664	1	755.664	1.471	0.241
	$P_{(KAPM \geq 0.5MPK)}$ (%)	9.525×10^{-5}	1	9.525×10^{-5}	0.006	0.941
Expertise * time pressure	MCs	3323.274	1	3323.274	0.016	0.901
	MPK	3981.274	1	3981.274	0.009	0.927
	APM	192.203	1	192.203	0.374	0.548
	$P_{(KAPM \geq 0.5MPK)}$ (%)	0.002	1	0.002	0.123	0.730
Error	MCs	3738059.633	18	207669.980		
	MPK	8407766.567	18	467098.143		
	APM	9248.447	18	513.803		
	$P_{(KAPM \geq 0.5MPK)}$ (%)	0.303	18	0.017		
Total	MCs	16703007.000	22			
	MPK	30694124.000	22			
	APM	57532.208	22			
	$P_{(KAPM \geq 0.5MPK)}$ (%)	0.456	22			
Revised total	MCs	4272444.773	21			
	MPK	9990443.818	21			
	APM	10689.083	21			
	$P_{(KAPM \geq 0.5MPK)}$ (%)	0.309	21			

a. $R^2 = 0.125$ (Adjusted $R^2 = -0.021$); b. $R^2 = 0.158$ (Adjusted $R^2 = -0.018$);
c. $R^2 = 0.135$ (Adjusted $R^2 = -0.009$); d. $R^2 = 0.019$ (Adjusted $R^2 = -0.144$)

Eye-Tracking Data

Table 12. The ANOVA of the eye tracking data in experiment 2

Source	Response	SS	Dof	MS	F	P-value
Modified models	AOI AR	253.899a	19	13.363	5.812	0.000
	GLP	12562.626b	19	661.191	5.282	0.000
Intercept	AOI AR	333.255	1	333.255	144.932	0.000
	GLP	43636.335	1	43636.335	348.582	0.000
Expertise	AOI AR	40.525	1	40.525	17.624	0.000*
	GLP	7.758×10^{-8}	1	7.758×10^{-8}	0.000	1.000
Time pressure	AOI AR	.048	1	0.048	0.021	0.885
	GLP	2.048×10^{-7}	1	2.048×10^{-7}	0.000	1.000
AOIs	AOI AR	130.743	4	32.686	14.215	0.000*
	GLP	8963.364	4	2240.841	17.901	0.000*
Expertise * time pressure	AOI AR	1.125	1	1.125	0.489	0.486
	GLP	5.939×10^{-8}	1	5.939×10^{-8}	0.000	1.000
Time pressure * AOIs	AOI AR	31.404	4	7.851	3.414	0.012*
	GLP	1395.524	4	348.881	2.787	0.031*
Expertise * AOIs	AOI AR	34.586	4	8.646	3.760	0.007*
	GLP	1618.946	4	404.737	3.233	0.016*
Expertise * time pressure * AOIs	AOI AR	1.062	4	0.265	0.115	0.977
	GLP	161.425	4	40.356	0.322	0.862
Error	AOI AR	206.945	90	2.299		
	GLP	11266.425	90	125.183		
Total	AOI AR	818.520	110			
	GLP	67829.011	110			
Revised total	AOI AR	460.845	109			
	GLP	23829.051	109			

a. $R^2 = 0.551$ (Adjusted $R^2 = -0.456$); b. $R^2 = 0.527$ (Adjusted $R^2 = 0.427$); * $P < 0.05$

The number of glace and glance duration of AOIs of participants are recorded and processed, the represent index- AOI AR, GLP-are calculated. ANOVA (see Table 12) shows that there is no significant difference in factors under different time pressures and GLP values under different expertise. There is no significant interactive effect between other factors except time pressure and AOIs.

First, there are significant differences in AOI AR and GLP values for all players with different AOI. Secondly, when there is no time pressure, the AOI AR value of players' control buttons area is the highest, followed by the unit information area, minimap, resource bar and home city button. Under the time pressure, the AOI AR value of players' minimap and unit information increased significantly, the AOI AR value of the minimap reached the highest, while the AOI AR value of the control button decreased to the second. The AOI AR value in the resource bar decreased slightly, while the AOI AR value of the Home City button does not change significantly (see Fig. 10(a)).

In all cases, the AOI AR values of expert players' control buttons, minimap and unit information are significantly higher than those of casual players, while there is no significant difference in AOI AR values of the other two AOIs (see Fig. 10(b)). Meanwhile, the GLP values of expert players are lower than those of casual players in all areas except the control buttons area, especially in the resource bar.

In general, among combinations of factors with significant differences, AOI AR is most significantly influenced by the interactive effect of expertise of players and AOIs, and AOI AR is greatly impacted by AOIs.

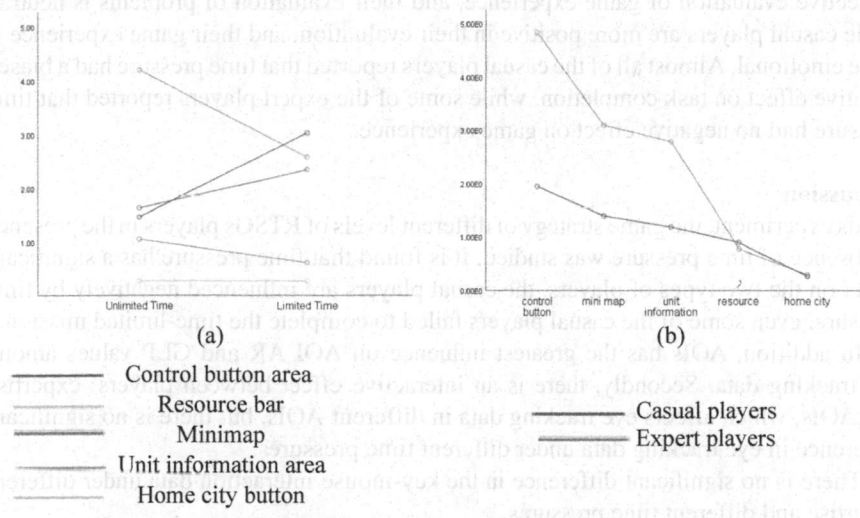

(a)   (b)

──────── Control button area
──────── Resource bar
──────── Minimap   ──────── Casual players
──────── Unit information area   ──────── Expert players
──────── Home city button

Fig. 10. The eye-tracking data in experiment 2

Subjective Evaluation
The modified GUESS-18 combined with 5-scale Likert questionnaire [14] was used for evaluation at the end of experiment 2. The result is depicted in Fig. 11.

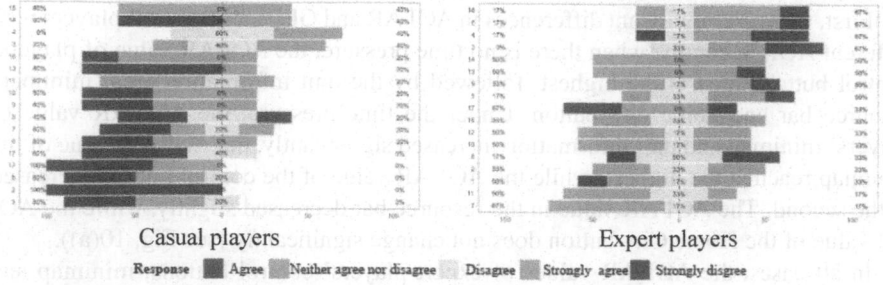

Casual players   Expert players

Response ■ Agree ■ Neither agree nor disagree Disagree ■ Strongly agree ■ Strongly disagree

Fig. 11. The distribution of players' subjective evaluation score in experiment 2

On the whole, the evaluation of casual players tends to be a high degree of positive, while the game experience evaluation of expert players rarely tends to be "strongly agree" or "strongly disagree", with a balanced distribution of positive and negative comments. This reflects the difference in game experience between expert players and casual players from the perspective of subjective evaluation: expert players are more rational in their subjective evaluation of game experience, and their evaluation of problems is neutral, while casual players are more positive in their evaluation, and their game experience is more emotional. Almost all of the casual players reported that time pressure had a biased negative effect on task completion, while some of the expert players reported that time pressure had no negative effect on game experience.

Discussion

In this experiment, the game strategy of different levels of RTSGs players in the presence or absence of time pressure was studied. It is found that time pressure has a significant effect on the two types of players, the casual players are influenced negatively by time pressure, even some of the casual players failed to complete the time-limited mission.

In addition, AOIs has the greatest influence on AOI AR and GLP values among eye tracking data. Secondly, there is an interactive effect between players' expertise and AOIs, which affects eye tracking data in different AOIs, but there is no significant difference in eye tracking data under different time pressures.

There is no significant difference in the key-mouse interaction data under different expertise and different time pressures.

According to the subjective evaluation, there is a difference in time pressure between expert players and casual players. Almost all casual players thought that time pressure had a negative impact on their game experience, while some expert players thought that time pressure had no negative impact on their game experience.

7 General Discussion

The method of the eye tracking and key-mouse interaction data combined was applied in this paper to explore the effect of players' expertise and HUD layouts on the PX in RTS gameplay, participants were also required to choose the most suitable HUD layout for them. The study conclusion of Caroux using subjective evaluation was proved in experiment 1: there are differences in HUD layout choices among game players with different expertise, and the differences between various layouts are more significant for expert players.

On the basis of Experiment 1, whether players would change their game strategies under different time pressure levels was further explored in experiment 2. The eye-tracking data and key-mouse interaction data of participants during the experiment, as well as the subjective evaluation filled in after the experiment were also recorded. Regarding to duration, there is significant difference in expert players under various time pressure. In the mission time-limited, expert players spent shorter time than casual players, several casual players even failed to finish the mission time-limited, from the perspective of duration proved that the game strategy had a certain change under time pressure. At the same time, it was also found that there was an impact of the interactive effect between time pressure and AOIs on players' eye-tracking data. However, key-mouse interaction data did not show a significant correlation with the changes in the game strategy, and the subjective evaluation of time pressure for different levels of players also existed certain differences. Expert players are more likely to shift game strategy. For example, manipulations of the combat units' training are increased, and manipulations of the resources collection related are decreased to complete the mission as fast as possible; Casual players, on the other hand, couldn't easily shift their game strategy, resulting in a relatively long time spending on mission accomplishment. It is shown that there are differences in the comprehension of RTS game mechanics between players with different levels in another way.

8 Conclusion

In this paper, the effect of different HUD layout forms of RTS games with different expertise on PX was studied by the method combined eye-tracking technology with key-mouse interaction data recording, which further proves the previous conclusions from the perspective of interactive experience. Furthermore, whether there are differences between the game strategies of players of different levels under different time pressures were studied and verified.

However, there are still many limitations in this study. Firstly, due to the time limitation, the first experiment was relatively short, and participants were not required to play a RTS game completely, only the task "age upgrade" was completed, resulting in a certain gap between the experimental results and the results of the complete RTS game. In addition, due to objective conditions, expert players are hard to find, so there is still a gap from the ideal results. At the same time, as the main interaction of the game, there are several limitations in the key-mouse interaction data record, resulting assumptions could not be proved. However, from the information input way, the diversity in the interaction between different levels of the players may be explored through the method of combining key-mouse interaction data recorded more reasonably with eye-tracking data and experience videos recorded.

In conclusion, although there are several limitations and deficiencies, the method used in the study on the different levels of professional players RTSG PX still provided the approach for PX and other monitoring activities related to HCI of the research for part of the scene. It is hoped that there will be more accurate recording methods of interaction devices in the future to study user experience in different fields better from the perspectives of physiology, behavioral performance, and subjective evaluation.

References

1. Toth, A.J., Conroy, E., Campbell, M.J.: Beyond action video games: differences in gameplay and ability preferences among gaming genres. Entertain. Comput. **38**, 100408 (2021)
2. Wang, D.: The Definition of video game art. J. Southwest Univ. Natl. (Humanit. Soc. Sci.) **12**, 356–359 (2005)
3. Hou, W., Bai, X.: HCI in real-time strategy games: a study of principals and guidelines for designing 3D user interface. In: 7th International Conference on Computer-Aided Industrial Design and Conceptual Design, pp. 1–6. IEEE, Hangzhou (2006)
4. Qin, H., Rau, P.P., Salvendy, G.: Measuring player immersion in the computer game narrative. Int. J. Hum.-Comput. Interact. **25**(2), 107–133 (2009)
5. Jennett, C., Coxa, A.L., Cairns, P., et al.: Measuring and defining the experience of immersion in games. Int. J. Hum. Comput. Stud. **66**(9), 541–661 (2008)
6. Fang, X., Zhang, J., Chan, S.S.: Development of an instrument for studying flow in computer game play. Int. J. Hum.-Comput. Interact. **29**(7), 456–470 (2013)
7. Fang, X., Chan, S.S., Brzezinski, J., et al.: Development of an instrument to measure enjoyment of computer game play. Int. J. Hum.-Comput. Interact. **26**(9), 868–886 (2010)
8. Phan, M.H., Keebler, J.R., Chaparro, B.S.: The development and validation of the game user experience satisfaction scale (GUESS). Hum. Factors: J. Hum. Factors Ergon. Soc. **58**(8), 1217–1247 (2016)
9. Caroux, L., Isbister, K.: Influence of head-up displays' characteristics on user experience in video games. Int. J. Hum. Comput. Stud. **87**, 65–79 (2016)
10. Kalar, D., Green, C.: Assessing interfaces supporting situational awareness in multi-agent command and control tasks. In: Shumaker, R. (ed.) VAMR 2013. LNCS, vol. 8021, pp. 277–284. Springer, Heidelberg (2013). https://doi.org/10.1007/978-3-642-39405-8_31
11. Gong, D., Yan, Y., Yao, Y., et al.: The high-working load states induced by action real-time strategy gaming: an EEG power spectrum and network study. Neuropsychologia **131**, 42–52 (2019)
12. Kim, Y.H., Kang, D.W., Kim, D., et al.: Real-time strategy video game experience and visual perceptual learning. J. Neurosci. **35**(29), 10485–10492 (2015)
13. Sanchez, J.L.G., Vela, F.L.G., Simarro, F.M., et al.: Playability: analysing user experience in video games. Behav. Inf. Technol. **31**(10), 1033–1054 (2012)
14. Keebler, J.R., Shelstad, W.J., Smith, D.C., et al.: Validation of the GUESS-18: a short version of the game user experience satisfaction scale (GUESS). J. Usability Stud. **16**(1), 49–62 (2020)

First Person vs. Third Person Perspective in a Persuasive Virtual Reality Game: How Does Perspective Affect Empathy Orientation?

Asha Kambe[✉] and Tatsuo Nakajima

Waseda University, Okubo 3-4-1, Shinjuku-ku, Tokyo, Japan
{asha.k,tatsuo}@dcl.cs.waseda.ac.jp

Abstract. Persuasive games, which use immersive technology to address social issues, appeal to player empathy by making them feel and understand the suffering of others. However, it remains ambiguous what type of empathy the player feels and for whom when experiencing a specific situation. We hypothesized that visual information regarding a distressed person obtained by the player influences the player's empathic orientation towards the person, whereby we note that other-oriented empathy is a more useful psychological state for developing prosocial attitudes than self-oriented empathy. The purpose of this study was to preliminarily investigate which player perspective (first-person perspective vs. third-person perspective) is more effective in promoting other-oriented empathy towards a virtual character in persuasive VR games and to provide insight into the design of such games. In a between-subjects experiment (N = 12), participants played a persuasive VR game from each perspective, and their empathy orientation was investigated using a questionnaire. The results show that there was no significant difference in empathy orientation between the two conditions. The explanation may be that self-oriented empathy is mixed with attitude as a player, such as paying attention to the progress of the game.

Keywords: Virtual reality games · Empathy · Perspective

1 Introduction

In recent years, persuasive games using virtual reality (VR) have drawn increasing research attention; persuasive games that appeal to player empathy, when combined with immersive technology, allow the player to "step into" any environment [4, 15, 16]. Persuasive games have been designed to solve problems across different domains [10, 23]. The purpose of such games is to convey persuasive messages that intentionally aim to affect player responses. In persuasive VR games that focus on social issues, the game appeals to user empathy by making the user feel and understand the suffering of others. In such a game, the player acts out an assigned role in the game world, and this experience deepens the understanding of the player who feel distress through empathy. In this way, such games are expected to deepen the understanding of those who subsequently find themselves in similar positions in the real world and to provide clues that may help

X. Fang (Ed.): HCII 2022, LNCS 13334, pp. 375–386, 2022.
https://doi.org/10.1007/978-3-031-05637-6_23

people solve social issues [4, 8, 16]. However, there are many questions regarding the detailed process of empathy arousal, and it remains unclear how players behave in the game world or with whom players empathize [17].[1]

1.1 Background

Appealing to empathy is a persuasive strategy that causes a person to consider someone else's situation and feelings. Empathy has been shown to have clear benefits in nursing [22], conflict resolution [2], and discrimination issues [24]. However, empathy is a complex psychological state for which a unified definition is lacking, even among researchers [6].

Since VR can immerse a game player in any virtual world regardless of the limitations of time and space, a player can experience another person's situation by placing him- or herself in the other person's environment. This phenomenon can occur because VR evokes a sense of "being there" in the player [7]. Through such experiences, it is expected that VR can be used to help players consider the feelings of others, i.e., to promote empathy [3]. In VR works that arouse the player's empathy, 360-degree video and persuasive games have been used; works such as The Displaced [13], Project Syria [8], Clouds Over Sidra [1], and Permanent [16] have been produced. The experiences provided in such works are designed to allow players to engage in perspective-taking [5] and provide the ability to imagine another person's viewpoint; such experiences have been suggested as a means to encourage social behaviour when used in VR [18, 32]. It has been found that the effect of empathy arousal is higher in VR environments than in 2D environments [12, 26], and the VR empathy arousal effect has been found relevant to the medical field [29] and to social issues [26]. It has also been found that such effects continue into daily life [12].

However, in recent years, the VR field has been criticized for its unclear and superficial definition of empathy, and it is argued that empathy arousal in fact involves far more complicated matters than the physical implementation of having players "stand in another's shoes" alone [17]. Kors et al. argue that in designing VR programs to elicit empathy arousal, it is not always optimal to design from the first-person perspective (1pp). A player who is physically "in another person's shoes", e.g., in distress, does not necessarily involve the experience of literally "putting oneself in another person's shoes" [17]. When a player plays a role in a VR game, the player brings his or her own experience and personality to the role. As the player focuses on playing, he or she may lose awareness of the meta-view that the player is experiencing another person's situation. The boundary between self and others may become blurred, and players may think primarily in terms of their own needs and be unaware of the feelings of others (e.g., "What 'I' need in this situation is _____"). Additionally, the mixing of self and others is considered to be more conspicuous with 1pp, in which the character's and player's physical positions are the same. As this self-oriented empathy grows stronger, there is a risk that the self and others will become mixed and, therefore, that it will be impossible to correctly understand the feelings and desires of others. In contrast, it is also

---

[1] Please note that this paper provides a more detailed description of our previous poster presentation [14].

argued that other-oriented empathy is a motivation to help others in need [2]. Empathy follows the development of the ability to distinguish between the self and others [21]; thus, nurturing the cognitive ability to distinguish between the self and others enables prosocial behaviours that help others [30]. It is therefore important for players to distinguish between the self and others and to use their imagination in relation to empathy. To achieve this outcome, it is first necessary to consider how the player interprets and behaves in the assigned role so to distinguish between self- and other-oriented empathy in empathy arousal.

The relationship between a player and a given role in persuasive games remains unclear. Particularly in recent persuasive games, roles assigned to the players are becoming more diverse, and a role is not necessarily that of one who feels distress (who is intended to be understood) [13, 23]. In game studies, Tavinor argues that the player character acts as an "epistemic and agential proxy" for the player that enables the player to "step into" a fictional world (i.e., a game world) to play games and experience a narrative [27, 28]. Matsunaga categorizes the attitudes of such players towards the player character into two types [20]. The first is the self-involving type. In this attitude, the player imagines him- or herself in a particular situation in the fictional world, thereby forming his or her own motivations and acting on them [25]. Therefore, there is a possibility that self-oriented empathy becomes stronger, and it is easy to confuse oneself and others since the player imagines that he or she has entered the fictional world. In the second attitude type, known as the mimicry type, the player becomes a specific character that already exists in the fictional world. Matsunaga refers to third-person role-playing games and adventure games as genres in which this attitude is conventionally held [20]. This view suggests a relationship between the player's perspective and the player's attitude. In addition, the mimicry type may be an attitude that makes it easier to distinguish between the self and other because the player "pretends" to be the other and understands the other from a third-person perspective.

1.2 Player Perspectives and Empathy

In this study, we focused on the visual information regarding a distressed person that a player receives during play and hypothesized that this information affects the player's empathic orientation towards that person. Regarding the relationship between the player and the given role, we assigned the role of the person who is distressed to the player and investigated arousal empathy from two perspectives: the first-person perspective (1pp) and the third-person perspective (3pp). The characteristic visual information regarding each perspective is summarized below to clarify the definition of these perspectives as used in this study.

- 1pp (First-Person Perspective):

  In 1pp, the player's viewpoint coincides with that of the assigned role, and the player shares the role's view. Especially in VR games, the player's head movements are generally tracked. Thus, the physical positions of the player and the player character are felt to be consistent. In this study, since the player is in the position of the one who feels the distress, the player can see the visual information related to the player character.

- 3pp (Third-Person Perspective):

   In 3pp, the viewpoint of the player is different from that of the given role. The player is located near the player character in the manner of a floating ghost. Therefore, the player can see the surrounding environment, including the player character. Furthermore, the player can see the facial expressions, gestures, and other attitudes of the assigned role, which can make it easier to imagine the psychological state of the player character.

Persuasive VR games that enable players to objectively view those who feel distress include INJUSTICE [4], which places the player in the role of a witness to racism, and Permanent [16], which places the player in the role of a reporter covering victims of a natural disaster. Similarly, in the 3pp used in this research, the player is placed in the position of being able to objectively view the one who feels distress. However, the player is assigned to the role of the one who feels distress.

In this study, we empirically investigated the effect of the difference in player perspectives on empathy orientation by comparing 1pp and 3pp for the same player character. More specifically, we addressed the following two research questions.

- RQ1: Is the empathic orientation of the player's personality consistent with the orientation demonstrated while playing persuasive VR games?
- RQ2: Are there differences in empathic orientation between 1pp and 3pp in persuasive VR games?

To the best of our knowledge, no previous research has separately measured the orientations of empathy evoked by persuasive VR games. Thus, we preliminarily investigated differences in empathic orientation between personality and persuasive VR games using RQ1. Then, we clarified the differences in empathic orientation between 1pp and 3pp in persuasive VR games using RQ2. To validate the RQs, we conducted between-subject experiments (N = 12) in which participants played a persuasive VR game. Then, we collected data on the playing experience using questionnaires and interviews. The contribution of this study is to preliminarily investigate which perspective (1pp vs. 3pp) is more effective in arousing other-oriented empathy in persuasive VR games and to provide insight into the design of such games.

2   Method

To investigate the effect of perspective, we conducted a between-subject experiment using a standalone persuasive VR game in both 1pp and 3pp versions. Since there was no such available game, we created a VR game with both perspectives for the experiment. We used the Unity (version 2019.4.13f) game engine, C# and Oculus Quest.

2.1   Game Mechanics

Since it was found that interactive narratives improve player empathy [11], we adopted an interactive narrative for the game [31]. More specifically, we designed the story to branch depending on player choices.

The game consists of a conversation mode and an exploration mode. In the conversation mode, a window in which conversation logs are displayed in Japanese appears in the lower area of the display screen (termed the text scene). In certain scenarios, the player must choose what action the player character will take. In such scenes, two options are displayed, and the player needs to select one of them by using the controller (termed the choice scene). The game has a total of four choice scenes. Figure 1 shows screenshots of sample scenes from both perspectives. In the exploration mode, the player character can move around, talk to other characters, and examine objects. In this way, the player can gather clues and progress through the story.

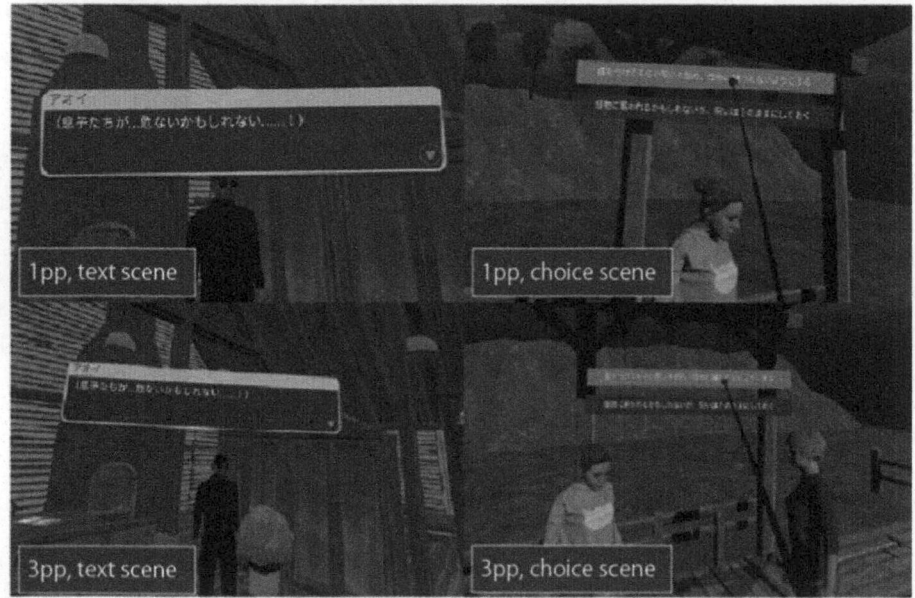

Fig. 1. Screenshots of the game

2.2 Narrative

Since nonfictional scenarios may cause individual differences in empathy measurement due to the influence of previous knowledge and experience, a fictional scenario was adopted so that the story would be unknown to all participants. The adopted scenario was created based on the TRPG scenario "Who's the Swampman?" [19]. Our scenario was inspired by Swampman, a thought experiment that provides players numerous opportunities to think through philosophical questions.

The player is given the role of the protagonist, Aoi, and controls her. Aoi is involved in an incident and seeks the truth to protect her children. Finally, she is forced to choose between protecting her children at the expense of many others or protecting many others at the expense of her children.

2.3 Perspective

In our persuasive VR game, we implemented 1pp and 3pp viewpoints. In 1pp, the virtual camera is located at the player character's eye position. By operating the camera viewpoint using a joystick, the camera can be rotated as if the player character is moving his or her body. In 3pp, the camera is located on a sphere of 3 m with a radius centred on the eyes of the player character. The camera can be moved around the sphere by controlling the camera viewpoint with the joystick. In addition, the camera can rotate on its own axis. To prevent VR sickness, spherical movement in the vertical direction is limited.

Game content is almost the same between the two perspectives. It includes character motions, the position of the conversation log window, the story, and other aspects of game content. The only difference is the virtual position of the player depending on the perspective in game mechanics. This difference leads to differences in the visual information that the player receives. For example, the player with 1pp cannot see some of what the player in 3pp can see (e.g., the motion of the player character). The differences are listed below.

- 1pp (First-Person Perspective)

  - A conversation window appearing from the player character feels like it is coming from the player's body.
  - When the player chooses to be wounded in one of the choice scenes, the player's view shakes due to the dragging of the feet during movement.
  - In one scene, being preyed on is represented by a darkening of vision.

- 3pp (Third-Person Perspective)

  - The player character has two types of standby motion, relaxed and tense, and these motion types can be seen to change depending on the scene.
  - The player can see a conversation window appearing from the player character body.
  - If the player chooses to be wounded in one choice scene, the player character will move as if painfully wounded, and the waiting and moving motions will change to limping. The 3pp player can see these motions.
  - In one scene, predation is expressed using swallowing sounds.

3 Experiment

3.1 Participants

The participants in the experiment were 12 students (1 female, 10 males, and 1 non-respondent) of a Japanese university (mean age: 23.6 years). All had experience with VR. Based on the results of a pre-experimental survey, the participants were assigned to either perspective condition (1pp vs. 3pp) so as to counterbalance each group regarding empathy orientation. The experiment was conducted in a university laboratory. After his experiment, one participant (a male) who stated "I was too sick to do the experiment (VR sickness)" was excluded from the data analysis because it is highly possible that the data on this participant were not collected accurately. As a result, we successfully collected data from 11 participants. There were 6 participants in the 1pp condition and 5 participants in the 3pp condition.

3.2 Experimental Procedure

The experiment was conducted according to the following procedure.

1. Explanation: An overview of the VR game and its operation was provided (approximately 5 min).
2. Tutorial: In the VR environment, the participants practised operating the game (approximately 3 min).
3. Gameplay: Participants played the game from the assigned perspective (25–40 min).
4. Questionnaire and interview: After the participants completed the questionnaire, a semi-structured interview was conducted (20–35 min).

3.3 Data Collection

Pre-experimental Survey. Prior to the experiment, we investigated the empathic orientation of the participants' personalities. Perspective-taking [5] was conducted on a person in a presented image for measurement. Participants completed the online task of writing a diary for the person shown in the image. After completing the task, they answered a questionnaire that consisted of four questions that measure the participants' empathy orientation and requested free writing regarding their thoughts. The four-item questionnaire measured four psychological states that involve empathy (the details are below). These questions were rated on a 5-point Likert scale (1 = I do not think so, 5 = I think so). The results of this measurement were used as the empathic orientation of the participants' personalities.

To measure empathy that distinguishes between empathy for oneself and others, we used the definition proposed by Batson et al. [2]. According to this definition, empathy is divided into four psychological states, which are defined in Table 1.

Table 1. Four items that measure psychological states related to empathy

Psychological state	What the state involves
Imagine-self Perspective (ISP)	Imagining how one would think and feel in another's situation or "shoes"
Imagine-other Perspective (IOP)	Imagining how another person thinks or feels given his or her situation
Emotion Matching (EM)	Feeling as another person feels
Empathic Concern (EC)	Feeling for another person who is in need

ISP and EM are classified as self-oriented empathy, while IOP and EC are classified as other-oriented empathy. In addition, ISP and IOP are classified as cognitive/perceptual psychological states, while EM and EC are classified as affective/emotional states [2].

In-Game Score. The results of all four choice scenes were collected.

Post-experiment Survey. After the gameplay, questionnaires were completed, and interviews conducted. The content of these evaluations was the same as in the pre-experiment survey and measured the empathic orientation towards Aoi in each choice scene.

4   Results and Discussion

4.1   Questionnaire Results

Four items describing the psychological state of empathy were used as the index of empathic orientation. As investigating statistically significant differences in a between-subjects design with a total of 11 participants does not meet the requirements for a parametric statistical test, we chose parametric tests.

Regarding RQ1, the Wilcoxon signed-ranks test was used to compare the personal subjective answers regarding the empathic orientation of each participant between the pre- and post-experiment. The results were considered significant when $p < 0.05$. Table 2 shows the sample means, standard deviations, and p values. As shown in the table, ISP, EM, and EC in the VR game were significantly greater than personality-derived empathy.

Table 2. Comparison of empathic orientation between personality and persuasive VR game

Item	Personality	VR game	p-value
ISP	2.50 ± 1.06	2.80 ± 1.04	0.007
IOP	3.84 ± 1.15	1.85 ± 0.58	0.085
EM	2.34 ± 1.17	1.90 ± 0.52	0.008
EC	2.34 ± 0.92	2.45 ± 0.82	0.006

Regarding RQ2, we used the Mann–Whitney U test to compare the subjective answers concerning empathic orientation between the two viewpoint conditions (1PP/3PP). The results were considered significant when $p < 0.05$, the same as RQ1.

Table 3 shows the sample means, standard deviations, and p values of the means for each variable of empathy in the four choice scenes. As shown in the table, there was no significant difference between the two groups in the variables related to empathy in the choice scene. In addition, there was no difference in the choice results between the conditions.

Table 3. Comparison of empathic orientation between 1pp and 3pp

Item	1pp	3pp	p-value
ISP	3.71 ± 1.44	3.80 ± 1.04	1.000
IOP	3.17 ± 1.00	2.85 ± 0.58	0.662
EM	3.67 ± 1.09	2.90 ± 0.52	0.247
EC	3.38 ± 1.05	3.45 ± 0.82	0.931

In 3pp, the player can see the player character's movements, which cannot be seen in 1pp. However, there was only one response that mentioned this difference in the interview ("I did not want to see a scene in which Aoi gets hurt (3pp)"). It was unclear to what extent the players had seen the unique information available in 1pp and 3pp.

4.2 RQ1

The psychological state related to empathy in the persuasive VR game significantly increased ISP, EM, and EC compared to the states related to personality. The reason for the significant increase in self-oriented empathy (ISP, EM) could be that the role assigned to the player is that of a distressed person and the player is manipulating that person. The significantly higher emotional empathy (EM, EC) could be caused by experiencing the game for a long time (approximately 40 min) in the immersive VR environment. The results of these empathic indices (ISP, EM, and EC) were significantly higher in the VR game, which could be explained by the difference in the amount of information between the photographs and the VR game. However, that IOP was lower in the VR game was contrary to our expectations, although there was no statistically significant difference. We believe this result occurred because taking control of the actions of the given role enabled the player to identify with the player character and thus lose the feeling that the player character was an other rather than oneself. To be certain regarding this surmise, it is necessary to investigate whether the degree of controllability changes the orientation of empathy. IOP is a psychological state in which you imagine the feelings of others, taking into account their backgrounds and ways of thinking so that you can truly understand their needs. Therefore, the low IOP result suggests that persuasive VR games may not be the best way to understand what others need. On the other hand, the persuasive VR game significantly improved the psychological state of EC, which is a motivation to work for others. Thus, it could be that the persuasive VR game is effective regarding the opportunity to learn about others and develop a motivation to take action for others.

4.3 RQ2

There are two likely causes for the lack of a significant difference in the orientation of empathy between 1pp and 3pp in the persuasive VR game. The first is that self-oriented empathy was mixed with the player's attitudes as "a player". The second is that there was little visual information regarding the role available to the 3pp players.

Regarding the first cause, we observed three play styles during the experiment: "What I would do (ISP, self-oriented empathy)", "What I would do in this role (IOP, other-oriented empathy)", and "What I would do as a player". Not all players had one attitude; some players had different attitudes depending on the situation; some had an attitude in between. The third attitude is that of the player who plays while paying attention to the progress of the game, such as the player who responds positively to "choose an option that seems to be interesting to develop (3pp)" or "choose an option that does not clog the story (1pp)". This attitude occurred for players in both groups. It is the attitude of the player who knows that the story is in a game and is therefore not an attitude that results in a player immersing him- or herself in the story and creating self- and other-oriented empathy. This attitude may distract from the fact that the player characters are in distress and thus diminishes the sense of crisis regarding social issues that players are expected to feel. As an element that emphasizes the fictional nature of the story, intervention in the story world (i.e., interactivity) [9], a typical element of such game, should be considered. Certain players provided answers in the interviews that suggested their attitudes as players were mixed with self-orientation, which may have resulted in a high measurement of self-oriented empathy. Therefore, when measuring empathy orientation, it is necessary to separate self-oriented empathy from player attitude.

Regarding the second cause, in this study, we hypothesized that the difference in visual information obtained by the player due to the virtual position of the player between 1pp and 3pp would change player empathy. The reason why there was no significant difference in empathy orientation may have been the narrowness of the differences in visual information between the 2 versions. Future game design improvements should include adding facial expressions to the main character and increasing movement. Such improvements would strengthen and distinguish the characteristics of perspectives so as to magnify the influence of each condition. In addition, they would encourage players to approach the game used in the experiment as if it were a general persuasive VR game. As a result, the information specific to perspective would have a larger effect on player empathy, and the empathy would be more easily measured.

Several important limitations of the present research should be mentioned. The first is the small power of the analysis due to the very small sample of users ($N = 12$) in a between-subjects design (6 participants per condition). Second, the possible effect of sex difference between the protagonist and the player should be considered. Most of experiment participants were male and played the role of a female character.

5 Conclusion

Our research provides preliminary insight regarding the effect of perspective on empathic orientation in persuasive VR games. Participants played a persuasive VR game from one of two perspectives (1pp or 3pp), and their empathy orientation was investigated using a questionnaire. First, it was found that persuasive VR games are optimal for evoking emotions that truly deepen player understanding of what others need. However, such games do elicit emotions that motivate the player to learn about others and take action for them. Second, the results showed that there was no significant difference in empathy orientation between the two perspectives. We hope that the identification of empathy arousal depending on perspective will support the development of a potentially efficient use of such games to promote empathy.

References

1. Arora, G., Milk, C.: Clouds over sidra. https://www.with.in/watch/clouds-over-sidra/. Accessed 18 June 2021
2. Batson, C.D., Ahmad, N.Y.: Using empathy to improve intergroup attitudes and relations. Soc. Issues Policy Rev. **3**(1), 141–177 (2009). https://doi.org/10.1111/j.1751-2409.2009.010 13.x
3. Bujić, M., Salminen, M., Macey, J., Hamari, J.: "Empathy machine": how virtual reality affects human rights attitudes. Internet Res. **30**(5), 1407–1425 (2020). https://doi.org/10.1108/INTR-07-2019-0306
4. Cho, J., Won, Y., Kothari, A., Fawaz, S., Ding, Z., Cheng, X.: INJUSTICE: interactive live action virtual reality experience. In: Proceedings of the 2016 Annual Symposium on Computer-Human Interaction in Play Companion Extended Abstracts, pp. 33–37. ACM (2016). https://doi.org/10.1145/2968120.2968121
5. Coke, J.S., Batson, C.D., McDavis, K.: Empathic mediation of helping: a two-stage model. J. Pers. Soc. Psychol. **36**(7), 752–766 (1978). https://doi.org/10.1037/0022-3514.36.7.752
6. Cuff, B.M., Brown, S.J., Taylor, L., Howat, D.J.: Empathy: a review of the concept. Emot. Rev. **8**(2), 144–153 (2016). https://doi.org/10.1177/1754073914558466
7. Cummings, J.J., Bailenson, J.N.: how immersive is enough? A meta-analysis of the effect of immersive technology on user presence. Media Psychol. **19**(2), 272–309 (2016). https://doi.org/10.1080/15213269.2015.1015740
8. De La Pena, N.: Project Syria. Emblematic Group, USC School of Cinematic Arts, MxR Studio, U.S.A. (2014)
9. Frome, J.: The ontology of interactivity. In: The Philosophy of Computer Games Conference (2009)
10. Ganesh, A., Ndulue, C., Orji, R.: PERMARUN - a persuasive game to improve user awareness and self-efficacy towards secure smartphone behaviour. In: Conference on Human Factors in Computing Systems - Proceedings, pp. 1–7. ACM (2021). https://doi.org/10.1145/3411763. 3451781
11. Hand, S., Varan, D.: Interactive stories and the audience: why empathy is important. Comput. Entertain. **7**(3), 1–14 (2009). https://doi.org/10.1145/1594943.1594951
12. Herrera, F., Bailenson, J., Weisz, E., Ogle, E., Zaki, J.: Building long-term empathy: a large-scale comparison of traditional and virtual reality perspective-taking. PLoS One **13**(8), e0204494 (2018). https://doi.org/10.1371/journal.pone.0204494
13. Ismail, I., Solomon, B.S.: The Displaced. The New York Times Magazine, U.S.A. (2015)
14. Kambe, A., Nakajima, T.: Have the same perspective as someone else, so am I the person?: the effect of perspective on empathic orientation in virtual reality. In: 20th International Conference on Mobile and Ubiquitous Multimedia (MUM 2021). ACM (2021)
15. Kors, M.J., Ferri, G., Van Fer Spek, E.D., Ketel, C., Schouten, B.A.: A breathtaking journey. On the design of an empathy-arousing mixed-reality game. In: Proceedings of the 2016 Annual Symposium on Computer-Human Interaction in Play, pp. 91–104. ACM (2016). https://doi.org/10.1145/2967934.2968110
16. Kors, M.J., et al.: The curious case of the transdiegetic cow, or a mission to foster other-oriented empathy through virtual reality. In: Proceedings of the 2020 CHI Conference on Human Factors in Computing Systems, pp. 1–13. ACM, New York (2020). https://doi.org/10.1145/3313831.3376748

17. Kors, M.J., Van Der Spek, E.D., Ferri, G., Schouten, B.A.: You; the observer, partaker or victim. Delineating three perspectives to empathic engagement in persuasive games using immersive technologies. In: Proceedings of the 2018 Annual Symposium on Computer-Human Interaction in Play Companion Extended Abstracts, pp. 493–501. ACM (2018). https://doi.org/10.1145/3270316.3271547

18. Levett-Jones, T., et al.: Measuring the impact of a 'point of view' disability simulation on nursing students' empathy using the Comprehensive State Empathy Scale. Nurse Educ. Today **59**, 75–81 (2017). https://doi.org/10.1016/j.nedt.2017.09.007

19. ma34. NumaOtoko ha Dare da? (in Japanese, "Who's the Swampman?"). https://ux.getuploader.com/trpgma34/download/13. Accessed 13 Jan 2021

20. Matsunaga, S.: Video Ge-mu no Bigaku (in Japanese, "The Aesthetics of Videogames"). Keio University Press Inc. (2018)

21. Matsuo, Y., Matsushita, H.: A review of Hoffman's theory for empathic arousal. Bull. Train. Res. Cent. Clin. Psychol. **6**, 104–112 (2017). https://doi.org/10.15027/23564

22. Moyers, T.B., Houck, J., Rice, S.L., Longabaugh, R., Miller, W.R.: Therapist empathy, combined behavioral intervention, and alcohol outcomes in the COMBINE research project. J. Consult. Clin. Psychol. **84**(3), 221–229 (2016). https://doi.org/10.1037/ccp0000074

23. Ndulue, C., Orji, R.: STD PONG: changing risky sexual behaviour in Africa through persuasive games. In: ACM International Conference Proceeding Series, pp. 134–138. ACM (2018). https://doi.org/10.1145/3283458.3283463

24. Olapegba, P.O.: Empathy, knowledge, and personal distress as correlates of HIV-/AIDS-Related stigmatization and discrimination. J. Appl. Soc. Psychol. **40**(4), 956–969 (2010). https://doi.org/10.1111/j.1559-1816.2010.00606.x

25. Robson, J., Meskin, A.: Video games as self-involving interactive fictions. J. Aesthet. Art Critic. **74**(2), 165–177 (2016). https://doi.org/10.1111/jaac.12269

26. Schutte, N.S., Stilinović, E.J.: Facilitating empathy through virtual reality. Motiv. Emot. **41**(6), 708–712 (2017). https://doi.org/10.1007/s11031-017-9641-7

27. Tavinor, G.: The Art of Videogames. Blackwell (2009)

28. Tavinor, G.: What's my motivation? Video games and interpretative performance. J. Aesthet. Art Critic. **75**(1), 23–33 (2017). https://doi.org/10.1111/jaac.12334

29. Tong, X., Gromala, D., Ziabari, S.P.K., Shaw, C.D.: Designing a virtual reality game for promoting empathy toward patients with chronic pain: feasibility and usability study. JMIR Serious Games **8**(3), e17354 (2020)

30. Ueda, M., Katsurada, E.: A review of research on empathic development: necessity of theories including positive empathy. Jimbun Ronkyu: Humanit. Rev. **69**(1), 71–90 (2019)

31. Van Lent, M.: Guest editor's introduction: interactive narrative. IEEE Comput. Graph. Appl. **26**(3), 20–21 (2006). https://doi.org/10.1109/MCG.2006.59

32. Van Loon, A., Bailenson, J., Zaki, J., Bostick, J., Willer, R.: Virtual reality perspective-taking increases cognitive empathy for specific others. PLoS ONE **13**(8), e0202442 (2018). https://doi.org/10.1371/journal.pone.0202442

Does "Left-Behind" Cause Rural Adolescents to Spend More Time Playing Video Games in China?
Evidence from China Education Panel Survey

Siyuan Wang[1]([⊠]) [iD], Lihanjing Wu[1] [iD], and Xiao Liang[2]

[1] Central China Normal University, Wuhan 430070, Hubei, People's Republic of China
{wangsiyuan0420,Lihanjing}@mails.ccnu.edu.cn
[2] Peking University, Beijing 100871, People's Republic of China
liangxiao2018@pku.edu.cn

Abstract. Video games have become more prevalent in adolescents' lives to entertain. Previous studies suggest rural left-behind adolescents are vulnerable to being absorbed in video games. To characterize a causal relation between "left-behind" and the time of playing video games among rural adolescents, we used representative data from China Educational Panel Survey (CEPS) and Propensity Score Matching (PSM) method. The sample includes 1166 rural left-behind adolescents and 1156 rural non-left-behind adolescents. Results demonstrated significant differences in the individual and family characteristics of rural left-behind adolescents and rural non-left-behind adolescents; rural left-behind adolescents spend more time playing video games on weekends, not on weekdays. The findings have implications for parents and educators who should give adequate care and supervision to rural left-behind adolescents on weekends.

Keywords: Left-behind adolescents · Video games · Propensity score matching

1 Introduction

China has undergone the most rapid industrialization and urbanization since the 1980s, so it is common for migrant workers to find jobs in wealthier cities [1]. However, due to economic restrictions and China's hukou system, nearly 70% of children of migrant workers do not migrate with their parents [2]. Rural left-behind children refer to children under 18 who are left by their parents in their original rural residence and unable to live with both or one of their parents [3]. Data shows that the number of left-behind children in rural China was 6.97 million in 2018, which is still considerable [4]. Given the change in family structure caused by parents' absence, rural left-behind children are at increased risk of behavioral and psychological problems [5].

With the greater availability of the internet, playing video games has become the most prominent way for children and adolescents to entertain [6]. According to China Internet Network Information Center, compared with 2019, the percentage of children aged 6 to 18 who play video games increased by 1.5% to 62.5% in 2020, and adolescents are the primary group playing video games [7]. Displacement theory explains that using the internet or screen may replace other activities, such as learning and doing sports [8]. In addition, time management on the internet is an essential indicator for assessing adolescent internet addiction [9]. Excessive time spent on the internet can be detrimental to adolescents' physical and mental health. Barrense-Dias et al. indicated that obesity in adolescents was associated with excessive time use of the internet [10]. Trumello et al. found that internet addiction was significantly and negatively associated with the parent-child relationship [11]. Empirical studies have shown that rural children prefer to play video games more than urban children [12], and internet addiction has rapidly become a prevalent concern among left-behind adolescents in China [13].

Left-behind children are more easily exposed to internet addiction than non-left-behind children [14]. Among the factors affecting adolescents playing video games, parent-child separation is a risk factor, leading to lousy parent-child relationships and adolescents' video games addiction [15]. Self-determination theory states that the basic drive of human beings is to seek the satisfaction of psychological needs [16]. Parent-child separation makes rural left-behind adolescents unable to meet their basic psychological needs for a long time in their lives, so they are likely to turn to video games to seek compensation [17]. Previous studies indicated that the lack of parental support and supervision would positively predict adolescents' internet gaming disorder [18, 19].

Extant studies examining the effects of internet use on adolescents are mainly divided into two main scenarios: weekdays and weekends. Some researchers have demonstrated that adolescents tend to play computer games longer on weekends than on weekdays [20], and weekend internet use is a more vital predictor of overweight and internet addiction in adolescents than weekday internet use [21, 22]. The fact is that compared to weekdays, teenagers have much spare time and lack adequate supervision on weekends, which tends to make game playing longer on weekends than on weekdays [23]. Therefore, it is worth exploring whether the time spent playing video games during weekends and weekdays differed between the left-behind and non-left-behind adolescents.

In this study, we used the baseline data from China Education Panel Survey (CEPS) to explore the following two questions: (1) Does "left-behind" affect rural adolescents to spend more time playing video games in China? (2) Whether there is a difference in the time spent playing video games on weekends and weekdays between left-behind rural adolescents and non-left-behind rural adolescents.

2   Method

2.1   Data

The data used in this study came from the CEPS from 2013 to 2014. CEPS is a nationally representative large-scale longitudinal survey of 19,487 junior high school seventh and ninth-grade students in 28 counties (districts). The survey collected students' demographic characteristics, family background, information on internet use, and physical and mental health [24].

2.2 Variables

Dependent Variable. CEPS questionnaire designed two questions that measure adolescents' time playing video games on weekdays and weekends. We use the two questions to generate the dependent variables in our study: weekday minutes and weekends minutes. Weekdays minutes is defined as the average time an adolescent spent on the internet and playing video games per day from Monday to Friday in the last week; weekends minutes is defined as the average time an adolescent spent on the internet and playing video games per day in last weekend.

Independent Variable. CEPS asked respondents whether they live with their parents and the type of household registration (i.e., rural or urban). Based on the two questions, we constructed the core independent variable "Rural left-behind adolescents (yes = 1)".

Other Control Variables. According to previous studies, we controlled several factors that may influence adolescents' time spent on the internet and playing video games. These factors include:

Individual-Level Variables. Gender (male = 1), grade (grade 9 = 1), whether a student is an only child (yes = 1), and academic achievement (dummy variables for "academic achievement is average" and "academic achievement is excellent" with "academic achievement is poor" as the reference group).

Family-Level Variables. Education level of parents (dummy variables for "high school education" and "higher education" with "middle school education or below" as the reference group), parent-child relationships, and family income (dummy variables for "family's economic level is wealthy" and "family's economic level is average" with "family's economic level is poor" as the reference group).

School-Level Variable. Whether a school is a boarding school (yes = 1).

After excluding observations with missing values for any variable, the final analysis sample consisted of 2322 rural adolescents, of which 1166 were rural left-behind children and the remaining 1156 were rural non-left-behind children.

2.3 Analysis Approach

Descriptive Statistics Used to Describe the Differences Between Rural Non-left-behind Children and Rural Left-Behind Children. First, the present study used descriptive statistics to demonstrate the differences between rural left-behind children and rural non-left-behind children in terms of individual characteristics and family background, which helps understand whether the basic characteristics of the two groups matched. The results are reported in Table 1.

Ordinary Least Squares (OLS) Model and Propensity Score Matching (PSM) Estimation to Identify the Effect of Left-Behind. Second, we conducted estimates based on two different approaches to assess the effect of "left-behind" on rural adolescents' time spent playing video games. We first used the OLS model. However, due to the unbalanced selection into "left-behind" and "non-left-behind" groups, the OLS estimation can be biased seriously. Therefore, the OLS model can only provide a crude estimation of "left-behind" treatment effects.

The OLS model is shown in formula (1) and (2):

$$Weekdays\ minutes_i = \alpha + \beta \cdot left\text{-}behind_i + \gamma \cdot X_i + \varepsilon_i \tag{1}$$

$$Weekends\ minutes_i = \alpha + \beta \cdot left\text{-}behind_i + \gamma \cdot X_i + \varepsilon_i \tag{2}$$

Weekdays minutes_i and *Weekends minutes_i* are the amount of time (per day) that rural adolescents spend playing video games on weekdays and weekends, respectively. *Left-behind_i* is a dummy variable for whether rural adolescents are left behind at home, and X_i is a set of control variables.

To address and alleviate the problem in OLS estimation, we further use the Propensity Score Matching (PSM) method to adjust for observed characteristics. Relative to OLS, PSM can more effectively match the background information of the treatment and non-treatment groups and mitigate the selective bias. Whether an adolescent is left behind is not a random process but is influenced by individual characteristics and family backgrounds. However, we cannot observe the results of the same individual in both left-behind and non-left-behind conditions at the same time. In order to accurately estimate the effect of left-behind, we need to deal with the particular bias problem. Therefore, the research conclusions will be mainly based on PSM results. The net effect of left-behind on time rural adolescents spent playing video games is recorded as the Average Treatment Effect on the Treated (ATT) in the PSM model, which is as follows:

$$ATT = E\{E[Y_{1i} - Y_{0i}|D_i = 1, p(X_i)]\} \tag{3}$$

Y_{1i} and Y_{0i} denote the time spent playing video games in the two cases of rural adolescents i left-behind and non-left-behind, respectively. D_i is a dummy variable that indicates whether rural adolescent i is left-behind, with $D_i = 1$ if rural adolescent i is left-behind and $D_i = 0$ otherwise. $p(X_i)$ is the propensity score, which indicates the probability that rural adolescent i is left-behind while controlling for sample characteristic covariates X.

PSM is divided into four steps: firstly, select the appropriate covariates that predict the individuals' propensity into the treatment group (i.e., the control variables above). Secondly, calculate the propensity scores of each individual, which were generated by predicted values using logit regression. Third, match samples based on propensity scores. Additionally, the k-Nearest Neighbors Matching (k-NNM) (k = 3) was used to generate the primary estimate for the effect of "left-behind" on individuals' time spent playing video games, and the Radius Matching (RM) (caliper = 0.2) was used to conduct a robustness test for the results. Finally, by comparing the results of two matching methods, the net effect of left-behind on the time of rural adolescents playing video games was obtained.

3 Results

3.1 Descriptive Data of Rural Adolescents

Table 1 shows significant differences between rural left-behind adolescents and rural non-left-behind adolescents regarding individual and family characteristics. Specifically, in terms of individual characteristics, the proportion of attending boarding schools was lower in the rural left-behind group, and the proportion of only children was higher. At the same time, we find no statistically significant differences in gender, grade, and academic achievement between the two groups. Regarding family characteristics, the families of rural left-behind adolescents are more likely to have more social capital and higher income (if we take parents' education level as a proxy for family social capital, as other studies have done), but the parent-child relationship in such families is often weaker. Moreover, the proportion of rural left-behind adolescents' parents (both mother and father) with high school or higher education was higher than that of rural non-left-behind adolescents; and the proportion of rural left-behind adolescents' families with the average and wealthy income was also significantly higher than that of rural non-left-behind adolescents. Finally, the parent-child relationship of rural non-left-behind adolescents was better than that of rural left-behind adolescents.

Table 1. Descriptive data of rural adolescents

Variables	Rural non-left-behind children (N = 1156)	Rural left-behind children (N = 1166)	Difference
	Mean	Mean	
Weekdays minutes (per day)	7.51	7.84	−0.33
Weekends minutes (per day)	31.16	42.85	−11.69***
Gender (male = 1)	0.51	0.51	0
Grade (grade9 = 1)	0.50	0.49	0.01
Whether to board (yes = 1)	0.65	0.48	0.17***
Whether an only child (yes = 1)	0.17	0.25	−0.08***
Academic achievement			
Poor	0.30	0.31	−0.01
Average	0.31	0.28	0.03
Excellent	0.39	0.41	−0.02
Education level of mother			
Middle school education or below	0.87	0.83	0.04***
High school education	0.12	0.15	−0.03**
Higher education	0.01	0.02	−0.01*

(continued)

Table 1. (*continued*)

Variables	Rural non-left-behind children (N = 1156)	Rural left-behind children (N = 1166)	Difference
	Mean	Mean	
Education level of father			
Middle school education or below	0.83	0.77	0.06^{***}
High school education	0.16	0.19	-0.03^{**}
Higher education	0.01	0.04	-0.03^{***}
Parent-child relationship	2.71	2.61	0.10^{***}
Family income	1.80	1.68	0.12^{***}
Poor	0.36	0.25	0.11^{***}
Average	0.61	0.70	-0.09^{***}
Wealthy	0.03	0.05	-0.02^{**}

Notes: (1) $^*p < 0.05$, $^{**}p < 0.01$, $^{***}p < 0.001$

3.2 Factors Affecting the Time Rural Adolescents Spent Playing Video Games

To explore the factors influencing rural adolescents to play video games, we used OLS regression to analyze the specific factors affecting the time rural adolescents spent playing video games, and the results are shown in Table 2. The results of the OLS regression (Table 2) suggested that rural left-behind adolescents spend significantly more time playing video games on weekends than rural non-left-behind adolescents after we control for other variables that may also have an effect on adolescents' time spent playing video games. In addition, some control variables in the OLS regression model can also provide valuable conclusions. For example, boys spent more time playing video games on both weekdays and weekends than girls, and the mothers' education level of higher education significantly and positively predicted the number of time adolescents spent playing video games on weekdays and weekends. In contrast, the parent-child relationship significantly and negatively predicted the amount of time students spent playing video games on weekends.

3.3 The Effect of "Left-Behind" on the Time Rural Adolescents Spent Playing Video Games

We used OLS regression to estimate whether being left behind significantly affects rural adolescents' time spent playing video games after controlling for other factors that may affect rural adolescents' time spent playing video games. Then, the propensity score matching was used for further analysis. The specific results are shown in Table 3.

The PSM results show that after adjusting for observed characteristics, including individual and family factors, rural non-left-behind children spend significantly less time playing video games on weekends than rural left-behind adolescents. At the same time, there is no difference on weekdays. i.e., whether or not left-behind is an essential

Table 2. Results based on OLS estimation

Variables	Weekdays minutes (Per day)	Weekends minutes (Per day)
Whether to be left behind (yes = 1)	0.05	3.95***
Gender (male = 1)	4.01***	6.25***
Grade (grade9 = 1)	0.34	0.81
Whether to board (yes = 1)	−1.92	−0.44
Whether an only child (yes = 1)	−0.87	1.95
Academic achievement		
Average	−3.29**	−1.90
Excellent	−3.84***	−3.84***
Education level of mother		
High school education	1.42	0.33
Higher education	4.03***	2.43**
Education level of father		
High school education	0.95	0.96
Higher education	−0.04	−0.58
Parent-child relationship	−1.93	−3.97***
Family income		
Average	0.73	0.79
Wealthy	0.66	0.17
N	2322	
Adj R^2	0.04	0.05

Notes: (1) **p < 0.01, ***p < 0.001

Table 3. ATT effects based on "whether to be left-behind"

Outcome variables	PSM	
	k-Nearest neighbor matching	Radius matching
Weekdays minutes (per day)	−1.68	−0.02
Weekends minutes (per day)	7.90***	11.04***
N	2322	

Notes: (1) ***p < 0.001 (2) k = 3, caliper = 0.2

factor affecting the time spent playing video games by rural adolescents. Notably, the effect size (when weekends minutes as the dependent variable) became larger when using both k-Nearest Neighbor Matching and Radius Matching, compared with OLS regression.

4 Discussion

The present study explored whether "left-behind" causes rural adolescents to spend more time playing video games in China. And whether there is a difference in the time spent playing video games on weekends and weekdays between left-behind and non-left-behind rural adolescents. The results of the OLS regression and the PSM estimation indicated that rural left-behind adolescents spend more time playing video games than rural non-left-behind adolescents on weekends, not on weekdays in China. Firstly, this result is consistent with previous research showing that left-behind children are more susceptible to playing video games than non-left-behind children [25]. According to Self-determination theory, the emotional needs of left-behind teenagers are difficult to be satisfied due to the lack of parental companionship [26]. Thus, they will play computer games to meet their own needs.

Secondly, this observation aligns with the "Weekend" effect: weekends are the primary time of the week for teenagers to have free time compared to weekdays, and teenagers can choose more of what they want to do [27]. Therefore, since rural left-behind adolescents lack parental supervision and care during weekends, they will spend significantly more playing games than rural non-left-behind adolescents. However, during weekdays, adolescents are mostly in school under the supervision of teachers and do not have much time for entertainment [28], so there is no significant difference between the two in terms of the time they spend playing computer games.

Overall, the results suggest that being "left-behind" causes rural adolescents to spend more time playing video games on weekends, not on weekdays. This result should arouse parents' attention, who should give left-behind children enough care and supervision to regulate the length of time left-behind adolescents play video games. However, it is essential to point out that all items are based on adolescent self-report. In the future, more pathways (e.g., multiple informants and tracking video games' software) to assess the length of playing video games should be considered to confirm the present study results.

References

1. Shen, M., Gao, J., Liang, Z., Wang, Y., Du, Y., Tallones, L.: Parental migration patterns and risk of depression and anxiety disorder among rural children aged 10–18 years in China: a cross-sectional study. BMJ Open 5(12), e007802 (2015)
2. Wang, M., Sokol, R., Luan, H., Perron, B.E., Victor, B.G., Wu, S.: Mental health service interventions for left-behind children in mainland China: a systematic review of randomized controlled trials. Child Youth Serv. Rev. 117, 105304 (2020)
3. Duan, C., Zhou, F.: Studies on left behind children in China. Popul. Res. 25(1), 29–36 (2005)
4. Wu, H., Cai, Z., Yan, Q., Yu, Y., Yu, N.N.: The impact of childhood left-behind experience on the mental health of late adolescents: evidence from Chinese college freshmen. Int. J. Environ. Res. Public Health 18(5), 2778 (2021)

5. Li, X., et al.: Sustained effects of left-behind experience during childhood on mental health in Chinese university undergraduates. Eur. Child Adolesc. Psychiatry **30**(12), 1949–1957 (2020). https://doi.org/10.1007/s00787-020-01666-6

6. Guo, J., et al.: The relationship between Internet addiction and depression among migrant children and left-behind children in China. Cyberpsychol. Behav. Soc. Netw. **15**(11), 585–590 (2012)

7. National Study on Internet Use of Minors 2020. http://www.cnnic.cn/hlwfzyj/hlwxzbg/qsnbg/202107/t20210720_71505.htm. Accessed 15 Oct 2021

8. Anderson, D.R., Huston, A.C., Schmitt, K.L., Linebarger, D.L., Wright, J.C.: Early childhood television viewing and adolescent behavior: the recontact study. Monogr. Soc. Res. Child Dev. **66**(1), 1–147 (2001)

9. Grohol, J.M.: Too much time online: internet addiction or healthy social interactions? Cyberpsychol. Behav. **2**(5), 395–401 (1999)

10. Barrense-Dias, Y., Berchtold, A., Akre, C., Surís, J.C.: The relation between internet use and overweight among adolescents: a longitudinal study in Switzerland. Int. J. Obes. **40**(1), 45–50 (2016)

11. Trumello, C., Babore, A., Candelori, C., Morelli, M., Bianchi, D.: Relationship with parents, emotion regulation, and callous-unemotional traits in adolescents' Internet addiction. Biomed. Res. Int. **2018**, 1–10 (2018)

12. Ning, K., Zhu, Z., Xu, Z.: Internet, time allocation decision and rural teenager health. NanKai Econ. Stud. **4**, 81–104 (2019)

13. Cao, Q., An, J., Yang, Y., et al.: Correlation among psychological resilience, loneliness, and internet addiction among left-behind children in China: a cross-sectional study. Curr. Psychol. (2020). https://doi.org/10.1007/s12144-020-00970-3

14. Ge, Y., Se, J., Zhang, J.: Research on relationship among internet-addiction, personality traits and mental health of urban left-behind children. Glob. J. Health Science **7**(4), 60 (2015)

15. Yan, W., Li, Y., Sui, N.: The relationship between recent stressful life events, personality traits, perceived family functioning and internet addiction among college students. Stress Health **30**(1), 3–11 (2014)

16. Ryan, R.M., Deci, E.L.: Self-determination theory and the facilitation of intrinsic motivation, social development, and well-being. Am. Psychol. **55**(1), 68 (2000)

17. Li, D., Zhang, W., Li, X., Zhou, Y., Zhao, L., Wang, Y.: Stressful life events and adolescent Internet addiction: the mediating role of psychological needs satisfaction and the moderating role of coping style. Comput. Hum. Behav. **63**, 408–415 (2016)

18. Cuong, V.M., Assanangkornchai, S., Wichaidit, W., Minh Hanh, V.T., My Hanh, H.T.: Associations between gaming disorder, parent-child relationship, parental supervision, and discipline styles: findings from a school-based survey during the COVID-19 pandemic in Vietnam. J. Behav. Addict. **10**(3), 722–730 (2021)

19. Xie, X.C., Guo, Q.T., Wang, P.C.: Childhood parental neglect and adolescent internet gaming disorder: from the perspective of a distal—proximal—process—outcome model. Child Youth Serv. Rev. **120**, 105564 (2021)

20. Lee, M.S., et al.: Characteristics of Internet use in relation to game genre in Korean adolescents. Cyber Psychol. Behav. **10**(2), 278–285 (2006)

21. Berchtold, A., Akre, C., Surís, J.C.: The relation between internet use and overweight among adolescents: a longitudinal study in Switzerland. Int. J. Obes. **40**(1), 45–50 (2016)

22. Xu, J., et al.: Personal characteristics related to the risk of adolescent internet addiction: a survey in Shanghai China. BMC Public Health **12**(1), 1–10 (2012)

23. Huston, A.C., Wright, J.C., Marquis, J., Green, S.B.: How young children spend their time: television and other activities. Dev. Psychol. **35**(4), 912 (1999)

24. Zheng, L., Weng, Q., Gong, X.: Does preschool attendance affect the urban-rural cognition gap among middle school students? Evidence from China Education Panel Survey. J. Chin. Sociol. **8**(1), 1–22 (2021). https://doi.org/10.1186/s40711-021-00150-1

25. Li, W., Garland, E.L., Howard, M.O.: Family factors in Internet addiction among Chinese youth: a review of English-and Chinese-language studies. Comput. Hum. Behav. **31**, 393–411 (2014)

26. Fard, Z.S., Mousavi, P.S., Pooravari, M.: Predictive role of parental acceptance, rejection and control in the internet addiction of the female students. Int. J. Appl. Behav. Sci. **2**(3), 42–51 (2015)

27. Yeung, W.J., Sandberg, J.F., Davis-Kean, P.E., Hofferth, S.L.: Children's time with fathers in intact families. J. Marriage Fam. **63**(1), 136–154 (2001)

28. Hartanto, A., Toh, W.X., Yang, H.: Context counts: the different implications of weekday and weekend video gaming for academic performance in mathematics, reading, and science. Comput. Educ. **120**, 51–63 (2018)

Games in Education and Learning

Validating Learning Games, a Case Study

Alessandro Canossa[✉], Alexis Lozano Angulo, and Luis Laris Pardo

The Royal Danish Academy, 1435 Copenhagen, Denmark
acan@kglakademi.dk

Abstract. Serious games (or transformational games) are used to operate transformations on players that range from transferring knowledge to changing players'
sense of self. Since these games have other purposes besides entertainment, it is
necessary to validate them with a whole new set of methods other than the parameters utilized for traditional software or digital games such as stability, usability,
or playability. Most researchers working with serious games provide a section on
validation, but often the methods are developed ad-hoc for each specific case. We
propose a validation methodology able to pinpoint accurately to which specific
game interactions support specific knowledge transfer. We developed a method to
probe both experimental validity (internal and external validity) and test validity
(construct-, content-, criterion-, concurrent-, predictive-, and face validity). In this
article, we demonstrate how such a methodology can be developed and we use
it to validate the impact of the knowledge-transfer game SubSyst Simulator, a
clicker game designed to allow experimentation with concepts of circular economy, sustainable food production and consumption. The method proposed was
able to identify granularly areas where the game was successful at transferring
the intended knowledge as well as aspects of the learning objectives that were
less successful and finally recommend changes to maximize the impact of the
knowledge transfer process. The advantage of the method proposed is the ability
to identify specifically which elements in the game need to be iterated over to
guarantee a successful and enjoyable learning experience.

Keywords: Computer games · Edutainment · Educational games · Game based
learning · Games for learning · Game data analytics

1 Introduction

Serious games are being used in more and more contexts to operate player transformations ranging from skill and/or knowledge acquisition all the way to changing players
sense of self [5]. This widespread adoption is not always followed by scientific trials to
validate the impact and intended effects of these games. The term "validation" itself is
not always used in a consistent manner. As reported by Kato [13] serious games can be
used both as interventions to impact outcomes and as measures to assess performance.
This entails that these games can be validated in at least two ways: a) do they achieve
the effects that they intended to (experimental validity); and b) do they measure the
effect correctly (test validity). These two types of validation are orthogonal as a game

X. Fang (Ed.): HCII 2022, LNCS 13334, pp. 399–413, 2022.
https://doi.org/10.1007/978-3-031-05637-6_25

can provide a good measure for a certain effect while not being particularly successful at achieving the intended effect. For example a game can be successful at assessing student's knowledge but it might not perform very well at transferring said knowledge. Both types of validity are important but obviously indicate very different things. Experimental validation refers to studies that provide adequate evidence that a certain game has the intended effect or transformation (behavior change, knowledge acquisition, etc.). Test validation refers to subjective assessments and correlational studies that show how a certain game measures precisely the values it intended to measure. With this work we propose an iterative methodology for experimental validation of games designed for knowledge transfer, and we apply it to the game SubSyst Simulator [2]. Future work will have to assess the generalizability of such methodology.

1.1 Experimental Validity

Experimental validity refers to whether a game has the effect it was designed for. Experimental validity is expressed in terms of internal and external validity. Internal validity refers to whether a game operates the transformations it was designed to do and whether or not there is sufficient evidence to support the claim that it makes a difference (statistical significance). External validity refers to whether the claimed effects of a game will transfer to target audiences and contexts not included in the experimental study considered for the internal validation, or how generalizable is the effectiveness as it cannot be taken for granted that a game's effectiveness can be assumed valid for every context and type of audience. Internal and external validity are both components of experimental validity and allow researchers to assert the effectiveness of their serious games supported by evidence, at the same time it allows the same researchers to acknowledge the limits of both their effectiveness and their generalizability.

1.2 Test Validity

Serious games are used with the objective of generating a transformation in users [5]. However, it may be unclear which criteria validate this kind of interactive media as an evaluation tool of the performance of players within a certain domain. Games can convey concepts from different areas of knowledge. In this sense, the affordances of gameplay mechanics have led to the development of interactive simulators. Several of these digital tools have been designed, for example, to train individuals in acquiring skills from areas like medicine. When using a serious game to measure the user's competence or behavior, it is essential to understand the components of test validity. Construct validity measures how successful a game is in achieving its transformational objectives. Here it is important to consider what type of knowledge the game is meant to convey or what behavioral change it tries to achieve. Content validity is achieved when a serious game has conveyed information relevant to a specific knowledge domain. Subject matter experts may have to decide how high or low is the content validity of the game. Criterion validity evaluates how the simulation performance translates to outcomes in real situations. This validity component can also be constituted by its concurrence and prediction measures. Concurrent validity refers to how a simulation relates to other tests measuring the same competences. Predictive validity entails a long lasting value of the game's content; when a player's improved performance lasts for a medium or long term in reality after the gameplay sessions, the predictive validity of the simulation is high. Face validity or consensus includes how experts and users perceive the value of the simulation, and if the serious game deploys critical concepts adequately. Increasing face validity may require an iterative process, where the game's development is guided by qualitative and empirical judgements.

1.3 Software Validity

Additionally, since games are software products, there is a third family of validation procedures that applies, namely stability, usability and, specifically for games, playability. Stability testing is a range of activities designed to validate if a software product can function without crashes, beyond established time frames and under high stress levels. Also referred to as Quality Assurance, it entails stress testing, recovery testing, failover testing, resource leaks, error handling verification and variable de-initialization. Generally, the testing activities include the repetitive execution of tests and the comparison of the outcomes. Usability is a measure of product use whereby users achieve concrete objectives in varying degrees of effectiveness, efficiency and satisfaction, within a specific context of use [15]. Playability, also referred to as Player Experience, has been defined as the degree to which a game is fun to play and provides satisfactory experience, with an emphasis on the interaction style and plot-quality of the game; the quality of gameplay [17]. Playability is assessed either experimentally with playtests or with the use of heuristics [6].

2 Previous Work

2.1 Serious Games Validation

Our purpose is not just to design a methodology finalized to experimental validation for a serious game focused on knowledge transfer, but also to use the validation method to help designers refine their game to maximize the potential impact. Gee et al. [22] presented a review of assessment frameworks but all of those frameworks focused on the users' performance and do not provide designers with any information about what to improve to make their game more impactful. Even their proposed GRAND assessment framework consists of a set of questions that basically amounts to a list of heuristics and best practices.

We collected a sample of nine relevant research articles that conducted serious games experimental validation [1, 3, 4, 8, 10, 12, 16, 18, 20]. The articles were collected from the ACM Digital Library using a combination of these keywords: *"serious games, games for impact, persuasive games, educational games, evaluation, impact, validation"*. Subsequently we classified the articles based on types of experimental manipulation, whether they had a control group, if the study entailed a classroom learning scenario, if questionnaires were administered to assess increased knowledge, if they used telemetry and game logs and finally which analytical method was utilized to obtain the results (Table 1). Six out of nine experiments adopted a pre and post questionnaire. Five experiments adopted a *within subjects* design protocol while two adopted a *between subjects* protocol. One group analyzed the data with Wilcoxon signed rank test, while three groups used dependent samples t-test. Based on this survey we developed the method explained in Sect. 4.

Table 1. Summary of methods and findings from the nine research articles selected.

Paper #	1	3	4	8	10	12	16	18	20
Experimental manipulation	Open tasks in real world	Mixed reality with toys	Recreation historical places and items	Real items to simple math operations	Leave AR game in class and test different scenarios	Discuss guidelines on the game, teach about invasive species	Usability learning for undergrad	Using games for data visualization literacy	Teach loops and arrays in an interactive visual way
Open quest.	X				X				
Contr.group							X		X
Classroom learning	X	X	X	X	X		X	X	X
Pre and post quest.	X		X	X			X	X	X
Videos	X				X				
Telemetry					X	X			
Analytical method	Qualitative analysis	Test accuracy (Likert scales)	Comparing pre and post test questionnaires (wilcoxon)	Assessing existing knowledge, telemetry and post questionnaire	t-test based on amount of errors made	No results	Comparing pre and post test questionnaires	Assessing existing knowledge, telemetry and post questionnaire	Comparing pre and post test questionnaires

3   Design Methods

The game SubSyst Simulator was designed following practices borrowed from two fields: frameworks for serious games design and Evidence-Centered Design. In the development of serious games there are two frameworks that have emerged recently as effective tools: the Transformational Framework by Sabrina Culyba [5] and the Triadic Game Design framework by Casper Harteveld [11] we found them to be complementary and utilized both. Evidence-Centered Design (ECD) is a framework that analyzes participants' tasks and actions to derive and inform the evidence and rules that build statistical models to infer the competencies to be measured [21], we found this approach extremely beneficial for two reasons: a) it allowed us to identify simulation variables directly linked to actions in the game that built towards skills, learning objectives and global objectives, and b) sections and items for the assessment questionnaires could be derived directly from the same global objectives and learning objectives.

3.1 Triadic Game Design

Triadic Game Design [11] considers three worlds: reality, meaning and play. The world of reality relates to the domain concepts and subjects addressed in the game. The world of meaning refers to the value and messages deployed by the game. Finally, the world of play refers to the affordances of the game's genre and gameplay mechanics. This triadic framework was used to coherently design the Subsyst Simulator. In this case, the world of reality consists of knowledge about circular economy for food. This subject matter was abstracted into a model of reality. The pillars of this model are the relationships between food, energy, and waste. The world of play (the content and mechanics of the game) was construed based on the model of reality. The world of meaning sees the game as a medium to deploy value or affect the previously mentioned player transformations.

3.2 Transformational Framework

The Transformational Framework [5] can be used as a holistic tool for game development. It has been used by Schell Games and a number of other developers to understand the complexities of a game intended to generate a change in players. The framework focuses on eight criteria: the higher purpose of the project, the audience and its context, player transformations, the barriers preventing such transformations, the domain or subject-matter, expert resources, prior works and the assessment of the transformations. In case of the Subsyst Simulator the transformation was focused on knowledge transfer in a classroom scenario. Culyba elaborated on the Three Hallmarks of a Transformational Game consisting of intention, transfer, and persistence. In this sense, this project's game was designed with the intention of increasing the player's knowledge about food systems. To deploy this transformation, the game visualizes the relationships of food production, consumption and waste processing. The value of the game persists if the intended transformations happen and remain after the gaming session.

3.3 Evidence Centered Design

According to ECD [21], the following are the game's global competencies derived from the Ellen MacArthur Foundation and FAO's reports: 1) Visualize the potential of cities to transform themselves from black holes consuming food, energy, and other resources to regenerative engines of food systems and bioeconomy; 2) reflect about how can resources be "looped" into productive use after consumption or disposal, supporting natural regeneration; and 3) reflect on ways in which the economic, social and environmental costs of food production and food consumption can be reduced. From the three global objectives 12 learning objectives were derived and a skill map was developed. The skill map was then linked to player actions and gameplay mechanics (see Fig. 2). Since the game relies on players' failure to teach important concepts, it is clear that it cannot be used to assess players' performance, therefore we also needed to generate a questionnaire to assess players' knowledge; the skill map was utilized also for this purpose (the full questionnaire is divided in 3 sections that mirror the global objectives; the items, the answers and the scoring table are included in Table 1). Subsequently, the game economy system was developed including include the following systems: food resources; energy resources; processed waste resources; food and energy production methods (small-scale production, industrial scale production, and an agroecological or efficiency method); waste processing methods (waste collection, recycling, composting, and upcycling); socio-economic variables (money, public approval or number of "likes", and population count); and environmental variables (pollution and unprocessed waste, natural capital, and bee population count). The game was balanced using Machinations, an online game design platform [7]. This tool was useful to understand and finetune the general balance and flow of in-game resources. Based on the skill and action graph obtained through the ECD method, we proceeded to define the 36 most important variables that compose the competency model, see Fig. 1. Finally all these game events were instrumented and tracked through telemetry to allow for exploratory analyses and correlations between players' behavior in the game and their performance with the questionnaire.

Fig. 1. Comprehensive list of the 36 variables tracked.

4   Method for Experimental Validation

Looking at the methods utilized to validate the previous work reviewed in Sect. 2.1, we developed an iterative validation methodology. We selected to collect pre-test and post-test questionnaires as well as a *within subjects* protocol to map existing knowledge and any possible improvement after playing the game [9, 19], we chose to randomize the order of the second questionnaire to minimize the risk of habituation. We implemented a telemetry tracking system to collect granular player behavior, we analyzed questionnaire data both with Wilcoxon and with t-test because there are no outstanding outliers and the data is somewhat normally distributed, and t-tests are more appropriate for relatively small sample sizes. The questionnaire was derived from the same global objectives and learning objectives defined during the ECD process that was used to design the game systems and interactions (Fig. 2).

After taking the initial questionnaire participants were asked to play the game for at least 30 min and, the day after, take the questionnaire again, but with items randomized. Only two of the nine examined studies chose to have a control group [4, 8] therefore we also chose to maximize the number of participants and not have a control group. Inspired

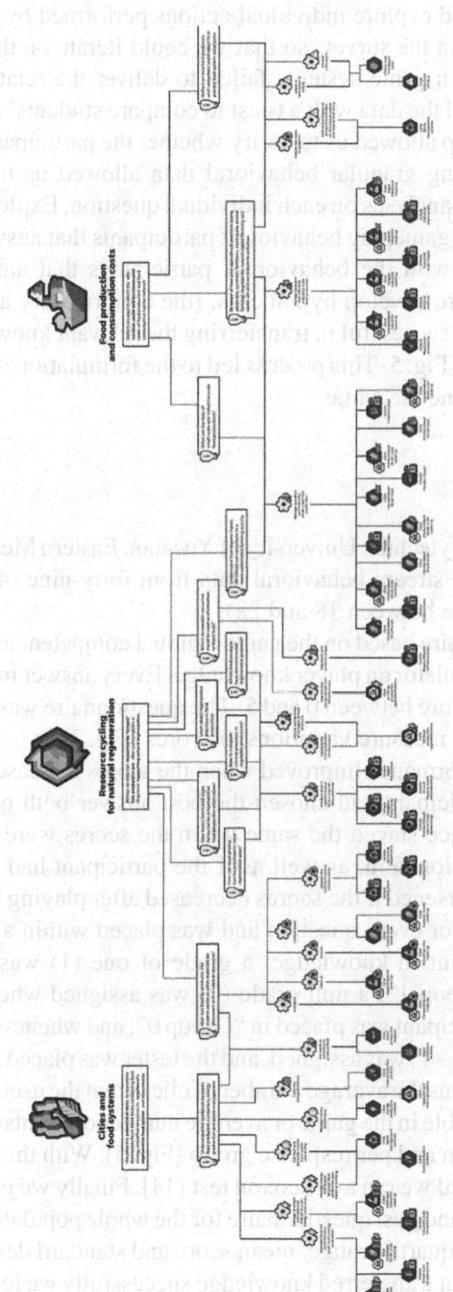

Fig. 2. Skill map defining 3 global objectives (top layer), 13 learning objectives (second layer), 23 skills (third layer) and 50 player actions or game events (fourth layer) according to the ECD framework.

by [12, 20] we decided to implement a remote data collection and telemetry system, collecting data regarding the 36 variables identified through the ECD process and listed in Fig. 1, in this way we could explore individual actions performed by players related to each individual questions in the survey, so that we could iterate on the game design and accurately pinpoint which game systems failed to deliver the related knowledge. Villanueva et al. [20] analyzed the data with a t-test to compare students' results, we also elected to use t-test. This setup allowed us to verify whether the participants' knowledge had been increased. Collecting granular behavioral data allowed us to conduct both exploratory and confirmatory analyses on each individual question. Exploratory analysis consists of comparing logged gameplay behavior of participants that answered correctly in the second questionnaire with the behavior of participants that answered wrong. This comparison allowed us to develop hypotheses, (the confirmatory analysis) on the reason why the game was not successful in transferring the relevant knowledge. Logged behavioral data can be seen in Fig. 5. This process led to the formulation of very concrete suggestions on how to fine tune the game.

5   Results

The game was tested at the Polytechnic University of Yucatan, Eastern Mexico. A telemetry system was configured to stream behavioral data from forty-nine (49) participants (30 males and 19 females, age between 18 and 28).

Furthermore, a questionnaire based on the game's global competencies was designed to assess the impact of the simulator on player knowledge. Every answer in this evaluation tool gave each participant a score between 0 and 5. The questionnaire was applied before and after playing the game to measure variations in scores (Fig. 3).

For each participant, performance improved when the scores increased after playing the simulation, or if the participant had chosen the best answer both before and after playing the game. Performance stayed the same when the scores were equal between each application of the questionnaire, as well as if the participant had not chosen the best answer. Performance worsened if the scores decreased after playing the game. Each participant received a grade for every question and was placed within a group. If there was an observed improvement in knowledge, a grade of one (1) was assigned, and the tester was placed in "Group 1"; a null grade (0) was assigned when performance stayed the same, and the participant was placed in "Group 0"; and whenever performance worsened, a minus one grade (-1) was assigned, and the tester was placed in "Group -1". Behavioral data was collected as the average number of clicks that the users made for each of the actions they have available in the game or average number of events triggered in the game, subdivided per question and per response group (Fig. 5). With the definitions and the data formatted as explained we ran a Wilcoxon test [14]. Finally we produced a table comparing the results for pre and post questionnaire for the whole population, calculating p-values, median score, inter quartile range, mean score and standard deviation (Fig. 4). In order to select questions that transferred knowledge successfully we looked first at the p-values, higher p-values represent less successful participant performances. Therefore, we flagged as problematic questionnaire items with p-values greater than or equal to 0.428. Subsequently we looked at median delta and mean delta and last at the spread

SECT. 1	CITIES AND FOOD SYSTEMS	
Q. 1	Between the following options, which scenario reflects a more sustainable society?	Score
a	Sustaining future human generations through economic growth and the intensive use of natural capital.	1
b	Prioritizing environmental and human wellbeing, necessarily limiting economic growth.	3
c	Sustaining economic growth, the human population, and the environment.	5
Q. 2	Factors influencing a food product's environmental impact are:	
a	The machinery, soil, fertilizers, and food used to grow crops or feed farm animals.	1
b	The greenhouse gases emitted from product transportation and waste.	3
c	The resources used for food production, processing, distribution, food preparation and waste disposal.	5
Q. 3	Considering the following options, what is the most sustainable way in which waste can be processed?	
a	Recycling plastic waste	1
b	Collecting waste in landfills	3
c	Composting	3
d	Upcycling waste	5
SECT. 2	KEEPING RESOURCES IN USE AND REGENERATING NATURAL SYSTEMS	
Q. 4	Which option is an agroecology cycle with the greatest potential to regenerate the environment and use the least amount of resources?	
a	1) Crops grow. 2) Crops are efficiently harvested with machinery. 3) Farmers apply artificial fertilizers. 4) New crops can grow faster.	1
b	1) Crops grow. 2) Inedible crop parts are transported for waste disposal. 3) Organic waste is processed to produce compost. 4) New crops can grow using compost.	3
c	1) Crops grow. 2) Livestock eat crop by-products. 3) Livestock fertilize the soil. 4) New crops can grow	5
Q. 5	Which of these practices has the greatest potential to regenerate the environment?	
a	Using chemical products to protect and increase crop yields.	0
b	Using food by-products to feed livestock, and manure to fertilize crops.	3
c	Nurturing insect farms and algae farms with organic waste.	5
Q. 6	From the following resources, which one may be used to increase crop yields and rebuild farming soils?	
a	Biogas	0
b	Artificial fertilizers	3
c	Compost and organic fertilizers	5
Q. 7	How may unprocessed waste be transformed in the most sustainable way and re-used as a resource?	
a	Recycling materials, such as plastic.	1
b	Using organic waste as nutrients for insect farms.	5
c	Using organic waste to produce compost and biogas.	5
Q. 8	Which of the following activities is the most sustainable practice?	
a	Producing meat to feed a large amount of the population.	1
b	Using organic fertilizers to grow crops and rebuild soil quality.	3
c	Developing insect farms to feed the human population.	5
d	Cultivating or harvesting algae for food.	7
Q. 9	Which of these options processes the greatest amount of waste and generates energy?	
a	Agroecology	1
b	Solar energy	1
c	Biogas production	5
SECT. 3	FOOD PRODUCTION AND CONSUMPTION COSTS	
Q. 10	Which of the following production methods could lead to the greatest farming soil degradation?	
a	Organic fertilizers and compost	0
b	Small-scale farming	3
c	Artificial fertilizers	5
Q. 11	Which of these foods use the most intensive amount of energy for production?	
a	Algae	1
b	Insects	2
c	Vegetables	4
d	Meat	5
Q. 12	Which of these food types generate the smallest quantities of greenhouse gases in their production?	
a	Algae	5
b	Insects	4
c	Vegetables	1
d	Meat	0
Q. 13	Which is the most dangerous potential outcome of both small-scale and industrial scale food production?	
a	Extinction process	0
b	Lost livestock	1
c	Plague	3
d	Soil degradation	5
e	Sick farm animals	5
Q. 14	Which of these food types could feed the greatest number of people?	
a	Algae	1
b	Insects	2
c	Vegetables	4
d	Meat	5

65-72 points scored	Top achievement medal
51-64 points scored	Middle achievement medal
<50 points scored	Low achievement medal

Fig. 3. Questionnaire sections, items, multiple choice answers and scoring table.

(inter quartile range and standard deviation) and complemented our observations based on how many participants improved or decreased their scores. The analysis of the results can be seen in Fig. 4.

Question	p-val	Median pre	IQR pre	Mean pre	SD pre	Median post	IQR post	Mean post	Sd post	Mean Delta	Median Delta
Q 1	0,47	5	2	4,06	1,42	5	3	3,78	1,52	0,28	0
Q 2	0,009	1	4	2,71	1,83	5	2	3,73	1,56	-1,02	4
Q 3	0,017	3	3	2,55	1,65	3	2	3,2	1,59	-0,65	0
Q 4	0,428	3	2	3,37	1,13	5	2	3,37	1,33	0,00	2
Q 5	0,067	5	0	4,22	1,26	6	1	3,8	1,78	0,42	1
Q 6	0,167	5	0	4,31	1,67	6	3	4,04	1,79	0,27	1
Q 7	0	1	1	4,10	1,69	5	1	4,51	1,32	-0,41	4
Q 8	0,003	3	2	3,73	1,45	5	4	4,43	1,68	-0,70	2
Q 9	0,037	1	4	2,71	2,00	5	4	3,29	2	-0,58	4
Q 10	0,33	5	2	3,31	2,28	5	5,25	3,27	2,27	0,04	0
Q 11	0,067	5	0	4,57	1,00	6	1	4,16	1,5	0,41	1
Q 12	0,11	4	4	3,24	1,84	4,5	3,25	3,51	1,73	-0,27	0,5
Q 13	0,68	5	2	3,80	1,99	5	5	3,08	2,11	0,72	0
Q 14	0,91	4	2,25	3,14	1,32	2	4	2,8	1,59	0,34	-2

Fig. 4. Performance of participants for the pre- and post-questionnaire (p-value, median, inter quartile range, mean and standard deviation) subdivided according to the 3 global objectives. The exact wording of the 14 questions can be seen in Fig. 3.

5.1 Analysis

Based on the scores from Fig. 4 we identified the items which revealed the most serious failures in knowledge transfer (questions 13 and 14), light failures (questions 1, 6, 11) or qualitative anomalies (questions 4 and 12) in participant performance. The results show considerable improvements for questions 2, 3, 5, 7, 8, 9 and 10. At this point we needed to understand why the remaining items did not show improvement, which skills and actions they corresponded to and to modify the game to address that portion of knowledge that did not seem to transfer. The questionnaire scores and the telemetry data were correlated to help support a detailed understanding of those questions where the performance improved (knowledge was acquired); those where performance did not change; and those where the participant performance decreased (the game created confusion). For this purpose, we conducted exploratory and confirmatory analyses mentioned in Sect. 4.

Questions 2, 12, and 14 are here analyzed as examples to describe the exploratory approach we adopted (as seem in Fig. 5). The three questions were chosen because they show the best performance (question 2), no improvement (question 12), or worst performance (question 14). In question 2, we identified the variables with the widest proportional difference between the averages of Groups −1, 0, and 1. For example observing the behavioral variables "Insect Small-scale" and "Energy Small-scale", it can be noted that participants from Group −1 (those who decreased in performance) produced Insect Small-scale and Energy Small-scale in higher quantities, compared to the participants in other groups. This behavior suggests that participants with lower-score answers in question 2 were probably concentrated on clicking these variables' buttons; in other words, they were busy trying to survive in the simulation, which prevented some learning opportunities, it in fact not uncommon that gameplay can distract players from absorbing intended knowledge. In question 12 the average production of "Algae Small-scale" for players who did not show any improvement is less than half of the amount produced by players that improved their performance in the questionnaire. Players that did not answer correctly tended to avoid the production of Algae Small-scale. In question 14, we can see that players belonging to group −1 (worsened questionnaire performance) interacted more with variables related to algae and a lot less with production of meat and therefore triggered less cataclysms. Once the game session ended, algae may have been one of the strongest variables, thus creating a bias and leading some players to lower-score answers (this question is analyzed in more detail later).

This method helped us to better understand how users may have learned using our game and where the game failed to transfer knowledge. It also supported the generation of hypotheses – found in Sect. 6 (Discussion) – about ways to improve the knowledge-transfer potential of the game.

6 Discussion

We observed the critical variables that stood out (manifesting significant differences between the gameplay data of players in Group 1 and Group −1) during the exploratory analysis for each of the questions with *serious failures* (13 and 14) *light failures* (1, 6, 11) and *other anomalies* (4 and 12). Based on these observations we found opportunities to holistically improve the knowledge-transfer performance of the simulation.

6.1 Light Failures

Question 1: we observed that the "extinction process" and the "low food yield quality" cataclysms – which are linked to environmental variables (natural capital and bees) – were never triggered by players in group −1, but they were exposed to several cataclysms related to food, energy or waste processing, meaning that these events could be used to improve the players' performance. Suggestions: not all players experienced the cataclysms related to a drop in the natural capital or bee count. The affordances for increasing the players' knowledge could improve if the threshold for these events was lowered and triggered earlier in the game. Adding a 'pause' feature could also give players more time to better understand the status and events within the simulation. Showing hints to alternative paths for economic growth, once cataclysms happen, could support a clearer knowledge-transfer process.

Question 6: we noticed that group −1 upgraded the small-scale production of vegetables almost four times more, and the industrial production of vegetables and waste composting infrastructure approx. three times more than group 1. Suggestions: The participants of group −1 clearly interacted more times with the variables and gameplay mechanics which should lead to the answer with the highest score. Nonetheless, their score decreased. Therefore, the simulation could improve if the composting process and

	Q2						Q12						Q14					
Count of ClickInteraction	Average			Standard deviation			Average			Standard Deviation			Average			Standard Deviation		
Row Labels	-1	0	1	-1	0	1	-1	0	1	-1	0	1	-1	0	1	-1	0	1
Cataclysm Algae Industrial	0.38	0.40	0.32	0.46	0.00	0.81	0.24	0.64	0.29	0.44	0.92	0.64	0.30	0.38	0.38	0.66	0.87	0.50
Catac. Meat Industrial	0.25	0.40	0.26	0.62	0.00	0.60	0.29	0.73	0.05	0.39	0.65	0.22	0.15	0.31	0.44	0.37	0.48	0.45
Catac. Energy Industrial	0.50	0.70	0.35	0.53	0.00	1.02	0.35	1.00	0.24	0.47	1.10	0.62	0.25	0.54	0.63	0.55	0.88	0.50
Catac. Insects Small-scale	0.50	0.30	0.26	0.46	0.00	0.69	0.18	0.73	0.19	0.39	0.79	0.51	0.25	0.46	0.25	0.55	0.78	0.45
Catac. Recycling	0.50	0.40	0.39	0.61	0.00	0.88	0.35	0.73	0.29	0.47	0.65	0.64	0.35	0.38	0.50	0.67	0.65	0.51
Algae Small-scale	117.63	73.30	129.19	110.22	956.72	306.67	67.00	213.27	112.57	77.78	390.68	311.25	134.05	157.08	59.75	314.17	370.45	90.49
Algae Small-scale Upgrade	6.25	4.40	7.29	9.62	0.00	24.99	1.82	16.64	5.05	3.23	31.90	12.73	5.45	9.08	5.81	13.16	28.32	11.84
Algae Industrial Upg.	5.50	4.30	5.94	6.91	0.00	16.73	2.35	13.00	4.19	5.26	20.72	9.48	4.65	8.23	4.44	10.08	19.33	7.35
Energy Small-scale Upg.	8.75	7.80	8.81	8.32	1.41	20.47	5.24	19.45	5.62	5.80	26.44	7.69	6.45	11.92	8.56	7.65	24.95	10.24
Waste collection Upg.	7.13	9.00	7.13	7.40	3.54	15.20	5.35	16.09	4.76	4.86	19.95	6.46	5.50	9.69	8.25	6.02	18.20	9.75
Waste collection	843.13	285.20	296.35	516.07	88.97	837.81	169.65	886.09	216.81	290.38	1077.35	466.25	270.60	568.77	257.38	498.67	1068.96	360.47
Compost Upg.	5.00	8.20	8.48	7.92	0.00	30.29	2.88	23.00	3.95	5.53	39.45	8.58	4.15	13.92	7.56	7.80	37.55	11.43
Insect Industrial Upg.	5.88	4.50	8.77	8.92	0.00	27.43	3.59	22.45	2.87	6.91	36.01	5.90	3.30	14.85	6.56	6.71	34.23	10.49
Insect Small-scale	250.88	16.50	85.90	342.91	67.18	208.04	49.41	303.36	31.33	86.72	557.05	58.80	48.50	258.46	31.56	82.94	520.25	61.59
Insect Small-scale Upg.	4.75	3.50	4.45	7.21	0.00	11.44	1.47	12.82	2.14	2.72	15.64	5.31	2.95	6.00	4.63	6.10	12.75	9.75
Energy Industrial Upg.	12.25	13.70	13.48	12.00	0.00	33.14	8.06	30.00	8.86	8.53	42.88	14.49	8.55	20.23	13.69	14.12	40.20	15.12
Meat Small-scale	240.25	196.50	111.87	125.07	135.06	453.65	156.47	195.64	121.10	335.45	339.60	309.96	204.60	136.00	93.44	419.43	306.67	148.75
Meat Small-scale Upg.	3.13	5.20	6.77	8.42	0.00	17.87	2.88	16.09	2.90	6.58	22.81	7.13	3.50	7.46	7.50	7.84	20.43	11.64
Meat Industrial Upg.	2.25	4.60	8.87	8.12	0.00	37.82	3.41	23.55	1.05	7.88	50.10	3.54	2.10	14.92	6.44	5.67	47.00	11.26
Recycle Upg.	7.00	8.70	8.00	7.99	0.71	28.29	3.29	20.27	4.38	5.88	36.67	9.53	4.40	13.62	6.63	8.32	34.93	9.91
Energy Small-scale	984.75	175.40	391.77	1170.73	259.51	952.41	199.24	1291.64	191.52	327.20	1947.46	437.11	252.90	988.08	232.13	503.70	1882.58	267.58
Upcycle Upg.	3.88	6.10	7.65	7.64	0.00	26.85	3.53	18.45	3.14	5.96	35.80	7.25	2.90	12.00	7.19	5.84	33.27	10.52
Veggies Small-scale	122.00	26.70	52.06	80.85	127.99	143.09	56.35	56.36	80.90	99.93	69.24	128.62	81.10	33.69	49.81	142.02	63.19	76.72
Veggies Small-scale Upg.	5.38	4.60	6.45	9.03	0.00	26.20	1.71	19.18	2.33	3.44	35.63	4.79	3.55	9.23	6.13	6.36	32.39	12.21
Veggies Industrial Upg.	1.88	2.80	4.94	4.79	0.00	17.45	1.59	11.09	2.24	4.86	22.69	5.79	2.90	6.31	3.50	6.61	21.01	6.79
Unlock Algae Small. Upg.	0.88	0.80	0.52	0.97	0.00	0.85	0.47	0.64	0.81	0.72	0.52	0.51	0.75	0.54	0.63	0.60	0.66	0.72
Unlock Algae Industrial Upg.	0.75	0.80	0.52	0.85	0.71	0.89	0.47	1.00	0.52	0.62	0.52	0.81	0.55	0.54	0.75	0.50	1.13	0.86
Unlock Algae Flocculation	0.13	0.40	0.23	0.32	0.00	0.60	0.18	0.36	0.24	0.39	0.50	0.40	0.20	0.23	0.31	0.52	0.44	0.48
Unlock Energy Small. Upg.	0.88	1.00	0.90	0.27	0.00	0.22	0.94	1.00	0.90	0.24	0.00	0.30	0.90	1.00	0.94	0.31	0.00	0.25
Unlock Energy Biogas	0.88	0.40	0.48	0.64	0.00	0.75	0.47	0.64	0.52	0.51	0.50	0.48	0.65	0.38	0.50	0.88	0.51	0.52
Unlock Meat Agroecology	0.25	0.20	0.23	0.32	0.00	0.60	0.18	0.36	0.19	0.39	0.50	0.36	0.20	0.23	0.25	0.52	0.44	0.45
Unlock Compost	0.38	0.80	0.42	0.54	0.00	0.66	0.35	1.09	0.29	0.49	0.50	0.40	0.40	0.46	0.63	0.68	0.48	0.51
Unlock Insect Biowaste	0.25	0.50	0.35	0.40	0.00	0.88	0.24	0.64	0.33	0.44	0.52	0.44	0.25	0.46	0.44	0.55	0.48	0.63
Unlock Veggies Agroecology	0.13	0.50	0.29	0.36	0.00	0.69	0.18	0.55	0.29	0.39	0.52	0.44	0.25	0.23	0.44	0.55	0.38	0.51
Unlock Insects Small. Upg.	0.75	0.50	0.58	0.85	0.00	0.86	0.53	1.00	0.43	0.51	0.52	0.48	0.55	0.69	0.56	0.69	0.51	0.50
Unlock Insects Industrial Upg.	0.63	0.60	0.58	0.75	0.00	0.99	0.41	1.09	0.48	0.62	0.52	0.50	0.35	0.69	0.81	0.49	0.48	0.51
Unlock Energy Industrial Upg.	0.88	0.70	0.58	0.51	0.71	0.41	0.71	0.82	0.52	0.47	0.40	0.51	0.65	0.69	0.63	0.49	0.48	0.50
Unlock Meat Small. Upg.	0.38	0.70	0.71	0.56	0.00	0.58	0.59	1.18	0.43	0.49	0.52	0.48	0.45	0.62	0.94	0.60	0.48	0.63
Unlock Meat Industrial Upg.	0.25	1.00	0.48	0.83	0.00	0.97	0.59	0.73	0.43	0.51	0.50	0.40	0.40	0.46	0.81	0.75	0.51	0.51
Unlock Recycle	0.63	0.70	0.81	0.51	0.71	0.44	0.47	0.82	0.67	0.51	0.40	0.48	0.70	0.46	0.69	0.47	0.52	0.48
Unlock Upcycle	0.50	0.50	0.39	0.61	0.00	0.67	0.41	0.73	0.29	0.49	0.50	0.40	0.40	0.38	0.50	0.68	0.48	0.51
Unlock Veggies Small. Upg.	0.63	0.50	0.55	0.64	0.00	0.81	0.41	0.82	0.52	0.49	0.47	0.50	0.65	0.38	0.56	0.81	0.48	0.52
Unlock Veggies Industrial Upg.	0.25	0.50	0.42	0.54	0.00	0.88	0.41	0.55	0.33	0.49	0.52	0.46	0.30	0.31	0.63	0.47	0.44	0.52
Catac. Veggies Industrial	0.25	0.20	0.13	0.27	0.00	0.47	0.06	0.45	0.10	0.24	0.52	0.30	0.15	0.15	0.19	0.37	0.38	0.40
Catac. Veggies Small.	0.63	0.50	0.19	0.53	0.00	0.60	0.18	0.55	0.33	0.39	0.52	0.44	0.45	0.15	0.31	0.69	0.38	0.48
Total Participants	8	10	31				17	11	21				20	13	16			

Fig. 5. Example of behavioral tracking for question 2, 12 and 14 showing average clicks or average number of events triggered for participants whose performance worsened (group −1), stayed the same (group 0) or improved (group 1).

vegetable upgrades were linked, and if this symbiosis was clearly described. For example, if the player invests in composting, it should be possible to easily produce more vegetables.

Question 11: on average, group −1 invested more in the vegetable, insect, or algae upgrades, compared to meat production. On the other hand, group 1 upgraded the small-scale meat production slightly more and the industrial meat production two times more than group −1. Suggestions: group −1 diversified its food production. Therefore, players could clearly visualize meat's resource consumption if the energy demand significantly increased every time meat production was upgraded.

6.2 Serious Failures

Question 13: we focused our observations on cataclysms related to food production. We were surprised to notice that group −1 triggered this type of cataclysms approximately three or four times more than group 1, on average. Suggestions: The simulation could improve by concretely describing the consequences of cataclysms. More specifically, the "Sick farm animals" cataclysm could be renamed as "Mad cow disease" and include words like "dead cattle". The "Soil degradation" cataclysm could be referred to as "Desertification". The "Plague" cataclysm could be instead referenced as "Fungal infection". Lessening the impact of some cataclysms, like the lost insect livestock and altered algae metabolism, and in contrast, increasing the severity of cataclysms linked to meat and vegetable production could benefit the knowledge transfer affordances. Finally, removing references to "farming" and "small-scale" processes in the cataclysms linked to small-scale vegetable production and industrial meat production could avoid mixing concepts and confusing users.

Question 14: we observed that group −1 diversified its food production, where meat was the most intensely produced food type on a small-scale. We also noticed that group −1 produced every small-scale food type approximately two times more than group 1. Suggestions: Group −1 diversified and intensified its food production, and still did not achieve the highest score in question 14, overall. We observed that food is currently represented in an abstract way as food units in the simulation. Implementing the name "Food Portion" in the top menu and food type descriptions could help players achieve a higher awareness about the food yield provided by each food type.

6.3 Other Anomalies

Question 4: This item's best answer lists the steps of an agroecology cycle with the greatest potential to regenerate the environment and use the least amount of resources: "1) Crops grow. 2) Livestock eat crop by-products. 3) Livestock fertilize the soil. 4) New crops can grow." We observed that group −1 unlocked the vegetable agroecology infrastructure approx. one and a half times more and the cattle agroecology infrastructure almost two times more than group 1. On the other hand, group 1 upgraded the industrial production of meat approx. five times more, and the small-scale production of vegetables almost four times more than group −1. Group 1 also had a 33% chance of triggering the soil degradation cataclysm, while Group −1 did not experience this event.

Suggestions: even though participants within group −1 more likely to unlock agroecology infrastructures, they were not able to answer correctly. The cataclysms related to food production could include information describing agroecology processes more in detail. The probability for these events to happen should be increased as well, since these participants were also less likely to encounter these cataclysms. In relation to the questionnaire, question 4 and its options should be rephrased to convey a clearer connection with the use of agroecology in the simulation.

Question 12: group −1 produced algae, insects, and vegetables to a similar degree on average to group 0 and 1. There are no behavioral markers differentiating participants that answered correctly versus participant that answered incorrectly. Suggestions: the most correct answer for this item is "Algae" – which generates the smallest quantities of greenhouse gases, yet several participants chose insects as the alternative which generates the least amount of greenhouse gases. Since the participants were from Mexico and the Mexican gastronomy includes the use of insects, we considered that this could have generated a cultural bias affecting performance. Modifying the text of cataclysms related to algae and insects, by embedding more concrete consequences to their greenhouse gas emissions could lessen this bias.

7 Conclusions

The method designed to validate the knowledge transfer potential of SubSyst Simulator has shown clear success of the game as a learning tool while at the same time pointing out in details the systems, interactions and mechanics where the game can be improved and its impact increased even more. Future work could include repeating the experiment with a control group and analyzing the result using Analysis of Covariance (ANCOVA) to compare the difference in pretest versus posttest improvement while accounting for control conditions. At the same time, in order to prove the potential generalization of the proposed framework, it will be necessary to focus on applying the method to other knowledge transfer games.

References

1. Aloba, A., et al.: From board game to digital game: designing a mobile game for children to learn about invasive species. In: Extended Abstracts Publication of the Annual Symposium on Computer-Human Interaction in Play, pp. 375–382, October 2017
2. Angulo, A.L., Pardo, L.L., Canossa, A.: Subsyst simulator: an interactive infographic for knowledge transfer. In: Proceedings of the 13th International Symposium on Visual Information Communication and Interaction, pp. 1–5 (2020)
3. Barbatsis, K., Economou, D., Papamagkana, I., Loukas, D.: 3D environments with games characteristics for teaching history: the VRLerna case study. In: Proceedings of the 29th ACM International Conference on Design of Communication, pp. 59–66, October 2011
4. Benitti, F.B.V., Sommariva, L.: Evaluation of a game used to teach usability to undergraduate students in computer science. J. Usability Stud. 11(1), 21–39 (2015)
5. Culyba, S.: The Transformational Framework: A Process Tool for the Development of Transformational Games. ETC Press (2018)

6. Desurvire, H., Wiberg, C.: Game usability heuristics (PLAY) for evaluating and designing better games: the next iteration. In: Ozok, A.A., Zaphiris, P. (eds.) OCSC 2009. LNCS, vol. 5621, pp. 557–566. Springer, Heidelberg (2009). https://doi.org/10.1007/978-3-642-02774-1_60
7. Dormans, J.: Machinations: elemental feedback structures for game design. In: Proceedings of the GAMEON-NA Conference, vol. 20, pp. 33–40, August 2009
8. Eagle, M., Barnes, T.: Wu's castle: teaching arrays and loops in a game. In: Proceedings of the 13th Annual Conference on Innovation and Technology in Computer Science Education, pp. 245–249, June 2008
9. Ellen MacArthur Foundation. Cities and Circular Economy for Food. Ellen MacArthur Foundation (2019). https://www.ellenmacarthurfoundation.org/assets/downloads/Cities-and-Circular-Economy-for-Food_280119.pdf. Accessed 4 June 2020
10. Gäbler, J., et al.: Diagram safari: a visualization literacy game for young children. In: Extended Abstracts of the Annual Symposium on Computer-Human Interaction in Play Companion Extended Abstracts, pp. 389–396, October 2019
11. Harteveld, C.: Triadic Game Design: Balancing Reality, Meaning and Play. Springer, London (2011). https://doi.org/10.1007/978-1-84996-157-8
12. Kang, S., et al.: ARMath: augmenting EverydaLife with math learning. In: Proceedings of the 2020 CHI Conference on Human Factors in Computing Systems, pp. 1–15, April 2020
13. Kato, P.M.: What do you mean when you say your serious game has been validated? Experimental vs. Test Validity, 25 April 2013. http://www.webcitation.org/6gt9POLIu
14. Kloke, J., McKean, J.: Nonparametric Statistical Methods Using R. CRC Press, Boca Raton (2014)
15. ISO 9241-11: Guidance on Usability, also issued by the International Organization for Standardization (1998)
16. Powers, D.M., et al.: Language teaching in a mixed reality games environment. In: Proceedings of the 1st International Conference on Pervasive Technologies Related to Assistive Environments, pp. 1–7, July 2008
17. González Sánchez, J.L., Padilla Zea, N., Gutiérrez, F.L.: Playability: how to identify the player experience in a video game. In: Gross, T., et al. (eds.) Human-Computer Interaction – INTERACT 2009, pp. 356–359. Springer, Heidelberg (2009). https://doi.org/10.1007/978-3-642-03655-2_39
18. Schrier, K.: Using augmented reality games to teach 21st century skills. In: ACM SIGGRAPH 2006 Educators Program, p. 15-es (2006)
19. Scialabba, N.: Food wastage footprint & Climate Change. Food and Agriculture Organization of the United Nations (2015). http://www.fao.org/3/a-bb144e.pdf. Accessed 4 June 2020
20. Villanueva, A., Zhu, Z., Liu, Z., Peppler, K., Redick, T., Ramani, K.: Meta-AR-App: an authoring platform for collaborative augmented reality in STEM classrooms. In: Proceedings of the 2020 CHI Conference on Human Factors in Computing Systems, pp. 1–14, April 2020
21. Yarnall, L., Haertel, G.: CIRCL primer: evidence-centered design. In: CIRCL Primer Series (2016). http://circlcenter.org/evidencecentered-design
22. Gee, D., et al.: Assessing serious games: the GRAND assessment framework (2014)

Do We Speak the Same Language?
The Effect of Emojis on Learners
in an Online Learning Environment

Wad Ghaban(✉)

University of Tabuk, Tabuk, Saudi Arabia
wghaban@ut.edu.sa

Abstract. Emojis are quickly spreading in text-based communication. Accordingly, most students and teachers in an online learning environment integrate their online text communication with emojis to explain or support their perspective. However, because of the variation in students and teachers' age, gender and culture, it was essential to ensure that students and teachers have the same understanding of used emojis. Consequently, we ran our study to ask students and teachers about their interpretations of the most common emojis. The results show moderate agreement between students and teachers. For example, 👌 was interpreted as 'perfect' by students and 'punishment' by teachers. This variation in interpretation must be resolved to ensure acceptable online communication between students and teachers.

Keywords: Online learning · Motivation · Emoji · Interpretation · Misunderstanding

1 Introduction

Online learning has become very popular in recent years, especially during the COVID-19 pandemic in 2020. By that time, most countries had gone into lockdown and were social distancing. Thus, education in most countries was forced online. Most researchers have shown the benefits of online learning as a replacement for traditional learning during the pandemic. However, one of the major limitations of online learning is the lack of physical interaction and body language [13]. Hence, social interactions and informal contact between students and teachers in online learning are essential to motivate students. [8] note that the use of nonverbal interactions with text when contacting students can help to represent facial expressions, for instance. For example, students and teachers can use emoticons, stickers and emojis to represent their feelings, thoughts and opinions.

An emoji is defined by [15] as a graphic icon that can be identified by a Unicode character. This icon has a certain meaning. Thus, it is expected to be interpreted similarly by different users. However, [1] argued that the presentation

X. Fang (Ed.): HCII 2022, LNCS 13334, pp. 414–426, 2022.
https://doi.org/10.1007/978-3-031-05637-6_26

of an emoji can vary across platforms. A smiley icon on an iPhone can be presented as a sad icon on another platform. Furthermore, some researchers claimed that the interpretation of emojis might diverge between users, even if they are using the same platform [2]. This distinction can occur because of a user's age, gender, culture and context [2]. For example, the 'wow' emoji 👌, known as the 'okay' sign, is considered the most important gestural icon and is interpreted as a positive sign. However, in some Asian countries, this emoji can be interpreted as 'fine' in some places or 'less' in others. It also means 'zero' in Tunisia. In some countries, such as Greece and Turkey, this sign can represent rude intentions [8].

Because of variations in the interpretation of emojis, we conducted this research. The aim is to ensure that all students and teachers in the online learning environment have the same understanding and interpretation of the most-used emojis. We ran our research in two stages. In the first, we asked teachers about the most common emojis they used. Then, we used the results from the first stage to ask 84 students and 18 teachers about their interpretations and their understanding of the emojis. We then measured the agreement between students and teachers. The results reveal moderate agreement between students and teachers that could improve the quality of communication.

2 Background

A lack of motivation is considered a major issue in online learning for several reasons, including feelings of isolation. Hence, a social presence is vital in online learning [8]. However, researchers have argued that text communication may not be enough for students because of the lack of body language and facial expressions. Consequently, non-verbal communication is recommended and became very popular in any communication channel. For example, emoticons, the use of special characteristics to represent the emotions associated with a situation, were used in text-based communication as early as 1980 [8]. For example, people usually posted a smiley face as :) and a sad face as :(. Emoticons were followed by emoji, the small graphic icon that can represent a wide range of concepts, ideas and feelings, such as a picture of animals, flowers and a variety of facial expressions [14]. Many papers and users mix emojis and emoticons. According to [14], this can happen for two reasons. The first is the similarity in the spelling of both emojis and emoticons, and the second is because some programs, such as Microsoft Word, automatically convert emoticons – for example :) – to emojis (e.g., ☺). Emojis have been very popular in recent years. Indeed, [5] demonstrated that at least 50% of posts on Instagram include emojis. Furthermore, [12] indicated there are now more than 1,282 available emojis.

[14] show that people use emojis in online communication for several reasons. For example, they use them to express feelings, avoid misunderstandings and have fun. Meanwhile, [7] note that using emojis can be helpful in strengthening users' opinions and adjusting the tone of a conversation.

However, researchers also have argued there are variations in the use and understanding of emojis between users, according to factors such as age, gender and context. For example, [6] demonstrate that emojis are used frequently among females. [7] proved females use emojis more than males. Younger children use emojis even more. Moreover, users varied in their usage of emojis based on their personalities. [9] highlight that users who score highly in conscientiousness and are more self-controlled are usually less likely to use emojis. If they do use them, they usually prefer positive emojis, such as ☀. In contrast, highly introverted users prefer to represent themselves using emojis. Highly extroverted users usually prefer to use positive emojis. Neurotic users have unstable emotions, which render their use of emojis different. However, if they do use emojis, they usually prefer to use negative emojis, such as ☹. Highly agreeable users prefer to use emojis, such as ❤.

Emojis vary based on the context. [3] analysed texts on Instagram and found familiar emojis used frequently based on the image. For example, images alluding to gyms are usually integrated with the emoji 💪.

In addition, the usage of emoji varies among continents. As [10] indicated, Asia has the highest usage of emojis at 26.3%, followed by South America at 20.9%. Europe came in third place with 16.7% and, finally, Australia with 13.7%. In addition, the kind of emoji changes based on the region. For example, North Americans, Western Europeans and Russians usually employed emojis lacking explicit emotion. They used emojis that represent weather, such as ☀, or natural occurrences, such as the palm tree 🌴. Conversely, South Americans, Indians and the Chinese used more positive emojis, such as smiling faces with sunglasses 😎, the winking face 😉 and the closed-eyes kissing face 😚. In third world countries, like Saudi Arabia and Jordan, the dominant emojis are unhappy faces, such as loudly crying faces 😭 and sleepy faces 😪.

[4] illustrate that the use of emojis in text-based communication has a positive effect on users. In their results, the users were happier when they used emojis in marketing and advertisements. Thus, users make more purchases regarding existing emojis, especially positive ones. However, the understanding of emojis can vary between users. According to [14], users usually interpreted emojis as positive if they were in asynchronous communication and negative if they were in synchronous communication. Furthermore, users understand emojis differently based on their culture. One example is two yellow hands placed or clapped together 🙏, which represents an apology in Japan. In India, the same emoji is used for praying [8]. In addition, the presence of emojis also varies between platforms, considered another reason for the distinct interpretations of emojis [11]. Because of all these variations in the presentation and the interpretation of emojis, it was essential to understand whether the students and teachers agreed on the meaning of emojis when they were presented in the online learning platform or in text-based communication channels.

3   Research Question

Based on what is mentioned above, it is clear that emojis are spreading quickly and have become an essential part of online communication. Therefore, it is important to investigate the usage of emojis in online learning. Correspondingly, this paper will try to answer the following questions:

- How popular are emojis in online learning environments?
- What are the most common emojis used in online learning?
- Do students and teachers interpret emojis in the same way?

4   Methodology

This paper investigates whether students and teachers interpret emojis in the same way. Because of the lack of information related to the most popular emojis used in the online learning environment and the difficulty in evaluating all emojis, we ran our study in two separate stages. First, to understand teachers' usage of emojis, we asked 73 teachers from four different schools in Saudi Arabia, aged between 21 and 40, to complete a questionnaire related to emojis. The questionnaire comprised two sections. The first section obtained demographic information about the teachers, such as their age, gender, country where they were born, and how many years they had lived in Saudi Arabia. The second section of the questionnaire used to ask teachers about the most common emojis they usually used. Also, as we believed that the culture and place of residence can influence the use of emojis and their meanings, and as the appearance of emojis is different from one platform to another, we also asked the teachers about which platform they used. The second stage of the questionnaire used the most common emojis chosen by the teachers in the previous stage and the ones mentioned in the existing literature. The questions that are provided to the teachers are as follows:

- Age
    - Less than 20
    - Between 21 and 30
    - Between 31 and 40
    - More than 41
- Gender
    - Male
    - Female
    - Other
- Where did you born?
    - Saudi Arabia
    - Egypt
    - Jordan
    - Others, ...
- How many years do you live in Saudi Arabia?
    - less than 2 years
    - Between 3 and 5 years
    - Between 6 and 10 years

> • More than 11 years
> – How many devices you used in online learning platforms?
>   ....
> – Which device you are used in online learning?
>   • Apple iPhones
>   • SAMSUNG phones
>   • LG phones
>   • others, please specify ....
> – Are you using emojis in contacting with students?
>   • Yes
>   • No
>   • I don't know
> – Mention or draw at lease 5 emojis that you are commonly used in online learning?

Before commencing our data collection, we obtained an ethical agreement from schools, parents, students and teachers to participate in our study and clarified the purpose of the study. The participants were informed that all data were encrypted and saved securely. The final sample included 84 students (25 boys and 59 girls) from six different primary school students in Saudi Arabia aged 9–11 years and a sample of 18 teachers (all female) who taught the students different modules. Table 1 shows information about the participants. At the time the study was conducted, the primary school was running remotely and all classes were conducted online via Zoom. Further, teachers and students used a WhatsApp group for each module to exchange materials and assignments.

Table 1. The statistics related to the participants

		Device used			Country			How many years live in Saudi Arabia			
		Apple iPhone	Samsung phone	Other	Saudi	Jordan	Egypt	Less than two years	3–5 years	6–10 years	More than 11 years
Students	Boys	2	4	19	10	1	14	1	7	0	17
	Girls	14	2	43	23	18	18	2	4	13	40
Teachers	Girls	13	6	14	5	3	10	1	3	6	8

All students and teachers in this study were familiar with online classes and how to interact with each other online, as they had conducted their classes online in 2020 and 2021. Thus, in 2021, we asked students and teachers to complete a questionnaire to obtain similar demographic information to that obtained in the first stage. After that, we printed 24 of the most common emojis separately on A5 paper (Fig. 1 shows the chosen emojis) and presented this paper to each teacher and student individually and in a different order. We presented the A5 paper three times for the learners on three different occasions (the first by 14th

November 2021, the second by 28th November and the third by 12th December). Each time, we presented 10th. Emojis and asked the students and teachers to answer the following questions for each emoji:

- Have you ever seen or used this emoji before?
- In 10 words or less, what do you think this emoji means?
- In one or two words, how would you describe this emoji if you had to use it?
- Evaluate this emoji as either positive, neutral or negative.

Fig. 1. The emojis used in the study

5   Results

In the first stage, the teachers were asked about the communication platform and channel used by the teachers. Of the teachers, 38% used Samsung phones, 60% used Apple Phones and 2% used Hawaii tablets. Further, 73% of the teachers claimed that they used two devices in the online lesson. For example, they used their personal computers and laptops to present the lessons, and they used their phones to communicate with the students and answer their questions via the chat box integrated into the online learning platform, such as Zoom and Microsoft Teams. Further, 90% of teachers also used WhatsApp and Messenger to discuss students' mistakes or to motivate them either individually or in a class group. We asked the teachers about the most preferable and usable emojis. The answers included various face and gesture emojis to show how much they liked and disliked the students' work. Further, some of the teachers claimed that the most common emojis varied depending on the students' gender. For example, to like the work accomplished by a male student, the teachers would use a thumb-up or a flexed arm. However, in the case of a female student, the teachers would use a face emoji with a heart or just a heart. The teacher also used some other special icons, such as red and yellow circles, to get students to pay attention and give warnings. Table 2 and Fig. 2 show the top 10 most commonly used emojis.

Table 2. The most common used emoji based on teachers' questionnaire

The emoji	The percentage of usage
	10%
	12%
	15%
	17%
	20%
	26%
	27%
	40%
	30%
	33%
	34%
	39%
	40%
	40%
	42%
	43%
	50%
	54%
	55%
	59%
	60%
	63%
	64%
	64%
	70%
	73%
	73%
	80%
	88%
	88%
	100%

In the second stage, we asked teachers and students about their emoji usage and found that both teachers and students frequently used emojis in their contact and collaboration with others. We also asked both the teachers and students about their interpretations of the commonly used emojis. Figure 3 shows two examples of the participants' answers about the meaning of emojis. The findings showed that most of the teachers and students agreed on the meaning of most of the emojis. However, they interpreted a few emojis differently. For example, all

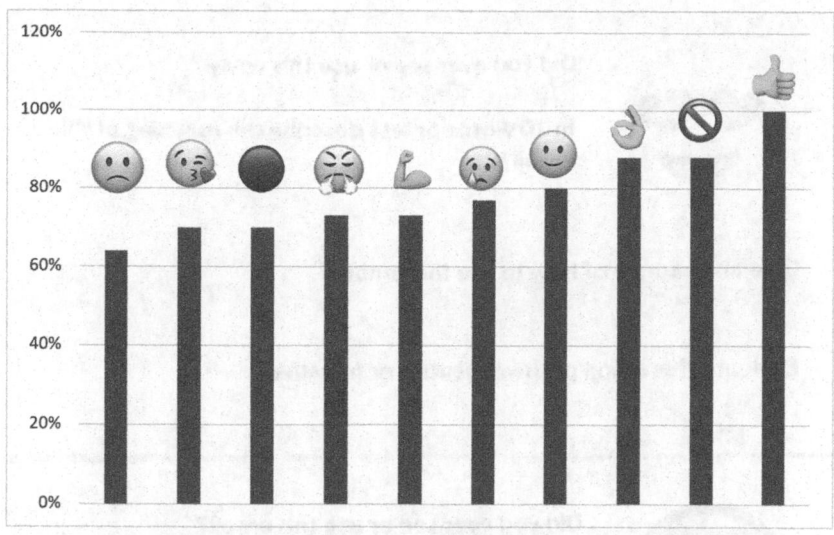

Fig. 2. The emojis used in the study

of the teachers agreed that the smile emoji is a positive emoji and it means 'well done' when it is posted for a student. However, some of the students interpreted this emoji to mean that their answer was acceptable, but not perfect, and could be better. Regarding the tears of joy emoji, all the students said it was a sign of happiness, but two of the teachers used this emoji when the students were making too much noise to show that they were crying from anger. Students reported posting a sleep face to indicate that they were feeling tired or sleepy. However, some of the teachers understood that to mean the student was sick. Most of the teachers claimed that they did not understand the meaning of the anxious face with sweat, but they believed it to be negative. However, the students often used that emoji to indicate that they did not know the answer when called upon by the teacher. While most of the teachers and students agreed on the meanings of the face emojis, there were some differences in their interpretations of the gesture emojis. For instance, the students interpreted the crossed fingers 🤞 emoji as a request by the teacher to pay attention or focus. However, the teachers used this gesture to wish the students luck. The students and a few of the teachers interpreted the pinched fingers 🤌 emoji as a sign to wait or be patient. However, other teachers used this emoji to indicate a punishment or notify the student of a mistake. Additionally, while students interpreted the ok-hand 👌 emoji to mean perfect, the teachers interpreted it as wishing good luck or, contrastingly, as a punishment. Table 3 shows interpretations for each emoji mentioned by the teachers and students.

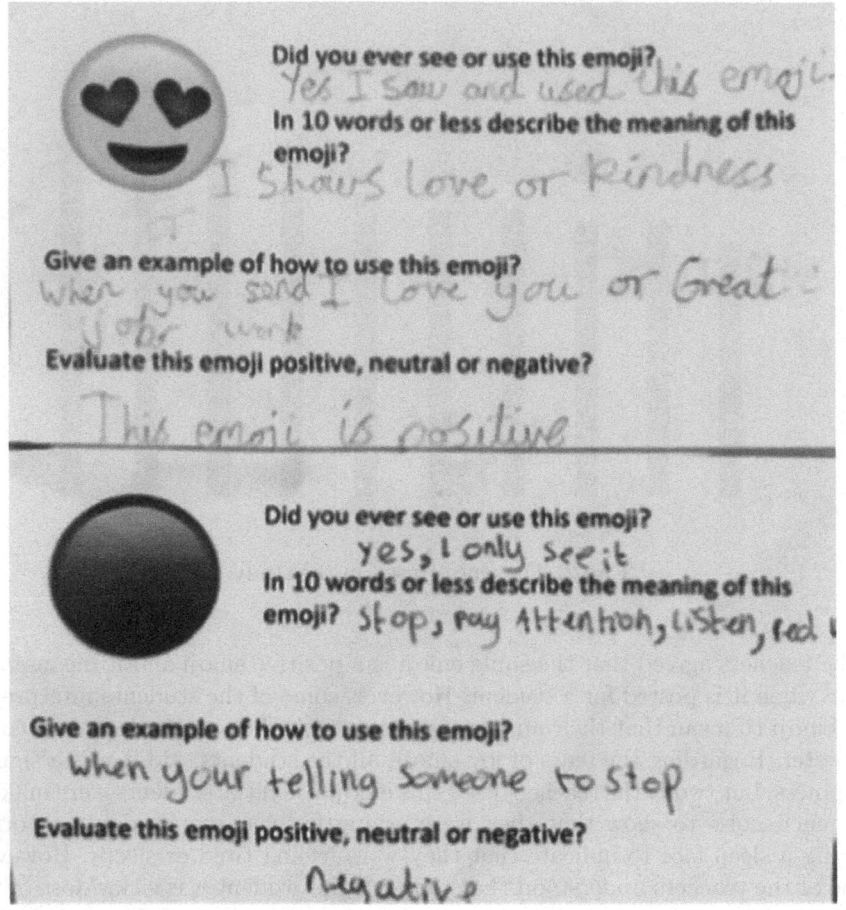

Fig. 3. An example of participants' answer for questionnaire

We also asked the participants to evaluate each emoji as either positive (1), neutral (0) or negative (−1). To analyse the agreement between students and teachers, we used the interclass correlation coefficient. Thus, we first measured the agreement between the teachers and the students as separate groups. We found strong agreement between the student group (0.91) and the teacher group (0.88). In the next step, we measured the agreement between the students and the teachers. The results showed an agreement of 0.73, indicating moderate agreement between the students and the teachers.

Table 3. The interpretation of the most used emojis

The emoji	Students			Teachers	
	Victory	Winning		Good job	
	Attention	Focus	Be happy	Good luck	
	Silly	by mistake	sorry	Happy	
	Surprised	Amazed	Disbelief	Surprised	
	Pray	Belief		Pray	
	Good job		Like	Like	
	Grateful	happy	Shy	happy	
	Pray	Hope	Luck	Pray	Wishing luck
	relief	sorry	by mistake	sorry	
	shocked	surprised		shocked	
	Love it			Love it	
	Good job	Nice work		Good	
	Bad	Mad	Horrible	Bad	
	Wait	Few minutes	Be patient	Wait	Punishment
	Exhausted	Tired	Not good	Give up	
	Sweating	Tired		Tired	Enough
	Funny	Laugh	Silly	Funny	Sad
	How come	I don't understand	Hard	Difficult	Need explain
	Satisfy	Happy	Like	Happy	
	Excellent	Well done	Proud of you	Good job	Perfect
	Angry	very bad	Trouble	Angry	
	Sad	Sorry		Sad	
	Love	very good		Like	
	Mad	Bad behaviour	Horrible	Bad	
	Sorry			sorry	
	Perfect	very good	delicious	luck	punishment
	very bad	Terrible		bad	
	I can	Brilliant	Well done	Work hard	
	Not allowed			Not allowed	
	Pay attention	Important	Stop	Warning	important
	Attention			To be informed	

6   Discussion

The use of emojis is very popular in online communication, including interactions between students and teachers in the online learning environment. However, [14] show that the interpretation of emojis varies depending on factors such as age, gender and culture. Therefore, we examined whether any differences existed in the students' and teachers' understandings of emojis. Therefore, first, we investigated the most commonly used emojis in online learning platforms, and second, we selected a sample of emojis and asked the students and teachers about the meanings of these emojis.

The results confirmed the results from the literature. For example, our results confirmed the results obtained from [10] as the most common used emojis in Saudi Arabia is crying loudly 😭 and the joy crying from the happiness 😂.

The results also show that most teachers use both face and gesture emojis and that most of the teachers and students agreed on the meanings of the face emojis, such as the 😕, 😖 and 👍. However, there are still variations in the interpretation of some emojis, such as 👌 and 👏.

The difference in interpretation can be explained, as suggested by [7], by the age difference between the students and the teachers. Most of the teachers in our study were older than 25 years, while the students were between 9 and 11 years of age. Thus, their interests and the way they usually communicated differed. The participants' cultures might also have affected the results. Some of the participants were from Jordan and Egypt. However, as some of them had lived in Saudi Arabia for more than 10 years, they gained some of the Saudi culture. For example, the emoji 👌 was interpreted by some of the students and teachers as good or perfect as in Saudi culture, while others interpreted this emoji to mean that you did something bad. Further, the emoji 😂 is also interpreted differently. Some explained it as a crying face, and others explained it as tears of joys.

Various factors limit the generalisation of the results from this study. First, this paper examined only a few emojis because we used the ones most commonly used by a limited number of teachers. Other teachers may choose different emojis. Second, the data obtained from the results may be inaccurate, as they can be affected by various factors. For example, variations between teachers' and students' backgrounds can affect the results. Third, the results of this study may not be reliable, as they are based on a subjective questionnaire. Therefore, future studies should collect a sample of the chats conducted between teachers and students to obtain and analyse frequently used emojis. Using this method, we can analyse more realistic data. Further, future studies could be controlled by examining teachers and students with the same background. After collecting data, we can also analyse and find the most common emoji by using clustering and then evaluate each cluster by using sentiment analysis. Further, we can also find out the most acceptable emoji for users based on their personality. By using the most favourite emoji for each students, we can improve their motivation and engagement.

7   Conclusion

In recent years, online learning, through which learners can have their lessons at any time and in any place, has become very popular, especially during the COVID-19 lockdowns. However, one of the main limitations of online learning is the lack of motivation experienced by learners as a result of feeling isolated. For this reason, social interaction between learners and teachers in the online environment is very important. Emojis are usually incorporated into this kind of interaction to help students explain their ideas or to assist in sharing their viewpoints. However, students and teachers vary in age and gender. They also come from different countries with different backgrounds. As a result, the meaning and interpretation of emojis vary between users based on their age, gender, personality and culture. For example, [14] discovered that males and females use emojis differently. Furthermore, emojis are more popular among younger children than adults.

For the above reasons, it was important to build a strong understanding of emojis and how they are interpreted by students and teachers. For that, we ran our study in two stages: (1) we asked teachers about the most common emojis, and then (2) we asked students and teachers to evaluate and interpret a sample of emojis. The results show that students and teachers enjoy using emojis when talking with each other and that they interpret most emojis equally. However, there are some variations in the interpretation of emojis between boys and girls. This can be explained by different factors, such as the difference in age between students and teachers. Also, students and teachers come from different countries and various backgrounds.

The results of our study cannot be generalised, as our results are based on subjective measurements that were obtained from a sample of students 9–11 years old. Also, we used a very small number of emojis that are considered to be the most common. Therefore, future studies should be conducted with a larger sample and participants of different ages. Furthermore, we may be able to use one of the machine learning algorithms to measure how students' and teachers' interpretations of emojis are similar. The results from these studies can be combined to identify the most suitable emojis for students based on, for instance, their age and personality. These emojis can later be used to motivate students by posting emojis that are easier to understand and preferred by students.

References

1. Annamalai, S., Salam, S.: Undergraduates' interpretation on WhatsApp smiley emoji. Jurnal Komunikasi, Malays. J. Commun. **33**(4), 89–103 (2017)
2. Ares, G., Vidal, L., Jaeger, S.R.: How do consumers use emoji in a food-related context? Insights for the design and interpretation of emoji questionnaires. J. Sensory Stud. **36**(4), e12663 (2021)
3. Barbieri, F., Ballesteros, M., Ronzano, F., Saggion, H.: Multimodal emoji prediction. arXiv preprint arXiv:1803.02392 (2018)
4. Das, G., Wiener, H.J., Kareklas, I.: To emoji or not to emoji? Examining the influence of emoji on consumer reactions to advertising. J. Bus. Res. **96**, 147–156 (2019)
5. Eisner, B., Rocktäschel, T., Augenstein, I., Bošnjak, M., Riedel, S.: emoji2vec: learning emoji representations from their description. arXiv preprint arXiv:1609.08359 (2016)
6. Herring, S.C., Dainas, A.R.: Receiver interpretations of emoji functions: a gender perspective. In: Proceedings of the 1st International Workshop on Emoji Understanding and Applications in Social Media (Emoji2018), Stanford, CA (2018)
7. Herring, S.C., Dainas, A.R.: Gender and age influences on interpretation of emoji functions. ACM Trans. Soc. Comput. **3**(2), 1–26 (2020)

426   W. Ghaban

8. Kousar, A., Memon, S., Simming, I.A.: The pragmatic analysis of 👍, 👍, 👍 emojis by ESL learners in verbal modalities: a case study of whatsapp chat. IJCSNS **20**(10), 199 (2020)
9. Li, W., Chen, Y., Hu, T., Luo, J.: Mining the relationship between emoji usage patterns and personality. In: Proceedings of the International AAAI Conference on Web and Social Media, vol. 12 (2018)
10. Ljubešić, N., Fišer, D.: A global analysis of emoji usage. In: Proceedings of the 10th Web as Corpus Workshop, pp. 82–89 (2016)
11. Miller, H., Kluver, D., Thebault-Spieker, J., Terveen, L., Hecht, B.: Understanding emoji ambiguity in context: the role of text in emoji-related miscommunication. In: Proceedings of the International AAAI Conference on Web and Social Media, vol. 11, pp. 152–161 (2017)
12. Miller, H.J., Thebault-Spieker, J., Chang, S., Johnson, I., Terveen, L., Hecht, B.: "Blissfully happy" or "ready tofight": varying interpretations of emoji. In: Tenth International AAAI Conference on Web and Social Media (2016)
13. Sher, A.: Assessing the relationship of student-instructor and student-student interaction to student learning and satisfaction in web-based online learning environment. J. Interact. Online Learn. **8**(2), 102–120 (2009)
14. Tang, Y., Hew, K.F.: Emoticon, emoji, and sticker use in computer-mediated communication: a review of theories and research findings. Int. J. Commun. **13**, 27 (2019)
15. Tigwell, G.W., Flatla, D.R.: Oh that's what you meant! reducing emoji misunderstanding. In: Proceedings of the 18th International Conference on Human-Computer Interaction with Mobile Devices and Services Adjunct, pp. 859–866 (2016)

Multisensory Collaborative Play: Online Resources for Parents of Children with Autism Spectrum Disorder

Mohamad Hassan Fadi Hijab(✉) , Bilikis Banire, and Dena Al-Thani

Information and Computing Technology Division, College of Science and Engineering, Hamad Bin Khalifa University, Doha, Qatar

{mhhijab,bobanire,dalthani}@hbku.edu.qa

Abstract. Switching from face-to-face learning to online learning due to the COVID-19 pandemic is challenging for students especially for children with autism spectrum disorder (ASD). Parents and caregivers of children with ASD struggle when adjusting to the new situation due to the lack of online support-ive educational resources. This paper explores two different mediums for online learning resources; which are mobile applications and videos. The strengths and limitations of 11 mobile applications and two websites on educational videos were highlighted and compared using customized rubrics adapted from existing stud-ies. Findings show that the existing applications require content enhancements, dynamic children-directed layout design and free access to a number of the con-tents. The reviewed videos on two different websites have quality content but lack explicit subject categorization as well as filtering features to help parents and care-givers access desired videos. Evaluation of online learning experience for children with ASD is still in its infancy and requires further research, especially in content development.

Keywords: Multisensory · Autism Spectrum Disorder · Collaborative play · Online learning

1 Introduction

COVID-19 pandemic in 2020 enforced all educational institutions around the world to a complete lock-down affecting more than 94% of the learners in 190 countries (De Giusti 2020). There is a pressing need to keep the educational sector active; hence, educational institutions shifted from on-campus learning to online learning. The teachers and students have to adapt to the new learning conditions that are challenging for most of the students as online courses require a detailed and more organized plan for teachers to deliver the information (Xhelili et al. 2021). A recent study showed that students suffer from many problems during these periods such as lack of information and the absence of suitable learning conditions (Bao 2020). The shift in mode and medium of learning has posed several challenges for students with special needs, specifically children with Autism Spectrum Disorder (ASD) and their parents. Children with ASD experience difficulties with the new learning technique and in many cases, their parents would have limited access to the internet or technological resources. Some parents lack enough knowledge in handling online learning sessions with their children.

ASD is a lifelong neurodevelopmental condition with several apparent symptoms (Salhia et al. 2014). These symptoms include difficulties in social communication and interaction, language usage and comprehension problems, repetitive and limited behavioural patterns, and challenges in perceptual processing. All that hinders social imagination. ASD is an increasingly prevalent disorder; in 2018, the Centers for Disease Control determined that approximately 1 in 59 children in the United States are diagnosed with ASD (Baio et al. 2018). Qatar is no different from the rest of the world. A recent study conducted by the Qatar Biomedical Research Institute revealed that ASD is present in 1.14% or one in every 87 children in Qatar (Alshaban et al. 2019). For this reason, governmental and non-governmental efforts were put in place to support children with ASD, and therefore, Qatar announced its national autism plan (NAP) 2017–2018.

The literature on teaching children with ASD reveals that multisensory tools have the potential to support a good learning outcome (Broadbent et al. 2018; Foxe and Schroeder 2005). Multisensory involves the combination of two or more sensory stimulations. Teachers often use multisensory tools to reach the desired goal of educating their students with ASD (Broadbent et al. 2018). For example, to introduce an apple, the teacher will bring different coloured apples; the student can see the colour and shape (visual), smell it (olfactory), touch it (tactile), taste it (gustatory), and lastly hear the teacher (auditory). Hence using a multisensory teaching technique can assist children with ASD to acquire many targeted skills in one session. For children with ASD, it is essential to support them in managing information with multisensory stimulations since they exhibit sensory processing disorder (Mallory and Keehn 2021). Thus, understanding how multisensory resources are utilized for online learning resources is imperative.

Also, the challenges of online learning include the ability to access some basic technological tools such as the internet and laptops to receive the necessary information. For example, among South African citizens, the majority of them lie under uneven income distribution with a high cost of computers and the internet (Venter and Daniels 2020). Despite the challenges of online learning, there are online educational platforms that allow students with various disabilities to access multisensory learning content online during the pandemic (Bjekić et al. 2014). These online platforms are commonly accessed via videos or mobile applications. Video can be accessed through organization websites or YouTube channels. Existing mobile applications on smart devices support children with ASD with several skills such as matching pictures, scheduling, communication via PECS images; and providing information on ASD for parents. Despite the lack of mobile applications targeting users with ASD (Hijab et al. 2021), recent research agrees that the existing digital tools can enhance the learning progress of children with special needs and help them achieve academic excellence and enhanced social skills (Gushchina et al. 2020).

Training caregivers and parents is essential in improving therapies and educational workshops for children with ASD (White et al. 2021). A recent study concludes that there is no difference between training parents in-person and remotely (Hao et al. 2021). Therefore, online learning can serve as a good avenue to educate parents of children with ASD on supporting their wards during online learning. The rise of the COVID-19 pandemic has led to an increase in the number of studies to support online learning for students with ASD. The work of Aristovnik et al. (2020) aims to assist the educational community in understanding the impact of the pandemic on learners to enhance online learning in the future. Another study by Martinho et al. (2021) discussed the psychological effect of the COVID-19 pandemic on learners' experience by comparing both online and face-to-face learning.

In this light, the online learning solutions targeting children with ASD need to be further explored and developed. Furthermore, there is a need for the design of online resources to support parents of children with ASD in supporting their children during online learning. This study aims to explore online learning resources for parents of children with ASD and conduct a quality and content comparison between the commonly used multisensory online support platforms. The study will cover two platforms separately: Mobile applications targeting educational content for children with ASD and videos from websites or YouTube channels that focus on teaching parents how to support children with ASD. The videos considered in this study mainly cover multisensory workshops and educational information regarding ASD in general. The comparison of the online resources will be conducted using a set of checklists and rubrics adopted from studies on multisensory learning contents (Neumann and Herodotou 2020; Sugar et al. 2010). To the best of our knowledge, no study has compared the existing online multisensory educational platforms for children with ASD. Highlighting the gaps and advantages of the existing platforms will help software developers or organizations in designing and developing build better platforms in the future.

2   Method

This section describes the inclusion criteria used in selecting existing educational content on Google Play (Android) applications and websites (or YouTube) videos targeting children with ASD, parents, caregivers, or specialists. Next, the sources searched are highlighted followed by the labelling of the applications and videos. Finally, the process of assessing the searched data is described.

2.1   Inclusion Criteria

The following are the inclusion criteria used for shortlisting the online learning resources for children with ASD and their parents:

- It targets users with ASD or their families.
- It consists of educational content.
- It can be freely downloaded and used.
- For videos, they must be developed by specialists or expertise in the field.

Any application or video that doesn't meet its inclusion criteria is excluded.

2.2   Searching Sources

To date, the Apple store has over 1.96 million applications available for download (93.8% free for download), and 3.18 million applications available on Google Play

Store (Android) for download where 96.7% are free (42 matters 2022). However, the scope of this study is only on the educational application on Google Play Store. The keyword used for the search was: "Education for Autism". The search was conducted on the 28th of November, 202 and the first 100 results from the Google Play Store were reviewed.

YouTube is considered the most powerful free media streaming and video sharing platform that exists online (Prestianta 2021). Hence, YouTube was the only search engine targeted in this paper. The same search keywords used for mobile applications were used on YouTube channels (not individual videos). The inclusion criteria were also used in selecting the video channels. The search was conducted between the 28th of November 2021 and the 4th of December 2021.

2.3   Applications and Videos Labeling

After gathering all the results, video labelling was done to determine the final videos and applications to be analyzed. The applications were labelled and classified into 12 main categories based on their description and published category: Sensory, Language, Education, Communication, Schedule handler, Cognitive, Information, Anxiety, Development, Motor, Social Skills, and Health and fitness. In total, 16 educational applications and six main channels designed for children with ASD met the inclusion criteria. Among the video channels, only two were created as playlists and videos for educating parents and caregivers on teaching, playing, and handling children with ASD.

2.4   Data Assessment

In the process of analyzing the included applications and video channels, two separate rubrics were for each platform. The mobile application rubric was adapted from several studies (Lubniewski et al. 2017; Stoyanov et al. 2016; Walker 2011; Walker and Schrock 2011) and it covered four main sections: Application overview, design features, functionality, and content. The Application Overview consists of general information regarding the included applications. The design features highlight the application's layout, graphics, and auditory elements. The performance, ease of use, and navigation are discussed under the functionality section. Finally, the content discusses the targeted age, available levels, language, type of skills, and the ability to engage the teacher of children with ASD. The primary rubrics used to evaluate the educational videos were based on 4 categories: Channel overview, Video overview, Content, Targeted audience (Sugar et al. 2010). The channel overview describes the general statistics of the YouTube channel, the video overview describes the quality of the sound and images, the existence of transcription, and the video bumper which is a short video that introduces the video at the beginning and summarizes it at the end. The content highlights the type of the video, the target skills, screen movement, narration, and the supplementary tool used in the video. Finally, the target audience is to specify the age and category of the audience as either parents, caregivers or children with ASD.

3 Results

3.1 Educational Mobile Applications

Search Results

The analysis of 100 android applications showed that only 16 applications focused on educating parents of children with ASD and these applications were included in the pre-analysis phase. All the 16 applications except one were released in the last five years and updated at least once. A quick review was conducted on all the 16 applications to identify relevant applications to this study. Five of the 16 applications were removed because of several reasons like duplicated applications, unable to access the application's features unless purchasing its full version, and not a learning application (assessment application). Therefore, the total number of applications analyzed is 11 android applications.

Application Assessment

This section highlights the overview of the applications, design features, functionality evaluation, and contents of the application. The oldest application was released in 2013 and the newest in 2021, hence our analysis was divided into two groups: Group 1, having the applications released when the COVID-19 pandemic started in 2019 till 2021, and group 2, having the applications released before the pandemic (between 2013 and 2018).

Application Overview

The majority of the applications were included in group 1 (55%, 6 out of 11). Among these applications, only one out of six stopped their updates in 2019, and others (5, out of six) still get updates. In group 2, only two applications didn't get updated since the release date (2017). Similarly, two applications stopped getting updates in 2019. Table 1 displays the application name, the year of release, and the last updated date until the search was done.

Considering the number of downloads, applications in group 1(113,000) reached a higher number of downloads than applications in group 2 (85,000). The top-three downloaded applications out of the 11 have more than 50,000 downloads each (two

Table 1. Release and last update year of the applications

App name	Release	Update	Minimum number of downloads
Autism Read & Write	2013	2019	10,000
Autism Speech Sequencing ZApps 1.0	2017	2017	10,000
Autism Learning Games: Camp Discovery Pro	2017	2017	5,000
Jade	2018	2021	50,000
TEAPP - Autism and videogames	2018	2019	10,000
Otsimo I Speech and Language Therapy SLP	2019	2021	50,000
Autism Teaching kids the first 701 Words with ABA	2019	2019	1,000
AutiSpark: Kids Autism Games	2020	2021	50,000
Mr PECS - Autism Speech Therapist	2020	2021	10,000
Talking ABA Cards - Kids Language Therapy, Autism	2020	2021	1,000
Simple sentence builder	2021	2021	1,000

applications in group 1 and one application in group 2). Understanding the users' satis-faction when rating the application is an important factor to be considered for detailed analysis. The users rated the application differently and the rating scores were standard-ized for a fair comparison. Thus, the total number of users who rated the application was multiplied by their rating scores to get a cumulative rating score. Among the six applications in group 1 "*AutiSpark: Kids Autism Games*" achieved the highest rating score of 4.2/5 and a cumulative rating score of 1676.4, and "*Autism Teaching kids the first 701 Words with ABA*" has the lowest rating score of 3.3/4 and cumulative rating score of 23.1. In group 2, the highest rating score was achieved by "TEAPP – Autism and videogames" with 4.1/5 and "Jade" achieved the lowest rating score with 3.3/5, however, the highest cumulative rating score was achieved by "*Jade*" with 775.5 and the lowest by "*Autism Learning Games: Camp Discovery Pro*" with 64.6.

Figure 1 shows the distribution of the rating scores (over five) and cumulative ratings among all the applications.

Design Features
The design feature is divided into three sections: layout consistency, graphics with ani-mations, and lip-sync (synchronization of audio and video) The assessment of each design feature was characterized as 'applicable', 'somewhat applicable' and 'not appli-cable' where 1, 0.5 and 0 values were used respectively to represent each assessment. These assessment values were averaged to estimate the design feature score. Only six out of 11 applications (three applications in each group) were above average scores (0.5), and five others were below average. Lastly, five applications lack lip-sync, quality graphics and animations (resolution, link between graphics and animations, and inclu-sion of animation), and others achieved the full score in design features. Among the 11 applications, only three (one out of six in group 1 and two out of five in group 2) lack layout consistency, and others have consistent layout design.

Functionality
The Mobile Application Rating Scale: user version (uMARS) questionnaire is used to measure the functionality feature of the applications. The uMARS (Stoyanov et al.

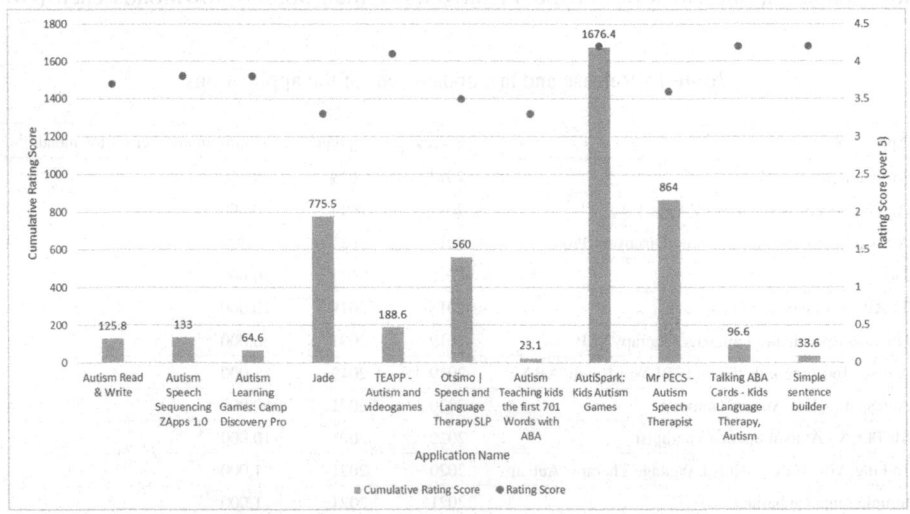

Fig. 1. Rating score and cumulative rating of the applications

2016) is a simple and reliable tool that can be used by end-users to assess the quality of mobile applications. It includes 4 objective quality subscales (engagement, functionality, esthetics, and information quality) and 1 subjective quality subscale. For this study, only the functionality subscale was used on the 11 included applications. The functionality was divided to three questions: performance, ease of use, and navigation. The performance means the ability of the application's component (buttons and menus) to perform (1 if application is broken, and 5 perfect and timely response). The "ease to use" refers to the ability to learn the application clearly and easy (1 if the application is complex and confusing, and 5 if the user could be able to use the application immediately). Lastly, the navigation consists of the screen movements and links between the screens (1 if there is no logical connection between screens, and 5 if the connection was perfectly logical). These questions are scored out of five, where five is the highest and one is the lowest. The minimum, maximum and mean are calculated over five. Table 2 highlights the functionality mean score of each application.

Table 2. The distribution of the functionality features of the applications

App name	Performance	Ease of use	Navigation	Functionality mean
Autism Read & Write	5.0	4.0	3.0	4.0
Autism Speech Sequencing ZApps 1.0	2.0	2.0	2.0	2.0
Autism Learning Games: Camp Discovery Pro	2.0	2.0	2.0	2.0
Jade	3.0	4.0	2.0	3.0
TEAPP - Autism and videogames	4.0	4.0	4.0	4.0
Otsimo I Speech and Language Therapy SLP	4.0	3.0	3.0	3.3
Autism Teaching kids the first 701 Words with ABA	4.0	4.0	4.0	4.0
AutiSpark: Kids Autism Games	5.0	4.0	4.0	4.3
Mr PECS - Autism Speech Therapist	3.0	3.0	3.0	3.0
Talking ABA Cards - Kids Language Therapy, Autism	4.0	4.0	3.0	3.7
Simple sentence builder	5.0	4.0	3.0	4.0
Min	2.0	2.0	2.0	2.0
Max	5.0	4.0	4.0	4.3
Mean	**3.7**	**3.5**	**3.0**	**3.4**
Variance	1.2	0.7	0.6	0.7
Standard deviation	1.1	0.8	0.8	0.8

Content

Five main criteria were used in reviewing the content of the videos: users' age, available game levels, application's language, tools used to achieve a targeted skill, application accessibility to teachers/parents/caregivers. All the analyzed applications were directed to all ages of children with ASD. Five out of the 11 applications have more than five levels (46%) whereas group 2 applications have only one game level. Three applications were having one level (two in group 1; one in group 2). Around 64% of the applications (seven out of 11) were only delivering the application in one language which is English. The remaining four applications allow users to choose one out of two available languages in the application. Flashcard (two-sided cards with an image on one side and information on the other side) is one of the tools used in the application. Six applications used flashcards only and five applications used both flashcards and random words. One of the applications aims to teach children with ASD letters and word formation by using Text-to-Speech and encouraging them to read each letter separately. None of these mobile applications are free except for only four applications that offer restricted access to a few functionalities and students' progress. Figure 2 shows the tools used in the analyzed android applications.

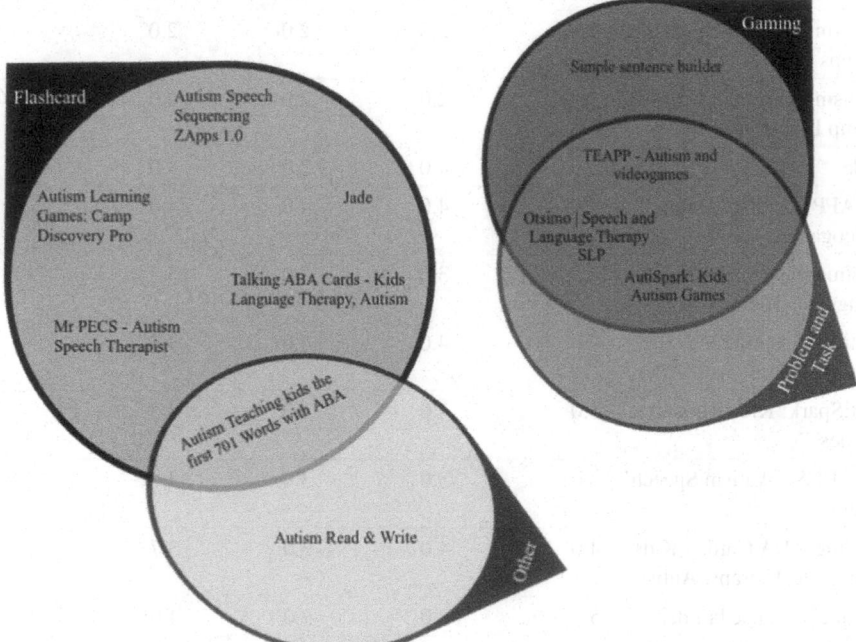

Fig. 2. Distribution of tools used in the applications.

3.2   Educational Videos

Search Results

Six YouTube channels emerged after a direct and backward search was carried out on YouTube. Results of the direct search consist of four active channels from the first page of the YouTube channels, and the backward search retrieved two active channels by going through the subscribed channels and the accepted channels. Among the six channels, only two were considered for analysis as the others were not delivering educational content to parents and caregivers or specialists. The excluded channels are the ones on talk-show, meetings, interviews videos with parents of children with ASD and specialists talking about their experiences. The two channels analyzed in this paper are: *"Early Autism Project Malaysia*[1]*"* and *"Learn Autism*[2]*"*. Both channels are targeting audiences who are parents and caregivers of children with ASD and specialists working in the ASD field.

"Early Autism Project Malaysia" (EAP) has both a website and a YouTube channel. It delivers videos containing Applied Behavioural Analysis (ABA material in Malay) content. This online platform was founded by Wisconsin Early Autism Project (WEAP) in September 2006. Their videos were developed to raise awareness about ASD, and provide resources, tips, facts, entertainment and inspiration to support parents, caregivers and specialists supporting individuals with ASD.

"Learn Autism" (LA) is a team of experts in the field of ASD: a University professor diagnosed with ASD at the age of four, board members of several autism societies, a speech-language pathologist with more than 45 years of experience in the autism field, an occupational therapist with more than 15 years of experience, early childhood special educator with more than 10 years of experience, ABA specialist with more than 20 years of experience, and a child with ASD. LA aims to deliver a comprehensive series of videos directed to parents, caregivers and specialists to guide them in teaching and communicating with children with ASD.

Videos Assessment

Video Overview
Both channels divided their videos into categories that are delivered as courses. EAP YouTube channel consists of 12 categories with 74 videos and six extra talk show sessions. These videos are offered for free on YouTube and their official website. On the other hand, LA had 131 videos divided into 24 categories where 27 videos belong to more than one category. These videos only exist on the official website for $24.99 per annum: only eight videos are fully available for free on YouTube, and 30 previews of the videos are available for free on YouTube. Table 3 highlights the overview of the two channels.

---

[1] YouTube channel: www.youtube.com/user/autismmalaysia; Website: www.autismmalaysia.com.

[2] YouTube Channel: www.youtube.com/c/LearnAutism; Website: tv.learnautism.com.

Table 3. Channels overview

	Categories	Videos	Starting year	Viewers on YouTube	Total videos duration (HH:MM:ss)	Payment
EAP	12	74	2012	621,310	16:58:24	Free
LA	24	131	2019	2,979	12:48:08	$24.99 for full access

These two channels have common topics and categories to support the living and learning experience of children with ASD. This experience includes setting up a home for children with ASD, general information regarding relevant therapeutic treatment, such as ABA, and social skills. Both channels have professional and quality content with video bumpers to introduce and summarize the topic of the video. However, for EAP, their webinars and Instagram live videos are not of good quality in terms of filming and resolution when compared to other learning videos. All the videos are transcribed on both channels, and the main language is English. EAP transcribed all their videos to English and Malay except for the webinars and Instagram live videos, while LA transcribed all their videos from English to Arabic, except for six videos which were in other languages (Arabic, Italian, and Spanish). It is important to mention that both channels are still uploading videos and updating their channel.

Content
The contents of the videos were analyzed using five parameters: type of the video, targeted skills, screen movement, narration type, and the usage of supplementary tools. Only educational videos were compared while webinars, live videos, and personal experiences were removed (EAP: n = 7; LA: n = 10).

Video Type: All EAP videos have information about ASD and educational content. While most of the videos for LA are also about the information on ASD and 86% (103 out of 120) of the video are on educational content. In LA, 12 videos mainly focus on education using a play-based approach and a scenario where a specialist intervenes in the teaching approach.

Targeted Skills: Diversity in targeted skills are observed in both channels and most of the videos combine different aspects of learning skills, hence, falling within more than one category. Most of the videos on the EAP channel targeted social and behavioural skills (64%, 47 out of 73) specifically patience and self-improvement. Meanwhile, the LA channel mainly presents experts to provide information (66%, 79 out of 120) on specific skills. It also provides educational videos on communication language and behavioural skills (32%, 38 out of 120). Multi-sensory stimuli such as visual and auditory were used to teach sensory processing skills in the videos. In the EAP videos, colours and shapes were used to teach scheduling and learning requests while LA used Mr. Potato's head (a toy in form of a human) to teach body parts. Figure 3 displays the distribution of the targeted skills for both EAP and LA. Seven videos in EAP and five in LA were targeting other skills: LA focused on scheduling skills similarly to EAP, they focused also on COVID and tracking the enhancement of the child with ASD.

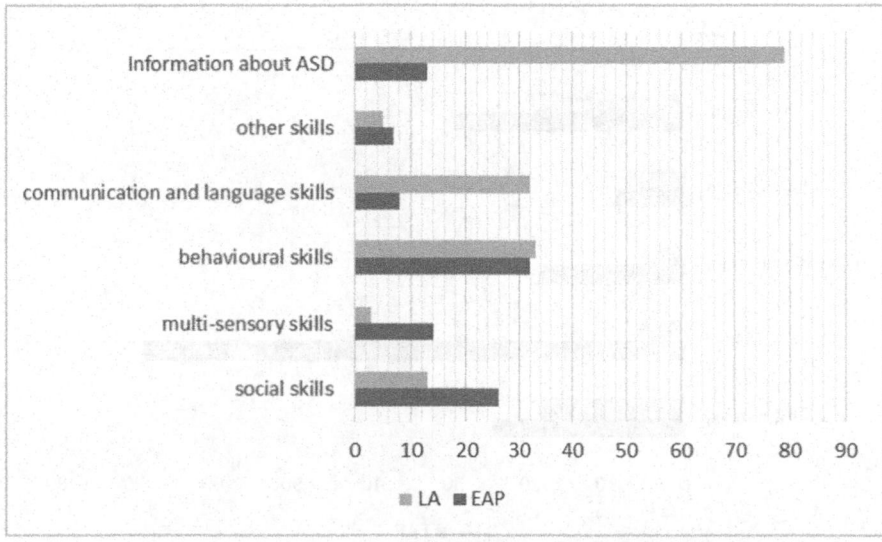

Fig. 3. Main contents and targeted skills in the channels' videos

Screen Movement: Fixed screens were used in all videos from both channels. All narration in LA videos were explicit but only 19% (14 out of 73) of the videos of EAP were explicit and the remaining were mixed between explicit and implicit narration. Visual and sensory tools are important for teaching and learning in general (Nuere and de Miguel 2020). This is the reason to employ some supplementary tools during sessions. Each channel has its unique way of delivering its video content as they used different tools. The supplementary tools used in both channels include studios, slides, toys, playing, and educational rooms as shown in Fig. 4.

Narration Type: EAP narrates their video in a standard structure which includes discussing a specific behaviour, acting the behavioural scenes (good or bad behaviour), proposing a multiple choice question as a quick quiz, and illustrating a scenario summarizing the video's topic. To achieve comprehensive video content, EAP uses slides, an educational and playing room (this is where the sketch recording takes place), and toys (such as play-dough, stories, food, paint, and puzzles...) as supplementary tools. On the other hand, LA presents its video contents without any supplementary tool. However, two of the 24 categories focus on real-life examples using supplementary toys. The first category is when a special education teacher demonstrates how she teaches children with ASD new skills using toys such as Mr. Potato Head, board games, card games, stories, car ramp, and dolls. These videos had a detailed explanation of the steps to introduce the toy to the child with ASD till the end of the session showing each step and its corresponding targeted skill. The second category showed a child with ASD with his mother playing and then a specialist will comment on what happened and give her feedback. These videos included supplementary tools such as educational and playing room, Mr. Potato Head, and card game.

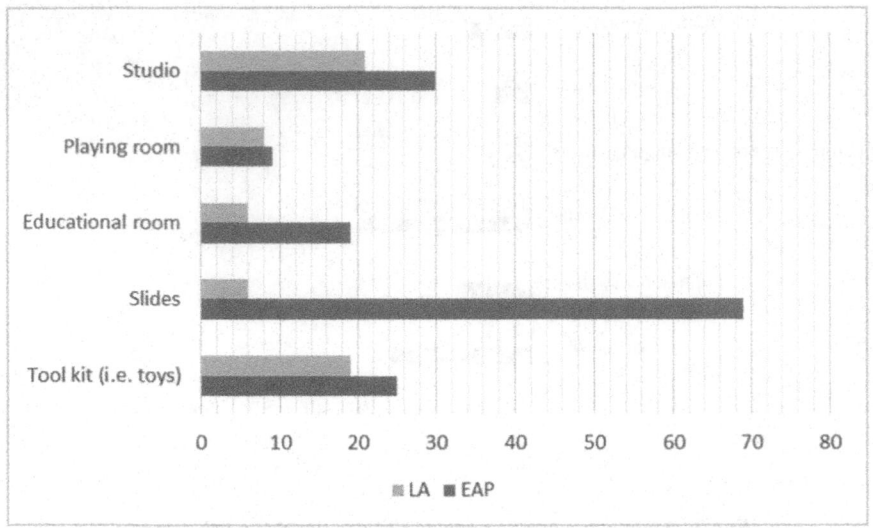

Fig. 4. Distribution of the supplementary tools on the channels' videos

Supplementary Tools: The inclusion of supplementary learning toys and games is referred to as learning through play. The two channels use learning through play in several videos. In EAP, learning through play was used in several videos to teach specific skills such as turn-taking, sensory processing, game tolerance, and focusing on interactive play. In LA, the importance of using the concept of learning through play was explained by a special needs teacher to inform parents and other stakeholders of ASD.

Targeted Audience
All the videos on both channels were mainly directed to parents and caregivers. EAP focuses more on teaching specific skills in children with ASD using real-life examples. Also, the video content was designed with simple expressions that can easily be understood by parents and caregivers. In the LA channel, their videos consist of a hybrid of technical and non-technical content from professional and specialized team members. Hence, they delivered most of their videos in a well-explained way for both parents, caregivers and specialists.

Targeting children with ASD regardless of the age group can be observed in both channels. However, some videos encourage the parents and caregivers to use a specific supplementary tool based on the children's capability of focusing and engaging. In EAP, a specialist recommended upgrading the level of the used toy based on the child with ASD, for example using board games or advanced sports games with a set of rules to follow. Similarly, in LA specialist suggests that children with ASD may get bored of learning the Mr. Potato head and body parts if it is often used. So, the children should be provided with something more advanced.

4 Discussion and Implication

This paper highlights the current situation of online learning for children with ASD on two platforms: mobile applications and website videos. The main findings from the analysis of 11 educational mobile applications and two websites' videos are discussed in this section.

4.1 Educational Mobile Applications

The educational mobile applications for children with ASD developed between 2013 and 2021 (n = 11) were categorized into two groups: before and after the Covid-19 pandemic. Six applications developed during the COVID19 pandemic between 2019 and 2021) were categorized as group 1 and five applications developed between 2013 and 2018 were categorized as group 2. All the applications were updated at least once in the last two years. The rating score for the applications developed during the pandemic is higher than the applications developed before the pandemic. This rating assessment reflects the quality enhancement of the applications released during the pandemic.

The performance score of the application was estimated based on the audio quality, ease of use and responsiveness of the application. Six applications in group 1 and one application in group 2 achieved performance scores above average. However, one application in group 1 and two applications in group 2 had a lower performance score due to poor navigation features. In general, five applications in group 1 and one application in group 2 had performance scores above average. The evaluation of the mobile applications in this study revealed that "*AutiSpark: Kids Autism Games*" has the best functional design while "*Autism Learning Games: Camp Discovery Pro*" and "*Autism Speech Sequencing ZApps 1.0*" have the least functional design.

Many of these applications are designed for a specific age group but "*Otsimo | Speech and Language Therapy SLP*" allows parents/caregivers to specify the age and desired skill training required, and creates the curriculum based on the requests of the parents/caregivers. The application of games for vocabulary learning was common to all the applications analyzed in this study. "*Simple sentence builder*" is an educational application that uses games to teach writing skills where users listen to a story and fill in sentences using icons and images. The stories are built-in and the teacher can't access them. This application is delivered only in English and has up to 3 game levels. Also, three applications used games to teach problem-solving skills to users with ASD. "*TEApp - Autism and videogames*" consists of more than five game levels and languages where the children can perform some tasks by matching images and other educational activities to learn new skills with restricted access for the teachers. "*Otsimo | Speech and*

Language Therapy SLP" application allows teachers to monitor the learning progress of their students on vocabulary but the application requires a paid subscription. *"AutiSpark: Kids Autism Games"* is a game with more than five game levels delivered in English. The application consists of short games in different categories such as matching, sorting, vocabulary, letters, puzzles, patterns, colouring and flashcards. Also, it has videos on daily activities to help children understand good and bad behaviour in doing in carrying out these activities such as washing hands, wearing and lacing shoes, eating, and brushing teeth. Similarly, many videos regarding social and communication skills such as welcoming guests, communicating and playing with a friend. This application also required a paid subscription to unlock its full functionalities.

4.2 Educational Videos

The two websites (EAP and LA) analyzed in this paper have YouTube channels for publishing their videos. Both channels had specialized members in their teams but LA has more professionals and therapists. In general, EAP has longer videos addressing different skills while LA presented its video in chunks to address different skills separately. Both channels transcribed the majority of their videos from English to another language (Arabic for LA and Malay for EAP).

The majority of the videos were about giving information to parents, caregivers, and specialists about ASD in general. This is because some parents could be new to ASD and aim to know more about it. The information delivered by the specialists in the videos was mainly on introducing ASD, available treatments such as ABA, and the existing therapy techniques. EAP highlighted the importance of the existing treatments and therapy. Instead, LA discussed the techniques and treatments used by specialists and professional therapists as well as their roles in supporting children with ASD.

Both EAP and LA channels targeted the same skills. For example social skills, language and communication skills, and multisensory skills. However, the content used by each channel for teaching each skill differs. Social skills were delivered in EAP using videos on how to handle 'no' as an answer and stories on appropriate manners in the public. LA videos were delivered by specialists on the importance of using some available tools to achieve specific social skills such as morning routines such as brushing teeth, washing face and being patient. Language and communication skills were more focused in LA than in EAP videos. LA focused on the use of language for effective communication, its importance and how to enhance such skill. Lastly, multisensory skills were mainly focused on using learning through play techniques. This technique was used by EAP in their acting scenes to illustrate the usage of the existing multisensory tools and their goals. Instead, LA used more than one category to demonstrate targeted skills with specific tools (Mr. Potato head, baby doll, mini cars…). These videos by LA were delivered by teachers of children with ASD who has many years of experience in the field.

Considering screen movement as a parameter for assessing the applications, both channels used fixed screen movement in all their videos. The screen was static and even for real-life examples, the camera was fixed on a specific position. This static screen was used for an explicit video narration on both channels. However, EAP used some both explicit and implicit narration when they needed to switch to some assistive tools such as explanatory slides. There was no restriction on the age group targeted by the videos delivered from both channels. However, in some videos, they recommended the usage of some techniques or tools based on the ages and skills of children with ASD. Similarly, the videos of both channels are targeting parents, caregivers, or specialists and the content was delivered in a simple language to suit all users.

4.3 Implications

The implication of the findings in this study is addressed from four perspectives. Defined taxonomy of online resources, accessibility of resources, emphasis on teaching multisensory skills, and enhancing applications' design features.

Defining the taxonomy of the video content can reduce the search time for a specific content which makes the application easy to use. Most of the videos gave information about ASD and introduced some skills in separate videos but did not categorize the videos by targeted skills. This uncategorized video approach can make information seeking challenging and time-consuming. Therefore, there is a need for definitive categorization of videos where users can find information on a specific skill based on the category. This categorization will ease and reduce search time which could make information seeking challenging.

The videos analyzed in this study gave a brief description of multisensory skills and the available tools and toys that could be used to enhance the skill. These videos teach the parents and caregivers more about targeting and enhancing these skills for children with ASD. The importance of learning through play has been identified as a good approach to teaching multisensory skills. Therefore, stakeholders in the ASD field who engage in teaching children with ASD need to consider several toys with multisensory stimulation.

Accessing the progress of children with ASD is the ability of the teacher, parent, or caregiver to track the achievements and learning curve of the child. The existing applications do not provide this assessment feature for teachers, parents, or caregivers unless with a paid subscription. Hence, there is a need for free access to educational applications for tracking the learning progress of children with ASD.

Design features used in educational mobile applications for children with ASD over the last four years and during the Covid-19 pandemic (between 2019 and 2021) have been enhanced to ease online learning. Also, consistent layout designs including animations and attractive images, videos, and features have been improved better than applications developed before 2019. This is due to the existence of more focused and directed research on children with ASD.

This study could be the starting point for further studies comparing educational applications and videos for children with ASD on a larger scale. Also, highlights on the situation of the existing mobile applications and videos to achieve better results in the future. Researchers are giving attention to the design of online learning resources for children with ASD but the videos available as teaching resources for parents, caregivers, and specialists with ASD need to be freely accessible to support them in an urgent situation like the Covid-19 pandemic.

5   Conclusion

Prior to the pandemic of COVID-19, children with ASD often learn in a face-to-face classroom. However, during the pandemic, learning was mostly online and this is challenging for children with ASD as well as their parents and caregivers. Most parents do not have the expertise to manage their children during online learning. Thus providing huge support for parents and caregivers in teaching their children is imperative.

This paper highlights the existing supportive resources for parents and caregivers of children with ASD. It is evident that the main supportive resources are delivered through mobile applications and online videos. The online resources designed to educate parents and children with ASD are remarkable but the full versions of some of the resources are not available for free. The videos are of good quality designed by professionals and the contents are well delivered. Having the ability to filter the videos by targeted skill is an important feature that could be used by parents and caregivers who want to teach and enhance a specific skill in their children. The analysis of educational mobile applications for children with ASD is limited to only android applications in this study. Exploring similar applications on both android and IOS platforms is an important direction for future studies.

Acknowledgment. This study was made possible by NPRP grant # NPRP13S-0108-200027 from the Qatar National Research Fund (a member of Qatar Foundation). The findings achieved herein are solely the responsibility of the author[s].

References

42matters: Google Play vs the IOS App Store I Store Stats for Mobile Apps. 42matters (2022). https://42matters.com/stats

Alshaban, F., et al.: Prevalence and correlates of autism spectrum disorder in qatar: a national study. J. Child Psychol. Psychiatry **60**(12), 1254–1268 (2019). https://doi.org/10.1111/jcpp. 13066

Aristovnik, A., et al.: Impacts of the COVID-19 pandemic on life of higher education students: a global perspective. Sustainability **12**(20), 8438 (2020). https://www.mdpi.com/2071-1050/12/ 20/8438

Baio, J., et al.: Prevalence of autism spectrum disorder among children aged 8 years—autism and developmental disabilities monitoring network, 11 sites, United States, 2014. MMWR. Surveill. Summ. **67**(6), 1–23 (2018). http://www.cdc.gov/mmwr/volumes/67/ss/ss6706a1.htm? s_cid=ss6706a1_w

Bao, W.: COVID-19 and online teaching in higher education: a case study of Peking University. Hum. Behav. Emerg. Technol. **2**(2), 113–115 (2020). https://doi.org/10.1002/hbe2.191

Bjekić, D., Obradović, S., Vučetić, M., Bojović, M.: E-teacher in inclusive e-education for students with specific learning disabilities. Procedia – Soc. Behav. Sci. **128**, 128–133 (2014). https://lin kinghub.elsevier.com/retrieve/pii/S1877042814022228

Broadbent, H.J., White, H., Mareschal, D., Kirkham, N.Z.: Incidental learning in a multisensory environment across childhood. Dev. Sci. **21**(2), e12554 (2018). https://doi.org/10.1111/desc. 12554

Foxe, J.J., Schroeder, C.E.: The case for feedforward multisensory convergence during early cortical processing. NeuroReport **16**(5), 419–423 (2005). http://journals.lww.com/00001756-200504040-00001

De Giusti, A.: Policy brief: education during COVID-19 and beyond. Revista Iberoamericana de Tecnología en Educación y Educación en Tecnología (26), e12 (2020). https://teyet-revista.info.unlp.edu.ar/TEyET/article/view/1456

Gushchina, O., et al.: Structural model of learning success formation among first-year students of informatics. Universidad y Sociedad **12**(2), 325–329 (2020). https://www.scopus.com/inward/record.uri?eid=2-s2.0-85100910440&partnerID=40&md5=da914ad54ab46ddd51413647641e6472

Hao, Y., Franco, J.H., Sundarrajan, M., Chen, Y.: A pilot study comparing tele-therapy and in-person therapy: perspectives from parent-mediated intervention for children with autism spectrum disorders. J. Autism Dev. Disorders **51**(1), 129–143 (2021). https://doi.org/10.1007/s10803-020-04439-x

Hijab, M.H.F., Al-Thani, D., Banire, B.: A multimodal messaging app (MAAN) for adults with autism spectrum disorder: mixed methods evaluation study. JMIR Formative Res. **5**(12), e33123 (2021). https://formative.jmir.org/2021/12/e33123

Lubniewski, K.L., McArthur, C.L., Harriott, W.A.: Evaluating instructional apps using the app checklist for educators (ACE). Int. Electron. J. Elementary Educ. **10**(3 Special Issue), 323–329 (2017)

Mallory, C., Keehn, B.: Implications of sensory processing and attentional differences associated with autism in academic settings: an integrative review. Front. Psychiatry **12** (2021). https://doi.org/10.3389/fpsyt.2021.695825/full

Martinho, D., Sobreiro, P., Vardasca, R.: Teaching sentiment in emergency online learning—a conceptual model. Educ. Sci. **11**(2), 53 (2021). https://www.mdpi.com/2227-7102/11/2/53

Neumann, M.M., Herodotou, C.: Evaluating YouTube videos for young children. Educ. Inf. Technol. **25**(5), 4459–4475 (2020). https://doi.org/10.1007/s10639-020-10183-7

Nuere, S., de Miguel, L.: The digital/technological connection with COVID-19: an unprecedented challenge in university teaching. Technol. Knowl. Learn. **26**(4), 931–943 (2020). https://doi.org/10.1007/s10758-020-09454-6

Prestianta, A.M.: Mapping the ASEAN YouTube uploaders. Jurnal ASPIKOM **6**(1), 1 (2021). http://jurnalaspikom.org/index.php/aspikom/article/view/761

Salhia, H.O., et al.: Systemic review of the epidemiology of autism in arab gulf countries. Neurosciences **19**(4), 291–296 (2014). https://pubmed.ncbi.nlm.nih.gov/25274588

Stoyanov, S.R., Hides, L., Kavanagh, D.J., Wilson, H.: Development and validation of the user version of the mobile application rating scale (UMARS). JMIR mHealth uHealth **4**(2), e72 (2016). http://mhealth.jmir.org/2016/2/e72/

Sugar, W., Brown, A., Luterbach, K.: Examining the anatomy of a screencast: uncovering common elements and instructional strategies. Int. Rev. Res. Open Dist. Learn. **11**(3), 1–20 (2010)

Venter, I.M., Daniels, A.D.: Towards Bridging the Digital Divide: The Complexities of the South African Story, pp. 3250–3256 (2020). http://library.iated.org/view/VENTER2020TOW

Walker, H.: Evaluating the effectiveness of apps for mobile devices. J. Spec. Educ. Technol. **26**, 59–63 (2011)

Walker, H., Schrock, K.: Educational App Evaluation Rubric, p. 4 (2011)

White, L.C., et al.: Brief report: impact of COVID-19 on individuals with ASD and their caregivers: a perspective from the SPARK cohort. J. Autism Dev. Disord. **51**(10), 3766–3773 (2021). https://doi.org/10.1007/s10803-020-04816-6

Xhelili, P., Ibrahimi, E., Rruci, E., Sheme, K.: Adaptation and perception of online learning during COVID-19 pandemic by Albanian University students. Int. J. Stud. Educ. **3**(2), 103–111 (2021). https://ijonse.net/index.php/ijonse/article/view/49

Students' Status Toward the New Gamified Learning Method: An Exploratory Study

Lan Jiang, Fan Zhao$^{(\boxtimes)}$, Xiaoxue Wang, and Jingshun Zhang

Florida Gulf Coast University, Fort Myers, FL 33965, USA
fzhao@fgcu.edu

Abstract. Virtual reality has been applied in assisting teaching and facilitating learning in different disciplines of education, yet how VR can be used to assist and even to enhance student learning of hospitality management remains unknown to us. This study aims to examine student learning experiences with virtual reality technology and their behavioral intentions in a hospitality classroom. A Virtual Reality (VR) hotel tour simulation was designed and developed to examine student learning experiences. A total of 220 college students participated in the current study and 209 valid responses were collected and analyzed using the structural model. The findings of the current exploratory study suggested that the use of VR was well received by students as being useful in learning hospitality concepts. The findings suggested that perceived usefulness and perceived enjoyment were significantly positive indicators of students' intention to take and recommend the class, while perceived ease of use and the flow experience were not significant factors.

Keywords: Virtual reality · Hospitality education · Student learning · Structural equation modeling

1 Introduction

As virtual reality (VR) becomes more pupolar in education, many educational researchers and practitioners start to not only integrate it in learning and instruction but also engage in the systematic research and evaluation of VR. This trend is well reflected by the increasing number of VR publications. In the past five years, the number of articles with "Virtual Reality" in the titles, according to an advanced search in "Web of Science," reaches to 351 within the field of education. In the year of 2020 alone, there were 147 educational articles published with VR in their titles. In the field of hospitality, according to a review article on hospitality journal publications, this number also started to increase rapidly since 2016 [1].

According to Steuer [2], virtual reality is related to Social Presence Theory and provides the sense of being in an environment which provides users both physical immersion and psychological presence [3]. Therefore, VR becomes increasingly essential to understand users' social needs in establishing and developing virtual learning [4–6]. From the lens of educators, Wang and Stork [7] defined virtual reality as "any technology that provides its users an interactive computer-generated experience through text, audio, visual, spatial and/or speed messages within a simulated environment that engages its users in multi-sensory interactions and reactions for learning" (p. 89). By this definition, VR has been applied in assisting teaching and facilitating learning in different aspects of education such as computer science, foreign languages learning, art and music [7–9].

While VR being adopted in different tourism areas such as cruises, museums, and theme parks, the tourism practioners tried to apply VR as a method for destination marketing [10] and interactive advertising [11]. However, the significance of adopting VR in the hospitality education receives relatively less attention. A thorough understanding of whether VR can be adopted in hospitality education could assist hospitality educators and researchers in designing future classes and revealing research gaps. Therefore, this study is aim to examine student learning experiences with virtual reality technology and their behavioral intentions in a hospitality classroom. Specifically, this study aims in addressing these research questions: how well will students adopt VR technology in the classroom? what are the impacts of their VR experience on their behavioral intention? will their VR experience positively associated with their intention taking this class?

2   Literature Review

2.1   Effectiveness of Virtual Reality-Based Learning

Although effects of VR on learning, according its rich literature, vary greatly and with different foci, a few recent studies on VR are enlightening for understanding VR-based learning. Abdjul et al. [12] reported their study of virtual laboratory-based learning in physics with high school students. They found that student learning activities increased significantly, which contributed to the improved student learning outcomes. Wijayanti and Ikhsan [13] reported their study of VR laboratory for chemistry education with ten-grade students. They concluded that the experiment student group with the VR laboratory understood the learning material better than the control student group "because students from the experiment class can repeat practical activity freely" (p. 15). Shi et al. [14] conducted a study on a game-based immersive virtual reality with seventh graders for learning mathematics. The findings of their studty suggested students with VR learning environment had significant improvements in math learning.

In addition, Lund and Wang [15] conducted a study on VR to examine the impact on university student learning motivation and performance. The study showed that student learning motivation and performance were significantly influenced by VR. Again, in the university with pre-service teacher students, Johnston and Collum [16] explored the use of VR at ten colleges in the U.S. and Puerto Rico. Their study found the use of VR improved pre-service teachers' performance and understanding of classroom management.

These results of VR on learning have revealed many contributing factos including VR's unique functionalities. VR affords different communication methods including those in text, image, audio and video formats [7]; provides consistent and stable immersive learning environments that can be used repeatedly to meet student learning needs [17]; offers unique 3D social and physical presence that promotes situated learning and experiential learning [18] and unique learning experience to avoid risks and dangers existing in realistic environments for learning [19]. The presentation of VR gives its users with detailed explorations of the problems to seek for solutions from multiple perspectives [14, 20, 21]. Therefore, how these VR functionalities can be used to assist and even to enhance student learning of hospitality management remains unknown to us, which triggered this study of exploring the adoption of VR in the hospitality education.

2.2 Adoption of Virtual Reality

Technology Acceptance Model (TAM)
TAM is one of the most commonly used frameworks in user-based evaluation [22]. It is a variation of the theory of reasoned action to predict the acceptance attitude of new technology from an organization's perspective [23]. It then became a popular theoretical method to explain group behaviors toward the acceptance of new technology [24]. With the continuous development of new technologies, such as Internet technology, smart phone, etc., after 1990s, TAM has been widely adopted to examine and predict technology acceptance of individual uers [25].

The TAM framework explains users' attitude towards a technology and the usage effects of the technology [22]. It provides an explanation of how the external features of a technology affect users' perceptions and attitudes that influence the actual use intention of the technology. When users approache a new technology, the perception of how this technology enhances the performance and productivity influences the users' attitude on the use intention of this technology [26]. The user's subjective opinion affects the usefulness [27]. Positive outcomes observed by the user will raise the user's attitude about using this technology as well as the intention of using the technology [28]. Ease of use of a technology decreases users' physical and mental efforts to adapt a new method to complete desired tasks [29]. The more the user believes the easy and effortless of a technology, the higher degree of the user's positive perception will increase [30]. In the hospitatlity field, reseachers also demonstrated that TAM could help understand the technology acceptance behavior [31]. Additionally, as to the students' perspectives of VR technology acceptance in education, previous studies show that both perceivd ease of use and perceived usefulness have positive influence on behaviors' intention [32]. Thus, we propose the following hypotheses.

H1: Perceived usefulness while experiencing the in-class VR hotel tour positively influence students' intentions to recommend this class.
H2: Perceived ease of use while experiencing the in-class VR hotel tour positively influence students' intentions to recommend this class.

Despite of the wide applications of TAM in academic research, there is a limitation identified by Van der Heijden [33] that when the use of technology is unavoidable or limited, the variables in TAM are appropriate to explain users' acceptance behaviors; however, if there are more options with other overwhelming factors, the users' decisions of technology adoption may not be limited to the variables in TAM. Therefore, in some cases, the original TAM variables may not be sufficient to explain and predict the acceptance attitude toward certain technologies including VR technology [34]. In our study, we extend the TAM framework with additional two variables: Perceived Enjoyment and Flow Experience.

Perceived Enjoyment

Perceived enjoyment refers to the extent to which a person perceived satisfied and enjoyed [35, 36]. Perceived enjoyment has been consistently examined as a significant factor to individuals' behavior [37, 38]. In the past decades, researchers in both fields of information technology and hospitality have observed and investigated the impact of perceived enjoyment on behavioral intentions [39–41]. Many studies have examined perceived enjoyment as an significant factors to better understand virtual experience [38, 42, 43]. Dickinger et al. [42] demostrated a significantly positive link between perceived enjoyment and individuals' adoption intentions, which is consistent with Van der Heijden [33]'s findings. Goh and Yoon [43] examined influence of the key hedonic factors to virtual world acceptance and their results confirmed that perceived enjoyment is a significant indicator of intention of using a hedonic virtual world. Similarly, So et al. [38]'s study also confirmed the significantly positive impact of perceived enjoyment on behavioral intention. Therefore, the following hypothesis was proposed:

H3: Perceived enjoyment while experiencing the in-class VR hotel tour positively influence students' intentions to recommend this class.

Flow Experience

Researchers used flow experience framework to better understand individuals' behavior on adoption of new technologies [44]. Flow was defined as "the holistic sensation that people feel when they act with total involvement" [45]. Ghani [46] pointed out the close relationship between the flow experience and satisfaction because individuals in a flow state can immerse themselves in such state and filter out all irrelevant perceptions. Researchers have shown that the flow experience can enhance adoption intention and satisfaction in virtual environments [47, 48]. Faiola and Smyslova [47] suggested flow as a significant factor of virtual experiences, which was also confirmed by Nah et al. [48]. Followed the researchers who found a significant relationship between flow experience and consumers return intentions [44, 49], Hsu, Chang, Kuo, & Cheng [50] also confirmed this finding. Therefore, we propose the following hypothesis:

H4: Flow experience while experiencing the in-class VR hotel tour positively influence students' intentions to recommend this class.

3 Methodology

3.1 Instruments Design

The major purpose of the current study was to examine student learning experiences with virtual reality technology and their behavioral intentions in a hospitality classroom. Specifically, two major questions were developed: (1) What are student learning experiences with VR technology in the classroom? (2) What are the effect of student learning experiences with VR technology on their behavioral intention? To answer these two major questions, following hypotheses were also used to guide and test the effects of student learning with VR in the classroom.

The research team designed a VR hotel tour simulation, in which users can obtain a digital first-person point of view, though the collaboration with specialists in VR technology. The VR tour utilized images and sounds to make participants feel like physically present in a real full-service hotel. A workshop lasting about 15 min was conducted to introduce the basic instruction of the tour and the VR devices that were provided by the research team. Students then experienced the hotel tour under the research team's instructions (see Fig. 1). A survey was used during the hotel tour with some questions answered before their VR experience and some questions after the VR experience.

Fig. 1. Students using VR in the classroom and some VR App senarios

The questionnaire has two parts. The first part (used before the VR hotel tour) gathered the background information, including students' demographic information (i.e. gender and major) and their past experience with VR technology. For example, "Have you used VR before?", "What was the major purpose when you used VR", "Do you like to use VR in your course learning?" Then students' self-evaluation on their learning ability was asked, such as "confidence in using VR" and "confidence of learning with Technology." The second part (used after the VR hotel tour) collected student's feedback for the VR hotel tour. Adapted from previous literatures [51, 52], fifteen items using Likert scale from 1 = strongly disagree to 7 = strongly agree were used to collect student's perceptions of VR technology experience. Table 1 presented the measurement of the constructs.

Table 1. Survey Questions.

PU	PU1	I learned something new during VR use Q5-2
(Perceived Usefulness)	PU2	The experience increased my productivity Q5-3
	PU3	Using VR can support my learning Q5-24
PEU	PEU1	Learning to operate with VR is easy Q5-22
(Perceived ease of use)	PEU2	Remembering how to operate with VR is easy Q5-27
	PEU3	I find the VR system easy to use Q5-28
PE	PE1	Using VR was captivating Q5-8
(Perceived Enjoyment)	PE2	Using VR was entertaining Q5-11
	PE3	Using VR was fun Q5-15
FL	FL1	It stimulated my curiosity to learn new things Q5-5
(Flow)	FL2	When experiencing VR, I feel in control Q5-7
	FL3	Using VR contributed positively to my overall visitor experience Q5-18
BI	BI1	VR increased my interest to take this class Q5-19
(Behavior Intention)	BI2	I want to use VR again in this class Q5-20
	BI3	I would recommend the class to others after the VR Q5-23

3.2 Sampling

Convenience sampling was adopted in this study due to the restricted environment with VR devices and nature of the VR hotel tour. A total of 220 college students participated in the current study and 209 valid responses were collected, which met the criterion that sample size for structural equation modeling is 200 cases [53]. Fifty-five percent of the respondents were female and majority of them have never used VR before (57.9%). For those who used VR, sixty percent used it for gaming and only thirty percent of them used VR for learning. Most students (89.9%) stated they like to use VR in their course learning.

3.3 Data Analysis

A two-step approach was used in the current study to analyze the data, which is consistent with many previous studies [54]. In the first step, confirmatory factor analysis was conducted in accessing the measurement scale's reliability. Then the structural model was analyzed to verify the hypotheses in the second step. SPSS 26 package and AMOS 21 software package were used for data analysis. The following section shows the results of the analyses.

4 Results

Table 2 presented the reliability and validity results for the measurement items. According to [55], reliability can be confirmed when the Cronbach's alpha value were higher than 0.7 for all constructs. Addiontionaly, all the average variance extracted (AVE) for each construct were higher than 0.5 and the composite reliability (CR) was higher than 0.7, both confirming convergent validity [55, 56]. Therefore, as shown in Table 2, the model in the study had satisfactory discriminant validity.

Table 2. Confirmatory factor analysis.

Construct	Factor mean	Standard deviation	Cronbach's alpha	Average variance extracted	Compostie reliability
PU	5.636	1.277	0.869	0.559	0.792
PEU	5.839	1.172	0.907	0.674	0.861
PE	6.008	1.158	0.908	0.573	0.801
FL	5.619	1.239	0.846	0.571	0.799
BI	5.648	1.342	0.912	0.621	0.831

Followed Fornell and Larcker's [57] suggestion, the square root of the AVE for each of the constructs was compared with the construct inter-correlations to confirm the discriminant validity of the scales. As can be seen in Table 3, the construct inter-correlations were less than the square root of the AVE, suggesting that discriminant validity of the measurement model scales was established.

Table 3. Constructs inter-correlation and average variance extracted (AVE).

Construct	PU	PE	FL	PEU	BI
PU	**0.748[a]**				
PEU	0.669	**0.820**			
PE	0.726	0.625	**0.756**		
FL	0.710	0.718	0.737	**0.756**	
BI	0.732	0.643	0.692	0.698	**0.788**

[a]The bold diagonal elements are the squre root of the AVE.

Structural model was used in assessing hypothesized relationships based on Anderson and Gerbing [56]'s two-step approach. The results of the structural model (R^2 for Behavior Intention = 0.77) showed the χ^2/d.f. = 2.9, met the fit threshold of 5.0 or less, CFI (comparative fit index) = 0.92, RMSEA (root mean square error of approximation) = 0.073, NNFI (non-normed fit index) = 0.91, demonstrating a good fit of the model. The results showed that wo path coefficients (PU and PE) were significant at a $p < 0.001$ level, suggesting hypothesis 1 ($\beta = 0.62$, $p < 0.001$) and hypothesis 3 ($\beta = 0.15$, $p < 0.001$) were supported, while Hypothesis 2 ($\beta = 0.55$, $p > 0.05$) and hypothesis 4 ($\beta = 0.20$, $p > 0.05$) were not supported, as shown in Fig. 2.

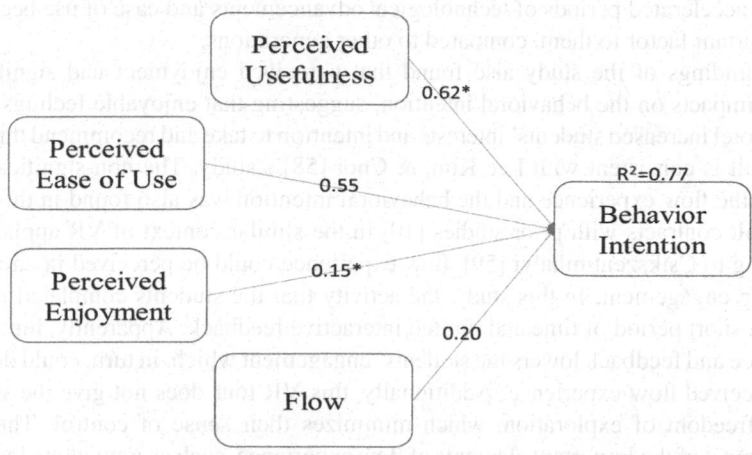

Fig. 2. Structural model analysis (*$p < 0.001$)

5   Conclusions and Discussions

The virtual reality hotel tour provides opportunities for hospitality educators in providing unique experience and capturing the attention of potential hospitality major students. By incorporating the VR hotel tours in entry-level hospitality courses (i.e. introduction to hospitality industry), hospitality educators can develop a better understanding on how to adopt virtual reality in hospitality education. The current study attempted to use the TAM framework to examine students' virtual experience and their intentions during their virtual hotel tour in the classroom, and identified factors that influence students' engagement in the virtual environment.

The current study has both theoretical and practical contribution. Theoretically, the study validated the Technology Acceptance Model (TAM) for understanding students' perception of virtual reality experience and the framework, and it also expanded the TAM framework by incorporating the flow theory and hedonic construct (i.e. perceived enjoyment) to examine users' virtual experience. The developed framework offers a new avenue for hospitality educators to better understand factors that motivate students' engagement in hospitality courses. With adequate reliability and validity of the measurement for constructs used in the study, the development of the measurement scales can be used for further study, contributing to the theoretical progress of the framework. The developed model first examined how the TAM factors (PU and PEU) contributed to the behavioral intention. The results showed that PU was a significantly positive indicator of students' intention to take and recommend the class, while PEU was not a significant factor of students' intention. This is consistent with Huang et al. [10]'s findings. To be specific, the functional aspect of VR hotel tour increased students' interests in the class, however PEU may be a necessary condition when designing VR hotel tour instead of a sufficient criterion to enhance students' intention. Another possible reason for the non-significant result of PEU is that generation Z (those who born after 1996) grew up during the most accelerated periods of technological advancements and ease of use becomes a less important factor to them, compared to other generations.

The findings of the study also found that perceived enjoyment had significantly positive impacts on the behavioral intention, suggesting that enjoyable feelings during the VR hotel increased students' interests and intention to take and recommend this class. This result is consistent with Lee Kim, & Choi [58]'s study. The non-significant link between the flow experience and the behavioral intention was also found in this study. This result contracts with prior studies [10] in the similar context of VR applications. According to Csikszentmihalyi [59], flow experience could be perceived in an activity with deep engagement. In this study, the activity that the students completed is a VR tour with short period of time and limited interactive feedback. Apparently, limited VR experience and feedback lowers the students' engagement which, in turn, could decrease their perceived flow experience. Additionally, this VR tour does not give the students enough freedom of exploration, which minimizes their sense of control. Therefore, missing most of the important elements of flow experience, such as immediate feedback, a sense of control, and merger of action and awareness, explains this non-significant relationship in the results.

Practically, this study explored the possibility of incorporating virtual reality experience into hospitality education. The results of this exploratory study indicated that the use of VR hotel tour was well received by students as being useful in learning hospitality concepts. By integrating VR experience, hospitality courses can be more enjoyable and attracting to students. Of courses, hospitality educators should examine the opportunities and identify the best ways of integrating VR into hospitality courses, building a connection between the concepts learned in the virtual environment and their success in the classroom as well as in the real hospitality world.

Therefore, for future studies, the research team will improve the VR hotel tour with embedded learning elements, in order to examine the effectiveness of virtual reality-based learning. For example, multiple information items lead to the learning of hospitality concepts can be used in the VR hotel tour, where students need to complete the preset-missions.

Same as other studies, this study has several limitations. First of all, convenience sampling was used in this exploratory study and sample size was limited. Larger samples should be used in the future study to make the results to be more generalized. Second, as said above, the current study mainly focused on the acceptance and hedonic experience of virtual reality hotel tour. Future studies should examine the effectiveness of virtual reality-based learning.

References

1. Wei, W.: Research progress on virtual reality (VR) and augmented reality (AR) in tourism and hospitality. J. Hosp. Tour. Technol. 10(4), 539–570 (2019)

2. Steuer, J.: Defining virtual reality: dimensions determining telepresence. In: Biocca, F., Levy, M.R. (eds.) Communication in the Age of Virtual Reality, pp. 33–56. Lawrence Erlbaum Associates, Hillsdale (1995)
3. Gutiérrez, M., Vexo, F., Thalmann, D.: Stepping into Virtual Reality. Springer, Heidelberg (2008)
4. Bruner, J.: The Relevance of Education. Harvard University Press, Cambridge (1971)
5. Govindasamy, T.: Successful implementation of E-learning pedagogical considerations. Internet High. Educ. 4, 287–299 (2002)
6. Spiro, R., Feltovich, P., Feltovich, P., Jacobson, M., Coulson, R.: Cognitive flexibility, vonstructivism, and hypertext; random access instruction for advanced knowledge acquisition in unstructured domains. Educ. Technol. 31(5), 24–33 (1995)
7. Wang, C., Stork, M.: Virtual reality through the lens of educators. Int. J. Smart Technol. Learn. 2(2/3), 89–95 (2020)
8. Cargill-Kipar, N.: My dragonfly flies upside down! using second life in multimedia design to teach students programming. Br. J. Edu. Technol. 40, 539–542 (2009)
9. Greenberg, J., Nepkie, J., Pence, H.: The SUNY oneonta second life music project. J. Educ. Technol. Syst. 37, 251–258 (2009)
10. Huang, Y., Backman, S., Backman, K., Moore, D.: Exploring user acceptance of 3D virtual worlds in travel and tourism marketing. Tour. Manag. 36, 490–501 (2013)
11. Grigorovici, D., Constantin, C.: Experiencing interactive advertising beyond rich media: impacts of ad type and presence on brand effectiveness in 3D gaming immersive virtual environments. J. Interact. Advert. 5(1), 22–36 (2004)
12. Abdjul, T., Ntobuo, N., Payu, C.: Development of virtual laboratory-based of learning to improve physics learning outcomes of high school students. Jurnal Pendidikan Fisika Indonesia 15(2), 97–106 (2019)
13. Wijayanti, J., Ikhsan, J.: Virtual Reality Laboratory for Chemistry Education: The Effect of VR-Lab Media on Student's Cognitive Outcome (2019)
14. Shi, A., Wang, Y., Ding, N.: The effect of game–based immersive virtual reality learning environment on learning outcomes: designing an intrinsic integrated educational game for pre-class learning. Interact. Learn. Environ. 1–14 (2019)
15. Lund, B., Wang, T.: Effect of virtual reality on learning motivation and academic performance: what value may VR have for library instruction? Kansas Libr. Assoc. Coll. Univ. Libr. Section Proc. 9(1), 4 (2019)
16. Johnston, V., Collum, D.: Understanding diversity and the educational needs of students with exceptionalities: a case study of simSchool. Int. J. Smart Technol. Learn. 2(2–3), 198–216 (2020)
17. Scoresby, J., Shelton, B.: Visual perspectives within educational computer games: effects on presence and flow within virtual immersive learning environments. Instr. Sci. 39(3), 227–254 (2011)
18. Dawley, L., Dede, C.: Situated learning in virtual worlds and immersive simulations. In: Spector, J., Merrill, M., Elen, J., Bishop, M. (eds.) Handbook of Research on Educational Communications and Technology, pp. 723–734. Springer, New York (2014). https://doi.org/10.1007/978-1-4614-3185-5_58
19. Tichon, J., Burgess-Limerick, R.: A review of virtual reality as a medium for safety related training in mining. J. Health Saf. Res. Pract. 3(1), 33–40 (2011)
20. Aqlan, F., Elliott, L., Zhao, R.: Measuring problem-solving skills with virtual reality. Ind. Eng. 52(2), 40–45 (2020)
21. Hwang, W., Hu, S.: Analysis of peer learning behaviors using multiple representations in virtual reality and their impacts on geometry problem solving. Comput. Educ. 62, 308–319 (2013)

22. Davis, F.: Perceived usefulness, perceived ease of use, and user acceptance of information technology. MIS Q. **13**, 319–340 (1989)
23. Davis, F.: A technology acceptance model for empirically testing new end-user information systems: Theory and results. Doctoral dissertation, Massachusetts Institute of Technology (1985)
24. Lim, C., Khine, M.: Managing teachers' barriers to ICT integration in Singapore schools. J. Technol. Teach. Educ. **14**(1), 97–125 (2006)
25. Wixom, B., Todd, P.: A theoretical integration of user satisfaction and technology acceptance. Inf. Syst. Res. **16**(1), 85–102 (2005)
26. Igbaria, M., Schiffman, S., Wieckowski, T.: The respective roles of perceived usefulness and perceived fun in the acceptance of microcomputer technology. Behav. Inf. Technol. **13**(6), 349–361 (1994)
27. Karahanna, E., Straub, D.W.: The psychological origins of perceived usefulness and ease-of-use. Inf. Manag. **35**(4), 237–250 (1999)
28. Subramanian, G.: A replication of perceived usefulness and perceived ease of use measurement. Decis. Sci. **25**(5–6), 863–874 (1994)
29. Saadé, R., Bahli, B.: The impact of cognitive absorption on perceived usefulness and perceived ease of use in on-line learning: an extension of the technology acceptance model. Inf. Manag. **42**(2), 317–327 (2005)
30. Segars, A.H., Grover, V.: Re-examining perceived ease of use and usefulness: a confirmatory factor analysis. MIS Q. **17**(4), 517 (1993). https://doi.org/10.2307/249590
31. Wang, Y., Qualls, W.: Towards a theoretical model of technology adoption in hospitality organizations. Int. J. Hosp. Manag. **26**(3), 560–573 (2007)
32. Shin, D.H., Biocca, F., Choo, H.: Exploring the user experience of three-dimensional virtual learning environments. Behav. Inf. Technol. **32**(2), 203–214 (2013)
33. van der Heijden, H.: User acceptance of hedonic information systems. MIS Q. **28**(4), 695–704 (2004). https://doi.org/10.2307/25148660
34. Manis, K., Choi, D.: The virtual reality hardware acceptance model (VR-HAM): extending and individuating the technology acceptance model (TAM) for virtual reality hardware. J. Bus. Res. **100**, 503–513 (2019)
35. Hamari, J., Sjöklint, M., Ukkonen, A.: The sharing economy: why people participate in collaborative consumption. J. Am. Soc. Inf. Sci. **67**(9), 2047–2059 (2016)
36. Venkatesh, V.: Determinants of perceived ease of use: integrating control, intrinsic motivation, and emotion into the technology acceptance model. Inf. Syst. Res. **11**(4), 342–365 (2000)
37. Liu, Z., Park, S.: What makes a useful online review? Implication for travel product websites. Tour. Manag. **47**, 140–151 (2015)
38. So, K., Kim, H., Oh, H.: What makes Airbnb experiences enjoyable? The effects of environmental stimuli on perceived enjoyment and repurchase intention. J. Travel Res. **60**(5), 1018–1038 (2020). https://doi.org/10.1177/0047287520921241
39. Chen, Y., Shang, R., Li, M.: The effects of perceived relevance of travel blogs' content on the behavioral intention to visit a tourist destination. Comput. Hum. Behav. **30**, 787–799 (2014)
40. Kim, J., Ahn, K., Chung, N.: Examining the factors affecting perceived enjoyment and usage intention of ubiquitous tour information services: a service quality perspective. Asia Pac. J. Tourism Res. **18**(6), 598–617 (2013)
41. Lee, W., Xiong, L., Hu, C.: The effect of Facebook users' arousal and valence on intention to go to the festival: applying an extension of the technology acceptance model. Int. J. Hosp. Manag. **31**(3), 819–827 (2012)
42. Dickinger, A., Arami, M., Meyer, D.: The role of perceived enjoyment and social norm in the adoption of technology with network externalities. Eur. J. Inf. Syst. **17**(1), 4–11 (2008)

43. Goh, S., Yoon, T.: If you build it will they come? An empirical investigation of facilitators and inhibitors of hedonic virtual world acceptance. In: 2011 44th Hawaii International Conference on System Sciences, pp. 1–9. IEEE (2011)

44. Skadberg, Y., Kimmel, J.: Visitors' flow experience while browsing a Web site: its measurement, contributing factors and consequences. Comput. Hum. Behav. **20**(3), 403–422 (2004)

45. Csikszentmihalyi, M.: Beyond Boredom and Anxiety. Jossey-Bass, San Francisco (2000)

46. Ghani, J.: Flow in human computer interactions: test of a model. Hum. Factors Inf. Syst. Emerg. Theor. Bases **3**, 291–311 (1995)

47. Faiola, A., Smyslova, O.: Flow experience in second life: the impact of telepresence on human-computer interaction. In: Ozok, A.A., Zaphiris, P. (eds.) OCSC 2009. LNCS, vol. 5621, pp. 574–583. Springer, Heidelberg (2009). https://doi.org/10.1007/978-3-642-02774-1_62

48. Nah, F., Eschenbrenner, B., DeWester, D., Park, S.: Impact of flow and brand equity in 3D virtual worlds. In: Cross-Disciplinary Models and Applications of Database Management: Advancing Approaches, pp. 277–297. IGI Global (2012)

49. Chang, H., Wang, I.: An investigation of user communication behavior in computer mediated environments. Comput. Hum. Behav. **24**(5), 2336–2356 (2008)

50. Hsu, C., Chang, K., Kuo, N., Cheng, Y.: The mediating effect of flow experience on social shopping behavior. Inf. Dev. **33**(3), 243–256 (2017)

51. Jung, T., tom Dieck, M.C., Lee, H., Chung, N.: Effects of virtual reality and augmented reality on visitor experiences in museum. In: Inversini, A., Schegg, R. (eds.) Information and Communication Technologies in Tourism, pp. 621–635. Springer, Cham (2016). https://doi.org/10.1007/978-3-319-28231-2_45

52. Huang, Y., Backman, K., Backman, S., Chang, L.: Exploring the implications of virtual reality technology in tourism marketing: an integrated research framework. Int. J. Tour. Res. **18**(2), 116–128 (2016)

53. Kline, R.: Principles and Practice of Structural Equation Modeling (3. Baskı). Guilford, New York (2011)

54. Wallace, L.G., Sheetz, S.D.: The adoption of software measures: a technology acceptance model (TAM) perspective. Inf. Manag. **51**(2), 249–259 (2014)

55. Hair, J., Sarstedt, M., Pieper, T., Ringle, C.: The use of partial least squares structural equation modeling in strategic management research: a review of past practices and recommendations for future applications. Long Range Plan. **45**(5–6), 320–340 (2012)

56. Anderson, J., Gerbing, D.: Structural equation modeling in practice: a review and recommended two-step approach. Psychol. Bull. **103**(3), 411 (1988)

57. Fornell, C., Larcker, D.: Evaluating structural equation models with unobservable variables and measurement error. J. Mark. Res. **18**(1), 39–50 (1981)

58. Lee, J., Kim, J., Choi, J.Y.: The adoption of virtual reality devices: the technology acceptance model integrating enjoyment, social interaction, and strength of the social ties. Telematics Inform. **39**, 37–48 (2019)

59. Csikszentmihalyi, M.: Finding Flow: The Psychology of Engagement with Everyday Life. Basic Books, New York (1997)

Understanding School Children's Playful Experiences Through the Use of Educational Robotics - The Impact of Open-Ended Designs

Jeanette Sjöberg[1]([✉]) [iD] and Eva Brooks[2] [iD]

[1] Halmstad University, Kristian IVs väg 3, 301 18 Halmstad, Sweden
jeanette.sjoberg@hh.se
[2] Aalborg University, Kroghstraede, 3, 9220 Aalborg, Denmark
eb@hum.aau.dk

Abstract. The use of digital technology in school settings is increasing every year, where one aspect of digital technology is robotics in education. In relation to that and of uttermost importance is the issue of how to design teaching and learning activities that includes robot technology in education. In this paper we investigate how open-ended designs can allow children to playfully explore robotics in educational settings, drawing from workshops carried out with three third grade classes of Danish school children, aged 9–10 years old, that interact with robotics in a cross-case study. By the use of video recordings, the unit of analysis focuses on the activities with a special interest on children's interactions with the robots and with each other. The research questions posed in the study are: (1) What happens when school children use robotics designed for open-ended interactions? And (2) In what ways do children's playful experiences unfold while engaged with robotics? The study applies a qualitative approach and the theoretical framework used describes open-ended designs as resources to develop playful experiences. In doing so, Vygotsky's theory on mediation, Hutt's studies into children's play with novel objects, and Bird and Edwards' digital play framework are used as an analytical framework. The results of this study imply that by using an open-ended design in the teaching activity with the robot, which included an exploratory and problem-solving approach, conditions were created for playful and collaborative learning.

Keywords: Collaboration · Educational robotics · Open-ended designs · Playfulness · Problem-solving · School children

1 Introduction

The use of digital technology in school settings is increasing every year, not least in view of how technology has become increasingly entrenched in curricula around the world [1], where one aspect of digital technology is robotics in education [2, 3]. There are a variety of robotics, such as for example physically coded robots, introductory programmable robots, computer-programmable robots, and kit-based robots. When it

X. Fang (Ed.): HCII 2022, LNCS 13334, pp. 456–468, 2022.
https://doi.org/10.1007/978-3-031-05637-6_29

comes to robotics in education, some types of robotics are better suited than others. A group of researchers has developed a so-called *EduRobot Taxonomy* [4], where they divide educational robotics into the following three categories: *build bots* (e.g., maker bots and robot kits), *use bots* (e.g., turtles, walking robots and drones) and *social bots* (e.g., humanoids and toys). Both the robotics found under build and use bots have been used in educational settings for quite a long time (since the 1970s more or less) and traditionally exclusively with a focus on engineering learning within STEM (Science, Technology, Engineering and Math) subjects. Social bots are more recent, though its use in education has increased significantly in recent years [e.g., 5, 6].

However, the use of robots in education remains largely unknown to both researchers and educators [7]. Despite increased efforts in investigating the educational impact of educational robotics referring to its potentials and limitations [8], research underlines that the use of robotics in education tends to be narrow [e.g., 9]. A perspective on this relates to the fact that the majority of contemporary educational robotic activities do not fully meet formal educational requirements, but rather exploit technical innovations [10]. Thus, just adding robotics to a teaching situation in order to show technicalities without any higher educational aim, makes it difficult to tie robot activities to general pedagogical goals. As a consequence, other approaches have been adopted for the introduction of robots in school settings, where, e.g., research points to the benefits of using children's creativity in these contexts [cf. 11]. Additionally, research on the identification of potentially influential factors on student success in using open-ended design scenarios is scarce [12].

To this end, we aim to widening up this narrow perspective by investigating how open-ended designs can allow children to playfully explore robotics in educational settings. Our main concern is that the educational robotics that exist and are used in educational contexts have limited opportunities for interaction and/or learning. Therefore, we want to demonstrate the inclusion of playful learning that we claim could offer a greater area of use for robotics in education. To support the aim, we have posed the following research questions: (1) What happens when school children use robotics designed for open-ended interactions? And (2) In what ways do children's playful experiences unfold while engaged with robotics?

1.1 Robotics in Education

As a support for what is usually called the 21st century skills (collaboration, communication, critical and/or computational thinking, and creativity), robot technology has come to be used more frequently in education [9], and research has pointed out the great promise robotics holds as a learning technology [e.g., 7]. However, the use of robotics in education has been most frequent as a support for teaching STEM (Science, Technology, Engineering and Math) subjects, programming in particular, and has mostly been outcome focused [13, 14]. This is basically the case despite research pointing at the fact that children's development of cognitive, conceptual, language and social (collaborative) skills are positively influenced by working with programmable robots [e.g., 9, 15–17] and that the use of robots in teaching thus could be broader and more creatively inclined [e.g., 11]. Furthermore, there is a lack of focus in research on playfulness in relation to robotics in education, which potentially could be an opening for an increased use of robotics in additional school subjects.

In a longitudinal Italian study, an innovative program teaching the basics of robotics was implemented in a primary school curriculum as a subject for a period of five years. The results show that the students who completed the entire robotics program attained higher levels of competence and achieved the skills that were planned for them quicker and more in-depth, compared to students in classes from the same school and the countrywide average who had not participated in such a program [18]. During the robotic teaching activities, such as exploring robot design and programming, the students have reportedly shown great curiosity and passion, as well as acquired important life skills like collaboration and problem-solving. In another study, focusing on educational robotics (ER) in the stage of secondary education, questionnaires from a total of 158 students and 61 teachers were collected and analyzed. The questionnaires were sent out just after the students' and teachers' participation in an ER competition, with the aim of capturing their perceptions and assessments about its impact in the learning process [19]. The results show that "ER generates high motivation in students. Likewise, the autonomy in decision-making provides appropriate conditions to develop creativity and autonomous work" [19, p. 13]. These examples support the idea that an exploratory and problem-solving approach in the inclusion of robots in education can foster the development of students' cognitive and social skills [e.g., 15, 20].

1.2 Open-Ended Design

In designing new interactive play environments, it is of vital importance to understand the dynamic social context in which play takes place, since play usually is a social experience [21]. The same goes for designing open-ended learning environments, which includes playfulness and creativity. In a previous study we conducted with school children in the same age group as in the current study, our results showed that the open-ended design of the educational activities deployed, which included smart mobile technology, fostered collaborative interactions among a group of Swedish school children [22]. In the current study we have been inspired by user-centered design-activities and -processes focusing on open-endedness enabling play and creativity. Mattelmäki, Brandt and Vaajakallio [23] has defined the concept of open-ended as follows: "Being open-ended means that they can allow and inspire new individual interpretations for various participants in the collaborative design processes, which include users, designers and other stakeholders" [23, p. 79]. They have examined the concept of open-ended interpretations in user-centered design processes and discuss different kinds of formats that can be used to work with representations of field research findings and insights in ways that can be considered open-ended. On another note, Bartholomew and Strimel [12] has conducted a study in which they examined both qualitative and quantitative data from 706 middle school students, working in small groups, as they completed an open-ended design challenge. Drawing from both questionnaires and student interviews, their results suggest "that students are familiar, comfortable, and receptive to open-ended design problems and enjoy working through them" [12, p. 766]. Furthermore, the results show that the students got better rankings on their final design products when faced with more experiences of open-ended design problems in school, which seems to suggest that "one way of increasing student success is by affording students more opportunities for completing open-ended design problems in school settings" [12, p. 766].

2 Theoretical Approach

To address the matters of children's open-ended interactions and playful experiences when interacting with robotics, we have developed a analytical framework deriving from concepts based on Vygotsky's [24] theory of mediation, Hutt's [25] studies into children's play with novel objects, and Bird and Edwards' [26] digital play framework. The concept of mediation argues that people's learning is mediated by symbolic tools, which regulate their activities. This formed the foundation for Vygotsky's analytical model for mediated activity, which comprises a triangular unity consisting of the subject (person) and object as opposing ends of the base of the triangle, and the tools placed at the top (Fig. 1) [24, 27]. Further, the triangle points to the fact that people use tools to realize a certain object. When a person acquires insights into the use of a certain tool, the object of the activity changes [24].

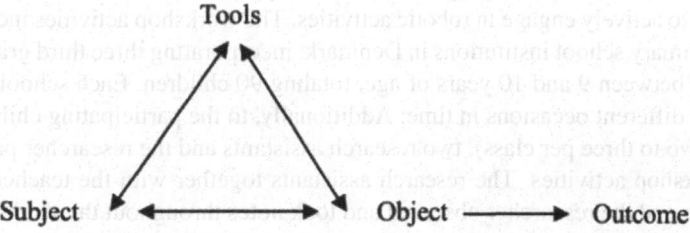

Tools

Subject ◄——————— **Object** ———————► **Outcome**

Fig. 1. The mediating activity model as proposed by Vygotsky [24].

Hutt's theory based on children's play with novel objects suggests two categories of children's play activities. These are based on the author's findings demonstrating the ways a child responds when confronted with new objects to play with. While in the first category the child examines the object to explore "what can this *object* do?", the second category is characterized by diverse exploration or play questioning "what can *I* do with this object?" [25, p. 16]. In their article, Bird and Edwards [26] present a digital play framework to understand the ways children learn to use technology through play. They elaborate on Hutt's categories by defining the first category as epistemic activity in which children explore functionalities of specific technologies, and the second category as ludic activity where children generate new content by means of technology. When epistemic and ludic activities include relational aspects, the movement between the two activities becomes complex as the activity then deals with both relational and content aspects competing for attention [28, 29]. This means that participants need to monitor both their own and the others' epistemic processes, which could influence movement from epistemic to ludic activity. In the present study, children are carrying out a collaborative activity including robotics, where it can become difficult for them to channel diverging and potential opposing stances toward epistemic and ludic engagement. Bird and Edwards [26] underline that ludic activity only emerges once epistemic activity is mastered. However, the children can always return to epistemic issues and thus develop their learning. In relation to Vygotsky's mediating activity model (Fig. 1), we have used robotics (Ozobots) as the tool to observe children's engagement with the Ozobot robots as an epistemic object. This is to say, how the children during the activity by means of questioning, discussing, and determining functionalities and values of the robots moved to a ludic activity with the object. This is in line with Hutt et al. [30], who in their article identified and categorized both epistemic and ludic activities.

3 Methodology

The present study is based on a cross-case study, which included three cases, which were designed as workshop activities focusing on children's interaction with robotics. The workshop setup was arranged in an open-ended way intended to promote children's playful engagement with robotics. The robotics used in the study were Ozobots, which is a versatile robot designed to enhance interest in programming. As part of the open-ended workshop design, we complemented the robotics with fairytale scenarios. This combination of traditional and digital tools was supposed to invite a broader spectrum of children to actively engage in robotic activities. The workshop activities included two different primary school institutions in Denmark, incorporating three third grade classes of children between 9 and 10 years of age, totaling 90 children. Each school class was involved at different occasions in time. Additionally, to the participating children, their teachers (two to three per class), two research assistants and the researcher participated in the workshop activities. The research assistants together with the teachers assisted the children and the researcher observed and took notes throughout the workshops. The data collected included video observations, informal conversations with the children and their teachers, observational notes, and pictures.

3.1 Procedure

The workshop activity was divided into different phases. The first phase briefly introduced the activity showing the Ozobot robot and exemplifying a couple of fairytale scenarios. The task for the children was to, in their groups, interpret the fairytale and to use creative material to reproduce the storyline and to code the Ozobot representing the main character of the fairytale. The fairytales were selected by the researchers and made up of classic fairytales, for example H. C. Anderson's "The Ugly Duckling" and European folklore tales such as "Goldilocks and the Three Bears". In this paper, we focus on the empirical material deriving from two groups who at different occasions in time were engaged with H. C. Andersen's fairytale of "Little Red Riding Hood", and "What the Old Man Does is Always Right". In line with Ozobot's coding scheme based on colors and sequences, the coding was carried out analogously with different colored sharpies. Other props consisted of creative material such as foam clay, crayons, markers, LEGO, cardboard, paper, yarn, glue, tape, scissors and post-its (Fig. 2). The different groups of children each had a workstation, which was equipped with a fixed camera facing the center of the table, which recorded the activities taking place around the table. The teachers had divided the children into groups beforehand.

After the general introduction, the children went to their workstation, where either the research assistants and teachers or the children themselves read the fairytales out loud (Fig. 3). As some of the fairytales were relatively new to the children, the research assistants, and the teachers' discussed parts of the fairytales together with the children, for example how a marketplace functioned at the time when a specific fairytale was produced or what kind of motives that could be foundation for a fairytale character's choice of action. In this way, the children could draw upon these discussions to imagine how, for example, a horse could be sold for a basket of eggs. After this, the children were introduced to the task, the Ozobot robots and the creative material, which formed the start of their group work. In the final phase of the activity, the children presented their reproduction of the fairytales and demonstrated how they had coded Ozobot as the main character of the plot.

Fig. 2. Coding scheme, sharpies and other creative material such as wooden brix and foamclay.

Fig. 3. Children reading their fairytale.

3.2 Ethical Considerations

Teachers and parents were informed about the study in writing. The teachers distributed the information and a consent form to the parents. All parents agreed to let their child participate by signing the informed consent form. The signatures included the parents' approval of us using videos and photos for scientific purposes. At the workshop, we again informed the children about their right to withdraw from the workshop activity at any time if they felt uncomfortable or for any other reason did not want to participate. Aligned with ethical guidelines, all names of the schools and participants are anonymized.

3.3 Analysis

The analysis was carried out by using the analytical concepts of *epistemic* and *ludic* activity. These concepts are associated with actions as identified by Hutt et al. [30] and elaborated by Bird and Edwards [26]. The actions related to epistemic activity are: exploration, problem-solving, and skill acquisition. The actions related to ludic activity are: symbolic and innovation (Table 1). Thus, the analytical procedure was deductive through which we categorized the data from video observations of the children engaged in coding and interpretative activities with robotics, fairytales, and creative material. Deductive analysis starts with the analytical concepts chosen to approach the data, which in this study were based on Vygostsky's [24] concept of tool-mediated activity positioned with the play actions identified by Hutt [25] represented by object of epistemic and ludic play [26]. The data were categorized based on the children's engagement with the Ozobot robots and the analogue material, sorted by means of children's questioning, followed by ordering the outcomes in relation to the five actions. Inspired by Bird and Edwards [26], we then applied an inductive approach to clarify indicators for the playful experience of children's engagement with robotics framed by an open-ended design.

4 Results

Using the analytical framework, we have identified a set of indicators for children's playful experiences with robotics through workshops that were designed for open-ended interactions. The indicators are summarized and explained in Tables 1 and 2 (Figs. 4, 5, 6 and 7).

Table 1. Indicators for playful experiences with robotics through open-ended designed workshop: scenario 1 (inspired by Bird & Edwards, 2015)

Object of activity	Actions	Indicators associated with playful experiences while engaged with robotics through open-ended designed workshop	
		Robots, Little red riding hood (fairytale), creative material	Examples
Epistemic play	Exploration	Holding the Ozobot in one hand while investigating the sensors of the robot.	Benjamin asks: *how does it work? How can I get the colors in correct order when I shall program the robot?*
		Drawing lines with the markers on a white sheet of paper.	Carl is concentrated while learning how the markers work. He turns to Benjamin and says: *Give the robot to me, we test how it works.* Both boys laughing out loud.
		Locating different codes on the coding guidelines.	Peter discusses with the research assistant about how different color combination creates different ways for the robot to move forward, backward, spin, dance, etc.
	Problemsolving	Coding with markers and placing the robot on the coded line.	Carl is busy with drawing a long line to form a circle with tight curves while at the same time letting the robot move forward on the line.
		Reconstructing props.	Benjamin and Carl identify that Ozobot (Little red riding hood) could not get into the grandmother's house, which they built of wooden bricks. Benjamin, then, makes a total reconstruction of the house and informs the other group members what he has done, and that Ozobot now perfectly can get into the house.
	Skill acquisition	Deliberate dividing the circle into smaller parts. Using the coding scheme and decides how the Ozobot should move. Sharing what learnt with each other.	Benjamin and Carl demonstrate to each other how the coding scheme works and how the robot picks up the code and moves in different ways depending on the coloring.
Ludic play	Symbolic	Deliberate connecting coding and fairytale	Benjamin, Carl and Peter create props to reproducing of the fairytale and fit them into the coding they have done.
	Innovation		Explaining for the teacher assistant how it all comes together, e.g. how they have decorated Ozobot to look alike little red riding hood and how they have changed grandmother's house so that Ozobot can move into it.

Table 2. Indicators for playful experiences with robotics through open-ended designed workshop: scenario 2 (inspired by Bird & Edwards, 2015)

Object of activity	Actions	*Indicators associated with playful experiences while engaged with robotics through open-ended designed workshop*	
		Robots, What the old man does is always right (fairytale), creative material	Examples
Epistemic play	Exploration	Testing the foamclay.	Max, David, Anton, and Marie collectively investigate the foamclay in terms of what can be possible to use it for, e.g. creating the animals of different sizes included in the fairytale (hens, lamb, cow, ets.).
		Locating different codes on the coding scheme	Max, David, Anton, and Marie are concerned that the coding of Ozobot fits to the characters and the props of the fairytales that they have created. David investigates the coding scheme and how they differ in color combinations.
	Problemsolving	Trying different creative material to solve.	Max puts glue under the cow's hooves and cut circles of thick paper so that the cow, which is made by foamclay can stand up more secure compared to without this solution.
		Intentional but random coding.	The teacher assistant reminds the group that they also should do some coding to finalize their reproduction of the fairytale. Max grabs the coding markers and draws a line in between the characters and props.
	Skill acquisition	Sharing learnt actions with the group members.	David has put efforts into creating an as authentic lamb as possible with the foamclay. When having finished it, he
			demonstrates for the other group members how he dimensioned it so that it could stand up properly. He also shows the others that he decorated the lamb so that that one could see that it was a kind and sweet lamb. The four group members clap their hands, smile and laughs.
Ludic play	Symbolic Innovation	Creation of imaginary props.	Marie has created a basket of apples and shows to the others how she has made them to look rotten. David decorates the pigs in an imaginary way with feathers and shows it to the others. They all laugh.

(1) What happens when school children use robotics designed for open-ended interactions? And (2) In what ways do children's playful experiences unfold while engaged with robotics?

Fig. 4. Children's epistemic play – exploration.

Fig. 5. Children's epistemic play – problem-solving.

Fig. 6. Children's epistemic play – skill acquisition.

Fig. 7. Children's ludic play – symbolic/innovation.

5 Discussion

In this paper, we set out to investigate how open-ended designs can allow children to playfully explore robotics in educational settings. In the current study, the content in the teaching activity was the subject of programming, where the Ozobot was the tool; a *user bot* in Catlin et al. [4] category scheme. By adding a playful element through the fairytale, conditions were created for the children to explore different possibilities for problem solving and collaboration, and the participating children showed enthusiasm, creativity, and engagement. Hence, the results show that by using an open-ended design in the teaching activity with the robot, which included an exploratory and problem-solving approach, conditions were created for playful and collaborative learning [e.g., 11]. Consequently, the study provides useful insights into what is happening when children use robotics designed for open-ended interactions. This was shown through certain indicators of the children's actions and interactions with the robotics, the fairytales, and the creative material, which combined evidently evoked and shaped an open-ended setting and playful experiences. This was shown in the children's epistemic play actions where they explored the robots' and the material's functionalities, solved problems, and experienced how, for example, the robot could identify and handle sharp corners. Through this the children developed skills by demonstrating what they learnt for each other or for the research assistant.

Children's ludic play emerged as a result of the epistemic play. Here, they tried out playful ideas, such as decorating a pig with feathers, and by connecting Ozobot together with the fairytale and props, the children's creativity started to shine. The two groups exemplified in the result section, approached the task differently. The group who had the fairytale of the little red riding hood, started out with exploring the robot and the coding and kept that focus throughout the activity, the reproduction was secondary. Their way of working was merely pairwise. Conversely, the other group, having the fairytale of what the old man does is always right, was primarily exploring the creative material and focused on reproducing the fairytale by carefully creating characters and props. The four of them worked together, but by the end when they started the programming, it was one of the boys who concentrated on this task. This is to say that the open-ended design offered the children flexibility and through the openness they could choose their own focus and how to carry out the task. As such, this contributed to a relaxed and playful atmosphere. The playfulness was shown through children's movement between full concentration and laughs, through sharing thoughts and creations and in such situations being supported by their group members, leading to many smiles and 'high fives'.

Aligned with Bird and Edwards [26], the analytical framework and the way it provides descriptions of how an open-ended design can contribute to engagement and playful learning, can be used by teachers as an observation tool. It is possible to, for example, contemplate the range of play behavior that emerges while children are occupied in an activity.

5.1 Contribution and Implications for the Field

This study provides teachers with a framework for the use of robotics in school activities to create an increased interest for the subject at hand. The open-ended design affords the teacher the possibility to tie robot activities to general pedagogical goals, rather than just adding a robot to a teaching situation to show technicalities without any higher educational aim. This is done partly through the description of an open-ended way by combining robotic and creative activities leading to engagement and playful ways of learning. Furthermore, the framework includes a guide for teachers to integrate robotics in their teaching activities, which consists of indicators from epistemic and ludic play providing the teachers with opportunities to identify children's learning by means of robotics. In this article, we have applied Bird and Edward's digital play framework in another context, namely robotics, however more studies are needed to validate the framework in different school settings.

References

1. Brooks, E., Sjöberg, J.: Playfulness and creativity as vital features when school children develop game-based designs. Designs for Learning (Forthcoming)
2. Malinverni, L., Valero, C., Schaper, M.M., Garcia de la Cruz, I.: Educational robotics as a boundary object: towards a research agenda. Int. J. Child-Comput. Interact. **29**, 100305 (2021)
3. Brooks, E., Sjöberg, J.: Children's programming of robots by designing fairytales. In: Brooks, E., Dau, S., Selander, S. (eds.) Digital Learning and Collaborative Practices: Lessons from Inclusive and Empowering Participation with Emerging Technologies, pp. 158–174. Routledge, London (2021)
4. Catlin, D., Kandlhofer, M., Holmquist, S.: EduRobot taxonomy: a provisional schema for classifying educational robots. In: Robotics in Education 2018 (2018)
5. Johal, W.: Research trends in social robots for learning. Curr. Robot. Rep. **1**(3), 75–83 (2020). https://doi.org/10.1007/s43154-020-00008-3
6. Pachidis, T., Vrochidou, E., Kaburlasos, V. G., Kostova, S., Bonković, M., Papić, V.: Social robotics in education: state-of-the-art and directions. In: Aspragathos, N.A., Koustoumpardis, P.N., Moulianitis, V.C. (eds.) RAAD 2018. MMS, vol. 67, pp. 689–700. Springer, Cham (2019). https://doi.org/10.1007/978-3-030-00232-9_72
7. Cheng, Y.-W., Sun, P.-C., Chen, N.-S.: The essential applications of educational robot: requirement analysis from the perspectives of experts, researchers and instructors. Comput. Educ. **126**, 399–416 (2018)
8. Bascou, N.A., Menekse, M.: Robotics in K-12 formal and informal learning environments: a review of literature. In: ASEE Annual Conference and Exposition, Conference Proceedings, vol. 2016 (2016). https://doi.org/10.18260/p.26119
9. Rusk, N., Resnick, M., Berg, R., Pezalla-Granlund, M.: New pathways into robotics: strategies for broadening participation. J. Sci. Educ. Technol. **17**(1), 59–69 (2008). https://doi.org/10.1007/s10956-007-9082-2
10. Mondada, F., et al.: Bringing robotics to formal education: the Thymio open-source hardware robot. IEEE Robot. Autom. Mag. **24**(1), 77–85 (2017)
11. Barreto, F., Benitti, V.: Exploring the educational potential of robotics in schools: a systematic review. Comput. Educ. **58**(3), 978–988 (2012). https://doi.org/10.1016/j.compedu.2011.10.006
12. Bartholomew, S.R., Strimel, G.J.: Factors influencing student success on open-ended design problems. Int. J. Technol. Des. Educ. **28**(3), 753–770 (2017). https://doi.org/10.1007/s10798-017-9415-2
13. Bertel, L.B., Rasmussen, D.M.: On being a peer: what persuasive technology for teaching can gain from social robotics in education. Int. J. Conceptual Struct. Smart Appl. (IJCSSA) **1**(2), 58–68 (2013)

14. Daniela, L., Lytras, M.D.: Educational robotics for inclusive education. Technol. Knowl. Learn. **24**(2), 219–225 (2018). https://doi.org/10.1007/s10758-018-9397-5

15. Ioannou, A., Makridou, E.: Exploring the potentials of educational robotics in the development of computational thinking: a summary of current research and practical proposal for future work. Educ. Inf. Technol. **23**(6), 2531–2544 (2018). https://doi.org/10.1007/s10639-018-9729-z

16. Bruni, F., Nisdeo, M.: Educational robots and children's imagery: a preliminary investigation in the first year of primary school. Res. Educ. Media **9**(1), 37–44 (2017)

17. Bertel, L.B., Dau, S., Brooks, E.: ROSIE: robot-supported inclusive education - a play- based approach to STEM education and inclusion in early childhood transitions. In: Proceedings of the ESERA 2019 Conference (2020)

18. Valzano, M., Vergine, C., Cesaretti, L., Screpanti, L., Scaradozzi, D.: Ten years of educational robotics in a primary school. In: Scaradozzi, D., Guasti, L., Di Stasio, M., Miotti, B., Monteriù, A., Blikstein, P. (eds.) Makers at School, Educational Robotics and Innovative Learning Environments. LNNS, vol. 240, pp. 283–289. Springer, Cham (2021). https://doi.org/10.1007/978-3-030-77040-2_38

19. Arís, N., Orcos, L.: Educational robotics in the stage of secondary education: empirical study on motivation and STEM skills. Educ. Sci. **9**, 73 (2019). https://doi.org/10.3390/educsci9020073

20. Atmatzidou, S., Demetriadis, S.: Advancing students' computational thinking skills through educational robotics: a study on age and gender relevant differences. Robot. Auton. Syst. **75**, 661–670 (2016)

21. de Valk, L., Bekker, T., Eggen, B.: Designing for social interaction in open-ended play environments. Int. J. Des. **9**(1), 107–120 (2015)

22. Sjöberg, J., Brooks, E.: Collaborative interactions in problem-solving activities: school children's orientations while developing digital game designs using smart mobile technology. Int. J. Child-Comput. Interact. **33**, 100456 (2022)

23. Mattelmäki, T., Brandt, M., Vaajakallio, K.: On designing open-ended interpretations for collaborative design exploration. CoDesign **7**(2), 79–93 (2011). https://doi.org/10.1080/15710882.2011.609891

24. Vygotsky, L.S.: Mind in Society: The Development of Higher Psychological Processes. Harvard University Press, Cambridge (1978)

25. Hutt, C.: Exploration and play in children. Paper Presented at the Symposia of the Zoological Society of London, London (1966)

26. Bird, J., Edwards, S.: Children learning to use technologies through play: a digital play framework. Br. J. Educ. Technol. **46**(6), 1149–1160 (2014). https://doi.org/10.1111/bjet.12191

27. Wertsch, J.V.: Vygotsky and the Social Formation of Mind. Harvard University Press, Cambridge (1985)

28. Damşa, C., Ludvigsen, S., Andriessen, J.: Knowledge co-construction – epistemic consensus or relational assent? In: Baker, M., Andriessen, J., Järvelä, S. (eds.) Affective Learning Together. Social and Emotional Dimensions of Collaborative Learning, pp. 97–119. Routledge, London (2013)

29. Barron, B.: Achieving coordination in collaborative problem-solving groups. J. Learn. Sci. **9**, 403–436 (2000). https://doi.org/10.1207/S15327809JLS0904_2

30. Hutt, S., Tyler, C., Hutt, C., Shristopherson, H.: Play, Exploration and Learning. A Natural History of the Preschool. Routledge, London (1989)

Videogame Design Using a User-Centered Approach to Teaching Projectile Motion

Julian F. Villada[1] and Maria F. Montoya[2]([⊠])

[1] Universidad Tecnológica de Pereira, Pereira, Colombia
jfvillada@utp.edu.co
[2] Exertion Games Lab, Monash University, Melbourne, Australia
maria.montoyavega@monash.edu

Abstract. The teaching of physics as a university course presents different challenges, within which the lack of interest and motivation to study physics in students is one of the most prominent. It has been identified that this demotivation is due to the disconnection that relates physical phenomena with the daily life. In addition, students need to construct proper mental representations to meaningfully learn scientific concepts and understand the physical world. Thus, some authors have proposed virtual simulators of several scientific phenomena as an alternative teaching tool. In the last decade, animations and video games in virtual reality have been proposed for the teaching of physics and other science subjects, such as chemistry and geometry, where authors have noticed the improvement in the assimilation of content. Virtual environments (VE) are proposed since they motivate students and bring them closer to reality, allowing them to visualize the phenomenon and modify it. Despite the increasing popularity of VE as a teaching tool, there is no clear evidence to establish a guide on their design for different learning contexts. Therefore, in this work, we propose a methodology to the design of a videogame for college teaching of the physical concept called projectile motion. Our proposal is based on user-centered design and videogame design to engage students with problem-solving activities in a game-like environment making learning more exciting and enjoyable for them. Finally, we present the first version of the video game improved by following 2 playtest with stakeholders.

Keywords: Serious videogames · Virtual learning environment · Projectile motion

1 Introduction

Teaching physics as a college course presents different challenges, within which the student's lack of interest and motivation to study physics is one of the most prominent [1]. It has been identified that this demotivation is due to the disconnection that relates physical phenomena with daily life.

In addition, the traditional instruction leaves aside qualitative analysis of this subject and emphasizes quantitative aspects, which most students fear [2]. These methodologies are less effective than research practice and interactive teaching-learning methods [3].

© The Author(s), under exclusive license to Springer Nature Switzerland AG 2022
X. Fang (Ed.): HCII 2022, LNCS 13334, pp. 469–483, 2022.
https://doi.org/10.1007/978-3-031-05637-6_30

However, engineering programs continue trusting in those methods to transmit scientific knowledge [4].

Researchers have proven that students must construct proper mental representations to meaningfully learn scientific concepts and understand the physical world [5]. That is why some authors have proposed simulators that present a model of the phenome-non studied or information and associated graphics on the screen. Simulations allow students to make variations of the simulation parameters for each phenomenon, analyze results, and recognize physical processes without facing difficulties in mathematical calculations [6–8].

In the last decade, animations and video games in virtual reality (VR) have been proposed to teach physics and other science subjects, such as chemistry and geometry [9]. Several authors note improvements in the assimilation of content and the rapid growth of the learning curve applying virtual environments in education, currently called virtual learning environments (VLEs) [10], going from 2D, 3D, and VR. VLEs are proposed since they motivate students, it brings them closer to reality, allowing them to visualize the phenomenon and modify it.

Some of the more frequently proposed VLEs by researchers and teachers are video games [10–12] since computer games are essentially based on computer simulations which usually are informal with explicit goals and rules, and are designed for entertainment [13]. Educational games in different contexts have become popular in the last decade since the cost of hardware and the availability of software are increasingly smaller barriers. Cheng et al. [14] discuss the use of serious games in science education, showing that most games are adventure or role-playing games. Bahadoorsingh et al. [15] and Huang [16] have investigated serious learning games for engineering students. Particularly, physics games propose simulations of theoretical equations and phenomena and interactive digital experiments that can be too expensive, dangerous, or complicated in real life. The MechGames project proposed by [13] aims to blend simulations and games to teach key concepts of the Dynamics course. Other works like [17] and [18] combined mixed and virtual reality to teach different physics concepts for engineers. Similarly, educators have used commercial games to teach physics and foster students' understanding of the underlying physical principles more thoroughly than traditional physics lessons from a book [19]. The authors in [20] and [21] used modern videogames that incorporate accurate physics in their game engines to teach projectile motion, one of the essential concepts in high schools and colleges' physics courses.

Projectile motion is a two-dimensional kinematic movement that describes a curved path. This motion is analyzed by making two assumptions: 1) the free-fall acceleration g is constant over the range of motion and is directed downward, and 2) the effect of air resistance is negligible. With these assumptions, the path of a projectile, which we call its trajectory, is always a parable [22].

The study of this motion is present in the curriculum of most of the engineering programs of the world. Despite many attempts by educators to include hands-on activities, students still face misconceptions and learning difficulties [23]. Although the VLEs present several advantages as learning tools, there is not enough evidence to establish a guide on their design for different learning contexts [10].

Therefore, this work presents a design methodology of a videogame in VR for teaching the physics concept called projectile motion. We propose a user-centered design approach combined with prior research on game design theory and learning strategies. Our goal is to engage students with problem-solving activities in a game-like environment that simulates a real word situation, making learning more exciting and enjoyable for students. Moreover, stakeholders in the HCI field will benefit from our game design proposal since we present a practical case study in the use of serious games to teach physics, considering the specific needs of end-users.

2 Methodology

The videogame aims to explain the physics concept of parabolic movement, one of the key concepts of kinematics. It was developed using a user-centered design methodology called Usability and Accessibility Engineering Process Model (MPIu+a) [24]. Our main goal using this model was to know the user's needs, in our case, physics students of first semesters from the local university. That is why we designed and applied a survey asking for the students' game experience, motivation to study physics, and the strategies to study physics.

2.1 Survey for University Students of the Physical I Course

An online questionnaire was conducted to establish the limitations and motivations of the students of the physics I course when learning the concept of parabolic movement, and in this way, design a videogame to teach it. Additionally, the questionnaire inquired about the gaming experience of the students, their most liked video games, and experiences with VR.

For the design of this questionnaire, the authors carried out a literature review to find that users' different gaming experiences are relevant when designing gamified systems. We also found that various investigations give importance to knowing the student's motivation to play. Based on our findings, we created the questionnaire with the following sections:

- First section: This section ask for the demographic data of the participant such as name, identification number, age, gender.
- Second section: request the game experience and the participant's practice with classic games played in our country, such as parks, dominoes, and rounds. This section is also geared towards finding participants' motivation to play and what they like to do while playing.
- Third section: the section asks for participants' experience with video games and VR.
- Fourth section: request students' perception of the physics I course, based on standard questionnaires such as [25].
- Fifth section: this section requests the student's perception of projectile motion and the strategies students use when learning it.

This questionnaire was rewritten online using Google Forms. Physics 1 students from the Technological University of Pereira (Pereira, Colombia) were volunteers and could access it to answer their questions virtually. The survey results were analyzed using the *Personas* technique to create a model of the possible user's profiles of the videogame. Each Persona role represents a grouping of behaviors, interests, and motivations identified in the end-user questionnaire results. We created the user profiles considering the following capacities, needs, and abilities that are decisive for the usability of the interactive system:

- Gaming experience: if the student has had experience with virtual reality, played video games, and how many hours he spends playing video games.
- The student's perception of the physics course, if he finds it attractive, he cares about learning and enjoys it, or on the contrary, he does not find it relevant or interested in learning.

2.2 User-Centered Design Using the MPIu+a Model

We decided to design the video game following the MPIu+a user-centered design methodology. This methodology has three main stages (Fig. 1): requirements analysis, prototyping, and evaluation [24]. We present the first and second stages in this work, leaving the evaluation for future work.

Requirement Analysis: In this stage, we were focused on knowing the stakeholders through the designed questionnaire and the classification of the students into the Personas profiles. In this stage, we also established the goals of our systems, such as the functional objective to reinforce the concept of parabolic movement through a video-game; and the usability objective to ensure that the videogame will be easy to learn, effective, and enjoyable for its users. Finally, according to the MPIu+a model, the developers need to define the technology that would be used for the system development. Since our interactive system is a videogame, we developed it on the worldwide known platform called Unity 3D. This platform allows to run the game on different operating systems, from Microsoft, Linux to Android, and allows create 3D and VR content with a vast number of free assets.

Prototyping: Following the MPIu+a model we developed two prototyping stages. The first stage was low-fidelity fast prototyping [26], using the storyboard technique, the game mechanics proposed by Shell [27], and the learning mechanics presented in [28]. Once the design team approved the rapid prototyping, the slow prototyping continued, using the programming of the videogame using Unity 3D and iterative playtesting.

Playtesting: Playtesting is an iterative technique used to improve the designed interactive system [29]. Playtest sessions have been used in VLE to ensure not only that learning occurs as a result of gameplay, but also that the proper intrinsic integration of properties, concepts, and strategies within the game's mechanics [30].

Therefore we developed two playtest once we considered that the videogame was complete, which means, the videogame had all the features planned in the fast prototyping. The first playtesting session was held with two university professors who teach the physics 1 course. The second session was developed with two UTP systems engineering program students who already see parabolic motion in their physics 1 course.

The experimental protocol developed for each playtesting section is described in the following Table 1:

Table 1. Playtesting experimental protocol

Tasks	Observations	Time
Introduction to the session		
Signing the consent form		10 min
Explanation of the VR headset use A general explanation of the videogame	Difficulties using the headset, first reactions to the videogame	5 min
Free gaming	Natural interaction with the videogame, likes and dislikes	5 min
Users' recommendations		10 min
Questions		10 min

Playing with Teachers: the authors carried out this playtest with two professors, each one in separate periods at a physics laboratory of the university. The videogame was played using the head-mounted display Oculus Quest 2 and its controls. The authors recorded a general video of the entire session and created an analysis document with observations that they considered essential to improve the learning mechanics. In the analysis document, the researchers registered all the general comments made by professors and their questionnaire answers. This questionnaire inquired about how the videogame explained the concept of parabolic motion from a VR perspective, the graphics used, and the presented equations. Once the playtesting ended, the authors analyzed the documentation and determined the improvements for a new videogame version. Finally, we implemented the videogame changes and programmed a new playtesting section with the students.

Playing with Students: the authors carried out this playtest with two students in separate periods at a physics laboratory of the university. The videogame was played using the head-mounted display Oculus Quest 2 and its controls. As the previous playtesting session, the researchers recorded a general video of the entire session and created an analysis document with the discussions that they considered essential to improve the game and learning mechanics. In the analysis document, the researchers also registered all the general comments made by the students and their questionnaire answers. For example, the student's questionnaire inquired about the graphics, sound, character placement, control manipulation, and game difficulty. Once the play-testing was ended, the authors analyzed the documentation and determined the improvement for a final videogame version.

3 Results

This section shows the physics students' survey analysis and survey results proposed in the methodology. Additionally, the videogame design results are presented following the steps of the MPIu+a methodology. Finally, we show the playtesting results based on the comments and suggestions of the participants.

3.1 Survey for University Students of the Physical I Course

The survey was solved by 93 students from the local university who were coursing the first semester of 2021. The authors recruited voluntary students of physics 1 with the help of the faculty of basic sciences of the university and the professors who teach this course. The questionnaire only was developed if the student agreed with the in-formed consent. The students were 33 women and 60 men who filled out the questionnaire in its entirety, with an average age of 20.8 years ± 3.35 years. The participants were from 14 different programs: mechanical technology, mechanical engineering, mechatronics engineering, agro-industrial process engineering, manufacturing engineering, chemical technology, industrial chemistry, environmental management, industrial engineering, electrical engineering, electronic engineering, and systems engineering, and bachelor of mathematics and physics.

Game Experience: Participants answered different questions about the importance of various features in a game. The results highlight that the game must have an elaborate story (70%), the game should allow to practice, see the progress and become better (71%). Also, the game must allow acquiring powers, special weapons, or great prizes (80%) and have constant challenges (76%). On the other hand, the actions they perform most frequently while playing were also questioned (see Fig. 1), where they want to make careful and highly planned plays (87%) and work together (47%) (see Fig. 1).

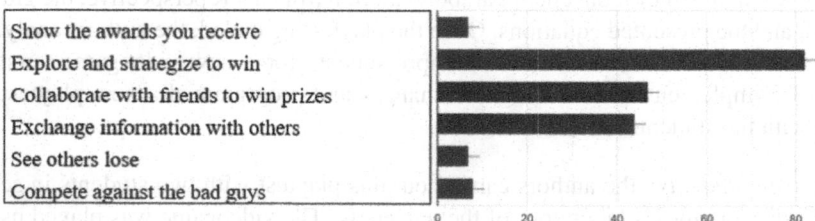

Fig. 1. Student's preferred actions to do while playing videogames

Regarding the student's experience with video games, 93% of players have played a videogame, 53% used a computer or tablet and 47% used a console. The most popular video games were League of Legends, Call of Duty, FIFA, and Mario cart. However, only 24% of these students play video games every day, and only 11% consider themselves serious gamers (see Fig. 2). Similarly, only 23% of the survey participants have played video games using VR and all reported some difficulty using the technology, mainly blurred vision and dizziness.

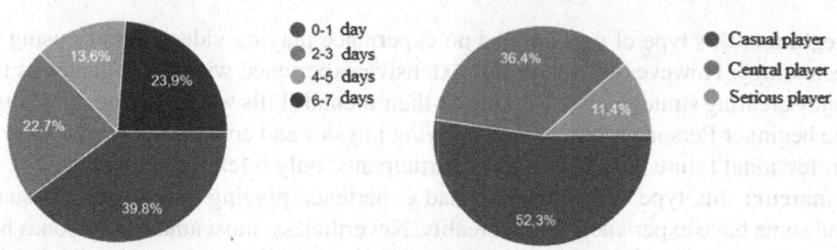

Fig. 2. Left: How many days per week do the students play video games. Right: How do the students consider themselves as players.

Physics Perception and Motivation to Study Physics: Most students were interested in learning the concepts of the physics course. 90% of the participants believe that learning physics will bring them professional benefits, so they make an effort and prepare to do well on tests. Similarly, 82% of the students surveyed express interest and enjoyment in studying physics and consider it relevant to their lives. The students were asked about the type of strategies they use when faced with a physics problem, where 60% usually use equations with known variables and search similar problems in books or class notes (Fig. 3). Finally, the survey revealed that 58% of the students surveyed think that projectile motion is a complicated physical concept to understand and is cumbersome to determine the variables involved.

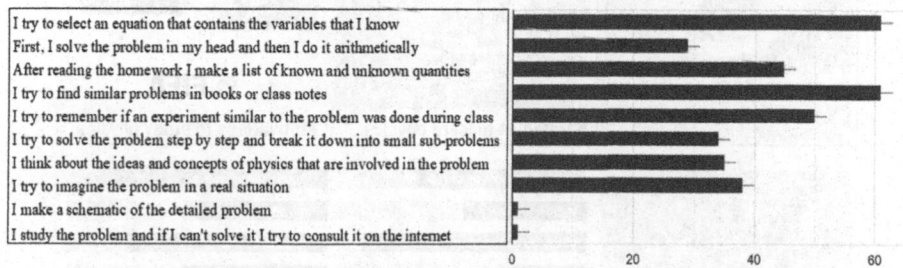

Fig. 3. Student's strategies to learn physics

3.2 Projectile Motion Videogame Design Using User-Centered Design

Following the MIPu+a model, we classify the final users of our systems based on the questionnaire results. Since the questionnaire revealed the likes and motivations of the students to play video games, as well as the limitations and needs when studying physics, we created the student's profiles using this information through the "Persons" technique. We build the following profiles grouped into three Personas: beginner, amateur, and experienced. Each persona role represents a grouping of behaviors, interests, and motivations identified in the end-user questionnaire results. This information was summarized on an infographic card, as shown in Fig. 4.

- **Beginner:** this type of user has had no experience playing videogames or using VR technology. However, they have had extensive experience with board games as they enjoy creating strategies and working on their mental skills while playing. In addition, the beginner Persona is attracted to studying physics and considers it essential for his professional future. Of the 93 survey participants, only 6 fell into this category.
- **Amateur:** this type of Persona has had experience playing video games casually, and some have experienced virtual reality. Nevertheless, most amateur Personas have no interest in physics, do not care to learn it, or believe it is not essential for their professional future. Of the 93 survey participants, 16 fell into this category.
- **Expert:** this type of Persona role is considered a serious gamer who plays video games competitively, with high frequency, and using high-level equipment. Additionally, this type of student believes that physics is important for their professional development and is interested in studying and understanding physics concepts. Of the 93 survey participants, 71 fell into this category.

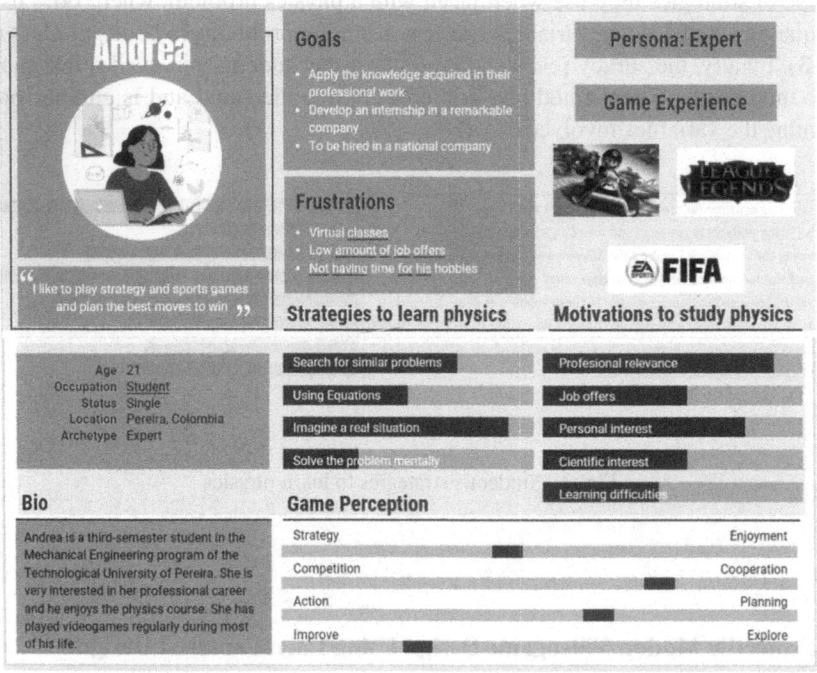

Fig. 4. Example of Persona role. This card shows the main features of an Expert Persona, such as a short biography, their motivations to learn physics, and their game experience.

In the next subsections, we explained in detail the results of the fast and slow prototyping, as well as the iterative process to improve the videogame using the playtest sessions.

Fast Prototyping: According to the MIPu+a model and the videogame design recommendations of [27], the fundamental elements of the game were proposed as follows:

History: The proposed videogame is a project designed to uniquely and attractively explain the projectile motion to any university student through a sport such as a basketball. The user is the game's protagonist, and its success is based on learning the concept in a realistic environment with multiple stimuli. First, the videogame incorporates a calibration stage called "Training," where a virtual teacher explains projectile motion's general concepts and equations. Then, the students are transported to the main scene in a basketball court, where they perform ball shooting from different positions to earn points and win the game. A correct ball shooting requires calibration of angles and velocity by the player; that is why the videogame performs constant feedback of the kinematics of the shooting. Finally, the videogame was called "Parabolic basketball" and it is in Spanish since it is the official language of Colombia.

Storyboard: Through a series of sketches, we draw the concepts of projectile motion that would be useful for the virtual reality explanation of this phenomenon. Also, the game mechanics, the functionality of the buttons, and the general history of the video game can be seen in Fig. 5.

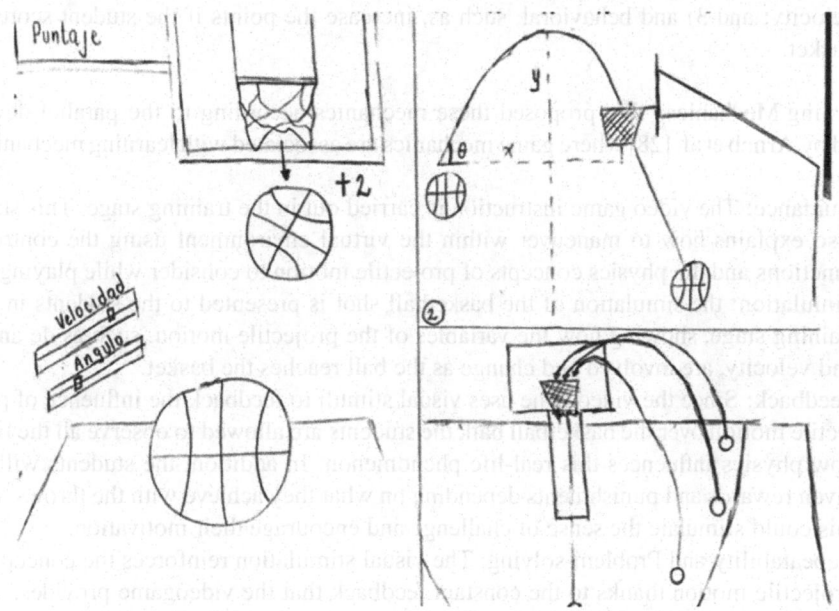

Fig. 5. Storyboard of the videogame main scene

Game Mechanics: According to [27] we present the game mechanics as:

- Space: In the proposed game, the interactions will occur in an empty basketball stadium, where the main character will be alone in front of the basketball board.
- Time: It is a dimension to determine the duration of actions within the game. For example, the training will last 2 min, the duration of each level will depend on the time that each student takes to hit all the shots. The ball takes 1 s to reach the basket and the time for the change of launch position is 4 s.
- Objects: the elements that intervene in the interaction of the players. Each object has attributes that characterize them, such as the characters, the items they can use and grab, the powers, etc. In our game, the most important objects are 1) the character who is a basketball player and he sees himself in a first-person view; 2) the basketball ball that is an interactive element, which is round, orange, and it can be caught and bounced; and 3) the board, that is placed in a fixed spot, and its distance depends on the game difficulty.
- Actions: the verbs that define the game mechanics. The main activity performed by the main character is throwing the ball. He will also be able to grab the ball and change its speed and release angle. Moreover, the character will earn points and win or lose the game.
- Rules: the rules establish the consequences of game actions. We choose the rules for our videogame following Parlett's rule analysis [17]. This model considers three types of rules: 1) fundamental, such as the game can only be played if the student made the training stage; 2) operational, such as the constant adjustment of the ball angle and velocity; and 3) and behavioral, such as, increase the points if the student scores a basket.

Learning Mechanics: We proposed these mechanics according to the parallel developed by Arnab et al. [28] where game mechanics are associated with learning mechanics:

- Guidance: The video game instruction is carried out in the training stage. This stage also explains how to maneuver within the virtual environment using the control's functions and the physics concepts of projectile motion to consider while playing.
- Simulation: the simulation of the basketball shot is presented to the students in the training stage, showing how the variables of the projectile motion, such as de angle and velocity, are involved and change as the ball reaches the basket.
- Feedback: Since the videogame uses visual stimuli to feedback the influence of projectile motion over the basketball ball, the students are allowed to observe all the time how physics influences this real-life phenomenon. In addition, the students will be given rewards and punishments depending on what they achieve with the throws, and this could stimulate the sense of challenge and encourage their motivation.
- Repeatability and Problem-solving: The visual stimulation reinforces the concept of projectile motion thanks to the constant feedback that the videogame provides. The students are encouraged to explore the influence of the angle and velocity over the ball every time they want to score a basket.

Slow Prototyping: This prototyping was done together with an expert in video-game programming, through the Unity 3D platform using C# as the programming language.

The digitalization of the game mechanics took two months to be finished. Figure 6 are shown the main scene in the virtual scenario.

Playtesting: the sessions revealed vital information to improve the game and learning mechanics of the videogame. Bellow has described the insights taken from the playtesting sessions with the educators and the students.

Playing with Teachers: Figure 7 shows the two teachers who volunteered for this playtest session. It is worthy to clarify that the videogame was made in Spanish since is the official language of Colombia. Discussing and analyzing the interviews and the playtest documents, the following considerations for the videogame emerged:

- In other to skip the training scene if the student already saw the conceptual explanation, was necessary to add a skip button at the start of the videogame.
- The training scene needed to explain the projectile motion equations clearer, thus, adding an equation's simulation frame per frame was proposed. We also decided to add a voice command to explain the equations simulation.
- It was proposed to integrate an explanation of the control's functions into the training scene, such as using the trigger to release the ball and using the joystick to move the avatar (Fig. 8). Moreover, the functions of other buttons of the controls were blocked in other avoid confusion in the commands.

Fig. 6. Virtual programming of the videogame "Parabolic Basketball."

Playing with Students: Before the playtest session with the students, all the improvements proposed in the discussions of the first playtest were made. We designed several

Fig. 7. Session of playtesting with volunteer teachers. Left: the first teacher is making a shooting. Right: the second teacher is changing the parameters (Speed "Velocidad", Angle: "Angulo")

GeoGebra (31) simulations (see Fig. 8) of the parabolic motion with the equations and trajectories of the object that were placed as gifs in the conceptual explanation part of the training scene.

Fig. 8. Left: Simulation of projectile motion made in GeoGebra. Right: Instructions in Spanish to use the controls.

Once the expert programmed the improvements, we carried out the session with two students, as shown in Fig. 9. We focus special attention on the student's game perception, interaction with the commands, challenge generated by the videogame, and degree of immersion and playability. Discussing these observations, we made the following improvement considerations:

- Delete the scoring function of the training scene since those points do not count to the final score to win the game.
- Add to the main scene a previous observation of the ball shooting trajectory to allow students to change the throw's parameters according to the ball's final position. Also, we decided to add to the main scene visual and auditory feedback every time the student scores a basket. Finally, the score to win the game was increased due to the students won easily. Once a student wins or loses the game, a final result is shown and saved in the game.
- We observed that some balls were shooting without releasing the buttons, so calibration of the shooting needed to be done.

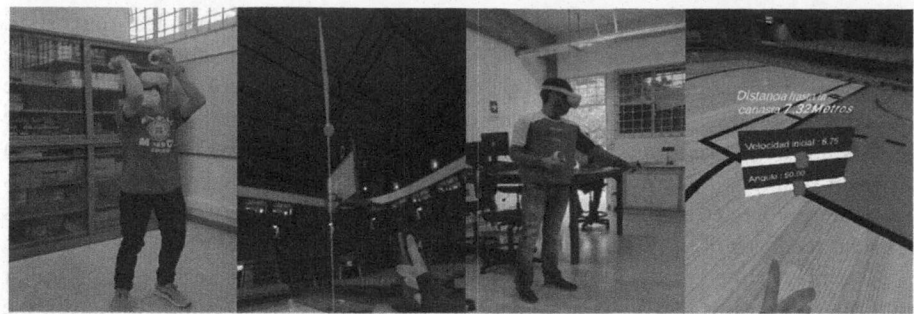

Fig. 9. Session of playtesting with two students: Left: The first student is making a shoot observing the ball trajectory. Right: The second student is changing the parameters observing the final distance of the ball (Speed "Velocidad", Angle: "Angulo")

All the improvements proposed in the discussions of this playtest were made. For instance, Fig. 10 shows the trajectory of the ball in each throw, the score that appears on the board, and the final result of the game session. Finally, we obtain a more elaborate and robust videogame, and as result, it is ready to be evaluated in a pilot study.

Fig. 10. Final improvements of the videogame. Left: an accurate trajectory of the ball. Right: visual feedback of the final score of the students.

4 Conclusions

Our work proposes the use of a user-centered methodology to develop a video game for teaching a concept of college physics, such as the parabolic movement. Our main contribution is the use of novel technological tools in the field of education as a complement to traditional teaching. In addition, we present a practical case study in the use of serious games for physics' teaching, in which, making use of design techniques from the HCI field, a suitable prototype can be ensured for students.

The survey revealed that most students of the physics course had experience playing video games, however, only a low percentage reported experience with virtual reality. On the other hand, most of the students expressed that it would be useful for them to learn this concept through real-life phenomena.

The MIPu+a model was beneficial when determining the students' learning needs. Furthermore, the authors were available to know the student's features thanks to the creation of the Personas profiles, and they also could propose accurate content for the videogame. Finally, the videogame was called "Parabolic Basketball", in which the players are transported to a basketball court and have to perform ball shooting from different positions to earn points and win the game. A correct ball shooting requires calibration of angles and velocity by the student, that is why the videogame performs constant feedback of the kinematics of the shooting.

The playtesting revealed that the students required a training scene to be familiar with the concepts of parabolic movement and the controls of the game. Moreover, the playtesting allowed the designers to improve the game's feedback and provide a better way to present the key concepts of the parabolic movement. Finally, we consider that the videogame is ready to be tested in a pilot study with college students.

References

1. Guichot Reina, V.: Historia de la educación: reflexiones sobre su objeto, ubicación epistemológica, devenir histórico y tendencias actuals. Rev. Latinoam. Estud. Educ. 2(1), 11–51 (2006)
2. Gaspard, P.: On the Relationship of Theory and History in Pedagogy, an Introduction to the West German Discussion on the Significance of the History of Education (1950–1980). (Studia pedagogical; new series 6). JSTOR (1985)
3. Abubakar, S.M., Danjuma, I.M.: Effects of explicit problem-solving strategy on students achievement and retention in senior secondary school physics. ATBU J. Sci. Technol. Educ. 1(1), 123–128 (2012)
4. Veloo, A., Nor, R., Khalid, R.: Attitude towards physics and additional mathematics achievement towards physics achievement. Int. Educ. Stud. 8(3), 35–43 (2015)
5. Docktor, J.L., Strand, N.E., Mestre, J.P., Ross, B.H.: Conceptual problem-solving in high school physics. Phys. Rev. Spec. Top.-Phys. Educ. Res. 11(2), 020106 (2015)
6. García Barneto, A., Gil Martín, M.R.: Entornos constructivistas de aprendizaje basados en simulaciones informáticas (2006)
7. Sánchez, A., Sierra, J.L., Martínez, S., Perales Palacios, F.J.: El aprendizaje de la Física en Bachillerato: investigación con simuladores informáticos versus aula tradicional. Enseñ. Las Cienc. Extra 1–4 (2005)
8. Ortega-Zarzosa, G., Medellín-Anaya, H.E., Martínez, J.R.: Influencia en el aprendizaje de los alumnos usando simuladores de física. Lat.-Am. J. Phys. Educ. 4(1), 20 (2010)
9. Bagozzi, L., Tarchi, C., Falsini, P., Fiorentini, C.: 'Slow Science': building scientific concepts in physics in high school. Int. J. Sci. Educ. 36(13), 2221–2242 (2014)
10. Wang, R., Lowe, R., Newton, S., Kocaturk, T.: Task complexity and learning styles in situated virtual learning environments for construction higher education. Autom. Constr. 113, 103148 (2020)
11. Kolb, D.A., Goldman, M.B.: Toward a typology of learning styles and learning environments: an investigation of the impact of learning styles and discipline demands on the academic performance, social adaptation and career choices of MIT seniors (1973)
12. Bellotti, F., et al.: Designing serious games for education: from pedagogical principles to game mechanisms. In: Proceedings of the 5th European Conference on Games Based Learning, pp. 26–34 (2011)

13. Liao, Y., Liu, S.: MechGames: Teaching and Learning Dynamics Through Computer Simulations and Games (2020)
14. Cheng, M.-T., Chen, J.-H., The Chu, S.-J., Chen, S.-Y.: The use of serious games in science education: a review of selected empirical research from 2002 to 2013. J. Comput. Educ. **2**(3), 353–375 (2015)
15. Bahadoorsingh, S., Dyer, R., Sharma, C.: Integrating serious games into the engineering curriculum-a game-based learning approach to power systems analysis. Int. J. Comput. Vis. Robot. **6**(3), 276–289 (2016)
16. Huang, W.: Evaluating the effectiveness of head-mounted display virtual reality (HMD VR) environment on students' learning for a virtual collaborative engineering assembly task. In: 2018 IEEE Conference on Virtual Reality and 3D User Interfaces (VR), pp. 827–829 (2018)
17. Kuhn, J., Lukowicz, P., Hirth, M., Poxrucker, A., Weppner, J., Younas, J.: gPhysics—using smart glasses for head-centered, context-aware learning in physics experiments. IEEE Trans. Learn. Technol. **9**(4), 304–317 (2016)
18. Bogusevschi, D., Muntean, C., Muntean, G.-M.: Teaching and learning physics using 3D virtual learning environment: a case study of combined virtual reality and virtual laboratory in secondary school. J. Comput. Math. Sci. Teach. **39**(1), 5–18 (2020)
19. Klein, P., Gröber, S., Kuhn, J., Müller, A.: Video analysis of projectile motion using tablet computers as experimental tools. Phys. Educ. **49**(1), 37 (2014)
20. Jurcevic, J.S.: Learning projectile motion with the computer game "Scorched 3D". Phys. Teach. **46**(1), 48–49 (2008)
21. Mohanty, S.D., Cantu, S.: Teaching introductory undergraduate physics using commercial video games. Phys. Educ. **46**(5), 570 (2011)
22. Halliday, D., Resnick, R., Walker, J.: Fundamentals of Physics. John Wiley & Sons (2013)
23. Wee, L.K., Chew, C., Goh, G.H., Tan, S., Lee, T.L.: Using tracker as a pedagogical tool for understanding projectile motion. Phys. Educ. **47**(4), 448 (2012)
24. i Saltiveri, T.G.: MPIu+a. Una metodología que integra la Ingeniería del Software, la Interacción Persona-Ordenador y la Accesibilidad en el contexto de equipos de desarrollo multidisciplinares. Universitat de Lleida (2007)
25. Glynn, S.M., Brickman, P., Armstrong, N., Taasoobshirazi, G.: Science motivation questionnaire II: validation with science majors and nonscience majors. J. Res. Sci. Teach. **48**(10), 1159–1176 (2011)
26. Kurniawan, S.: Interaction design: beyond human–computer interaction by Preece, Sharp, and Rogers (2001), ISBN 0471492787. Springer (2004)
27. Schell, J.: The Art of Game Design: A Book of Lenses. CRC Press (2008)
28. Arnab, S., et al.: Mapping learning and game mechanics for serious games analysis. Br. J. Educ. Technol. **46**(2), 391–411 (2015)
29. Choi, J.O., Forlizzi, J., Christel, M., Moeller, R., Bates, M., Hammer, J.: Playtesting with a purpose. In: Proceedings of the 2016 Annual Symposium on Computer-Human Interaction in Play, pp. 254–265 (2016)
30. Denham, A.R.: Improving the design of a learning game through intrinsic integration and playtesting. Technol. Knowl. Learn. **21**(2), 175–194 (2016)
31. García, J.G. ., Izquierdo, S.J.: GeoGebra, una propuesta para innovar el proceso enseñanza-aprendizaje en matemáticas. Revista electrónica sobre tecnología, educación y sociedad, **4**(7), (2017)

Serious Games

A 'Serious Games' Approach to Decisions of Environmental Impact of Energy Transformation

Jakub Binter[1]([🖂]) [ID], Silvia Boschetti[1] [ID], Tomáš Hladký[1] [ID], Hermann Prossinger[2] [ID], Timothy Jason Wells[1] [ID], Jiřina Jílková[1] [ID], and Daniel Říha[1,3] [ID]

[1] Faculty of Social and Economic Studies, University of Jan Evangelista Purkyně, Ústí nad Labem, Czech Republic
jakub.binter@ujep.cz
[2] Department of Evolutionary Anthropology, University of Vienna, Vienna, Austria
[3] Faculty of Humanities, Charles University, Prague, Czech Republic

Abstract. As software technology becomes more and more present in our lives, its use has arched from purely purposeful (such as complex computations), to purely fun-related (such as video-games). We can combine both in so-called 'serious games'. These can serve as means of training, instructing, tutoring, teaching, and also as a basis for data collection in various scenarios. Data collection and analysis is the primary one we pursue in our proof-of-concept presentation. Our 'serious gaming' is the gamification of an environment-related challenge. We intend to use the *Serious Game for Energy Science* scenario and populate it with formalized task models. Gamers will be exposed to videos that could modify their behavior. Graphically, the game will not be very complex so as to keep the focus on input information. The environment will be visualized in five levels, from bucolic to devastated. Use of videos picturing current states of environmental situations will be used to increase immersion while players will, in the game, make economically or environmentally driven choices. A teamed second player will be constrained by the first player's decisions, and the first player needs to consider consequences for his/her follower. The imagery of environmental impact will also be used to track psycho-physiological responses to the real world via in-game cinematics by the use of wearables. The insights gained will be discussed, post statistical analyses, of psychological implications with all players in a town-hall meeting.

Keywords: Serious games · Environment · Sustainability · Coal region · Neural networks · Heat maps · Decision dilemmas

1 Introduction

The technological advances in the era 4.0 revolution will cause an irreversible impact on multiple levels of our everyday lives. The technological advances mostly affect the economic, social, political and cultural environments in current 'Western' societies. Concurrently, an unparalleled amount of resources is invested in the entertainment industry.

X. Fang (Ed.): HCII 2022, LNCS 13334, pp. 487–495, 2022.
https://doi.org/10.1007/978-3-031-05637-6_31

Gaming is financed at highest levels; small wonder, since 2.7 billion players generate 160 billion US dollars in revenue [13]. The gaming industry is, therefore, a stand-alone economic force that creates many novel approaches and produces standards for other, comparable fields. These other fields are beginning to take advantage of the gaming industry's potential contributions—from sharing to debate to motivation. Currently, they are mainly implemented in the field of education, where game-based activities have been gaining popularity. Pupils find suitably programmed educational games exciting, pleasurable, enjoyable, and motivating; their use also increases the amount of information that the pupils can recall [12].

Indeed, game design, if incorporated correctly, is motivating and engages the majority of these gaming individuals. In one study [3], the evaluation reached slightly more than 2/3; specifically, 67.7%. In other words, a considerable majority of pupils found game-based learning motivating, irrespective of their personal characteristics (such as age, biological sex, and so on). One of the most pronounced variations in ways to create engagement is to what degree some agency can become manifest. The agency constitutes the impact that an individual can have on the environment via his/her decisions and actions [11].

Fig. 1. A composite image of the region of study and its current ecological status. A: The map of where this region is located within the Czech Republic (top of the page is north). B: An image of a smoke-infested town. The cooling towers in the image emit water vapor, not smoke. The smoke infestation is evidenced by the hazy sky. C: An open-pit mine where lignite (the most environmentally damaging form of coal) is mined. The landscape is scarred by the removal of topsoil and vegetation. The image has been composed of individual images, each with its own creative commons imaging rights.

Such approaches have been implemented successfully to acquire abilities in health-related training (including resuscitation), in various battlefield related instructions and in other training assignments, as well as in natural science lessons (primarily, but not limited to, physics, biology and chemistry). Since game development is an expensive undertaking that usually involves cooperation of programmers with design studio creatives and may take many years to achieve state-of-art levels, many short-cuts have been developed to alleviate these problems as much as possible. For example, urban planning was streamlined by using the game *SimCity* [8]. Other examples include the use of *The Sims* or *Farmville* for studying and exemplifying social interactions [5].

Games do not need to be complex to allow for enjoyable and engaging experiences. Indeed, many games benefit from a traditional board-game like designs or are directly based on such games, such as *Terraforming Mars*, *Gloomhaven*, and *Heroes of Might and Magic*. Historically, 'serious board games' such as *Chess* or *Tafl* were considered important yet fun-including. At the same time, these provided covert systematic training of military tactics (evidenced in the capture or protection of valuable play pieces—often called kings) so as to resemble real-world challenges.

1.1 Coal Mining and Electrical Power Generation

Although the Industrial Revolution should not always be perceived as negative, the resulting environmental impacts due to the search for and exploitation of resources have been—and remain so to this day—devastating. The increased urgency of the dilemmas that accompany energy production and consumption is a case in point. Consider coal; surface mining devastates large landscapes (Fig. 1), while subterranean mining produces enormous heaps of tailings. Since the transportation of raw resources such as coal is expensive, coal-fired power plants are often located close to the mines and the electrical power generated must then be distributed over enormous distances via overland cables [9]. Large regions in every heavily industrialized country then suffer from the production-oriented infrastructure decisions; underlying these is economic reasoning—the professed goal of maximizing productivity. As has become well-known, the attendant down-sides are air pollution, water pollution and the destruction of local landscapes [1].

The Ústí nad Labem Region, located along the north boarder of the Czech Republic, is an exemplary case (Fig. 1). The production-oriented politics during the communist regime supported coal mining and was willing to transform the region into the "battery" (in the electrical storage-cell sense) of the republic. Now, after the fall of the Iron Curtain, the region is economically, socially and environmentally devastated—only partly ascribable to the economic collapse that accompanied the disappearance of state communism. Unintentionally, perhaps, this region now serves as the ideal natural laboratory setting for investigating the possible mechanisms that may bring about a change—in the direction of environmental improvement and healing the scars produced earlier (Fig. 1). Whether a change can be achieved is one of the issues we investigate with the serious game concept we present in this paper.

It has been argued that coal mining has, for a myriad of reasons, a limited future (despite the almost unlimited reserves still underground) and so the political intention is for it to be abandoned within next decade. As cleaner sources of energy are preferable, the Ústí nad Labem Region will have to undergo a transformation. Despite these 'objective' realizations by those in the upper echelons of power, there is also a strong grass-roots political opposition wanting to maintain the current status quo, fearing both economic hardships (particularly unemployment and its attendant social stresses) and the region's subsequent drifting towards unimportance.

There are known undertakings that can make individuals (and groups) more likely to re-orientate themselves towards environmentally friendly options and at the same time reject environment-harming behaviors. One undertaking we highlight involves education. One discussion topic involves the evaluation of economic interests, the (environmental and developmental) consequences if they are disregarded, and how possible confrontations occur when environmental impacts override these concerns about the short-term economic distresses (primarily the specter of unemployment). It has been suggested that higher education can further the acceptance of the primacy of environmental concerns [10]. Harring & Jagers identify mediating factors, namely the trust in the provided information and the inhabitants' willingness to change the norms they abide by in their everyday life. This approach assumes, again, that more highly educated people are the ones to be convinced. What about those with low levels of education and precarious economic situations?

2   Aim

The aim of this article is to describe a 'serious-game' creation that will be used as a diagnostic tool in cases involving political changes. The reason is that gamification of activities garners increased attention and tends to become popular among both adolescents and adults alike. The proposed game is designed to stay simplistic so as to avoid being distracted by other game elements. The main element it must include in its in-game cinematics is the one that is employed to affect the decision-making process. During the cinematics, data about stress-levels will be collected via wearables and gaze directions will be measured via eye-trackers. Players will also be able to affect other players by employing suggested interventions.

A further novelty in this game is its inclusion of a second player who is known (and emotionally attached—such as being a friend or a relative) to the first player. This second player takes over the game after the first one has left the game scenario. He/she mimics the carry-over effect of environmental burdens between generations.

3   Materials and Methods

3.1   Participants

Because the largest fraction of target participants will be from economically lower-class members of the society, recruiting them will be challenging. We intent to recruit them by distributing flyers and by online advertising. We aim for chance samples collected using a snowball-contacting technique for the preliminary rounds of game testing.

The participants will be asked to come to the laboratory for psycho-physiological measures of Jan Evangelista Purkyně University in Ústí nad Labem, Czech Republic or to our mobile laboratory, and will also be requested to bring along an accompanying person (a family member or a friend), who will then be the second player in the game and will, as described above, simulate the generation carry-over-effect(s).

In order to compare gamer behavior in different sub-regions of the Ústí nad Labem environs, we will use a mobile laboratory. Typically, the specific groups of people we want to target don't participate in scientific research projects for a myriad of subjective/personal and location-related reasons. The mobile laboratory allows us to gain data about inhabitants in those localities. In this mobile laboratory we will be able to test several respondents simultaneously. The sub-regions will be chosen based on the distributions of income levels of the inhabitants. These levels are identifiable using publicly available information.

The financial loss caused by replacement of the current technological processes involved in electrical energy production is the most prevalent argument for avoiding the use of novel, fancy, 'environment-friendly' methods when attempting to recruit inhabitants with low economic status. Longevity of the ecosystem is intended to be included as a key element in the decision-making strategies of the game, alongside with the simulation of imminent economic loss.

Our incorporating a twist during mid-game has been rarely used previously. As mentioned above, we will ask participants to let a friend or relative take over the scenario once they have reached the end of their part of the game. The reason to have another person continue the game is to motivate the first gamer to make decisions not only geared towards his/her financial gain while gaming, but also how the subsequent consequences as a prior impact the friend's ability to successfully continue the game when he/she takes over the scenario.

3.2 Pre-participation Procedures

The game will be limited to 30 min of playing time (that excludes the in-game cinematics). Total time is estimated to be 60 min per player. Each player will first fill out a questionnaire, submit to calibration procedures of all attached devices (wearables) and be instructed in game technicalities.

Prior to the commencement of the game, we will use responses in questionnaires to determine self↔other differences in general beliefs about the environment, along with the gamer's personal economic situation, his/her well-being, his/her delayed reward tendency, and his/her closeness to another individual. Subsequent, post-game analyses will include these measures of influences.

During the game physiological responses—galvanic skin response (GSR), heart rate variability (HRV), and eye tracking (actually gaze orientation)—during the in-game cinematics will be collected in real time. These responses are needed in order to evaluate the emotional responses to the information provided as the game ensues.

The galvanic skin response: measuring electrical conductance of the skin using electrodes placed on a patient's body. Increase of sweat production is considered to be a signal of emotional excitement and is mainly under control of sympathetic inputs. The heart rate variability results mainly from parasympathetic inputs to the heart via the sinoatrial node.

It has been shown that the HRV can be related to decision making [7]; there are such claims also for the GSR. The combination of both constitutes a powerful tool for subsequent analyses [4]. Gaze orientation will be used to spot the triggering of visual representations that the responses can be attributed to.

3.3 Game Design

The development of a 3D virtual reality game is beyond the financial resources of the university department; remarkably, such large resources are not a necessary prerequisite. Rather, we pursue the option of an interactive computer-animated board game with branching options accompanied by additional visual presentations.

The environment we focus on will be the Ústí nad Labem Region; it will be incorporated as a play-board map showing the distribution of 5 levels of pollution and of devastation. The middle level—level three—will be the one all players begin with and will be considered base level. Based on their own behavior and the behaviors of their group—this models collaboration—the environment will become (positively or negatively) affected. Feedback will be visual; after reaching a new level, there will be audiovisual in-game cinematics. The cinematics will include a voiceover to increase the engagement of the players [2]. It is to be expected that the personal values of players will mirror their in-game decisions [13].

In order to offer direct feedback of each individual's actions to all other participants, any changes will be displayed both graphically and numerically in real time. Specifically, extent of pollution, levels of financial gain, time remaining and amount of remaining resources will be presented. Further information available will be that of actions of other gamers who have been influencing the displayed effects. Such a game construct forces a gamer's involvement with the (economic and environmental) behaviors of others. Each gamer will have the possibility to suggest a trajectory (in the form of an intervention) three times per game and respond to a suggested trajectory by voting for, or against or ignoring the suggested intervention. The subsequent gamer behavior need not abide by the vote. One publication has described and evaluated decision-making and engagement in games such as our proposed one [6].

All decisions will be executed by mouse click on the elements of the action-panel located at the bottom of the screen. The actions triggered by the gamers will involve matters such as an increase or decrease of mining activities, conversion rates of coal-burning to electrical power, sales of which will be represented in local currency and actually paid to the gamer.

All along, the amount of resources available will be limited; all players together, by necessity, will share these. The consumption of electricity by the city during a 5-min-period of clean gaming time initiates the necessity of mining coal and causes the loss of already produced electrical energy, at the same time providing a gamer with his/her own financial gain. If the gamer fails to provide even a minimal amount of resources, the game will terminate and all resources and financial gain will be lost.

3.4 Stimuli

Audiovisual stimuli will be presented to the participants during gaming. An introductory sequence will describe the situation. Factual information about the state of the region will be provided by a voice-over while the in-game cinematics are active. Consequently, there will be in-game cinematics while the pollution will increase or decrease. Since the group of players share the in-game environment, the cinematics will be triggered at the same time for each player. This is important for psycho-physiological measures (collected as described above). All levels will undergo pre-testing on groups of volunteers to ensure representation levels.

Introductory Sequence.   The introductory sequence will rely on historical photographs and paintings depicting the region with a voice-over highlighting the strategic and natural resource importance before the Industrial Revolution. The timeline will continue through the Industrial Revolution and recent times highlighting the pollution, impact of coal mining; stills will appear on the screen for 5 s duration. The total time of the introductory sequence will be 4 min.

The five levels of pollution and devastation. Each lasts 2 min.

Level 1: This representation consists of stills of pristine nature, namely green trees in intact forests interspersed with green fields, and traversed by clean, clear rivers. No industrial buildings will be displayed.

Level 2: This representation consists of stills that will highlight a life-style that is less oriented towards high-energy consumption, with ubiquitous pedestrians in parks, cyclists rather than automobiles and abundant nature in the city-scape environs reminiscent of the times before the industrial revolution.

Level 3 (the base level level): This representation consists of stills of the current state of the region: unattractive and unsustainable environs and a city life geared towards consumption by those with adequate income.

Level 4: This representation consists of stills that highlight the high-energy consumption life-style. Motorized transportation via automobiles and trucks using fossil fuels (refined petroleum products) will be pictured; factories and coal mines will be abundantly present.

Level 5: This representation will depict the deplorable state from the 1990s of the almost complete devastation of nature with factories ubiquitous in smoke-infested cities.

3.5   Statistical and Evaluation Methods

Questionnaires consist of queries with response options that can vary from query to query. The responses will be feature vectors resulting from concatenation of one-hot encoded responses.

Physiological response data will be time-series data. For each participant, at each time point, a multivariate response vector is recorded. One mode of analysis will be the use of SVD (singular value decomposition) of each participant's matrix separately, and one of a grand matrix of all participants. Subsets of the singular values will be used to identify smoothed responses, fraction of noise, as well as possible clustering of responses.

Level-change responses will be time series of ordinal numbers, which can again be one-hot encoded prior to a suite of analyses.

Feature vectors from the questionnaires can be dimension-reduced by using autoencoders, which are a class of unsupervised artificial neural networks. The dimension-reduced feature vectors cluster, and these clusters not only show interdependencies but also characteristics of inhabitants in the Ústí nad Labem Region. In fact, the analyses of the clusters are the most reliable method of identifying social strata and political subgroups within the population (and the extent of their emotional responses).

The analyses of the level-change responses will be the most challenging and will require the most advanced, up-to-date neural network methods. We expect to find feedback mechanisms between first and second player pairs, as well as interdependencies among player pairs.

4 Discussion

There are several distinctive features of the proposed study that we believe will shed light on the prevailing mechanisms involved in the interplay of environment-oriented goals, agreement/disagreement with interventions and possible contradictions with economic goals. Even though the game is designed to be simplistic and focuses on a selection of variables, the novel approaches as to the existence of their interrelatedness, which can be detected by neural networks, will provide unexpected insights.

The method of including physiological parameters reflecting—at least in part—environmental and pollution awareness has, to our knowledge, not been heretofore utilized. The physiological reaction of a body is non-conscious, and therefore very informative about the value system producing an individual's reaction. This method is typically used in behavioral research dealing with individual responses. Thus we predict that this method of inclusion of physiological data will provide a basis that can be used to further our knowledge not only about how individuals perceive the treatment of our environment but also which motivations lead either to its conservation or to its devastation.

To encourage motivations, we intend to use real, actual financial incentives for participation. Further motivation beyond the financial aspect is the dependency of the gain possibilities of the second player on the first player's (prior) behavior. To be more concrete: if the first player decides to maximize the financial incentive by minimizing environmentally friendly decisions, the second player will not be able to completely reverse the first player's strategy, no matter what the decisions the second player intends to make.

The conclusion of the study will be a type of town-hall meeting—a group session discussing motivations for decisions in the variously chosen scenarios. Therefore, the game itself is not only a tool in its own right but will also provide a basis for focused and pertinent questions that the individuals will be able to respond to. The project will further our knowledge about the comparability of gaming to real-world scenarios of threats to the environment.

We hope to understand the motivations of our participants using the game scenario and its development. Beyond environmental action implications, we hope to gain insights about how political groupings (clusters) come about and how they are also based on psycho-physiological responses.

It is widely accepted in democratically organized societies that decisions relating to modifications of the environment and redefinitions of the concept of progress are largely driven by emotions, rather than by acceptance of prognoses derived by experts and communicated by them (the much-hated 'top-down' political ruling scenario). The psycho-physiological responses promise to reveal—at least to some extent—how emotions drive the gaming behavior. And the emotionally driven strategies are arguably not independent of the economic and aspirational characteristics of the social strata from which the majority of participants come. The 'serious games' approach, along with the collection of social-standing and psycho-physiological data will contribute to unravelling the many complexities that are inter-twined with necessary, but not always acknowledged, redirections of economic development.

Future variants of our design would include computer-controlled co-players (driven by artificial intelligence) to enable testing of single individuals.

Acknowledgements. This article was authored with the support of the Doctoral School: Applied and Behavioral Studies project (Grant Number: CZ.02.2.69/0.0/0.0/16_018/000272), University of Jan Evangelista Purkyně, Ústí nad Labem, Czech Republic. D.Ř. is further funded by the Ministry of Education, Youth and Sports, Czech Republic and the Institutional Support for Long-term Development of Research Organizations, Faculty of Humanities, Charles University, Czech Republic (Grant COOPERATIO "Arts and Culture").

References

1. Anpilova, Y., Yakovliev, Y., Drozdovych, I.: Landscape and geological factors of water and ecological conditions technogenesis of Donbas at the post-mining stage. In: Geoinformatics: Theoretical and Applied Aspects. Vol. 2020, No. 1, pp. 1–5 (2020)
2. Byun, J., Loh, C.S.: Audial engagement: effects of game sound on learner engagement in digital game-based learning environments. Comput. Hum. Behav. **46**, 129–138 (2015)
3. Chapman, J.R., Rich, P.J.: Does educational gamification improve students' motivation? If so, which game elements work best? J. Educ. Bus. **93**(7), 315–322 (2018)
4. De La Cruz, J., Shimizu, D., George, K.: Using EEG for the analysis of heat stress on quick decision-making. In: 2021 IEEE 12th Annual Information Technology, Electronics and Mobile Communication Conference (IEMCON), pp. 0299–0304. IEEE (2021)
5. Deterding, S., Dixon, D., Khaled, R., Nacke, L.: From game design elements to game-fulness: defining "gamification". In: Proceedings of the 15th International Academic Mind-Trek Conference: Envisioning Future Media Environments, pp. 9–15 (September 2011)
6. Flood, S., Cradock-Henry, N.A., Blackett, P., Edwards, P.: Adaptive and interactive climate futures: systematic review of 'serious games' for engagement and decision-making. Environ. Res. Lett. **13**(6), 063005 (2018)
7. Forte, G., Morelli, M., Casagrande, M.: Heart rate variability and decision-making: autonomic responses in making decisions. Brain Sci. **11**(2), 243 (2021)
8. Gaber, J.: Simulating planning: SimCity as a pedagogical tool. J. Plan. Educ. Res. **27**(2), 113–121 (2007)
9. Hanlon, W.W.: Coal smoke and the costs of the industrial revolution (No. w22921). National Bureau of Economic Research (2016)
10. Harring, N., Jagers, S.C.: Why do people accept environmental policies? The prospects of higher education and changes in norms, beliefs and policy preferences. Environ. Educ. Res. **24**(6), 791–806 (2018)
11. Laamarti, F., Eid, M., El Saddik, A.: An overview of serious games. Int. J. Comput. Games Technol. (2014)
12. Taub, M., Sawyer, R., Smith, A., Rowe, J., Azevedo, R., Lester, J.: The agency effect: the impact of student agency on learning, emotions, and problem-solving behaviors in a game-based learning environment. Comput. Educ. **147**, 103781 (2020)
13. Vuong, Q.H., et al.: On the environment-destructive probabilistic trends: a perceptual and behavioral study on video game players. Technol. Soc. **65**, 101530 (2021)

A Configurable Serious Game for Inhibitory and Interference Control

Houda Chabbi[1]([✉]), Sandy Ingram[1], Florian Hofmann[1], Vinh Ngyuen[2], and Yasser Khazaal[2]

[1] School of Engineering and Architecture, University of Applied Sciences and Arts Western Switzerland, Fribourg, Switzerland
houda.chabbidr@hes-so.ch
[2] Department of Psychiatry, Addiction Medicine, University of Lausanne, Lausanne, Switzerland

Abstract. Psychological disorders are often associated with a lack of inhibitory and interference control. In this paper, we present the software architecture design of a configurable serious game dedicated to inhibitory and interference control tests. The proposed architecture is based on generic components that are reusable across different game platforms and modes. Our design enables mental health practitioners to easily configure the serious game to adapt it to their test objectives and patients' profile. The proposed game facilitates the tracking and analysis of inhibitory and interference control and their evolution over time, as data is logged over different gaming sessions. As a proof of concept, we implement a pilot application based on the proposed architecture, in both the 2D and VR modes. The developed application implements a gamified Stop Signal task (SST) augmented with interferences. We report the results of an empirical study assessing the perceived usability of the 2D and VR pilot games, using a standard usability test.

Keywords: Serious game · SST · Usability · Go stimuli · Game design · Inhibition control · Software game architecture · eHealth · Virtual reality

1 Introduction

Many psychological disorders are associated with a lack of impulse control and inhibition capacity. These capacities are further impaired when, during an inhibition task, the person is confronted with interference and more specifically with salient stimuli associated with his psychopathology [1]. The person should then resist interference caused by irrelevant information that could disrupt the proper performance of a task.

Many tests are used in neuropsychology to assess inhibition disorders. In particular, the Stop Signal Task (SST) has been widely studied to assess a person's ability to inhibit a dominant response. In an SST test, participants are instructed to respond as quickly as possible to a repetitive Go stimulus, except when an Stop Signal appears, in which case the participant must withhold responding. The participant's reaction time is then used to assess inhibitory efficiency.

© The Author(s), under exclusive license to Springer Nature Switzerland AG 2022
X. Fang (Ed.): HCII 2022, LNCS 13334, pp. 496–507, 2022.
https://doi.org/10.1007/978-3-031-05637-6_32

In this paper, we propose to combine SSTs with interference control tests that assess a person's ability to resist irrelevant stimuli interfering with a carried-out task. Towards this aim, we present the design and implement a configurable serious game enabling both practitioners and cognitive researchers to conduct inhibitory and interference control tests. Designed by a team of mental health and IT professionals, the developed game can be used to improve and track the evolution of inhibitory and interference control. Participant activity and associated game session parameters are logged for analysis purposes after every game session. Our work is motivated by several factors. First, gamified SSTs were found to motivate participants' engagement [2]. Second, inhibitory capacity is affected by stimulus salience and contextual relevance; an interference involving an invitation for a drink is typically more relevant for a population suffering from alcohol use disorder than that of smoking. Therefore, it is important to allow therapists to choose the kind of needed interferences. Existing software games dedicated to SSTs tests do not integrate interferences that can be tailored to the participant's profile and psychopathology. Given the impact of salient interferences on inhibition control, we propose a game design that integrates configurable interferences in SSTs and enables practitioners and researchers to easily configure game parameters to the targeted participant profile as well as the game session objectives. For valid post-test analysis and assessments, the type, duration, and timestamps of the different interferences to which the user was subjected, are logged and analysed along with participant response times. Third, the configurable aspect of the proposed game, also covers the ability to apply the same game scenario in different application modes such 2D and VR, enabling researchers to easily reproduce experiments and compare the perceived user experience and performance across different modes. We present hereafter a software architecture design enabling the sharing of a custom game scenario and generic game components across different game instances. The proposed game design is utilized to implement a prototype for both the 2D and VR modes and conduct a small-scale usability study.

The rest of the paper is organized as follows: Sect. 2 positions the multidisciplinary work reported in this paper with respect to the state of the art. Section 3 describes the game and its control execution flow. Section 4 describes the core components of the software game architecture. Section 5 presents the implemented pilot application. In Sect. 6, we present the outcome of a small-scale usability. Section 7 concludes the paper and summarizes future work.

2 Related Work

Using software games in psychotherapy and in cognitive tests is not new [3–7] and has served different purposes including SSTs and video games dedicated to children suffering from obsessive-compulsive disorder. Games specifically designed for inhibition control tests can also be found in the literature [8–12]. The design of a game using cartoon characters and based on stop-signal tasks (SSTs) is proposed in [8]. In terms of experiment and instrument validity, gamified SSTs have been found to impact behavioral performance in the comparative study reported in [12]. Nevertheless, the association between overweight and inhibitory control was still observed, as it was the case in non-gamified experiments. The article reports that the findings observed using serious games were valid in comparison with those observed in laboratory and Web-based experiments.

The work presented in this paper addresses three main limitations of existing SST games. First, no games have yet been proposed and tested supporting both SSTs and interference control tests. Second, none of the existing studies are designed to help health professionals in easily adapting game features and environments to different therapeutic contexts. Games described in [13, 14] allow testers to configure the task execution scenario but the configuration remains limited and requires programming skills. Finally, the games proposed for SSTs are not virtual therefore losing the reported benefits of immersive virtual games [15].

In this paper, we present a modular software framework to build configurable games dedicated to both SSTs and interference control tests. The therapist can specify different therapeutic game parameters (such as the SSTs frequency, fixation time and the interference signal type) as well as the game mode (2D or VR). The game is then built with the specified parameters. Configurable game settings enable health professionals and researchers to compare the effect of different experimental settings and personalize the game to its experimental context and target participant.

3 Game Description

Our game design is driven by SST test protocols and was developed with health professionals following a participatory design approach. The test protocol directly impacts gameplay, game mechanics as well the game development process.

To avoid overloading the player, limit the learning curve, and prevent the impact of unintended cognitive interferences, gameplay structures were purposely kept simple and interaction styles limited. To ensure consistent behavior across different game modes, the game is developed as a first-person perspective where the player is fixed and cannot move inside the environment. Two main user roles were identified for the design of our inhibition and interference control game. The first user role, fulfilled by the therapist or a researcher, is responsible for describing the game scenario and analysing its output. The therapist can typically customize the game scenario according to a patient's profile. The second user role is nothing but the actual game player. We describe hereafter, the game mechanics, and the performance evaluation metrics.

3.1 Game Mechanics

Game mechanics are directly derived from the SST test protocol: the player is expected to react to the appearance of a recurrent event during a period defined in the game scenario. Nevertheless, if the recurrent event appearance is followed by a Stop Signal, the participant should not act on this event. Figure 1 represents the game mechanics as a finite state machine. In the proof-of-concept prototype developed based on the proposed software game architecture, the player task consisted of stamping a paper appearing on a desk, only when the paper is not associated with a red border (representing the Stop Signal). As much as the SST task is repetitive, the introduction of interference provides a way to make the game more interesting for the player while making inhibition control exercises harder. This is especially true since the interferences can take different forms based on the player profile (patient pathology) and the test objectives. The parametrizable interferences whose types and probability of appearance are specified in the customized game scenario, trigger a surprise effect, and increase game challenge. The player is expected to resist those interferences and focus on reacting to the GO stimuli.

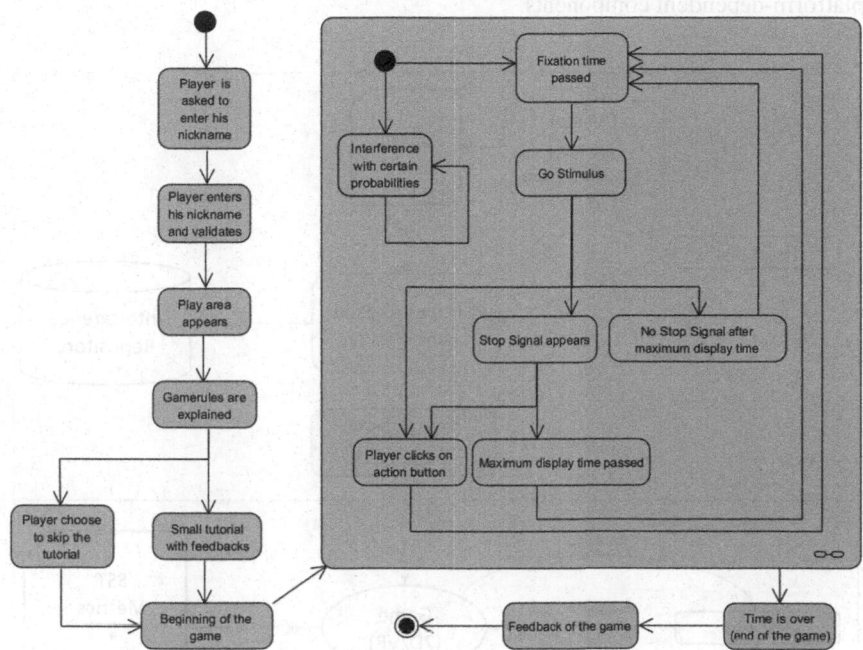

Fig. 1. Representation of a game mechanics as a finite state machine

3.2 Performance Evaluation Metrics

Performance evaluation metrics help therapists in analysing patients' inhibitory capacity over time, and researchers in HCI and cognitive sciences in conducting topic-related research studies using quantitative and objective data. During a game session, a score is calculated according to the commission errors and omission errors. This game score is communicated to the player at the end of the game. Furthermore, the player's reactions, and reaction times as well as the times of all the events that appeared in the game environment are systematically recorded. Each personalized scenario is associated with the player evaluation metrics. Further analysis can then be conducted using the performance evaluation metrics, the game score, in combination with the set scenario parameters.

4 Game Software Architecture

We propose a software game architecture that ensures consistent behavior across different game modes and development platforms and enables valid comparative analysis by proposing generic reusable components and limiting platform-dependent ones, which also reduces development code. The resulting game generation (and handling) process involves three communicating core components represented in Fig. 2 below: the configurator of a custom scenario, the creation of generic game components, and the generation of platform-dependent components.

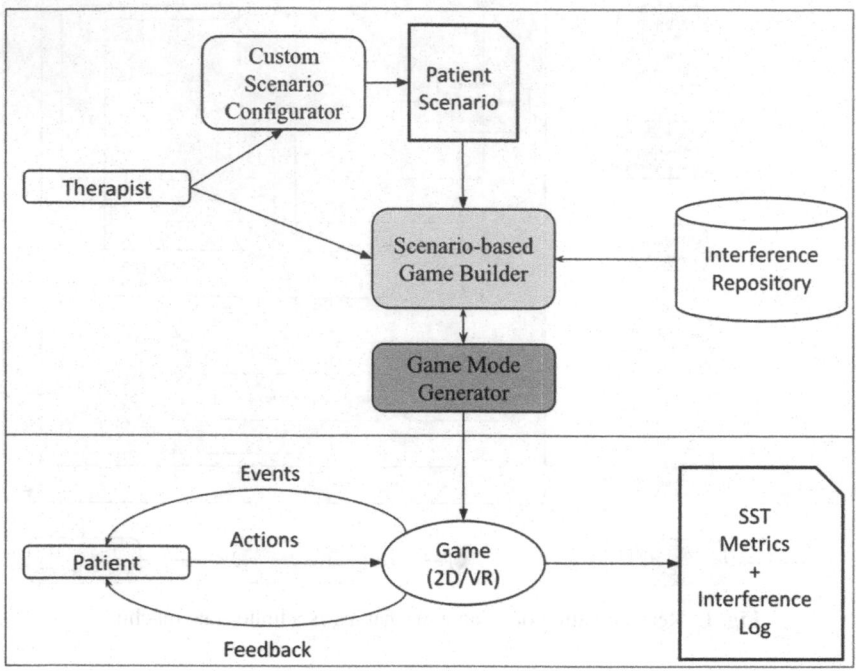

Fig. 2. Core architectural components

4.1 Game Scenario Configurator

The configurator allows a therapist (respectively a researcher) to describe a custom game scenario for a specific patient (respectively an experiment participant). It is worth noting that the resulting configuration file (saved in JSON format) can be reused in different game sessions and modes (2D and VR) and for different participants. The different types of configurable parameters are described hereafter, and their relative timing represented in Fig. 3.

The following global game parameters are mandatory and should be specified by the therapist or researcher:

- the total duration of the game session,
- the fixation time: which refers to the time between the appearance of the target object and the GO stimuli to which the player can react,

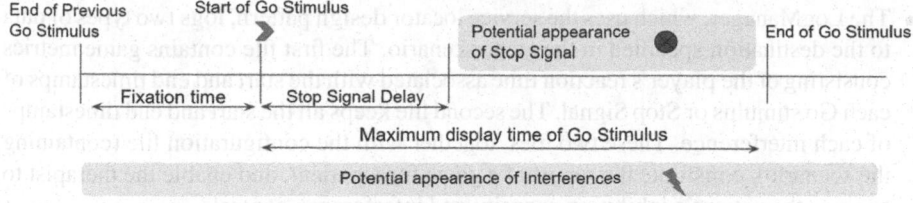

Fig. 3. Relative timing of the configurable game parameters

- the maximal display time of the GO stimuli if not clicked.
- the SSD (Stop Signal Delay) which refers to the delay time before a Stop Signal can be triggered.
- and finally, the desired frequency for the appearance of the Stop Signal.

Interference-related parameters are optional. Interference stimuli constitute cognitive distractions that a player will be confronted with during a game. Depending on the player's profile, the therapist can specify from a predefined list, which interference(s) to activate. A scenario may have zero, one, or a mix of several interference types. For each chosen interference, the name, frequency of appearance, and duration should be specified. Four adaptable categories of interferences are identified:

- Auditory interferences can consist of a voice message or a noise that will be played according to the therapist's scenario during the game. The interference duration and the corresponding audio file should be provided.
- Static (visual) interferences can consist of an image, a textual message, or a video that appears on a predefined flat surface of the game scene, according to the parameters of the therapist's scenario. For this interference, the data source file (and the video duration if applicable) should be specified.
- Animated visual interferences can consist of moving objects that appear in the player's space. This category is more complex to establish because it needs a 3D model object with its animation. The current framework does not support this type of interference in a generic way; it must be directly implemented in the specific game instance.
- "Ambient" interferences can consist of a change in the ambient sound or a luminosity during the game. The volume and intensity are parameterizable.

4.2 Scenario-Based Game Builder

The GameBuilder consumes the output of the scenario configurator to instantiate different platform-independent generic components listed and described hereafter:

- The (Singleton) GameManager implements the GameStateMachine logic represented in Fig. 1 and orchestrates other components accordingly.
- The StorageManager is used by other components to retrieve and store data using the locations specified in the custom game scenario.
- The SceneManager is responsible for loading the 3D game scene used in all game modes.

- The LogManager, which uses the service locator design pattern, logs two types of data to the destination specified in the game scenario. The first file contains game metrics consisting of the player's reaction time associated with the start and end timestamps of each Go stimulus or Stop Signal. The second file keeps all the start and end timestamps of each interference. These two files, together with the configuration file (containing the scenario), constitute the report of a game for a patient, and enable the therapist to analyze the patient's inhibition capacity and interference control.
- The InterferenceManager handles the apparition and disappearance of interferences based on the game's custom scenario. The interference objects corresponding to the therapist's desired interferences, are instantiated, and integrated into the loaded game environment. To be able to instantiate static visual interferences in a generic way, the proposed design choice is to define fixed flat spaces in the generic game scene, in which interferences can appear.

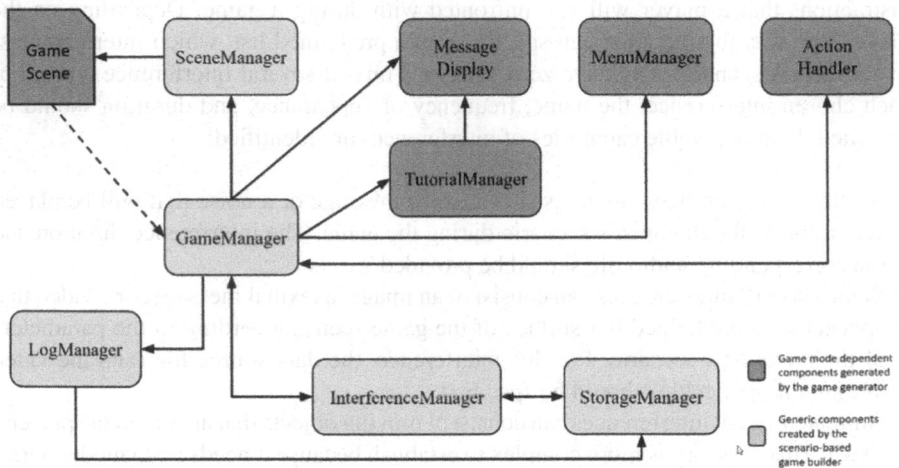

Fig. 4. Interaction between generic and platform-dependent components

4.3 Game Mode Generator

Starting from the same custom scenario configurations, the game generator generates all the platform-dependent components. Menus, message display, user input handling, and the tutorial indeed differ depending on the chosen game mode (2D vs VR) and resulting development platform. A common interface is defined for each platform-dependent component. The MessageDisplay component renders messages destined to the user on the target platform. The ActionHandler notifies the GameManager when a platform-dependent user input event is triggered.

Figure 4 represents the interaction between generic and platform-dependent components.

5   Implementation of a Pilot Application

We implemented two pilot applications using the Unity Engine: a game in 2D mode running on Windows, and its equivalent in VR mode application using the Oculus Quest headset. In the virtual reality (VR) game mode, the participant is in a virtual isolated environment. In the desktop mode (2D), the external environment surrounding the participant remains present.

The pilot application targets inhibitory and interference control tests in cigarette dependency contexts. Figure 5 presents side by side, the 2D and VR user interfaces, built using the same game configuration parameters.

Fig. 5. Snapshots of a same scenario-based game in two modes. (a) 2D mode Menu. (b) 2D game where a Stop Signal was triggered (the paper has a red outline). (c) VR mode menu with the interaction of the player. (d) Beginning of the VR game.

Three interferences were configured and used by both game modes: a generic "ambient" interference consisting of changing the scene lighting, an "auditory" interference type consisting of a voice message inviting the player to smoke, and an "animated" interference consisting of a falling cigarette. Table 1 summarizes the SST and interference representations of our pilot application.

Table 1. SST and interferences of the pilot application

Parameter	Representation/significance
Stimulus object	White paper sheet
Go stimulus	Appearance of a white paper
Stop signal	Red frame around the paper sheet
Action	Paper stamping (via a key press in 2D and a click on a joystick button in VR)
Interferences	Scene lighting, falling cigarette, vocal invitation to smoke

6 Usability Study

A usability study was conducted on the 2D and the VR prototypes with a total of 12 participants, with the objective of assessing the game's perceived ease of use, identifying usability issues, and getting design insights for the next game version.

6.1 Usability Evaluation Methods

Participants were invited to play the game without any prior information. Half of the participants were suggested the 2D version of the game and the other half the virtual version of the game. The 6 participants that played the VR game version had zero or very little experience with VR games. For consistency, the same game scenario is used in both game modes. In both modes, each participant was invited to play a very short tutorial game session. In the tutorial game, the player gets immediate feedback on the correctness of the undertaken actions. To get a preliminary assessment of the game's perceived ease of use and user experience and be able to compare participant answers, participants were requested to respond to the User Experience Questionnaire (UEQ) [16]. The UEQ consists of twenty-six items grouped into six sub-categories to assess the perceived attractive, pragmatic (covering efficiency, dependability, and perspicuity), and hedonic (encompassing novelty and stimulation) qualities of our pilot application. Using this questionnaire, score values higher than 0.8 should be considered as positive whilst noting that values exceeding 2 are very rarely observed in practice.

6.2 Results and Discussion

The 2D and VR game modes achieved comparable and positive scores (of 1.69 and 1.82 respectively) for their perceived pragmatic quality as reported in Table 2. The VR and 2D games which were based on the same game scenario, were both perceived as highly comprehensible and easy to use. The attractiveness quality was perceived as positive for both game modes whilst noting that the score of the VR game was higher than that of the 2D game (1.8 vs 1.21). Participants specifically reported being "amused" and "surprised" by both the animated and the vocal interferences. The perceived hedonic quality of the VR game version was 0.95 as compared to that of the 2D version which had a lower and neutral score of 0.5. The difference between the score of the 2D and VR version, for both the attractive and hedonic qualities, can be explained by the immersive nature of VR games. A/B testing experiments with a larger number of participants are required to confirm that gamifying SSTs using VR instead of 2D yields a better user experience. More importantly, a comparative analysis of game scores is important to assess the impact of each mode on cognitive test goals. The comparatively low score values obtained for the hedonic qualities can be attributed to the test duration which was perceived as lengthy; boredom and progressive loss of interest in carrying out the SSTs was unanimously reported and observed. Knowing that test duration is constrained by cognitive test validity, design efforts will be put into how to increase user engagement and reduce the boredom effect during a game session (Fig. 6).

Table 2. Pragmatic and Hedonic quality of the 2D and VR game

	2D game	VR game
Attractiveness	1.21	1.8
Pragmatic quality	1.69	1.82
Hedonic quality	0.50	0.95

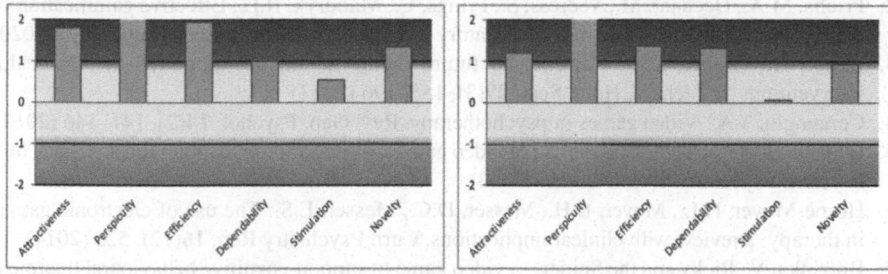

Fig. 6. Pragmatic and Hedonic quality: Left for the 2D game, Right for the VR game

The small-scale study conducted helped identify specific usability issues reported by participants. In the tutorial, the fact that green frames appear alongside with red frames, made some participants expect a green frame for sheets that should be stamped. Furthermore, the feedback during the tutorial game was not noticeable, especially as people were focused on the "desk" where Go stimuli objects were landing. In subsequent game versions, we aim for a better coherence between the tutorial and game interferences, and a grouping of feedback and game structures. Furthermore, in the VR version, it was not straightforward that only one joystick button was actionable, which can explain the relatively low (however positive) score of the dependability aspect of the VR mode, in comparison with other aspects of the pragmatic quality.

7 Conclusion and Future Work

In this paper, we present the architecture design of a configurable game dedicated for inhibitory and interference control. The proposed game design enables mental health researchers and practitioners to easily parametrize a game session by choosing interferences and setting other test parameters such as SSTs frequencies. Starting from the same custom game scenario, the proposed design facilitates the generation of 2D and a VR version of the same game, thus enabling comparative studies.

As part of our future work at the software architecture level, we plan to extend the proposed design to support an AR mode with the constraint of laying 3D game objects on top of the real world in a consistent manner. Other generalizations are being considered, such as proposing customisable game environments. In the long run, our concept is to build a shared open-source repository of reusable game assets that can expand over time. Such repository would typically allow a therapist to create, reuse, and share a list of reusable interferences that can be augmented, shared, and reused by therapists. This repository along with anonymized experimental data can help the research community assess which types of SSTs, interferences, and experiment parameters are adequate for a specific gaming context.

References

1. Friedman, N.P., Miyake, A.: The relations among inhibition and interference control functions: a latent-variable analysis. J. Exp. Psychol. **133**(1), 101–135 (2004)
2. Friehs, M.A., Dechant, M., Vedress, S., Frings, C., Mandryk, R.L.: Effective gamification of the stop-signal task: two controlled laboratory experiments. JMIR Serious Games **8**(3) (2020)
3. Barak, A., Grohol, J.M.: Current and future trends in internet-supported mental health interventions. J. Technol. Hum. Serv. **29**(3), 155–196 (2011)
4. Ceranoglu, T.A.: Video games in psychotherapy. Rev. Gen. Psychol. **14**(2), 141–146 (2010)
5. Griffiths, M.D.: The therapeutic use of video games in childhood and adolescence. Clin. Child Psychol. Psychiatry **8**(4), 547–554 (2003)
6. Horne-Moyer, H.L., Moyer, B.H., Messer, D.C., Messer, E.S.: The use of electronic games in therapy: a review with clinical implications. Curr. Psychiatry Rep. **16**(12), 520 (2014)
7. Brezinka, V.: Ricky and the Spider – a video game to support cognitive behavioural treatment of children with obsessive-compulsive disorder. Clin. Neuropsychiatry **10**(3), 6–12 (2013)
8. Craven, M.P., Groom, M.J.: Computer games for user engagement in attention deficit hyperactivity disorder (ADHD) monitoring and therapy. In: 2015 International Conference on Interactive Technologies and Games, pp. 34–40 (2015)
9. Verbruggen, F., Logan, G.D., Stevens, M.A.: STOP-IT: windows executable software for the stop-signal paradigm. Behav. Res. Methods **40**(2), 479–483 (2008)
10. Crepaldi, M., et al.: The use of a serious game to assess inhibition mechanisms in children. Front. Comput. Sci. **2** (2020)
11. Crepaldi, M., et al.: Antonyms: a computer game to improve inhibitory control of impulsivity in children with attention deficit/hyperactivity disorder (ADHD). Information **11**(4), 230 (2020)
12. Schroeder, P.A., Lohmann, J., Ninaus, M.: Preserved inhibitory control deficits of overweight participants in a gamified stop-signal task: experimental study of validity. JMIR Serious Games **9**(1), e25063 (2021)
13. De Leeuw, J.R.: jsPsych: a JavaScript library for creating behavioral experiments in a web browser. Behav. Res. Methods **47**(1), 1–12 (2015)
14. Peirce, J.W., et al.: PsychoPy2: experiments in behavior made easy. Behav. Res. Methods **51**(1), 195–203 (2019)

15. Lumsden, J., Edwards, E.A., Lawrence, N.S., Coyle, D., Munafò, M.R.: Gamification of cognitive assessment and cognitive training: a systematic review of applications and efficacy. JMIR Serious Games **4**(2), e11 (2016)
16. Laugwitz, B., Held, T., Schrepp, M.: Construction and Evaluation of a User Experience Questionnaire. In: Holzinger, A. (ed.) USAB 2008. LNCS, vol. 5298, pp. 63–76. Springer, Heidelberg (2008). https://doi.org/10.1007/978-3-540-89350-9_6

AWATO: A Serious Game to Improve Cybersecurity Awareness

Lauren S. Ferro[1(✉)], Andrea Marrella[1], Tiziana Catarci[1], Francesco Sapio[1],
Adriano Parenti[2], and Matteo De Santis[2]

[1] Sapienza, University of Rome, Rome, Italy
{lsferro,marrella,catarci,sapio}@diag.uniroma1.it
[2] Red Hog Studio, Rome, Italy
{adriano.parenti,matteo.desantis}@redhogstudio.com
http://www.redhogstudio.com/

Abstract. The role of human factors in cybersecurity is an under-explored area that has a lot of potential towards mitigating attacks. As a result, an SLR that explored human factors in cybersecurity, focusing on phishing, revealed five key human factors that were persistent with phishing related attacks or issues. Based on the results of the SLR, further explorations into threat modelling were conducted to determine how to classify human factor related behaviour and the decisions that are likely behind them or lead towards human error. From here, this information was used to develop a human factor-centred threat model called STRIDE-HF that was implemented into a game called Another Week at the Office (AWATO). The results of further testing of AWATO revealed that is an effective tool for improving users awareness of good cybersecurity practices.

Keywords: Serious game · Cybersecurity · Threat modelling

1 Introduction

Technology has provided us with a luxury to connect with the world and those in it. However, at the same time it has created new and innovative ways that make us and our data vulnerable to exploitation and cyber-attacks because of our behaviour (e.g., norms, lack of knowledge, etc.) - the human factor (e.g., Dupont [9]. In fact, one such modern and popular cyber-attack that human error leads to the success of is phishing.

Phishing is one of the most common and effective cyber-attacks that takes advantage of human factors. Phishing is a continual threat that shows no signs of slowing down, and it is frequently successful due to user vulnerabilities, particularly human factors. To be successful, a phishing attack must be well-prepared. Phishing attacks that are more targeted examine people, their behaviour, or their online posts to collect important information for developing a focused and credible attack. It is also crucial to understand that phishing does not just happen via email [6].

X. Fang (Ed.): HCII 2022, LNCS 13334, pp. 508–529, 2022.
https://doi.org/10.1007/978-3-031-05637-6_33

Similarly to phishing, many other attacks also happen from the outside in. One approach to address these issues is by using threat models [29]. Given that threat models seek to categorise and identify potentially harmful interactions and respond appropriately, the primary argument is that threats should be understood in the context of human factors and how they can be taught to the average user to improve their behavior and attitudes toward cybersecurity practices, notably phishing. As a consequence, by applying threat modelling approaches, it is feasible to work toward building better user-centred security policies and processes to reduce security threats and handle problems in a number of ways (e.g., changing the design of user interface elements, file sharing and management, or password policies). This viewpoint is consistent with the focus of a recent systematic literature review on phishing [8], which found numerous major areas of concern when it comes to cybersecurity hygiene, including habits, attitudes, and processes that can contribute to a successful phishing assault. One such issue is a lack of tools and training resources to educate users about cybersecurity practices and to make the general public aware that they may be a phishing target, as well as the implications of supposedly alarming information getting into the wrong hands.

Using video games to tackle this problem is one method that is in line with current technology (and proposed in the SLR) and can be readily updated and adjusted based on the goal of usage. A strategy like this may combine theory with a way of putting it into practice in a fun and, more importantly, participatory atmosphere. As a consequence, it can help to raise user understanding of safe cybersecurity behavior and how to identify human component problems that contribute to it. To address this issue, we iterated on a previously developed serious game geared toward threat modelling. This iteration focuses on threat modelling of phishing-related behavior and analysing improvements in users' initial knowledge and awareness, attitude, and behavior against phishing, as well as whether it can be improved with the use of a serious game. Furthermore, the game provides the player with an overview screen that displays not just the user's competence in spotting and categorising threats, but also areas where they might improve.

2   Background

Cybersecurity attacks are successful because people are ignorant of their vulnerabilities and the implications and consequences of cybercrime. Because social media users reveal so much about their lives online, attackers may more easily collect information about them and then use it to "convince" them of their identity and intentions. This form of attack is known as "phishing," and it continues to do significant damage. Despite the fact that experts are engaged to secure a system from outside threats, to profile an attacker, and to uncover vulnerabilities in order to protect a system through threat modelling, systems are nevertheless vulnerable due to human error. Therefore, we must explore methods to recognise harmful human behavior in order to safeguard systems and their users from themselves.

2.1 Phishing

Phishing is one of the most effective cyberattacks. Various authors define phishing in slightly different ways. In this article, we adopt the definition of phishing proposed by Lastdrager in his literature survey on phishing attacks [20], where phishing is defined as: "a scalable act of deception whereby impersonation is used to obtain information from a target".

A phishing attack begins with a message, as shown in Fig. 1. This communication (e.g., an email) seems to be from a real organisation (e.g., a bank), sounds urgent, promises to contain crucial information, and directs victims to a website that is a clone of the original (e.g., a clone of their own bank website). In the message, the victims are asked to provide personal information on the website. For example, they must login to the website to update their profile information. Most victims are unlikely to question the credibility of the website; so, they open it and submit the essential information, which is unfortunately stolen by the attackers, who can use it, for example, to get access to the victims' bank accounts and steal their money.

Phishing is frequently successful because of user weaknesses or human qualities that lead to future errors. To be effective, a phishing attack must be planned, which entails evaluating people, their behavior, their online posts, and even watching them online in order to acquire usable information to be used in a targeted approach. Furthermore, attackers analyse target websites to optimise the efficacy of their attacks. For example, by knowing at what time servers are down for (regular) maintenance, their content, and so on. On the one hand, having information about victims allows attackers to send personalised messages; for example, soccer enthusiasts may receive an email with an offer to purchase their club's clothing (in this case, the phishing website aims to steal their credit card information). On the other hand, knowledge about the target website might boost the trustworthiness of phishing communications. For example, if a website is planned for maintenance, its users may receive an email instructing them to unlock their accounts after the maintenance. Therefore, to achieve this, the user needs to click on a link and log in to the website (in this scenario, the phishing website seeks to steal users' credentials).

Phishing does not simply occur through email. In a number of circumstances, consumers receive bogus phone calls or text messages that appear to be from a

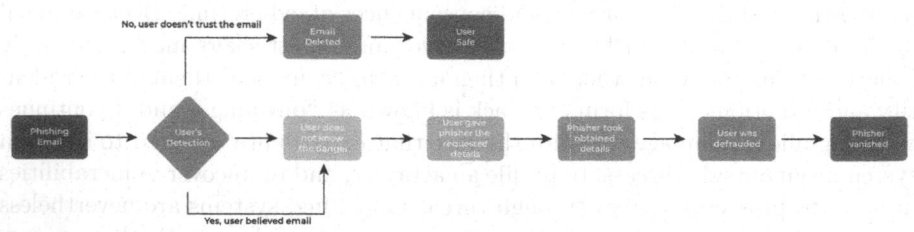

Fig. 1. An overview of a phishing attack as presented by Nmachi and Win [24]

company with which they have an account or service. As a result, some users are reluctant to investigate or question their veracity, and they unknowingly transfer their personal information to fraudsters, hackers, and other harmful individuals. Furthermore, increasingly sophisticated and diverse assaults are offered in response to ongoing upgrades to defensive measures against phishing attempts. A comprehensive overview of the variants of phishing attacks is reported by Chiew et al. [6], where a classification of the main components characterising this attack is derived. This classification first identifies the *"medium"* that is used to start the attack, namely, the Internet, SMS, and voice. Each medium may use a *vector*, i.e., the vehicle for launching the attack. Examples of vectors for the Internet are e-mail, eFax, instant messaging (e.g., social network messages), and websites. The last layer of this categorisation is called *"technical methods"* and it reports all of the technological options accessible to launch a phishing assault, such as JavaScript obfuscation, man-in-the-middle, and SQL injection. Each vector can utilise one or more of these technological tools to carry out the assault. A phishing assault, according to this classification, is highly intricate and may be carried out in a number of ways. As a result, a new nomenclature for distinct sorts of phishing attempts has emerged.

2.2   Threat Modelling

Threat modelling is a way of identifying human variables in cybersecurity that is similar to user profiling and modelling with the exception that the emphasis is on the attackers behaviour rather than the victim. In general, a threat refers to any unauthorised method that gains access to sensitive information, networks, and applications. These are a few common threats that can be addressed by using threat modelling, such as dealing with malware, phishing, denial of service (DoS/DDoS), hacking, insider threats, and so on. There are many different types of threat modelling approaches, frameworks, and techniques [15]. For example, one of the most popular models is STRIDE, which is a methodology introduced by Praerit Garg and Loren Kohnfelder at Microsoft [29] to classify vulnerabilities. Others include DREAD (Damage, Reproducibility, Exploitability, Affected Users, Discoverability) [21], which is used to rate, compare, and prioritise the severity of risk presented by each threat that is classified using STRIDE. In addition, others such as P.A.S.T.A (Process for Attack Simulation and Threat Analysis) [34], Trike [26], OCTAVE (Operationally Critical Threat, Asset, and Vulnerability Evaluation) [2,30] all have various approaches to assessing and planning for attacks from different approaches (i.e., risk or context centred). Lastly, one other method to consider are attack trees [15,29], which are diagrams that depict attacks on a system in tree form. In these cases, the "root" of the tree represents the goal of the attack, and the "leaves" are different ways to achieve that goal.

The STRIDE method is a mnemonic for six types of security threats [29]. The STRIDE threats are the opposite of some of the properties you would like your system to have. For example, the threat of Spoofing violates the property of authenticity. Tampering violates integrity, and so on. In addition, STRIDE supplies the foundation of our theoretical model known as STRIDE-HF (Spoofing, Tampering, Repudiation, Information Disclosure, Denial of Service, and Elevation of Privilege - Human Factor) (See: [11]). STRIDE has also been used to address many concerns within cybersecurity (e.g., [5,18,22,25]) as well as variations such as STRIDE-per-element and STRIDE-per-interaction [29]. Moreover, Khan et al. [18] differentiate the two variations by describing STRIDE-per-element as a more complex method because it analyses the behavior and operations of each system component; and STRIDE-per-interaction as a simpler method to perform because it provides protection strategies sufficient enough to protect a system. However, the general version of STRIDE includes elements that are typical in many cybersecurity-related situations.

2.3   Games and Cybersecurity

Considering the direction of this research, we also investigated educationally and entertainment orientated games. From an educational perspective, several games have been developed over the last decade in an effort to help users understand the importance and necessity of cybersecurity concepts and practices, as well as to aid security specialists in making better security judgements [13,31]. For example, games like Cyberspace Odyssey [13], CyberCIEGE [16], CounterMeasures [17], SecurityCom [32], CyberVR [36], Anti-Phishing Phil [28], PhishGuru [19], CyberPhishing [14], NoPhish [4], Smells Phishy? [3], Phish Phinder [23], PHISHY [7], Bird's Life [37], and StrikeCom [33] are examples of the serious games and gamified approaches intended for educating users about phishing and cybersecurity issues. Few of these games are described in more detail below:

While instructional games exist, many more have been developed to promote different areas of cybersecurity, most notably hacking. A few examples are Watch Dogs (series), Cyber Manhunt, Midnight Protocol, Hacknet, Uplink, Code 7: A Story-Driven Hacking Adventure, Hacker Evolution series (Untold, Duality, Duality: Inception), NITE Team 4-Military Hacking Division, Yolo Space Hacker, and Hacker Simulator. As a result, games with a cybersecurity theme tend to put the player in the shoes of an attacker rather than someone attempting to protect a system. Those that do not focus on hacking may include elements that compromise other aspects of cybersecurity, such as espionage or eavesdropping, in order to gather information to apprehend the attacker. In fact, many games designed to entertain (rather than educate) their players centre on the concept of hacking, providing a safe setting for players to romanticise the idea of hacking into government organisations.

Overall, it is crucial to highlight that many of these games (e.g., Veneruso et al. [35,36]) have touched on relevant and popular forms of cyber assaults as defined by Verizon [1]. However, given the breadth of all these games across various contexts, there is currently no single game that specifically aims to address various cybersecurity-related topics through the lens of human factors and how to address them via threat models with the intention of improving them at the time this paper exists (e.g., the behaviour of users).

3   Another Week a the Office - AWATO

Another Week at the Office (AWATO) is a serious game where you play the role of a recently hired security analyst who must identify errors caused by human error within AWATOcorp. It is a typical office space where employees are currently working towards the launch of a new and innovative product set for to unveil at the end of the week. Therefore, it is the role of a player to ensure the integrity and authenticity of the data and a successful product launch. To do this, the player must identify threats such as opening a dangerous attachment in an email (e.g., Fig. 2) and then classify them using the STRIDE-HF model. The more threats that the player can identify, the more likely the launch will be successful.

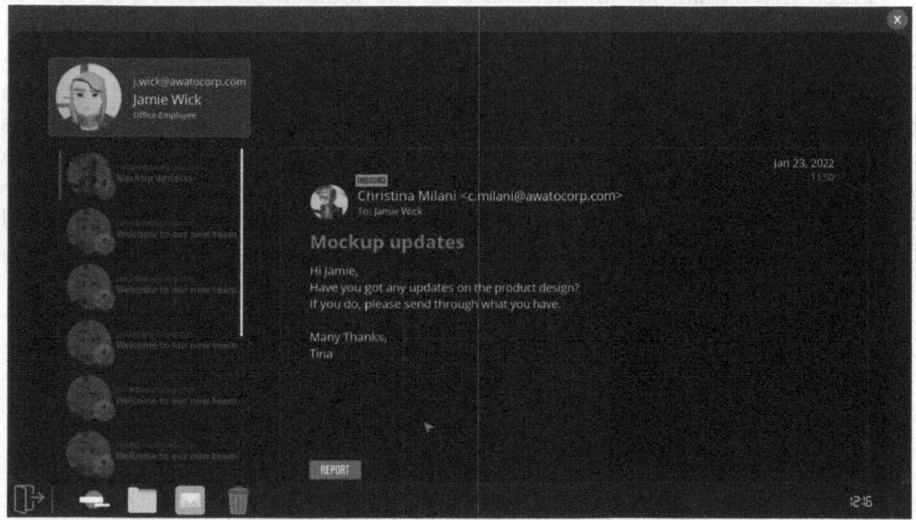

Fig. 2. Screenshot of a characters emails

This is the second iteration of AWATO (previous version [12]). The development of the second version was partly influenced by a systematic literature review (SLR), which was conducted [8] (as part of related work to this project). The SLR highlighted numerous relevant factors that subsequently influenced the iteration of the game (e.g., prominent human factors). Therefore, in the second iteration we considered the issues raised within the SLR: *raising the awareness of human factors in cybersecurity, lack of training, better design indications*, and *anticipating phishing variants*; and the five key human factors.

- **Lack of Knowledge:** is represented by players exchanging sensitive information to fraudulent calls/emails.
- **Lack of Resources:** not having enough resources (e.g., time, tools, people, etc.) to complete task.
- **Lack of Awareness:** not paying attention that unauthorised people are accessing AWATOcorp.
- **Norms:** are represented by actions that friends/colleagues would generally engage with. This includes sharing passwords, login details, leaving computers unattended without a password lock, and not discarding of sensitive information properly.
- **Complacency:** a feeling of self-confidence that can lead to a lack of awareness of potential dangers.

These five human factors were used as the foundation of STRIDE-HF[1] as opposed to all of them to implement into AWATO. As a result, in order for AWATO to create situations where the human elements would have ramifications for the game's objectives, the following interactions were built for each human aspect. Finally, because the game's goal is to increase a user's awareness of improper cyber practices, it needed a mechanism to categorise the human aspect (and behavior) with the implications that it may have on a system. The STRIDEHF framework was used to create this classification and iterated based on the SLR and subsequently implemented into AWATO (Fig. 3).

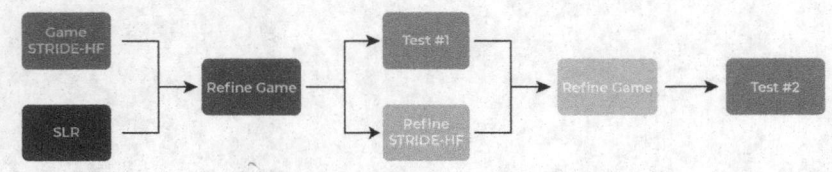

Fig. 3. Overview of the game's development

4   Game Design of AWATO

AWATO was developed using Unreal Engine 4[2] and the interaction was created using both Blueprints and C++. The game environment consists of a total 9 interactble rooms. Within all of these rooms, players need to search for post-it notes, look at trash items (that are found in the trash bin), monitor conversations, and the characters' computers. To add to the immersion of the game, the characters walk around the environment and interact with each other as shown in Fig. 4.

---

[1] It will be possible in future version of AWATO to add other human factors and related in-game behaviours.

[2] www.unrealengine.com.

Fig. 4. Screenshot of characters talking in the 3D environment

4.1   Game Narrative

The narrative design of the conversations and emails is a significant game design component in AWATO. The goal was not to make it easy for the player to notice harmful emails all of the time, as it is in reality. However, the relationships between the characters and the links, as well as these ties and the game's events, are a more essential component of the game's story. Problems, disputes, and friendships are presented and discussed in the email, discussions, Fig. 5, and written (e.g., post-it notes and newspaper articles, trash) material. Furthermore, all story aspects represent scenarios that occur in the workplace, whether they are crucial and detrimental to the office's cybersecurity or if they are linked to events that occur in the characters' lives (in and out of the office). As a result, AWATOcorp contains a backstory that adds dimension to the plot and characters and contributes to a more immersive experience.

AWATO has 99 post-it notes, 200 trash papers, and 258 emails. Post-it notes and trash documents were generated randomly and appeared in various locations around the game. These documents include both non-sensitive information (e.g., appointment calendars, reminders, song lyrics, shopping lists, and notes to other characters) and dangerous information (e.g., pin numbers, access codes, and private details). Another important aspect of the interaction to emphasise was the use of pre-and post-survey questions. The decision was taken to include the survey questions into the game's storyline in order to increase the player's immersion and prevent them from having to interact with several platforms (i.e., Google Forms). To accomplish this, the questions were inserted into the first interaction between the player and the CEO (Edlyn Firth) during a job interview, as seen in Fig. 6.

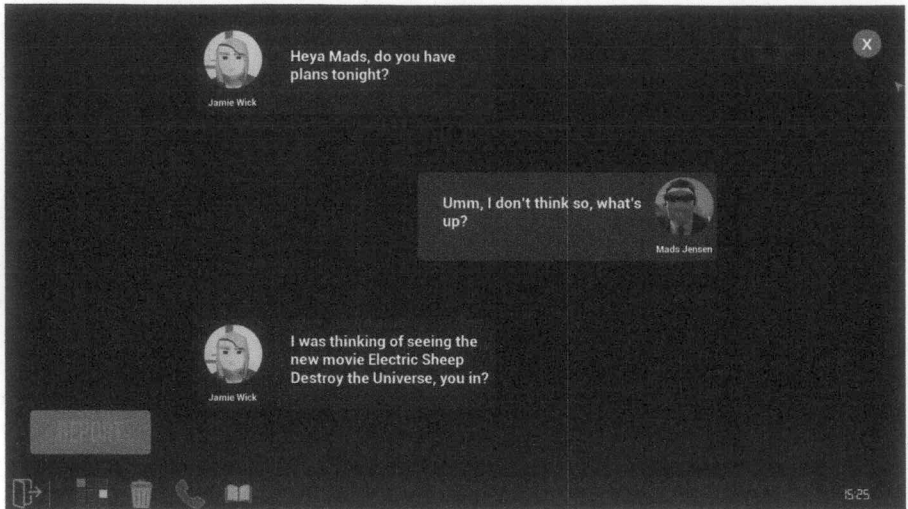

Fig. 5. Screenshot of conversations between characters

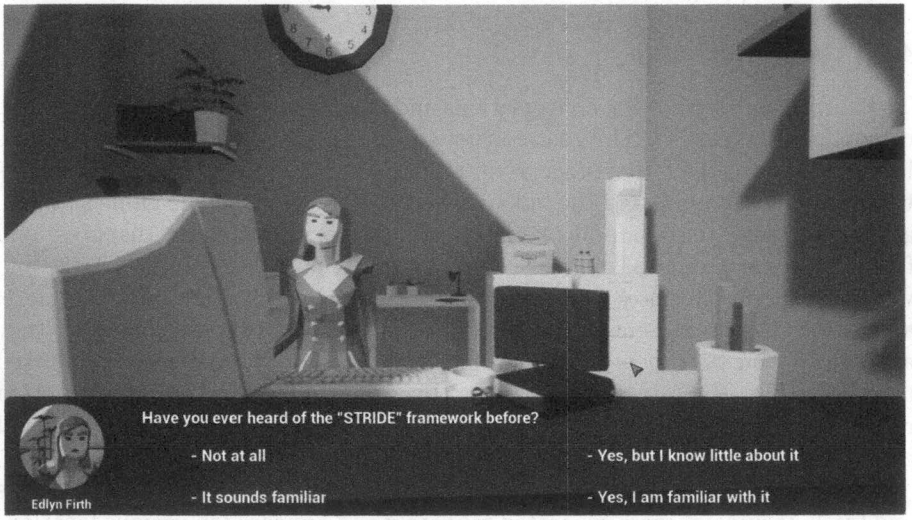

Fig. 6. Screenshots from the starting interview (with survey questions)

4.2 Game Mechanics

The game's interaction is based on the player clicking on in-game objects (post-its, trash cans, and computers), and subsequently classifying them using STRIDE-HF. Each character has their own PC (including the player). This is the central hub that connects a player to most of the gameplay. Here, the player can access each of the characters PC and observe their interaction with files (whether they have been scanning files that they download), their emails (e.g. if they have been engaging in phishing scams, or sharing sensitive information), and lastly to see if anti-virus software is updated. Throughout the game, NPCs will receive emails[3] that consist of the following information:

- **General Communication (positive):** in these instances, emails between users are not dangerous and often follow general everyday conversations.
- **General Communication (negative):** these types of emails also follow general everyday conversations; however, they reveal sensitive information (e.g. passwords, account details, privileged information).
- **Spam Emails:** contain your typical phishing scams where people are asking for details from a user.

For a player to interact with computers, they need to use a password that is given to them at the beginning of the game (and is accessible through the pause menu). The player needs the password to access the other character's computers to check emails and to see whether the antivirus is updated. In addition to the computers of the other characters, the player must access their own computer to accomplish numerous activities, such as classifying the reported faults, listening to phone calls between the characters, and reviewing the manual if they are having difficulty.[4]

4.3   Game Conditions

At the end of each day, a player is presented with a summary report, as show in Fig. 7. At the end of the game, the player is presented with another but more detailed summary report that is shown in Fig. 7. The end game summary report contains:

- The outcome of the game: Failure, Delayed, or Success.
- The amount of threats that were classified that day.
- Areas that are suggested for the player to improve their understanding on. This is based on the threats that they failed to classify/classify correctly throughout the game.

For now, the player is only presented with a percentage regarding the areas that they should focus on. In future versions of AWATO, the user will be provided with more specific documentation to help them continue learning.

4.4   Collecting Data and Input from AWATO

Considering the amount of different forms of interaction, we collected not only answers to the pre and post game questions, but also the time spent on reading the corporate manual, classifying threats, overall time spent playing the game, as well as every item they interacted with.

---

[3] The emails were created within an excel spreadsheet and implemented into the game via Blueprint scripts in the Unreal Engine.

[4] The handbook (corporate manual) is also shown to the player at the start of the game, following "the interview".

Fig. 7. End of the game stat screen.

5 STRIDE-HF in AWATO

To use the STRIDE-HF approach to classify threats (described in [11]), the player must first understand workplace culture and/or how workers interact with one another and the system. To predict the types and severity of human behavior-related security concerns, the security analyst must first understand workplace culture. For example, if the workplace environment is relaxed and employees freely share information, the probability that particular behaviours may be abused as attack vectors increases. Assume that one employee transfers a malicious file to a coworker, who subsequently uploads it to a server. As a result, security requirements must be adaptable as well as monitored and enforced on a frequent basis. Understanding behavior, on the other hand, is not the only way to address human component issues. For example, if a workplace is at high risk of getting phishing emails but does not have an antivirus or a download limit, the system permits certain behaviours to occur (e.g., downloading potentially unsafe files and opening them without scanning them). As a result, the system is being exposed needlessly. Another factor to consider is the work environment. The ubiquity of open-plan office buildings raises the risk of unintentional threats such as information disclosure, repudiation, and denial of service. This is because of the simplicity with which conversations may be overheard, the regularity with which computers are left unattended and, in certain circumstances, unlocked, and the frequency with which sensitive material is shown on-screen for anyone to examine.

The threats in the game were designed to be connected to human factors, with a focus on phishing-related difficulties (e.g., predominantly email and password/pin based failures). Where classic STRIDE concerns arose, for example, we examined the likelihood of the same "deliberate" issue arising by accident. For example, someone "tampering" with cables to get something to function but inadvertently disconnecting the servers. An example of these are also presented in Table 1.[5]

---

[5] While many of the issues have similar STRIDE elements and human factors, the way that they are presented in-game varies.

Table 1. Example of how in-game actions are classified with STRIDE-HF in AWATO

Issue	STRIDE element	Human factor
Passwords on post-notes	Norms	Information Disclosure
Sharing ID Cards	Norms	Information Disclosure
Sharing bank account details	Norms	Information Disclosure
Unplugging hardware (e.g., Printer, Router)	Lack of Awareness	Denial of Service
Leaving key-locked doors open	Norms	Tampering
Pranks (e.g., changing passwords on employees computers)	Norms	Denial of Service
Lost ID cards (unreported)	Lack of Awareness	Information Disclosure
Forgetting/leaving documents with sensitive information in various locations	Lack of Awareness	Information Disclosure
Not disposing of sensitive (printed) files (e.g., by shredding)	Complacency	Information Disclosure

- **Phishing Scams**: Some NPCs will send replies to phishing emails, which then expose the system to vulnerabilities. Therefore, it is important that the player identifies these early on.
- **Updating (patches, antivirus)**: It is important that the player pay attention to which NPC has updated their anti-virus software.
- **Reporting email attachments and other security issues** (see Fig. 8): when players receive files in-game from various sources (including those from AWATO) they need to make sure that they read the file, even if it is from a trusted source (e.g., a friend or colleague).
- **Sharing/losing passwords**: the player must find out who is sharing passwords and locate "lost" passwords that are left around the environment (e.g. in the kitchen, on the floor, in the trash, etc.) like in Fig. 8.
- **Tampering**: some employees may accidentally tamper with equipment or even files without being aware that it is an issue. Therefore, it is important that the player checks the details in post-it notes and emails.
- **Sharing sensitive information**: during email or phone conversations, NPCs may accidentally reveal sensitive content to others, such as in Fig. 5.

Fig. 8. Screenshots of unsafe (right) and safe (left) post-it note.

Based on the description of STRIDE-HF the following behaviours were classified accordingly (in Table) within AWATO. It is important to remember that the "most likely" human factor *and* STRIDE combination were chosen for the behaviours.

5.1 STRIDE-HF Matrix

As mentioned previously, one of the main objectives for the player to do in AWATO is to identify bad behaviour of users. For example, if an NPC is constantly responding to spam emails then it is up to the player to realise this, report it, and subsequently classify the issue in STRIDE-HF Matrix. As users categorise the threats, the columns and rows are highlighted in red or green. This was intended to assist the player in identifying the related STRIDE and human factor factors. The purpose of highlighting a correct or wrong column and/or row was to offer some direction to the player rather than have them meaninglessly click on random squares if they did not know the solution. If the player is doubtful, they can make a more educated judgement with the correctness of the information being made evident through visual feedback (Fig. 9).

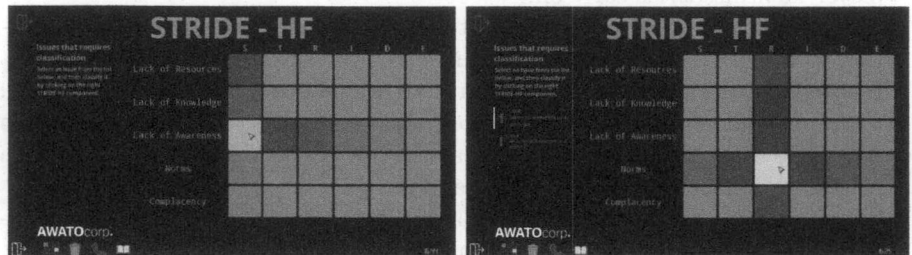

Fig. 9. In-game screenshot of the STRIDE-HF Matrix when the player makes a *correct* (left) and *incorrect* (right) classification

6 Results

At the beginning of the game, participants were asked a series of questions to gauge their cybersecurity practices and knowledge as part of an in-game interview with AWATOcorp's CEO (Edlyn Firth). Questions consisted of basic demographics, knowledge of STRIDE and human factors, as well as some general cybersecurity practices that were rated on a 7-point Likert scale questions (Fig. 10).

The test run consisted of 19 participants (26% female, 74% male) with a majority of the participants being aged between 18–24 years old (74%) and the rest between the ages of 25–30 (21%), and over 30 (5%).

1. Age Group
2. Which gender do you identify yourself as?
3. How do you evaluate your computer skills?
4. How safe would you rate your cyber security practises?
5. Have you ever heard of the "STRIDE" framework before?
6. Do you know what "Human Factors" are?
7. Have you ever heard of the Dirty Dozen in the context of "Human Factors"?

The following questions were based on a 7-point Likert scale:

8. I keep my devices updated with the latest software.
9. I always scan files I download from the internet for virus.
10. I write down password on paper (e.g. post-it notes, etc.).
11. I share or have shared login details with colleagues, friends or family.
12. When I am away from my computer, I lock it (e.g. PIN).
13. My Devices (phone, computer, laptop and tablets) are PIN protected.
14. I generally create strong passwords.
15. I use two factor authentication.
16. I use a personal device in general at work (e.g., mobile).
17. I often backup my devices.
18. I consider myself knowledgeable about using the computer.
19. I use safe cybersecurity practises.

The following questions concluded the interview process:

20. Are you ready to start?
21. Do you remember the PIN I gave you at the beginning?
22. Did you write it down?

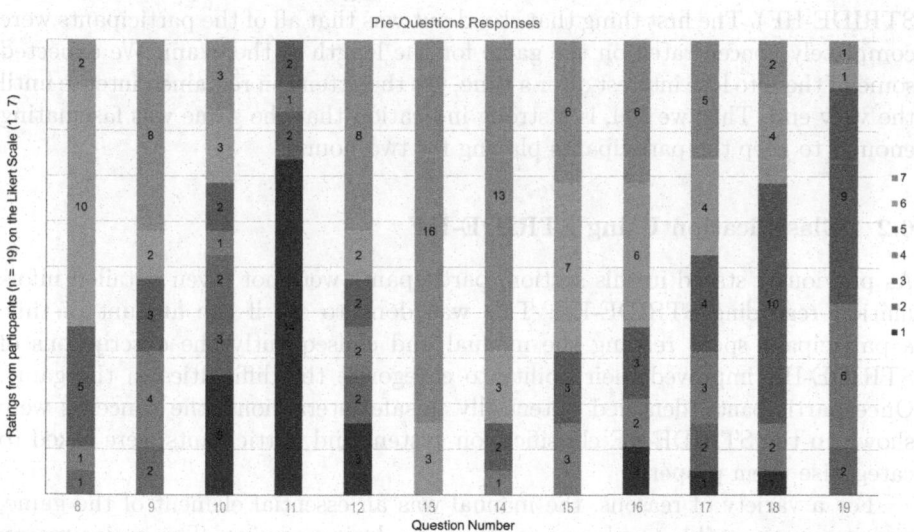

Fig. 10. Results from the pretest questionnaire

Based on the answers to these pre-test questions, the following observations were made:

- Most participants rated their computer skills as being medium (58%).
- Few participants had heard of STRIDE (74%) or the "Dirty Dozen" (89%).
- The level of safe cybersecurity practices were distributed with users identifying as mostly having low (37%) or medium (47%) safe practices.
- On average most participants kept their computers up-to-date, with few (11%) doing it always.
- While a majority of participants identified as using strong passwords (68%), scanning files that they download from the internet (42%)lock their devices when they are not in use (42%), very few identified as engaging with good cybersecurity practices (5%). Suggesting that they know what good practices consist of but perhaps make trade-offs for efficiency or complacency. However, this level of ignorance is what can potentially trap unsuspecting users.
- Given the amount of players who wrote down the password given to them at the beginning of the game (79%), it is plausible to assume that if they do not use a password manager then they write down new passwords albeit on the computer (e.g., in an application like Notepad) or physically (e.g., in a notebook, on a post-it, etc.).
- Most of responses do suggest that participants engage with safe cybersecurity practices (e.g., two-factor login, locking devices, scanning for viruses, etc.).

6.1 Results During Gameplay

Screen sharing through Google Meet was used to watch participants during games. We were able to observe what the participants were doing and how they interacted with various aspects in this manner (e.g., trashcans, post-it notes, and STRIDE-HF). The first thing that stood out was that all of the participants were completely concentrated on the game for the length of the exam. We expected some of them to lose interest after a time, yet the attention remained intense until the very end. This, we feel, is a strong indication that the game was fascinating enough to keep the participants playing for two hours.

6.2 Classification Using STRIDE-HF

As previously stated in this section, participants were not given detailed information regarding STRIDE-HF. This was done to see if the amount of time a participant spent reading the manual and consequently the descriptions of STRIDE-HF improved their ability to categorise the difficulties in the game. Once participants identified potentially unsafe interactions, the concerns were shown in the STRIDE-HF classification system and participants were asked to categorise them properly.

For a variety of reasons, the manual was an essential element of the game, and it was accessible to players at any time during gaming. The major reason for this is that it is similar to what a new employee is likely to receive when they start a job. The handbook detailed the AWATOcorp policy, indicating what the player should and should not do (even though this interaction was not possible during gameplay) to increase immersion in the position that the participant was adopting. Furthermore, the handbook included information about STRIDE-HF, which the participant was asked to use to categorise the hazards. Participants studied the instructions for an average of 395 s (6.6 min).

While there are not large differences, observing Fig. 11, it is clear that the more time that a participant spent reading the manual did have a slight impact on the amount of misclasifications and misreported issues they made during gameplay. Lastly, it did not appear to have influenced the amount of correctly classified issues, with the amount of correctly classified issues not presenting with any trends. Therefore, other investigations are needed to determine what is influencing this.

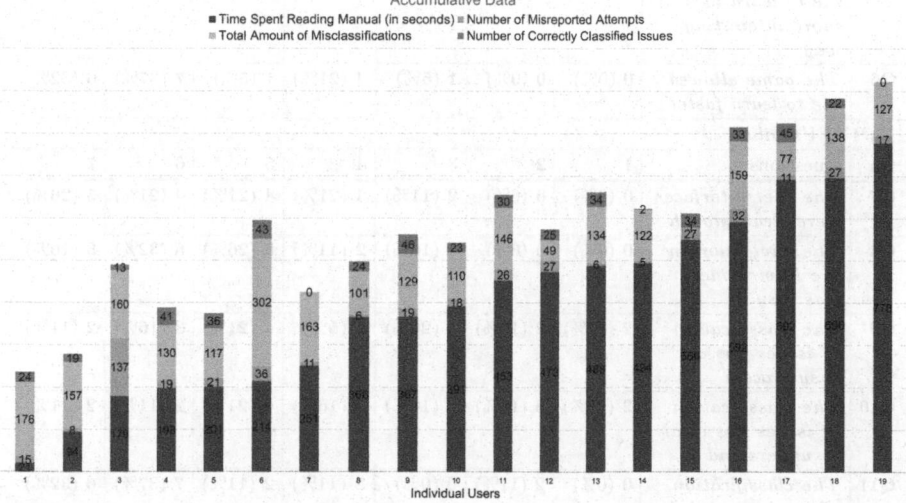

Fig. 11. Time spent reading the manual versus the number of misclassifications and misreporting of issues during gameplay

6.3 Results of the Post-game Questionnaire

Participants were also asked several questions during an in-game follow-up from AWATOcorp's CEO (Edlyn Firth), similar to how they were at the start of the game. The goal of these questions was to figure out how the user felt about the experience. Once again, we used a Likert scale, in which the format of the seven-level items ranged from *Strongly Agree* to *Strongly Disagree*. The questions, along with their answers, can be found in Table 2, whereas Fig. 12 gives a more visual representations on how the participants answered the questions.

The internal consistency of the questionnaire (only the post test) has been evaluated by Split-Half Reliability [27]. For each participant, we partitioned the

Table 2. Test – post questionnaire about participants' perception of the experience

Qn	Questions	1	2	3	4	5	6	7
Part 1: Likeability								
Q1	I enjoyed playing the game	1 (5%)	0 (0%)	1 (5%)	0 (0%)	8 (42%)	6 (32%)	3 (16%)
Q2	I believe AWATO is an engaging experience	0 (0%)	0 (0%)	0 (0%)	2 (11%)	4 (21%)	7 (37%)	6 (32%)
Q3	I will recommend AWATO to other people	0 (0%)	1 (5%)	1 (5%)	2 (11%)	4 (21%)	4 (21%)	7 (37%)
Part 2: Learnability								
Q4	I have learned by playing the game	0 (0%)	0 (0%)	2 (11%)	1 (5%)	3 (16%)	4 (21%)	9 (47%)
Q5	The game allowed me to learn in a more interesting way	0 (0%)	0 (0%)	0 (0%)	3 (16%)	2 (11%)	8 (42%)	6 (32%)
Q6	The game allowed me to learn faster	0 (0%)	0 (0%)	1 (5%)	4 (21%)	1 (5%)	7 (37%)	6 (32%)
Part 3: Usability								
Q7	The user interfaces were clear enough	0 (0%)	0 (0%)	2 (11%)	4 (21%)	4 (21%)	4 (21%)	5 (26%)
Q8	The navigation in the Environment was easy	0 (0%)	0 (0%)	3 (16%)	2 (11%)	5 (26%)	6 (32%)	3 (16%)
Q9	The classification of issues was an easy process	2 (11%)	2 (11%)	5 (26%)	1 (5%)	4 (21%)	3 (16%)	2 (11%)
Q10	The classification of issues was clear to understand	2 (11%)	3 (16%)	3 (16%)	3 (16%)	4 (21%)	2 (11%)	2 (11%)
Q11	The classification of issues provided good feedback when I was classifying wrongly	0 (0%)	2 (11%)	0 (0%)	2 (11%)	2 (11%)	7 (37%)	6 (32%)
Part 4: Preferences								
Q12	Having the characters moving around made the world feel more alive	0 (0%)	1 (5%)	0 (0%)	3 (16%)	2 (11%)	3 (16%)	10 (53%)
Q13	I enjoyed playing AWATO	1 (5%)	0 (0%)	1 (5%)	2 (11%)	1 (5%)	7 (37%)	7 (37%)
Q14	I like playing videogames	1 (5%)	0 (0%)	0 (0%)	1 (5%)	2 (11%)	4 (21%)	11 (58%)
Q15	I believe AWATO can be considered a videogame	1 (5%)	0 (0%)	0 (0%)	2 (11%)	3 (16%)	7 (37%)	6 (32%)

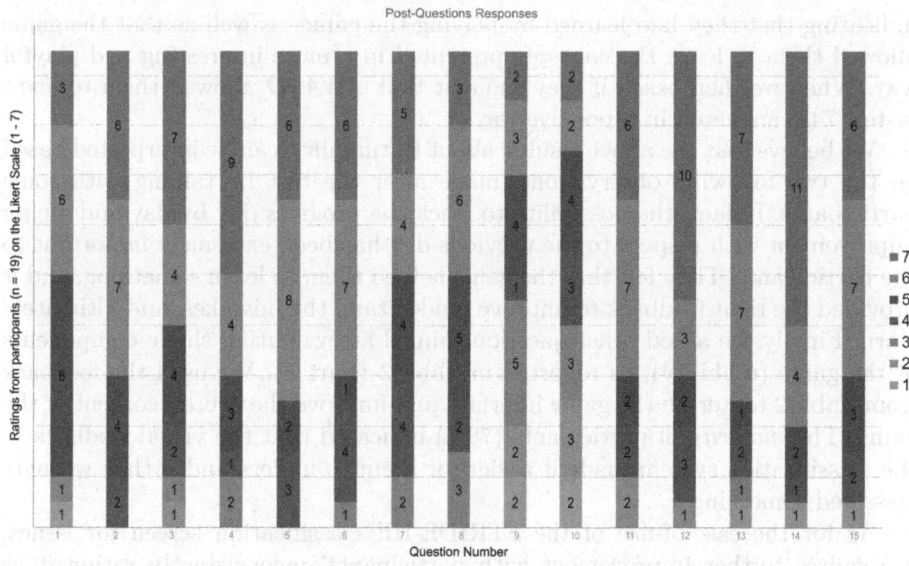

Fig. 12. Overview of the results from the post-game survey

questions into *odd* and *even*, and summed the scores for each half. Then, we computed the correlation between the two halves. Finally, in order to get a better estimate of the reliability of the full test, we applied the Spearman-Brown correction (see Table 3), thus leading to the final value of the *Cronbach's Alpha* of .94, which is an excellent result.

Table 3. Test: post - questionnaire reliability

Correlation Coefficient	.8946051882
Spearman–Brown correction	.9443710951

The first three questions, shown in Table 2 (Part 1) aimed to establish whether participants liked the game and would recommend it to other people (likeability). 90% of participants enjoyed playing[6]; and 10% disliked it. 89% of the participants think that *AWATO* is more engaging than a traditional lecture, but only 79% would recommend the game to other people, while 11% are indifferent. The second set of questions in the Table 2 (Part 2) is intended to confirm participants' perceptions of learning outcomes (learnability). The *majority* of participants felt that the game offered a good educational experience, with 84%

---

[6] Positive results refer to participants who gave a rating of between 5–7 on the Likert scale; neutral (or indifferent) results for who gave a rating of 4; negative results for those who gave a rating of between 1–3.

indicating that they had learned by playing the game, as well as that the game allowed them to learn the concepts presented in a more interesting and playful way. When we then asked if they thought that *AWATO* allowed them to learn faster, 74% answered in a positive way.

We believe that the above results, about learnability, can be interpreted based on the two following observations, made after the test by talking with some participants. In fact, the possibility to track the progress day by day and see an improvement with respect to the previous day has been extremely important to the participants. They felt that the game helped them to learn something, and it provided the right feedback to improve, understand the mistakes, and ultimately learn. Finally, we asked other questions aimed at evaluating single components of the game (usability), as reported in Table 2 (Part 3). We used the feedback from Table 2 to iterate the game interface and improve the overall content of the game. The *majority* of participants (79%) indicated that the visual feedback in the classification system made it easier for them to understand if they wrongly classified something.

As for the ease-of-use of the STRIDE-HF classification screen for issues, it requires further improvement with participants' inconsistently rating it as being between being difficult and easy to understand and use. The last part of the questionnaire concerned the attitude of the participants toward gaming. However, we did not uncover any correlation between these two answers and the likeability or learnability parts of the questionnaire. In addition to these quantitative questions, participants were also asked to share verbally or in the chat their thoughts and feedback on the game. These are discussed in the next section.

7 Discussion

AWATO offered several purposes. The first step was to put STRIDE-HF through its paces to see if it could be used to threat model human behavior in order to avert harmful cyber attacks. Second, to address issues that were raised in the SLR, and third, to investigate if a serious game could be developed to teach people about cybersecurity vulnerabilities and to explain how to threat model these issues using Human Factors. Initial findings show that AWATO is capable of achieving these goals.

The key drawback of AWATO is that further empirical testing is needed to verify the serious game's efficacy as an educational tool and a long-term resource for educating people beyond what we have examined. The outcomes of the study suggest potential, but we feel that further development will need expert assistance if AWATO is to become a more powerful instrument (i.e., from threat modellers and security analysts). Furthermore, while STRIDE-HF is primarily a theoretical model based on current research, a more comprehensive examination of the STRIDE-HF framework for inclusion in AWATO is required to guarantee that the STRIDE and the accompanying HF components are appropriately reflected in the STRIDE-HF matrix.

The evaluation procedure's results are favourable. Participants praised AWATO, saying it was a fun way to learn and that they would recommend it to others. The game's narrative was highly appreciated, and participants enjoyed the location, tale, and the fact that the place was dynamic with people moving around. Several locations will need to be updated in the future. More testing and refinement of STRIDE-HF are necessary to make the classification system more intelligible. Furthermore, we should offer the NPCs greater behaviours so that they respond to the player's decisions. This means that the game will become considerably more exciting. Furthermore, we should give the NPCs more characteristics so that they respond to the player's decisions. This means that the game will become considerably more exciting. Furthermore, AWATO might be turned into a diagnostic tool, giving organisations a simple way to evaluate the current level of knowledge among their employees.

8 Conclusion

We can conclude that AWATO has shown the capacity to educate users while also offering a tool to aid users in comprehending the threat modelling process. It is apparent that consumers respond positively to the use of an interactive educational tool, and in some circumstances, prefer it to traditional content. Future options include extending AWATO to add customisable elements, allowing it to be more directed towards a training setting that mimics the work environment of where the serious game is being played; this might also incorporate other profile factors such as personality. This also reflects what was proposed by Egelman and Peer [10] who introduced a new paradigm of psychographic targeting of privacy and security mitigation. Given this, it is expected that AWATO will eventually serve as a way to inform users about human error-related issues and their impact on a work environment, with the goal of influencing a user's real-life behavior and/or opening up a dialogue between employees about practising safe cybersecurity and improving workplace conditions to accommodate it.

References

1. 2020 data breach investigations report: official—verison enterprise solutions. https://enterprise.verizon.com/resources/reports/dbir/. Accessed 20 Oct 2020
2. Alberts, C.J., Behrens, S.G., Pethia, R.D., Wilson, W.R.: Operationally critical threat, asset, and vulnerability evaluation (OCTAVE) framework, version 1.0. Technical report, Carnegie-Mellon University Pittsburgh PA Software Engineering Institute (1999)
3. Baslyman, M., Chiasson, S.: "Smells phishy?": an educational game about online phishing scams. In: 2016 APWG Symposium on Electronic Crime Research (eCrime), pp. 1–11. IEEE (2016)
4. Canova, G., Volkamer, M., Bergmann, C., Borza, R.: NoPhish: an anti-phishing education app. In: Mauw, S., Jensen, C.D. (eds.) STM 2014. LNCS, vol. 8743, pp. 188–192. Springer, Cham (2014). https://doi.org/10.1007/978-3-319-11851-2_14

5. Chen, X., Liu, Y., Yi, J.: A security evaluation framework based on stride model for software in networks. Int. J. Adv. Comput. Technol. **4**(13), 269–278 (2012). July

6. Chiew, K.L., Yong, K.S.C., Tan, C.L.: A survey of phishing attacks: their types, vectors and technical approaches. Expert Syst. Appl. **106**, 1–20 (2018)

7. Gokul, G.J., Pandit, S., Vaddepalli, S., Tupsamudre, H., Banahatti, V., Lodha, S.: Phishy-a serious game to train enterprise users on phishing awareness. In: Proceedings of the 2018 Annual Symposium on Computer-Human Interaction in Play Companion Extended Abstracts, pp. 169–181 (2018)

8. Desolda, G., Ferro, L.S., Marrella, A., Catarci, T., Costabile, M.F.: Human factors in phishing attacks: a systematic literature review. ACM Comput. Surv. (CSUR) **54**(8), 1–35 (2021)

9. Dupont, G.: The dirty dozen errors in maintenance. In: The 11th Symposium on Human Factors in Maintenance and Inspection: Human Error in Aviation Maintenance (1997)

10. Egelman, S., Peer, E.: The myth of the average user: improving privacy and security systems through individualization. In: Proceedings of the 2015 New Security Paradigms Workshop, pp. 16–28 (2015)

11. Ferro, L.S., Marrella, A., Catarci, T.: A human factor approach to threat modeling. In: Moallem, A. (ed.) HCII 2021. LNCS, vol. 12788, pp. 139–157. Springer, Cham (2021). https://doi.org/10.1007/978-3-030-77392-2_10

12. Ferro, L.S., Sapio, F.: Another week at the office (AWATO) – an interactive serious game for threat modeling human factors. In: Moallem, A. (ed.) HCII 2020. LNCS, vol. 12210, pp. 123–142. Springer, Cham (2020). https://doi.org/10.1007/978-3-030-50309-3_9

13. Graham, K., et al.: Cyberspace odyssey: a competitive team-oriented serious game in computer networking. IEEE Trans. Learn. Technol. **13**(3), 502–515 (2020)

14. Hale, M.L., Gamble, R.F., Gamble, P.: CyberPhishing: a game-based platform for phishing awareness testing. In: 2015 48th Hawaii International Conference on System Sciences, pp. 5260–5269. IEEE (2015)

15. Hussain, S., Kamal, A., Ahmad, S., Rasool, G., Iqbal, S.: Threat modelling methodologies: a survey. Sci. Int. (Lahore) **26**(4), 1607–1609 (2014)

16. Irvine, C.E., Thompson, M.F., Allen, K.: CyberCIEGE: gaming for information assurance. IEEE Secur. Priv. **3**(3), 61–64 (2005)

17. Jordan, C., Knapp, M., Mitchell, D., Claypool, M., Fisler, K.: Countermeasures: a game for teaching computer security. In: 2011 10th Annual Workshop on Network and Systems Support for Games, pp. 1–6. IEEE (2011)

18. Khan, R., McLaughlin, K., Laverty, D., Sezer, S.: Stride-based threat modeling for cyber-physical systems. In: 2017 IEEE PES Innovative Smart Grid Technologies Conference Europe (ISGT-Europe), pp. 1–6. IEEE (2017)

19. Kumaraguru, P., et al.: School of phish: a real-world evaluation of anti-phishing training. In: 5th Symposium on Usable Privacy and Security (SOUPS 2009). ACM (2009). https://doi.org/10.1145/1572532.1572536

20. Lastdrager, E.E.H.: Achieving a consensual definition of phishing based on a systematic review of the literature. Crime Sci. **3**(1), 1–10 (2014). https://doi.org/10.1186/s40163-014-0009-y

21. LeBlanc, D., Howard, M.: Writing Secure Code. Pearson Education (2002)

22. Marback, A., Do, H., He, K., Kondamarri, S., Xu, D.: A threat model-based approach to security testing. Softw. Pract. Exp. **43**(2), 241–258 (2013)

23. Misra, G., Arachchilage, N.A.G., Berkovsky, S.: Phish phinder: a game design approach to enhance user confidence in mitigating phishing attacks. arXiv preprint arXiv:1710.06064 (2017)
24. Nmachi, W.P., Win, T., et al.: Mitigating phishing attack in organisations: a literature review. In: CS & IT Conference Proceedings, vol. 11. CS & IT Conference Proceedings (2021)
25. Ruffy, F., Hommel, W., von Eye, F.: A STRIDE-based security architecture for software-defined networking. In: ICN 2016, p. 107 (2016)
26. Saitta, P., Larcom, B., Eddington, M.: Trike v1 methodology document. Draft (2005, work in progress)
27. Salkind, N.J.: Encyclopedia of Research Design, vol. 1. SAGE, Newbury Park (2010). https://doi.org/10.4135/9781412961288
28. Sheng, S., et al.: Anti-phishing phil: the design and evaluation of a game that teaches people not to fall for phish. In: 3rd Symposium on Usable privacy and security - SOUPS 2007, pp. 88–99. ACM (2007). https://doi.org/10.1145/1280680.1280692
29. Shostack, A.: Threat Modeling: Designing for Security. Wiley, Hoboken (2014)
30. Sosonkin, M.: Octave: operationally critical threat, asset and vulnerability evaluation. Polytechnic University, April 2005
31. Tioh, J.N., Mina, M., Jacobson, D.W.: Cyber security training a survey of serious games in cyber security. In: 2017 IEEE Frontiers in Education Conference (FIE), pp. 1–5. IEEE (2017)
32. Twitchell, D.P.: SecurityCom: a multi-player game for researching and teaching information security teams. J. Digit. Forensics Secur. Law 2(4), 1 (2007)
33. Twitchell, D.P., Wiers, K., Adkins, M., Burgoon, J.K., Nunamaker, J.F.: StrikeCom: a multi-player online strategy game for researching and teaching group dynamics. In: Proceedings of the 38th Annual Hawaii International Conference on System Sciences, pp. 45b–45b. IEEE (2005)
34. UcedaVelez, T., Morana, M.M.: Risk Centric Threat Modeling. Wiley Online Library (2015)
35. Veneruso, S., Ferro, L.S., Marrella, A., Mecella, M., Catarci, T.: A game-based learning experience for improving cybersecurity awareness. In: ITASEC, pp. 235–242 (2020)
36. Veneruso, S.V., Ferro, L.S., Marrella, A., Mecella, M., Catarci, T.: CyberVR: an interactive learning experience in virtual reality for cybersecurity related issues. In: Proceedings of the International Conference on Advanced Visual Interfaces, pp. 1–8 (2020)
37. Weanquoi, P., Johnson, J., Zhang, J.: Using a game to improve phishing awareness. J. Cybersecur. Educ. Res. Pract. 2018(2), 2 (2018)

Designing Social Exergame to Enhance Intergenerational Interaction and Exercise

Emiran Kaisar, Shi Qiu[(✉)], Rui Yuan, and Ting Han

Department of Design, Shanghai Jiao Tong University, Shanghai, China
{imarsemiran,qiushi11,YuanRui-design,hanting}@sjtu.edu.cn

Abstract. This paper describes a social exergame, aiming at promoting intergenerational interaction between older adults and young people, in which an older adult and a young person team up as a pair to reach the goals. Different interactions and mechanisms were designed for older adults and young people in consideration of their variations in mental and physical abilities. Motion capture by webcam was implemented and used as an interaction mechanism for older adults to play the exergame, while young people using NEONEO balance ball, a tangible interaction device, to control the game character. Although they were given different tasks, there are requirements for communication and cooperation within the pair (older adults and young people). The design process and system implementation were presented. And the Evaluation scheme was designed to test if the exergame could provide a way for intergenerational interaction between young and old, which will be of benefit for both generations. Contributions of this paper include knowledge of designing and implementing such exergame and the study on this topic can be the reference for other researchers in the relevant area.

Keywords: Intergenerational interaction · Active aging · Social exergame · Social interaction · Older adults

1 Introduction

With the growth of the aging population worldwide, studies concerned with older adults' physical and mental well-being are getting more attention. Intergenerational interactions provide a way for older adults to keep track of social norms and culture in the present society which are beneficial to their daily life and mental health [1]. In the case of young people, an improvement of prosocial behavior and communion was expected through intergenerational interaction [2].

Fuchsberger et al. [3] argued that game-play between old and young provide a new way of intergenerational interactions which is beneficial to both generations. Joint playing can provide older adults and young people with opportunities to communicate and solve problems together which deepens relationships [4].

Familiarity design was suggested in consideration of older adults' perceived difficulty in adapting to new technologies [5]. Thus, in our exergame, the motion capture was deployed that takes in older adults' posture information and mapping it to the game

X. Fang (Ed.): HCII 2022, LNCS 13334, pp. 530–541, 2022.
https://doi.org/10.1007/978-3-031-05637-6_34

character which can be perceived more easily by older adults, compared with other interaction mechanisms. In the meantime, the exergame should be challenging for young people so that they can play with older adults without getting bored. In other words, one of the purposes of this exergame is to appeal to both generations and provide them a new way to interact with each other.

In previous studies, we conducted systematic reviews [6, 7] regarding Socially Assistive Systems (SASs), to summarize research findings that using design intervention to promote social interaction for people with special needs (typically older adults and people with disabilities [7–10]. Next, we implemented a NEONEO balance ball [11] to establish intergenerational interaction between older adults and young people. In the pilot test, we found that different tasks and challenges should be allocated to the old and young so that they can cooperate to carry out missions. Therefore, in this paper, we implemented an exergame based on previous findings and designed an evaluation scheme to test if the exergame could provide a way for intergenerational interaction between older adults and young people.

2 Related Work

Researchers recruited five intergenerational pairs to play two Wii games, and record their gameplay and downtime conversation. Their study on the record materials using conversation analysis (CA) revealed that joint gameplay can facilitate intergenerational interaction and prosocial behaviors in young people [12]. Hausknecht et al. [13] discussed the possible design approaches for intergenerational collaboration within the game genre of Alternate Reality Games (ARGs) and argued that such games should require different skills so that both generations can contribute to their gameplay. The effects of video gameplay were explored in a program involving intergenerational interaction sessions over two months where each pair of participants (older adults and young people) were randomly assigned to either the video-game condition or the non-video-game condition. The researcher used a pre-post-test in this research to collect data related to attraction, intergroup anxiety, attitudes, and game enjoyment and found improvements in intergroup anxiety and attitudes in the video-game condition compared to the non-video-game condition [14].

Xu et al. conducted a three-week experiment to compare the effects of playing exergame among young-old and old-old, and results of a two-way ANOVA revealed that older adults, in young-old condition, felt more motivated to play exergame compared to those who are in old-old condition [15]. In addition, more trust and prosocial behaviors were observed in the exercise group compared to the control group [16]. Seaborn et al. argued that shared activity within older adults and young people will generate empathy that is beneficial to society. Two versions of intergenerational shared action games were implemented for experiments. They used Interpersonal Reactivity Index to capture dispositional empathy after experiments and found that their intergenerational shared action games have positive effects on social presence and empathy [17].

In conclusion, researchers had presented the value of joint game play between old and young. And this paper focuses on the design and implementation of the exergame and the effects of the exergame on intergenerational interactions.

3 Concept Design

3.1 Design Goals

There are differences between older adults and young people with their physical and mental abilities. So, the design and mechanism of the exergame should be considered for both generations. Two main goals are presented to achieve this mechanism.

- Allocate different tasks to older adults and young people that suit their abilities and enhance their interactions through the game.
- Find a cheap and feasible pipeline for implementing an exergame platform that supports different interactions between players and the game.

3.2 Scenarios

Our design goals and concept can be well presented in scenario Fig. 1, where older adults and young people play the exergame in the same physical space. However, it is not limited to this particular context, because online cooperative interactions are also considered.

Ling Plays Exergame with Her Grandson Xiao Ming

Ling (65 years old) just got retired from her job at a bank, and she now spends most of her time taking care of her grandson, Xiao Ming (7 years old). Although they spend lots of time together, their communication seems to be restricted to a few casual topics like "How have you been lately?" and "What did you do today?" Ling wants to talk more but doesn't know how to break through these restrictions.

It is a Saturday afternoon. Xiao Ming receives a gift from his parents. It is an exergame Fig. 1(1). He set up the game immediately and connects it to the TV screen Fig. 1(2). He thinks the mechanism of the game is very easy so he invites his grandmother to play with him Fig. 1(3)–(4). He always wants to play with Ling, but most of his games are hard for Ling to understand. This time, he is excited because he could be able to teach and guide his grandmother, which gives him a feeling of pride. Ling hesitates at the beginning, but afterward, she realizes that this might be good a chance to enhance their interactions.

- "Grandma, we cooperatively control that bird in the game and we cannot let those boxes hit on the bird." said Xiao Ming.
- "Ok, but how do we control the bird?".
- "When you wave your arms like a bird before the webcam, that bird on the screen will go up, and it will go down if you stop. And I will control the horizontal movement of the bird."
- "I think I got it!" Ling smiled.

It is a happy and different experience for both Ling and Xiao Ming Fig. 1(5). Xiao Ming talks about games with Ling as if she was one of his regular friends at school, and Ling also gives him feedback.

– "I think we need to have priority when escaping from those boxes." -Xiao Ming said.
– "You are right! Some boxes are much more dangerous than others." Ling said.
– "I will give you a signal to which direction we should move."
– "Ok, I will pay close attention." Ling said to Xiao Ming happily.

After a few times of playing together, their cooperation improves and they get good grades in the game Fig. 1(6). After all, this exergame provides them a way to talk about things beyond the game and casual stuff.

Fig. 1. User scenarios: (1) Xiao Ming's parents buy him an exergame, (2) Xiao Ming connects exergame with TV, (3)–(4) Xiao Ming explains the game to his grandmother, (5) Xiao Ming and grandmother play together, (6) they cooperate very well and get good grades in the game.

4   System Implementation

The Unity engine is the platform to create the exergame, in which the game characters are controlled by two kinds of interactions. Tangible prototype (NEONEO Balance Ball) is for young people, whereas older adults' interaction with the game is through motion capture by the computer's webcam. Figure 2 presents a real setup of the scene in which our team members adjust and debug the game.

Fig. 2. Debugging the game in the laboratory.

4.1   Tangible Interaction

Hardware as shown in Fig. 3, where the player standing on it, can change the tilt direction and angle of the acrylic board to connect with the game character. The design and implementation (NEONEO Balance Ball) are derived and improved from our previous research [11].

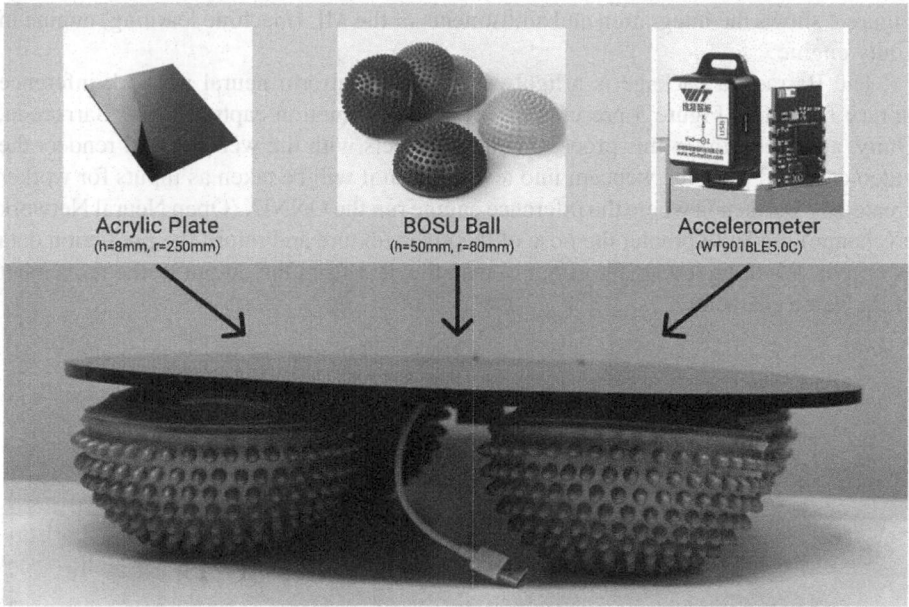

Fig. 3. Tangible interaction device that detects movements and transmits signals.

4.2 Motion Capture

The ML (machine learning) engine, Barracuda [18], was used in this project, which makes motion capture with webcam possible. In this way, familiarity and tailored design can be achieved for older adults [5], in consideration of their physical and mental abilities.

Fig. 4. Integrate ML (machine learning) engine into the game.

Figure 4 shows the integration and adjustments of the ML (machine learning) engine in Unity engine.

The Barracuda package is a lightweight cross-platform neural network inference library for Unity. Figure 5 presents the workflow of motion capture using Barracuda, Unity, and webcam. In this process, Unity connects with the webcam and renders the video captured from the webcam into texture, then it will be taken as inputs for worker created by Barracuda where the inference engine run the ONNIX (Open Neural Network eXchange) model to predict the pose of the given texture and return the prediction data as output. We designed an algorithm to map the data from the output to the movement of the game character.

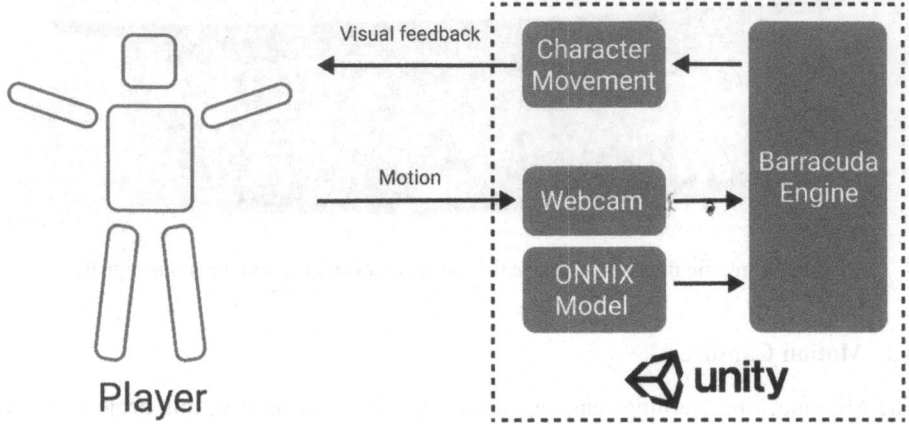

Fig. 5. The workflow of the motion capture in the game.

In this game, a game character is controlled cooperatively by a team, made up of an older adult and a young person. In the beginning, the team will choose a game character as presented in Fig. 6, and these characters are from Unity Asset Store [19], among them

Fig. 6. The team chooses their game character at the beginning.

are Lilly, Jack, and Larry. And then the game begins in which the vertical movement of the game character is related to the adult's swing of arms. In addition, the older adult can swing his/her arms faster or slower to achieve a certain vertical speed of the game character. The movement of the older adult is captured by webcam and only the motion of arms is referenced, and then transmitted to the game. On the other hand, the young person is responsible for the horizontal movement of the bird, controlling the tilt direction and angle of the acrylic board (NEONEO Balance Ball). The main goal of the team is to keep the game character away from obstacles and stay alive as long as possible Fig. 7. The background of the game scene is established with Unity assets from Unity Asset Store [20]. The game will end when the game character hits the obstacle, and there will be a team performance and their rank, comparing them with other teams (old-and-young-team) based on their duration time in the game.

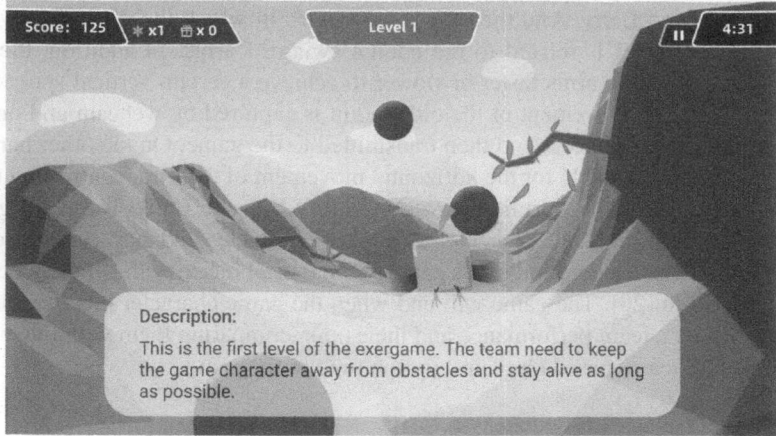

(1)   The first level of the exergame.

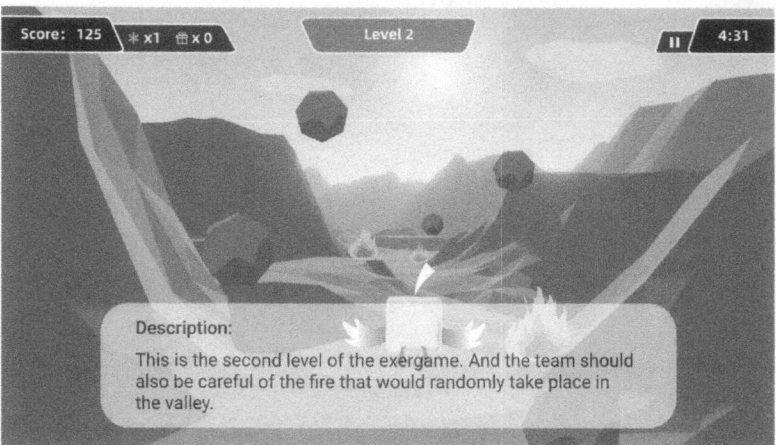

(2)   The second level of the exergame.

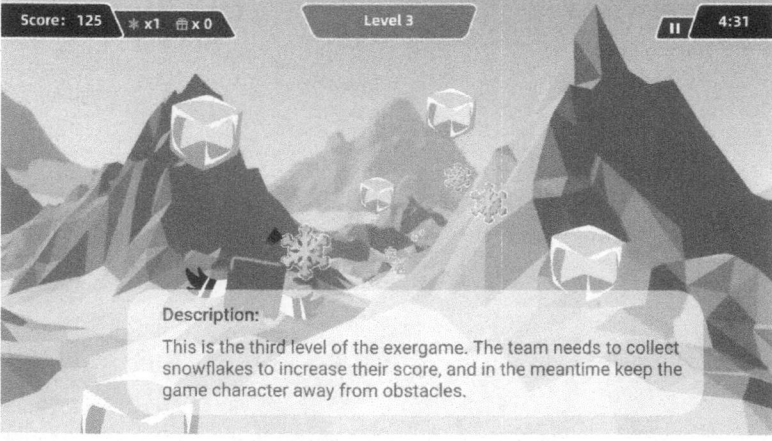

(3)   The third level of the exergame.

Fig. 7. Three levels and corresponding scenes.

5 Evaluation Scheme

The objective of this preliminary experiment is to evaluate the usability of the modified system, observing whether the intervention of this social exergame could efficiently establish social connectedness and raise positive feelings between young people and older adults. Ten pairs of participants will be recruited for the system evaluation. One pair consists of a young adult participant and an older adult participant. Young adult participants are recruited from Shanghai Jiao Tong University (SJTU) via the website of tongqu.sjtu.edu.cn and older adult participants are majorly recruited from the neighborhood committee near the SJTU campus. We will conduct the experiment in a usability lab of the NEO Bay nearby the SJTU campus.

Both quantitative and qualitative data will be collected through the user experiment. Before the test, all the participants should sign the informed consent. Then, we collect the participants' demographic information as well as their social activities in daily routines through the subjective questionnaires. After that, they are invited to experience social exergame for 12 min and complete the three questionnaires. The overall experiment is expected to last 45 min and all the participants will receive 50 RMB as the reward.

Intrinsic Motion Inventory would be adopted to evaluate the subjective experience of the participants related to the exergame play, which contains a total of 45 items categorized in seven subscales [21]. We selected six subscales due to their high relevance to the purpose of this experiment, including Interest/Enjoyment, Perceived Competence, Effort/Importance, Pressure/Tension, Value/Usefulness, Relatedness.

User Experience Questionnaire would be given to participants to fill after the exergame play for the assessment of the prototype. The questionnaire consists of pairs of contrasting attributes that may apply to the product.

Post-Game questionnaire [22] will be adopted to evaluate the social engagement of participants in the exergame play. It consists of three factors, cooperation (COOP), communication (COMM), and partner preference (PARPREF) (see Table 1). And there are 12 randomly ordered questionnaires.

Table 1. Post-Game questionnaire.

Subscales	Items
COOP	1. My partner and I worked well together 2. The game was easier when I cooperated with my partner 3. My partner and I played individually 4. My partner and I shared tips with each other when playing the game
COMM	1. I communicated well with my partner during the game 2. My partner was responsive 3. I understood what my partner was trying to tell me 4. It was difficult to communicate with my partner (cited from [24]) playing
PAR PREF	1. Playing alone would be more effective than playing as a pair 2. The age of my partner made the gameplay interesting 3. I didn't enjoy playing with my partner 4. I would feel more comfortable playing without a partner table

Attachment

Video: https://www.bilibili.com/video/BV1xu411d729/.

Acknowledgments. This work is supported by the [Shanghai Pujiang Program] under Grant [2020PJC071]; [Shanghai Jiao Tong University] under Grant [WF220543011] and facilitated by Shanghai Jiao Tong University.

References

1. Lloyd, J.: The state of intergenerational relations today. ILC-UK, no. October, pp. 1–31 (2008)
2. Kessler, E.-M., Staudinger, U.M.: Intergenerational potential: effects of social interaction between older adults and adolescents. Psychol. Aging **22**(4), 690–704 (2007)
3. Fuchsberger, V., Sellner, W., Moser, C., Tscheligi, M.: Benefits and hurdles for older adults in intergenerational online interactions. In: Miesenberger, K., Karshmer, A., Penaz, P., Zagler, W. (eds.) ICCHP 2012. LNCS, vol. 7382, pp. 697–704. Springer, Heidelberg (2012). https://doi.org/10.1007/978-3-642-31522-0_104
4. Williams, S., Renehan, E., Cramer, E., Lin, X., Haralambous, B.: 'All in a day's play' – an intergenerational playgroup in a residential aged care facility. Int. J. Play **1**, 250–263 (2012). https://doi.org/10.1080/21594937.2012.738870
5. Zhang, H., Wu, Q., Miao, C., Shen, Z., Leung, C.: Towards age-friendly exergame design: the role of familiarity. In: CHI PLAY 2019 - Proceedings of the Annual Symposium on Computer-Human Interaction in Play, pp. 45–57 (2019). https://doi.org/10.1145/3311350.3347191
6. Qiu, S., An, P., Kang, K., Hu, J., Han, T., Rauterberg, M.: Investigating socially assistive systems from system design and evaluation: a systematic review. Univ. Access Inf. Soc. (0123456789) (2021). https://doi.org/10.1007/s10209-021-00852-w
7. Qiu, S., An, P., Kang, K., Hu, J., Han, T., Rauterberg, M.: A review of data gathering methods for evaluating socially assistive systems. Sensors **22**(1), 82 (2022)
8. Qiu, S., Hu, J., Han, T., Osawa, H., Rauterberg, M.: Social glasses: simulating interactive gaze for visually impaired people in face-to-face communication. Int. J. Hum.-Comput. Interact. **36**, 1–17 (2019). https://doi.org/10.1080/10447318.2019.1696513
9. Qiu, S., Hu, J., Han, T., Osawa, H., Rauterberg, M.: An evaluation of a wearable assistive device for augmenting social interactions. IEEE Access **8**, 164661–164677 (2020). https://doi.org/10.1109/ACCESS.2020.3022425
10. Qiu, S., An, P., Hu, J., Han, T., Rauterberg, M.: Understanding visually impaired people's experiences of social signal perception in face-to-face communication. Univ. Access Inf. Soc. **19**, 1–18 (2020). https://doi.org/10.1007/s10209-019-00698-3
11. Kaisar, E., Ding, R.B., Han, T., Qiu, S.: NEONEO balance ball: designing an intergenerational interaction exergame for in-home balance training. In: Gao, Q., Zhou, J. (eds.) HCII 2021. LNCS, vol. 12787, pp. 78–89. Springer, Cham (2021). https://doi.org/10.1007/978-3-030-78111-8_5
12. Zhang, F., Schell, R., Kaufman, D., Salgado, G., Jeremic, J.: Social interaction between older adults (80+) and younger people during intergenerational digital gameplay. In: Zhou, J., Salvendy, G. (eds.) ITAP 2017. LNCS, vol. 10298, pp. 308–322. Springer, Cham (2017). https://doi.org/10.1007/978-3-319-58536-9_25
13. Hausknecht, S., Neustaedter, C., Kaufman, D.: Blurring the lines of age: intergenerational collaboration in alternate reality games. In: Romero, M., Sawchuk, K., Blat, J., Sayago, S., Ouellet, H. (eds.) Game-Based Learning Across the Lifespan. AGL, pp. 47–64. Springer, Cham (2017). https://doi.org/10.1007/978-3-319-41797-4_4

14. Chua, P.H., Jung, Y., Lwin, M.O., Theng, Y.L.: Let's play together: effects of video-game play on intergenerational perceptions among youth and elderly participants. Comput. Hum. Behav. **29**(6), 2303–2311 (2013). https://doi.org/10.1016/j.chb.2013.04.037

15. Xu, X., Theng, Y.-L., Li, J., Phat, P.T.: Investigating effects of exergames on exercise intentions among young-old and old-old. In: Proceedings of the 2016 CHI Conference Extended Abstracts on Human Factors in Computing Systems, pp. 2961–2968 (2016). https://doi.org/10.1145/2851581.2892296

16. di Bartolomeo, G., Papa, S.: The effects of physical activity on social interactions: the case of trust and trustworthiness. J. Sports Econ. **20**(1), 50–71 (2019). https://doi.org/10.1177/1527002517717299

17. Seaborn, K., Lee, N., Narazani, M., Hiyama, A.: Intergenerational shared action games for promoting empathy between Japanese youth and elders (2019). https://doi.org/10.1109/ACII.2019.8925483

18. Introduction to Barracuda (2020). https://docs.unity3d.com/Packages/com.unity.barracuda@1.0/manual/index.html

19. KUBIKOS - Animated Cube Mini BIRDS. https://assetstore.unity.com/packages/3d/characters/animals/birds/kubikos-animated-cube-mini-birds-137343

20. Low Poly Modular Terrain Pack. https://assetstore.unity.com/packages/3d/environments/low-poly-modular-terrain-pack-91558

21. McAuley, E., Duncan, T., Tammen, V.V.: Psychometric properties of the intrinsic motivation inventory in a competitive sport setting: a confirmatory factor analysis. Res. Q. Exerc. Sport **60**(1), 48–58 (1989). https://doi.org/10.1080/02701367.1989.10607413

22. Rice, M., Yau, L.J., Ong, J., Wan, M., Ng, J.: Intergenerational gameplay, pp. 2333–2338 (2012). https://doi.org/10.1145/2212776.2223798

Toward the Design of a Gamification Framework for Enhancing Motivation Among Journalists, Experts, and the Public to Combat Disinformation: The Case of CALYPSO Platform

Catherine Sotirakou(✉) ⓘ, Theodoros Paraskevas ⓘ, and Constantinos Mourlas ⓘ

Faculty of Communication and Media Studies, National and Kapodistrian University of Athens, Athens, Greece

{katerinasot,tsparaskevas,mourlas}@media.uoa.gr

Abstract. This paper presents the preliminary outputs of the EU project CALYPSO which aims to create a crowdsourcing ecosystem for citizens to volunteer to combat disinformation campaigns by participating in a game for good. CALYPSO seeks to enhance fact-checking through the participation of different actors with different levels of responsibilities and privileges forming communities of practice. These communities will involve professional journalists, experts, and ordinary citizens in an attempt to combine their respective strengths and through collaboration to early detect and fact-check suspected cases of disinformation in real-time. For this crowdsourcing platform to work efficiently, this paper proposes gamification as a means of motivating digital readers to become members of a dedicated community of practice in the domain of disinformation.

Keywords: Disinformation · Gamification · Citizen journalism

1 Introduction

One of the main obstacles when debugging disinformation is that fake news appears and disappears rapidly (Mercier 2020), therefore a crucial element to effectively combat false content is to detect it within minutes of its publication to be able to quickly restore the truth and minimize the impact of fake news on society. Furthermore, many newsrooms cannot afford to employ professional fact-checkers or to pay for sophisticated fact-checking services while previous research shows that journalists often lack the necessary up-to-date news verification training and skills (Shapiro et al. 2013). Against these backdrops, this work combines citizen journalism (Gillmor 2004), communities of practice, and gamification techniques to build a gamified crowdsourcing platform for detecting and verifying falsities.

Taking into account that the success of a crowdsourcing platform depends highly on the participation and devotion of the user to solve a real-life problem, the usability and the user experience are of the utmost importance. Therefore, for the design of the platform, we follow a user-centered approach. Firstly, we review existing systems on crowdsourcing providing gamification especially by giving non-real rewards (Yang et al. 2021, Morschheuser et al. 2017, Choi et al. 2014). Then, we conduct a focus group with master's students in the field of media studies as well as interviews with professional journalists and experts. The participants configure the gamification strategy by mentioning the most favorable type of rewards and explaining how game elements could positively affect their involvement in the community of practice. Except for the gamification guidelines, the user roles, tasks, and scenarios are defined in the user requirements phase resulting in a functional prototype of the final platform.

For evaluation purposes, two case studies in two European partner countries (Greece and Poland) will be implemented, to test not only the effectiveness of the platform to combat disinformation but to measure also user engagement and user satisfaction for participating in a gamified way in a community trying to reduce the emerging disinformation trends in these countries.

2   Related Work

2.1   News Verification

The deliberate spread of fake news negatively affects millions of people across the globe and deteriorates democracy and social cohesion. Disinformation campaigns serve many financial and political interests (Marwick et al. 2021; Shu et al. 2017) and as the covid-19 pandemic has vividly showcased false information has the potential to expose the public to immediate danger[1]. News organizations try to combat disinformation by employing fact-checking techniques alongside their traditional reporting routines. Fact-checking refers to the effort of combating fake news, that is "news that is intentionally elaborated to deceive their readers" (Allcott and Gentzkow 2017:213). Furthermore, the news verification process consists of checking "whether the information is true through the analysis of its sources, including the search for evidence that proves the facts" (Pinto et al. 2019:495). News fact-checking is carried out daily by qualified staff working for journalism organizations, or dedicated fact-checking organizations, such as Politifact[2], Snopes[3], and Factcheck[4].

Fact-checkers decide whether a news story is true based on their journalistic skills, prior knowledge, by asking experts for advice, and by implementing a plethora of digital tools on their analysis. According to Pinto et al. (2019), a casual fact-checking workflow inside a news outlet includes four main actors with their corresponding responsibilities, namely the reader who requests specific news verification, the journalist who selects the news for verification and does the research, the specialist whose job is to perform specialized content analysis and advise the journalist, and the author who published the false story who is contacted for an explanation. Meanwhile, the fact-checking process can either be an in-house procedure or news outlets and companies outsource it to

---

[1] https://www.bbc.com/news/world-53755067.

[2] https://www.politifact.com/.

[3] https://www.snopes.com/.

[4] https://www.factcheck.org/.

specialized fact-checking organizations. Finally, in the work Pinto et al. (2019), the role of the reader is essential to the news verification process, since one-third of the selected news for fact-checking arrived at the news desks by a reader's email.

Since the volume of false or misleading news is massive whereas the human and financial resources of news organizations are limited, professional fact-checkers can only fact-check a small portion of potential fake information by themselves (Allen et al. 2020). As a solution, collaborative fact-checking platforms such as Truly Media[5], Check[6], and specialized material and workshops like the First Draft verification curriculum[7] and the International Fact-Checking Network (IFCN) Codes and Principles[8] are offered to journalists. Apart from platforms intended only for media professionals, there are some recent initiatives that involve members of the public in the fact-checking process, giving them responsibilities like finding potentially fake news, filtering, analyzing, and verifying the stories. Some of these platforms are the Truthsetter[9], Our.news[10], and Public Editor[11] where the users rate and verify potentially fake stories, while CaptainFact[12] provides the same functionalities for YouTube videos. In general, these initiatives use a website or a mobile app for the main functionalities with Our.news and CaptainFact also providing a browser plugin.

2.2 Citizen Journalism and Communities of Practice

Collaborative fact-checking platforms are beginning to appear in an effort to engage the public to join forces with professional fact-checkers. Citizen or participatory journalism has been investigated by researchers who refer to citizen journalists as "ordinary people" who carry out activities supporting news production through digital tools (Gillmor 2004; Glaser 2003; Lasica 2003a, b). Furthermore, citizen journalism is defined as "the act of a citizen, or group of citizens, playing an active role in the process of collecting, reporting, analyzing and disseminating news and information. The intent of this participation is to provide independent, reliable, accurate, wide-ranging and relevant information that a democracy requires" (Bowman and Willis 2003:9). Other studies refer to participatory journalism as "pro/am journalism" (De Rosnay and Révelli 2006) or "collaborative journalism" between journalists and amateur professionals. However, except for having citizens do the actual reporting, many news organizations in the past have used crowdsourcing as a means to outsource a heavy workload to their readers. Crowdsourcing is defined as "taking a function once performed by employees and outsourcing it to an undefined (and generally large) network of people in the form of an open call." (Howe 2006:1). More toward community building, dedicated communities of practice have worked efficiently in many fields. According to Smith and McKeen

---

[5] https://www.truly.media.
[6] https://meedan.com/check.
[7] https://firstdraftnews.org/training/.
[8] https://ifcncodeofprinciples.poynter.org/know-more.
[9] https://truthsetter.com/.
[10] https://our.news/.
[11] https://www.publiceditor.io/.
[12] https://captainfact.io/.

(2004) a community of practice (CoP) is broadly defined as "a group of people with a common interest who work together informally in a responsible, independent fashion to promote learning, solve problems, or develop ideas".

A new term for this collaborative phenomenon has started to appear called "crowd-checking", emanating from an analysis of Reddit's[13] political fact-checking subreddit. According to the findings, crowd-powered fact-checking is a prominent approach and could help build a sustainable model for fact-checkers. On the downside, having the public verify fake information is susceptible to mistakes and manipulation. Several experiments such as TruthSquad[14] and FactcheckEU[15] have highlighted the need for collaboration with journalists to ensure the quality of the information. Within this frame, crowdsourcing combined with collaborative journalism seems a promising model for the development of fact-checking communities and digital literacy.

2.3 Gamification

There is extensive prior work on the use of game design elements in real-world contexts for non-gaming purposes, to engage people to commit to certain activities. According to Borges and his colleagues (2014:216) gamification can be defined as "the use of game-based elements such as mechanics, aesthetics, and game thinking in non-game contexts aimed at engaging people, motivating action, enhancing learning, and solving problems". Previous research has shown that gamification elements when used correctly could foster human motivation and performance in regard to a given activity (Feng et al. 2018; Sailer et al. 2017; Stanculescu et al. 2016). Gamification techniques have been used successfully in many fields such as education (Boada et al. 2015), the workspace (Morschheuser and Hamari 2019), and governance (Harviainen and Hassan 2019), with a vivid discussion over the last years to implement it for media literacy skills and especially fact-checking (Mantzarlis 2018).

In fact, fact-checking organizations such as First Draft have used serious games to raise public awareness concerning fake news. Particularly in the field of media literacy, gamification techniques, in the form of serious games, have been implemented successfully many times in order to educate the public regarding misinformation. Bad news[16] is an online game developed in 2019 by the Social Decision-Making Laboratory of the University of Cambridge. The players are presented with a set of texts, images, and twitter posts and are asked to spread misinformation about them, thus familiarising themselves with the most common misinformation techniques (Roozenbeek and Van der Linden 2019). A subsequent study on the game confirmed that participants were significantly more successful at recognizing misinformation after playing the game and felt more confident about their abilities (Basol et al. 2020). Another example is Go Viral[17], a 5-min browser game, where players learn about Covid-19 misinformation and are then

---

[13] https://ifcncodeofprinciples.poynter.org/.

[14] https://blog.newstrust.net/2010/08/truthsquad-results.html.

[15] https://eufactcheck.eu/.

[16] https://www.getbadnews.com/#intro.

[17] https://www.goviralgame.com/en.

asked to distinguish real news from misleading information (Basol et al. 2021). Furthermore, MAthE is a news verification game for Greek users, developed by the Aristotle University of Thessaloniki. Users of MathE were asked to determine if an article is fake and were given sources for fact-checking tools, like reverse image search engines and fact-checking sites. The majority of the participants (70%) stated that they learned about the existence of fact-checking tools (Katsaounidou et al. 2019). Lastly, examples of gamification applications for media literacy come from the Media and Information Literacy Lab (MilLab[18]) in Georgia, where educational games like "Dr. Fake" and "Measure the Truth and Your Nose" encourage students to verify false claims and develop an informed news consumption. The results of such approaches seem to be promising, and open new horizons for the development of crowd-checking and community building in the domain of fact-checking.

This work builds upon these premises and proposes the CALYPSO platform as a means to empower "people, communities and nations to participate in and contribute to global knowledge societies" (UNESCO 2013). It will establish a dedicated community of practice comprising of members of the general public, experts, reporters and professional fact-checkers, who will discover and debunk fake news. More specifically, the goal is to involve the audience in the process of promptly detecting harmful content, and, through a digital platform, to source citizens' contributions to false and misleading news articles. After the early detection of these stories, journalists will take over and debunk the falsehoods with the help of experts when needed. In that respect, we will build a dedicated web-based platform. To successfully deliver these goal, CALYPSO is designed using state-of-the-art techniques in the fields of user-centered design, gamification and creating and maintaining communities of practice.

3   Analysis

3.1   Study Design

CALYPSO's interface has been developed following a user-centered design (UCD) approach. To gather insights about the different user roles we conducted a focus group with 20 master's students following the course: "User-Centered Design Methodology for Web-Based Interactive Environments" and interviews with open questions. These interviews were conducted with five media professionals, four of whom were journalists from the collaborating news outlets and one expert in the fields of migration, education, and religion. Based on the answers of the participants, we examined both the usability and UX goals of CALYPSO. Specific diagrams were designed and shown in Sect. 3.3 of the paper.

3.2   User Requirement Analysis

This section contains the results of the user requirements analysis beginning from the role of the *User/Reader* who will search and flag potentially misleading news stories. The results of the focus group with the MSc students are presented in Table 1 below.

---

[18] http://millab.ge/en/mil-resources/game_quizzes/any/any/any/1/.

Table 1. Focus group results.

Actions	Preferences
Registration	The responders prefer an option that includes signing in with email instead of only using a Facebook or Gmail account
Flagging	Both desktop/laptop and mobile phones, and a browser plugin is necessary
Profile	Only the achievements appearing on a user profile, (i.e. no false flags)
Motivation	Personal gain (portfolio), learning fact-checking tools, personal satisfaction, being a member of a community, looking good inside a community
Gamification	Points, levels, badges, "top5" leaderboards

The interviews revealed how the *Journalists* would like to use the platform and their personal taste concerning the Content Management System (CMS) along with how to assign the fake stories for fact-checking and more.

Chat: The responders recognized the need for a chat to communicate with other journalists and experts, but they would prefer if it was outside the platform. Also, they underlined the importance of very strict rules and policies followed by penalties for policy violation.

Fact-Checking Education: The journalists stressed the need for fact-checking education, along with clear, short, and easy-to-follow tutorials and guidelines. They suggested the tutorials and other media literacy content be published on the website to train the readers as well.

Assignment of Flagged Stories: The participants prefer the assignment to be automatic.

Gamification: The responders disliked the option of gamification since it will be part of their professional duties.

Fact-Checker's Dashboard: The responders mentioned they would like to use a writing pad where they would write their findings and keep notes. Also, they would like to be able to access their own statistics (number of finished fact-checks), other journalists' records, and the overall statistics of the platform including the number of registered and active users, pending flags, and so on.

Additionally, the responders suggested some further matters to consider when designing the platform, such as using a text similarity function for flagged articles so that the system would recognize the same story published on different outlets, have a flag limit at the first levels, and penalizing the users who repeatedly send false flags and spam the system.

Taking into consideration all the user requirements we designed a use case diagram depicted in Fig. 1.

The above diagram describes the interaction between the system and its environment. The participating actors are *Readers, Journalists, Experts* as well as the *Administrator*

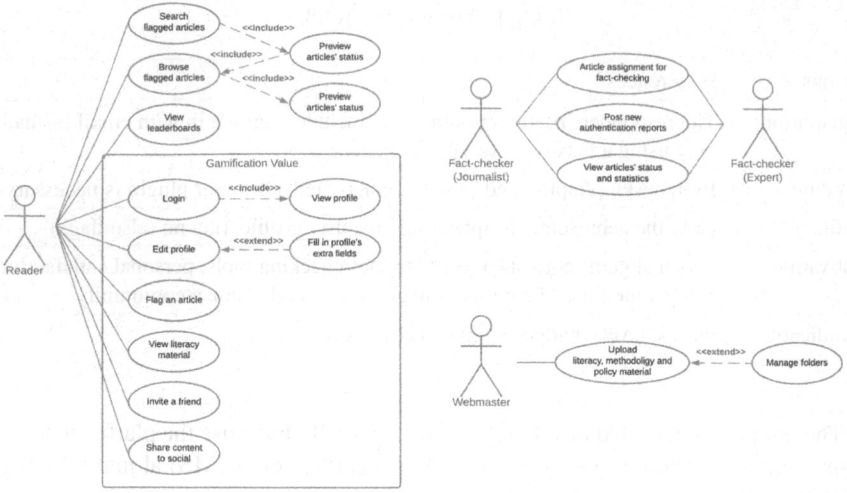

Fig. 1. Use case diagram

of the platform that manages data and policy issues. These actors participate in classes of interaction with the system. The classes included in the square box are related to the gamification mechanics of the platform, namely the activities for which the *User* is awarded points, badges, or levels.

3.3 Platform Design

Based on the resulting user preferences that are visualized in detail in the following illustration (see Fig. 2), the system consists of three components, namely a web-based application, a web browser extension (for Chrome), and a mobile app (Android, IOS), where the user will create an account and start flagging suspected online news as "fake". The functionality of the system is described in the following user scenario:

Mobile Phone: When a *User* reads a news item that they think is misleading and might be false, they will click the share button on their mobile phone and choose the app. The system will then send the link to the web-based platform and then it will be stored in the platform's database. When multiple flags are accumulated concerning the same article, the media organization partner along with experts if needed will verify it, and debunk it if necessary.

Computer: If the *User* reads a news article via a web browser on their computer they will click the add-on button that will provide the same functionality as the app.

To be able to use the above tools, the user will have to register on the CALYPSO website with their email. After the registration, the *User* will have to create their profile and pick one of the following options: basic *User, Journalist,* or *Expert* (for this category a pop-up list with several fields like climate, health, education, etc. will appear for the user to select their expertise). Furthermore, if a *Reader/User* flags a fake story correctly,

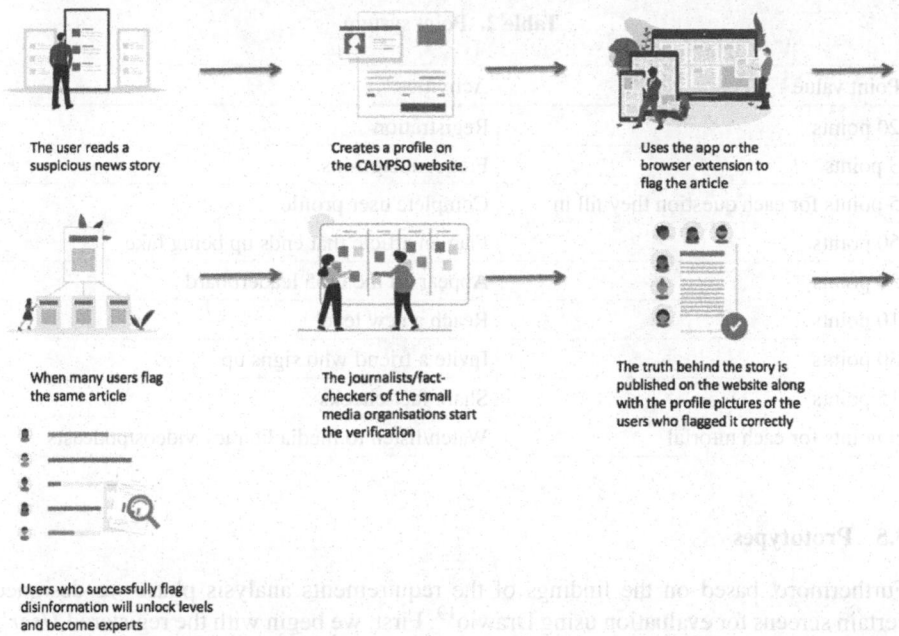

The user reads a
suspicious news story

Creates a profile on
the CALYPSO website.

Uses the app or the
browser extension to
flag the article

When many users flag
the same article

The journalists/fact-
checkers of the small
media organisations start
the verification

The truth behind the story is
published on the website along
with the profile pictures of the
users who flagged it correctly

Users who successfully flag
disinformation will unlock levels
and become experts

Fig. 2. A figure showing the logic behind the CALYPSO platform.

their profile picture will appear on the published fact-check next to the *Journalist's* name
and they will receive points for their successful flag. This way each *User's* contribution
will appear on the platform promoting a sense of belonging to a vivid community of
fact-checkers and encouraging participation.

3.4   Game Design

To enhance user engagement and build a trustworthy community of fact-checkers, the
project will introduce gamification elements into the system. The implementation of
gamification techniques in the platform will harness the motivational power of games in
order to create intrinsic motivations, promote participation, persistence, and goal-setting,
engage users to promptly detect more suspected cases of disinformation, provide a sense
of belonging, and a friendly user experience. The gamification framework is developed
based on current literature and best practices in the field, to ensure that the implemented
game elements will be translated into concrete guidelines to both assist and incentivize
the creation of a highly engaged community of practice. To that end, a point and badge
collecting system will be used where registered *Users* will collect points for every article
they flag if the latter is later determined to be fake from the *Journalist*. A detailed point
system is presented in Table 2.

Table 2. Point system

Point value	Activities
20 points	Registration
3 points	Frequent sign-ins
5 points for each question they fill in	Complete user profile
50 points	Flag an article that ends up being fake
50 points	Appear on the top5 leaderboard
10 points	Reach a new level
30 points	Invite a friend who signs up
15 points	Share fact-checks
5 points for each tutorial	Watch/listen to media literacy videos/podcasts

3.5 Prototypes

Furthermore, based on the findings of the requirements analysis phase we designed certain screens for evaluation using Drawio[19]. First, we begin with the registered *User's* profile screen where they could see all their achievements illustrated (see Fig. 3). On the left side of this screen, the *User* checks their status, collected points and badges, their history, and rank, while on the center, they can view all their achievements in multiple pie chart illustrations. At the bottom of the screen, the *User* can click the green button and learn how to "play the game", earn more points, view the remaining badges and levels. That way the *User* will be intrigued into playing and be loyal to the platform. Finally, on the right side, the *User* sees an overview of their achievements, flags, and invites.

Based on the interviews with the *Journalists*, the following screens were designed (see Fig. 4 and Fig. 5). When a *Journalist* accepts to verify a flagged news story, this story appears on the homepage of the platform as "In Progress", after it is finished there are three available labels "True", "False", and "Undefined" in the case of important information still missing as shown in Fig. 4. On the right side, a registered *User* sees the leaderboards and some profile statistics.

The *Journalist's* dashboard (see Fig. 5) consists of a notepad, information concerning the flagged story, as well as a list of the available *Journalists* and *Experts* for assistance if needed appear on the left side. On the right side, a *Journalist* can view overall statistics regarding flagged content.

4   Discussion

Effectively debugging disinformation within minutes of its publication through a crowd-sourcing digital platform, able to quickly restore the truth and minimize the impact of fake news on society needs a precise and accurate design. The platform needs to utilize

---

[19] https://github.com/jgraph/drawio-desktop/releases/tag/v16.5.1.

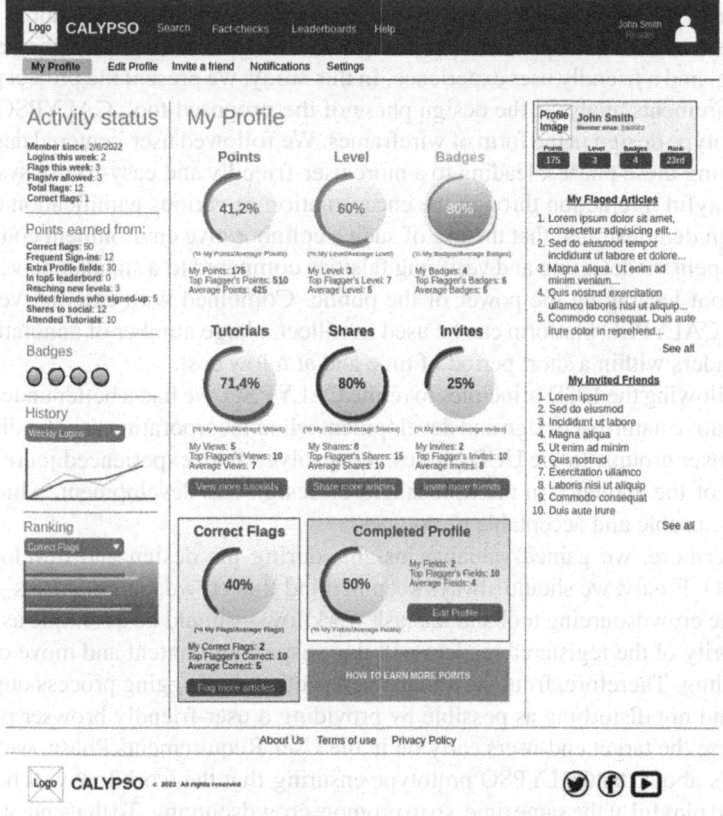

Fig. 3. Registered users' profile screen

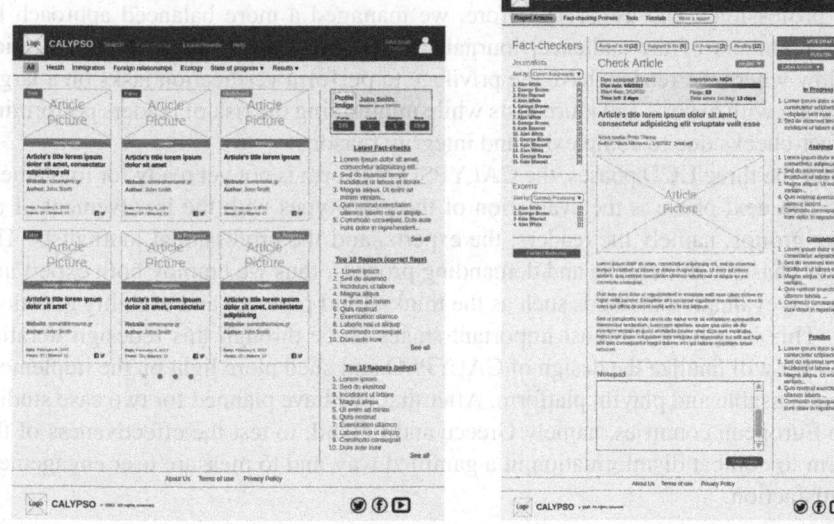

Fig. 4. Homepage of CALYPSO

Fig. 5. Fact-checker's dashboard

the power of crowdsourcing to facilitate the annotation of false information, by creating intrinsic motivations, promoting participation and goal-setting, providing a sense of belonging, and a friendly user experience. In this study, we present the project planning, user requirements analysis, the design phase of the proposed tool, CALYPSO, and the final prototype design in the form of wireframes. We followed user-centered design principles during these phases, leading to a more user-friendly and easy-to-use system with a more playful interaction through the encapsulation of various gamification elements. Our design demonstrated that the use of such a collaborative environment could reduce the time spent on detecting and verifying falsities compared to a standalone verification tool without leveraging the power of the public. Combined with external verification tools, the CALYPSO platform can be used to collect a large number of annotations from online readers within a short period of time and at a low cost.

By following the UCD principles to refine CALYPSO, we had a better understanding of the iterative nature of design and development when incorporating user feedback from different user groups. In the UCD phases, we involved both experienced journalists and members of the audience in multiple stages of design and development, which helped us achieve usable and acceptable prototypes.

Furthermore, we gained valuable insights during the design and development of CALYPSO. Firstly, we should always keep in mind that crowdsourcing tasks—in terms of both the crowdsourcing tool and the task workflow—should be as simple as possible. The majority of the registered readers will flag suspicious content and move on to their news reading. Therefore, from the clients' perspective the flagging process oughts to be as easy and not disturbing as possible by providing a user-friendly browser plugin. By considering the target end-users early on in the User Requirements Phase, we collected user needs about the CALYPSO prototype ensuring that the workflow will be easy-to-follow and playful at the same time, so to promote crowdsourcing. To that end, we divided the complex workflow of news verification into simple annotation through flagging for the readers and moved the more difficult steps (i.e., image verification, text analysis) to the professional end-users. Therefore, we managed a more balanced approach by mixing members of the audience, journalists, and experts into the news verification workflow where the readers have the privilege to perform verification tasks on a larger scale along with experts and journalists while minimizing the risk of readers performing false fact-checks due to complexity and integrity reasons.

After the three UCD phases, the CALYPSO platform is not yet ready for implementation. The next phase is the evaluation of the prototypes with the involvement of all the user groups, namely the readers, the experts, and the professional journalists. The redesign phase is an iterative and demanding process, thus we employ both expert and user-based evaluation methods such as the think-aloud protocol and usability questionnaires. This is one of the most important stages since through this redesign iterative process we will finalize the design of CALYPSO and shed more light on the implementation of a usable and playful platform. After that, we have planned for two case studies in two European countries, namely Greece and Poland, to test the effectiveness of the platform to combat disinformation in a gamified way and to measure user engagement and satisfaction.

Acknowledgments. Co-funded by the CNECT/2020/5464403 programme of the European Union under grant agreement LC-01682258.

References

Allcott, H., Gentzkow, M.: Social media and fake news in the 2016 election. J. Econ. Perspect. **31**(2), 211–236 (2017)

Allen, J., Arechar, A.A., Pennycook, G., Rand, D.G.: Scaling up fact-checking using the wisdom of crowds (2020). https://doi.org/10.31234/osf.io/9qdza

Basol, M., Roozenbeek, J., van der Linden, S.: Good news about bad news: gamified inoculation boosts confidence and cognitive immunity against fake news. J. Cogn. **3**(1), 1–9 (2020)

Basol, M., Roozenbeek, J., Berriche, M., Uenal, F., McClanahan, W.P., van der Linden, S.: Towards psychological herd immunity: cross-cultural evidence for two prebunking interventions against COVID-19 misinformation. Big Data Soc. **8**(1), 1–18 (2021)

Boada, I., Rodriguez-Benitez, A., Garcia-Gonzalez, J.M., Olivet, J., Carreras, V., Sbert, M.: Using a serious game to complement CPR instruction in a nurse faculty. Comput. Methods Progr.ams Biomed. **122**(2), 282–291 (2015)

Borges, S.S., Durelli, V.H.S., Reis, H.M., Isotani, S.: A systematic mapping on gamification applied to education. In: Proceedings of the 29th Annual ACM Symposium on Applied Computing, pp. 216–222. ACM Press, Gyeongju (2014)

Bowman S., Willis C.: We media: how audiences are shaping the future of news and information. The Media Center at the American Press Institute (2003). http://www.flickertracks.com/blog/images/we_media.pdf

Choi, J., Choi, H., So, W., Lee, J., You, J.: A study about designing reward for gamified crowdsourcing system. In: Marcus, A. (ed.) DUXU 2014. LNCS, vol. 8518, pp. 678-687. Springer, Cham (2014). https://doi.org/10.1007/978-3-319-07626-3_64

De Rosnay J., Révelli C.: La Révolte du pronétariat. Des mass média aux médias des masses, Paris, Fayard (2006)

Feng, Y., Ye, H.J., Yu, Y., Yang, C., Cui, T.: Gamification artifacts and crowdsourcing participation: examining the mediating role of intrinsic motivations. Comput. Hum. Behav. **81**, 124–136 (2018)

Gillmor D.: We the Media. Grassroots Journalism by the People, for the People. O'Reilly Media, Inc., New York (2004)

Glaser M.: Journalists debate closure of another blog. Online Journalism Review (2003). http://www.ojr.org/ojr/glaser/1051593413.php

Harviainen, J.T., Hassan, L.: Governmental service gamification: central principles. Int. J. Innov. Digit. Econ. (IJIDE) **10**(3), 1–12 (2019)

Howe, J.: The rise of crowdsourcing. Wired Mag. **14**(6), 1–4 (2006)

Katsaounidou, A., Vrysis, L., Kotsakis, R., Dimoulas, C., Veglis, A.: MAthE the game: a serious game for education and training in news verification. Educ. Sci. **9**(2), 155 (2019)

Lasica, J.: What is participatory journalism? Online Journalism Review (2003a). http://www.ojr.org/ojr/workplace/1060217106.php

Lasica, J.: Participatory Journalism Puts the Reader in the Driver's Seat. Online Journalism Review (2003b). http://www.ojr.org/ojr/workplace/1060218311.php

Mantzarlis, A.: Fact-checking 101. In: Journalism, Fake News & Disinformation: Handbook for Journalism Education and Training, pp. 85–100 (2018)

Marwick, A., Kuo, R., Cameron, S.J., Weigel, M.: Critical disinformation studies: a syllabus. Center for Information, Technology, & Public Life (CITAP), University of North Carolina at Chapel Hill (2021). http://citap.unc.edu/critical-disinfo

Mercier, H.: Fake news in the time of coronavirus: how big is the threat. The Guardian (2020). https://www.theguardian.com/commentisfree/2020/mar/30/fake-news-cor onavirus-false-information

Morschheuser, B., Hamari, J., Koivisto, J., Maedche, A.: Gamified crowdsourcing: conceptualization, literature review, and future agenda. Int. J. Hum. Comput. Stud. **106**, 26–43 (2017)

Morschheuser, B., Hamari, J.: The gamification of work: lessons from crowdsourcing. J. Manag. Inq. **28**(2), 145–148 (2019)

Pinto, M.R., de Lima, Y.O., Barbosa, C.E., de Souza, J.M.: Towards fact-checking through crowdsourcing. In: 2019 IEEE 23rd International Conference on Computer Supported Cooperative Work in Design (CSCWD), pp. 494–499. IEEE (2019)

Roozenbeek, J., Van der Linden, S.: Fake news game confers psychological resistance against online misinformation. Palgrave Commun. **5**(1), 1–10 (2019)

UNESCO: Global MIL Assessment Framework (2013). http://www.unesco.org/new/en/commun ication-and-information/media-development/media-literacy/unesco-global-mil-assessment-framework/

Sailer, M., Hense, J.U., Mayr, S.K., Mandl, H.: How gamification motivates: an experimental study of the effects of specific game design elements on psychological need satisfaction. Comput. Hum. Behav. **69**, 371–380 (2017)

Shapiro, I., Brin, C., Bédard-Brûlé, I., Mychajlowycz, K.: Verification as a strategic ritual: How journalists retrospectively describe processes for ensuring accuracy. Journal. Pract. **7**(6), 657–673 (2013)

Shu, K., Sliva, A., Wang, S., Tang, J., Liu, H.: Fake news detection on social media: a data mining perspective. ACM SIGKDD Explor. Newsl. **19**(1), 22–36 (2017)

Smith, H.A., McKeen, J.D.: Creating and facilitating communities of practice. In: Holsapple, C.W. (ed.) Handbook on Knowledge Management 1, vol. 1, pp. 393–407. Springer, Heidelberg (2004). https://doi.org/10.1007/978-3-540-24746-3_20

Stanculescu, L.C., Bozzon, A., Sips, R.J., Houben, G.J.: Work and play: an experiment in enterprise gamification. In: Proceedings of the 19th ACM Conference on Computer-Supported Cooperative Work & Social Computing, pp. 346–358 (2016)

Yang, C., Ye, H.J., Feng, Y.: Using gamification elements for competitive crowdsourcing: exploring the underlying mechanism. Behav. Inf. Technol. **40**(9), 837–854 (2021)

FIST FIX: Soft Hard Combination Product Design for Hand Rehabilitation After Stroke

Tianyu Zhou and Ting Han[✉]

School of Design, Shanghai Jiao Tong University, 800 Dongchuan Road, Minhang District, Shanghai 200240, China
hanting@sjtu.edu.cn

Abstract. Celebrate stoke, as the number one killer of middle-aged and elderly people, presents five characteristics in China: high incidence, high disability rate, high mortality rate, high recurrence rate and high economic burden. Of these, more than half of stroke patients have impaired upper limb motor function. The FIST FIX is designed to help stroke patients in Brunnstorm stage III, IV and V. The patient performs the job therapy according to the interactive interface by wearing a wireless glove sensor. In a control group experiment of 20 individuals, both groups received routine occupational therapy, patients using FIST FIX for extra target oriented repetitive exercise training achieved 12.7% higher scores than controls on the FMA-UE scale, concurrent with an 12.1% lower score on the subjective mood inventory PHQ-9. It improves the progress of rehabilitation of stroke patients and reduces the propensity for post-stroke depression.

Keywords: Cerebral stroke recovery · Hand motor dysfunction · Game-based motivation · Industrial design

1 Introduction

1.1 Stroke Status in China

According to the China Stroke Prevention Report 2018, the standardized prevalence of stroke in residents older than 40 years increased from 1.89% in 2012 to 2.19% in 2016. Extrapolating the 12.42 million existing stroke patients in residents aged $\geq$40 years [1], meanwhile, the recurrence rate of stroke is also higher, and a study conducted in 35 hospitals showed that the recurrence rate is as high as 17.1% at 1 year after first-ever stroke [2]. Therefore, the prevention and treatment of stroke is a complex process that is continuous and requires the close cooperation between patients of medical families, and the economic and time costs and medical resources required will be further expanded in the future.

1.2 Rehabilitation of Stroke Patients

Hospital treatment for stroke patients like: surgery, physical therapy and rehabilitation exercise are the most effective methods to reduce the disability of patients due to stroke.

Stroke pathological processes can be divided into three phases according to the time of onset: acute phase, post-acute phase, chronic phase. According to the definition of AHCPR (The Agency for Health Care Policy and Research), the acute phase of stroke refers to the 48 h before admission for surgical treatment and inpatient rehabilitation after the onset of acute stroke, the post-acute phase refers to the phase after the acute phase, and finally the chronic phase. Stroke medical units, such as stroke center and other related institutions are places where acute phase patients first travel to. These institutions have full equipment and professionals, so that the patients are treated and recovered most timely and effectively as expected. Upon diagnosis determination in the rehabilitation phase and without clinical medical contraindications, the relevant institution may start acute phase rehabilitation for the patient. Stroke rehabilitation at this stage mainly emphasizes early activity as well as proper swing.

Therefore, in many hospitals in China, the principle of early activity and acute phase rehabilitation has been followed. If the patient itself meets the conditions of no aggravation of the primary neurological disorder after 48 h of stable vital signs, the rehabilitation treatment would start. The appropriate timing and rehabilitation method should be chosen during the overall rehabilitation process, the evaluation of rehabilitation should be carried out throughout the course of treatment [3]. Different rehabilitation programs should be developed for different conditions with the patient population, step through and require the patient to participate actively in the cooperation of the family, supplemented by the routine medication and the necessary surgical treatment. According to the interview with the rehabilitation doctors of Renji Hospital in Shanghai, the main body is divided into three phases at the treatment level:

First Level Rehabilitation. Patients' early routine treatment in hospital for surgery or department of Neurology and early rehabilitation are collectively referred to as first level rehabilitation in stroke rehabilitation. These mainly contain medical therapy versus rehabilitation operations in the soft paralysis phase of patients, and the rehabilitation process is mainly concerned with preventing stroke recurrence and corresponding complications, encouraging patients to try and initiate autonomous activities. Since this phase is mainly a bed ridden phase and patients need to promote recovery of muscle tone and emergence of active activities in limbs on the hemiparetic side, rehabilitation is mainly through patients' acceptance of relevant physiotherapy and patients' active participation, as well as correct limb placement and conversion of posture.

Secondary Rehabilitation. Aimed at patients within 4 to 12 weeks of stroke onset in order to suppress spasticity while gradually promoting motor recovery on the affected side of the patient. A therapeutic process that targets the strengthening of active motor function of the affected limb is called secondary rehabilitation. Secondary rehabilitation is generally performed in the rehabilitation medicine department in rehabilitation specialized or general hospitals, which is mainly divided into physical therapy, occupational therapy, cognitive therapy, psychotherapy, and so on. At the same time, it is important during rehabilitation to initially reduce the degree of muscle spasticity in the hemiplegic limbs, as well as to avoid strengthening abnormal movement patterns (flexor spastic pattern in the upper limbs and extensor spastic pattern in the lower limbs).

Tertiary Rehabilitation. Standardized community rehabilitation treatment can effectively promote the recovery of motor function and improve the living ability of patients [4]. Patient can return to the community hospital or home for subsequent rehabilitation operations when they completed primary and secondary rehabilitation and treatment in the hospital. The hospital's rehabilitation physician could train the patient's family through rehabilitation preaching and homework treatment arrangements, etc., to help the patient in community or home-based rehabilitation. Tertiary rehabilitation therefore refers to rehabilitation in the community or at home of stroke. Among them, the rehabilitation takes a long time and is boring with less relevant equipment.

In this subject, the FIST FIX is designed to support patients in Tertiary rehabilitation.

2 Concept of FIST FIX

2.1 Haptic Devices for Hand Rehabilitation After Stroke

Many different kinds of haptic devices have been used in clinical settings such as Reha-Slide and Bi-Manu-Track [5]. During fieldwork at Shanghai Sunshine rehabilitation center, it was found that pneumatic power assist rehabilitation gloves using mirror therapy have a very mature product and theoretical support [6]. In recent years, the interactive rehabilitation products which are distinguished from traditional instruments become the emerging roles [7]. The rehabilitation and assisted robotics team in Advanced Manufacturing Institute of Ningbo Institute of materials technology and engineering, Chinese Academy of Sciences completed a prototype of three degrees of freedom wrist motor function rehabilitation training system based on scenario interaction (see Fig. 1).

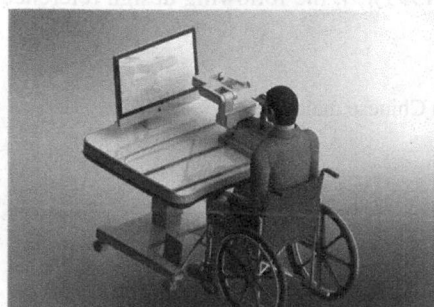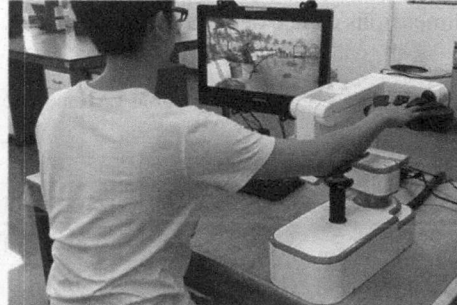

Fig. 1. A prototype of three degrees of freedom wrist motor function rehabilitation training system based on scenario interaction.

In view of the characteristics of stroke patients in the community rehabilitation stage, the design concept of FIST FIX is different from the above functional auxiliary devices.

2.2 Hardware of FIST FIX

To meet the requirements of low-cost, lightweight, digital interaction and so on in community or home-based scenarios, the FIST FIX employs potentiators as the input of finger movement. The first prototype incorporated Arduino combined with hc-08 Bluetooth with the mpu6050 gyre for PCB design and incorporated a rechargeable battery composition (see Fig. 2).

Fig. 2. The hardware of FIST FIX prototype.

The dimensional design of the hardware section needs to take into account the dimensional coverage in terms of ergonomics. With reference to the human dimensions of chinese adults(GB/T 10000-1988)[8] and general rules of using percentiles of the body dimensions for products design(GB/T 12985-1991)[9], the following design reference dimensions can be derived (Tables 1 and 2).

Table 1. Hand size in Chinese males.

Age subgroups	36–60						
Percentile	1	5	10	50	90	95	99
Hand length	164	170	173	182	193	196	202
Hand width	73	76	77	82	87	89	91
Index finger length	60	63	64	63	74	76	79
max finger II breadth	17	18	18	19	20	21	21
finger II breadth	14	15	15	16	18	18	19

Due to the fact that hand size needs to be taken into account for the vast majority of patients, but because the male to female ratio in stroke patients is approximately 1.3:1–1.7:1. Therefore take the default male to female ratio of 1.5:1 in terms of the male to female weight in the dimensions of the designed product. The hand length was 190 mm and fitted with finger cuff fixation to leave a 10 mm elastic space, encompassing patients

Table 2. Hand size in Chinese females.

Age subgroups	36–55						
Percentile	1	5	10	50	90	95	99
Hand length	154	158	161	171	180	183	189
Hand width	68	70	72	76	81	82	85
Index finger length	57	60	61	66	71	73	76
max finger II breadth	16	16	16	17	19	19	20
finger II breadth	13	14	14	15	16	17	17

with 180 mm–200 mm hand length. At the same time, the width was taken to be 85 mm, and since the present product was not loaded by clasping the hand, the hand width aspect could satisfy the vast majority of patients by the method of arm immobilization.

2.3 Challenges from the User's Point of View in Software

According to the interviews with rehabilitation physicians of Renji Hospital and the survey of stroke patients, the software interaction design needs to consider several key factors: the interface readability is strong, the game mechanism is interesting, the feedback of rehabilitation process is needed, and multisensory modalities are also popular.

2.4 Software of FIST FIX

Followed the above interview contents as well as the survey results, relevant design steps were used, such as brainstorm and draft drawing. After conducting the interaction line diagram as well as the low fidelity interface design, patients in community rehabilitation were surveyed to the three game forms in a questionnaire form, and the final interaction form consisting three types of interactive games called 'Piano fix', 'Squeeze Lemon' and 'Wu Song Fights the Tiger' was determined.

The software part of FIST FIX was developed by Unity, 2019 3.4f1. Three-dimensional modelling was done with 3ds max. The web side data presentation communicating with unity was via Python. The FIST FIX usage flow is shown below (see Fig. 3).

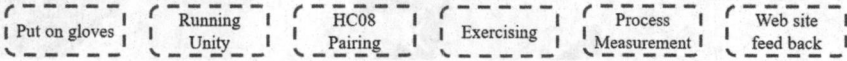

Fig. 3. The usage flow of FIST FIX prototype.

In the design of interactive interface, the Squeeze Lemon is an interactive game that presents the contraction range of five fingers of the patient from time to time. The patient will pass the game by completing the action of grasping for 5 times. Patients can always see the maximum movement range of each finger during exercise (see Fig. 4).

Fig. 4. The squeeze lemon interface.

The second interactive game is called the Piano Fix. Patients will see the mapping of their hands through the screen in 3D scene. At the same time, the patient will contract his fingers when the notes fall according to the music to simulate the activity of playing the piano. The maximum movement amplitude of each finger during the activity is also recorded (see Fig. 5).

Fig. 5. The Piano Fix interface.

Wu Song tiger fighting part adds elements of traditional Chinese culture on the basis that patients are familiar with hand movement. Taking Wu Song's story of fighting the tiger as the background, it is presented in the way of hand control shadow play.

The design of this part blurs the mapping of finger movement, so that patients can appropriately increase movement in the process of exploration (see Fig. 6).

Fig. 6. Wu Song Fights the Tiger interface.

Of course, during these games, potentiometer data representing finger movement is transmitted to unity. After filtering, it is transmitted to the server through python, and the visual chart is generated on the web page (see Fig. 7). It contains task overview, exercise progress, maximum exercise range, training history, diagnosis and treatment suggestions from doctors. Patients, family members and doctors are able to view this site at the same time.

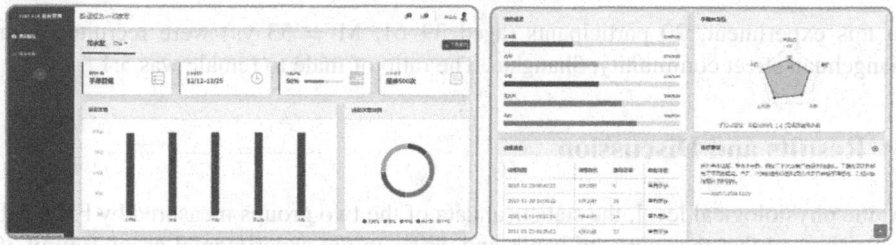

Fig. 7. The FIST FIX web site.

3 Test Methodology

3.1 Research Questions

The purpose of this work is to explore whether software interaction can have a better effect on the rehabilitation of stroke patients in the environment of community rehabilitation or family rehabilitation. According to the analysis of patients' pain points and the medical interviews during the preliminary investigation, this work is willing to measure the effect from both physiological and psychological perspectives. It can be summarized as two questions.

RQ1: Compared with traditional occupational therapy, is there any difference in the physiological improvement of patients by interactive soft and hard combination products.

RQ2: Whether patients are psychologically more inclined to accept interactive rehabilitation products and the reasons.

3.2 Experiment Design

In order to test the difference between soft and hard combination products and traditional occupational therapy in hand rehabilitation, the experiment of this work is divided into objective and subjective parts. In the objective part, Fugl-Meyer Assessment Upper Extremity Scale (FMA-UE) was used to score the participants before and after the intervention. In the subjective part, PHQ-9 scale was used to measure whether participants had a better psychological experience.

The experimental process is divided into four steps: Firstly, the participants were measured by the wrist and finger parts of FMA-UE scale (30pts total) and PHQ-9 scale. Then the experimental group was randomly selected according to the ranking of scores of FMA-UE scales. Thirdly, both groups received routine occupational therapy. The experimental group was intervened for four weeks, the Piano Fix of Fist Fix was used as the target oriented repetitive exercise training [10] added on this basis. 30 min each time, once a day, 5 days a week. Finally, four weeks later, the two groups were scored with FMA-UE scale and PHQ-9 scale.

3.3 Participants

In this experiment, 20 participants (aged 39–61, M = 53 ys) were recruited from Jiangchuan street community, Shanghai. The ratio of male to female was 5:1.

4 Results and Discussion

At the physiological level, the statistical data of the two groups measured by FMA-UE scale showed that the scores of hands and wrists in the experimental group (out of 30 points) were 12.7% higher than those in the control group after four weeks (see Fig. 8).

On the subjective scale level, before the experiment, the average scores of the experimental group and the control group in the PHQ-9 scale were 10.7 (min 8, Max 13) and 11 (min 8, Max 13) respectively. After four weeks of intervention, the average score of PHQ-9 in the experimental group decreased by 12.1% (from 10.7 to 9.4) compared with that at the beginning (see Fig. 9). In contrast, the control group decreased by 5.4% (from 11 to 10.4) (see Fig. 10).

Through the above experimental results, it can be seen that the interactive products of soft and hard combination are helpful in occupational therapy for stroke patients undergoing home rehabilitation or community rehabilitation. In the interview with the experimental group after the experiment, it is found that the average age of the selected participants is relatively young. Therefore, the adaptability to interactive products is very high. In the feedback, they mainly mentioned that the data feedback such as the maximum movement amplitude after each exercise is a factor that encourages them to exercise. 70% of the participants in the experimental group agreed that this game based occupational rehabilitation made them more interested in exercising themselves in the community.

However, when analyzing the data, it was found that with the increase of age, the scores of PHQ-9 and FMA-UE were lower than those of younger participants. Because

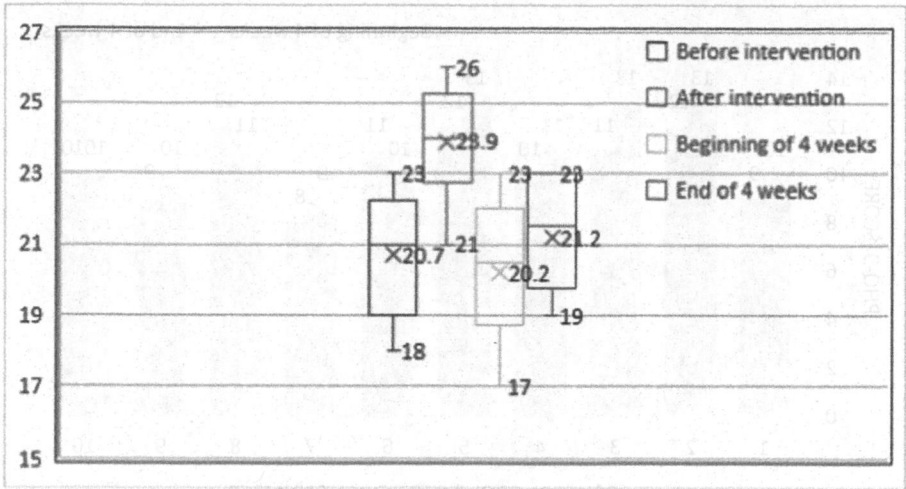

Fig. 8. The results of wrist and finger parts of FMA-UE scale (30pts total).

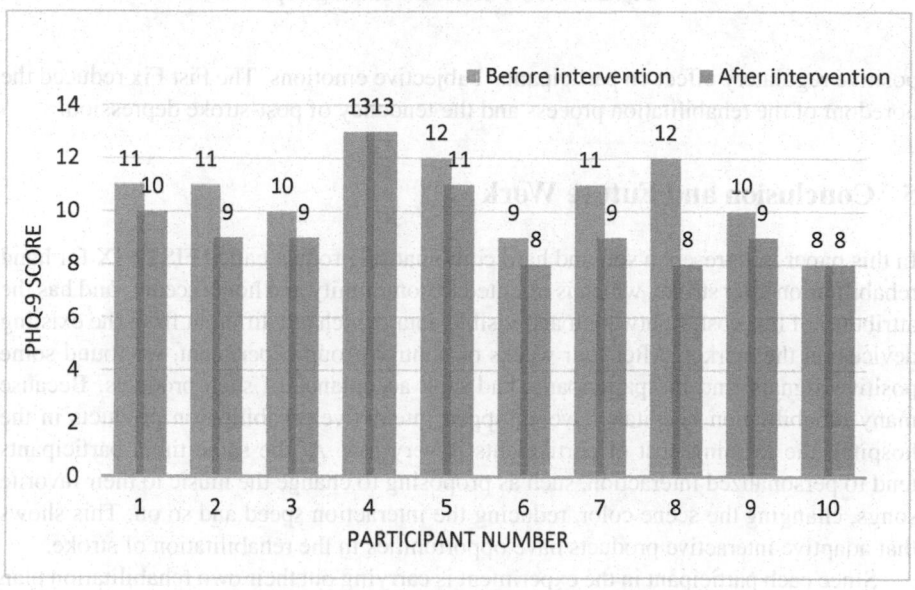

Fig. 9. PHQ-9 scores in experimental group.

the average age of the participants recruited in this work is 53 years old, the sample size is small and the intervention time is short, and the participants are carrying out their own rehabilitation process at the same time. Therefore, it can only be confirmed that in community rehabilitation or home rehabilitation, the FIST FIX can assist the rehabilitation of stroke patients with lower age. At the same time, this work also has a

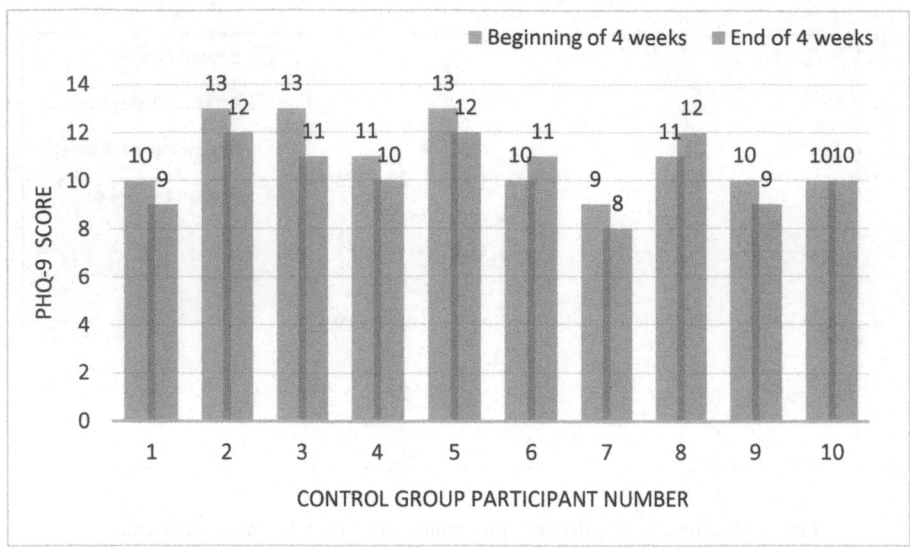

Fig. 10. PHQ-9 scores in control group.

positive regulatory effect on participants' subjective emotions. The Fist Fix reduced the boredom of the rehabilitation process and the tendency of post-stroke depression.

5 Conclusion and Future Work

In this paper, we present a soft and hard combination product called FIST FIX for hand rehabilitation after stroke, which is oriented to community and home scenes, and has the attributes of low cost, lightweight and visible data, which are different from the existing devices on the market. After four weeks of control group experiment, we found some positive signals, and the participants had high acceptance of such products. Because many rehabilitation hospitals have equipped interactive rehabilitation products in the hospital, the learning cost of participants is very low. At the same time, participants tend to personalized interaction, such as proposing to change the music to their favorite songs, changing the scene color, reducing the interaction speed and so on. This shows that adaptive interactive products have opportunities in the rehabilitation of stroke.

Since each participant in the experiment is carrying out their own rehabilitation plan at the same time, we cannot determine whether it is psychological factors that lead to the acceleration of physical rehabilitation or the amount of exercise that leads to the acceleration of rehabilitation. But in terms of the results, the experimental group has made more progress than we expected, especially the subjective scale found that this work has effectively improved the tendency of post-stroke depression, which is an important contribution to the psychological nursing of rehabilitated patients. Because of privacy, we don't know whether each participant has someone to accompany and supervise the rehabilitation in the family, so the impact of this variable on the experiment is unknown, but it can be improved by the sample size. Therefore, in the future, we intend to further verify its effect through more sampling after improving the wearing comfort and software. And study the logic behind it from a more medical perspective.

Acknowledgments. The authors would like to thank the Department of rehabilitation, Renji Hospital for medical guidance on this work, and the medical theoretical support for this work by the nursing professional teacher at Shanghai Jiao Tong University School of medicine, as well as the project funding support provided by the entrepreneurial School of Shanghai Jiao Tong University.

References

1. Wang, L., et al.: Stroke prevention and control in china is still facing great challenges - summary of the "China stroke prevention and control report 2018". Chin. Cir. J. **2**(15) (2019)
2. Zhou, J., et al.: Meta-analysis of the effect of virtual reality technology on function in stroke patients. Chin. J. Rehabil. Med. **36.5**(6) (2021)
3. Wang, L.: Effect of timing of rehabilitation treatment on prognosis of stroke patients. Hebei Med. **20**(11), 4 (2014)
4. Li, L.: The effect of standardized community rehabilitation treatment for stroke patients. Health Horiz. **1**(1) (2020)
5. Ivanova, E., Lorenz, K., Schrader, M., et al.: Developing motivational visual feedback for a new telerehabilitation system for motor relearning after stroke. In: HCI 2017 - Digital Make-Believe (2017)
6. Thieme, H., et al.: Mirror therapy for improving motor function after stroke. Cochrane Database Syst. Rev. **50** (2018). https://doi.org/10.1002/14651858.CD008449.pub3
7. Sun, Z., Zhang, L., Wang, T.: Progress in the application of virtual reality technology in the field of geriatric rehabilitation medicine. Chin. J. Rehabil. Med. **35.4**(6) (2020)
8. The Standardization Administration of the People's Republic of China.: General rules of using percentiles of the body dimensions for products design.GB/T 12985-1991.1991
9. The Standardization Administration of the People's Republic of China.: Human dimensions of Chinese adults. GB/T 10000-1988.1988
10. Zhang, Y., Hu, J., Song, W., et al.: Effect of goal-directed repetitive exercise training on upper limb motor function of stroke patients. Chin. Rehabil. Theory Pract. **22**(12), 4 (2016)

Augmented and Virtual Reality Games

An Augmented Reality Update of a Classic Game: "Where in the World is Carmen Sandiego?", Case Study

Annette Marie Chabebe Rivera[1]([✉]), Wenyu Wu[2], and Chengqi Xue[2]

[1] School of Mechanical Engineering, Southeast University, SEU, Santo Domingo, República Dominicana
annchabebe@gmail.com

[2] School of Mechanical Engineering, Southeast University, SEU, Nanjing, China
{wuwenyu.design,ipd_xcq}@seu.edu.cn

Abstract. 37 years after its original launch, it is proposed a study comparing the Augmented Reality (AR) prototype of the game "Where in the World is Carmen Sandiego?" with this classic edutainment game. The main goal of the experiment is to determine if there is a significant difference between the 13th mission (last level) of the game, and it was done with a sample of 20 individuals aged between 5 and 7 years. The results could be a promising future for both, gaming and education areas. The author used 3 investigation tools to reach the answer: Perceived Understanding, Perceived Usability and a version of the PSSUQ (Post-Study System Usability Questionnaire). A big constraint for this study was the COVID-19 pandemic that the world is living at the time it was completed, however, the use of technology played a big role to make it possible.

Keywords: Carmen Sandiego · Edutainment game · Augmented Reality (AR) · PSSUQ

1 Introduction

Educational gaming might seem as very attractive to game developers, mostly because parents are happy to buy games that would help the educational process, however, the revenue that those developers could have is not as high as other categories, such as, competition or adventure. Since the genres often work as intended and as the consumers would buy them for, they work as a certain escape from reality when life becomes too daunting to endure at times.

In the mid-1990s, "edutainment" was a popular concept among teachers and computer-based designers, which is similar to "educational gaming", but does not imply the same. The first concept goes from what appears to be a regular game, but includes education in it, therefore, the user will learn while completing the game, but the main purpose does not look like the educational process itself. Since the process takes place in the more traditional setting of a classroom which sometimes the children grow to ignore or dislike, the freedom of an open world game makes it a much more enjoyable operation.

© The Author(s), under exclusive license to Springer Nature Switzerland AG 2022
X. Fang (Ed.): HCII 2022, LNCS 13334, pp. 569–585, 2022.
https://doi.org/10.1007/978-3-031-05637-6_37

Also, the word "edutainment" has a second half more akin to entertainment rather than gaming, and that happens to be because at the time, gaming wasn't either as strong or as marketable as it is today, making it a rather bold idea then. That's particularly because it was both a growing industry and a rather trialed one for the popularity of some violent games, in the minds of the parents. The second concept, "educational gaming" refers specially to games or apps that are exclusively designed with the purpose of education or learning: they might be fun or interactive, but the goal is clearly established.

Augmented Reality (AR) could be defined as a real-time direct or indirect view of the physical real-world that has been enhanced/augmented by adding virtual computer-generated information and components [1]. AR icons are a representation of the real-life items used for the intended purposes. And as such they're able to be seen but unable to be touched, because the use or interaction is to be done by the player. Which is precisely the desired experience that the developers wish their users to have.

Since the term "icon" has been around for a long time, there is lack of recent literature defining the term. An icon is a sign which exemplifies its object in a simplified manner [2]. Townsend says that icons should clearly depict, indicate and distinguish commands and operations, and also suggest and indicate the command's intention [3]. Definitions which the author can get behind as well as adding a bit to them: An icon is and should always strive to be the simplest portrayal of an object in order to be most effectively consumed. Icons are also the smallest part of the visual communication excluding written word which is why they're so important for our understanding of what surrounds us, whether that is crude reality or augmented reality.

Symbols are those signs which "represent their objects, independently alike of any resemblance or any real connection, because dispositions or factitious habits of their interpreters ensure their being so understood" [4].

In the early 1980s, the availability and growing popularity of personal computers allowed the birth of the consumer software industry. Educators and technologists saw an opportunity to use this new medium to help children learn, and a niche industry of educational software was born (Shuler, 2012). Among the games that were produced and designed, our subject of analysis was created. Carmen Sandiego series first debuted in 1985 [5], created with the idea of a computer game that would get kids interested in geography, but with the main purpose of entertainment. Had it not succeeded, this paper wouldn't exist. Nor the desire to make it or the AR game prototype which will be elaborated upon in a moment. But since it succeeded, it has become a new avenue for teaching the younger generation about such an encompassing subject as geography is. As it involves the location of places no one would visit if they didn't know of their existence as well as a bit of their rich history before travelling there.

2   Background and Starting Point

Considering the importance of the Carmen Sandiego series, as it has both a cult-like following as well as many different iterations of all characters involved and the story, they're in; the author decided to use the game "Where in the World is Carmen Sandiego?", where the titular character made her first appearance. In this game, the player is a gumshoe detective who must catch the slyest of the thieves, Carmen Sandiego. In all her usual escapades, Carmen leaves various clues the player must decipher to identify Carmen's next geographic location. Almost like if she was either taunting or testing young detective. The clues are mostly true facts about real geographic locations and deciphering the clues assists the player in learning geographic locales. And right here is where the improved learning process takes place, as the player, in this instance the children, must solve the riddle by themselves in order to progress. The gameplay in Carmen Sandiego is typical of edutainment; drill and practice activities disguised as games [6]. Instead of a different, surreal world, these exercises open the young minds of the children to real places in their own world which they wouldn't know existed or wouldn't probably learn of them whilst being so young.

Fig. 1. Original game screenshot

As a rather general description, this experiment wants to determine how an old edutainment game interface can be translated to the modern Augmented Reality (AR) design, and how much does it affect the comprehension and understanding of the icons and symbols. The comparison will not only be made with the graphics but will also consider testing methods that are widely known, such as the PSSUQ. It's also particularly obvious, but the author understands that the graphics need to be at least seeable in order for the child to be immersed in the game and focused on the task at hand, the "cleverly learning" aspect of the game. If the game is visually intolerable, it will obviously not be able to hold their interest and attention in the long run. With all the technological advancements, the quality standards for games have risen dramatically, leaving aside Augmented Reality (AR) games which were barely a genre, let alone almost an industry in the 1990's.

From the selected game, the study will be focused on the last level, where the player should try to successfully catch Carmen Sandiego, using the clues and following the rules of the game. For this experiment the author considered the same components of the original game, but they had to be updated to the times that we're living. The thirteenth and last level of the game was purposefully chosen since it is the most complete level of the game as it has all the different mechanics to be learned throughout the playthrough, and the purpose was to evaluate the players having an experience as complete as possible. From the storytelling aspect, the author isn't worried about the plot being "spoiled" as it's a well-known franchise ever since its conception. Also, it's a remake with updated graphics of a pre-existing game and concept. There's hardly anything else left to "spoil". Another important aspect is that in this level, the players get to see Carmen Sandiego herself instead of her lackeys as in the other levels. Which also could work as a selling point for this new Augmented Reality (AR) iteration. These lackeys with their generic designs are harder to recognize for the target audience (children 5–7 years old), and this could have led to player biases, to avoid them, an iconic character was chosen. Therefore, the characters used are the ones displayed at the Netflix Carmen Sandiego TV series, mostly because the kids would be familiar with them, these were extracted from a copyright-free source.

Fig. 2. AR prototype screenshot

The main components were designed for understanding, if the player would always take the "right way", therefore, there are not wrong scenarios in this prototype because what was designed was the required for the comparison experiment. In further versions of the game the many different scenarios shall be added to have a more complete game experience with a more open world feel to it.

Even though there were some modifications to give context to the dialogs, most of them remain the same of the original game, because they are not the subject of analysis of the experiment. Any other variables that are not mentioned were not accounted for during the experiment because they were deemed irrelevant.

Fig. 3. Carmen Sandiego appearing in AR version

3   Design of the Experiment and Results

The sample of this study consists of 20 participants (60% female, 40% male), aged between 5 and 7 years old (on average, the age is 6.05 years, SD = 0.80). The survey/interview was conducted by the author with the help of a parent/tutor via video call. The average of the self-rated experience with phone on a scale from 1 to 5 was 4.4 (SD = 0.66), being 1 low and 5 high, and having boys (4.25, SD = 0.7) with lower average than girls (4.5, SD = 0.67), there is a detailed table containing all the data in Appendix 1. The reading ability follows the distribution of the Table 1, showing that 75% of the interviewed kids can read:

Table 1. Reading ability

Gender	Knows how to read				
	Yes	% Yes	No	% No	Total
Female	9	45	3	15	12
Male	6	30	2	10	8
Total	15	75	5	25	20

On 20 participants aged 5-7 years old.
The evaluated points were:

1. Perceived understanding: "I can understand how this game works"
2. Perceived Usability: "I can play this game easily"

3. PSSUQ (Post-Study System Usability Questionnaire), with the components:

  a. System Usefulness
  b. Information Quality
  c. Interface Quality

To evaluate the Perceived Understanding, and other aspects of the study, some steps were taken:

- The original game was installed in the author's personal computer, and TeamViewer (program) access was granted to the parents of the subjects, so they could be able to play the 13th mission of "Where in the world is Carmen Sandiego?".
- The access to the prototype was granted to the kids according to their language, meaning that they would evaluate the Spanish or English version with the language that they would feel most comfortable.
- With the help of the parents/tutor the author taught/gave a demonstration to the players how the AR camera worked.

The scale was from 1 to 7, and the comparison was between the original videogame and the AR version. The perceived understanding of the original videogame decreased after the players completed the test, from an average of 3.2 (SD = 1.12) to 2.95 (SD = 0.66). The participants opinion varied in the AR version: the starting point was 5.6 (SD = 1.2) and increased to 5.9 (SD = 0.88) for the comprehension of how the game works. Figure 1 contains the summary of this category, and Appendix 2 contains the detailed data (Fig. 4).

Perceived Understanding

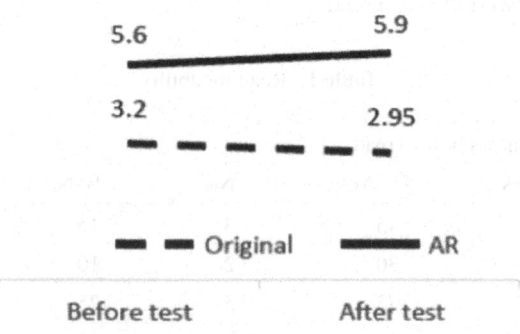

Fig. 4. Participants perceived understanding

The evaluation of the Perceived Usability was done using two different methods. One, using a computer emulator to play the original game and the other, using a cell phone or tablet to play the prototype. The participants had to evaluate how easily they could play the videogames using a scale from 1 to 7, where 1 means strongly disagree and 7 strongly agree. The participants completed the evaluation before and after testing the games.

The results obtained with the Perceived Usability, the values assigned to the original videogame decreased after the players completed the test, and the rate given to the AR version increased after the test was completed. To be more specific, the average values went from 2.9 (SD = 0.85) to 2.7 (SD = 0.64) and 5.6 (SD = 1.2) to 5.9 (SD = 0.99) at the original and the prototype, respectively. Figure 2 is a graphic of the answers of how easily the game can be played, and Appendix 3 is a table containing all the detailed data (Fig. 5).

Perceived Usability

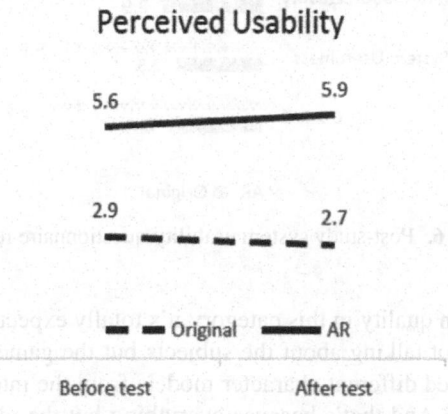

Fig. 5. Participants perceived usability

Before presenting the results of the PSSUQ (Post-Study System Usability Questionnaire), it is important to emphasize how important this questionnaire is in the industry. The PSSUQ has excellent internal consistency ($\alpha = 0.80$), as well as satisfactory inter-rater reliability (ICC = 0.67). The PSSUQ presents validity, with a high and significant correlation with an overall usability evaluation question ($r = 0.84$, $p < ;0.05$). The PSSUQ presents discriminative validity, distinguishing applications with distinct quality [7]. The modifications of the original questionnaire come in the following areas:

- The questions were modified to help the kids better understand them, specifically, the wording (e.g., instead of "system", "game", instead of "how do you explain?", "what do you think?").
- The scale was inverted to have an accurate value, since kids could think that the best would be the highest rates, as well as doing the opposite could lead to fake positive results. Usually, a 1 means strongly agree and a 7 a strongly disagree. Figure 3 summarizes the responses.

Graphically its easy jump to a conclusion, however, we need to evaluate one by one the results of the PSSUQ.

First category: interface quality. It is a measure of the level of comfortability the player has with the things they can see on the screen. More precisely, it is a rate of the quality of the images, sound, functions and capabilities the game has, as well as the level of happiness it provides to the player. The average answer at this category for the original game was 2.9 (being 3 a "slightly disagree" rate; SD = 0.91) and 6.7 for the AR prototype (7 means "strongly agree"; SD = 0.69) (Fig. 6).

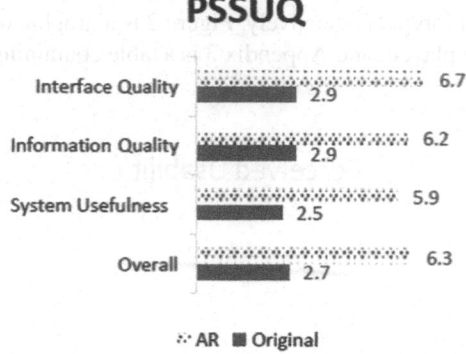

Fig. 6. Post-study system usability questionnaire results

The obvious dip in quality in this category it's totally expected to occur because of the age difference. Not talking about the subjects but the games compared with each other. The original used different character models from the intended by the author in their current iteration. And that's because everything but the plot in and of itself was different at the time of the original's launch. The images and their color grading were designed in accordance with the hardware's available capacity at that stage. Now the most recent one, the AR one, was revamped almost entirely by the author and their team to create a more marketable product according to current times.

Second category: information quality. This category takes into consideration the data given by the game, as well as the internal help, hints and how easy it is for the user to find information in said game when it's needed. Like the other categories, the interviews were performed asking specific questions to the players and watching them play. The average punctuation of the prototype was 6.2 (SD = 0.89) and the original game got 2.9 (SD = 0.95). Even in this apparently unrelated topic, the graphical update makes its presence known. Since the visual quality increased, the readable information also got boosted to match, with that the audio quality grew with the usage of better sound hardware and certain editing techniques.

Third category: system usefulness. How easy and simple the game is to play, the comfortability while playing it and the learning process, were part of the elements evaluated in this category. The players rated section with the help of their parents/tutors, similarly to the others, as well as the guide of the author. The average answers were 2.5 (SD = 0.96) and 5.9 (6 means "agree"; SD = 0.86) for the original version and the augmented reality prototype, respectively. These results are no surprise since the systems in which the games are or would be played, should this prototype see itself being finished and commercialized. In the original iteration, the game was to be played in the available hardware and maybe out of convenience was adapted to recent hardware but the graphics, as previously pointed out, remained the same, faithful to the original. The most recent product of the author and their team will allow itself to be downloaded as an app for smartphones or tablets, making it far more accessible than ever before. As such is way more on with the times and that speaks volumes to its usefulness. On the other hand, the usefulness for the intended purpose, the numbers are to be trusted since the evaluation was conducted with a sample chosen at random.

Chiong and Shuler [8] propose that even though younger children often experience difficulties in using apps on smartphone devices, like uncontrolled swiping, tapping icons incorrectly, accidentally exiting the app and/or not being able "to read" – author's note – gaming instructions, many of them still find themselves motivated to continue using the device.

This could be noticed in the results of the questionnaire and the other evaluates' scenarios, the questions of the PSSUQ can be seen on Appendix 4 while the answers are detailed on Appendixes 5 and 6.

4 Discussion and Limitations

The main goal of this study is to determine how an old edutainment game interface can be translated to the modern Augmented Reality (AR) design, and how much does it affect the comprehension and understanding of the icons and symbols. Which has been determined to be an increase so substantial that it makes this a worthy pursuit or at least a considerable endeavor to be partaking. For this, the author translated the icons and symbols to an AR version. The characters used are the ones displayed at the Netflix Carmen Sandiego TV series, mostly because the kids were going to be familiar with them. And that resemblance makes this prototype more likely to be highly marketable, as we human beings have learned to embrace that said familiarity.

The result of the evaluated categories is that the augmented reality game appears to be more visually attractive, easier to play, the player was able to complete it quickly, the provided information was helpful, and the game was clear, pleasant and likeable; when compared to the same game in its original version, that was released to the public in 1985.

There were some limitations in the study and should be acknowledged. The first one is that due to the COVID-19 pandemic that the world is living during the study period, the interviews were done at a distance, using video call technologies. The second one is that part of the data was reported by the parents: even though the author herself did most of the questions and could see what was happening, the parents and/or tutors played an important part. The author does not expect that they would over-report or under-report the players skills or their likeability of the game, but it is worth noting and acknowledging their participation. Since the parents are obviously adults that can convey complex thoughts in order to fulfill the author's requirements for information during and after the game testing.

5   Conclusions and Further Path

Acquiring new knowledge is a very important part of the development of individuals. Kids nowadays are required to learn more things than all the previous human generations in history, however, this process could be described as boring or not interesting by many students. As well as quite a daunting challenge if taken head-on. Luckily, an edutainment game is a platform where kids can be motivated to complete learning activities, such as games that will provide new areas of knowledge. Because the impetus for making this entire study was to find for more creative ways to make learning as interesting as it could possibly be. That in turn helping the future generations of humanity develop a "continuous learning" mentality, which is of great importance to both face life's challenges as well as having fun whilst doing it. For life's challenges it's what makes it interesting and worthwhile.

The comparison of two different versions of the last level of the edutainment game "Where in the World is Carmen Sandiego?" (Original game versus Augmented Reality prototype) gave a good result for the AR prototype. None of the evaluated characteristics were outperformed by the original version. And even though that was the expected conclusion, it wasn't totally the intended one, meaning the data wasn't skewed in favor of one or the other. It just happened to be the case for the reasons previously explained. A detailed comparison between the changes made to the original game can be seen on Appendix 7.

It is difficult to find games that are exclusively designed with the "educational" purpose; however, this study creates a breach where new games could be created as remakes of their original versions. As Charsky said, "there has been a parallel progression from developing edutainment to creating other games" [9]. It is important to review that progression and see that augmented reality can do a lot for successful edutainment games. And how to honor the legacy of the previously great games with an even greater revamp.

Acknowledgments. I would like to express my gratitude to my supervisor Xue Chengqi and professor Wenyu Wu, for their guidance during this research and feedback. My gratitude is also extended to my family and friends, who with their support and words of encouragement made everything possible.

Appendix 1

See Table 2.

Table 2. Participant's data

Participant	Gender	Age	Experience with phone (1 low - 5 max)	Knows Carmen Sandiego?	Knows how to read?	Spanish or English prototype?	Prototype or Demo first?
						Participants	
1	Female	7	5	Yes	Yes	English	Prototype
2	Male	7	5	Yes	Yes	English	Demo
3	Female	5	5	Yes	No	English	Prototype
4	Male	6	4	No	Yes	English	Demo
5	Female	7	4	Yes	Yes	Spanish	Prototype
6	Male	6	5	No	Yes	Spanish	Demo
7	Female	5	3	No	No	Spanish	Prototype
8	Male	5	4	No	Yes	Spanish	Demo
9	Female	5	5	Yes	No	Spanish	Prototype
10	Female	6	4	Yes	Yes	Spanish	Demo
11	Female	6	5	Yes	Yes	Spanish	Prototype
12	Male	5	5	Yes	No	English	Demo
13	Female	6	4	No	Yes	Spanish	Prototype
14	Male	6	3	Yes	Yes	Spanish	Demo
15	Female	6	4	Yes	Yes	Spanish	Prototype
16	Female	7	5	Yes	Yes	Spanish	Demo
17	Female	7	5	Yes	Yes	English	Prototype
18	Male	7	4	Yes	Yes	English	Demo
19	Female	7	5	Yes	Yes	Spanish	Prototype
20	Male	5	4	No	No	Spanish	Demo

Appendix 2

See Table 3.

Appendix 3

See Table 4.

Appendix 4

See Table 5.

Table 3. Perceived understanding

Perceived Understanding: "I can undestand how this game works"							
Before test				After test			
Demo (Original Videogame)		Prototype (AR Version)		Demo (Original Videogame)		Prototype (AR Version)	
Participant	Points	Participant	Points	Participant	Points	Participant	Points
1	5	1	7	1	4	1	7
2	2	2	6	2	3	2	6
3	4	3	5	3	4	3	6
4	3	4	5	4	3	4	5
5	4	5	7	5	3	5	7
6	5	6	7	6	2	6	7
7	5	7	3	7	4	7	4
8	2	8	6	8	2	8	6
9	3	9	5	9	3	9	6
10	3	10	6	10	3	10	6
11	4	11	7	11	2	11	7
12	1	12	6	12	3	12	6
13	2	13	6	13	4	13	6
14	3	14	5	14	3	14	5
15	2	15	4	15	2	15	6
16	3	16	6	16	3	16	6
17	4	17	6	17	3	17	6
18	3	18	7	18	3	18	7
19	2	19	5	19	2	19	5
20	4	20	3	20	3	20	4

Table 4. Perceived usability

Perceived Usability: "I can play this game easily"							
Before				After			
Demo (Original Videogame)		Prototype (AR Version)		Demo (Original Videogame)		Prototype (AR Version)	
Participant	Points	Participant	Points	Participant	Points	Participant	Points
1	4	1	7	1	3	1	7
2	2	2	6	2	2	2	5
3	3	3	5	3	3	3	5
4	4	4	5	4	3	4	6
5	3	5	7	5	3	5	7
6	3	6	7	6	3	6	7
7	4	7	3	7	2	7	5
8	3	8	6	8	3	8	6
9	2	9	5	9	2	9	5
10	2	10	6	10	2	10	7
11	3	11	7	11	3	11	7
12	1	12	6	12	2	12	6
13	2	13	6	13	2	13	6
14	3	14	5	14	4	14	6
15	2	15	4	15	2	15	6
16	3	16	6	16	3	16	6
17	4	17	6	17	3	17	6
18	3	18	7	18	3	18	7
19	2	19	5	19	2	19	5
20	4	20	3	20	4	20	3

Table 5. PSSUQ

	Category	Number	Question
Overall	**System Usefulness**	1	It's easy to play this game
		2	The game was simple to play
		3	I was able to complete the game quickly
		4	I felt comfortable using this game
		5	It was easy to learn how to pay the game
		6	I believe I can learn playing this game
	Information Quality	7	When I comitted an error the game helped me fix it
		8	When I made a mistake playing the game, I could recover easy and quick
		9	The information provided in the game was clear
		10	It was easy to find the information I needed
		11	The information helped me complete the game
		12	The organization of the game was clear
	Interface Quality	13	The interface of the game was pleasant
		14	I liked using the interface of this game
		15	This game has all the functions and capabilities I expect it to have
		16	Overall, I am happy with the game

Table 6. PSSUQ demo answers

	System Usefulness						**Information Quality**						**Interface Quality**			
Participant	Q1	Q2	Q3	Q4	Q5	Q6	Q7	Q8	Q9	Q10	Q11	Q12	Q13	Q14	Q15	Q16
1	2	3	3	1	2	3	4	3	3	3	4	2	1	1	2	3
2	3	2	2	1	3	2	3	2	4	2	3	3	2	1	3	3
3	1	1	1	2	4	3	3	4	3	3	2	2	2	2	3	2
4	4	3	4	1	2	3	2	3	2	4	1	4	2	3	2	4
5	3	4	3	2	3	2	4	1	1	3	3	3	1	2	3	1
6	2	4	3	3	3	4	3	3	2	2	2	2	1	1	2	3
7	3	3	2	2	1	3	2	2	3	1	1	1	2	1	4	2
8	1	2	3	3	2	2	1	1	4	3	2	3	3	2	1	1
9	4	1	2	3	3	1	3	5	3	2	3	2	2	3	2	4
10	3	1	3	4	4	3	4	3	3	2	4	3	1	3	3	3
11	2	3	1	3	3	2	2	3	2	3	3	3	2	2	2	3
12	1	2	4	2	2	1	1	2	2	4	2	3	2	1	4	2
13	4	2	2	1	3	2	3	4	3	2	1	4	3	4	2	3
14	3	3	3	3	4	1	3	1	4	1	2	2	1	3	3	2
15	3	1	2	2	3	2	2	3	3	3	3	3	2	2	2	4
16	2	2	1	4	2	3	4	2	2	2	2	2	3	1	3	3
17	1	2	3	3	3	2	1	4	1	1	1	4	2	1	2	4
18	2	3	4	1	3	2	3	3	2	2	2	1	1	2	3	2
19	3	4	5	2	2	3	2	1	3	3	3	2	2	3	4	3
20	4	3	3	2	1	1	3	2	4	2	2	3	1	2	2	3

Appendix 5

See Table 6.

Appendix 6

See Table 7.

Table 7. PSSUQ prototype answers

PSSUQ															
Prototype (AR Version)															
System Usefulness						Information Quality						Interface Quality			
Participant Q1	Q2	Q3	Q4	Q5	Q6	Q7	Q8	Q9	Q10	Q11	Q12	Q13	Q14	Q15	Q16
1 5	6	7	6	7	6	6	6	6	7	6	5	6	7	7	6
2 6	7	5	6	7	6	6	6	6	7	6	5	6	7	7	6
3 4	5	6	7	6	6	6	5	6	6	6	6	6	7	6	7
4 6	6	6	5	6	5	5	7	7	6	5	6	6	7	6	7
5 7	6	5	6	5	7	7	6	6	5	4	7	7	6	5	7
6 5	7	6	6	7	6	7	5	5	7	7	6	5	6	7	6
7 6	7	7	7	6	7	6	4	7	7	6	7	6	6	6	6
8 7	7	6	7	6	7	5	7	6	6	6	7	7	6	6	6
9 6	5	6	6	7	4	7	6	7	7	6	7	7	5	7	5
10 6	6	7	4	7	6	7	5	6	5	6	4	7	6	7	6
11 5	7	7	6	5	5	6	4	7	6	5	6	6	7	6	7
12 6	5	6	6	6	7	5	5	7	7	7	7	7	6	7	7
13 7	6	6	5	5	7	6	6	6	7	6	7	7	5	6	6
14 4	7	7	7	7	6	7	7	4	6	6	7	6	6	7	7
15 6	6	6	6	6	6	6	5	7	6	5	7	7	7	6	7
16 5	6	5	5	5	5	6	6	6	5	7	7	6	4	6	7
17 7	5	4	7	4	6	5	4	5	6	6	7	7	6	6	7
18 6	4	6	6	7	6	7	7	6	7	6	7	7	6	5	7
19 6	6	7	7	6	5	6	5	3	6	6	6	7	5	6	6
20 5	5	7	7	5	6	5	7	7	6	5	6	7	7	6	7

Appendix 7

See Table 8.

Table 8. Items comparison

ITEM	ORIGINAL	AR	DESCRIPTION
DeeJay			The voice of the Gizmo Tapper, and team support
Zack			The male support agent
Ivy			The female support agent
Carmen Sandiego			The sly wanted criminal
Chief			The head of ACME Detective Agency
Location	GREAT BRITAIN	⊙ ACME Headquarters	Current team location
Photo Puzzle	WANTED!		Wanted criminal poster puzzle
Battery meter		90% ▭	Battery of the Gizmo Tapper
World map		⊕	World map access, to track down the criminal's next stop
Clues viewer		⊙	Place to find the clues left by the criminal (In AR changes with the phone's camera)

Appendix 8

ITEM	ORIGINAL	AR	DESCRIPTION
Communicator		There's not enough to recognize the culprit. You should go look for clues while we are here, this could lead us to our next destination.	Team communication and support
ACME photo fax			Device that receives the fragments of the criminal's picture
Photograph taking		CLICK!	Team's photographer taking the criminal's picture
Clues counter		Clues left: 1	Clues left to find in the current location
Clues			Clue to the criminal's next stop

References

1. Carmigniani, J., Furht, B.: Augmented reality: an overview. In: Furht, B. (ed.) Handbook of Augmented Reality, pp. 3-46. Springer, New York (2011). https://doi.org/10.1007/978-1-4614-0064-6_1
2. Burks, A.W.: Icon, index, and symbol. Philos. Phenomenol. Res. **9**(4), 673–689 (1949). https://doi.org/10.2307/2103298
3. Barker, H.A., Chen, M., Grant, P.W., Jobling, C.P., Townsend, P.: Computer-aided control system design (1986)
4. Nöth, W.: The criterion of habit in Peirce's definition of the symbol. Trans. Charles S. Peirce Soc. **46**(1), 82–93 (2010). https://doi.org/10.2979/tra.2010.46.1.82
5. Craddock, D.L.: The making of Carmen Sandiego. Kotaku: gaming reviews, news, tips and more (2017). https://kotaku.com/the-making-of-carmen-sandiego-1804490410
6. Collins, A.: Design issues for learning environments. In: Vosniadou, S., De Corte, E., Glaser, R., Mandl, H. (eds.) International Perspectives on the Psychological Foundations of Technology-Based Learning Environments, pp. 347–361. Lawrence Erlbaum Associates, Hillsdale (1996)
7. Rosa, A.F., Martins, A.I., Costa, V., Queirós, A., Silva, A., Rocha, N.P.: European Portuguese validation of the post-study system usability questionnaire (PSSUQ). In: 10th Iberian Conference on Information Systems and Technologies (CISTI), Aveiro, pp. 1–5 (2015). https://doi.org/10.1109/CISTI.2015.7170431

8. Chiong, C., Shuler, C.: Learning: is there an app for that. In: Investigations of Young Children's Usage and Learning with Mobile Devices and Apps. The Joan Ganz Cooney Center at Sesame Workshop, New York, pp. 13–20 (2010)
9. Charsky, D.: From edutainment to serious games: a change in the use of game characteristics. Games Cult. **5**, 177–198 (2010). https://doi.org/10.1177/1555412009354727
10. De Rosa, A.S., Farr, R.: Icon and symbol: two sides of the coin in the investigation of social representations (2001)
11. Fombona, J., Pascual, M.A., Madeira, M.F.: Augmented reality, an evolution of the application of mobile devices. Pixel-Bit. Revista de Medios y Educación **41**, 197–210 (2012)
12. Griffiths, M.: Online video gaming: what should educational psychologists know? Educ. Psychol. Pract. **26**, 35–40 (2010). https://doi.org/10.1080/02667360903522769
13. Papadakis, S., Kalogiannakis, M.: Mobile educational applications for children: what educators and parents need to know. Int. J. Mob. Learn. Organ. **11**(3), 256 (2017). https://doi.org/10.1504/IJMLO.2017.085338
14. Plavšić, M., Bubb, H., Duschl, M.: Ergonomic design and evaluation of augmented reality based cautionary warnings for driving assistance in urban environments (2009)
15. Roberts, D.C., Snarski, S., Sherrill, T., Menozzi, A., Clipp, B., Russler, P.: Soldier-worn augmented reality system for tactical icon visualization. In: Head- and Helmet-Mounted Displays XVII; and Display Technologies and Applications for Defense, Security, and Avionics VI (2012). https://doi.org/10.1117/12.921290
16. Sonderegger, A., Sauer, J.: The influence of design aesthetics in usability testing: effects on user performance and perceived usability. Appl. Ergon. **41**, 403–410 (2010). https://doi.org/10.1016/j.apergo.2009.09.002

A Data-Driven Design of AR Alternate Reality Games to Measure Resilience

Reza Habibi[⊠][iD], Sai Siddartha Maram[iD], Johannes Pfau[iD], Jessica Wei[iD],
Shweta K. Sisodiya[iD], Atieh Kashani[iD], Elin Carstensdottir[iD],
and Magy Seif El-Nasr[iD]

University of California, 1156 High Street, Santa Cruz, CA 95064, USA
{rehabibi,samaram,jopfau,jecwei,sksisodi,atkashan,
ecarsten,mseifeln}@ucsc.edu
https://engineering.ucsc.edu/departments/computational-media

Abstract. Games have been used to study psychological phenomena in the past. Further, Alternate Reality Games (ARGs) have also been discussed as great platforms to study psychological constructs such as team dynamics, social communication or coordination, personality, and emotions. In this paper, we introduce a new ARG we developed called *LUX*. *LUX* is developed as a new team-based Alternate Reality Game used to study the construct of coping and resilience within small groups of undergraduate/graduate students. We used a design research approach to develop *LUX*, where we developed and tested prototypes based on their ability to: (a) engage participants over time, and (b) collect granular data to study coping and resilience. To assess these prototypes, we developed a novel methodology that combines three methods: (i) qualitative coding of participants' interaction outlining team work, exhibition of emotions, solution development, and submissions, (ii) process discovery, where a model of how participants interacted and solved process is developed from log data, (iii) a process visualization highlighting problem solving and team work with bottlenecks and time sinks, and (iv) a method to identify coping from process visualizations. We present *LUX*, the methodology, and results from using this methodology to evaluate one of the playtests.

Keywords: Alternate Reality Games · Game design · Resilience · Process mining · Team dynamics

1 Introduction

Games, for many years, have been used to understand psychological constructs [13,28]. Alternate Reality Games (ARGs) were poised as a new form of games that can have an impact on how we study and understand psychological and social phenomena [44]. ARGs are games that embed participants in a fictional narrative that unfolds through interaction with real-world applications, such as mobile phones, text messages and social networks. ARGs have the potential to fundamentally alter how psychological research is conducted by allowing researchers to observe participants in a (semi-)controlled manner via real-world temporal interactions, embedding participants in situations resembling those encountered in the real world. Further, ARGs enable us to collect multidimensional data about hundreds to potentially thousands of participants' actions and the context in which they occur. Unlike laboratory experiments, ARGs can engage participants for an extended period of time.

In this paper, we propose developing and using ARGs to study coping and resilience and demonstrate this by the deployment and evaluation of an ARG tailored to this context, called *LUX*. The term resilience is commonly understood to describe how people face and deal with adverse situations; specifically, resilient individuals can be defined as those who adapt to unpleasant experiences [20,38,40]. In psychology, Block and Block [3] studied resilience defining the construct of "ego-resilience", adding the prefix "ego" to suggest that resilience is a construct based on individual differences. Individuals who score high on the ego-resilience scale tend to have coordinated cognition, emotion, and behavior, which aids in their adaptation to novel or demanding situations, conflict, or change. Individuals who are ego-resilient alter their behavior in reaction to situational circumstances, choose and employ problem-solving strategies flexibly and properly, and effectively regulate emotions, particularly anxiety. A necessary mechanism for resilience is coping [6], defined as the ability to apply cognitive and behavioral strategies to exert control over, and manage the demands of, stressful situations [18].

By designing an ARG that lays ground for process mining on communication, we aim to address limitations with the current methods used for studying coping and resilience. Typically, resilience and coping have been studied using methods, such as surveys, interviews, and observations in a controlled environment, e.g., a lab [9,48]. Constructing lab experiments provides experimental control, but lab experiments also pose several limitations. They are not scalable and are often not ecologically valid [32]. They also do not capture longitudinal events, which are important for coping and resilience. Surveys and interviews focus on self-report and cognitive processes rather than behavioral processes. Using an ARG, as discussed above, provides us with a method to collect data longitudinally in an ecologically valid environment.

Studying coping through an ARG necessitates addressing some key research questions on methodology and design. First, we need to design the environment such as it mimics realistic scenarios, and allow collection of granular process data. We, thus, designed *LUX* around engaging small teams in solving puzzles communicating through the instant messaging platform *Discord*[1]. We used *Discord*, because it allows textual and verbal communication and collection of data which fits our requirements. To design the mechanics of *LUX*, we took a design research approach, where we used playtesting results to help us tune the game towards engaging participants over long periods of time in a conflict that elicits

---

[1] https://discord.com.

coping mechanisms. Towards that end we leverage previous work on motivation and design, such as the work on gamification [47], agency, competition, and self determination theories (Ryan & Deci, 2000 [39]; Deci & Ryan, 1985 [12]), e.g., [1,34].

While previous work has contributed design lessons and guidelines for developing games and ARGs to motivate long engagement, to our knowledge, previous work does not discuss methods for evaluating and tuning game design to measure process-based behavioral constructs, such as resilience and coping. This is, thus, the focus and contribution of the paper.

Specifically, we target the research question of: how to develop a methodology that allows us to identify coping strategies and assess the design in terms of its engagement and ability to collect the data necessary for the research? We propose a new methodology composed of four phases: (i) data collection and processing, (ii) qualitative coding of participants' interaction outlining team work, emotions, and problem-solving activities, (iii) generating process visualizations of how the participants' played the game, highlighting bottlenecks and time sinks, and (iv) a method for identifying design issues and coping patterns based on process visualizations.

This paper is then divided into the following sections. Section 2 discusses previous work. Section 3 introduces *LUX*. Section 4 delves deeply into the proposed methodology. Section 5 details the study and results of using the methodology on data generated from playtesting *LUX*. We conclude the paper by discussing limitations and future work and present the conclusion.

2   Previous Work

Most previous work measuring psychological constructs, such as coping, resilience, or adaptability, have mostly focused on self-report instruments, such as surveys [9,48] and interviews [14,48]. A good example of this is the work of Carver et al. [7], who developed a multidimensional inventory to measure coping. There are few works that focused on behavioral measures of constructs, such as coping. For example, Ewart et al. developed the Social Competence Interview (SCI), where they subjected participants to a 10-min stressor and then used a behavior coding system to assess the behavior. The behavior codes were derived from 70 interpersonal competence measures [46] that can be coded using a reliability metric, which includes behaviors connected to emotions and affect, such as "speaks rapidly". They found that SCI can provide a reliable and valid assessment of important dimensions of social competence and coping, including interpersonal skills, social impact on others, and the individual's orientation to a stressful problem [14]. However, to the best of our knowledge, no work investigated measuring coping behaviors through log data from a game or digital platform.

While previous work investigated the development of Alternate Reality Games to measure and understand similar psychological constructs [14,33,35, 50], the capabilities of Alternate Reality, Virtual Reality, and Serious Games as tools to study or support coping strategies remain still under-investigated. In the past, ARGs have been developed and used to raise awareness and to teach or engage community in a discussion. These examples present good lessons for design, narrative and ways to engage participants over time. A good example of that is *World Without Oil*, which places its players in a situation where they must work together, survive, and reflect on how an oil crisis might affect their lives [23]. The results show the variation of narratives of how people accomodated to living without oil for 32 weeks. Another interesting example is the work of Rodríguez and Jareda [36] who developed an ARG using participatory design to support mothers whose children have been diagnosed with autism spectrum disorder. A good example of an ARG used within an educational environment is ARGOSI [24]- an Alternate Reality Game that was developed to introduce first year students to the university life, and to traditional methods of introducing students to university life. Seif El-Nasr et al. constitute another example where they used game environments to investigate social psychology and social believability [13]. They created a novel gaming architecture that includes semi-autonomous, socially realistic characters with distinct personalities, a scenario system, and a Wizard of Oz interface via which psychologists can access and manipulate the characters' behaviors.

3   LUX - An ARG Designed to Study Resilience

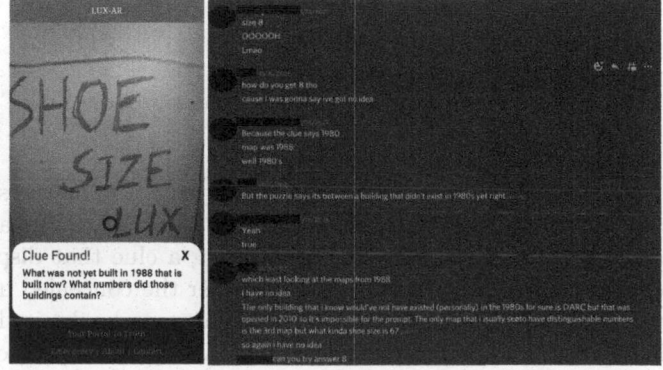

Fig. 1. Participants using the LUX AR application to unlock puzzles (left) and discussing how to solve the puzzle on Discord (right).

In this paper, we propose *LUX* – an Alternate Reality Game to study coping within small teams, specifically first year undergraduate students. The game was constructed to be a cooperative as well as competitive multi-player team-based game to target coping within social settings. The narrative of the game revolves around the founding principles of University of California at Santa Cruz

(UCSC) - as a university. Specifically, UCSC was founded on the principle of making a utopian campus in the woods, where every student could thrive in harmony, learn at their own pace, without pressure or worry about grades. Using this as a context, the game starts with a recruitment message from a group of people who believe in the grand vision and goals of the university founders. They seek support to return the university to its original values. Upon acceptance, participants are added to Discord (Fig. 1), where the game unfolds. The game is composed of multiple episodes, where each episode consists of a series of puzzles. Participants are challenged in teams of three to solve these puzzles by finding clues scattered on campus (see Fig. 2). Each puzzle reveals information about the university history, both factually and geographically.

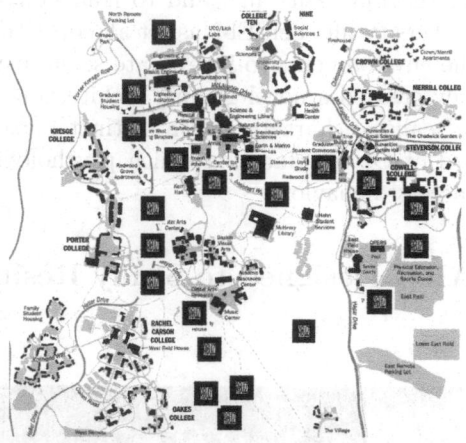

Fig. 2. A map showing the distribution of AR markers across the UCSC campus.

Players are provided with clues towards finding the AR markers, by a bot within Discord that implements the game logic and storyline. Using an AR app, they can scan the AR marker (see Fig. 1), revealing a clue that displays information to solve a puzzle. Participants must decipher the concealed information contained in these clues in order to solve the challenge and submit the solution to the bot. If they submit the proper answer, they will proceed to the next level of the game; their score will also increase accordingly.

3.1   Data Collected

Since *LUX* was developed to identify and understand the process of coping, it is essential for us to collect enough data that allows us to see this process. All data collected through player interaction consists of the following: chat data collected via Discord, which includes all communication between team members and bots; and action data collected via the augmented reality application, which includes

Fig. 3. Images from participants scanning clues located at different locations through the AR application and communicating results via Discord.

clues scanned and application logs. Additionally, we computed the following from the chat data: cumulative score, puzzle solved, hint requested, and time spent playing the game (Fig. 3).

3.2 Design Approach

To develop *LUX*, we used a design research approach, where we iteratively designed the game through multiple playtests. Every iteration builds on the lessons learned through the playtest of the previous iteration. In particular, we used the iterations to assess the ability of the current design to engender conflict, motivate users to interact for a longer period of time (a week or longer), and collect granular process data showing team dynamics and coping. Through the iterations, we encountered design problems, and we developed solutions to address them. We note that these solutions were developed based on design lessons deciphered from previous work. Below, we discuss the goals we used to assess the prototypes in more detail.

Data Integrity and Completeness Goal. During our first playtest, we found that the game was not collecting the complete account of participants' interaction. For example, we found that interaction data, where participants coordinated how they would solve a puzzle together, were not collected. Since the puzzles were located in the same space, participants decided to meet physically and opted to communicate using face-to-face modality rather than Discord. To address this problem, we used three methods. First, we used narrative to encourage participants to communicate discreetly through Discord. For example, we added narrative that urges participants to be discreet and private, just as the underground organization that recruited the players would not discuss *LUX* agenda publicly. Second, we altered the manner in which the clues and puzzles were presented. We dispersed clues at various locations throughout campus, which would ensure participants are not in the same location when picking up concurrent clues. Third, we defined participants' roles in such a way to engender communication with the bot and also with each other requiring coordination to solve the puzzle.

Gamification and Motivation - Engagement Goal. To boost participant engagement with the game, we developed and tuned our game mechanics given elements of Self Determination Theory (SDT) (tackling intrinsic motivation) and used PBL (Points, Badges and Leaderboards) as extrinsic motivators. Specifically, previous work discussed *competence* as a critical dimension of game engagement [8,10,11,25,43,49]. According to Sweetser et al. [49], the game should maintain an appropriate pace and challenge participants to instill feelings of competence and efficiency. Additionally, it should provide participants with the opportunity to develop new abilities while receiving positive feedback, and should be confronted with difficulties appropriate to their skill level. Given lessons from previous works, we tuned our puzzles' design to pace difficulty over time and levels. We used a variation of puzzles that required different skill levels, including: simple in-game actions, deduction, and, for more complex puzzles, lateral thinking.

We took inspiration from Lai et al.'s work [27], where they restricted access of specific resources to a specific member in the team to achieve a common objective. They observed that this type of constraint encouraged players to communicate and collectively manipulate a geometric shape, which in our case translates to collectively solving a problem. We, thus, used a similar approach and assigned participants roles with restricted abilities. Specifically, participants can take on the following roles: "Headmaster", "Gatekeeper" and "Acolyte". The "Headmaster" is responsible for assigning the roles "Gatekeeper" and "Acolyte" to other members in the team preventing team members to choose their own roles. In order to balance the efficiency of teams progressing through the narrative, we gave different roles abilities that other team members cannot do, and where puzzles requires all abilities to be present to be solved. For example, we enforced that only "Acolyte" is allowed to ask for hints and "Gatekeeper" is allowed to ask the bot questions. Despite having the question unlocked, the teams will have to wait for their "Acolyte" to come online and ask hints. Similarly, even after solving the puzzle, teams have to wait for their "Gatekeeper" to come online and submit the answer. This then ensures some level of coordination to solve a puzzle. The "Headmaster" was reset every 24 h to allow different participants take different roles.

In addition to adding roles and pacing our puzzles, we also included extrinsic motivational elements in our design. Gamification work identified Points, Badges and Leaderboards (PBL) as important extrinsic motivational elements that can be added to any game [5,15,31,52]. For our game, we added points as rewards; teams gain points for solving puzzles, but they can also lose points for solving puzzles late. Teams can also gain points for communicating over *Discord*. Additionally, we added a leaderboard and visualized it in a separate channel to incite competition and motivate players to play. We also announced that winners will receive an unknown prize (gift card). We chose not to resolve the nature of the prize to maintain a sense of mystery and uncertainty.

4 Methodology for ARG Evaluation and Identification of Coping

To assess the design and identify coping, we developed a novel methodology. Specifically, we propose the use of a combination of *process discovery* [51] and the concept of *user journey maps* [22]. *Process discovery* denotes algorithms that compute process models from event log data. A user journey map is a graphical representation of the user's journey as they interact with a product from start to finish. Visualizing a process model of a team's interaction represents what we call a *team process map*. This map can also indicate time spent on activities and transitions between activities; such time indicators can be used to identify bottlenecks or issues. Researchers can then use the *team process map* to identify coping processes and events as well as evaluate the design. The Study section will discuss an implementation of this methodology for *LUX*. We specifically use this as an example to show case the methodology and how it can be used to formatively evaluate the design as well as identify coping events.

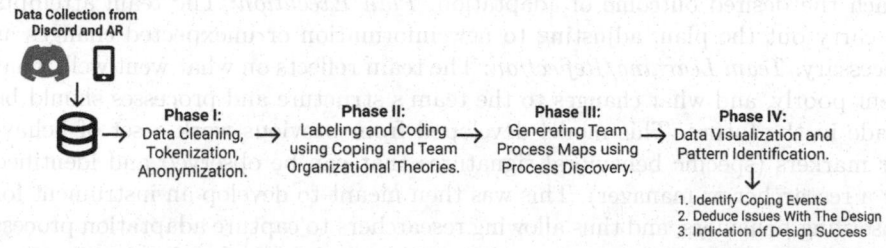

Fig. 4. Process chart outlining data analysis, process mining, and visualization.

Figure 4 shows the proposed methodology, composed of four phases. Below, we discuss the different phases of the methodology.

Phase I: Data Cleaning. In this phase, data needs to be exported, processed, and cleaned. Empty cells need to be either filled or removed. Then the data needs to be tokenized, e.g., emojis or Gifs in chat data need to be replaced by text tokens. Data also needs to be anonymized and participant information redacted.

Phase II: Labeling - Qualitative Coding. To achieve the appropriate level of abstraction in the sequential data and to make it easier to comprehend and compare, we first developed a set of labels. We used a combination of coping theories [20, 38, 40] and team organizational theories [4, 16, 37, 45] to develop a set of labels that can be used and generalized across applications. We also added labels for game actions.

For coping theories, our research showed that emotions constitute an important factor in coping [42], e.g., "Positive Emotion", "Negative Emotion" or "Confusion". Similarly, actions indicating asking for resources or help constitute another important dimension of coping. Thus, labeling both displays of emotion and requests for assistance from the data would be important.

Since social settings and team work depict further important elements of the interaction, we investigated models for team dynamics to enable us to develop behavior markers from important team behaviors that are related to coping. Studying team processes to understand adaptation, team learning, coordination or innovation requires an in-depth study of team activity. Previous work has already started discussing the different team processes that is captured under such teamwork [2]. By studying adaptation as a process, previous work identified cognitive, affective, and motivational processes that underlie team adaptation, and thus coping. To further solidify the process of adaptation we adopted Rosen et al.'s work [37]. Figure 4 shows the processes identified by the researchers to fall under the team adaptation process. The processes include four stages: *Situation Assessment*: The team starts collecting information about their environment, including identifying and assigning meaning to cues and ensuring good communication. *Plan Formulation*: The team formulates a plan of action in order to reach the desired outcome of adaptation. *Plan Execution*: The team attempts to carry out the plan, adjusting to new information or unexpected changes as necessary. *Team Learning/Reflection*: The team reflects on what went well, what went poorly, and what changes to the team's structure and processes should be made in the future. This model developed from previous work a set of behavior markers (specific behavioral signatures that can be observed and identified by a researcher or manager). This was then meant to develop an instrument for observing behaviors, and thus allowing researchers to capture adaptation process through these observed behaviors. Examples include a marker for coordination: articulated information about their status, needs and objectives as often as necessary (and not more), and a marker for reactive conflict management: utilized negotiation or mediation strategies for conflict resolution [37]. Such behavior markers are close to what we need to develop labels for team dynamics and adaptation within an ARG. Thus, we used this model as a base to develop our labels.

Given these different types of criteria, we developed an initial set of labels. We initiated an assessment by asking three researchers to code a segment of the data qualitatively using the labels as code. We then discussed the labels addressing aspects where the labels were not clear or confusing or may have several meanings.

We then finalized the set of labels to the ones displayed in Table 1. In total, we had 17 labels. It is then expected as part of the methodology for researchers to use this label set to label the data. To establish reliability, different researchers should independently code the log data, followed by the calculation of inter-rater reliability using Fleiss' Fixed-Marginal Multirater Kappa [17].

Table 1. The definition of the codes we used to label the collected data. Items from previous work are highlighted in bold and accompanied by the particular reference.

Labels	Description
Asking for Puzzle	Participants request new puzzles from the bot.
Asking for Hint	Participants request hints to solve puzzles from the bot.
Cue found	Participants searching for cues [4, 37].
Acquiring information	Collecting data in order to solve the puzzle/problem.
Deciphering Information	Participants drawing information from clues after discussion with team members.
Meaning Ascription	The process of assigning meaning and relevance to cues by classifying or synthesizing them based on existing knowledge [41].
Submitting Answer	Sending the solution to the puzzle to the bot.
Discussion	When team members argue about a puzzle or hint towards a solution [45, 4, 16].
Conflict Management	Sometimes a plan runs into unanticipated changes in the agenda and revisions must be made mid-execution to the existing strategy [29].
Awareness	Team/individual knowledge or perception of a situation or fact in the game [41].
Encouragement	Giving **team members support, confidence, or hope** in order to help them solve puzzles or problems is giving them support.
Backup Behavior	Can take many forms, such as providing a teammate with verbal feedback, assisting a teammate behaviorally in carrying out actions, or completing a task for a teammate [37].
Mutual Monitoring	A cognitive process in which team members observe their fellow team members' actions and behaviors in order to catch and correct performance [30, 26].
Coordination	The ability to use a team to work together in order to solve a puzzle or problem [26, 16, 29].
Positive Emotion	Pleasan t or desirable situational responses to e.g. solving puzzles or gaining success in the game. (Messages, GIFs, reactions, and etc.)
Negative Emotion	Undesirable situational responses, e.g. to a failure during the game (Messages, GIFs, reactions, and etc.)
Confusion	Uncertainty about a puzzle or game situation; lack of comprehension.

Phase III: Generating Team Process Maps. To generate Team Process Maps, we used a process called *Process Discovery*, introduced above, which is a set of algorithms under the area of Process Mining. Process Discovery describes algorithms that focus on discovering a process model from log data. In this paper, we used a software called *Disco*[2], which implements a process discovery algorithm called *fuzzy miner*. *Fuzzy Miner* uses fuzzy algorithms to develop a process model from log data [21].

Once we develop a process model, we will then need to visualize it. We can use many different types of visualizations, including Petri nets, dependency graphs, flow graphs, etc. In this paper, we used the process visualization provided by *Disco*, where the process model is shown as a dependency graph. This in many ways resembles user journey graphs showing the user journey as they interact with a product [19]. The graph starts with start and ends with an end state. Nodes represent intermediate states that are connected by edges with a time value associated with each transition. Note: other process mining software can

---

[2] https://fluxicon.com/disco/.

be used here or one can also implement their own. Since the paper is not focused on the actual algorithm or visualization system, we will not provide more details on process mining algorithms. Interested readers are referred to the books and materials referenced above.

In addition to generating a team process map, we also generated time indicators. Using the time-stamps, one can indicate time spent for each event and to transition between events. This can allow us to color code bottle-necks or delays highlighting them. For a game, if players spend more time in specific transitions or events, this may signify places where the team is encountering a design problem or a coping problem.

We investigated several options for visualizing team process maps. We then decided to develop visualizations one per team per day. This was essential to conserve time and also remove sleep time from our timing indicators. It also gives us a meaningful way to get deeper into their process.

Phase IV: Identifying Coping and Design Issues. The generated visualizations with time indicators are then used in three ways to address our research question and measure efficacy of solutions discussed above. First, they are used to identify coping events when they happen – addressing our RQ. Since multiple researchers can see the visualizations and these visualizations can be validated, this can account for both validity and reliability of the event and process identified. Second, the process map with the time indicators can also be used to deduce issues with the design, such as bottlenecks, pain points, churn, etc. Third, the process map can also give us an indication if the design is working. For example, we can see if the motivation strategy encouraged teams or not.

5   Study

In this study, we are interested in our ability to use the methodology outlined above to (a) identify and highlight coping and (b) assess the design of *LUX*.

5.1   Procedure

We recruited participants through an on-boarding event on campus. We sent advertisements through mailing lists and slack workspaces used by students on campus. During the on-boarding event, we introduced the game and posed an ice breaker puzzle. We then asked participants to form a team with three members to start the game, resulting in three teams in total: two teams with three members each and one team with four members - a total of ten participants. Four identified as female, six identified as male. All participants signed the user agreement consenting to us collecting their data through playing *LUX*.

Given the data from the playtesting logs, we then applied the methodology discussed above, shown in Fig. 4. We followed the phases discussed above. Phase I: we cleaned the data, tokenized it and removed any participant identifying data. Phase II: we labeled the data using the labels shown in Table 1. Phase III: we generated and visualized the team process maps. Phase IV: we identified coping and design issues from the generated maps. Results are discussed below.

5.2 Results

One team didn't engage with the game. Two teams played the game with a total of six participants. We will discuss results from the two teams here.

Data Coding - Phase II Results. Three members of the research team coded a total of 200 utterances independently that resulted in *good* inter-rater reliability ($\kappa = 0.71$) [17]. Our codes and frequencies are shown in Fig. 5. For Team 1, the most frequently occurring event was "Meaning Ascription" in which they deduced meaningful patterns from clues in order to solve puzzles, and the second most frequent event was "Coordination" where they made arrangements towards solving a puzzle or problem. The most frequently occurring occurrence for Team 2 was "Positive Emotion" as a response to playing the game or submitting the correct answer to the puzzles.

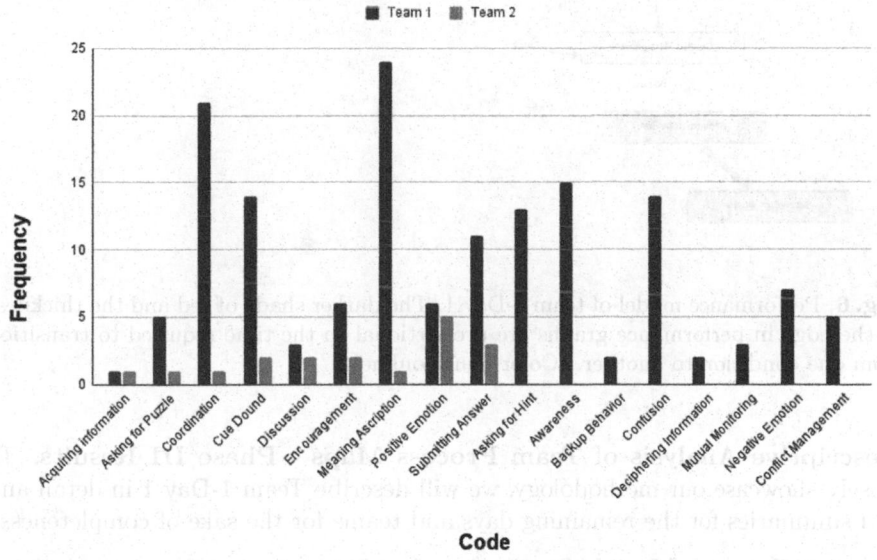

Fig. 5. Frequency of labels among two teams during playtesting session.

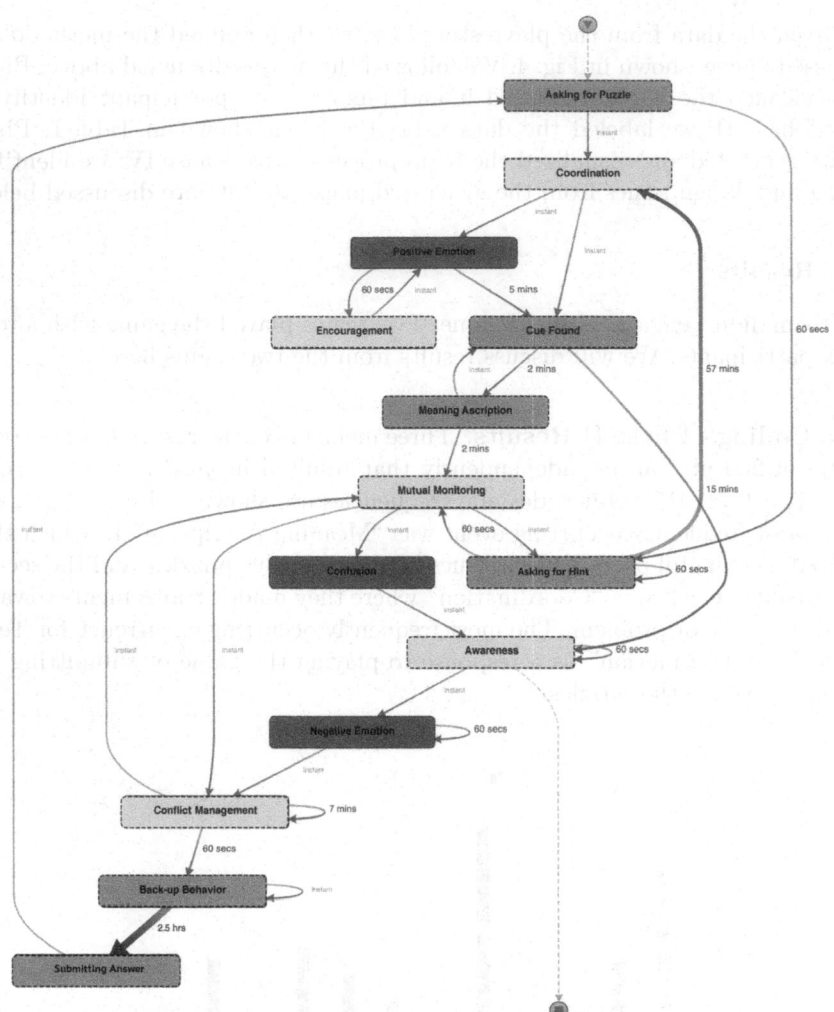

Fig. 6. Performance model of team 1-Day 1. The darker shade of red and the thickness of the edge in performance graphs are proportional to the time required to transition from one condition to another. (Color figure online)

Descriptive Analysis of Team Process Maps - Phase III Results. To closely showcase our methodology, we will describe Team 1-Day 1 in detail and add summaries for the remaining days and teams for the sake of completeness.

Team 1 Process Model: On the first day, Team 1 spent four hours solving one puzzle. The model is depicted in Fig. 6. The team employed a multi-tiered approach to problem solving and management. We broke down that approach into three layers. In the puzzle solving layer denoted by green boxes the team requested the puzzle from the bot indicated in the figure as "Asking for Puzzle", then discovered the clue indicated as "Cue Found", deciphered the meaning indicated as "Meaning Ascription", then asked for a hint from the bot, denoted by "Asking for Hint", and finally solved the puzzle by "Submitting Answer".

The team coordination and management layer denoted by yellow boxes includes several actions that the team may take over time, such as "Coordination", which happened two times throughout the day. They started coordinating by finding clues for the puzzle and then they asked for a hint. For instance, player1 stated: *"So gatekeeper and Acolyte. The headmaster has discovered the following. Standing at the location specified revealed this"*. The team also engaged in overseeing each other, shown as "Mutual Monitoring". In this part of the game, team members observed each others' actions and behaviors in order to catch and correct performance. This occurred 3 times during this day. A good example of this is when the "Headmaster" tried to use the "Gatekeeper" role abilities, but was notified by another team member that it was a wrong move. The team also engaged in "Backup Behavior" at this instant to try to fill in the role of the missing team member. Team encouragement is also another team coordination and management mechanism observed, shown as "Encouragement". This is where a team member was observed to give support, confidence and hope to their team. Moreover, "Conflict Management" was used 3 times during Day 1 in order to plan for unanticipated changes, similarly to instances of situation awareness ("Awareness").

In the emotion layer, denoted by red boxes, team 1 engaged in the expression of emotions as reactions to specific events happening throughout the game. Examples include "Positive Emotion" at the start of the game, "Confusion" resulting from trying to submit an answer but not being able to due to role mismatch, and "Negative Emotion" as a result of facing a conflict. For example, when players become aware that they do not have all of their team members available to begin the game (Player1 sent: *"I see, well our gate keeper just left campus :/. Mb. Plyaer2: damn smh gatekeeping us. If he doesn't see it in the next 40 mins we can't complete it today."*).

In Day 2, Team 1 spent 7 h solving one puzzle and used the same procedure as on day one for puzzle solving, team coordination, and management. They did, however, experience a range of emotions as they encountered numerous obstacles when attempting to solve the second puzzle. They encountered "Confusion" 8 times. For instance, they discovered that they lack a clue when an accident occurred with the clue and it was removed from its location. Player1: *"Is this the correct clue at the specified location?. [Clue image]. Because the pillar seems to have been erased. Lmao I used the app too and couldn't find anything either. The image cannot be scanned"* and as result they spent most of their time on this problem.

In Day 3, team 1 started working on another puzzle. They repeated the same flow, but stopped playing in the middle of the day. This was the end of their engagement with the game.

Now that we discussed Team 1's flow, let's discuss how they spent their time. For Day 1, the team spent the majority of their time engaging in "Backup

Behavior" (red arrow in Fig. 6). This was due to one team member not present at the time. They attempted to resolve the problem for 2.5 h before they finally presented the solution. On Day 2, they spent 2.3 h in confusion and 3.5 expressing negative emotions, because they could not find the clues in the locations that they were supposed to be at. On Day 3, the team spent 3.5 h in coordination.

Team 2 Process Model: Team 2 didn't engage with the game until Day 3. On that day, they started by solving one puzzle. They worked their way through the first puzzle, "Asking for Puzzle", then "Cue Found", and ultimately deciphered the meaning from the cue displayed. They proceeded through an "Encouragement" state in the second layer, where they evaluated the game's scoreboard and discovered they were in second position (Player1: *"TeamAloy! I'll be on campus today, prepared to assist with the puzzles. Who's up for claiming the leaderboard's top spot ?! "*). In terms of overall emotional reactions, they gravitated toward positive emotions, where they attempted to solve the puzzle and claim a place on the leaderboard. After spending 5 h answering the first puzzle, they ceased playing the game.

Identifying Coping - Phase IV. We identified coping by inspecting team process models for instances of "Confusion" since this event denotes a conflict or a struggle. Once we've identified a state of confusion, we followed the path to determine how a team dealt with or resolved the issue. For instance, as illustrated in Fig. 6, team 1 attempted the problem that emerged on Day 1 using backup behavior and then submitted the puzzle. Following definitions and criteria aggregated from background work, this series of events classifies as an incidence of coping [6, 18].

For team 1, we identified a total of four coping and eleven confusion events, the last of which did not result in a coping pattern. Team 2 did not encounter any instances of confusion and no coping patterns were detected.

Identifying Design Success and Issues. Using the process model visualization, we identified the following states as possible indicators of a design's success or failure: "Positive Emotion", "Negative Emotion", "Encouragement", points of no interaction, and just leaving the game. We then traced the event back to the log data to determine what elicited that response from participants. As an illustration, consider "Encouragement" and "Leaderboard". Using descriptive analysis of team 2 chat we identified "Encouragement" where they found their rank on the "Leaderboard" (Player1: *"Good morning, @Team Aloy ! I'll be on-campus today, ready to help with the puzzles. Who's ready to take 1st place on the leaderboard !?"*). Another example of design success occurred during team 1's discussion on Day 3, when they began forming teams and assigning responsibilities to team members based on their roles (Player1: *"hit us uuuuuppppp @[player2] I wish to be assigned the role of Gatekeeper unless of course [player3] doesn't want to be Acolyte twice then I'll be Acolyte"*)

6   Limitations and Future Work

The methodology was effective at pointing out coping and design issues in a scalable and easy to use way. However, the study discussed here has several limitations. First, this is our first set of playtests with the game. They were scheduled for a shorter duration than our later playtests. For these initial playtests, our longest session lasted five days, which is still insufficient time to collect enough data to focus on individual and group changes over time. As future or current work, we are playtesting the game for two weeks and intend to deploy it at a later time for a month. The second limitation is the number of participants and teams currently represented in this study. We only had 6 active players in total and analyzed a total of 200 lines of chat. This is very limited and doesn't given us enough information on motivation or coping behaviors. As a result, the mentioned findings require additional research to verify in a larger groups.

One of the limitations of the methodology itself is the time induced for manual coding and labeling the data. With a large dataset this would become a definite bottleneck. For future work, we intend to look at semi-automated or sentiment analysis methods [53] to process the data and intend to extend the methodology in the future. Further, the user journey graphs used and shown in this paper are limited as they cannot show the multi-dimensional interaction between the layers discussed. Therefore, in future work, we will examine various techniques and algorithms for visualizing and analyzing a player's in a multi-dimensional visualization showing interactions between the different dimensions.

7   Conclusion

Resilience and coping are difficult to quantify using methods like as surveys and interviews [9,48], because such methods are often limited to self reports and do not capture behavioral and longitudinal aspects of such constructs. In this paper, we proposed a new method for studying these constructs using ARGs and process mining, evaluated on a prototype called *LUX*. We designed game mechanics to engage people in conflict and elicit coping mechanisms comparable to those found in real-world situations. Additionally, we proposed a new methodological approach to studying team dynamics and behavior to identify coping as well as assess the design. We presented our game and a study we conducted using the proposed methodology, where we analyzed team behaviors and activities using team process maps of qualitative codes mapping their team behaviors, puzzle solving activities as well as emotional reactions. We discussed some results indicating ability of our method to deduce coping events and team dynamics leading coping or failure of coping. We also showed the use of the method to deduce issues in the design. Future work will address methodological limitations as well as extend the current ARG design collecting more data to expand our results. We believe LUX, the proposed methodology and the study constitute a good first step addressing this new area of research around the use of ARGs to study the psychological construct of coping and resilience.

Acknowledgement. This work is funded by James S McDonnell Foundation (Grant Title: A Methodology for Studying the Dynamics of Resilience of College Students).

References

1. Aparicio, A., Vela, F.L., González-Sánchez, J., Isla-Montes, J.L.: Analysis and application of gamification, October 2012. https://doi.org/10.1145/2379636. 2379653
2. Baard, S.K., Rench, T.A., Kozlowski, S.W.: Performance adaptation: a theoretical integration and review. J. Manag. **40**(1), 48–99 (2014)
3. Block, N.: Readings in Philosophy of Psychology, vol. 1. Harvard University Press (1980)
4. Burke, C.S., Stagl, K.C., Salas, E., Pierce, L., Kendall, D.: Understanding team adaptation: a conceptual analysis and model. J. Appl. Psychol. **91**(6), 1189 (2006)
5. Cameron, J., Pierce, W.D., Banko, K.M., Gear, A.: Achievement-based rewards and intrinsic motivation: a test of cognitive mediators. J. Educ. Psychol. **97**(4), 641 (2005)
6. Campbell-Sills, L., Cohan, S.L., Stein, M.B.: Relationship of resilience to personality, coping, and psychiatric symptoms in young adults. Behav. Res. Ther. **44**(4), 585–599 (2006)
7. Carver, C.S., Scheier, M.F., Weintraub, J.K.: Assessing coping strategies: a theoretically based approach. J. Pers. Soc. Psychol. **56**(2), 267–83 (1989)
8. Chen, H.L., Lattuca, L.R., Hamilton, E.R.: Conceptualizing engagement: contributions of faculty to student engagement in engineering. J. Eng. Educ. **97**(3), 339–353 (2008)
9. Clark, K.K., Bormann, C.A., Cropanzano, R.S., James, K.: Validation evidence for three coping measures. J. Pers. Assess. **65**(3), 434–455 (1995). https://doi.org/10. 1207/s15327752jpa6503_5
10. Csikszentmihalyi, M., Csikzentmihaly, M.: Flow: The Psychology of Optimal Experience, vol. 1990. Harper & Row New York (1990)
11. Deci, E.L., Olafsen, A.H., Ryan, R.M.: Self-determination theory in work organizations: the state of a science. Annu. Rev. Organ. Psych. Organ. Behav. **4**, 19–43 (2017)
12. Deci, E.L., Ryan, R.M.: Intrinsic motivation and self-determination in human behavior. In: Perspectives in Social Psychology (1985)
13. El-Nasr, M.S., Gray, M., Nguyen, T.H.D., Isaacowitz, D., Carstensdottir, E., DeSteno, D.: Social gaming as an experimental platform. In: Foundations of Digital Games Workshop on Social Believability (2014)
14. Ewart, C.K., Jorgensen, R.S., Suchday, S., Chen, E., Matthews, K.A.: Measuring stress resilience and coping in vulnerable youth: the social competence interview. Psychol. Assess. **14**(3), 339 (2002)
15. Filsecker, M., Hickey, D.T.: Incentives in educational games: a multilevel analysis of their impact on elementary students' engagement and learning (2013)
16. Fleishman, E.A., Zaccaro, S.J.: Toward a taxonomy of team performance functions (1992)
17. Fleiss, J.L.: Measuring nominal scale agreement among many raters. Psychol. Bull. **76**(5), 378 (1971)
18. Folkman, S., Moskowitz, J.T.: Coping: pitfalls and promise. Annu. Rev. Psychol. **55**, 745–774 (2004)

19. Følstad, A., Kvale, K.: Customer journeys: a systematic literature review. J. Serv. Theor. Pract. **28**(2), 196–227 (2018). https://doi.org/10.1108/JSTP-11-2014-0261
20. Garmezy, N.: Resilience in children's adaptation to negative life events and stressed environments. Pediatr. Ann. **20**(9), 459–466 (1991)
21. Günther, C.W., van der Aalst, W.M.P.: Fuzzy mining – adaptive process simplification based on multi-perspective metrics. In: Alonso, G., Dadam, P., Rosemann, M. (eds.) BPM 2007. LNCS, vol. 4714, pp. 328–343. Springer, Heidelberg (2007). https://doi.org/10.1007/978-3-540-75183-0_24
22. Howard, T.: Journey mapping: a brief overview. Commun. Des. Q. Rev. **2**(3), 10–13 (2014)
23. JafariNaimi, N., Meyers, E.M.: Collective Intelligence or Group Think? Engaging Participation Patterns in World Without Oil. Association for Computing Machinery, New York (2015)
24. Jones, R., Whitton, N.: ARGOSI: alternate reality games for orientation, socialisation and induction, January 2009
25. Kiili, K., Lainema, T.: Foundation for measuring engagement in educational games. J. Interact. Learn. Res. **19**(3), 469–488 (2008)
26. Kozlowski, S.W.: Training and developing adaptive teams: theory, principles, and research (1998)
27. Lai, K., White, T.: How groups cooperate in a networked geometry learning environment. Instr. Sci. **42**(4), 615–637 (2013). https://doi.org/10.1007/s11251-013-9303-4
28. Madsen, K.E.: The differential effects of agency on fear induction using a horror-themed video game. Comput. Hum. Behav. **56**, 142–146 (2016)
29. Marks, G., Steenbergen, M.: Understanding political contestation in the European union (2002)
30. McIntyre, R.M., Salas, E.: Measuring and managing for team performance: emerging principles from complex environments. Team Effectiveness Decis. Making Organ. **16**, 9–45 (1995)
31. Mekler, E.D., Brühlmann, F., Opwis, K., Tuch, A.N.: Do points, levels and leaderboards harm intrinsic motivation? An empirical analysis of common gamification elements. In: Proceedings of the First International Conference on Gameful Design, Research, and Applications, pp. 66–73 (2013)
32. Mitchell, G.: Revisiting truth or triviality: the external validity of research in the psychological laboratory. Perspect. Psychol. Sci. **7**(2), 109–117 (2012)
33. Olbrish, K.: The ABC's of ARGs: alternate reality games for learning. ELearn **2011**(8) (2011). https://doi.org/10.1145/2016016.2019544
34. Przybylski, A.K., Rigby, C.S., Ryan, R.M.: A motivational model of video game engagement. Rev. Gen. Psychol. **14**(2), 154–166 (2010)
35. Razavi, M., Yamauchi, T., Janfaza, V., Leontyev, A., Longmire-Monford, S., Orr, J.: Multimodal-multisensory experiments (2020)
36. Rodríguez, N.L., Jareda, M.E.M.: Design process of an alternate reality game (ARG) as a strategy to foster social support and well-being of mothers of children with ASD. In: 2019 IEEE 7th International Conference on Serious Games and Applications for Health (SeGAH), pp. 1–7 (2019). https://doi.org/10.1109/SeGAH.2019.8882440
37. Rosen, M.A., Bedwell, W.L., Wildman, J.L., Fritzsche, B.A., Salas, E., Burke, C.S.: Managing adaptive performance in teams: guiding principles and behavioral markers for measurement. Hum. Resour. Manag. Rev. **21**(2), 107–122 (2011)
38. Rutter, M.: Psychosocial resilience and protective mechanisms. Am. J. Orthopsychiatry **57**(3), 316–331 (1987)

39. Ryan, R.M., Deci, E.L.: Self-determination theory and the facilitation of intrinsic motivation, social development, and well-being. Am. Psychol. **55**(1), 68 (2000)
40. Ryff, C.D., Friedman, E.M., Morozink, J.A., Tsenkova, V.: Psychological resilience in adulthood and later life: implications for health. Annu. Rev. Gerontol. Geriatr. **32**(1), 73–92 (2012)
41. Salas, E., Prince, C., Baker, D.P., Shrestha, L.: Situation awareness in team performance: implications for measurement and training. Hum. Factors **37**(1), 123–136 (1995)
42. Scherer, R.F., Luther, D.C., Wiebe, F.A., Adams, J.S.: Dimensionality of coping: factor stability using the ways of coping questionnaire. Psychol. Rep. **62**(3), 763–770 (1988)
43. Shogren, K.A., Little, T.D., Wehmeyer, M.L.: Human agentic theories and the development of self-determination. In: Wehmeyer, M.L., Shogren, K.A., Little, T.D., Lopez, S.J. (eds.) Development of Self-Determination Through the Life-Course, pp. 17–26. Springer, Dordrecht (2017). https://doi.org/10.1007/978-94-024-1042-6_2
44. Shonin, E., Van Gordon, W., Singh, N.N.: Buddhist Foundations of Mindfulness. Springer, Cham (2015). https://doi.org/10.1007/978-3-319-18591-0
45. Smith-Jentsch, K.A., Zeisig, R.L., Acton, B., McPherson, J.A.: Team dimensional training: a strategy for guided team self-correction (1998)
46. Spitzberg, B.H., Cupach, W.R.: Handbook of Interpersonal Competence Research. Springer, Heidelberg (2012)
47. Stieglitz, S., Lattemann, C., Robra-Bissantz, S., Zarnekow, R., Brockmann, T.: Gamification. Springer, Heidelberg (2017)
48. Stone, A.A., Neale, J.M.: New measure of daily coping: development and preliminary results. J. Pers. Soc. Psychol. **46**(4), 892 (1984)
49. Sweetser, P., Wyeth, P.: GameFlow: a model for evaluating player enjoyment in games. Comput. Entertainment (CIE) **3**(3), 3 (2005)
50. Tabbakh, S.K., Habibi, R., Vafadar, S.: Design and implementation of a framework based on augmented reality for phobia treatment applications. In: 2015 International Congress on Technology, Communication and Knowledge (ICTCK), pp. 366–370. IEEE (2015)
51. Van Der Aalst, W.: Process mining: overview and opportunities. ACM Trans. Manag. Inf. Syst. (TMIS) **3**(2), 1–17 (2012)
52. Wang, H., Sun, C.T.: Game reward systems: gaming experiences and social meanings. In: DiGRA Conference, vol. 114 (2011)
53. Zad, S., Heidari, M., Hajibabaee, P., Malekzadeh, M.: A survey of deep learning methods on semantic similarity and sentence modeling. In: 2021 IEEE 12th Annual Information Technology, Electronics and Mobile Communication Conference (IEMCON), pp. 0466–0472. IEEE (2021)

Implicit Interaction Mechanisms in VR-Controlled Interactive Visual Novels

Cristóbal Maldonado[1], Francisco J. Gutierrez[1]([✉]), and Victor Fajnzylber[2]

[1] Department of Computer Science, University of Chile, Beauchef 851,
West Building, Third Floor, Santiago, Chile
{cmaldona,frgutier}@dcc.uchile.cl
[2] Communication and Image Institute, University of Chile,
Avenida Capitán Ignacio Carrera Pinto 1045, Ñuñoa, Chile
vfajnzylber@u.uchile.cl

Abstract. Virtual reality (VR) environments are increasingly being addressed by Human-Computer Interaction researchers and practitioners, due to the recent and rapid development of affordable hardware targeted to the mass market. In that respect, implicit interactions are the go-to paradigm for conceiving VR applications, particularly in simulation and gaming. However, to the best of our knowledge, there is still a significant gap in literature regarding models and practical guidelines to assist designers and software developers when building interactive applications in this domain. As a way to provide a common ground for designing interactive applications in VR environments, this paper presents a formal conceptualization of implicit interaction mechanisms. To do so, we propose a set of formal models and we show a working example implementing such interaction mechanisms in an interactive visual novel, i.e., a video game comprising a compelling narrative extended by the interaction within an immersive environment, which in this case corresponds to a VR world. As a way to gauge user acceptance of the produced video game, we conducted a controlled user study measuring perceived immersion and player experience with a particular focus in the implementation of the proposed implicit interaction mechanisms. The obtained results are highly promising, highlighting the understandability and flexibility of the proposed mechanisms.

Keywords: Virtual reality · Implicit interactions · Gaming experiences · Design · Empirical study

1 Introduction

Virtual reality (VR) environments are increasingly being addressed by human-computer interaction researchers and practitioners due to the rapid advancements in producing affordable mass-market headsets and displays. Therefore, we are faced to a complex—yet exciting—endeavor, given that design guidelines and software development frameworks are not widely available yet [7].

In VR environments, users can interact with existing components in natural and immersive ways, in a similar way as they would in the real world [6]. Formally speaking, these interactions are mostly *implicit* in nature [4], i.e., they aim to capture and/or trigger user actions in unintentional ways [9]. Conversely, interactive systems in more "traditional" domains are structured around *explicit* interactions, where users consciously capture and/or trigger prompts through an interface (e.g., a button displayed on a screen) to mediate their intent to perform a specific action.

When conceiving implicit interactions in a VR environment, designers should aim to provide a sensory immersion to users. That is, favoring that users disconnect their senses from the real world in a way that they perceive to be fully engaged within such a virtual experience [2].

In this paper we explore how to design and develop implicit interaction mechanics in a particular kind of VR applications: interactive visual novels. According to Kleinman et al. [5], visual novels are a videogame genre where users, besides playing in a "traditional" way, walk through a progressive narrative, making decisions or performing certain tasks to move forward in the story. In particular, VR-controlled visual novels have to provide a sensory experience that enhances player involvement and immersion.

The rest of this paper is structured as follows. Section 2 reviews and discusses related work. Section 3 presents a set of conceptual models for designing implicit interaction mechanisms in VR-controlled interactive visual novels. Section 4 describes a worked example showing how the proposed models can be instantiated. Section 5 is devoted to study user acceptance, immersion, and player experience of a VR-controlled game instantiating the proposed implicit interaction mechanisms. Finally, Sect. 6 concludes this work.

2   Related Work

When designing immersive interactions, it is important that the system is aware of the context in which the actions are being triggered (e.g., by analyzing body language and intentions), and consequently adapting its behavior [8]. In the particular case of implicit interaction mechanics, Ju [4] argues that these need to identify patterns in user behavior as a way to increase their effectiveness and involvement.

Ju [4] states that implicit interactions require the attention and involvement of users, under certain conditions. In particular, interactions involve states and transitions, depending on how much attention and who takes the initiative for triggering the interaction. Following that line of reasoning, interactions can be classified as: (1) foreground/reactive, where the interaction is initiated by the user and requires the attention of the user (e.g., direct manipulation in a graphical user interface); (2) foreground/proactive, where the interaction is initiated by the system and requires the attention of the user (e.g., any kind of awareness notification); (3) background/reactive, where the interaction is initiated by the user and does not require their attention (e.g., schedule an email); and (4) background/proactive, where the interaction is initiated by the system and does not require the attention of the user (e.g., autosaving).

Following this taxonomy, explicit interactions are mostly foreground/reactive and, at times, proactive. Conversely, implicit interactions are classified in the other three groups (i.e., foreground/proactive and those in the background), given that the system is implicitly mediating the interaction. In any case, these kinds of interactions require the action of a user. For example, let us consider the case of a mobile phone. When it receives a call, the phone screen displays a message alerting the user (foreground/proactive), which prompts the user to take action (foreground/reactive). Then, when the call is ended, the user presses a button on screen (foreground/reactive) and the telephone internally stores information relative to the call, such as time and duration (background/reactive).

Finally, when exploring how to design gaming experiences, Kleinman et al. [5] argue that metagaming (i.e., any action outside the game environment that allows the player to advance in their goals [1]) risks the perception of immersion within the system. In particular, in the case of games that actively involve decision-taking to pursue in the narrative (as it is the case of visual novels), a popular design pattern is to allow the user to rollback to a previous point in the storyline, once the result of taking a certain path is known. In this case, this kind of user involvement is not perceived as a significant factor regarding immersion and player experience.

3   Formalizing Implicit Interactions in Virtual Reality

In general, to formalize interaction models we typically use a structured language, such as the one used in the study of automata theory, or UML activity diagrams. On the one hand, we have *states*, that represent atomic and concrete actions that form part of the interaction scenario. On the other hand, we have *transitions*, which correspond to pre- and post-conditions that structure the flow between states.

Inspired by the seminal work of Ju, broadly discussing the notion of implicit interactions [4], we propose a set of three formal models to structure these kinds of interactions in VR environments: (1) sequential input – sequential output, (2) sequential input – disruptive output, and (3) progressive rupture. We discuss in the following subsections the rationale behind each representation.

3.1   Sequential Input – Sequential Output

The purpose of this first model is to describe interaction scenarios that are structured as a sequential set of stages, which cannot be skipped, but can flow in both directions (i.e., either forward or backward). For instance, let us consider a proximity sensor that dynamically alters the weather in a VR environment: the different states correspond to the amount of rain that drops from the sky, whereas the transitions could be modeled after the distance between the position of a player and a specific point of interest in the environment.

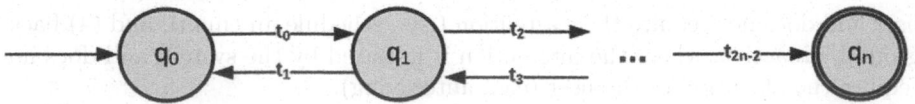

Fig. 1. Representation of the *Sequential Input – Sequential Output* model

The states, that are depicted in Fig. 1, are characterized as follows:

- The entry state, q_0, represents the inactive environment.
- States q_i ($i \in \{1, \ldots, n-1\}$) represent the different stages that are modeled within the environment.
- The final state, q_n, represents the output result in which we intend to leave the environment by the end of the interaction.

Likewise, the transitions (i.e., sequence of pre- and post-conditions) that link the different states are modeled as follows:

- From each state q_i ($i \in \{0, \ldots, n\}$), the interaction can only flow to the next state q_{i+1} or to the previous state q_{i-1}, if either of these exist.
- Once the final state q_n is reached, the interaction ends. In other words, this state does not have further transitions to disrupt the flow of the interaction.

Under this set of rules, it is possible to have states that force the interaction to flow in a specific direction, where the only viable transition is to advance the interaction to the following state. For instance, let us consider once again the example of modeling weather in a VR environment. We can define q_0 as the state with no rain in the scene. If the player moves closer to a treasure chest, we can alter the scene by making it rain softly: this is the transition between q_0 and q_1. Then, if the player moves away from the treasure chest, rain will stop falling, changing the interaction flow from q_1 to q_0. Conversely, if the player opens the treasure chest, rain will fall heavily: this would be the transition from state q_1 to q_2. If we define q_2 to be the final state, then the heavy rain will not be further affected by the position of the player in the scenario.

3.2   Sequential Input – Disruptive Output

In this model, we describe interaction scenarios that can be represented as a finite set of sequential stages, which cannot be avoided, but that under certain conditions the interaction flow comes back to the initial stage. For example, let us consider the case of a player that must concentrate on achieving a specific task: if he/she loses focus, then progress is lost and the task has to be restarted.

The states, that are depicted in Fig. 2, are characterized as follows:

- The entry state, q_0, represents the inactive environment.
- States q_i ($i \in \{1, \ldots, n-1\}$) represent the different stages that are modeled within the environment.

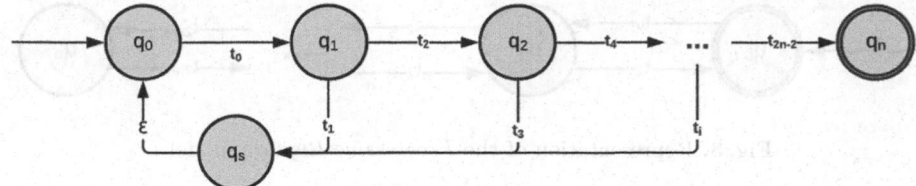

Fig. 2. Representation of the *Sequential Input – Disruptive Output* model

- The final state, q_n, represents the output result in which we intend to leave the environment by the end of the interaction.
- The state q_s represents a stage in the interaction where the environment necessary has to pass through, before reaching inactivity (similar to a *callback*). From now on, we will refer to this as a *special* state.

Likewise, the transitions that link the different states are modeled as follows:

- From the entry state q_0, the interaction can only flow to state q_1.
- From each state q_i ($i \in \{1, \ldots, n-1\}$), the interaction can only flow to the next state q_{i+1} or to the special state q_s, if either of these exist.
- From the special state q_s, the interaction will always flow to the entry state.
- Once the final state q_n is reached, the interaction ends. In other words, this state does not have further transitions to disrupt the flow of the interaction.

The special state q_s can be understood as a state where certain environment attributes are restarted, as a way to roll back to equilibrium. For example, let us consider the example of a player whose goal is to get out of a maze. We can define q_0 as the state where the player is located at the beginning of the maze. Once he/she moves forward in the environment, he/she finds several puzzles, each one corresponding to a different state. If the player correctly solves a puzzle, then he/she can move forward, unblocking a path to the following room. Conversely, if the player makes a mistake, then the special state q_s is called, which will reboot the gaming session and the player will be automatically warped to the beginning of the maze.

3.3 Progressive Rupture

Finally, in this model we describe situations in which the desired behavior is the environment equilibrium, and the user actions represent a disruption in such a behavior. For example, let us consider a video game where a player is required to follow a specific path in a forest. However, if the player moves away from the traced route, then the environment reacts with aggressive reactions that incite the player to regain the original path.

The states, that are depicted in Fig. 3, are characterized as follows:

- The entry—and final—state, q_0, represents the inactive environment.

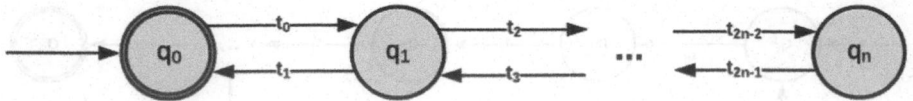

Fig. 3. Representation of the *Progressive Rupture* model

- States q_i ($i \in \{1, \ldots, n\}$) represent the different stages that are modeled within the environment.

Likewise, the transitions that link the different states are modeled as follows:

- From each state q_i ($i \in \{0, \ldots, n\}$), the interaction can only flow to the next state q_{i+1} or to the previous state q_{i-1}, if either of these exist.
- Once the final state q_0 is reached, the interaction may not immediately conclude, as it could resume if the transition to state q_1 is triggered. Therefore, this model might impose specific external conditions that have to be reached in order to stop the interaction.

Regarding this latter condition, and considering the example of the player finding his/her way out of the forest, the final state will be only activated when the player reaches the end of the trail. Therefore, if we define q_0 to represent the forest as a static environment when the player is at the beginning of the route, we can define q_1 to be a state where the environment will emit menacing sounds from animals, as the player walks in deeply into the forest. Furthermore, once the player reaches a specific milestone in the route, then state q_2 is activated and the environment will explicitly display raging animal shadows, inciting the player to run away and then dynamically change the environment as it was at the beginning of the interaction.

4 Instantiating the Implicit Interaction Models in a Visual Novel

In order to illustrate the application of the proposed models in a VR video game, we present the design of implicit interactions to control a visual novel. In this application, we show two instances of Sequential Input – Sequential Output, and then Sequential Input – Disruptive Output.

The first part of the interaction involves three non-playable characters (NPCs) talking to each other. Here, the player listens to unintelligible whispers. Once the player moves closer to these people (the zone marked in red in Fig. 4), then he/she will start listening to audible and understandable dialogue. This exemplifies an interaction following the Sequential Input – Sequential Output model, with just two states: (1) unintelligible whispers and (2) clear conversation, which corresponds to the final state. The transition between these two states corresponds to the relative position of the player with regard to the group of people.

Once the player enters the mentioned zone (in red, in Fig. 4), then the first stage of the interaction is complete. From now on, the dialogues will continue until they completion, since the conversation is not meant to be with the player, but rather with the other NPCs in the group. This is depicted in Fig. 5, exemplifying an implicit interaction modeled after sequential inputs and outputs.

Fig. 4. Non-playable characters talking to each other. (Color figure online)

When the dialogue among the NPCs is complete, one of them will turn to the player. If the player is located within the red zone, he/will be asked a question from the NPC; otherwise, the NPC will wait until the player is close enough. This triggers the second stage of the interaction, which instantiates the Sequential Input – Disruptive Output model. Here, the entry state is the NPC waiting until the player moves closer, which makes the interaction flow to the following state, where the NPC will formulate a question to the player (Fig. 6).

If the player moves away (transition), then the NPC will return to the initial state, waving goodbye. This latter action corresponds to the special state before returning to the beginning of the interaction. Otherwise, if the player responds, then the NPC will start interacting with the player (Fig. 7). Here we identify a transition (greeting) and a new state (the NPC talking directly to the player). In this new state, if the player is idle long enough or moves away from the NPC, then the special state is triggered.

Finally, if the player is actively involved in the interaction with the NPC, then it will flow to the following state, causing the NPC to move away. This wraps up the interaction scenario (Fig. 8).

Fig. 5. Non-playable characters talking to each other, once the player is close to the group.

Fig. 6. Non-playable character waiting for a response from the player.

5   Proof of Concept

In order to explore how potential users perceive and value the proposed implicit interaction mechanisms in a VR-controlled visual novel, we conducted a proof-of-concept study measuring perceived immersion and player experience. The game that was evaluated corresponds to the one instantiating the implicit interaction models described in Sects. 3 and 4.

Fig. 7. Non-playable character interacting with the player.

Fig. 8. Non-playable character leaving the environment.

5.1   Methods

In this subsection, we describe the empirical design that was followed to measure perceived immersion and player experience in the developed VR-controlled visual novel.

Participants. Through snowball sampling, we recruited 10 users, aged between 24 and 30 years old, balanced in gender, and who self-declared to enjoy playing videogames focused in the visual novel genre. None of the users had prior experience with VR technology. Complying with ethical standards when dealing with human subjects, the conducted study followed strict protocols and regulations. Participants had to provide explicit, informed, and free consent during enrollment. In particular, participants were informed that could experience dizziness during the game session, which is fairly common for novice users interacting with VR controls. All participants had the right to leave the experience at their own will, with no negative consequences. Collected data was anonymized and used only in the context of analyzing the reported experience. Given the current environmental conditions due to the COVID-19 pandemic, we carried out the experience respecting all sanitary protocols, ensuring that participants incurred in no health risks.

Materials. The game was implemented using the Unity game engine, running as a standalone executable file optimized for Oculus Quest. All participants used the same VR headset, as a way to control hardware conditions during the trial. Furthermore, in order to control for environmental conditions, all game sessions were held in the same room, with enough space for allowing natural movement.

Procedure. Participants were asked to complete individual and independent game sessions, facilitated by the first and second authors of this paper. At the beginning of each session, the facilitator explained the context of the study, i.e., evaluate a demo version of an interactive visual novel in VR. Given that none of the participants had prior experience with VR technology, they were asked to complete a tutorial as a way to get used to the controls and reduce potential novelty effect bias due to the use of unconventional technology (i.e., the Oculus headset). In order to ease the introduction to the game session, the tutorial was customized with some of the characters and scenarios that were part of the visual novel (cf. Sect. 4). The game demo lasted between 5 to 10 min. Afterwards, participants were asked to fill in a questionnaire measuring perceived involvement and player experience. This instrument was modeled after the first two modules of the Game Experience Questionnaire (GEQ) [3], which is an industry standard for evaluating player experience in video games.

5.2   Results

Despite our best efforts to control the execution of the experience, we cannot ensure the generalizability of the obtained results due to sample size limitations. Consequently, these results should be understood in the context of the studied groups. Next, we present aggregated results obtained from the GEQ questionnaire, as well as open comments captured at the end of the game session.

Questionnaire Dimensions. Scores are graded in a scale ranging from 0 to 4. The following tables show the aggregated results provided by participants at the end of the study. In particular, Table 1 reports the mean score for the core dimensions of player experience, as measured by GEQ.

Table 1. GEQ core module scores

Dimension	Mean score
Competence	2.81
Immersion	2.34
Flow	2.07
Tension/Annoyance	0.12
Challenge	1.63
Negative affect	0.79
Positive affect	3.24

According to the results, the interaction mechanics that were designed and developed, are considered as intuitive by users. Besides, they contribute to a positive player experience and immersion perception. Table 2 reports the mean score for the post-game dimensions of player experience, as measured by GEQ.

Table 2. GEQ post-game module scores

Dimension	Mean score
Positive experience	1.53
Negative experience	0.79
Tiredness	0.31
Returning to reality	0.78

Regarding the post-game dimensions, the experience is perceived as fairly positive by users. Finally, Table 3 reports the mean score for additional measures considering user perception of the developed implicit interaction mechanics in the game.

Table 3. Perception of implicit interaction mechanics

Dimension	Mean score
The interactions were engaging	3.41
The interactions were immersive	3.38
The interactions were natural	2.91
The interactions were useful	2.76

Open Comments. Broadly speaking, the sensation of users after interacting with the visual novel was fairly positive. In particular, most of the implicit interaction mechanisms provide cues to increase player engagement and immersion with the environment, which complements the narrative and game flow. Therefore, according to the opinion of evaluators, the developed implicit mechanics provide a clear purpose and ease the interaction with the game elements.

6   Conclusion

In this paper we propose a set of abstract implicit interaction mechanics, which can be instantiated in VR-controlled interactive visual novels. Using the models, we developed a video game using the Unity engine and deployed in standalone Oculus Quest VR headsets.

Regarding the formulation of the abstract models, sensory immersion in VR is one of the most critical aspects to consider, as it largely impacts player experience. In particular, implicit interaction mechanics can be adapted to address this concern. The proposed models are presented as activity diagrams or state-transition machines, which can help designers formalize implicit interactions and, therefore, develop engaging and playful experiences more easily.

In order to evaluate the perceived immersion and player experience of the prototype video game, we conducted a controlled user study in the form of a proof-of-concept. The obtained results are highly promising, highlighting the understandability and flexibility of the proposed mechanisms. Therefore, the proposed models can be effectively used as a first step for assisting in the analysis and initial phases of designing implicit interaction mechanics.

References

1. Baptista, G., Oliveira, T.: Gamification and serious games: a literature meta-analysis and integrative model. Comput. Hum. Behav. **92**, 306–315 (2019). https://doi.org/10.1016/j.chb.2018.11.030
2. Dawson, J.D.: A discussion of immersion in human computer interaction: the immersion model of user experience. Ph.D. thesis, Newcastle University, Newcastle upon Tyne, UK (2017). http://ethos.bl.uk/OrderDetails.do?uin=uk.bl.ethos.728321
3. IJsselsteijn, W., de Kort, Y., Poels, K.: The game experience questionnaire. Technische Universiteit Eindhoven (2013)
4. Ju, W.: The Design of Implicit Interactions. Synthesis Lectures on Human-Centered Informatics. Morgan & Claypool Publishers (2015). https://doi.org/10.2200/S00619ED1V01Y201412HCI028
5. Kleinman, E., Caro, K., Zhu, J.: From immersion to metagaming: understanding rewind mechanics in interactive storytelling. Entertain. Comput. **33**, 100322 (2020). https://doi.org/10.1016/j.entcom.2019.100322
6. LaValle, S.M.: Virtual Reality. Cambridge University Press (2020). http://vr.cs.uiuc.edu/
7. Salanitri, D.: Trust in virtual reality. Ph.D. thesis, University of Nottingham, UK (2018). http://ethos.bl.uk/OrderDetails.do?uin=uk.bl.ethos.748521

8. Schmidt, A.: Implicit human computer interaction through context. Pers. Ubiquit. Comput. **4**(2/3), 191–199 (2000). https://doi.org/10.1007/BF01324126

9. Serim, B., Jacucci, G.: Explicating "implicit interaction": an examination of the concept and challenges for research. In: Proceedings of the 2019 CHI Conference on Human Factors in Computing Systems, CHI 2019, pp. 1–16. Association for Computing Machinery, New York (2019). https://doi.org/10.1145/3290605.3300647

LegionARius - Beyond Limes

David A. Plecher(✉)(iD), Andreas Wohlschlager, Christian Eichhorn,
and Gudrun Klinker

Chair for Computer Aided Medical Procedures and Augmented Reality,
The Technical University of Munich, Munich, Germany
{plecher,klinker}@in.tum.de,
{andreas.wohlschlager,christian.eichhorn}@tum.de

Abstract. *LegionARius* is a real-time strategy game using Augmented
Reality (AR) to let players experience Roman and Germanic history in
their own home. Being rooted in the tradition of Serious Games (SG),
LegionARius aims at providing historically accurate knowledge about
ancient everyday life in an entertaining manner. The players have to
decide the destiny of a Roman cohort or a Germanic tribe living alongside
the fortifications of Limes during the second century AD. As Roman
commander or chief of a Germanic tribe they build, produce, trade and
use their environment to choose a path between peaceful coexistence and
war. With the help of AR the player can view and inspect the historically
accurate 3D models of Roman or Germanic buildings. In addition, the
player gets to know the historical context and background in a playful
way. This knowledge is not only expanded in the course of the game, but
is also a key element for success.

Keywords: Serious games · Augmented Reality · Serious AR game ·
Roman history · Limes · Latin · Historical

1 Introduction

In this paper we present the Serious AR-Game *LegionARius*. *Serious games* (SG)
are "digital games created with the intention to entertain and to achieve at least
one additional goal" [4], which in our case is knowledge transfer. We develop this
mobile educational application for students who want to learn about Roman-
Germanic history. It aims at providing insights about the daily life on both sides
of *Limes*, hence the construction and maintenance of Roman military camps
and the establishment of a Germanic settlements in the provinces north of the
Alps. We use *Augmented Reality* (AR) to bring Roman military buildings and
Germanic dwellings back to life, in a highly engaging way for the user. We base
our game design on the instructional ARCS-model developed by John Keller [7],
which includes four strategies to elicit and maintain motivation: attention, relevance, confidence, and satisfaction (ARCS).

LegionARius plays during the second century AD. In the year 15 AD, Roman
armies initially crossed the Alps in order to occupy considerable parts of today's

X. Fang (Ed.): HCII 2022, LNCS 13334, pp. 618–636, 2022.
https://doi.org/10.1007/978-3-031-05637-6_40

territory of Bavaria. Before the first half of the first century, these areas were incorporated as province *Raetia* into the Roman Empire. From the late first century on, the Romans established a permanent occupation of the territory. These troops lived in military camps, constructed by themselves, which differed considerably in size, the degree of fortification, camp internal infrastructure and the number of accommodated soldiers. During the second century AD the Romans started to fortify the northern border of the empire against the "Barbarians" in the north. They tried to protect it with watchtowers, earth banks, ditches, wooden palisades and stone walls. This so-called *Limes* (lat. path, border) was more than a military bulwark. It was permeable and flexible, intended to control people and goods crossing it in both directions. On the other side of *Limes* the Germanic tribes lived in their settlements comprising multiple long-houses (for families and livestock), grain silos, craftsman's facilities, meadows for grazing cattle and cultivated fields. In contrast to the Romans, these tribes produced their food on their own and through this had a logistical advantage. If uniting the Germanic clans were able to outnumber the Roman "occupying" forces. This is why Roman diplomacy tried to divide the clans to their own advantage.

Our goal is to examine which learning outcomes can be achieved by this modern educational approach of game-based learning and which general impact AR constitutes. Due to the Covid-19 pandemic and *LegionARius'* multi-player character, we couldn't carry out a survey yet, but plan to do so if circumstances will allow us to do so again. After this introduction we will give an overview of related work and a framework for the characterisation of SG, used to characterise *LegionARius*. In the following section we present details on the game itself. Finally, we will describe our vision for the final work and evaluation planned for the near future.

2 Related Work

2.1 Serious Games in the Cultural Sector

Christopoulos et al. use Virtual Reality (VR) and story-telling techniques to engage visitors of a museum in the ancient battle between the Greeks and the Persians at Thermopylae [2]. Based on the historical event, the authors aim at providing context to the battle and the battle's history itself as well as to point out cultural differences between the combatants. They try to accomplish the learning goals, by providing the player with an interactive game. The player visits the battle camps of the two parties, helping important officers to find and apply equipment and weapons. The evaluation took place in the form of observations during and semi-guided interviews after the visit. The persons questioned were all children in the age from nine to twelve. Questions about historical details could be answered mostly correctly, even those mentioned late during the virtual camp visits, which indicates high attention levels throughout the tour.

Martínez et al. try to reawaken a Roman villa in the Spanish city of Valladolid with the help of AR and integrated mini-games [10]. The authors created a virtual reconstruction of the building. The archaeological site, however, is still covered by a town garden. They intend to enhance the understanding of the remote past through the context, delivered by the interactive application, based on the present outline of the city. Intervening the virtual with the real world (using AR), users can even explore the villa's virtually reconstructed interior, as it could have looked like. Localisation and tracking are realised via GPS and the mobile devices' sensors. The authors try to improve the user experience by integrating components of SG. They let the user solve puzzles and answer questions, perform tasks, and offer complementing multimedia content. Martínez et al. did not carry out any evaluation of the potentially achieved learning success.

Djaouti et al. create a SG on the occasion of the 100th anniversary of the prehistoric *Gargas caves'* discovery [3]. The game can be played on a computer with a mouse, which can be used to reveal and trace rock engraving pictures from the cave. The engravings have to be discovered in a limited amount of time, adding a game element to the task. The authors also intend to provide the player with a notion of the difficulty, which real scientists experienced while exploring the cave.

HieroQuest [18] is a SG which deals with the intangible cultural heritage of the ancient Egyptians. Similar to an escape game, the player has to solve puzzles to find the way out of an Egyptian temple. In each room the player discovers new hieroglyphs, which he has to use to open the doors. This is done by assigning the transliterations to the hieroglyphs on the doors. In this way the player gets a basic knowledge of Egyptian hieroglyphs.

2.2 Framework for the Characterisation of Serious Games

Mortara et al. [11] contrast physical or *tangible* cultural heritage (e.g. historic sites, buildings, monuments, documents, etc.) with *intangible* cultural heritage (e.g. social values and traditions, customs, religious belief, language etc.), and state that the latter is "[...] difficult to preserve, and [...] SGs have the potential to maintain and communicate effectively, especially this immaterial legacy" [11]. They propose a characterisation of SGs in the cultural sector according to several characteristics: the educational objectives of the game, its genre and the context of use. After presenting some details on the framework proposed by Mortara et al. [11], we will use this characterisation scheme for SG in the cultural sector to analyse *LegionARius* according to its *educational objectives*, its *genre* and *context of use*. Table 1 takes the graphical illustration of the characterisation taxonomy presented in this section and applies a heat-map-like colourisation to it, indicating the classification of *LegionARius*.

Cultural awareness especially deals with immaterial heritage, like traditions, rules of behaviour and the history of a society. SGs can unite "tangible" and "intangible" elements, creating an extensive, and compelling experience, in which the player, for instance, can encounter not only places at a certain point of time but also characteristic sounds, as well as habits and religious events. Games in the category of *historical reconstruction* are focused on historic events, periods or processes, but can be also interwoven with archaeology, art and politics of that particular time. When only written records are the last witnesses of historical events, and physical relics do not exist anymore, SGs can show their strength. Then reconstructing not only the physical setting, but e.g. sounds, language and habits, let the player fully immerse into the historic event, and deliver information in a much more convincing way, enabling persisting knowledge. The games in the last category of educational objectives, *heritage awareness*, can be divided into *architectural/natural* and *artistic/archaeologic heritage awareness games*. The games in the first sub-category try to present realistic reconstructions of real places to convince the player of the importance of the architecture, art or nature prevalent in that particular site. Games in the second sub-category deal with a society's physical artefacts and enable the player to gain knowledge about history, art and archaeology.

The authors structure their analysis along a taxonomy consisting of the following categories: *cultural awareness, historical reconstruction, heritage awareness* comprising *artistic/archaeological heritage* and *architectural/natural heritage*.

Concerning *cultural awareness*, which is especially focused on immaterial heritage, *LegionARius* confronts the player with words from the Latin language, essential for the game. This can be terms describing parts or institutions of the military camp, places and buildings in the camp, food names and lastly military ranks. In addition, the daily habits and routines of life and service in the military, as well as spiritual beliefs, are illustrated, which essentially can be subsumed under "rules of behaviour in a society". Concluding we may say, that *LegionARius* does not focus on the aspect of cultural awareness, but aims at delivering a reasonable portion of immaterial Roman heritage from military and non-military perspective.

When it comes to the sub-category of *historical reconstruction*, it seems clear, that one of *LegionARius* main learning objectives can be found here. It intends to faithfully reconstruct the establishment and management of a legionary fortress in the Germanic lands, based on scientific findings. In the course of the game, the erected camp has to be adapted according to its development stage. Consequently, *historical reconstruction* is one of the main educational objectives of *LegionARrius*.

Architectural and natural heritage awareness are a minor part of *LegionARius*. Apart from historical buildings, it does yet not fully reconstruct the natural environment of the specific time, which however plays a key role in many ways. This concerns especially the erection of wells for water supply, mining of raw materials (for now only present in the menu) as well as the adaption of the camp layout to the landscape surrounding it. In comparison *LegionARius* aims at delivering *artistic and archaeological heritage awareness* to a somewhat greater extent. It tries to offer reconstructions of historical Roman military buildings, which therefore refers to architectural and in some degree also artistic aspects. Much of the presented content, like buildings, fortifications as well as artefacts of the legionaries daily life are based on archaeological results.

SGs make use of many different game genres, each of which should be applied in a specific scenario, achieving the best learning experience for the player.

According to the authors *action games*, though one of the most popular genres targeted at entertainment, is the least occurring genre amongst SGs. Its classic mechanics, grounding in quick reactions to game events, are not necessarily suitable for transferring knowledge. However, in order to promote the player's engagement, the integration of action-game-like elements in the form of sub-tasks or mini-games, Mortara et al. consider possible. *Strategy games* offer a gaming experience, which builds on planing and careful thinking. "However, this genre is suitable to raise awareness about the complexity of tactical thinking rather than actually teach or train such skill" [11]. Under the genre of *simulation games* the authors identified solely so-called *construction and management simulations*, which let the player build and maintain control over entities under resource constraints. This genre lets the player take the position of another person, experiencing difficult decisions and recognise the results of her/his actions. *Trivia games* present questions to be guessed by the player, and offer extra knowledge through the presented sample answers. In *puzzle games* it is all about solving riddles. The authors state, that besides online- and static in-museum games, all of the examined SGs for architectural/natural heritage belong to this category. Concerning the examined SGs *2D point-and-click adventures* and *3D real-time adventures* comprise the category of *adventure games*. Here puzzles have to be solved by combining information or utilising objects originating from different sources. They are "[...] particularly suited to implement the 'learning by doing' approach, [...] where the player learns by constructing knowledge while doing a meaningful activity. In this approach to education the learner [...] actively constructs new knowledge by finding information in the game, understanding it and then applying the new knowledge to fulfil tasks" [11].

Extensive parts of *LegionARius* can be clearly headlined *construction and management simulation* game, which are "[...] based on building, expanding or managing [historical] [...] communities or activities with limited resources" [11]. The player supervises the positioning of buildings and their modification, depending on constrained human labour, raw materials and food supply. Besides, the game makes also use of the *role-playing game* genre. If it comes to the actual camp management, the player experiences actively, by slipping into different roles of responsible servicemen and province officials, living their first-person difficulties. All this decision-making needs to be based on "[...] careful and skilful thinking and planning in order to achieve victory" [11] (in our case a higher score). Therefore *LegionARius* also borrows from the *strategy game* genre.

SGs can be also categorised by the context in which they are being used. Relating to this the authors distinguish *static set-up in public space*, *cultural tourism and augmented visit* as well as *stand-alone applications consumed at home or at school*. Games played in public space (e.g. a museum) have to deal with multiple constraints concerning space, time, number of players, suitability, and complexity. Here it should be possible that a considerably large number of visitors, each fulfilling vastly different prerequisites, when it comes to gaming experience and cognitive capabilities, can enter and/or leave the game in a short period. Players in private space have more time to acquaint with the specific

Table 1. Characterisation taxonomy for serious games with heat map indicating the classification of LegionARius (according to [11])

Learning Objectives		Game Genre	Context of Use
Cultural Awareness		Action Game	static set-up in public space
		Strategy Game	
Historical Reconstruction		Simulation Game	cultural tourism and augmented visit
		Role-Playing Adventure Game	
Artistic and Archeological Heritage Awareness	Architectural and Natural Heritage Awareness	Trivia Game	stand alone application consumed at home or at school
		Puzzle Game	
		Casual Game	
		Adventure Game	

game mechanics and therefore such games can be more complex. When applying SGs at school formal criteria like national curricular have to be taken into consideration as well as the age of the students. Besides games played in the public-static or at-home setting, there are mobile games augmenting cities, natural landscapes and archaeological sites, delivering complementing information along the player's way. The unbroken popularity of smartphones ensures, that e.g. exhibition visitors are ready to play and museums do not have to invest in additional hardware. Enriching the real tour with the virtual content, this kind of SG can have a profound influence on the visiting experience and through this on knowledge acquisition.

LegionARius is to be played on mobile devices, which add the augmented game content to the player's real environment. Therefore it is very possible that the game could be played as virtual experience before entering a museum, an exhibition or an archaeological excavation site - "[...] augment[ing] a real experience [...] with [...] cultural content encountered along their tour [...]", helping the visitor "[...] understanding and engaging more in a following real visit" [11]. Albeit to a lesser extent, *LegionARius* can be associated with the category of *cultural tourism and augmented visit. LegionARius* can be surely conceived a *stand alone application consumed at home or at school.* Intending the game for this use case, of course, would require the adherence of the historical content to national or regional curricula and adaption to the desired student level or age. Furthermore, the use of didactic and pedagogical theories during the creation of *LegionARius*, let it in principle be predestined for the use in the education sector. However, this is the first version of the game, a deeper didactic and pedagogical focus for later versions would be worth striving for.

Fig. 1. Screenshot of *LegionARius'* marker-based game-play - the Roman castrum at day

2.3   Serious Games Using Augmented Reality

In this section, we take a look at SG, that use AR in order to transfer knowledge to the player. AR is already being used in a variety of serious applications that deal with cultural heritage [13,17,20,21].

An example of a Serious AR-Game on the topic of cultural heritage, which also uses elements of classic board games is *Oppidum* [15]. This term initially described a fortified settlement of the Celts during the Iron Age. The game aims at providing knowledge about the Celts, while building a small Celtic village. In-game tasks and quizzes provide a competitive setting, which motivates the players to obtain the knowledge needed to gain so-called *Victory Points*. Beyond that, the player can develop new technologies, gather rune stones and explore her/his village. Finally, the players can challenge each other with so-called *Quiz Wars* and strive for victory.

Another SG in this category is *MathBuilder* [24], a collaborative AR game for the elementary school math classroom. Students play the game in teams, having the goal to erect buildings in an imaginative city. Each member of the group takes on another role (e.g. bricklayer, carpenter or painter) and tries to solve individual exercises. If answered correctly, she/he is rewarded with building materials specific to and needed for his role. After that, the students have to tackle more difficult group tasks, which require discussion between the students in order to erect the group's buildings finally.

Pathomon [23] is a social SG using AR, which involves teamwork by the players in order to reach their common goal, namely eradicating viruses in their environment, while acquiring knowledge about them. During the game, the players (taking the role of young scientists) have to find the right ingredients for producing antidotes against a particular virus. However, killing one of its kind, at a specific real-world location, does not eradicate the virus entirely. Some resistant viruses require team building to share knowledge about them and the collected ingredients for the antidotes. Experience points allow the players to develop more sophisticated antidotes over time.

On the Trail of Jack the Ripper [19] deals with the historical facts surrounding Jack the Ripper and the Whitechapel murders of 1888. AR is used to take players to the crime scenes in an immersive way and allow them to search for clues themselves. In the same manner, original sources are presented or letters handwritten by Jack the Ripper are made readable through an augmented printed form.

The last example is *DragonTale* [14]. This game teaches basic knowledge about Japanese Kanji. The player follows the story of a young girl and a little dragon. Kanjis can be detected in the game world and are used to solve riddles or to fight against enemies. One episode does also integrate AR. The goal is to build compound words by combining kanjis. Each kanji symbolizes a marker, so a 3D model representing the corresponding meaning is augmented on top of it.

2.4   Serious Games About Roman Imperial History

Ludus Magnus [16] is an open world SG for learning the Latin language. In contrast to many other SGs, special emphasis was put on the graphics. The students play as a young Marcomanne, that is enslaved by the Romans and has only one chance to free himself by becoming the best gladiator in the town. Along the story, the players learn the necessary fighting techniques (game element) of the different types of gladiators and the associated Latin terms and grammatical forms (learning element).

The puzzle adventure *Rome in Danger* is about an organisation of time-travelling investigators, that strive to defend the integrity of history [8]. The SG's primary audience are children in the age of between 11 and 14 years. Playing an agent of the so-called "Time Knights", they have to defend history (by solving history-related puzzles) against a villain from the future, called "Agent X", striving to change it.

The multi-player SG *The Siege of Syracuse* presents the siege of the Roman army of the Hellenistic city of Syracuse 212 BC [1]. It is a game for children between 9 and 15 years. Two players can choose between the Roman general Marcellus and Hippocrates from Syracuse. Their task is to control different types of war machines, to either attack (steering Roman siege ships) or defend the city walls. The game provides a presentation of the battle of Syracuse, information about Archimede's life and his inventions for defending the city.

In *Roma Nova*, 11 to 14 year old children can learn about Roman history in an interactive way [12]. The SG is based on a detailed 3D model of ancient Rome, developed during the *Rome Reborn* project [5], which contains hundreds of buildings. The player can move freely across the city and interact with authentic Roman characters. Talking to these characters or observing them during their daily business, the children gain knowledge about Roman history. Interactions with the conversational agents walking by, are based on question-answer-dialogues, which provide knowledge about imperial history. Knowledge can be transmitted in the shape of anecdotes presented as a personal story of the virtual Romans. Therefore keywords in these dialogues are automatically linked to definitions and explained, using modern terminology.

3 Near and Beyond Limes - Establishing Roman Military Camps and Germanic Settlements

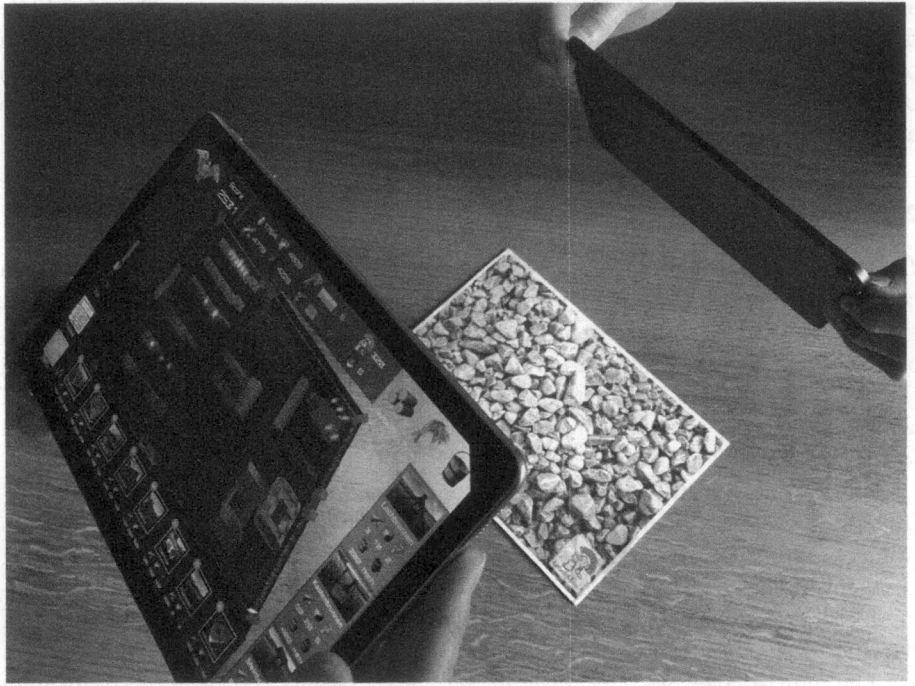

Fig. 2. Game-play: ground plane marker and two players

LegionARius is being developed using the Unity[1] cross-platform game engine. For now, all augmented content is handled using the Vuforia Engine[2]. The game is played on a marker or image target (see Figs. 1 and 2) that hosts a virtual ground plane on which camp buildings can be placed and manipulated via touch.

---

[1] https://unity.com (last access 02/10/22).
[2] https://developer.vuforia.com (last access 02/10/22).

We create low-poly, but historically accurate 3D models based on archaeological findings. While a prototype about the erection of a Roman military camp already exists, the part about the establishment of a Germanic settlement is currently still in development. Some of the knowledge provided about the historical buildings is being transferred via game-play, other information in the form of audio texts (see Fig. 3). The Roman game part is divided into two chapters:

Chapter I deals with the first development stage of every Roman military camp, the so-called field or marching camp. The player can activate overlays, which augment the field with coloured sections, carrying their respective Latin names, in order to place tents for their soldiers in the appropriate camp section and erect defensive earth walls around the camp. When later placing buildings, the player can use these camp sections to check if she/he has chosen the historically correct place in the camp. Wrongly placed buildings are dyed in red.

Fig. 3. Audio information on Roman grain silo *horreum*

Chapter II is about the so-called *castrum* (see Fig. 1), the Roman military camp designed for longer periods of time. The players have to take care of the water supply for the legionaries and can build wells with different deprecation rates and production volumes. In addition, constant food supply via the so-called *negotiatores* merchants has to be maintained. Before starting to erect camp buildings and fortifications, raw materials have to be extracted. Free legionaries can be assigned to the lumberjack's hut, the sawmill, the quarry and the lime kiln. Working legionaries consume more calories and water, which is one of the challenges the player is confronted with. The consumed amount is based on findings of historical sciences and determined in real-time for every soldier according to his workload. The legionaries' consumption is displayed to the user in litres of water and in kilos of grain, to ensure readable measures. Enriching visuals like smoking chimneys, lighting and fires at night as well as steam escaping the thermal baths, are coordinated by a day and night cycle.

Fig. 4. Low-poly 3D-model of Limes watchtower in last expansion phase

Finally, we decided to use AR to present our content to the player to leverage a few advantages unique to this technology. It is able to melt together the player's close environment with the game content, without locking out reality completely. What's more, we think that the relation between the user and the 3D-content, conceived via a portable device, gives an feeling of interaction, more *real* than a traditional computer game ever could convey. This goes for the direct manipulation of augmented game objects on the players' real desk, by just touching them through the display with their fingers. Here the immediate feedback of the virtual and animated content also plays a key role, as well as additional information shown next to the augmented objects.

In addition, we created the foundation-stone for the Limes fortifications, the watch towers, which can be erected by the player's deciding to take the Roman's side. There will be the possibility throughout the game, to customise and extend buildings. Therefore, we here also created several expansion stages for the watch towers (see Fig. 4). Starting from simple wooden scaffolding towers, the players can upgrade over half-timbered to stone towers.

Fig. 5. Look into the interior of an historically accurate 3D-model, based on archaeological excavations of a Germanic Longhouse in Feddersen Wierde, which the players are going to explore in Augmented Reality during the game.

In comparison to the Romans, historical sources on Germanic tribes are rather limited. In this initial stage of development, we rest the reproduction of the Games' Germanic buildings on archaeological excavations near Feddersen Wierde [6]. There it was possible to reconstruct the history of a whole antique Germanic peasant village, over a period of about 500 years (starting 50 B.C). As a step up from the first version of the game, we also tried to not only reconstruct the buildings facades, but also their interior. Playing the AR-version of *LegionARius*, it will be possible to take a look inside each building by only coming closer to the models with the gaming device (see Fig. 5).

The Germanic settlers lived in houses, which were approximately 20 m long, 5–6 m broad more than 2.4 m high. In comparison to the Romans, they particularly used transient building materials, which resulted in the need to rebuild their dwellings after one or two generations. This relatively simple construction method (e.g. there were no nails needed) had also advantages, because it enabled them to build their houses over a time frame of a few weeks only. The 1.5 high walls were made from widow or hazel rods winded around poles rammed into the ground. Upright oaken posts were fixed into holes into the soil, which were prone to draw humidity from the ground and rot over time. These wooden pillars carried the roof truss, which was covered with a thatch roof. The peasant family lived together with its livestock in the same building. The rear part of the dwelling was meant for the barn accommodating about 20 cows. The settlers prepared the ground inside the buildings with dried manure, which protects them from ground water and cold.

Fig. 6. Germanic long-stack charcoal kiln for producing the main wood-based fuel used for baking clay (for pottery), melting of bronze or working on iron ore.

In order to leave the Germanic dwellings there were 3 entrances, one on both long sides and another one on rear short side leading into the barn. The threshold was anchored with wooden nails into the ground and on both sides, poles bordering the low doors. Around the houses the inhabitants made ditches into which manure channels flowed directly from the barns. The settlers also build drainage ditches, fences and roads between the houses. In order to illustrate these settlements, we created a first prototype 3D-model of the Germanic settlement to see the dwellings in context of the landscape, their surroundings and neighbouring houses (see Figs. 6 and 7).

We are striving to also deepen the economic cycles encountered during the game. An example for this kind of extension of the gaming experience is the Germanic metalworking and craftsmanship, which could be verified during the archaeological excavations cited above. The main fuel used by the Germanic tribes was charcoal, which could be produced by themselves from wood accessible anywhere. In principle there are different ways to build charcoal kilns. In *LegionARius* players will be able to produce charcoal using a long stack. Charcoal was for example used for making pottery by baking clay in kilns with round stone cupola. Another use case was the working on iron ore and melting of bronze.

4 Future Work and Evaluation

We are currently working on some enhancements to the game concerning technical, immersion- and content-related issues. Beyond that we plan to carry out a survey, in which we want to reveal the long-term learning effects of the game.

4.1 Four Pillars of Immersion

In order to provide knowledge in an immersive setting, we want the players to be engaged with the historical content as much as possible. The four pillars we try to rest the player's attention upon are storytelling, recent AR technology, social interactions and identification through individualisation.

Story Telling: First, we want to utilise story telling. Gradually, the player will be introduced to different everyday issues, that she/he has to cope with. These tasks will be presented to the player by different characters, representing different ranks in the Roman army and civil provincial administration. Players opting for fulfilling the role of the tribal chief, will face different challenges when cultivating crops, building houses for their families and livestock, fostering diplomatic relations with other clans and trading goods, the tribe cannot produce on its own. These challenges faced by the player, will be also presented by different members of the Germanic community, each fulfilling a special role in the rural society.

Low-Poly Graphics and Tracking: In addition, we accompany the story telling with visually pleasing stylised graphics presented to the players via AR. In order to overcome the known limitations of the so-far used marker-based approach, we use other tracking techniques to integrate the player's environment into the game and to enable new ways of interaction with the augmented content. Emphasize can be placed on involving SLAM-based AR functionality for mobile devices. In this scenario markers don't need to be printed beforehand and the interaction with virtual content can become more diverse. In a previous project we developed EnvSLAM, where a SLAM algorithm is combined with a neural network which allows the application to get an understanding of the real environment through a segmentation neural network [9]. The game concept LegionARius could profit from letting virtual content interact with surrounding surfaces or even objects. Additionally, such functionality could be used in the museum to connect the virtual experience with the physical one. Another possibility would be to use the LiDAR scanner integrated in Apple's new iPad Pro. This enables players to literally touch history with their fingertips.

Fig. 7. 3D-Model of Germanic grain silo in last expansion phase, erected on wooden stilts in order to protect the supplies from pests, floods and moisture.

Social Interactions: Moreover, a big part of the player's experience will also rely on social interactions with her/his fellow players. Although all contestants will be occupied with their very own challenges during the game, there will open up multiple possibilities to forge alliances in order to overcome those difficulties together or fight each other in competition for limited resources. We strive to provide a setting in which the players expose human traits like behaving loyal or betraying each other to reach their goals. Actors in ancient times also had to operate in such unstable environments of fragile and changing alliances, which will be reflected by interactions among the players.

Identification Through Customization: Lastly, we want to enrich the player's experience by providing the possibility of customisation and individualisation. The players will not only have the possibility to adjust their camp or village to their liking, but also influence the development of single individuals in their community by training and education. Fostering certain characteristics and capabilities of her/his subordinates is not an end in itself, but can pay off in different ways like the production of special goods or deciding a battle already given up as lost. We expect that this helps her/him to identify with the soldiers or tribe, create intrinsic satisfaction (the "S" in the ARCS-model, meaning that people "feel good about their accomplishments" (Keller 1987, p. 6)) and improve the learning outcomes.

4.2   Sub-system Introduction and Extension

To create this immersive experience we are going to extend already existing and build new sub-systems on top, the player interacts with. These gameplay mechanics let the player face historical events, mine raw materials and erect buildings, produce goods and trade them, supply food and water to her/his subordinates as well as pursuing goals by applying diplomacy or force.

Food and Water Supply Cycle: In order to omit hunger, rebellion and epidemics, the most important part of the players efforts is to keep her/his people fed and supply a sufficient amount of liquids. Therefore, understanding the influence of weather on cultivation, food production techniques, its trade and the possibilities of drinking water acquisition are at the core of the knowledge the game provides. Here, strategic planning and close attention by the player are important, because critical shortages in this area lead to an early end of the game. Challenges like these can in *LegionARius* be overcome by "ability and effort rather than good luck" [4] and promote therefore confidence in success (the "C" in the ARCS-model).

Historic Events System: We are not only aiming at telling histories about the average ancient people's everyday life. In addition we want to show how big historical events influenced these individuals in peripheral regions of the Roman empire. In order to keep attention levels high (the "A" in the ARCS-model), a "widely accepted prerequisite of information processing" [4], we introduce a *historic event system.* The latter is used to interweave the big history on the imperial level with the northern provinces and triggers certain historical events according to the state of the game. The resulting effects on the player's situation will then force her/him to search for a practical solution and with it, they will implicitly delve into the historic event itself and its immediate and implicit effects.

Raw Materials Cycle and Construction System: Before constructing the Roman military camp or the Germanic settlement respectively, both parties need to extract a variety of raw materials. Here the player has to deal with the refinement and proper composition of ancient building materials to accomplish his goals. This ensures that the relevance (the "R" in the ARCS-model) of the provided information is clear and the player is "able to immediately recognize the functional significance of ... [the respective] in-game activity" [4]. Inevitably, she/he not only gets to know typical buildings and their purpose, but also the building materials used by the Romans and Germanic tribes to construct them. When the specific buildings are finally erected, side quests will be introduced to the player, which deepen the understanding and functioning of certain facilities.

Production and Trade Cycle: Thereafter, the players can start to use raw materials also for the production of goods. These can then be used and consumed by themselves or traded for products the respective parties are not able to produce on their own. Selling or exchanging goods can increase the budget of the community or enhance quality of life of the individuals. Therefore it constitutes an incentive for the player to pay attention to the production processes, the good's characteristics and their tradability on the market.

Diplomacy System and Battle Mode: Diplomacy was an extremely important way of ensuring supplies and security on both sides of Limes. The Germanic tribes had the advantage of growing their own food and preponderate when being united. That's why the Romans often tried to divide the tribes, by offering presents and goods to some and fighting others. If the players' diplomatic efforts should not bear fruits, they can decide for violence as measure of last resort and enter the so-called *battle mode*. This will be a 2D-top-down battle simulation in which the players can steer their soldiers and warriors to form historically accurate battle formations and attack their enemies by using the specific landscape surrounding them.

4.3 Future Evaluation

Due to the fact, that *LegionARius* is a multi-player game expecting up to four players to sit around a table and the obvious restrictions imposed on us by the Covid-19 pandemic, we were not able to carry out a survey yet. A remote survey was not possible either, because we then would loose the "laboratory conditions", if not being able to reliably monitor the execution of the experiment.

Generally, we are interested in answering two major questions with *LegionARius*: First, we want to examine the long-term learning effects, which can be achieved by such a serious learning game. Second, we will shed some light on the question, if AR indeed has any influence on the learning outcomes or if it solely impacts visuals and aesthetics of the game.

In order to determine the general learning outcomes of *LegionARius*, we want to provide the players with several questionnaires. There will be a pre-game-questionnaire asking for some basic data like gender, age, previous experiences with AR, interest in history, prior knowledge about the topic and gaming habits. A post-game-questionnaire is going to incorporate the so-called *Game Experience Questionnaire*, which "[...] allows researchers to obtain a reliable and valid indication of participants' subjective experiences associated with digital game-play" [22]. Additionally, it contains knowledge-related questions, which could be acquired during the game. In order to determine the long-term learning effects of *LegionARius*, we strive to question the same group of people after a certain amount of time again and compare the results between the two questioning rounds.

Finally, we will try to answer the question on learning impacts of AR by providing two versions of the game to the players. One group of players will have the chance to play a 2D isometric-top-down version of *LegionARius*, which will be based on the same game mechanics as the AR-version. This game will be presented as a two-dimensional playing experience, whereas the original title will make use of the possibilities offered by AR.

References

1. Christopoulos, D., Gaitatzes, A.: Multimodal interfaces for educational virtual environments. In: PCI 2009–13th Panhellenic Conference on Informatics, pp. 197–201 (2009)

2. Christopoulos, D., Mavridis, P., Andreadis, A., Karigiannis, J.: The ancient olympic games: being part of the experience. In: Proceedings of VS-Games (2011)
3. Djaouti, D., Alavrez, J., Rampenoux, O., Charvillat, V., Jessel, J.: Serious games & cultural heritage: a case study of prehistoric caves. In: Proceedings of 15th International Conference on Virtual Systems and Multimedia (VSMM 2009). IEEE Computer Society, Washington DC, pp. 221–226 (2009)
4. Dörner, R., Göbel, S., Effelsberg, W., Wiemeyer, J.: Serious Games - Foundations, Concepts and Practice. Springer, Heidelberg (2016). https://doi.org/10.1007/978-3-319-40612-1
5. Guidi, G., Frischer, B., Lucenti, I.: Rome reborn - virtualizing the ancient imperial Rome. In: International Archives of the Photogrammetry, Remote Sensing and Spatial Information Sciences - ISPRS Archives, vol. 36 (2007)
6. Haarnagel, W.: Die Grabung Feddersen Wierde: Methode, Hausbau, Siedlungsund Wirtschaftsformen sowie Sozialstruktur. F. Steiner (1979)
7. Keller, J.M.: Motivational Design for Learning and Performance: The ARCS Model Approach. Springer, Boston (2010). https://doi.org/10.1007/978-1-4419-1250-3
8. Learning, C.: Rome in danger, September 2008. sgschallenge.com/rome-in-danger/. Accessed 02 Oct 2022
9. Marchesi, G., Eichhorn, C., Plecher, D.A., Itoh, Y., Klinker, G.: EnvSLAM: combining SLAM systems and neural networks to improve the environment fusion in AR applications. ISPRS Int. J. Geo Inf. **10**(11), 772 (2021)
10. Martínez, J., Álvarez, S., Finat, J., Delgado, F., Finat, J.: Augmented reality to preserve hidden vestiges in historical cities. a case study. In: 3D Virtual Reconstruction and Visualization of Complex Architectures (2015). https://doi.org/10.5194/isprsarchives-XL-5-W4-61-2015
11. Mortara, M., Catalano, C., Bellotti, F., Fiucci, G., Houry-Panchetti, M., Petridis, P.: Learning cultural heritage by serious games. J. Cult. Herit. **15**(3), 318–325 (2014)
12. Panzoli, D., Peters, C., Dunwell, I., Sanchez, S.: A level of interaction framework for exploratory learning with characters in virtual environments. Stud. Comput. Intell. **321**, 123–143 (2010)
13. Pedersen, I., Gale, N., Mirza-Babaei, P., Reid, S.: More than meets the eye: the benefits of augmented reality and holographic displays for digital cultural heritage. J. Comput. Cult. Heritage (JOCCH) **10**(2), 1–15 (2017)
14. Plecher, D.A., Eichhorn, C., Kindl, J., Kreisig, S., Wintergerst, M., Klinker, G.: Dragon tale -a serious game for learning Japanese Kanji. In: Proceedings of the 2018 Annual Symposium on Computer-Human Interaction in Play Companion Extended Abstracts, pp. 577–583 (2018)
15. Plecher, D.A., Eichhorn, C., Köhler, A., Klinker, G.: Oppidum - a serious-AR-game about celtic life and history. In: Liapis, A., Yannakakis, G.N., Gentile, M., Ninaus, M. (eds.) GALA 2019. LNCS, vol. 11899, pp. 550–559. Springer, Cham (2019). https://doi.org/10.1007/978-3-030-34350-7_53
16. Plecher, D.A., Eichhorn, C., Naser, M., Klinker, G.: Ludus magnus - a serious game for learning the Latin language. In: Fang, X. (ed.) HCII 2021. LNCS, vol. 12790, pp. 51–61. Springer, Cham (2021). https://doi.org/10.1007/978-3-030-77414-1_5
17. Plecher, D.A., Eichhorn, C., Seyam, K.M., Klinker, G.: ARsinoë-learning egyptian hieroglyphs with augmented reality and machine learning. In: 2020 IEEE International Symposium on Mixed and Augmented Reality Adjunct (ISMAR-Adjunct), pp. 326–332. IEEE (2020)

18. Plecher, D.A., Herber, F., Eichhorn, C., Pongratz, A., Tanson, G., Klinker, G.: HieroQuest - a serious game for learning Egyptian hieroglyphs. Journal on Computing and Cultural Heritage (JOCCH) **13**(4), 1–20 (2020)
19. Plecher, D.A., Müller, A., Klinker, G.: On the trail of Jack the Ripper - a serious AR game about a cold case. In: GI VR / AR Workshop. Gesellschaft für Informatik e.V. (2021)
20. Plecher, D.A., Ulschmid, A., Kaiser, T., Klinker, G.: Projective augmented reality in a museum: development and evaluation of an interactive application. In: Argelaguet, F., McMahan, R., Sugimoto, M. (eds.) ICAT-EGVE 2020 - International Conference on Artificial Reality and Telexistence and Eurographics Symposium on Virtual Environments. The Eurographics Association (2020). https://doi.org/10.2312/egve.20201258
21. Plecher, D.A., Wandinger, M., Klinker, G.: Mixed reality for cultural heritage. In: 2019 IEEE Conference on Virtual Reality and 3D User Interfaces (VR), pp. 1618–1622. IEEE (2019)
22. Poels, K., de Kort, Y., IJsselsteijn, W.: FUGA-the fun of gaming: measuring the human experience of media enjoyment. Deliverable D3.3: Game Experience Questionnaire. TU Eindhoven, Eindhoven, The Netherlands (2008)
23. Rapp, D., Müller, J., Bucher, K., von Mammen, S.: Pathomon: a social augmented reality serious game. In: 10th International Conference on Virtual Worlds and Games for Serious Applications, VS-Games 2018 - Proceedings, article number 8493437 (2018). https://doi.org/10.1109/VS-Games.2018.8493437
24. van der Stappen, A., Liu, Y., Xu, J., Yu, X., Li, J., van der Spek, E.D.: Math-Builder: a collaborative AR math game for elementary school students. In: CHI PLAY 2019 Extended Abstracts: Extended Abstracts of the Annual Symposium on Computer-Human Interaction in Play Companion Extended Abstracts, pp. 731–738, October 2019. https://doi.org/10.1145/3341215.3356295

Research Status and Trends of the Gamification Design for Visually Impaired People in Virtual Reality

Shufang Tan, Wendan Huang, and Junjie Shang[✉] [iD]

Lab of Learning Sciences, Graduate School of Education, Peking University, Beijing, China
jjshang@pku.edu.cn

Abstract. This paper explores the current research status, issues, and future research trends of gamification of educational content related to spatial ability training in virtual environments for cognitive characteristics of people with visual impairment (PVI). Based on the Web of Science core collection, 29 related papers, including 20 gamification design cases, were selected and analyzed using the document content analysis method. The education content, techniques, and design in these previous work showed that: the current training tasks in gamification design mainly focus on navigation, orientation, and mobility training; sensory augmentation and sensory substitution with spatial audio and tactile interface are popular in interaction design for PVI, and it is controversial whether the information of different modalities complement each other or interfere with each other. Future research trends may include strategies of multimodal information for PVI, personalized dynamic adjustment of content and tasks, and standardized effectiveness evaluation methods.

Keywords: People with visual impairment · Gamification · Virtual environment · Spatial ability

1 Introduction

According to the World Health Organization's report, the global population of people with visual impairment (PVI) is estimated at 2.2 billion [1]. Due to the absence or limitation of vision, PVI have finite spatial ability. Spatial ability here refers to the ability to recognize, understand, remember and interact with our three-dimensional world [2]. When PVI lack spatial ability, they might experience cognitive decline, which undermines their quality of life and results in a high incidence of depression and anxiety [3].

To improve PVI's spatial ability, some educators use the traditional training method that combines tactile maps and realistic scenario training. Nevertheless, spatial ability training is often challenging because of the threats from uncertain surroundings posed in real life [4]. With the advent of virtual reality technology, patients can be immersed and educated in the diverse virtual training environment without facing unexpected danger in the physical environment. While a virtual training environment can solve the downsides

X. Fang (Ed.): HCII 2022, LNCS 13334, pp. 637–651, 2022.
https://doi.org/10.1007/978-3-031-05637-6_41

of the physical environment, the difficulty in the training process might undermine participants' motivation and result in frustration. So one of the critical issues that should not be overlooked is how to maintain the long-term learning willingness and self-efficacy of the visually impaired participants during the training in the virtual environment.

Using gamification can be helpful to this issue [5]. Gamification refers to using game design elements in non-game content [6]. But traditional gamification design in the virtual environment is not suitable for visually impaired people, because it mainly focuses on visual information and feedback, while the vision is no longer the dominant information receiving channel in this situation.

Therefore, the aim of this work was to give readers a complete, clear and concise overview of publications on the topic of gamification for PVI's spatial ability training in virtual environment. We especially focus on design cases, trying to find the commonalities and differences between them to show the research status and trends. The main research method used in this study is document content analyses. The research questions are listed below:

1. What are the most frequently gamified spatial ability training in current research?
2. In the absence of vision, what are the main interactions in these gamification designs?
3. What are the gamification goals and corresponding mechanisms in previous studies?
4. What technologies are closely related to gamification in this field?
5. What was the purpose of applying gamification in previous research? Does it work well?
6. What are the main problems with gamification in current research?
7. What is the development trend of gamification in this field?

For the research questions 1–5, the research is mainly carried out by retrieving the core literature in this field, and extracting and sorting out the content of the literature. The content analysis framework is shown in Fig. 1. Research questions 6 and 7 will be explored in the fifth section "Discussion and Conclusions" based on the completion of the research on the first five questions.

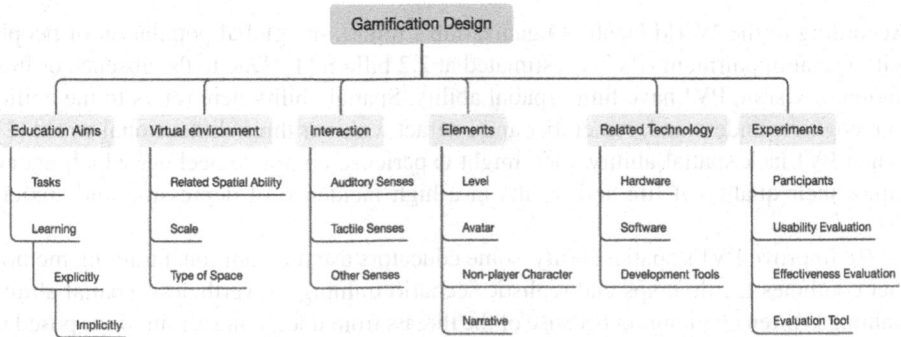

Fig. 1. The framework of document content analysis

2   Data Collection

The core collection of Web of Science was selected as the source of literature search, and the time period selected was 10 years span from January 2011 to December 2021. Taking consideration of different expressions of relative meanings, the search strategy was to use stemming and lemmatization to get literature, and then exclude the not relevant publications by checking their content. The search formula is TS = ("visually impair*" OR blind* OR "low vision") AND (space OR spatial) AND (virtual) AND (game* OR gamif*). 54 articles was obtained. 24 irrelevant articles were excluded, 1 without full text was excluded, and 29 articles were finally obtained. There are 3 review articles, 1 article about principles introduction, 1 article about a design project introduction, and 24 design research articles. As design research article is the majority type in this database, this study focuses on analyzing the research status of gamification design in multiple dimensions in 20 design cases covered by 25 design-related literatures. Details about these documents are in the appendix.

3   Results

To answer the research questions, with the framework in Fig. 1, the content in literature was analyzed according to the following dimensions: users, the theoretical basis of gamification design, scale and type of virtual environment, related spacial ability, interaction design, application of game mechanics and elements, usability and effectiveness evaluation.

3.1   Target Users and Theoretical Foundation for Gamification

Design for special groups often influences design content depending on the different categories of users. Therefore, this paper begins by analyzing the user characteristics in the studies. In terms of age, most studies do not target specific user ages, with a few targeting children and adolescents. As to the type of user's vision, in addition to gamified training systems designed exclusively for PVI, there are some that take non-visually impaired groups as users who can also use the system [7–9], trying to 'translate' between the different senses.

As far as the theoretical foundation is concerned, when the user group is visually impaired children, it is based on Piaget's classic theories of children's cognition. As children walk through space, they experience the concepts of space, time, and event logic simultaneously, and through these processes, children can understand and develop a mental map of the surroundings, which influences their subsequent cognitive functioning and understanding [10–12].The arrangement of the elements in the gamification design is based on Vygotsky's theories, such as the zone of proximal development and the scaffolding principle. For example, the scaffolding of audio prompts and previous experience of playing similar games in the real world can enable participants to achieve higher scores in virtual games [13].

3.2   Analysis of the Research Status

The application value of gamification in education is mainly reflected in four aspects: motivating learning, building learning environments, supporting learning styles, and enhancing learning effectiveness [14]. In practical design, motivating learning corresponds to game mechanics and narrative design; building learning environments is mainly related to game environment design; supporting learning styles is reflected in interaction, mechanics and environment design; and enhancing learning effectiveness is presented through learners' academic achievements in empirical researches.

Taking into account the specificity of spatially competent education for the visually impaired people, and in order to fit in the literature with the research methodology of design-based research, as well as for reference to subsequent research on gamification design, this study presents a content analysis from a design perspective in five areas: space environment design, interaction design, game mechanics and narrative design, development-related technologies, and usability evaluation, and answers the research questions 1–5 raised in the research design.

Space Environment Design and Education Aims. As the core of this study is spatial ability, the environment's design in different studies is mainly related to the spatial ability intended to be trained. The virtual environment is also a prerequisite that influences the rest of the gamification design. Thus, this study takes the design of the virtual space environment and the target spatial ability to be trained as the starting point for the content analysis.

Referring to Montello [15] and Hegarty's research [16], the scale of virtual environment is divided into three types in this study, including the space that can be touched by the hand without moving the body position (marked as spatial type A), the space that can be reached by walking (marked as spatial type B), and the large space that cannot be moved to by walking but can be imagined (marked as spatial type C). Of the 20 selected studies, 14 (70%) was on spatial type B, which the corresponding core spatial competence trained lies in orientation and mobility, which specifically involves determining one's position in the environment, knowing the direction one is facing and the direction in which one's body is moving, and deciding which route one should take in order to reach a certain destination. A prerequisite for these abilities is having a mental map of space [17, 18]. A spatial mental map is a map that collects information from various senses for route planning and walking, generating a spatial representation, then producing an accurate and stable spatial cognition.

The spaces are designed as mazes in studies that focus on training pathfinding skills, as architectural rooms that map the real world in studies that emphasize the effects of transferring spatial knowledge acquired in virtual environments to reality, and as fictional adventure or puzzle-solving spaces in studies that train the ability to find sound sources or avoid obstacles. The virtual environment's spatial type influences the design of corresponding gameplay.

Interaction Design. As analyzed in the section of space environment design and training objectives, the most common training in current relevant gamification designs lies in orientation and mobility, which presupposes the use of information from the external environment to create a spatial mental map. For sighted people, most of the information needed for the mental map is gathered visually. The main challenge for PVI is therefore to use other sensory channels to collect information, which places new demands on the interaction design. As a result, studies on interaction design have focused on two areas: firstly, the principles and methods of interaction design for sensory enhancement and sensory substitution in information transfer, mainly in the three modalities of auditory, tactile, and kinesthetic senses. The second area is the study of interaction hardware, which is designed primarily in relation to the combination of tactility and kinesthesia.

In general, concerning interaction design, there has been more research on the acquisition of information in both auditory and tactile modalities. And kinesthetic sense, as a sense that inevitably arises during changes in spatial position, is also integrated into the interaction design, including gestures and force feedback.

With regard to sound, the three main types used in gamification design are auditory display, earcon, and text to speech. Auditory display is recordings or imitations of specific sounds from reality, forming auditory interface elements that are reminiscent of the objects that make the corresponding sounds. Earcon is abstract and structured sound signals that map sequences of tones to actions or objects, connecting the sound and the action or object [7]. Examples of specific applications of auditory display in the literature include footsteps reflecting the material of the ground on which they are walking, chatter in a cafeteria, tinkling and knocking on doors [19], etc. Examples of the use of aural markers include the increase in pitch with the number of steps the user takes up the stairs, which should reflect the change in height [20].

One of the auditory-related interactions that have been studied in recent years is echolocation. Echolocation is the active production of a virtual sound by the user [21], which is propagated and reflected in the virtual environment and then heard by the user. It is more controllable than other forms of sounds that the user passively receives. Recent research has shown that room size and material and 90-degree turns can be detected by echolocation and that echolocation can support the construction of a mental map of the virtual space. However, there are limitations to the presentation of auditory-related information. In particular, the tendency for information to be confused or even overwritten by each other, making it impossible to simultaneously present multiple sound contents that need to be discerned in detail, such as two speaking voices [22]. Different ways of presenting information in the same sensory channel can also result in different cognitive loads. For example, sounds such as auditory display and earcon in virtual space can be helpful to reduce cognitive load and improve working memory to enhance people's ability to navigate, as opposed to verbal instructions [23].

Tactility has a unique advantage in that it may not occupy the auditory hearing channel. Wearable device research related to tactile is divided into two main categories: wearable devices and non-portable devices. There are many types of wearable devices, involving wristbands [24], headbands [25], belts [26], vests [27], shoe inserts [28], white canes [29] etc. Non-portable devices are relatively large or involve complex mechanics [9] and can only be used in specific contexts [17]. Actually, the logic of these studies is similar in that they all transfer visual coded information into tactile information delivered to the skin through vibrations or other movements of the wearable hardware.

Most current tactile interactions are still dominated by vibrations, such as The Sound of Vision project [7]. A relatively unusual idea in tactile sensory substitution research is the DualPanto project [9]. In the study, the tactile dimension is used to more aspects. Players can feel the orientation, distance and height of the virtual objects through the tactile senses of both hands, which solved the problem of the relative difficulty of continuously tracking the position of objects in virtual reality and controlling their relative and absolute position in space. It allowed two players to use it at the same time, making it suitable for competition and cooperation.

However, the transfer of tactile information also has its limitations. The signal from the vibration has certain limitations. Tactile vibrations alone tend to produce sensory decline as the affected area quickly becomes numb. To address this issue, the Goose-Bumps researchers used a changing frequency of skin poking to combat sensory degradation and set the contact surface between the wearable device and the skin to a distorted surface that may initially feel uncomfortable [24]. The tactile information of touch can be complex and challenging to understand, and its resolution, portability, and cost [13] are indeed current issues to consider for multimodal interaction in virtual environments for the visually impaired community. The finer tactile information requires constant hand interaction, which might lead to fatigue and hand occupation [28].

Gesture interaction is kind of special in interaction systerms for PVI. Well-designed gesture and sound interactions can complement each other. In the absence of visual information, these three principles can in fact be applied in the same way to sound effects and other interactions. Force feedback can present a small range of object shapes in a small space within reach of the hand, helping visually impaired people to learn mathematical knowledge such as spatial geometry [30]. When the objects touched by the hand are transformed into tactile maps, the visually impaired participant is trained to imagine and navigate large spaces [31]. However, without external assistance, the visually impaired group may face difficulties in learning gesture manipulation due to the inability to see the gesture examples. In addition, different types of body movement strategies may pose additional challenges for the design and usability of sports games in virtual worlds [20]. Therefore, if these relatively special interaction styles are to be used, usability testing will need to be tailored to ensure a smooth user experience.

Gamification Mechanics and Elements. The objectives of gamification in the studies lie in three main aspects. The first is to use the fun of the game in the virtual environment to enhance their motivation to train, to create problem-solving scenarios to motivate users to learn new assistive technologies or train their own abilities, and to reduce to some extent the initial unfamiliarity of use and the frustration caused by mistakes. The second aspect is the use of objectives in the game to conceal the purpose of learning and change the learning from explicitly to implicitly, promoting more independent exploration of space and reducing goal-oriented behaviors like over-learning and rote memorization. The third aspect is the use of the distribution of tasks in the game and the logical sequence between tasks to guide the player's exploration of space and progressive learning.

In the current literature, the mechanics of training games on the same spatial ability are relatively similar. In the case of orientation and mobility training, which accounts for the largest proportion, most designs use the mechanics of a scavenger hunt game, coupled with obstacle avoidance tasks. In the game, the items to be found are mostly in fixed locations, some in hidden locations. The obstacles or objects to be avoided are divided into three categories: obstacles that are fixed, obstacles that appear randomly and obstacles that have a moving path. Overall, there is a lack of variety in the game mechanics of these studies, and the differentiation and correlation between levels and task difficulty is not clearly designed. This may be due to the task of spatial training itself. However, it has been established that for spatial cognition, implicit learning is more effective when the learning purpose is not exposed and the game task does not correspond exactly to the learning purpose [20]. Therefore, gamification can actually be designed to include more gameplay and mechanics, as long as it promotes spatial exploration.

In terms of motivation, there are two types of motivation, the first being specialized designs for independent use by the visually impaired group, and the second being inclusive designs that emphasize the assistance, involvement or participation of non-visually impaired persons. The ideal situation for the first type is that the game-based training can be carried out entirely by the visually impaired themselves, thus enhancing their sense of self-efficacy and reducing the consumption of human resources. Most of the studies on spatial training for the visually impaired participants in virtual environments is single-player mode, with relatively few multi-player mode. On the other hand, for the second type, gamification is mainly used to enhance the connection and cooperation between the visually impaired and non-visually impaired groups to enhance social motivation. However, current designs do not take full advantage of the powerful intrinsic motivational approach of emotionally connecting the learner's player identity to the virtual world in which they are trained, which is commonly used in the field of gamification. For example, more design of avatars, connections to the virtual world, images of non-player characters, and relationships with participants could be used to create stronger emotional connections and motivations to facilitate training.

Relevant Technologies. Game engines, stereo simulation technologies, body sensors and open-source hardware are technologies that most commonly used in these studies.

In studies using sounds as the primary source of information, personalized head-related transfer function (HRTF) is used to obtain accurate representations of three-dimensional spatialized sound in virtual auditory environments [21]. HRTFs are transfer functions that define the acoustic basis of auditory perception of spatial sound sources and are often used to simulate free-field auditory conditions in virtual auditory displays. Technologies commonly used when gesture and body sensory interaction is involved are the Kinect and Leap Motion sensors.

The most commonly used tool for development over the last five years has been Unity 3D (about 64.28%) and the main platforms used are Android and Windows.

Usability Assessment and Validity Assessment. The test of usability in the studies may be multiple rounds. According to Sanchez and the rigorous practice in interaction design, the system or application designed is refined and iterated through the test of usability before the validity test is conducted [32]. The completion of tasks in the game is also used as a measure of the effectiveness of the system. In addition, because the game is played in a virtual environment, each step taken by the player can be recorded by the program in an electronic log, providing researchers with a more accurate, multi-dimensional, and less labor-intensive basis for assessing the behavior of visually impaired people during participation. For example, in the gamified virtual environment, logs and replays are given a higher priority, summarizing the actions players perform in the game and how they solve the problems they encounter [32]. These studies have yielded valid and optimistic findings in terms of users' motivation and competence enhancement. However, possible measurement bias due to the force majeure should be noted.

Electroencephalographic(EEG) studies were used in partially designed tests [23, 33, 34]. In an experiment, Sanchez found that when players heard auditory instructions describing where they were going, brain activity was limited to the auditory areas of the brain; when a person was asked to walk randomly in a virtual environment without any target destination, brain activity was not only in the auditory but also in the sensorimotor areas [34]. Balan found that when a blind person (whether congenital or acquired) navigates in the real world based on auditory sound cues, using the same brain areas (frontal cortex, parietal cortex, and hippocampus) used by sighted people to visually process spatial information, and on this basis he hypothesized that this might be due to the game's success in activating neuroplasticity in the brain, causing the brain to "rewire" its functions and thus adjusts compensatory abilities and helps PVI to deal with the problem of blindness [33]. The brain's function is rewired to adjust to different channels of information substitution. However, more brain science research is needed on how the brain uses the sensory information it receives to form spatial cognitive maps, and how visual signals are encoded into other sensory modalities to form spatial information that can be used by the brain to construct spatial cognition.

4 Discussion and Conclusion

4.1 Current Status of Research and Issues

This paper uses a content analysis method, focusing on the design research literature, to analyze and discuss the current status and trends of gamification related to spatial abilities of visually impaired people in virtual environments. The study reveals that gamification-related research has greatly applied in motivating spatial exploration, testing the validity of hardware and software, and enabling participants to construct more reliable mental models of space, and is better at facilitating implicit learning of spatial abilities in children with visual impairment.

With regard to research question 6, the current gamification of PVI for spatial ability training in virtual environment has some areas for improvement in terms of usability and validity assessment. First, usability assessment should receive more attention. Problems with system usability may lead to biased results of validity tests [32]. The format of these tests should be optimized for the age and cognitive level of the user. Each usability test leads to further iterations of the software and hardware by designers and developers to reduce the impact that the hardware and software itself may have on the final experimental results. In addition, the validity testing of gamified designs should be more rigorous. As much validity testing as possible needs to be included in the control experiments. Besides, special education professionals may be involved in the process of experimentation [17]. On the one hand, this situation may bring about the influence of off-site factors, and on the other hand, it may help to identify more problems. It is therefore recommended that the influence of special education professionals be controlled as much as possible in validation-related experiments, or that two groups of experiments be set up with or without special education professionals.

4.2 Future Trends in Relevant Research

Based on the results of the content analysis, it is possible to speculate future trends of research and answer research question 7, for example, focusing on the spatial abilities of elderly visually impaired groups, exploring how multimodal interaction information is combined and the neuroscience principles, and developing personalized and dynamically adapted gamified content. The details are discussed below.

Currently, there is a certain imbalance in the age of the target users of the studies. There are studies in the literature obtained that cover higher age visually impaired people [31], while there are no studies that address spatial ability training in the context of visual impairment in older age groups. However, the main reason of the increase of visually impaired people is due to the aging of the population [1]. The auditory abilities of older people may also decline with age, so alternatives to visual information may be more difficult for them. What's more, non-visual access to spatial information in the aging population should therefore also be explored.

The interaction between information from different modalities deserves further research. Currently, some researchers believe that multimodality leads to more cognitive load and that information from different sensory channels interfering with each other can lead to negative effects. Another researchers believe that well-designed multimodal interaction feedback can help visually impaired people to develop new channels of perception of spatial information processing by using neuroplasticity. When designing multimodal interactions, the different sensory channels should be presented in a way that complements the information presented in the other sensory channels, and further research is needed to determine what combination of presentations is 'appropriate'. Moreover, there may be differences in the ability of individuals to integrate and receive information from different modalities, and with the development of artificial intelligence, dynamic content adaptation and personalization techniques, it may be appropriate to measure this ability and match the presentation of modal information to different individuals.

Parametric and personalized dynamic adjustment of environmental complexity, task difficulty and content for different users in different states may be one of the future research trends. In other areas of gamification design, researchers are increasingly focusing on categorizing users according to player type and learning preferences, and presenting them with the most appropriate gamification content and format in order to maximize the effect. Gamification design for visually impaired people in virtual environments is also suitable to take advantage of its own parametric training environment, collecting user behavior data to determine the current state and matching the most appropriate training for PVI. For example, by incorporating emotion monitoring techniques to intersperse the much-needed and more challenging tasks for the visually impaired people with tasks they are good at in an appropriate and logical manner, the acquired helplessness that may arise during the training of difficult tasks can be avoided to some extent, and a measured rhythm can be reached to adjust the emotional experience during training. With the development of artificial intelligence and natural language processing technologies, elements such as non-player characters can be added to gamification designs.

4.3 Limitations and Future Work

As this study only selected literature from the Web of Science, there may be some omissions and the findings are somewhat limited. We intend to use a snowball method in future work to add and refine the study and, on this basis, propose a gamification design model that can be used as a reference for the corresponding researchers.

5 Appendix

See Table 1.

Table 1. List of selected article

No	Year	Literature title	Article type	No. of design cases	Author
1	2021	Echolocation as a Means for People with Visual Impairment (PVI) to Acquire Spatial Knowledge of Virtual Space	Design research	1	Andrade, Ronny; Waycott, Jenny; Baker, Steven; Vetere, Frank
2	2020	Virtual Reality Without Vision: A Haptic and Auditory White Cane to Navigate Complex Virtual Worlds	Design research	2	Siu, Alexa F.; Sinclair, Mike; Kovacs, Robert; Ofek, Eyal; Holz, Christian; Cutrell, Edward
3	2019	Hungry Cat-A Serious Game for Conveying Spatial Information to the Visually Impaired	Design research	3	Chai, Carmen; Lau, Bee; Pan, Zheng
4	2019	Loud and Clear: The VR Game Without Visuals	Design research	4	Baas, Berend; van Peer, Dennis; Gerling, Jan; e t.al
5	2019	ACCESSIBILITY AND SOME EDUCATIONAL BARRIERS FOR VISUALLY IMPAIRED USERS	Principles introcuction		Bogdanova, G.; Sabev, N.; Noev, N
6	2019	Virtual Interaction for Visually Impaired and Sighted People	literature review		Ivascu, Silviu; Moldoveanu, Alin; Moldoveanu, Florica; Morar, Anca; Balan, Oana

(continued)

Table 1. (*continued*)

7	2019	Virtual Showdown: An Accessible Virtual Reality Game with Scaffolds for Youth with Visual Impairments	Design research	5	Wedoff, Ryan; Ball, Lindsay; Wang, Amelia; Khoo, Yi Xuan; Lieberman, Lauren; Rector, Kyle
8	2018	Echo-House: Exploring a Virtual Environment by Using Echolocation	Design research	6	Andrade, Ronny; Baker, Steven; Waycott, Jenny; Vetere, Frank
9	2018	DualPanto: A Haptic Device that Enables Blind Users to Continuously Interact with Virtual Worlds	Design research	7	Schneider, Oliver; Shigeyama, Jotaro; Kovacs, Robert; e t.al
10	2018	An Audio and Haptic Feedback-based Virtual Environment Spatial Navigation Learning Tool	Design research	3	Wang, Carmen Chai; Theng, Lau Bee; Zheng, Pan
11	2017	Improving the Audio Game-Playing Performances of People with Visual Impairments Through Multimodal Training	Design research	8	Balan, Oana; Moldoveanu, Alin; Moldoveanu, Florica; Nagy, Hunor; Wersenyi, Gyorgy; Unnporsson, Runar
12	2017	Virtual Environments for Training Visually Impaired For A Sensory Substitution Device	Design research	9	Moldoveanu, Alin Dragos Bogdan; Stanica, Iulia. e t.al
13	2017	GooseBumps: Towards Sensory Substitution Using Servo Motors	Design project introduction	10	Olickel, Hrishi; Bhatnagar, Parag; Ong, Aaron CS; Perrault, Simon T
14	2016	Development of an Audio-Haptic Virtual Interface for Navigation of Large-Scale Environments for People Who Are Blind	Design research	11	Merabet, Lotfi B.; Sanchez, Jaime
15	2015	Multimodal Videogames for the Cognition of People Who Are Blind: Trends and Issues	Literature review		Sanchez, Jaime; Darin, Ticianne; Andrade, Rossana
16	2015	Audio Feedback Design Principles for Hand Gestures in Audio-Only Games	Design research	12	Wu, Wenjie; Rank, Stefan
17	2014	Virtual environments for the transfer of navigation skills in the blind: a comparison of directed instruction vs. video game based learning approaches	Design research	13	Connors, Erin C.; Chrastil, Elizabeth R.; Sanchez, Jaime; Merabet, Lo tfi B

(*continued*)

Table 1. (*continued*)

18	2014	Action video game play and transfer of navigation and spatial cognition skills in adolescents who are blind	Design research	13	Connors, Erin C.; Chrastil, Elizabeth R.; Sanchez, Jaime; Merabet, Lotfi B
19	2014	Navigational 3D audio-based game-training towards rich auditory spatial representation of the environment	Design research	14	Balan, Oana; Moldoveanu, Alin; Moldoveanu, Florica; Dascalu, Maria-Iuliana
20	2014	Audio Games-A Novel Approach Towards Effective Learning in The Case Of Visually-Impaired People	Literature review		Balan, Oana; Moldoveanu, Alin; Moldoveanu, Florica; Dascalu, Maria-Iuliana
21	2013	Development of an Audio-based Virtual Gaming Environment to Assist with Navigation Skills in the Blind	Design research	13	Connors, Erin C.; Yazzolino, Lindsay A.; Sanchez, Jaime; Merabet, Lotfi B
22	2013	Foot-Based Interfaces for Navigational Assistance of the Visually Impaired	Design research	15	Velazquez, R.; Bazan, O
23	2012	Teaching the Blind to Find Their Way by Playing Video Games	Design research	13	Merabet, Lotfi B.; Connors, Erin C.; Halko, Mark A.; Sanchez, Jaime
24	2011	User Centred Design and Development of an Educational Force-Feedback Haptic Game for Blind Students	Design research	16	Petridou, Maria; Blanchfield, Peter; Alabadi, Reham; Brailsford, Tim
25	2009	Enhanced perception for visually impaired people	Design research	17	Moeller, K.; Toth, F.; Wang, L.; Moeller, J.; Arras, KO; Bach, M.; Schumann, S.; Guttmann, J
26	2009	A Modality Replacement Framework for the Communication between Blind and Hearing Impaired People	Design research	18	Moustakas, Konstantinos; Tzovaras, Dimitrios; Dybkjaer, Laila; Bernsen, Niels Ole
27	2009	Blind Children Navigation through Gaming and Associated Brain Plasticity	Design research	13	Sanchez, Jaime; Tadres, Angelo; Pascual-Leone, Alvaro; Merabet, Lotfi

(*continued*)

Table 1. (*continued*)

| 28 | 2009 | Usability of a Multimodal Videogame to Improve Navigation Skills for Blind Children | Design research | 19 | Sanchez, Jaime; Saenz, Mauricio; Ripoll, Miguel |
| 29 | 2006 | 3D sound interactive environments for blind children problem solving skills | Design research | 20 | Sanchez, Jaime; Saenz, Mauricio |

Acknowledgement. This work was supported by the Key Education Research Project in 2020 Sponsored by Yuyue Educational Development Foundation in Center for Research on Pre-K12 Education of Peking University (No: JCJYYJ201902).

References

1. World Health Organization: World report on vision. https://www.who.int/publications/i/item/9789241516570. Accessed 19 Dec 2021
2. Mohler, J.L.: A review of spatial ability research. Eng. Des. Graph. J. **72**, 19–30 (2008)
3. World Health Organization: Vision impairment and blindness. https://www.who.int/newsroom/fact-sheets/detail/blindness-and-visual-impairment. Accessed 19 Dec 2021
4. Maidenbaum, S.: Sensory substitution training for users who are blind with dynamic stimuli, games and virtual environments. In: Proceedings of the 17th International ACM SIGACCESS Conference on Computers & Accessibility, pp. 355–356. Association for Computing Machinery, New York (2015). https://doi.org/10.1145/2700648.2811324
5. Sánchez, J., Darin, T., Andrade, R.: Multimodal videogames for the cognition of people who are blind: trends and issues. In: Antona, M., Stephanidis, C. (eds.) UAHCI 2015. LNCS, vol. 9177, pp. 535–546. Springer, Cham (2015). https://doi.org/10.1007/978-3-319-20684-4_52
6. Deterding, S., Dixon, D., Khaled, R., Nacke, L.: From game design elements to gamefulness: defining "gamification." In: Proceedings of the 15th International Academic MindTrek Conference: Envisioning Future Media Environments, pp. 9–15. Association for Computing Machinery, New York (2011). https://doi.org/10.1145/2181037.2181040
7. Ivascu, S., Moldoveanu, A., Moldoveanu, F., Morar, A., Balan, O.: Virtual interaction for visually impaired and sighted people. In: Roceanu, I., Belgian, D., Stefan, I.A., Moldoveanu, A., Matu, S.T. (eds.) New Technologies and Redesigning Learning Spaces, vol. I, pp. 209–214. Carol I Natl Defence Univ Publishing House, Bucharest (2019). https://doi.org/10.12753/2066-026X-19-028
8. Wedoff, R., Ball, L., Wang, A., Khoo, Y.X., Lieberman, L., Rector, K.: Virtual showdown: an accessible virtual reality game with scaffolds for youth with visual impairments. In: CHI 2019: Proceedings of the 2019 CHI Conference on Human Factors in Computing Systems. Assoc Computing Machinery, New York (2019). https://doi.org/10.1145/3290605.3300371
9. Schneider, O., et al.: DualPanto: a haptic device that enables blind users to continuously interact with virtual worlds. In: Proceedings of the 31st Annual ACM Symposium on User Interface Software and Technology, pp. 877–887. Association for Computing Machinery, New York (2018). https://doi.org/10.1145/3242587.3242604
10. Piaget, J.: The Construction of Reality in the Child. Routledge, Abingdon (1954)

11. Piaget, J.: The Child s Conception of the World. Routledge & Kegan Paul, Abingdon (1951)
12. Piaget, J.: Play, Dreams and Imitation in Childhood. W W Norton & Co., New York (1952)
13. Baas, B., et al.: Loud and clear: the VR game without visuals. In: Liapis, A., Yannakakis, G.N., Gentile, M., Ninaus, M. (eds.) GALA 2019. LNCS, vol. 11899, pp. 180–190. Springer, Cham (2019). https://doi.org/10.1007/978-3-030-34350-7_18
14. Zeng, J., Parks, S., Shang, J.: To learn scientifically, effectively, and enjoyably: a review of educational games. Hum. Behav. Emerg. Technol. 2, 186–195 (2020). https://doi.org/10.1002/hbe2.188
15. Montello, D.R.: Scale and multiple psychologies of space. In: Frank, A.U., Campari, I. (eds.) COSIT 1993. LNCS, vol. 716, pp. 312–321. Springer, Heidelberg (1993). https://doi.org/10.1007/3-540-57207-4_21
16. Hegarty, M., Waller, D.: A dissociation between mental rotation and perspective-taking spatial abilities. Intelligence 32, 175–191 (2004). https://doi.org/10.1016/j.intell.2003.12.001
17. Sanchez, J., Saenz, M., Ripoll, M.: Usability of a multimodal videogame to improve navigation skills for blind children. In: Assets 2009: Proceedings of the 11th International ACM SIGACCESS Conference on Computers and Accessibility, pp. 35–42. Assoc Computing Machinery, New York (2009)
18. Kreimeier, J., Götzelmann, T.: Two decades of touchable and walkable virtual reality for blind and visually impaired people: a high-level taxonomy. Multimod. Technol. Interact. 4, 79 (2020). https://doi.org/10.3390/mti4040079
19. Merabet, L.B., Sánchez, J.: Development of an audio-haptic virtual interface for navigation of large-scale environments for people who are blind. In: Antona, M., Stephanidis, C. (eds.) UAHCI 2016. LNCS, vol. 9739, pp. 595–606. Springer, Cham (2016). https://doi.org/10.1007/978-3-319-40238-3_57
20. Connors, E.C., Chrastil, E.R., Sanchez, J., Merabet, L.B.: Virtual environments for the transfer of navigation skills in the blind: a comparison of directed instruction vs. video game based learning approaches. Front. Hum. Neurosci. 8, 223 (2014). https://doi.org/10.3389/fnhum.2014.00223
21. Andrade, R., Waycott, J., Baker, S., Vetere, F.: Echolocation as a means for people with visual impairment (PVI) to acquire spatial knowledge of virtual space. ACM Trans. Access. Comput. 14, 4 (2021). https://doi.org/10.1145/3448273
22. Bogdanova, G., Sabev, N., Noev, N.: Accessibility and some educational barriers for visually impaired users. In: Chova, L.G., Martinez, A.L., Torres, I.C. (eds.) 13th International Technology, Education and Development Conference (INTED2019), pp. 9416–9421. IATED-Int Assoc Technology Education & Development, Valenica (2019). https://doi.org/10.21125/inted.2019.2333
23. Connors, E.C., Chrastil, E.R., Sanchez, J., Merabet, L.B.: Action video game play and transfer of navigation and spatial cognition skills in adolescents who are blind. Front. Hum. Neurosci. 8, 133 (2014). https://doi.org/10.3389/fnhum.2014.00133
24. Olickel, H., Bhatnagar, P., Ong, A.C.S., Perrault, S.T.: GooseBumps: towards sensory substitution using servo motors. In: Proceedings of the 2017 ACM International Conference on Interactive Surfaces and Spaces (ACM ISS 2017), pp. 425–428. Assoc Computing Machinery, New York (2017). https://doi.org/10.1145/3132272.3132293
25. Balan, O., Moldoveanu, A., Moldoveanu, F., Nagy, H., Wersenyi, G., Unnporsson, R.: Improving the audio game-playing performances of people with visual impairments through multimodal training. J. Vis. Impair. Blind. 111, 148–164 (2017)
26. Moeller, K., et al.: Enhanced perception for visually impaired people. In: 2009 3rd International Conference on Bioinformatics and Biomedical Engineering, vols. 1–11, pp. 1365+. IEEE, New York (2009)

27. Moldoveanu, A.D.B., et al.: Virtual environments for training visually impaired for a sensory substitution device. In: 2017 Zooming Innovation in Consumer Electronics International Conference (ZINC), pp. 26–29. IEEE, New York (2017)
28. Velazquez, R., Bazan, O.: Foot-based interfaces for navigational assistance of the visually impaired. In: 2013 Pan American Health Care Exchanges (PAHCE). IEEE, New York (2013)
29. Siu, A.F., Sinclair, M., Kovacs, R., Ofek, E., Holz, C., Cutrell, E.: Virtual reality without vision: a haptic and auditory white cane to navigate complex virtual worlds. In: Proceedings of the 2020 CHI Conference on Human Factors in Computing Systems (CHI 2020). Assoc Computing Machinery, New York (2020). https://doi.org/10.1145/3313831.3376353
30. Petridou, M., Blanchfield, P., Alabadi, R., Brailsford, T.: User centred design and development of an educational force-feedback haptic game for blind students. In: Gouscos, D., Meimaris, M. (eds.) Proceedings of the 5th European Conference on Games Based Learning, pp. 465–475. ACAD Conferences Ltd., Reading (2011)
31. Moustakas, K., Tzovaras, D., Dybkjær, L., Bernsen, N.O.: A modality replacement framework for the communication between blind and hearing impaired people. In: Stephanidis, C. (ed.) UAHCI 2009. LNCS, vol. 5616, pp. 226–235. Springer, Heidelberg (2009). https://doi.org/10.1007/978-3-642-02713-0_24
32. Sánchez, J., Sáenz, M.: 3D sound interactive environments for blind children problem solving skills. Behav. Inf. Technol. 25, 367–378 (2006). https://doi.org/10.1080/01449290600636660
33. Balan, O., Moldoveanu, A., Moldoveanu, F., Dascalu, M.-I.: Navigational 3D audio-based game- training towards rich auditory spatial representation of the environment. In: 2014 18th International Conference System Theory, Control and Computing (ICSTCC), pp. 682–687. IEEE, New York (2014)
34. Sanchez, J., Tadres, A., Pascual-Leone, A., Merabet, L.: Blind children navigation through gaming and associated brain plasticity. In: 2009 Virtual Rehabilitation International Conference, pp. 29+. IEEE, New York (2009). https://doi.org/10.1109/ICVR.2009.5174201

DropAR: Enriching Exergaming Using Collaborative Augmented Reality Content

Kieran Woodward$^{(\boxtimes)}$, Eiman Kanjo, and Will Parker

Department of Computer Science, Nottingham Trent University, Nottingham, UK
{kieran.woodward,eiman.kanjo,william.parker}@ntu.ac.uk

Abstract. Exergames are video games that require physical movement to play with AR presenting many opportunities for promoting physical activities as it can be used to engage players and encourage exploration. Multiplayer Augmented Reality (AR) games allow players to occupy a shared physical environment populated with interactive digital 3D models. We propose the use of an AR exergame whereby players unlock and place 3D models while walking. We have designed, implemented, and tested a casual exergame that creates innovative collaborative environments where multiple users can interact with the same computer-generated 3D models. Our results show the game successfully engaged participants in creating and viewing the shared augmented environment and encouraged them to stay physically active in order to explore existing models and place new models. These technological advances such as cloud anchors help to promote the mass adoption of collaborative AR technologies.

Keywords: Augmented Reality (AR) · Cloud anchors · Exergame · HCI · Gamification · Mixed reality and environments

1 Introduction

Augmented reality (AR) is an interactive experience to enhance the real-world environment by adding computer-generated objects to create an engaging experience. AR is a rapidly growing area of interactive design where virtual 3D models can be seamlessly integrated with a live camera feed of the real-world. With the ubiquity of smart mobile devices capable of producing innovative augmented reality environments, interactive AR games have significantly increased. AR applications present many opportunities for the future of Human-Computer Interaction (HCI), by revolutionizing the way content is presented by transforming the user's surroundings into an adaptable user interface.

Exergames are video games that require physical movement to play with AR presenting many opportunities for promoting exercise as it can be used to engage players and encourage exploration [7]. Exergames make physical activity more enjoyable for users by providing a fun gaming environment with gamification that motivates and engages people to participate in physical activity. The goal of exergames is to create games that are fun but also motivate players to be

X. Fang (Ed.): HCII 2022, LNCS 13334, pp. 652–663, 2022.
https://doi.org/10.1007/978-3-031-05637-6_42

more physically active but finding fun, sustainable physical activities that people will be motivated to participate in consistently and frequently is a challenging proposition. A previous exergame used advances in AI to promote engagement with physical activity through object recognition challenges [10]. However, while most location based games such as Pokemon Go [6] offer real-world gameplay utilising GPS that encourage players to exercise, the AR elements are a small feature of the game that offers little interactivity.

The vast majority of existing implementations of AR are not location specific and do not engage multiple players in creating new virtual worlds. This may be because that until recently GPS co-ordinates were used to display static 3D models over the smartphone camera view. However, this research explores a marker-less solution that allows AR content to be shared between multiple users at different times, utilising advances in cloud technologies such as real-time cloud anchors. Cloud anchors can be created by a user at a physical location by using their smartphone to capture the live scene and augmenting the place by adding virtual objects at specific places within the physical location. With this technological advancement, the potential use of new functional environments is expanding, greatly enriching HCI.

Some example use cases that are served by cloud anchors and AR content at different locations include:

1. Users creating a new cloud anchor (adding an AR model to a specific location).
2. Multiple users collaborating in the same AR environment using the cloud anchors.

Multiplayer augmented reality games allow players to occupy a shared physical environment populated with interactive digital 3D models. However, current available games fall short because of either limited synchronicity or limited opportunities for player movement. We introduce a Collaborative AR feature called "DropAR" for exergame whereby players view and collect 3D models through walking. As players collect 3D models by walking an increasing number of steps they can drop these models in the real-world for other players to view and interact with, creating a collaborative environment. Therefore, we have designed, implemented, and tested a casual exergame that creates innovative collaborative environments where multiple users can interact with the computer-generated 3D models.

2   Background

AR is increasing in popularity in recent years with advances in smartphones, immersive technologies, and Artificial Intelligence (AI). However, to create an engaging user experience through AR requires models where the user is a vital part of the application, adding objects and viewing objects from others. Advances in AR such as cloud anchors help resolve this fundamental challenge by allowing AR objects to be placed in the real-world and their position and orientation saved, allowing users to place new models and design the augmented interface themselves for others to view.

One of the first systems to embrace collaborative AR was Virtuoso [9], an educational application designed for studying the history of arts. Even though Virtuoso was a simple prototype with a small screen the results successfully demonstrated that AR learning techniques are effective for untrained users and that they promoted engagement. Gargalakos [3] found similar results when utilising AR in museums to allow students to playfully learn while interacting with digital exhibitions. Overall this work shows AR experiences significantly improved people's engagement and willingness to collaborate with the others.

The use of cloud anchors provides the unprecedented ability for people to share and view 3D models. LibrARy [4] aimed to create an AR based collaborative environment where multiple users can interact simultaneously with the same computer-generated content. Its main objective was to improve cooperation by enabling multiple users to access a shared space populated with 3D virtual objects to enrich collaboration through augmented interactions. However, there was little use for LibrARy with only the ability to simply place models and view previously placed models with no sense of purpose for the app. The ability to share 3D computer generated models provides unique collaborative opportunities including the ability for artists to share their work [1]. In particular, it offers digital artists to share their work in an interactive manner allowing people to view the art placed within the real world creating an augmented gallery, which is not traditionally possible with digital art.

Cloud anchors provide many opportunities for collaborative learning as an app enabled virtual black boards to be created and shared within an AR environment allowing people to collaboratively share notes [8]. Similarly, a translator app [5] enabled a shared educational virtual environment for active learning by enabling users to add notes to a virtual whiteboard along with the translation. By utilising these advances in AR the app was able to allow visual information sharing and discussion among students speaking different languages.

Cloud anchors can also be used for entertainment purposes as researchers have developed a multiplayer AR game, Brick [2]. Brick provides a room scale game where players collaborate to fill in a pattern of empty slots using digital "bricks" scattered about the room. Similarly, Pokemon Go combined augmented reality, exergaming and location based multi-player features [6]. It is the many technological advances, including the AR that were combined to make the game a success. This demonstrates the capabilities of mobile exergames relying on smartphones to create a stronger link between the game world and the real world, although the lack of cloud anchors within Pokemon Go prevents players from sharing their AR experience with others. Overall, there have been few attempts at utilising cloud anchors for gaming and while Brick and Pokemon Go demonstrate the potential of AR, the use of cloud anchors to promote exercise through an engaging exergame has not yet been explored.

3   System Design

The main objective is to develop a game that increases engagement and promotes physical activity by enabling co-located users to access a shared environment populated with 3D virtual models and to enrich gameplay between them through augmented interactions. Therefore, a mobile application has been developed for both Android and iOS that enables players to drop a 3d model within the augmented world for others to view. The application was developed using Flutter taking advantage of Google's ARCore and Apple's ARKit to enable the augmented reality functionality. Cloud anchors are then used to store the real-world location and positioning of the dropped models. By using the captured raw image and sensor data, AR metadata of the scene including the planes and camera pose is obtained and stored in association with the cloud anchor. The models and AR metadata are stored in an external database enabling all users to view the scene. The models available for players to drop are also stored within the database enabling them to be dynamically changes, creating the ability to continuously develop new gaming experiences.

The main functions of the AR cloud anchor-based exergame are shown below:

1. Floor recognition - Walking around with a smartphone to capture a floor and recognize the environment. When the floor is detected, a mesh is automatically generated for the 3D models to be placed within.
2. Generation of AR content downloaded from the remote server to enable the computer generated 3D models to be changed dynamically. By tapping the choose model button, a 3D model can be selected from the available models stored on the database. A model is then generated at the tapped position. The 3D model is anchored by environment recognition, and continues to be displayed in the virtual space as it is located even if the user moves.

The application is persuasive in nature in the way it promotes players to exercise whilst remaining unobtrusive. To accomplish this players will only have to interact with the app when placing a new model with the remaining functionality of scanning and visualising previously placed object functioning automatically in the background.

During the gameplay players unlock new 3d models by walking, where the further the player walks the more models they unlock. The aim of the game is for players to collect as many models as possible and place them within the environment for others to view. The ability for players to view and add to the shared AR environment allows them to collaboratively build the shared game environment.

A number of models were tested and user feedback was sought to ensure the available models were both relevant and interesting for the users to engage with. The feedback showed models related to nature and the environment were most suitable whilst remaining engaging and fun. A number of models were then explored resulting in the 8 selected models shown in Table 1 along with the proposed number of steps to unlock each model when the app is available to users.

Table 1. Description of the 8 models available within the app and the proposed number of steps to unlock each model.

Model Name	Image	Description
Oak Tree		A model of an oak tree allows players to add more scenic objects into the environment. This could be useful in more open areas to add more scenery to the AR world. This model is always unlocked.
Bee		One of the smallest of a collection of wildlife models. Can be used to place into the environment and as small decoration to blend into the real world. This model is always unlocked.
Bench		The bench model is another environment object that can be added to the AR world to increase variation in scenery. This model is always unlocked.
Owl		A 3D model of an owl gives the users another wildlife option, that also shows variation in size between models. This model is always unlocked.
Butterfly		The 3D model of a butterfly adds to the variety of insects that can be placed by the user. This model will be unlocked after walking 500 steps.
Fox		The fox model is currently the largest of the animal models. Users will be able to get up close to the model and see a fox up close. This model will be unlocked after walking 1000 steps.
Street Lantern		Similarly to the tree and the bench models, the street lantern adds more variety of scenery to the environment and combined with the other objects the user can start to develop a full AR scene. This model will be unlocked after walking 2000 steps.
Spider		The final model is a spider. On par in size with the bee model, the spider demonstrates variation in size. Close to what would be expected in the real world. This model will be unlocked after walking 5000 steps.

3.1   User Interface

Initially 4 models are available when playing the app, with more becoming unlocked when players walk an increasing number of steps, encouraging players to exercise more to unlock additional models.

When playing DropAR the screen mostly comprises of a real-time camera view allowing players to view where in the environment they wish to place a model. Upon first starting the app the player must scan the nearby environment for planes by slowly moving the phone, a tutorial helps players complete this action which enables the ability to place AR models in the environment.

A button at the bottom of the screen allows players to view the different models available to them that they have unlocked and select one to place in the augmented world, as shown in Fig. 1.

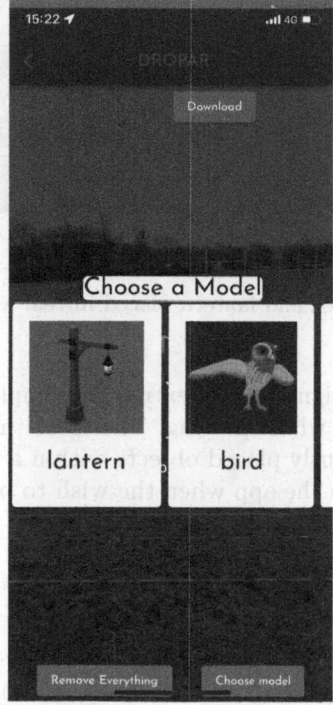

Fig. 1. Ability to select a 3D model from the available unlocked models.

To place the model players simply tap on the screen where they would like the model to be displayed, the model is then automatically added, taking advantage of the previously scanned planes as shown in Fig. 2. It is then possible to upload the placement of the model to enable other players to also view the model at this location or clear the model to place it elsewhere.

Fig. 2. 3D model fox and lantern placed in real world through AR.

The app has been designed to be extremely simple to operate as it should enable players to exercise whilst playing. Therefore the app automatically continuously scans for previously placed objects within a 100 m radius and players only need to interact with the app when the wish to place a new model.

4   System Testing and Evaluation

4.1   Methodology

We have implemented and tested the AR exergame DropAR. Participants over the age of 18 were recruited to test DropAR, completing a questionnaire before the experiment to express their current exercise levels and interest in exergames and AR. Participants were observed while playing the exergame and after the experiment each participant was interviewed to gather their feedback.

During the experiment participants were encouraged to walk around and drop AR models wherever they liked as well as hunt for models placed by previous players by visiting key locations. Participants were encouraged to walk around to unlock additional 3D models. All participants successfully used the application to collect and drop models within the AR environment.

4.2   Results

Pre-experiment Questionnaire. The results from the pre-experiment questionnaire indicate that the majority of participants were extremely interested (55%) or very interested (32.5%) in location based games. Participants believed this mobile app could encourage people to spend more time exercising, demonstrating the potential benefits of gamifying exercise. Finally, the majority of participants believed an AR-based exergame would greatly encourage families and children to visit new locations and help promote physical activity. Overall, this feedback shows the high demand for such an application to engage people with exercise and encourage them to visit new places.

In Situ Experiment. Our results show that the adoption of AR has created a collaborative gaming experience and facilitated playful experiences for large spaces. All Participants successfully used the game to walk around the open areas, placing new objects and viewing objects previously dropped by other players.

Participants were interviewed after playing the game to collect their feedback. The vast majority of participants reported that the game provided a more engaging experience while walking and encouraged them to walk further to collect and drop additional models. This is extremely positive as it successfully demonstrates the potential of using collaborative AR as an exergame to promote exercise.

Players also described their enjoyment regarding the multiplayer collaborative element of DropAR as it offered a unique gaming element that no participant had experienced before, even those who had played AR games previously. This collaborative element was found to actively engage players in order to search for new models that other players had dropped as well as encourage them to place models in unique and interesting places to create their own personal environments for others to view as shown in Fig. 3. All participants were highly interested in exploring what other people placed with them being fully emerged in environment. The immersion experienced was so high participants attempted to touch and physically interact with the virtual objects and one participant initially thought a physical object in the real world was a digital model placed by a previous player.

Additionally, participants liked the ability to unlock additional models through walking as they stated it encouraged them to walk further but believed more models could have been included. Participants expressed their desire for additional models as while 8 models have been included within the app once they are unlocked the majority of participants considered this insufficient. Participants particularly enjoyed the world building elements such as lights and benches to enable them to further develop their own spaces within the augmented world but additionally liked the elements of nature such as animals as decoration for their built environment. Players also expressed interest in the ability for them to design and develop their own models. While this is an interesting concept that would further engage players, it is a challenging proposition

Fig. 3. A selection of 3D models placed in the AR environment by participants.

to enable players to design their own 3d models within the app that can be placed for others to view.

Participants reported some technical issues regarding the app displaying models previously placed by other players, stating that sometimes the phone had to be held in a specific location for the model to appear. This is most likely due to the cloud anchors functioning best when viewing the model from the same position as the original player placed the model although this is not necessarily required it can aid the positioning aspect of the anchors. Additionally, participants reported that some models were slow to download so tapped multiple times due to this delay resulting in multiple models being placed once the model finished downloading. The time taken to place the model in the environment is impacted by multiple factors mainly the data connection speed and the size of the model. With the app being used in large open areas the signal available may vastly vary but most models remained small in size (under 1 MB) to ensure quick download. However, participants were grateful that not all models automatically upload and preferred the method implemented whereby players can only upload the last dropped model to prevent spamming objects in the augmented world.

5   Discussion and Limitations

The use of collaborative AR was received positively by players and succeeded in its aim to encourage people to walk more. All players carefully considered where to place the 3D objects in the augmented world and enjoyed this building aspect. While all participants played the game as intended, the limitation of only adding and uploading one model at a time helps to prevent players spamming the virtual world with objects, creating a more aesthetically pleasing environment for all. It was surprising that participants preferred the structural models in order to build their own augmented world as the majority of participants initially expressed interest for natural objects such as wildlife. After using the app players requested additional world building models showing the popularity of these models. This demonstrates players enjoyed creating their own unique spaced within the augmented world whilst also visiting other players' spaces where players would aim to improve the pre-existing space often by adding additional decorations. In the future, additional structural items will be added to the game to further promote this creativity aspect of the game.

Some technical challenges were encountered during the development and testing stages which impacted the performance of the app. Loss of GPS signal can impact the ability for the app to display previously placed models. Due to the open real-world nature of the trial it is not possible to control the signal strength but the cloud anchors successfully worked the vast majority of time showing these issues only appear occasionally and have little impact on the real-world performance of the app. Similarly, lack of data connection prevents players from being able to download new models, upload the dropped location or download the previously dropped models. The 3d models could be stored locally but this would prevent them from being continuously updated to provide new gaming experiences. The size of the 3D models impacts the time for the object to be downloaded and placed in the augmented environment. A larger tree model of size 13 MB was tested but in conditions with limited 4G connectivity this resulted in waiting 90 s for it to download which is not practical as users will become impatient. Therefore most models used within DropAR were under 1 MB in size but this severely limits the number of polygons and thus the complexity of the model. In general, a lack of connectivity has a severe impact on the app's performance as it removes all of the collaborative multiplayer aspects from the game. However, the vast majority of locations are covered by sufficient signal to download small 3D models and upload GPS co-ordinates but in the future a small number of models could be embedded within the app enabling play to continue when there is limited connectivity with additional models available with connectivity.

Furthermore, the frequent use of the camera and GPS have a significant impact on the temperature of the phone and subsequently battery life with the app draining around 20% power in 30 min when tested on an iPhone 11 pro, Google Pixel 3 and Samsung Galaxy 20+. The temperature of the phone was similarly problematic with the Android operating system occasionally closing the app when testing due to excessive heat. This issue can be negated by only using the app infrequently whilst walking but that may mean some previously dropped models may be missed. Due to the game's intensive use of camera, GPS and internet functionality it is challenging to reduce the high impact on phone temperature and battery life but with advancements in smartphone technologies battery life will continue to be improved.

Finally, a difference in appearance of the 3D models was experiences between the Android and iOS operating systems. Many of the GLB model files appeared significantly smaller on iOS and displayed different colours in comparison to the app running on Android devices. This is potentially due to the different architectures used by the Flutter libraries taking advantage of ARKit and ARCore but makes the development and management of 3D models challenging and time consuming as each model must be tested using both operating systems. Without updates to the libraries utilising ARKit and ARCore to improve model cross-compatibility, thorough testing is required for each new model.

Overall, the limitations experienced had very little real-world impact on the performance of the application when tested with all participants able to view the previously placed models and add new models to the augmented world. Participants enjoyed using the app to develop and explore the virtual world, encouraging exploration and therefore exercise to view the previously dropped models and unlock additional models by walking an increasing number of steps.

6   Conclusion and Future Work

AR represents a novel engaging approach towards developing new immersive experiences that provide collaborative and fun experiences by transforming the real-world into a user interface that everyone can contribute towards. Cloud anchors provide unique collaborative experiences, creating new means of social-isation and making exercising a collaborative and fun experience.

We have developed and deployed a novel AR world building game to accel-erate engagement with exergaming. This research provides an overview of the developed AR exergame from a design and technical perspective. It also dis-cusses how the game extends the current scope of AR games to include collab-orative gameplay. Our results show the game successfully engaged participants and encouraged them to exercise further. These advances help to promote the mass adoption of AR technologies but in the future it could be worth exploring alternative domains other than exergames such as utilising the technology for collaborative working.

The application will evolve by utilising the feedback gathered to improve the features and functionality of the app. In particular, new models will be added to ensure gameplay remains new and engaging with additional objects to enable players to build more complex environments. DropAR will continue to be trialled in additional locations to test its scalability and ensure its functionality can be adopted in a range of environments.

Overall, DropAR combines enriching gameplay with a multiplayer gaming experience. This research demonstrates the ability for collaborative AR to be used to promote physical activities and engage people with the outdoor environ-ment and that collaborative AR for exergaming is ready for more wide spread adoption.

References

1. Antunes, J.L., Bidarra, J., Figueiredo, M.: AR with cloud anchors. Int. J. Creat. Interfaces Comput. Graph. **10**(2), 29–40 (2020). https://doi.org/10.4018/ijcicg. 2019070103

2. Bhattacharyya, P., Jadhav, K., Hammer, J., Jo, Y., Nath, R.: Brick: a synchronous multiplayer augmented reality game for mobile phones. In: Conference on Human Factors in Computing Systems - Proceedings (2019). https://doi.org/10.1145/3290607.3313257

3. Gargalakos, M., Giallouri, E., Lazoudis, A., Sotiriou, S., Bogner, F.X.: Assessing the impact of technology-enhanced field trips in science centers and museums. Adv. Sci. Lett. 4(11–12), 3332–3341 (2011). https://doi.org/10.1166/asl.2011.2043

4. Ifrim, A.-C., Moldoveanu, F., Moldoveanu, A., Grădinaru, A.: LibrARy – enriching the cultural physical spaces with collaborative AR content. In: Chen, J.Y.C., Fragomeni, G. (eds.) HCII 2021. LNCS, vol. 12770, pp. 626–638. Springer, Cham (2021). https://doi.org/10.1007/978-3-030-77599-5_43

5. Meas, C., Tagai, K., Yuminaka, Y., Aoki, Y.: Augmented reality translator utilizing inter-device communication. In: Proceedings of International Conference on Technology and Social Science 2020 (2020)

6. Niantic: Pokémon GO (2021). https://pokemongolive.com/en/

7. Staiano, A.E., Calvert, S.L.: Exergames for physical education courses: physical, social, and cognitive benefits. Child Dev. Perspect. 5(2), 93 (2011). https://doi.org/10.1111/J.1750-8606.2011.00162.X, https://www.ncbi.nlm.nih.gov/pmc/articles/PMC3339488/

8. Tagai, K., Yuminaka, Y., Shimoda, T., Aoki, Y.: Active learning assistance systems utilizing AR-based virtual blackboards. In: ICTSS 2019, pp. 1–4 (2019)

9. Wagner, D., Schmalstieg, D., Billinghurst, M.: Handheld AR for collaborative edutainment. In: Pan, Z., Cheok, A., Haller, M., Lau, R.W.H., Saito, H., Liang, R. (eds.) ICAT 2006. LNCS (LNAI and LNB), vol. 4282, pp. 85–96. Springer, Heidelberg (2006). https://doi.org/10.1007/11941354_10

10. Woodward, K., Kanjo, E., Parker, W.: Towards the use of IoT and AI for pervasive exergames. In: 2021 IEEE Global Conference on Artificial Intelligence and Internet of Things (GCAIoT), pp. 1–6, December 2021. https://doi.org/10.1109/GCAIOT53516.2021.9692952, https://ieeexplore.ieee.org/document/9692952/

Author Index

Alejo, Hesiquio Mendez   180
Al-Thani, Dena   427
Ambati, Uday Sai Reddy   101

Baljko, Melanie   3
Banire, Bilikis   427
Barthet, Mathieu   160
Bartle, Richard   269
Bestard Lorigados, Elias   3
Binter, Jakub   487
Bock, Fabian   180
Boschetti, Silvia   487
Brandse, Michael   141
Brandt, Gregory   101
Brooks, Eva   456

Canossa, Alessandro   399
Carstensdottir, Elin   586
Castanho, Carla D.   69
Catarci, Tiziana   508
Chabbi, Houda   496
Chabebe Rivera, Annette Marie   569
Chen, Chien-Hsiung   234
Copeman, Matthew   309

De Santis, Matteo   508
Deng, Rong   180
Dullens, Vitor F.   69
Dürst, Martin J.   119

e Silva, Tiago B. P.   69
Eichhorn, Christian   618

Fajnzylber, Victor   605
Ferro, Lauren S.   508
Frachi, Yann   160
Fragulis, George F.   40
Freeman, Jonathan   196, 269, 309

Gao, Yichen   327
Ghaban, Wad   414
Gorman, Gregory   22
Goethe, Ole   289

Gou, Jiawen   340
Gutierrez, Francisco J.   605

Habibi, Reza   586
Han, Ting   530, 555
Helmefalk, Miralem   289
Hijab, Mohamad Hassan Fadi   427
Hladký, Tomáš   487
Hofmann, Florian   496
Huang, Wendan   637

Ingram, Sandy   496

Jiang, Lan   444
Jiao, Jiawei   354
Jílková, Jiřina   487

Kaisar, Emiran   530
Kambe, Asha   375
Kanjo, Eiman   652
Kashani, Atieh   586
Khazaal, Yasser   496
Klinker, Gudrun   618
Kollias, Konstantinos-Filippos   40
Krath, Jeanine   289
Kratky, Andreas   180
Kurta, Leah   196

LaLone, Nicolas   213
Laris Pardo, Luis   399
Lazaridis, Lazaros   40
Li, Erin   245
Li, Hongyu   234
Li, Hui   340
Li, Sean   245
Liang, Xiao   387
Linehan, Conor   22
Lozano Angulo, Alexis   399

MacCormick, Daniel   51
Machado, Thiago V.   69
MacKenzie, I. Scott   3
Maj, Anna   256

Maldonado, Cristóbal   605
Maram, Sai Siddartha   586
Maraslidis, George   40
Marrella, Andrea   508
Michailidis, Heraklis   40
Montoya, Maria F.   469
Mourlas, Constantinos   542

Nakajima, Tatsuo   375
Nery Bandeira, Ian   69
Ngyuen, Vinh   496

O'Shea, Zoë   269
Oliveira, Rennê Ruan A.   69

Palmquist, Adam   289
Pan, Xueni   269
Papangelis, Konstantinos   213
Papatsimouli, Maria   40
Paraskevas, Theodoros   542
Parenti, Adriano   508
Parker, Will   652
Pfau, Johannes   586
Plecher, David A.   618
Prossinger, Hermann   487

Qiu, Shi   530

Ribeiro, Gonçalo   84
Ribeiro, Tânia   84
Říha, Daniel   487
Rosenlund, Joacim   289

Sapio, Francesco   508
Sarmet, Mauricio M.   69
Schaffer, Owen   101
Seif El-Nasr, Magy   586

Shang, Junjie   637
Shen, Joanna   180
Shoji, Yoshiyuki   119
Sisodiya, Shweta K.   586
Sjöberg, Jeanette   456
Sotirakou, Catherine   542

Takahashi, Takuya   160
Takidaira, Shio   119
Tan, Shufang   637
Toups Dugas, Phoebe O.   213

Veloso, Ana Isabel   84
Villada, Julian F.   469

Wang, Feiqi   160
Wang, Siyuan   387
Wang, Xiaoxue   444
Wei, Jessica   586
Wells, Timothy Jason   487
Wohlschlager, Andreas   618
Woodward, Kieran   652
Wu, Jinchun   354
Wu, Lihanjing   340, 387
Wu, Wenyu   569
Wu, Zhanwei   327

Xue, Chengqi   354, 569

Yuan, Rui   530
Yuan, Xiaojun   245

Zaman, Loutfouz   51
Zhang, Jingshun   444
Zhao, Fan   444
Zhou, Tianyu   555

Printed in the United States
by Baker & Taylor Publisher Services

Printed in the United States
by Baker & Taylor Publisher Services